Assessment of Young Developmentally Disabled Children

Perspectives in Developmental Psychology

Series Editor: Michael Lewis
Rutgers Medical School
University of Medicine and Dentistry of New Jersey
New Brunswick, New Jersey

Assessment of Young Developmentally Disabled Children

Edited by

Theodore D. Wachs
Purdue University
West Lafayette, Indiana

and

Robert Sheehan
Cleveland State University
Cleveland, Ohio

Plenum Press • New York and London

Library of Congress Cataloging in Publication Data

Assessment of young developmentally disabled children / edited by Theodore D. Wachs and Robert Sheehan.
  p.   cm. — (Perspectives in developmental psychology)
  Includes bibliographies and indexes.
  ISBN 0-306-42733-8
  1. Developmentally disabled children. I. Wachs, Theodore, 1941–   . II. Sheehan, Robert, 1951–   . III. Series.
RJ135.A85   1988
618.92′8588 —dc19   88-2966
                                                                                          CIP

© 1988 Plenum Press, New York
A Division of Plenum Publishing Corporation
233 Spring Street, New York, N.Y. 10013

Printed in the United States of America

Contributors

Donald B. Bailey, Jr. • School of Education and FAMILIES Project, Carolina Institute for Research on Early Education of the Handicapped, Frank Porter Graham Child Developmental Center, University of North Carolina, Chapel Hill, North Carolina

Barbara A. Bain • Department of Communication Sciences and Disorders, University of Montana, Missoula, Montana

Kathryn Barnard • Department of Parent-Child Nursing, University of Washington, Seattle, Washington

Patricia Brandt • Department of Parent-Child Nursing, University of Washington, Seattle, Washington

Lois M. Brockman • Department of Family Studies, University of Manitoba, Winnipeg, Manitoba, Canada

D. Cech • Department of Physical Therapy, Chicago Medical School, North Chicago, Illinois

Carl J. Dunst • Family, Infant, and Preschool Program, and the Human Development Research and Training Institute, Western Carolina Center, Morgantown, North Carolina

Nancy Fieber • Meyer Children's Rehabilitation Institute, University of Nebraska Medical Center, Omaha, Nebraska

R. J. Gallagher • Department of Early Childhood Special Education, University of Cincinnati, Cincinnati, Ohio

Kathleen Gradel • Department of Special Education, University of Maryland, College Park, Maryland

Robert J. Harmon • Division of Child Psychiatry, University of Colorado School of Medicine, Denver, Colorado

Robert J. Hoffmeister • Center for the Study of Communication and Deafness, School of Education, Boston University, Boston, Massachusetts

Nancy C. Hubert • Sparks Center for Developmental and Learning Disorders, and the Department of Psychology, University of Alabama at Birmingham, Birmingham, Alabama

James V. Kahn • Department of Special Education, University of Illinois at Chicago, Chicago, Illinois

Diane Magyary • Department of Parent-Child Nursing, University of Washington, Seattle, Washington

Sean C. McDevitt • Western Behavioral Associates, Inc., 367 N. 21st Avenue, Phoenix, Arizona

R. A. McWilliam • Family, Infant, and Preschool Program, and the Human Development Research and Training Institute, Western Carolina Center, Morgantown, North Carolina

George A. Morgan • Human Development and Family Studies, Colorado State University, Fort Collins, Colorado

Lesley B. Olswang • Department of Speech and Hearing Sciences, University of Washington, Seattle, Washington

Michael D. Orlansky • College of Education, Ohio State University, Columbus, Ohio

Cordelia Robinson • Meyer Children's Rehabilitation Institute, University of Nebraska Medical Center, Omaha, Nebraska

Robert Sheehan • Department of Foundation and Curriculum, College of Education, Cleveland State University, Cleveland, Ohio

Rune J. Simeonsson • School of Education and FAMILIES Project, Carolina Institute for Research on Early Education of the Handicapped, Frank Porter Graham Child Development Center, University of North Carolina, Chapel Hill, North Carolina

Vaughan Stagg • Department of Psychology, Louisiana State University in Shreveport, Shreveport, Louisiana

Theodore D. Wachs • Department of Psychological Sciences, Purdue University, West Lafayette, Indiana

Jan L. Wallander • Sparks Center for Developmental and Learning Disorders, and the Department of Psychology, University of Alabama at Birmingham, Birmingham, Alabama

Sidney S. Zentall • Department of Special Education, Purdue University, West Lafayette, Indiana

Preface

Our knowledge of the cognitive and social-emotional functioning of developmentally disabled infants and preschoolers derives, in large part, from our assessment of such children. This book has been developed to familiarize readers with the characteristics of developmentally disabled children, and to introduce to readers aspects of measurement that are of relevance to the assessment of atypical infants and preschoolers.

The book has been developed with clinicians and prospective clinicians in mind. These are individuals who are committed to the care and education of developmentally disabled infants and preschoolers and the families of those children. The book has thus been written to provide support for the use of assessment data in planning early intervention programs.

Of special note in the development of this edited book is that it is divided into four major parts with interrelated chapters in each part. The authors of chapters in Parts II and III had access to the chapters in Part I *before* writing their chapters. The summary chapters found in Part IV were similarly written by authors having access to all chapters in Parts I–III. This approach to the development of an edited book was chosen as a way of ensuring an integration of major concepts throughout the book. This process is also a reflection of our belief that assessment is an interdisciplinary process, involving the synthesis of a number of diverse interests.

Part I of this book introduces the assessment process. In this section, we identify issues of development and measurement that are of particular relevance to all types of handicapped infants and preschoolers. Wachs and Sheehan provide an overview of the cognitive and socioemotional development of young developmentally disabled children, identifying many of the knowns and unknowns of development for this population. Simeonsson and Bailey discuss essential elements of the assessment process, including child variables, intervention variables, and outcome variables. Hubert and Wallander then articulate a model of instrument selection for the assessment of developmentally disabled infants and preschoolers. Stagg continues this theme by discussing clinical considerations in the assessment of young developmentally disabled children. In the last chapter in Part I, Sheehan analyzes numerous studies comparing parental and professional agreement in early childhood assessment and suggests a model for the involvement of parents in assessment.

Part II of the text, "Cognitive Assessment," includes six chapters discussing the specifics of infant and preschool cognitive assessment with various groups of handicapped infants and preschoolers. These groups include blind and visually impaired children, deaf and hard-of-hearing children, motorically impaired children, mentally retarded children, children with severe behavioral disorders, and multiply handicapped children.

Part III of the text, "Noncognitive Assessment," includes chapters dealing with the assessment of motoric behavior, the assessment of temperament, the assessment of motivation, the assessment of language, and environmental and biophysical assessment of developmentally disabled infants and preschoolers.

Part IV of the text is designed to guide links from assessment to treatment. The overview chapters in this final part emphasize the use of assessment data in intervention programs for handicapped children.

THE NATURE OF DEVELOPMENTAL ASSESSMENT

Definition

Any discussion of the assessment of development must begin with a definition of the term *assessment*. We define assessment as systematic, purposeful data-collection. Further, in this book, we restrict our use of the term *development* to psychological development. Rather than narrowly restricting our concept of psychological development to cognitive parameters, we prefer to operate within a *competence model*, including all those behavioral and intra- and interindividual factors that relate to the *child's ability to deal effectively with his or her environment*. Within this framework, the assessment of early development means the systematic, purposeful collection of data, reflecting both patterns of children's emergent abilities to comprehend and function in their environment and the factors associated with the emergence of these patterns.

The Role of Assessing Development in Our Culture

Historically, the emphasis in developmental assessment has been on describing current cognitive functioning and on predicting subsequent cognitive development. One assumption underlying the first usage is that a developmental test is necessary to confirm developmental delay. All too often, this is not the case. We have witnessed numerous efforts of clinicians to derive a scorable intelligence measure on the McCarthy scales for severely handicapped 6-year-olds. When asked why the test was being used, the answer is typically "To confirm developmental delay." Similarly, we have seen examples of clinicians who have been confronted with an infant whose performance on the Bayley scales was so low that the test did not yield a scorable index (a score indicating a norm group reference). These assessors have then attempted to derive an index score by dividing the infant's developmental age score (DA) by chronological age (CA) and multiplying by 100 ($DA/CA + 100 =$ Developmental quotient [DQ]). When asked why a DQ below 50 was needed, the answer was "To confirm developmental delay." Clearly, in these types of situations, the test only confirms the obvious.

In terms of the predictive function, although at least moderate continuity of performance is found between infant and childhood cognitive assessment (Bornstein & Sigman, 1986), we do not view the predictive function as necessarily primary for two reasons.

First, any type of mass cognitive screening would not be cost-effective as a means of detecting that small percentage of infants who would be truly at developmental risk. Second, as will be emphasized in this book, it is becoming increasingly clear that, to have the potential of predicting risk for children who are not obviously delayed, a *multidimensional approach* is necessary. A multidimensional approach involves the use of cognitive, biomedical, motivational, and environmental assessments.

Given the above, we view early assessment as more valid when used as a *descriptive and prescriptive procedure*. By descriptive and prescriptive, we mean using assessments that provide us with competence profiles for young children designated as being at risk. These profiles can be used to make decisions about which children need intervention, and to design the most effective intervention strategy for each child. The descriptive-prescriptive approach is seen as valid regardless of what specific assessment strategy is used (e.g., norm-referenced, criterion-referenced, or test adaptation).

The use of early assessment in a descriptive-prescriptive strategy is congruent with recent changes in our culture's attitudes toward handicapped infants and preschoolers. This change, though not widespread until the 1970s, was toward the provision of remedial educational services for infants and preschoolers who had been diagnosed as disabled. Previously, these children had received custodial care until they were of school age. However, the long-term consequences of severe early-childhood disability and the disadvantages of purely custodial care have become increasingly evident (Tjossem, 1976). The early intervention efforts for disadvantaged preschoolers (e.g., Head Start), begun in the 1960s, began to be directed toward young handicapped children with the Federal funding of P.L. 90-538, the Handicapped Children's Early Education Program (HCEEP).

The HCEEP models began funding in 1969, with the first three-year models being completed by 1972. Each of these models specified the entrance criteria for infants and children, using developmental data to support such decisions. As the models were intended to be replicated throughout the country and, as a consequence, had to be clearly explicated in rationale and practice, assessment data were also used to make programming decisions for children (in developing and modifying individual educational plans, or IEPs) and were also used to assess the efficacy of interventions. By the 1970s, therefore, two mandated purposes for early childhood assessment had evolved: assessment for program planning and assessment for program evaluation.

What has emerged from the above is an emphasis on the relevance of assessment data to clinical work with developmentally disabled populations. The question, then, becomes one of what types of assessment data, for what purposes, and for what populations. It is this question that this book was designed to answer.

REFERENCES

Bornstein, M., & Sigman, M. (1986). Continuity in mental development from infancy. *Child Development, 57,* 251–274.

Tjossem, T. (1976). *Intervention strategies for high risk infants and young children.* Baltimore: University Park Press.

Contents

III. Noncognitive Assessment

Foundations of the Assessment Process with the Developmentally Disabled

Any discipline in the sciences must be based on a firm foundation. When we discuss the assessment of developmentally disabled infants and preschoolers, we must be aware of the foundations in a number of related areas. Part I of this text is an attempt to highlight those foundations and to challenge assessors to use them as a referent in making decisions about the assessment process.

First, we must be cognizant of the patterns of growth and development that are shaping the young children whom we are assessing. In many instances, the developmental patterns that we witness in handicapped infants and preschoolers are identical to those of their nonhandicapped peers. In other instances, new developmental pathways are evident in individual handicapped children or in subgroupings of those children. In Chapter 1, Wachs and Sheehan explore the relevance of developmental patterns to the assessment process. Unfortunately, this is a foundation area about which more is unknown than is known. The authors highlight our knowledge base with regard to the cognitive development and the social-emotional-interpersonal development of children exhibiting a variety of handicapping conditions. As handicapping conditions become more complex, our knowledge base becomes less sure.

In addition to the foundation of children's growth and development, assessors must also be aware of the essential elements of the assessment process. In Chapter 2, Simeonsson and Bailey probe these issues, indentifying the various purposes of assessment and the need for nontraditional assessment approaches, depending on the desired assessment outcomes. These authors also highlight the complexity of assessment in the area of early intervention that is due to the tremendous heterogeneity of populations and the variability of definitions evident in the field. Chapter 2 also provides a carefully worded challenge to assessors to include the specification of intervention variables as well as of outcome variables.

In Chapter 3, Hubert and Wallander directly confront the inadequacies of applying classical test theory to the assessment of handicapped infants and preschoolers. The argument presented by these authors for an alternative strategy of instrument selection is a thoughtful application of decision theory principles to the early intervention area. Decisions about instrument selection should be heavily influenced by the type of decisions that assessors attempt to make for individual handicapped infants and preschoolers.

Once the diagnosis is made that a child is handicapped, the utility of standardized instruments, or the standardized administration of instruments becomes questionable. Stagg addresses this problem (in Chapter 4) by arguing that assessors should function as hypothesis testers, investigating the probable links between a child's impairments and the child's performance. He suggests that such an approach involves sequential probing and the frequent modification of instrumentation (either in the administration of an item or in the scoring of a response).

Classical test theory argues strongly for highly trained examiners and rigid protocols to ensure reliable assessment data. In Chapter 5, Sheehan questions this belief (for certain assessment purposes) by reviewing a large number of studies that compare the validity (and the reliability) of data generated from parent interviews. The data reviewed in this chapter are remarkable in their consistency, as they reveal a very systematic pattern in parents' estimation of their children's performance that is just slightly higher than that of trained examiners. Once again, Sheehan emphasizes a decision theory model in planning for the inclusion of parental report data in the assessment process.

Part 1 of this text represents a challenge to all early-childhood assessors. The chapters in this section make the point that there are no easy answers. There is no ''best instrument'' for all children and for all purposes. The authors in Part I are in agreement that too little attention has been paid to the purpose and context of assessment, and to the complexities of the various populations of handicapped infants and preschoolers that we assess. Answers to our dilemmas are to be found in a better phrasing of our questions and a more careful articulation of the purposes guiding our assessment efforts.

Developmental Patterns in Disabled Infants and Preschoolers

Theodore D. Wachs and Robert Sheehan

In the review of evidence on the pattern of cognitive and socioemotional development of the young developmentally disabled child, three factors combine to make the job difficult. First, as will become obvious, although for some disabilities, such as retardation, there is ample evidence on developmental patterns across the life span, for other groups, such as the mutiply handicapped, there are large gaps in our knowledge base, particularly below the age of 5 years. Often, only a single study represents our knowledge of development in critical areas. This problem is compounded by the all-too-common practice of aggregating data for different disability conditions under the labels of *handicapped* or *developmentally delayed*, and comparing the performance of a heterogeneous group of handicapped children to that of the nonhandicapped (i.e., Mundy, Seibert, & Hogan, 1984). As will become obvious, this assumption that all handicapping conditions are functionally equivalent in their developmental patterns does not appear to be justified by the data. Further, even when supposedly homogeneous handicaps are used, children with differing degrees of handicaps are very often clumped together. Thus, it is not uncommon to find studies in which the term *motor-impaired* is used to designate children with and without central nervous system (CNS) etiology (i.e., Fishman & Palkes, 1974). As a result, even when consistent relationships are found, the degree of generalizability is unclear, as distinctions based on the degree of the etiology of the handicap are rarely made.

PATTERNS OF DEVELOPMENT: THE VISUALLY IMPAIRED

Cognitive Development

In terms of cognitive development, the greatest emphasis has been on an analysis of the patterns of development of blind infants and toddlers within a Piagetian framework. In infancy, emphasis has been placed almost exclusively on the development of the con-

THEODORE D. WACHS ● Department of Psychological Sciences, Purdue University, West Lafayette, Indiana 47907.   ROBERT SHEEHAN ● Department of Foundation and Curriculum, College of Education, Cleveland State University, Cleveland, Ohio 44115.

cept of object permanence. The subject populations typically involve congenitally and totally blind infants. Much of the available evidence has come from the work of Fraiberg (1968) and Bigelow (1980). According to Fraiberg (1968), blind infants, although showing *similar sequences* of development, do show *delays* in the level of development of understanding of object permanence. Although there are discrepancies in the substages between Fraiberg and Bigelow, combining the two data sets results in the following developmental sequence. A comparison of Table 1 to the traditional Piagetian stages suggests that Stage 4 for the blind corresponds to the beginning of Piagetian Stage 3 object-permanence development for the sighted; that Stage 5 reflects the beginnings of Piagetian Stage 4 object permanence, and that Stages 6 and 7 signal the transition to higher levels of object permanence.

In this sequence, blind children appear to have particular difficulty with hidden displacements, involving the continuing search for an object after it has been sounded and then moved from the place where the original sound was made. In part, this difficulty in continuing to search for an object that has been moved may result from an inhibition of exploratory behavior by blind infants, as noted by Reynell (1978). An alternative explanation also exists, based on the nature of the procedure used for assessing object permanence in the blind. Drawing on her own work as well as data by Uzgiris and Benson (1980), Biglow (1980) hypothesized that the above pattern does not necessarily reflect a delay in the development of the concept of object permanence *per se* for the blind infant. Rather, delay is due to sounds initially being a less salient cue than visual stimuli in eliciting the object-permanence type of behavior (Bigelow, 1983). According to Bigelow, what may look like a cognitive delay in object permanence for the blind may, in fact, be due to procedural rather than cognitive factors (i.e., the use of sound rather than visual cues in assessing the blind).

Piagetian studies of the development of conservation in preschool blind children show a pattern similar to that seen in the sensorimotor period. Particularly in the development of the ability to conserve mass and volume, blind and nonblind preschoolers show *similar developmental sequences*; however, the blind perform at lower levels than the sighted (Gottesman, 1973). In contrast to the infancy data, methodological factors do not appear to be relevant, given evidence that there were no performance differences between

---

Table I. Proposed Stages in the Development of Object Permanence by Blind Infants[a]

Stage 1: Removal of object from hand—no protest.

Stage 2: Removal of object from hand—protest.

    Substage A: Turn hand in direction of object if touched after removal.

    Substage B: Reach of arm in direction of object if touched after removal.

Stage 3: After tactual contact with object, *random* search when object is removed.

Stage 4: Organized search pattern after tactual contact with object; i.e., search where object was last encountered.

    Substage A: Search in place where object sounded and not where last encountered.

Stage 5: Start of sound-induced search alone; i.e., hold fingers in grasp pattern with sound alone or pantomime object-activating movements following sounds.

Stage 6: Reach and recover on sound cue alone, but only if object remains where sounded.

Stage 7: Search for object in places other than sounded when object has moved after being sounded.

---

[a]Steps integrated from data of Fraiberg, Siegel, & Gibson, 1966; Fraiberg, 1968; Bigelow, 1980).

sighted preschoolers who could see the test material and sighted preschoolers who were blindfolded during the test sequence (Gottesman, 1973).

Moving from a Piagetian framework to other areas of cognitive functioning, Gottsman (1971) reported no differences between blind and sighted preschoolers on tests of haptic perception. This lack of difference in haptic functioning may reflect some type of CNS compensation, leading to enhanced development in nonvisual areas of the cortex, as suggested in infrahuman data by Rosenzweig (1955).

In terms of other domains of cognitive functioning, Reynell (1978) compared the development of blind and partially sighted children to that of sighted children in 6 developmental areas across the first 5 years of life. Her results indicate that, in the majority of areas, including social adaptation and the development of self-help skills, the understanding of object relations, the exploration of environment, verbal comprehension, and expressive language content, the blind are delayed anywhere from 1 to 2½ years but do *ultimately reach the level that the normal preschooler achieves earlier.* The delay in exploration documented by Reynell does not appear to be a function of delay in spatial representation, given case study data on this topic by Landau, Gleitman, and Spelke (1981). Rather, the evidence suggests either that sound is a less salient stimulus for triggering exploration, or that the delay in exploration may be due to the preference of the blind for oral over motor exploration (Burlingham, 1979; Fraiberg, 1975). Only in the case of expressive language functioning does the gap between the blind and the sighted remain.

What is unclear from Reynell's results is whether the apparent catch-up of the blind child is a *genuine developmental phenomenon*, or whether it is an artifact based on ceiling effects on the particular scales used by Reynell. Studies involving older blind children, using both psychometric (Smith & Mommers, 1975) and Piagetian (Gottesman, 1973) measures of cognitive functioning support the hypothesis that the catch-up may, in fact, be a genuine developmental phenomenon.

Overall, to the extent that the few studies in this area report a *reliable domain of knowledge*, the literature appears to be quite consistent in suggesting that the blind do eventually reach the cognitive levels attained by the sighted. Perhaps the one exception to this rule is blindness that is a function of a specific disease process, such as maternal rubella, which may predispose the child both to blindness and to retardation (Chess, Korn, & Fernandez, 1971).

Social-Emotional-Interpersonal Development

In terms of noncognitive development, almost without exception, most research in this area has been done within a psychoanalytic framework. What this means in practice is that the data base, which consists of either case studies or direct observation, is filtered through an analytic conceptual screen before interpretation. In contrast to the cognitive literature, which suggests parallel patterns of development, social-emotional-interpersonal development data indicate more *nonparallel, divergent developmental paths.*

There appears to be some agreement, from both the psychoanalytic (Sandler, 1963) and the nonpsychoanalytic literature (Als, Tronick, & Brazelton, 1980), that, at least for the first *2 months* of life, similarities in developmental pathways between blind and sighted infants outweigh any differences. Further, at least within the psychoanalytic literature, in terms of the development of stranger fears, during the age period when sighted infants show stranger avoidance behaviors, blind infants also appear to show discomfort or protest when picked up or held by a stranger (Fraiberg, 1975). However, the evidence generally indicates that, after 6 months of age, the developmental pathways of blind infants are different from the paths used by sighted infants (Fraiberg, 1968, 1975). Indeed, Burlingham (1979) hypothesized that after 6 months, behaviors that appear similar for the blind and the sighted may, in fact, reflect quite different processes for the two groups. Thus, although blind infants show the development of emotional bonds by 18 months of age, as indicated by such behaviors as selective affection, this behavior rarely appears spontaneously, as it does in the sighted infant (Fraiberg, 1968, 1975). In part, this may be due to the high level of passivity shown by blind infants (Scott, 1969). This passivity may be of such a degree that some blind infants may be labeled as motorically delayed when, in fact they have the motoric abilities appropriate to their age (Burlingham, 1979). Along the same lines, much of the activity of blind infants, particularly of those infants who are totally blind and who are deprived of emotional stimulation, appears to revolve around the mouthing of objects (Fraiberg & Freedman, 1969). However, unlike sighted infants, who use other schemes with objects, blind infants use objects almost exclusively for mouthing.

In the preschool-aged blind child, evidence also suggests the existence of divergent, nonparallel patterns of development. Psychoanalytic observers have stressed the difficulty that blind children have in separating from the mother at ages when sighted toddlers can handle separation (Fraiberg, 1968). This difficulty may be seen as a simple developmental delay, perhaps mediated either by lags in object permanence (Fraiberg, 1968) or by confusion about when the mother leaves, as the absence of sound does not necessarily mean that the mother has actually left (Fraiberg, 1975). However, a delay explanation would not explain why problems in separation tolerance for the blind *do not appear to relate to the quality of the mother–child relationship*, as they do for the sighted (Fraiberg, 1968).

A possible continuity in development is also seen in the fact that, like the blind infant, the blind preschooler has often been characterized as high passive. This passivity is shown in the blind preschooler's being less likely to show independence strivings (Fraiberg, 1968), being less likely to show attempts at social interactions (Scott, 1969), and being less likely to fight back when provoked (Burlingham, 1975). Using this data base, some analysts have gone so far as to hypothesize delays in ego development of the blind preschooler, which are associated with high levels of passivity (Sandler, 1963). Other analysts have also hypothesized delays in the development of the idea of self and increases in egocentrism by the blind preschooler (Sandler, 1963; Scott, 1969).

At least regarding passivity, there is partial support for the generalizability of this phenomenon from one of the few nonanalytic investigations in this area. Using both maternal and temperament ratings, plus direct observation of the classroom performance of infant and preschool blind children, Greenberg and Field (1982) reported that, in social situations, blind infants and preschoolers appear to require much more stimulation to reliably elicit responses than do nonhandicapped controls. These data could be viewed as congruent with analytic results characterizing the blind infant as more passive. However, the temperament data of Greenberg and Field indicate that blind infants and preschoolers are rated as more difficult by their parents than either nonhandicapped or retarded controls. At least in terms of this study, this pattern does not appear to fit with the picture drawn of the passive blind child. However, ambiguities in the concept of *difficult temperament* (Hubert & Wachs, 1985) make it hard to define exactly what characteristics parents may have been rating when they indicated that their blind preschoolers were more difficult.

Overall, to the extent that data primarily from one theoretical orientation represent a valid data base, the available evidence on the social-emotional-interpersonal development of the blind does suggest the existence of divergent developmental pathways, which may not be completely adaptable for the individual. These data would be congruent with analytic reports on the development of older blind children, which indicate continued problems in adaptation (Burlingham, 1979). These reports form a clear contrast to the data noted earlier for cognitive development, which suggest delays but the ultimate attainment of satisfactory levels of cognitive functioning. This pattern of evidence would seem to suggest that the focus of assessment of the blind should be more on noncognitive factors, as this area appears to be the area of greater risk.

PATTERNS OF DEVELOPMENT: THE DEAF AND HARD OF HEARING

Cognitive Development

Reviews of the available studies reveal a tremendous lack of data on the cognitive development patterns of the deaf before 5 years of age (Goetzinger & Proud, 1975; Meadow, 1975, 1980). As might be expected, given the nature of the sensory deficit, young hearing-impaired children are more likely to show delays in their *level* of language development, though their *pattern* of language development is often similar to that of hearing children (Geffner & Freeman, 1980; Schirmer, 1985). However, for cognitive development *per se*, the available evidence is either inconsistent or clouded by methodological problems. For example, a search of the literature on infancy reveals only one study comparing the cognitive development of deaf and hearing infants. Using Piagetian sensorimotor measures, Best and Roberts (1976) reported no significant differences between hearing and deaf toddlers on any sensorimotor scale except vocal imitation. However, as the infants used were older (2–28 months) than those that the test was designed for (a ceiling of 24 months), it is difficult to know whether these nonsignificant findings were due primarily to a ceiling effect.

Examining preschoolers in terms of global IQ, Chess *et al.* (1971) reported a significantly higher rate of mental retardation in their deaf rubella sample of preschoolers (aged 2.5–4 years) than is found in the general population; based on comparisons between nondeaf and deaf rubella children Chess *et al.* concluded that deafness, rather than rubella, was the major etiological factor. A higher rate of mental retardation is also found in children whose deafness was due to congenital cytomegalovirus infection; in this syndrome, both the deafness and the retardation appeared to be mediated by neurological damage (Eichorn, 1982). In contrast, Brunick (1981), using a deaf preschool population with less specific etiologies, reported that the deaf children showed normal cognitive performance on three separate intelligence scales.

Regarding specific cognitive abilities, Furth (1966) reported that 4- to 5-year-old deaf children lagged about 1 year behind their hearing counterparts on various acquisition and transfer tasks. Similarly, Lubin and Sherrill (1980) reported that 2- to 5-year-old deaf preschoolers were significantly below test norms on measures of creative thinking. In contrast, Blank and Bridger (1966) reported no significant differences between deaf and hearing children from ages 2 to 6 years, either on various tasks of cross-modal transfer or on the ability to use concepts to solve cross-modal transfer problems. Data at the infrahuman (MacDougall & Rabinovitch, 1971) and human levels (Sterritt, Camp, & Lysman, 1966) designed to test the sensory compensation hypothesis reported no significant differences between deaf and hearing subjects on various types of visual perception tasks.

Given the tremendous inconsistency of results, it could be argued, as Furth (1966) and Lubin and Sherrill (1980) have argued, that cognitive deficiencies appear *primarily* as a function of the *experiences* encountered by the young deaf child, rather than as a function of deafness *per se*. Experiential deprivation and inappropriate training are examples of the environmental factors implicated by these authors. However, as neither of these authors related variability in environment directly to variability in cognitive performance, this explanation can be viewed only as a hypothesis in need of testing. Further, data by Ashton and Beasley (1982) suggest, at least on certain types of tests, that physiological differences in CNS functioning may account for differing test performance between deaf and hearing children.

Given the inconsistency of results, perhaps the only conclusion that be *tentatively drawn* (besides the tremendous need for much more data for this age period) is that, although some young deaf children may show cognitive deficits, *impairments* in cognitive functioning are, at present, not clearly associated with deafness *per se*.

Social-Emotional-Interpersonal Development

As with cognitive development, the majority of evidence in this area is based on research with older deaf populations (Meadow, 1975, 1980). What evidence is available for infant and preschool children suggests that the social-interpersonal problems noted for older deaf individuals (Harris, 1978; Meadow, 1980) may have developmental antecedents at earlier ages. For example, social interaction problems documented for older deaf children (Meadow, 1980) may be only a later manifestation of earlier problems in social interaction. In one of the initial studies in this area, Van Lieshout (1973) reported that hearing preschool children were rated by their teachers as being more sociable and having more social interactions than deaf children; based on direct observation, it was found that deaf children spent more time in noninteraction situations than the hearing. Similar results were reported by Vandell and George (1981), using 4-year-old deaf and hearing dyads. Specifically, although there were no major differences between the groups in the *number of interaction attempts*, deaf preschoolers had a higher *failure rate* in terms of successfully initiating interactions than did hearing preschoolers. Comparing hearing preschoolers to both severely and profoundly deaf peers, Levy-Schiff and Hoffman (1985) reported significantly less social interaction in free play for the profoundly deaf group and significantly less peer response to interactions initiated by either the profoundly or the severely deaf children. These preschool patterns may be a later manifestation of even earlier problems, given the data by Greenberg and Field (1982) indicating that deaf infants and toddlers were rated by observers as less approachable than developmentally delayed or Downs syndrome infants.

It is difficult to attribute the above results to an inability in young deaf children to form interpersonal relationships. Levy-Schiff and Hoffman (1985) reported that even profoundly deaf children show a definite interest in social interactions. Studies by Freedman (1981) and Greenberg and Marvin (1979) clearly indicate that young deaf children have the capacity to form satisfactory interpersonal relationships. (The relevance to this question of data by Galenson, Miller, Kaplan, and Rothstein, 1979, who reported severe separation anxiety by younger deaf infants, must be viewed cautiously, given the selective sample used, the lack of appropriate controls, and the limited evidence on the quality of observations.) Nor do the results appear to be due to any type of bias against the deaf by hearing children. Although several studies indicate that children tend to play spontaneously with peers within the same hearing-status group (Arnold & Tremblay, 1970; Levy-Schiff & Hoffman, 1985), deaf children appear to have more success with hearing partners than with deaf partners (Vandell & George, 1981). It is still unclear if this pattern of difficulty in social interactions is due to any particular type of strategy used by deaf children to initiate interaction. Levy-Schiff and Hoffman (1985) reported that deaf preschoolers use less efficient modes of social interaction. In contrast, Vandell and George (1981) reported that the same strategies appear to be used by both deaf and hearing children.

The most promising explanation for deficits in social interaction among young deaf populations is that noted by Meadow (1975). Specifically, Meadow suggested that deaf children are limited to dealing with present actions and situations and thus are inhibited in their use of fantasy play, their use of role play, or their dealing with other individuals' future behavior. Data from Heider and Heider (1941) on the free-play behavior of deaf children clearly indicate an inhibition in the use of fantasy play, though more recent data by Greenberg and Marvin (1979) suggest that the degree of inhibition is a function of the level of communicative skills that the child possesses. There have been no direct attempts to deal with the young deaf child's problems in social interaction situations through such techniques as social skills training. However, Vandell, Anderson, Ehrhardt, and Wilson (1982) reported that attempts to make hearing preschool children more sensitive to the problems of deaf classmates typically lead to more failure in interactions between deaf and hearing preschoolers, rather than to fewer failures.

In terms of other areas of functioning, some research and theory are available on the personality development of the young deaf child. Schlesinger (1978; Schlesinger & Meadow, 1972) has attempted to analyze the personality development of young deaf children from an Eriksonian perspective. Although many of these data are based on case studies, Schlesinger has suggested problems in the development of autonomy and initiative by the young deaf child.

Although case study data (Freedman, Canady, & Robinson, 1971) also suggest that preschool deaf children have developed an adequate sense of identity and appropriate sexual identification, observational data of deaf children in interaction with their parents are not nearly as optimistic. Specifically, Schlesinger and Meadow (1972) reported that deaf children are rated as less flexible, less happy, less compliant, and less involved in mastery situations than are hearing preschoolers. Wedell-Monig and Lumley (1980), although not noting differential *responsivity* to the mother in a younger deaf population (13–29 months), did report a much greater degree of *passivity* in play in these infants, involving fewer interaction attempts with adults or with objects. This increased passivity is congruent with case study material (Schlesinger & Meadow, 1972), as well as with observational data indicating a higher stimulation threshold for deaf infants and toddlers (Greenberg & Field, 1982). This early passivity may be a precursor to the lower level of social maturity found in the preschool-aged deaf (Myklebust, 1964) and may also relate to higher failure rates in social interactions, as documented above. Wedell-Monig and Lumley also noted that, as deaf infants get older, there are even fewer interaction attempts by their mothers. These authors suggested that this may be due to the development of a negative cycle, with mothers attempting to initiate fewer interactions because of the child's passivity. Alternatively, the perception of mothers that their deaf infant or toddler is more difficult temperamentally (Greenberg & Field, 1982) may also help to account for the mothers' reluctance to initiate interactions.

Given the documented problems in social interaction and personality, it is surprising that more evidence of psychopathology in young deaf children is not available. Although problems in impulse control have been noted by age 5 years (Harris, 1978), deaf preschoolers do not appear to be at high risk for early major psychopathology, if rubella deaf can be said to be representative of the general population of deaf children (Chess et al., 1971). In part, this may be due to a lack of data on the development of psychopathology in deaf individuals (Altshuler, 1974). Alternatively, as Sanders (1980) suggested, the difficulty in diagnosing deafness in the infancy period may mean that the young deaf infant has a fairly normal period of parent–child interactions. These interactions may help to buffer the child against later psychopathology.

Overall, although deaf infants and preschoolers do not appear to be at any greater risk for psychopathology than nondeaf populations (given the limited evidence available), this population does appear to have problems in the development of social interactions and can be characterized as being highly passive with both people and objects. These developmental difficulties may be precursors of the later behavior problems exhibited by older deaf children. Combined with the data on cognitive functioning, these data suggest that a prime area of assessment of the young deaf child should be in the area of social interpersonal development, as, on a probability basis, this is where difficulties are most likely to be found.

PATTERNS OF DEVELOPMENT: THE MOTOR-IMPAIRED

Cognitive Development

Traditionally, problems in motor development have been assumed to be associated with deficits in cognitive functioning. The available evidence does appear to support this traditional view. In terms of infancy, data by Banham (1972) involving 19-month-old cerebral-palsied babies, and data by Fishman and Palkes (1974) using a group of 6- to 18-month-old infants with heterogeneous types of motor problems, clearly indicate that, as a group these infants show cognitive impairment. Comparison across studies indicates a greater degree of cognitive impairment in the cerebral-palsied group (mean IQ = 58.6) than in the group of children with heterogeneous etiologies (mean IQ = 84.5). In addition, the range of scores was also noteworthy. Specifically, for the cerebral-palsied group, the test standard deviation was 25.9; for the heterogeneous group, the IQs ranged from 44 to 106. Similar patterns of data are also found in children in the preschool age range. The overwhelming majority of cerebral-palsied preschoolers have IQs below 85 (Banham, 1976; Neilson, 1971), with mean IQs averaging approximately 68 (Cruickshank, Hallahan, & Bice, 1976a). A high incidence of retardation is found even in those types of cerebral palsy previously thought to be associated with normal intellectual functioning, such as cerebral palsy associated with extrapyramidal impairment (Marquis, Palmer, Mahoney, & Capute, 1982). For children with more heterogeneous types of motor disorders, although the overall IQ is higher (mean = 89.6), there is also a tremendous variability in scores (range = 39–129) (Fishman & Palkes, 1974). Discouragingly, there appears to be a significant degree of stability in intellectual performance for children with motor impairments (Banham, 1972; Fishman & Palkes, 1974), the highest degree of stability being shown in children tested after 2 years of age (Neilson, 1971) or in children with IQs of 80 and below (Fishman & Palkes, 1974; Neilson, 1971).

The above results must be qualified by a number of considerations. First, for almost all of the above studies, either the data base involved children who had been referred to some type of remediational center, or the description is so vague that it is impossible to know exactly how the sample was obtained. Thus, we may be dealing with a highly selected population. In the absence of more adequate baseline data, it is difficult to know how these children would compare on cognitive performance with children having motor impairments, who have *not been referred* to remediational centers. Second, most studies have used heterogeneous groups of children. For example, even in those studies using only cerebral-palsied children, distinctions are rarely made between the different etiologies or degrees of motor impairment. One exception is seen in studies indicating that young children with Duchenne muscular dystrophy may have greater impairment in verbal than in performance abilities (Liebowitz & Dubowitz, 1981), particularly in early stages of the disorder (Karagan, 1979). A second exception to this rule is seen in studies indicating a specific impairment in expressive language ("the cocktail party syndrome"—excessive but inappropriate verbalizations) in young spina-bifida children (Spain, 1974). More recent research involving older children with spina bifida strongly implicates increased distractibility by these children as a potential cause of this specific impairment (Horn, Lord, Lorch, & Culatta, 1985). The above data are clearly a model for future research, illustrating the importance of using homogeneous groups, so as to more precisely specify the nature and the etiology of cognitive impairments.

The necessity of looking at individual subgroups rather than heterogeneous groups assumes added importance when we recognize that not all motor impairment involves CNS damage. By assuming that the overwhelming majority of children with motor impairment also have cognitive impairment, we may well be overgeneralizing, given that most referred children are those whose motor impairments are due to CNS damage. A case report by Kopp and Shaperman (1973), of a child born without limbs suggests the necessity of taking care to avoid overgeneralization. Specifically, Kopp and Shaperman reported that, when tested on various Binet items at ages 2 and 3, this child was at or near age levels on most items. Kopp and Shaperman suggested that motor actions *per se* may not be necessary for the development of cognitive skills, and that distance receptors may be sufficient. Similarly, data by Spain (1974) indicate that over 80% of young children in a sample who had spina bifida but did not show obvious signs of hydrocephalus had IQ scores in the normal range; in contrast, only one third of young children with spina bifida *plus hydrocephalus* had IQ scores in the normal range. Hence, motor impairment *per se* may not necessarily predict deficiencies in cognitive functioning; these deficits may occur *primarily* when motor impairment is associated with damage to the central nervous system. Indeed, as in the case of Duchenne muscular dystrophy, the presence of cognitive deficits may signal the relevance of CNS factors to what had previously been viewed as primarily a muscular disorder (Karagan, 1979).

Given this conclusion, what are we to make of data from two studies in which cognitive deficits were shown by young children with motor impairments that were not related to CNS damage (Decarie, 1969; Wasserman, Allen, & Solomon, 1985)? These studies nicely illustrate a transactional perspective (Sameroff & Chandler, 1975) in terms of showing how motor impairments may lead to deficiencies in the child's *psychosocial environment*, which, in turn, lead to cognitive impairments. Specifically, in the Decarie (1969) study, many of her thalidomide infants had to have repeated and prolonged hospitalizations. There was substantial correlation between the amount of time spent in the hospital and level of cognitive deficit. Similarly, in the Wassermann *et al.* (1985) study, different styles of maternal interaction were found for physically handicapped versus nonhandicapped toddlers. The interaction patterns used by the mothers of the physically handicapped may be viewed as an attempt to compensate for their child's handicap, but certain aspects of the mother's style (i.e., lowered responsivity to the child) are more likely to impede than to facilitate cognitive development.

Overall, our conclusion must be that young children whose motor impairments are a function of CNS damage and who are referred for treatment are clearly at risk for cognitive deficits. Children whose motor impairments are not due to CNS damage may also be at potential risk because of deficiencies in the psychosocial environment that result from the motor impairment.

Social-Emotional-Interpersonal Development

As is true of the other developmental disabilities, much of the available evidence on social-emotional-interpersonal development is found primarily for children above preschool age (Cruickshank et al., 1976b; Richardson, 1969). Further, many of the available data are based on case reports or case studies, rather than on observations or experimental research. In case study results, a number of authors (Battle, 1977; Kogan, 1980) have emphasized the disruption of infant–parent interactions when the infant has some type of motor disability. This clinical conceptualization received some empirical support from a study with nonhandicapped infants, only some of whom had achieved locomotion (Gustafson, 1984). The results indicated that, as locomotion was achieved, the infants spent more time near adults and interacted more with adults. Thus, not only normal developmental functions (e.g., feeding and toileting) but also normal interaction patterns may be disrupted because of motoric problems. In addition, the repeated hospitalizations that are often associated with these problems may also influence the child's socialization patterns.

In preschool populations, case reports generally suggest a restriction of exploration and of learning through play interactions. It has been hypothesized, from the clinical literature, that these disruptions may lead to difficulties in establishing basic trust (Battle, 1977) as well as predispose to a longer duration of infantile behavior patterns, delays in impulse control, inadequate development of mastery behavior, and increases in isolate behavior, fears, negativism, and passivity (Freeman, 1967). However, the fact that both parents and teachers report higher rates than expected of behavior problems in young children with progressive motor disorders (Leibowitz & Dubowitz, 1981), where *major restrictions of physical activity have not yet occurred*, suggests some caution in generalizing from conclusions developed primarily from clinical studies. It may well be, as suggested by Seidel, Chadwick, and Rutter (1975), that CNS disorders leading to motor impairment predispose to greater vulnerability to environmental stressors. Within this framework, the *combination of predisposition and stress* is the major factor underlying behavior problems, rather than the motor disorder itself. Whatever the cause, these early disruptions may be the developmental precursors of the increased rate of psychiatric disturbances found with older *CNS motor-impaired children* (Rutter, 1978).

Given the above ambiguities, it is unfortunate that the validity of the case-study material can be neither supported nor negated by the available empirical data. Not only are there few empirical data available, but there are tremendous inconsistencies among these data. For example, Greenberg and Field (1982) reported that cerebral-palsied infants between 7 and 35 months were rated by their parents as having a more difficult temperament. In contrast, Heffernan, Black, and Poche (1982) reported that the temperament ratings of motorically impaired children are not different from what one would expect based on temperament norms (though these children are rated as less active and as having a shorter attention span). Differences between these studies may lie, in part, in the fact that Greenberg and Field looked specifically at cerebral-palsied children, whereas Heffernan *et al.* used a heterogeneous group including children having motor disorders other than cerebral palsy. In support of the clinical evidence, motorically impaired children appear to have a high sensory threshold (Greenberg & Field, 1982; Heffernan *et al.*, 1982) and are more distractible (Wasserman *et al.*, 1985), so that more stimulation is needed to elicit a response from the child. Obviously, this could disrupt normal parent–infant interactions, as suggested by the clinical literature.

Congruent with the clinical literature, young motorically impaired children were also rated by observers as less approachable (Greenberg & Field, 1982) and as less likely to display positive affect or to initiate social interactions (Wasserman *et al.*, 1985). However, in contrast to these data, Cruickshank *et al.* (1976b) reported that young cerebral-palsied twins were characterized as more cheerful, less stubborn, less excitable, and more patient than their non-cerebral-palsied co-twins. Complicating matters even further, Brooks-Gunn and Lewis (1982) reported that, while a heterogeneous group of motorically impaired infants and toddlers showed lower levels of positive affect and vocal interactions, these children were not notably different from normal controls on measures of positive affective interchanges or negative affect.

In summarizing data on the social-emotional-interpersonal development of motorically impaired children, many of the same problems found in the cognitive area apply. Not only is there a paucity of data, but heterogeneous groups are commonly used. The question of generalizability from these samples is rarely explored. For example, whether young motor-impaired children whose impairment is not due to CNS factors are at the same level of risk as young children whose impairment does have CNS involvement remains an open question; certainly, the data for older children suggests that great care must be taken in generalizing across populations (Seidel *et al.*, 1975). It seems clear that older (CNS-involved) motorically impaired children are at risk for various types of interpersonal and behavioral problems (Rutter, 1978). Whether the developmental precursors of these later problems are to be found in the disruption in parent–child interactions, as suggested by the clinical literature, cannot be established *conclusively*, given the variability of the occurring results within the studies and the possibility of alternative explanations. Different instruments, definitions, and population groups among the few empirical studies make it difficult to establish which conclusions can be taken as the most reliable. However, the regularity of concerns in the clinical literature, plus the one consistent finding in the empirical literature concerning higher stimulation thresholds for the motorically impaired children, does suggest, very tentatively, that the roots of later behavior problems in motorically impaired children may be found in the infancy and preschool periods.

PATTERNS OF DEVELOPMENT: THE BEHAVIORALLY AND EMOTIONALLY DISTURBED

Cognitive Development

Perhaps more than any other disability, childhood behavioral and emotional disability defies definition. In a recent review of empirical efforts, Achenbach and Edelbrock (1978) described a number of the childhood syndromes likely to appear in this population of children. These authors included over controlled and undercontrolled syndromes, as well as pathological detachment. They also included more specifically defined syndromes, such as aggressive, anxious, delinquent, depressed, hyperactive, schizoid, social withdrawal, somatic complaints, and uncommunicative. The great majority of these empirical studies dealt with children ages 10–15, although some studies included samples involving children as young as age 6.

Achenbach and Edelbrock (1978) also concluded, from their review, that the lack of independent criteria for categorizing disturbed children makes it difficult to establish the validity of such categorization schemes. Even within one of Achenbach and Edelbrock's syndromes (schizoid), enormous variations exists. Rutter (1972) commented that "Childhood schizophrenia has tended to be used as a generic term to include astonishingly heterogeneous mixture of disorders with little in common other than their severity, chronicity, and occurrence in childhood" (p. 315).

Review of the studies of disturbed children reveals that the disability most studied during the infancy and preschool years is infantile autism. The studies also reveal a sharp divergence between empirical findings and common perceptions about the cognitive abilities of autistic children.

The common perception held by many educators and laypersons alike is that a normal intelligence exists beneath the bizarre behavior exhibited by autistic children. As most measures of intelligence rely heavily on the establishment of some form of communicative relationship between a child and a tester (a relationship rarely witnessed with autistic children) autistic children are frequently viewed as untestable. Given the evidence of occasional "splinter skills," described by Barton, Alpern, Kimberlin, Allen, Yang, and Steele (1974) as "islands of competence," and given the fact that the face of the autistic child is often considered "intelligent," the autistic child is often considered untestable but as likely to have normal or greater than normal intelligence.

The common perception of normal intelligence in autistic children has also been fostered by our inability to define the etiology of autism. In the absence of hard neurological signs of brain impairment, the children are regarded as having normal brains that have somehow been constrained in their full expression.

Since the mid-1970s, some pieces of the autistic puzzle have begun to fit together, implicating neurological defect, possibly genetic in origin, in the etiology of autism. Folstein and Rutter (1977) reported that the presence of an autistic sibling is 50 times higher in families with an autistic child than in the general population. Folstein and Rutter (1977) also reported on a study of 21 same-sexed twin pairs, 11 monozygotic (MZ) and 10 dizygotic (DZ). There was a 36% pair wise concordance rate for autism in MZ compared to 0% concordance in DZ pairs. There was also an 82% concordance for cognitive abnormalities in MZ pairs and a 10% concordance for cognitive abnormalities in DZ pairs. This evidence certainly indicates that autism is more than a random emotional blockage in an otherwise normal individual.

DeMyer and associates have conducted a number of systematic studies of the cognitive abilities of autistic children. They have presented a sharp contrast to the suppositions of normal intelligence in autistic children. DeMyer et al. (1974) argued convincingly that most autistic children are testable when test items within their range of competence are used. They compared the initial IQ scores of autistic children to follow-up tests taken from 2 to 16 years later (M = 6 years). The general IQs correlated at .70. This correlation is similar to that found in the general population. The research of Clark and Rutter also supports this position that autistic children are testable, provided that the items being tested are within children's competence. Clark and Rutter (1979) found that success or failure on any item was best predicted by the intrinsic difficulty of that item rather than by the child's lack of cooperation.

DeMyer et al. (1974) concluded "Our findings strongly indicate that most autistic children have subnormal intelligence. For only a few will the IQ rise sufficiently to reach average levels even after treatment and several years of education" (p.43). DeMyer et al. also argued that autistic with IQs greater than 50 respond positively to early intervention. They further commented:

> This last result, while offering no hard and fast rules, does tend to suggest that we could use a <40 IQ as a guide for counselling parents about eventual outcome and the need for caution in expending too much of the family resources on treatment. Without exception children with >50 IQs should have treatment and education geared to their individual assets because some children in this group have a chance for borderline or even normal functioning. (p. 59)

In summary, systematic longitudinal study of young children with emotional and behavioral disorders is lacking, infantile autism being an exception. This subgroup of children is most likely to have serious retardation of cognitive abilities, despite evidence of occasional splinter skills and despite folk wisdom to the contrary. Churchill (1972) made the following comment regarding the success of treatment for autistic (and schizophrenic) children.

> Our overt experience is that the more colorful symptomatology of autism and schizophrenia decreases markedly during treatment while social and affective contact increases, and we are left with children who have a relatively hard and fast inability to learn particular precision skills, especially those prerequisiste for language competence. (p. 187)

Social-Emotional-Interpersonal Development

The noncognitive development of children with emotional and behavioral disorders is certainly implied, if not documented, by the diagnostic classifications of those children. Childhood psychosis is defined as impairment of communication, impairment of relationships, and impairment of object use (Churchill, 1972). The impairment of communication and relationships reflects a present and continuing disability in social and emotional development.

The narrow-band syndromes described by Achenbach and Edelbrock (1978) and empirically demonstrated in the literature paint a very disabling picture: aggressive, anxious, delinquent, depressed, hyperactive, immature, and so forth. These terms describe the characteristic behaviors of children labeled *behaviorally disturbed* or *emotionally disturbed*. Among severely disturbed children Barton, DeMyer, Norton, Allen, and Steele (1973) described infantile autistic children as most likely to make an unsatisfactory social adjustment. The level of social adjustment appears to be best predicted by language competence (Rutter & Lockyer, 1967a,b).

PATTERNS OF DEVELOPMENT: THE MENTALLY RETARDED

Cognitive Development

As is true in other types of handicapping conditions, *mental retardation* is a label for a wide variety of behavioral characteristics prompted by several etiologies. Zigler (1969) contributed to our understanding of mentally retarded children by distinguishing between children whose retardation is a function of cultural familial factors (nonorganic factors) and children whose retardation is a function of brain damage or genetic disability (organic factors).

Zigler's argument (1969) for a distinction between cultural-familial and organically retarded children, as well as his beliefs regarding the importance of motivation as a factor in understanding cultural familial retardation, has been largely unchallenged for 20 years. Recently, Spitz (1983) questioned the empirical basis of these beliefs and suggested that they lack a strong foundation. Though Spitz's comments (1983) are worth noting, they do not provide any alternative framework for understanding mental retardation.

The currently accepted definition of mental retardation is that found in the *Manual on Terminology and Classification in Mental Retardation* of the American Association on Mental Deficiency (AAMD): "Mental Retardation refers to significantly subaverage general intellectual functioning existing concurrently with deficits in adaptive behavior, and manifested during the developmental period" (Grossman, 1977, p. 11). As indicated by this definition, mentally retarded children are children with consistent skill deficits. They might be contrasted with learning-disabled children, whose profile of skills is much less consistent.

Researchers concerned with the intellectual development of mentally retarded children have primarily dealt with the ability of mentally retarded children to engage in Piagetian-type tasks. Inhelder (1968) described profoundly retarded children as differing from nonretarded children primarily in their *rate of development*, rather than in their *sequence of development.* Although some disagreement on this premise exists, the Weisz and Ziegler (1979) review clearly supports Inhelder's position in terms of retarded children's performance on Piagetian tasks. However, reviews of the empirical research on this issue also reveal that the bulk of the research on the cognitive capabilties of mentally retarded children is done with children whose chronological age is 6 or older, though the mental age of these children is usually in the infancy range. For example, 40 profoundly retarded children between the ages of 8 years, 8 months and 14 years, 10 months were tested on Piagetian tasks by Rogers (1977). The mental age range of these children was 11.5–23.5 months, and their average mental age was approximately 16 months. This study demonstrated normal stage progression of the mentally retarded children, though at a much delayed pace (for their chronological ages). The relationship between mental age and Piagetian task performance was significant, though there was no relationship between chronological age and performance on the Piagetian measures. These findings support the argument for rate differences but no qualitative differences in cognitive development. One qualitative difference worth noting was that performance across the Piagetian measure domains was uneven. Specifically, this pattern was different from that found in normal infants by Uzgiris and Hunt (1975).

A significant issue in this area is whether a retarded child of age 8 whose mental functioning is at age 2 is similar to a nonretarded infant of age 2. Addressing this question involves a comparison of retarded and nonretarded children on mental ages and chronological ages, a design used by Gruen and Vore (1972). The Gruen and Vore study used 10 children whose chronological age was 5, but no retarded children whose chronological age was less than 88 months; thus, the study is of limited usefulness for understanding the cognitive development of infant and preschool-aged mentally retarded children. The study reported more similarities than differences in performance in the youngest child when the children were matched for *mental age.*

Kahn (1976) tested 63 mentally retarded children ranging in age 42 to 126 months (mean of 66 months) on the Uzgiris and Hunt (1975) scales of sensorimotor development. He conducted scalogram analyses on the test results and confirmed that the performance of the retarded children was of a normal sequence (the index of consistencies ranged from .81 to 1.0). He also found high intercorrelations among the scales, though somewhat lower than those Hunt and Uzgiris found in nonretarded children. This finding was similar to that mentioned by Rogers (1977).

Studies exploring the usefulness of training mentally retarded children on Piagetian-type tasks are certainly found in the literature (see Wilton & Boersma, 1974, for a review of conservation training studies), though the absence of training studies for mentally retarded infants and preschoolers is notable. This absence is also evident in training studies in the area of memory, as is evident in the excellent review by Brown (1974).

One example of a training study of mentaly retarded children is to be found in Kahn's study (1978), demonstrating that progress toward object permanence can be accelerated in mentally retarded preschoolers through a 6-month training program. Although the sample was too small to permit generalizability (4 experimental subjects and 4 matched control children), it did yield a provocative finding that the children who had been trained in object permanence concepts, and who had shown accelerated performance, typically regressed in that performance during the year following the training. Regression of an ability such as object permanence is not an aspect of Piagetian theory that is discussed or even a phenomenon that would be explainable from Piagetian theory. More recent data with profoundly retarded children, involving the relation of training in cognitive skills (as reflected by the Uzgiris and Hunt Scales) to language skills, were presented by Kahn (1984).

Social-Emotional-Interpersonal Development

The noncognitive development of retarded infants and preschoolers has been the subject of several recent longitudinal studies. These studies are discussed at length in Keogh and Pullis's review (1980) of temperament influences on the development of exceptional children. In this review, the work of Thomas, Chess, and Birch (1968) and subsequent studies by one or more of these researchers are of critical importance. More recently, the longitudinal research of Brooks-Gunn and Lewis (1982), and of Cicchetti and Sroufe (1978), has provided a more detailed understanding of the behavioral interactions associated with the interpersonal development of retarded infants and preschoolers.

Clearly the noncognitive development of retarded children can be separated from their cognitive development only in theory. A conclusion common to the many studies in this area is that children's mental age is a better predictor of their noncognitive functioning than any other variable, including their chronological age. This is not to say that children's mental age, or level of mental retardation, is *the* mediator of childhood temperament. As a number of writers have noted (e.g., Bridges & Cicchetti, 1982), temperament is most typically assessed through the use of a parent questionnaire, and parents may perceive their handicapped children's temperament in a way unrelated to the children's behavior or directly related to the *bidirectional actions* of parent and child.

Thomas *et al.* (1968) were among the first to apply clinical skills and empirical efforts to the study of infant and preschool noncognitive development. The latest version of their instrument (Thomas & Chess, 1977) is widely used in studies in this area. Chess and Korn (cited in Keogh & Pullis, 1980) found through a parent survey that the temperamental characteristics of retarded and nonretarded children were similar when mental age was held constant. They also found that more retarded children exhibited signs of the difficult-child pattern than the nonhandicapped children (cited in Keogh & Pullis, 1980). This finding is contrary to the stereotype that mentally retarded children (particularly Down syndrome children) are placid, humorous, and easy children. Baron's study (1972) of 18 Down syndrome infants suggests that their similarity to mental-age-matched children was not without exception, yielding greater variability of infant temperament than Chess and Korn's research, though generally consistent with the earlier research. Thus, the temperament of a 4-year-old Down syndrome child is best predicted by his or her mental age, though exceptions are likely. Bridges and Cicchetti (1982) also found greater than normally expected variability in the temperament of Down syndrome infants, with a greater percentage of the Down syndrome infants being rated in the more difficult temperament categories. This result occurred with the Carey Infant Temperament Questionnaire and the comparison with nonretarded infants was made to the original Carey standardization sample. A more detailed discussion of this question of the tempermental patterns of retarded children can be found in Chapter 13 by McDevitt in this book.

A more detailed understanding of the noncognitive performance of retarded infants is provided by the work of Brooks-Gunn and Lewis (1982). In this longitudinal research,

Brooks-Gunn and Lewis studied the mother–infant interactions of 156 nonretarded children and 110 handicapped children, including 56 Down syndrome children, 20 developmentally delayed children and 34 physically handicapped children. The Down syndrome children are of interest in our present discussion. These researchers found that Down syndrome children were the least frequent smilers in free-play interactions with their mothers. Nonhandicapped children and other types of handicapped children reportedly smiled more. Down syndrome children also decreased in interactive smiling with age, in contrast to an increase in interactive smiling for nonhandicapped children.

The Brooks-Gunn and Lewis findings would appear to suggest the existence of an inherent depressed-affect pattern for Down syndrome children. Further aspects of this research, however, reveal a more complex pattern of noncognitive performance, as mothers of Down syndrome children vocalize and smile less to their infants than do mothers of nonhandicapped children. On this point, Brooks-Gunn and Lewis (1982) noted, "Thus mothers may be decreasing their responsiveness as they discover that their child is difficult. Interestingly, difficult infants are not necessarily less responsive, although the mothers may perceive them as such" (p. 184).

The noncognitive development of retarded children is coming to be viewed as a complex pattern of parent–child interaction. Brooks-Gunn and Lewis best summarized this view as follows: "[The] infant's capacity in part determines maternal responsiveness to maternal expression. However, the mother's perception of capacity or rate of [the infant's] acquisition also influences her behavior" (p. 185).

PATTERNS OF DEVELOPMENT: THE MULTIPLY HANDICAPPED

When considering the previous handicapping conditions, sufficient research related to the infancy and preschool years existed to warrant some degree of discussion. Unfortunately, this is not the case for the patterns of development of multiply handicapped children. The limited research that does exist related to multiply handicapped children is spread thinly throughout several literature bases. For example, research related to spina bifida children exists in neurological journals, but information related to the development of spina bifida children with additional handicaps (i.e., hydrocephalus) is occasionally found in the educational journals devoted to teaching the severely and profoundly handicapped. As yet, there are no journals devoted to *issues of development* for children with multiple handicapping conditions.

One researcher, in particular, has dealt with the measured developmental performance of multiply handicapped children. Dubose (1976) attempted to obtain standardized data across time on such children. She found, on a sample of 28 multiply handicapped children, strong consistency of IQ test performance across a three-year period. To obtain such data, when necessary, signs and gestures had to be substituted for oral instructions. VanderVeer and Schweid (1974) found similar consistency in a sample of 33 infants and preschoolers, though their description of the subjects is too vague to allow us to state with sureness that the subjects were multiply handicapped.

The work of Dubose (1976, 1977) illustrates the difficulties encountered in studying the development of multiply handicapped children. To study development, researchers typically turn to standardized measures. To obtain test data from multiply handicapped children, researchers must typically modify the test presentation or the desired test results, thus invalidating any norm-reference capabilities. This catch-22 situation must be remedied before we can make definitive statements about the patterns of development of multiply handicapped infants and preschoolers.

REFERENCES

Achenbach, T., & Edelbrock, C. (1978). The classification of child psychopathology: A review and analysis of empirical efforts. *Psychological Bulletin, 85*(6), 1275–1301.

Als, H., Tronick, E., & Brazelton, T. (1980). Stages of early behavioral organization. In T. Field (Ed)., *High risk infants and children.*

Altshuler, K. (1974). The social and psychological development of the deaf child: Problems, their treatment, and prevention. *American Annals of the Deaf, 119*(4), 365–376.

Arnold R., & Tremblay, A. (1979). Interaction of deaf and hearing preschool children. *Journal of Communication Disorders, 12*, 245–251.

Ashton, R., & Beasley, M. (1982). Cerebral laterality in deaf and hearing children. *Developmental Psychology, 18*, 294–300.

Banham, K. (1972). Progress in mental development of retarded cerebral palsied children. *Exceptional Children, 39*, 240.

Banham, K. (1976). Progress in motor development of retarded cerebral palsied children. *Rehabilitation Literature, 37*, 13–16.

Baron, J. (1972). Temperament profile of children with Down's syndrome. *Developmental Medicine and Child Neurology, 14*, 640–643.

Battle, C. V. (1977). Disruptions in the socialization of a young severely handicapped child. In R. P. Marinelli & A. E. Dell Orto (Eds.), *The psychological and social impact of physical handicap.* New York: Springer.

Best, B., & Roberts, G. (1976). Early cognitive development in hearing impaired children. *American Annals of the Deaf, 121*, 560–564.

Bigelow, A. (1980). *Object permanence for sound producing objects: Parallels between blind and sighted infants.* Paper presented to International Conference on Infant Studies. New Haven.

Bigelow, A. (1983). Development of the use of sound in search behavior of infants. *Developmental Psychology, 19*, 317–321.

Blank, M., & Bridge, W. (1966). Conceptual cross-model transfer in deaf and hearing impaired children. *Child Development, 37*, 29–38.

Bridges, F., & Cicchetti, D. (1982). Mother's ratings of the temperament characteristics of Down Syndrome infants. *Developmental Psychology, 18*(2), 238–244.

Brooks-Gunn, J. & Lewis, M. (1982). Affective exchanges between normal infants and handicapped infants and their mothers. In T. Field & A. Fogel (Eds.), *Emotion and early interaction.* Hillsdale, NJ: Erlbaum.

Brown, A. (1974). The role of strategic behavior in retardate memory. In N. Ellis (Ed.), *International review of research in mental retardation* (Vol 8). New York: Academic Press.

Brunick, P. (1981). Relationship between intellectual functioning and communicative competence in deaf children. *Journal of Communication Disorders, 30*, 3–13.

Burlingham. D. (1975). Special problems of blind infants. *Psychoanalytic study of the child, 30.*

Burlinghan, D. (1979). To be born blind in a sighted world, *Psychoanalytic Study of the Child, 34*, 5–30,

Caeg, W. (1970). A simplified method for measuring infant temperament. *Journal of Pediatrics, 77*, 188–194.

Chess, S., Korn, S., & Fernandez, P. (1971). *Psychiatric disorders of children with congenital rubella.* New York: Brunner-Mazel.

Churchill, D. (1972). The relations of infantile autism and early childhood schizophrenia to developmental language disorders of childhood. *Journal of Autism and Childhood Schizophrenia, 2*(2), 182–197.

Ciccletti, D., & Sroute, A. (1978). An organizational view of affect: Illustration from the study of Down Syndrome infants. In M. Lewis & L. Rosenblum (Eds.), *The development of affect.* New York: Plenum Press.

Clark, P., & Rutter, M. (1979). Task difficulty and task performance in autistic children. *Journal of Child Psychology and Psychiatry, 20*, 271–285.

Cruickshank, W., Hallahan, D., & Bice, H. (1976a). The evaluation of intelligence. In W. Cruickshank (Ed.), *Cerebral palsy: A developmental disability*. Syracuse, NY: Syracuse University Press.

Cruickshank, W., Hallahan, D., & Bice, H. (1976b). Personality and behavioral characteristics. In W. Cruickshank (Ed.), *Cerebral palsy: A developmental disability*. Syracuse, NY: Syracuse University Press.

Decarie, T., (1969). A study of the mental and emotional development of theThalidamide child. In B. Foss (Ed.), *Determinants of infant behavior* (Vol 4). New York: Barnes & Noble.

DeMyer, M., Barton, S., DeMyer, W., Norton, J., Allen, J., & Steele, R. (1973). Prognosis in autism: A followup study. *Journal of Autism and Childhood Schizophrenia, 3*, 199–246.

DeMyer, M., Barton, S., Alpern, G., Kimberlin, C., Allen, J., Yang, E., & Steele, R. (1974). The measured intelligence of autistic children. *Journal of Autism and Childhood Schizophrenia, 4*(1), 42–60.

Dubose, R. (1976). Predictive value of infant intelligence scales with multiply handicapped children. *American Journal of Mental Deficiency, 81*(4), 388–390.

Dubose, R. (1977). Assessing severely handicapped children. *Focus on exceptional children, 9*, 1–13.

Eichorn, S. (1982). Congenital cytomegalovirus infection: A significant cause of deafness and mental deficiency. *American Annuals of the Deaf, 127*, 838–843.

Fishman, M., & Palkes, H. (1974). The validity of psychometric testing in children with congenital malformations of the central nervous system. *Developmental Medicine and Child Neurology, 16*, 180–185.

Folstein, S., & Rutter, M. (1977). Infantile autism: A genetic study of 21 twin pairs. *Journal of Child Psychology and Psychiatry, 18*, 297–321.

Fraiberg, S. (1968). Parallel and divergent patterns in blind and sighted infants. *Psychoanalytic Study of the Child, 23*, 264–300.

Fraiberg, S., & Freedman, D. (1969). Some studies in the ego development of the congenitally blind child. *Psychoanalytic Study of the Child, 19*, 113–170.

Fraiberg, S., Siegel, B., & Gibson, R. (1966). The role of sound in the search behavior of a blind infant. *Psychoanalytic Study of the Child, 21*, 327–357.

Freedman, D. (1981). Speech, language and the vocal-auditory connection. *Psychoanalytic Study of the Child, 36*, 105–127.

Freedman, D., Canady, A., & Robinson, J. (1971). Speech and psychic structure. *Journal of the American Psychoanalytic Association, 19*, 765–779.

Freeman, R. (1967). Emotional reactions of handicapped children. *Rehabilitation Literature, 28*, 274–282.

Furth, H. (1966). *Thinking without languages: Psychological implications of deafness*. New York: Free Press.

Galenson, E., Miller, R., Kaplan, E., & Rothstein, A. (1979). Assessment of development in the deaf child. *Journal of the American Academy of Child Psychiatry, 18*, 128.

Geffner, D., & Freeman, L. (1980). Assessment of language comprehension of 6 year old deaf children. *Journal of Communication Disorders, 13*, 455–570.

Goetzinger, C., & Proud, G. (1975). The impact of hearing impairment on the psychological development of children. *Journal of Auditory Research, 15*, 1–60.

Gottesman, M. (1971). A comparative study of Piagetian developmental schema of sighted children with that of a group of blind children. *Child Development, 42*, 573–580.

Gottesman, M. (1973). Conservation development in blind children. *Child Development, 44*, 824–827.

Greenberg, M., & Marvin, R. (1979). Attachment patterns in profoundly deaf preschool children. *Merrill-Palmer Quarterly, 25*, 265–279.

Greenberg, R., & Field, T. (1982). Temperament ratings of handicapped infants during classroom, mother and teacher interactions. *Journal of Pediatric Psychology, 7*, 387–405.

Grossman, H. (1977). *Manual on terminology and classification in mental retardation*. Washington, DC: American Association on Mental Deficiency.

Gruen, G., & Vore, D. (1972). Development of conservation in normal and retarded children. *Developmental Psychology, 6*(1), 146–157.

Gustafson, G. (1984). Effects of the ability to locomote on infant's social and exploratory behaviors. *Developmental Psychology, 20*, 39–405.

Harris, R. (1978). Impulse control in deaf children: Research and clinical issues. In L. Liben (Ed.), *Deaf children developmental perspectives*. New York: Academic Press.

Heffernan, L., Black, F., & Poche, P. (1982). Temperament patterns in young neurologically handicapped children. *Journal of Pediatric Psychology, 7*, 415–423.

Heider, F., & Heider, G. (1941). Studies in the psychology of the deaf. *Psychological Monographs, 242*.

Horn, D., Lord, E. Lorch, F., & Culatto, B. (1985). Distractability and vocabulary deficits in children with spina bifida and hydrocephalus. *Developmental Medicine and Child Neurology, 16*, 180–185.

Hubert, N., & Wachs, T. (1985). Parental perceptions of the behavioral components of infant easiness-difficult-ness. *Child Development, 56*, 1525–1537.

Inhelder, B. (1968). *The diagnosis of reasoning in the mentally retarded*. New York: Day.

Kahn, J. (1976). Utility of the Uzgiris and Hunt Scales of Sensorimotor Development with severely and pro-foundly retarded children. *American Journal of Mental Deficiency, 80*(6), 663–665.

Kahn, J. (1978). Acceleration of object permanence with severely and profoundly retarded children. *AAESPH Review*, March, 15–22.

Kahn, J. (1984). Cognitive training and its relationship to the language of retarded children. In J. Berg (Ed.), *Perspectives and Progress in mental retardation*. Baltimore: University Park Press.

Karagan, N. (1979). Intellectual functioning in Duchenne muscular distrophy: A review. *Psychological Bulle-tine, 86*, 250–259.

Keogh, B., & Pullis, M. (1980). Temperament influences on the development of exceptional children. In B. Keogh (Ed.), *Advances in special education* (Vol. 1).

Kogan, K. (1980). Interaction systems between preschool handicapped or developmentally delayed children and their parents. In T. Field (Ed.), *High risk infants and children: Adult and peer interactions*. New York: Academic Press.

Kopp, C., & Shaperman, J. (1973). Cognitive development in the absence of object manipulation during infancy. *Developmental Psychology, 9*, 430.

Landau, B., Gleitman, H., & Spelke, E. (1981). Spatial knowledge and geometric representation in a child blind from birth. *Science, 213*, 1275–1278.

Leibowitz, D., & Dubowitz, V. (1981). Intellect and behavior in Duchenne muscular distrophy. *Developmental Medicine and Child Neurology, 23*, 577–590.

Levy-Schiff, R., & Hoffman, M. (1985). Social behavior of learning impaired and normally hearing pre-schoolers. *British Journal of Educational Psychology, 55*, 111–118.

Lubin, B., & Sherrill, C. (1980). Motor creativity of preschool deaf children. *American Annuals of the Deaf, 125*, 460–466.

MacDougall, J., & Rabinovitch, S. (1971). Early auditory deprivation and sensory compensation. *Developmen-tal Psychology, 5*, 368.

Marquis, P., Palmer, F., Mahoney, W., & Capute, A. (1982). Extrapyramidal cerebral palsy: A changing view. *Developmental and Behavioral Pediatrics, 3*, 65–68.

Meadow, K. (1975). The development of deaf children. In E. M. Hetherington, J. Hagen, R. Kron, & A. Stein (Eds.), *Review of child development research* (Vol. 5). Chicago: University of Chicago Press.

Meadow, K. (1980). *Deafness and child development*. Berkeley: University of California Press.

Mundy, P., Siebert, J., & Hogan, A. (1984). Relationship between sensorimotor and communication abilities in developmentally delayed children. *Merrill-Palmer Quarterly, 30*, 33–46.

Mykelbust, H. (1964). *The psychology of deafness*. New York: Grune & Stratton.

Neilson, H. (1971). Psychological appraisal of children with cerebral palsy. *Developmental Medicine and Child Neurology, 13*, 707–720.

Reynell, J. (1978). Developmental patterns of visually handicapped children. *Child Care, Health, and Devel-opment, 4*, 291-303.

Richardson, S. (1969). The effects of physical disability on the socialization of a child. In D. Goslin (Ed.), *Handbook of socialization theory and research*. Chicago: Rand McNally.

Rogers, S. (1977). Characteristics of the cognitive development of profoundly retarded children. *Child Devel-opment, 48*, 837–893.

Rosenzweig, M. (1966). Environmental complexity, cerebral change and behavior. *American Psychologist, 21*, 3321–332.

Rutter, M. (1972). Childhood schizophrenia reconsidered. *Journal of Autism and Childhood Schizophrenia, 2*, 315–337.

Rutter, M. (1978). Brain damage syndromes in childhood. In S. Chess & A. Thomas (Eds.), *Annual progress in child psychiatry and child development*. New York: Brunner-Mazel.

Rutter, M., & Lockyer, L. (1967a). A five to fifteen year follow-up study of infantile psychosis: 1. Description of the sample. *British Journal of Psychiatry, 113*, 1169–1182.

Rutter, M., & Lockyer, L. (1967b). A five to fifteen year follow-up study of infantile psychosis: 2. Social and behavioral outcome. *British Journal of Psychiatry, 113*, 1183–1199.

Sameroff, A., & Chandler, M. (1975). Reproductive risk and the continuum of caretaking casuality. In P. Horowitz (Ed.), *Review of Child Development Research* (Vol. 3). Chicago: University of Chicago Press.

Sandler, A. (1963). Aspects of passivity and ego development in the blind child. *Psychoanalytic Study of the Child, 10*, 343–360.

Schimer, B. (1985). An analysis of the language of young hearing impaired children in terms of syntax, semantics and use. *American Annuals of the Deaf, 100*, 15–19.

Schlesinger, H. (1978). The effects of deafness on child development: An Ericksonian perspective. In L. Liben (Ed.), *Deaf children: Developmental perspectives*. New York: Academic Press.

Schlesinger, H., & Meadow, K. (1972). *Sound and sign: Childhood deafness and mental health*. Berkeley: University of California Press.

Scott, R. (1969). The socialization of blind children. In D. Goslin (Ed.), *Handbook of socialization theory and research*. Chicago: Rand McNally.

Seidel, U., Chadewick, D., & Rutter, M. (1975). Psychological disorders in crippled children: A comparative study of children with and without brain damage. *Developmental Medicine and Child Neurology, 17*, 563–573.

Smits, B., & Mommers, M. (1976). Differences between blind and sighted children on WISC verbal subtests. *New Outlook for the Blind, 70*, 240–246.

Spain, B. (1974). Verbal and performance ability in preschool children with spina bifida. *Developmental Medicine and Child Neurology, 16*, 773–780.

Spitz, H. (1983). Critique of the developmental position in mental retardation research. *Journal of Special Education, 17*, 261–294.

Sterritt, G., Camp, B., & Lysman, B. (1966). Effects of early auditory deprivation upon auditory and visual information processing. *Perceptual Motor Skills, 23*, 123–130.

Thomas, A., & Chess, S. (1977). *Temperament and development*. New York: Brunner/Mazel.

Thomas, A., Chess, S., & Birch, H. (1968). *Temperament and behavior disorders in children*. New York: University Park Press.

Uzgiris, I., & Benson, J. (1980). *Infant use of sound in search for objects*. Paper presented to the International Conference on Infant Studies, New Haven, April.

Uzgiris, I., & Hunt, J. (1975). *Assessment in infancy: Ordinal scales of psychological development*. Urbana: University of Illinois Press.

Vandell, D., & George, L. (1981). Social interaction in hearing and deaf preschoolers: Successes and failures in initiations. *Child Development, 52*, 627–635.

Vandell, D., Anderson, L., Ehrhardt, G., & Wilson, K. (1982). Integrating hearing and deaf preschoolers. *Child Development, 53*, 1354–1363.

VanderVeer, B., & Schweid, E. (1974). Infant assessment: Stability of mental functioning in young retarded children. *American Journal of Mental Deficiency, 79*(1), 1–4.

Van Lieshout, C. (1973). *The assessment of stability and change in per interactions of normal hearing and deaf preschool children*. Paper presented to the International Society for the Study of Behavioral Development, Ann Arbor, August.

Wassermann, G., Allen, R., & Solomon, C. (1985). At risk toddlers and their mothers: The special case of physical handicap. *Child Development, 56*, 73–83.

Wedell-Monig, J., & Lumley, J. (1980). Child deafness and mother-child interaction. *Child Development, 55*, 766–774.

Weisz, J., & Zigler, E. (1979). Cognitive development in retarded and non-retarded persons: Piagetian tests of the similar sequence hypothesis. *Psychological Bulletin, 86*, 831–851.

Wilton, K., & Boersma, F. (1974). Conservation research with the mentally retarded. In N. Ellis (Ed.), *International review of research in mental retardation* (Vol. 8). New York: Academic Press.

Zigler, E. (1969) Developmental versus difference theories of mental retardation and the problem of motivation. *American Journal of Mental Deficiency, 73*, 536–566.

2

Essential Elements of
the Assessment Process

Rune J. Simeonsson and Donald B. Bailey, Jr.

The commitment to early intervention for handicapped infants and young children is reflected in the rapid growth of a variety of home- and center-based programs in recent years. Although the need for such programs has been established, documentation has been more difficult to achieve. Central to these problems has been the fact that the assessment instruments and procedures have been less than adequate to meet the unique demands of an immature population with limited functional skills that are often confounded by sensory and motor impairments. The special assessment problems associated with early intevention have been elaborated in a number of contributions to the literature (Bricker, 1978; Simeonsson, Huntington, & Parse, 1980). Although these assessments problems have had a negative effect in complicating the documentation of early intervention effects, they have had a positive effect in highlighting the need for alternative assessment instruments and procedures in broad (Bricker, 1978) as well as specific (Cicchetti & Sroufe, 1976) domains of development. Given this context, the purpose of this chapter is to (a) define the role of assessment with handicapped infants and young children, (b) discuss the particular problem of population variability in assessment, (c) review several models for specifying child characteristics; and (d) propose elements of an assessment approach for describing children in terms of their functional capabilities.

THE ROLE OF ASSESSMENT IN EARLY INTERVENTION

Assessment is defined in this chapter as the systematic use of direct as well as indirect procedures to document the characteristics of a target of interest. This target is often a single child, but it may also be a group of children or for that matter, an inanimate target, such as physical setting. Although it is beyond the scope of this chapter to review specific ecological assessment procedures, we support the trend toward more comprehensive assessment of the child's larger social and physical context (Bailey, Clifford, & Harms, 1982), a trend that is elaborated in Chapter 16 of this book.

RUNE J. SIMEONSSON and DONALD B. BAILEY, JR. ● School of Education and FAMILIES Project, Carolina Institute for Research on Early Education of the Handicapped, Frank Porter Graham Child Development Center, University of North Carolina, Chapel Hill, North Carolina 27599.

Purpose of Assessment

The purpose of the assessment of handicapped infants and young children is, in a general sense, the same as it is for any individual, namely, the derivation of information to facilitate decision making. In actuality, assessment is a process with many component parts, as displayed in Figure 1. Typically a problem, such as delayed development, presents itself in one form or another. A short screening process aids in the determination of whether a more detailed assessment is called for. The detailed assessment, usually consisting of a combination of interviews, observations, and direct testing, provides the core of information necessary for informal decision-making. Several kinds of decisions are likely to be made on the basis of assessment data. One type of decision is diagnostic, either confirming or disconfirming a diagnostic entity such as mental retardation or autism. A second type of decision pertains to the documentation of status, that is the definition of the child's current capabilities and/or deficits. Assessment for this purpose is likely to be made at an initial point and, to be repeated on one or more occasions following intervention to demonstrate progress. A third type of decision focuses on the prescription of an appropriate intervention matched to the assessed needs of the child. In early intervention efforts, these decisions are not mutually exclusive, and data from the same assessment may serve several purposes simultaneously. Unfortunately, the problems associated with assessing this population appear to be differentially limiting on the decisions that can be made. For example, assessment for prescribing individualized treatment can be highly informal and idiosyncratic, whereas the diagnosis or documentation of status requires assessment that is typically formal and standardized.

Interpreting Assessment Information

In order for assessment information to be used to make decisions regarding status, diagnosis, prescription, or progress, it must be interpeted. The two major strategies for interpreting assessment data are the norm-referenced and the criterion-referenced approaches to evaluation. The strategy adopted for a particular child may be dictated to some extent, by the purpose of the assessment, as we have just indicated. In instances where the characteristics and/or the performance of a child is to be compared or generalized to that of a peer group, normative measures are required. The identification of a child's characteristcs for the purpose of developing a treatment program, on the other hand, is often based on criterion-referenced measures, as the focus is idiosyncratic rather than normative. The advantages and disadvantages of each model have been discussed extensively elsewhere (see the introduction to this book, also see Ebel, 1978; Popham, 1978) and will not be addressed here.

When using assessment data to document child progress, however, neither approach has proved to be completely satisfactory, particularly when evaluating the progress of handicapped youngsters. For example, norm-referenced measures raise problems because normative groups typically contain few, if any, handicapped children; the large steps between items result in an inability to measure small gains; and the content of the instruments may not reflect what is being taught in early intervention programs. Criterion-referenced measures may be unwieldy because the number of criterion-specific items needed may be large, and measures may yield serious measurement problems when quantification procedures, such as percentage of items passed, are used as the criterion.

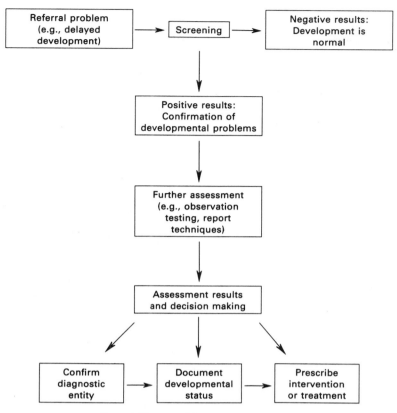

Figure 1. Elements of the assessment process.

In response to this situation, there have been several proposals for alternative documentation of the outcomes for children provided early intervention. As summarized in Table 1, the proposals seem to share a common orientation in what may be defined as an "expectancy-referenced" approach to documenting child progress.

The rate index of Brassell (1977) and the intervention efficiency index of Bagnato and Neisworth (1980) are essentially ratio indices of the amount of change shown by a child over a specified period of time. For example, the intervention efficiency index for Child A, who made 8 months of progress during a 10-month intervention period, would be .8, as opposed to an indes of 1.2 for Child B, who made 12 months of progress during the same period. The indices proposed by Simeonsson and Wiegerink (1975) and by Wolery (1983), on the other hand, require that the rate of change be qualified in terms of the functional capacity of the child. For example, the efficiency index for Child A, who at the beginning of intervention was progressing at a developmental rate on half that of her normal peers, would be 1.6, and for Child B, who at the beginning of intervention was progressing at a developmental rate, would be 1.2. Thus, Child A, made greater progress relative to her initial developmental status. Actual progress in intervention is compared to progress that would be expected on the basis of previous development.

Although each of these "expectancy-referenced" approaches does represent a posi-

Table 1. Approaches to Documenting Child Progress: Illustrations for
Two Children in a 10-Month Intervention Program

Approach	Variables	Child A $CA=12, DA=6$ $DQ=50$ Gain=8 months	Child B $CA=8, DA=8$ $DQ=100$ Gain=12 months
Developmental rate (Brassel, 1977)	$\dfrac{\text{Developmental gain}}{\text{Duration of intervention}}$	$\dfrac{8\text{ months}}{10\text{ months}}=.8$	$\dfrac{12\text{ months}}{10\text{ months}}=1.2$
Efficiency index (Simeonsson & Wiegerink, 1975)	$\dfrac{\text{Actual gain}}{\text{Ideal gain}} / \text{Devel. status}$	$\dfrac{8\text{ months}}{10\text{ months}} / .50=1.6$	$\dfrac{12\text{ months}}{10\text{ months}} / 1=1.2$
Intervention efficiency index (Bagnato & Neisworth, 1980)	$\dfrac{\text{Developmental gain}}{\text{Duration of intervention}}$	$\dfrac{8\text{ months}}{10\text{ months}}=.8$	$\dfrac{12\text{ months}}{10\text{ months}}=1.2$
Proportional change index (Wolery, 1983)	$\dfrac{\text{Develop. gain}}{\text{Duration interv.}} / \dfrac{\text{Pre-test DA}}{\text{Pre-test CA}}$	$\dfrac{8\text{ mos}}{10\text{ mos}} / \dfrac{6\text{ mos}}{12\text{ mos}}=1.6$	$\dfrac{12\text{ mos}}{10\text{ mos}} / \dfrac{8\text{ mos}}{8\text{ mos}}=1.2$

tive step to account for change in a child they are, in general, limited by a fundamental assumption pertaining to the relationship to age-equivalent performance and the duration of the intervention defined in terms of age. As we have pointed out elsewhere (Simeonsson, 1982) this assumption may yield numerically meaningful data but may not be defensible on conceptual grounds.

A more recently advocated approach, goal attainment scaling, however, is not tied to age-referenced data and may thus provide a viable "expectancy-referenced" means of documenting and evaluating child outcome in early intervention (Cooper, & Scheiner, 1982). Goal attainment scaling requires, first, the specifications of goals or objectives for intervention. Five possible outcome levels are generated for each goal, ranging from worst expected outcome (generally no progress at all or, in some cases, regression) to best expected outcome (the best outcome of intervention that is realistically possible). Each outcome level receives a numerical value ranging from -2 to $+2$ and can be weighted according to priorities. One of the particularly attractive features of this approach is that an index that is both numerically and conceptually meaningful can be derived from highly idiosyncratic data for individual children.

POPULATION AND DEFINITIONAL VARIABILITY IN ASSESSMENT

A persistent and pervasive problem in the field of early intervention is the hetero-geneity of populations and the attendant variability of the definitions used to describe them in clinical as well as research contexts. Children vary widely not only in terms of the nature and frequency of their handicapping conditions but also in terms of their sever-ity. The complexity of this situation is perhaps best exemplified by the difficulties that have been encountered in attempts to define "severely handicapped" populations. The issues discussed by Sontag, Smith, and Sailor (1977) and by Dollar and Brooks (1980) reflect the range of characteristics that are considered under this label. Central to those problems is the fact that the factors considered in arriving at definitions are not unidimen-sional but multidimensional. Furthermore, the dimensions may vary in the absolute versus relative status they reflect. Thus, structural characteristics such as sensory or mo-tor impairment constitute absolute status, whereas cognitive, motor, and other domains of functioning constitute status relative to development. The net effect, as we have dis-cussed elsewhere (Simeonsson, 1986), is that the categories currently used with excep-tional children reflect an arbitary focus on absolute dimensions in defining one group and relative dimensions in defining another group.

It can be argued that infants and young children with special needs have been, and will continue to be, identified for intervention services in spite of definitional problems. There is, however, a need to address these problems on the basis of pragmatic as well as scientific issues. Pressures for ensuring the accountability of early intervention will de-mand precision in the practical problem of identifying eligible children. In a scientific context, interest in inferring casual relationships between intervention and outcome will demand greater attention to the precise classification of child characteristics. The docu-mentation of the effectiveness, efficiency, and generalizability of interventions for special infants and children depends, at last in part, on the precision with which the population is defined.

A common problem in the identification of special children is the interchangeable use of definitional terms. Terms such as *handicapped, disabled,* and *impaired* are often combined arbitrarily with adjectives such as *mentally, physically,* or *emotionally* in the description of children. These terms should not be used interchangeably, as their mean-ings differ substantially. The World Health Organization (WHO, 1980) classification approach, in fact, builds on the premise that there is a hierarchical relationship between these sets of terms, so that a structural *impairment* (e.g., a skeletal impairment) may or may not result in a disability (e.g., a locomotor disability), which may or may not result in a label of handicap (e.g., "mobility handicap"). An approach such as this would obviously serve to reduce the semantic ambiguity pertaining to commonly used terms. A related semantic issue is the use of the prefix *multiple* to define children who have more than one identified problem. Holt (1977) emphasized that this prefix should not be auto-matically generalized from impairment to disability to handicap for a child. A child with multiple impairments is not necessarily multiply handicapped, and a child who is multi-ply handicapped may have only a single impairment.

The major issue in defining special children pertains to the conceptual framework within which they have been viewed. The commonly used system of categorizing chil-dren as mentally retarded, orthopedically impaired, and so on appears to be typological in nature; that is, children are assigned to one of a set of mutually exclusive categories. Kenden (1983) contrasted the categorical format to the dimensional format, in which classification is based on continuous rather than discrete variation. An examination of the classification system in use in the field of special education suggests that it is categorical in some respects and dimensional in others. The conceptual problems inherent in this situation and the practical implications for placement and intervention have undoubtedly been the impetus for recommendations of the use of cross-categorical as well as noncategorical approaches with special children in educational as well as medical contexts (Stein & Jessop, 1983).

Causal inference and generalizability are two major issues of scientific concern in regard to intervention for children. *Causal inference* refers to the question of whether outcomes are functionally related to intervention. For example, did the 6 hours per week of physical therapy *cause* the child to walk at an earlier age than he could have with no intervention? *Generalizability* addresses the issue of whether the effect of intervention is applicable to other children with similar characteristics and needs. For example, given that a motor-skill training-program was effective with a group of children with motor impairments, does it follow that the program will be effective with *all* motorically impaired children?

Empirical evidence that would answer these questions has been qualified by the methodological analytic limitations inherent in much of the research (Dunst & Rheingrover, 1981; Simeonsson, *et al.*, 1982). The equivocal nature of the evidence has resulted in significant debate (Bricker & Sheehan, 1981) and in recommendations of alternative approaches that would address these questions. Among these approaches are more comprehensive and sensitive assessment (Simeonsson *et al.*, 1980), including such domains as rhythmic habit patterns, state of arousal, sensorimotor functions, and temperament. Alternate research paradigms more suited to the unique problems encountered in the evaluation of early intervention programs have also been recommended (Sheehan & Keogh, 1982). These recommendations have resulted in increased attention to assessment strategies and evaluation models and should lead to more sensitive and relevant evidence on the effectiveness of early intervention. It is the premise of this chapter, however, that greater precision in defining special children is a neglected and needed component in improving the overall quality of the scientific findings. To this end, we will review several models that specify child characteristics, and we propose a specific method applicable to clinical as well as research settings.

MODELS FOR THE SPECIFICATION OF CHILD CHARACTERISTICS

Although the issue of definitions and classifications of children has not been without interest to the field, the focus has often been practical rather than theoretical. A representative issue, for example, has been how to classify children in a non- or cross-categorical manner for common educational placement. The major exception was the work headed by Hobbs (1975, 1978) on the status of classification of children. His ecological orientation to classification is an interesting, but apparently not widely adopted, approach based on theory. In considering alternative models for special children, we have therefore drawn on literature from fields other than education in which classification models have been developed. In reviewing the available models, several criteria were used to identify those that might be applicable to special childen. To be applicable, models should be comprehensive in scope, should focus on function and should be easy to use. Three models were identified that seemed applicable in this regard. These models—the global index approach, multiaxial classification, and the profiling of functional capacities—are reviewed below.

Global Index

One approach to defining the status of an individual is to assign a global index to reflect functioning from the most impaired to the most healthy level. This approach has been used in psychiatric settings to define severity of disturbance in adults (Endicott, Spitzer, & Fleiss, 1976). The premise of this approach is that individual functioning at a particular time can be documented in a single index, with values ranging from 1 (most impaired) to 100 (most healthy), thus conveying clinical meaningfulness. The Children's Global Assessment Scale (CGAS—Shaffer, Gould, Brasic, Ambrosini, Fisha, Bird, & Aluwahlia, 1983), adopted from the Global Assessment Scale (GAS—Endicott et al, 1976) consists of 10 levels of descriptions of functioning on a hyopthetical continuum, with the lowest level defined as "needs constant supervision" (10–1) and the highest as "superior functioning in all areas" (100–91). The use of intermediate values within a level (e.g., 37, 53, 76) is recommended to rate the actual functioning of the child. In a study using case vignettes with child psychiatry fellows (Shaffer et al., 1983), a correlation coefficient of .84 was obtained for interrater reliability. An analysis of the test–retest reliability of this global index yielded coefficients ranging from .69 to .95, revealing generally high consistency over time. The CGAS was also found to differentiate subgroups on the basis of severity. The assets of this approach are thus not only its general, global focus on functioning but also its relative simplicity. As the scale is designed to be non-syndrome-specific, the actual scale could be directly adopted for use with handicapped children.

Although differing somewhat in format, two other models have been reported that also yield single overall indices and may have heuristic value. The Patient Severity Index (Horn, Cashick, & Clayton, et al., 1980) appears in a matrix form in which seven variables characterizing the patient are rated on severity scales with rankings from 1 to 4 (e.g., low, moderate, major, and extreme). An overall severity index can be derived. An interesting, but very specialized model is the diagnostic index described by Preus and Rex (1983) for diagnosing children with Brackman–DeLange syndrome. Thirty separate characteristics are scored dichotomously and are added to yield a total score reflecting the presence or absence of the syndrome. The implication of this model is that commonly used, but vague, categories of exceptionality could be redefined in a similar manner to maximize the accuracy of identification.

Multiaxial Classification

The classification of individual characteristics on mutually exclusive axes is a practice that has also been explored in medical and psychiatric contexts. The premise of multiaxial classification systems is that the complexity of a person's problems or needs can be represented as numerical values on multiple axes. Meads (1983), for example, proposed a multiaxial format for classifying patients' reason for encounter within the context of World Health Organization efforts. Also of interest to WHO has been the multiaxial classification of child psychiatric disorders (Rutter, Shaffer, & Shepherd, 1975). The first axis of this classification system defines the psychiatric syndrome in terms of nine major categories. The second axis defines intellectual level, and the third permits the coding of biological factors in terms of the nature of the disorder. The fourth axis defines psychosocial variables. In an evaluation study, Rutter and his colleagues (1975) found multiaxial classification to be a reliable system of defining children with psychiatric disorders and to have greater clinical discriminability than the DSM-II system (American Psychiatric Association, 1968).

The value of a multiaxial approach to the classification of handicapped infants and young children lies in the fact that a common system could be used with all children, regardless of the nature or the severity of the handicapping condition. With a multiaxial system, it would thus be feasible to classify a very heterogenous group of special children along a number of axes in such a way that each child would be defined by a unique set of quantitative values. As an example of the summarizing and comparative utility of this approach, the multiaxial system described by Rutter and his colleagues is used to define the characteristics of three types of handicapped children in Table 2. As illustrated in the table, the commonalities among the mentally retarded, orthopedically impaired, and visually impaired youngsters are documented. The unique characteristics of each child are also evident by the codes assigned on the four axes, yielding a distinct summary index.

Profile of Functional Capacities

The profile approach to the documentation of individual characteristics has been used with some frequency in psychological and educational assessment. Common applications of this approach involve subscale analyses of intelligence and achievement tests. The popularity of this approach may be due in no small way to its value as a diagnostic tool. The use of profiles to identify or classify basic functional skills in children has,

Table 2. Illustration of Multiaxial Classification[a] of Three Handicapped Preschool Children

Child	First axis		Second axis		Third axis		Fourth axis	
	Code	Category	Code	Category	Code	Category	Code	Category
Mentally retarded	9.0	Manifestation of mental subnormality	3	Severe retardation	4.8	Other chromosome abnormality	0	Normal psychosocial variation
Motor impaired	1.0	Adaptation reaction	1	Mild retardation	8.1	Postnatal cerebral palsy	2	Excess of parental control
Visually impaired	0.0	Normal variation	0	Normal variation	9.1	Blindness	0	Normal psychosocial variation

[a]Rutter, Shaffer, and Shepherd (1975).

however, been limited. The premise of a profile approach to identify and classify hand-icapped children rests on the basis of a defined set of functional capacities, rather than on the nature or etiology of the handicapping condition.

Two models have been developed to facilitate the documentation of children's abili-ties and disabilities. Both of these models, developed in England, are based on a practical system developed for use in the classification of personnel in the armed forces. The earlier of these systems was proposed by Holt (1957) as a means of drawing "a profile of disabilities. The profiles will show the nature of help needed by the handicapped children and will allow the selection, from a group, of those children who will benefit from any particular form of assistance" (p. 226). The model is known as the PULHESTIB system, based on the initial letters of the nine functions that are assessed. These functions are (P) physique, (U) upper limits, (L) locomotion, (H) hearing, (E) eyes, (S) speech, (T) toilet, (I) intelligence, and (B) behavior. Each function is divided into four grades, with 1 representing normal functions and 4 complete absence or impairment of function. As Holt (1957) showed, the PULHESTIB system may be particularly useful in documenting the case history of a particular child. A similar system, known as PULSES, has been used in a study on treatment effectiveness in cerebral palsy (Goldkamp, 1984.)

A second model, proposed by Lindon (1963), involves a format that resembles Holt's system but was designed to emphasize positive functional capacities and to in-crease the sensitivity of the grading of each function. According to Lindon, "the PULTIBEC System was evolved as an attempt to fulfill the recognized need for a global, yet concise, system for coding the difficulties of children with multiple handicaps in functional terms" (p. 143). The functions assessed in this system are (P) physical capac-ity, (U) upper limits, (L) locomotive, (T) toilet, (I) intelligence, (B) behavior, (E) vision, and (C) communication. Each of these functions is graded from 1 to 6, the former denot-ing normality and the latter functional uselessness. A very useful feature of the PULTIBEC system is that several functions are subdivided to permit greater specification of function. Thus, the assessment of upper limits involves the arm and hands on both sides of the body, and locomotion involves a separate assessment of right and left limits. Furthermore, intermediate gradings of .5 are possible for upper and lower limits. Visual function is documented for each eye, and communication involves an assessment of both hearing and speech. The PULTIBEC profiles of the three hypothetical cases already used in the previous tables are illustated in Table 3.

The value of the PULTIBEC system is that it provides a "profile of a child's func-tional abilities which can be read at a glance" (Lindon, 1963, p. 126). The PULTIBEC profile can also be used to document change when repeated assessments are made of a child. A somewhat similar screening instrument (Perceptions of Developmental Skills Profile) has, in fact, been used to assess the prepost gains of handicapped preschool children (Bagnato, Neisworth, & Eaves, 1978).

Summary of Models

The three approaches reviewed in this chapter each have features that may be useful in improving the ways in which special children are defined and/or classified. The assets and limitations of each approach in this regard are summarized in Table 4.

One issue of importance to consider in the applicability of these appoaches is com-

Table 3. Illustration of the PULTIBEC System for Assessment of
Three Handicapped Preschool Children

Child	P	U Rt H	U Rt A	U Lt H	U Lt A	L Rt	L Lt	T	I	B	E Rt	E Lt	C H	C S
Mentally Retarded	3	2	2	2	2	2	2	3	5	2	1	1	1	3
Motor Impaired	4	6	6	3	3	6	3	6	4	2	1	1	2	5
Visually Impaired	2	1	1	1	1	1	1	2	2	2	6	6	1	1

prehensiveness. Each of the approaches has the flexibility of encompassing any type and severity of handicapping condition. The global index model seems, however, to be useful primarily in documenting the generic dimensions of functioning, whereas the other two approaches document functioning on multiple dimensions.

A second major issue to consider is the extent to which the dimensions used in defining child characteristics are permanent or developmental. The multiaxial approach involves classification on the basis of permanent characteristics, whereas the global index and the profile approach draw on permanent as well as developmental characteristics. The practical implication of these differences is that the classification of a child on the basis of a multiaxial approach is likely to remain unchanged over time, whereas some change is likely if the global index or the profile system is repeatedly used.

The nature of the classification system thus needs to be considered relative to the purpose of that classification. Classification may be carried out in order to determine eligibility for services as well as to document the characteristics of children for the purpose of drawing inferences about the generalizability of treatment effects. To this end, a global index approach may be very suitable to the identification and placement of children generally sharing similar characteristics. However, it is not likely to be a sensitive index in differentiating treatment effects. The multiaxial approach seems appropriate when a child's eligibility for, or provision of, services needs to be documented with particular reference to etiological factors. Such an approach would thus be applicable in medical or psychiatric settings. The arbitrary and nominal nature of some axes, however, would limit the usefulness of the multiaxial approach for the purpose of generalizing

Table 4. Comparison of Three Classification Models

Model	Nature of index	Focus of classification	Assets	Limitations
Global index	Single quantitative score (range) 0–100	Relative status characteristics	Comparisons across children can be made on the basis of single index; easy to comprehend	Single index may mask variability within and across children
Multiaxial	Four sets of digits	Relative and permanent status	Multiaxial nature portrays variability; model established in psychiatric, medical settings	Categories (axes) arbitrary; codes not numerically meaningful, making comparison of relative functioning impossible
Profile	Profile of ordinal values	Relative and permanent status	Values numerically meaningful; profile portrays relative functioning numerically and graphically	Functional areas are not equally important; hence, identical values in different areas may not reflect equal impact

treatment effects to other children. The profile approach, on the other hand, does not consider etiological factors and focuses on the variability of functional characteristics within and across children for eligibility and placement decisions. Furthermore, the profile approach, having a consistent ordinal format, should provide a basis for generalizing treatment effects relative to specific child characteristics. A useful classification system should thus emphasize permanent characteristics as the basis for classification.

ESSENTIAL ELEMENTS OF THE ASSESSMENT PROCESS

As we stated at the beginning of this chapter, an important, but inadequate, element of the assessment of handicapped infants and young children is the manner in which they are defined or classified. Lack of precision in definitional or classification systems has complicated both determination of eligibility and our ability to draw inferences about the generalizability of the findings. Given the issues and approaches pertaining to classification discussed in this chapter, we advocate far greater precision and systematization in the way in which handicapped infants and young children are defined. Such specification of child variables should be coupled with a specification of intervention variable and outcome variables as essential elements of the assessment process.

Specification of Child Variables

The interest in noncategorical and cross-categorical approaches in the field of special education and the recognition that the delivery of services to handicapped children is based on functional rather than etiological considerations provide support for the advocacy of a definitional system focusing on the functional characteristics of children. Furthermore, as we have already indicated, permanent, rather than developmental, dimensions would be the appropriate emphasis for classification, in that the defining characteristics of a child would remain stable over time. A profile system based primarily on permanent characteristics is thus advocated as an approach that can effectively represent the functional capacities of a child and that can be of practical utility as a classification index. The purpose of such a classification system should be to summarize in a global but concise manner the child's functional capacity. Although a large number of characteristics could be included, the use of a limited set of dimensions is important to ensure the practicality and simplicity of the system. The characteristics that seem essential in this regard are those pertaining to the integrity of the senses, upper and lower limb function, physical structure and tone, communication, and overall intellectual capacity. Drawing on Lindon's model, (1963), a six-level gradation seems necessary to adequately differentiate capacity in each of these functions.

Based on these considerations, we have developed the ABILITIES model summarized in Table 5 for defining the characteristics of handicapped infants and young children. The functions represented by the acronym are (A) audition; (B) behavior; (I) intelligence; (L) limb—arm—hand control; (I) interpersonal communication; (T) tonicity; (I) integrity—physical status; (E) extremities—lower; and (S) sight. Profiling of child characteristics on these dimensions should allow for documentation of the commonalities and the uniqueness of the children profiled. The applicability of this model is illustrated in Table 6 for the three hypothetical subjects shown in the earlier tables. An inspection of the table suggests that the potential value of a profile model is that it permits the classification of children along common dimensions in spite of differing etiologies and manifestations of handicapping conditions. Furthermore, the ABILITIES model, in contrast to the profile approaches of Lindon (1963) and Bagnato et al. (1978), reflects primarily permanent, rather than developmental, characteristics of the child. The utility of the ABILITIES model in specifying child characteristics systematically is being examined in research with handicapped youngsters.

Specification of Intervention Variables

A second important element associated with the assessment process is specifying intervention variables. As a frequent purpose of the assessment of handicapped children is to document child change as a function of treatment, it is essential that the dimensions of the intervention be detailed. The dimensions that should be specified include, but are not limited to, the duration, frequency, setting, and content of the intervention. Furthermore, the role of the child and the role of the interventionist in the intervention activities also need to be documented. The absence of such specification places substantial restrictions on the drawing of inferences about the generalizability of an intervention.

Specification of Outcome Variables

A third element of importance in the assessment of handicapped infants and young children is the selection and interpretation of the variables used to document intervention outcome.

Two considerations are important in this regard. First, outcome variables should be selected to match the focus of the interventions as closely as possible. Thus, if the focus of an intervention for a child is motor development, measures of intelligence or language are neither appropriate nor likely to reflect intervention outcomes. One or, preferably, several measures of motor functioning would be the outcome measures of choice. There are, of course, circumstances in which a battery of measures is administered, some of which are designed to assess generalization effects. The preoccupation with intelligence measures and the failure to select other measures sensitive to intervention in earlier research may be an unfortunate factor accounting for the difficulty of documenting the effectiveness of early intervention (Simeonsson, et al., 1982). Thus, we would advocate the inclusion of at least one outcome measure that is specifically matched to the focus of the intervention.

The second issue in regard to outcome variables pertains to the manner in which they are summarized and interpreted. Typically, the result of assessment yields outcome indices that reflect a child's representative performance. These outcome indices often take the form of a single value, such as a standardized score or an age equivalent. Although such values are frequently used to document outcome, they may fail to portray adequately the nature and the variability of the child's functioning or performance. Specification of the range, variability, and style of performance may yield information that complements or expands scores. Finally a description of the clinical and/or theoretical significance of the outcome index is also indicated because interventions are often proposed within a

Table 5. A Functional Definition of Child Status: The ABILITIES Model[a]

[a]Simeonsson and Bailey (1984). Symbol key: —×—, visually impaired: —○—, mentally retarded: —□—, motor impaired.

Table 6. Key to Table 5 (The ABILITIES Model)

Domain	Levels
A (Audition)	1. Normal 2. Suspected hearing impairment 3. Documented mild hearing impairment 4. Documented moderate hearing impairment 5. Documented severe hearing impairment 6. Documented profound hearing impairment; Deaf
B (Behavior)	1. Normal 2. Occasional expressions of unusual behavior 3. Occasional expressions of asocial/atypical behavior 4. Frequent expressions of asocial/atypical behavior 5. Frequent expressions of bizarre/atypical behavior 6. Constant expression of bizarre, atypical, out of control behavior
I (Intelligence)	1. Normal within expected rate of development for age 2. Slow (borderline) 3/4 rate of expected development for age 3. Mild MR—2/3 rate of expected development for age 4. Moderate MR—1/2 rate of expected rate of development for age 5. Severe MR—1/3 rate of expected development for age 6. Profound MR—1/4 rate of expected rate of development for age
L (Limbs-arms-hands)	1. Complete normal use 2. Some involvement but functional 3. Usable with minimal support 4. Usable with some support 5. Usable only with external support 6. Useless
I (Intentional communication)	1. Intentional communication adequate for age even if communication is nonverbval (e.g., signing, bliss symbols) 2. Intentional communication less than adequate for age but generally functional even if it is nonverbal 3. Limited use of idiosyncratic gestures/vocalizations 4. Ability to communicate very limited and/or setting specific 5. Only occasional evidence of some form of communication: primitive and basic in nature 6. No evidence of any form of intentional communication
T (Tonicity)	1. Normal 2. Variable but mostly normal 3. Mild degree 4. Moderate degree 5. Severe degree 6. Totally rigid/flaccid
I (Integrity of physical status)	1. Overall good health 2. Variable, more than normal health problems 3. Chronic but minor health problems 4. Chronic, controlled health problems 5. Chronic, uncontrolled health problems 6. Total incapacitation due to chronic health problems

(continued)

Table 6. (Continued)

Domain	Levels
E (Extremities—legs)	1. Complete normal use
	2. Some involvement but functional
	3. Usable with minimal support
	4. Usable with some support
	5. Usable only with external support
	6. Useless
S (Sight)	1. Normal
	2. Suspected visual impairment
	3. Documented mild visual impairment
	4. Documented moderate visual impairment
	5. Documented severe visual impairment
	6. Documented profound visual impairment; Blind

particular theoretical framework. The link between intervention and outcome should be evident in the presentation and interpretation of the outcome variables.

SUMMARY

This chapter has addressed elements that we feel are essential to the improvement of the assessment of young handicapped children. Although each of the elements can be considered individually, they are integrally linked in the implementation and evaluation of early interventions for children. The continued search for more effective and efficient interventions is contingent on improved precision in defining child characteristics, interventions, and outcome variables.

REFERENCES

American Psychiatric Association. (1968). *American psychiatry association diagnostic and statistic manual of mental disorders* (2nd ed.). Washington, DC: American Psychiatric Association.

Bagnato, S. J., Jr., Neisworth, J. T. (1980). The intervention efficiency index: An approach to preschool program accountability. *Exceptional Children 46*, 264–269.

Bagnato, S. J., Neisworth, J. T., & Eaves, R.C. (1978). A profile of perceived capabilities for the preschool child. *Child Care Quarterly, 7*, 327–335.

Bailey, D. B., Clifford, R. M., & Harms, R. (1982). Comparison of preschool environments for handicapped and nonhandicapped children. *Topics in Early Childhood Special Education, 2*(1), 9–20.

Brassell, D. R. (1977). Intervention with handicapped infants: Correlates of progress. *Mental Retardation, 15*, 18–22.

Bricker, D. (1978). Early intervention: The criteria of success. *Allied Health and Behavioral Sciences, 1*, 567–582.

Bricker, P. & Sheehan, R. (1981). Effectiveness of an early intervention program as indexed by child change. *Journal of the Division for Early Childhood, 4*, 11–27.

Cicchetti, D., & Sroufe, A. (1976). The relationship between affective and cognitive development in Down syndrome infants. *Child Development, 47*, 920–920.

Dollar, S. J., & Brooks, C. (1980). Assessment of severely and profoundly handicapped individuals. *Exceptional Education Quarterly, 1,* 87–101.

Dunst, C. J., & Rheingrover, R.M. (1981). An analysis of the efficacy of infant intervention programs with organically handicapped children. *Evaluation and Program Planning, 4,* 287–323.

Ebel, R. L. (1978). The case for norm-referenced measurements. *Educational Researcher,* 7(11), 3–5.

Endicott, J., Spitzer, R. L., & Fleiss, J. L. (1976). The Global Assessment Scale: A procedure for measuring overall severity of psychiatric disturbance. *Archives of General Psychiatry, 33,* 766–771.

Goldkamp, O. (1984). Treatment effectiveness in cerebral palsy. *Archives of Physical Medicine and Rehabilitation, 65,* 232–234.

Hobbs, N. (1978). Classification options. *Exceptional Children, 44,* 494–497.

Hobbs, N. (1975). *The future of children.* San Francisco: Jossey Bass.

Holt, K. S. (1957). A suggested medical classification of handicapped children. *Archives of the Diseases of Childhood, 32,* 226–229.

Holt, K. S. (1977). *Developmental pediatrics: Perspectives and Practice.* London: Butterworth.

Horn, S. O., Cashick, B., & Clayton, C. (1980). Measuring severity of illness; A reliability study. *Medical Care, 21,* 705–714.

Kenden, R. E. (1983). The principles of classification in relation to mental disease. In M. Shepard & O.L. Zangwill (Eds.), *Handbook of psychiatry: Vol. 1. General psychopathology,* Cambridge: Cambridge University Press.

Lindon, R. L. (1963). The Pultibec system for the medical assessment of handicapped children. *Developmental Medicine and Child Neurology, 5,* 125–145.

Meads, S. (1983). The World Health Organization's reason-for-encounter classification. *WHO Chronicle, 37,* 159-162.

Popham, W. J. (1978). The case for criterion-referenced measurements. *Educational Researcher,* 7(11), 6–10.

Preus, M., & Rex, A. P. (1983). Definition and diagnosis of the Brachmann-DeZange syndrome. *American Journal of Medical Genetics, 16,* 301–312.

Rutter, M., Shaffer, D., & Shepherd, M. (1975). *A multi-axial classification of child psychiatric disorders.* Geneva: World Health Organization.

Shaffer, D., Gould, M.S., Brasic, J., Ambrosini, P., Fisha, P., Bird, H., & Aluwahlia, S. (1983). A Children's Global Assessment Scale. *Archives of General Psychiatry, 40,* 1228–1231.

Sheehan, R., & Keogh, B. (1982). Design and analysis in the evaluation of early childhood special education program. *Topics in Early Childhood Special Education, 1,* 81–88.

Simeonsson, R. J., (1982). Intervention, accountability and efficiency indices: :A rejoinder. *Exceptional Children, 48,* 358–359.

Simeonsson, R. J. (1986). *Psychological and developmental assessment of special children.* Boston: Allyn & Bacon.

Simeonsson, R. J., Huntington, S. S., & Parse, S. A. (1980). Assessment of children with severe handicaps: Multiple problems, multivariate goals. *Journal of the Association for the Severely Handicapped, 5,* 55–72.

Simeonsson, R. J., & Wiegerink, R. (1975). Accountability: A dilemma in infant intervention. *Exceptional Children, 41,* 474–481.

Simeonsson, R. J., Cooper, D. H., & Scheiner, A. P. (1982). A review and analysis of the effectiveness of early intervention program. *Pediatrics, 69,* 635–641.

Sontag, E., Smith, J., & Sailor, W. (1977). The severely/profoundly handicapped: Who are they? Where are they? *Journal of Special Education, 11,* 5–11.

Stein, R. E., & Jessop, R. E. K., (1983). A noncategorical appoach to chronic childhood illness. *Public Health Reports, 97,* 354–362.

Wolery, M. (1983). Proportional change index: An alternative for comparing child change data. *Exceptional Children,* 1983, 50, 167–170.

World Health Organization. (1980). International Classification of Impairment Disabilities and Handicaps. Geneva: Author

3

Instrument Selection

Nancy C. Hubert and Jan L. Wallander

Assessment of developmentally disabled infants and preschoolers is a vital yet challenging task. Throughout the development of disabled children, assessments are conducted across numerous skill domains to aid in the multiple decisions that face affected parents and professionals. However, because of the great variation in the type, degree, and display of developmental disabilities, these children can seemingly defy standardized assessment. Nonetheless, professionals from many disciplines are repeatedly confronted with decisions, if not dilemmas, regarding how best is the selection of instruments for assessment. Three major types of considerations are involved in selecting an instrument: *practical considerations, psychometric considerations and consideration of the assessment objectives.* This chapter will discuss each of these, with the greatest emphasis placed on assessment objectives. The goal is to articulate a model or strategy for making decisions regarding the selection of assessment instruments for developmentally disabled children. The resulting model represents an attempt to integrate these three major types of considerations. Particular reference will be made to the assessment of cognitive abilities because of the authors' familiarity with this area; however, it is our belief that the discussion is applicable to the assessment of other abilities as well.

PRACTICAL CONSIDERATIONS

Numerous practical concerns impinge upon every assessment problem. They are immediately introduced by considering several of the parameters of most assessments: an assessment typically involves a procedure applied by a clinician in a particular setting to a client about whom questions have been raised. Each of these parameters gives rise to practical issues that need to be considered in selecting an assessment procedure. Some of these issues limit, or even dictate, this choice and must therefore be carefully considered before selecting a particular strategy. They may be thought of as primary issues. Other issues exist that should be considered after the primary issues have been dealt with appropriately. These secondary issues, though not unimportant, enter into the selection equation if alternatives remain following the satisfaction of the primary concerns. A final point before specifying some practical considerations in selecting assessment procedures

NANCY C. HUBERT and JAN L. WALLANDER • Sparks Center for Developmental and Learning Disorders, and the Department of Psychology, University of Alabama at Birmingham, Birmingham, Alabama 35233.

is that, in most cases, these represent dimensions on which instruments vary. For example, a particular procedure may be *more or less* suitable for physically handicapped children, costly, or appealing to consumers.

The primary practical considerations involve the suitability of the assessment procedure for the particular handicap displayed by the child. To determine this suitability necessitates a knowledge of the child's sensory and response capabilities and how these will meet the sensory and response demands required to complete the procedure. Sattler (1982) and Ulrey and Rogers (1982) have discussed this point in more detail. In brief, however, procedures may require the child to have basic sensory functions, such as vision and hearing. Required response capabilities might include speech, arm–hand use, independent sitting, and/or balance. All tests administered directly to the child require some ability to indicate reliably an affirmative and a negative response, even if only through minimal nonverbal means (e.g., eye gaze or head nod). Most tests however, require a much more varied and specific response repertoire. Certain types of tests, therefore, obviously cannot be used with certain disabilities: verbally administered tests are unsuitable for hearing impaired children, as are visual-performance tests for blind children. Either type of test may be unsuitable for physically impaired children, depending on the exact nature of the handicap. Timed tests are typically ill-advised for most disabled children. This problem of response capability can be handled in two primary ways: by adapting assessment procedures originally developed and standardized with a nonhandicapped population (e.g., estimating the intelligence of a severely multiply handicapped child using his or her affirmation of the examiner's pointing to alternative response pictures on the Peabody Picture Vocabulary Test) or by using measures specifically designed to meet the limited response capabilities of the child (e.g., using the Leiter International Performance Scale for nonverbal children). The first approach is more typical, but not without problems. When standardized procedures are varied, it becomes difficult to compare a child's performance to that of a normative reference group. On the other hand, failure to adapt assessment procedures is likely to produce a distorted picture of abilities.

Whereas the above concerns, related to sensory and response capabilities, are of primary importance, there are other practical considerations worthy of attention in selecting the most suitable instrument for a particular assessment task. Ease of application should certainly be considered. Tests for handicapped children may often be cumbersome to use, at times necessitating specialized equipment that may not be supplied by the publisher (e.g., the Reynell-Zinkin test for blind children). Others may require the presence of an aide or a parent (e.g., testing an 18-month-old infant with the Bayley). Still others involve a lot of materials, making them less portable (e.g., the Leiter). Because of their highly specialized nature, some tests suited to handicapped children may be used so infrequently that they necessitate constant relearning by the clinician. Such a test may be administered in a less standardized fashion, so that its reliability is jeopardized. A test well within the clinician's repertoire may therefore be preferable. Another practical concern is the amount of time a test will take. Not only can this be an issue for the clinician, but handicapped children often tire quickly. Adequate attention and motivation can become a problem. This may be a particular problem when assessing moderately to severely physically handicapped children. Closely associated with the amount of professional time required for administering and scoring a procedure is the overall cost, which includes the cost of materials.

The comprehensiveness of the testing manual should also be considered secondarily. Explicit procedural instructions, including how to adapt administration to handicapped children, make a manual more appealing as does the inclusion of sufficient information to facilitate an accurate interpretation of results. Cronbach (1970) discussed other requirements for a satisfactory manual. Finally, the appeal of the test to the parents or to teachers who will use the resulting information should be considered. Although a test may be technically and psychometrically appealing, it will be of little value if its results and implications are not well received. For example, a test containing ethnically biased items is likely to be questioned, not only by officials, but also by the child and his or her parents. It is likely that a face and content validity will be important in convincing the parent or others using the assessment information of the suitability of a particular test. That is, if the parent perceives the test to be "face" valid, in that it tests what it is supposed to test in the layperson's eyes, its results are likely to be better received by the parent.

PSYCHOMETRIC CONSIDERATIONS

Generally, an assessment is conducted not because of interest in the particular score that will be produced, but because the score represents a construct, such as intelligence or adaptation about which we want to learn something. In most cases, the construct in question represents a theoretical notion that is intangible and not directly observable. For example, we see not intelligence, but behaviors or test responses that are assumed to demonstrate the presence of intelligence. In this sense, there is always a certain distance between the construct and its measurement. For this reason, error will always be introduced when a construct is measured. Because of this figurative distance, it may also be debatable whether the instrument producing the score really represents the construct of interest or, in part, some other construct. Recognition of these potential problems in measurement has led to the development of psychometric theories and concern about the psychometric qualitites of assessment instruments. Because there are numerous excellent sources outlining these issues in varying detail elsewhere (e.g., Allen & Yen, 1979; Cronbach, 1970; Green, 1981), only a brief overview of the most basic concepts will follow.

Basic Concepts

Reliability

Reliability concerns the extent to which measurements are accurate or precise. According to classical test theory, *unreliability* refers to random error in measurement, that is, error that is not attributed to systematic biases in the measurement process. Furthermore, unreliability represents the discrepancy between "true ability" (true score) and the measurement of that ability (observed score). To the extent that measurement error is minimal (it can never be totally eliminated), an instrument is known to be reliable. Thus, reliability speaks to the degree of confidence that can be placed in any given assessment procedure.

Numerous sources of error can influence the measurement of abilities, necessitating the estimation of different types of reliability measurements. Of major importance is error attributable to factors uniquely present at the time of testing, estimated by test–retest correlations. Another type of error is introduced when we are forced to sample only a subset of all the potential items that might test the construct of interest. Questions also arise about how well this subset represents the total domain of items and is estimated by various internal-consistency coefficients.

Because error in measurement can never be completely eliminated, the goal is to assess its sources and to minimize its effects so as to potentiate the instrument's reliability. Classical test theory holds that the degree of reliability associated with an instrument affects its utility, in that accuracy of measurement relates directly to the degree of confidence that can be placed in the results of such measurement. In theory, because a measure cannot correlate more highly with another measure than it correlates with itself, an unreliable measure cannot be valid. In clinical settings, high reliability in assessment is regarded as extremely important (values in the range of .80 to .90 are typically cited as the minimum acceptable), particularly when an assessment is used to make critical decisions that might affect an individual's future. Less stringent criteria are generally applied in research situations, where group data are emphasized and approximations of characteristic variables may be regarded as adequate.

Validity

Validity can be defined as the agreement between a test score or measure and the quality or characteristic it is believed to measure. The *Standards for Educational and Psychological Tests* (American Psychological Association, 1974) defines three major types of validity: content, criterion-related, and construct validity.

Content validity refers to the extent to which an instrument provides an adequate representation of the conceptual domain it is designed to cover. A logical versus statistical approach is generally taken toward content validity. Weaknesses in a measure can arise from test items that do not adequately assess the domain of interest and that therefore lead to erroneous inferences on the basis of test scores. The characteristics of test items, such as their wording , the response format, and sampling, can significantly affect validity. Other factors that might influence test performance, such as anxiety, must also be considered in evaluating content validity.

Criterion-related validity signifies the extent to which a measure adequately predicts a criterion variable of interest. There are two types of criterion-related validity, defined by the length of time taken between the predictor and the criterion: *Predictive validity* refers to the relationship between an instrument and a criterion measure assessed at a future point in time. For example, the predictive validity of a preschool measure of intelligence may be evaluated in terms of the relationship between preschool scores and scores on a related cognitive measure in the elementary-school years. *Concurrent validity* is represented by the relationship between an instrument and a related criterion variable assessed at roughly the same time. A study of concurrent validity might involve an assessment of performance on an intelligence measure in the early school years related to the simultaneous assessment of academic achievement. The correlation between the predictor and the criterion expresses the degree to which the instrument is valid for making statements about the criterion. Such validity coefficients can vary considerably in numerical value, and inferences can be made in different ways, sometimes involving quite subjective evaluation.

Construct validity is an elusive concept at best. It is generally established through a long-continued interplay between measurement and the interpretation of the obtained measurements in light of the existing theoretical understanding of the construct. Evidence for construct validity is accumulated when measures of the construct "behave" according to theoretical expectations. Different types of evidence can therefore be used to argue for the construct validity of a measurement procedure. One type of data is the extent to which a measure defining the construct relates to other measures of the same construct, compared with measures of a different, presumably unrelated construct (Campbell & Fiske, 1959). For example, a measure of intelligence is expected to correlate considerably more with another measure of intelligence than with measures of physical ability or personality attributes. Another example of data relevant to building construct validity is the response of test scores that measure a construct to manipulations. For example, based on some theories that hold intelligence to be modifiable within certain limits, it would be reasonable to expect a "valid" measure of intelligence to improve following the completion of a credible remedial program. Thus, an evaluation of the construct validity of a measure follows from a theoretical understanding of the construct that the measure is supposed to represent. Evidence is cumulative, and, at any one point, a judgment is made only of the *extent* to which a measure appears to be construct-valid, subject to the acceptance of others reviewing the same data.

Normative Data

Many assessment questions reduce to one about how the individual is performing relative to a defined comparison group. Adequate normative data, or "norms," are required to address this question. *Norms* refer to the performance of a defined group of individuals on a particular assessment procedure and are based on the mean and distibution of scores obtained for that group. The adequacy of normative data depends to a large extent on the constitution of the normative sample, and on how this constitution relates to the specific assessment problem. Important questions include: (a) Does the normative sample adequately represent the population it is intended to represent, based on such characteristics as age, sex, and socioeconomic group? (b) Is the sample large enough so as to not be adversely affected by a few unrepresentative extreme scores? and (c) Does the normative sample include individuals with characteristics relevant to the questions addressed in the assessment problem at hand?

Application to Developmental Disabilities

Classical test-theory principles are frequently used as standard criteria for the evaluation and selection of the instruments used to assess clinical problems. This approach is praiseworthy, as it allows a standard procedure for describing and judging measurement methods, urges a data-based evaluation of assessment procedures, and maintains generally high standards for the validation of instruments. Among empirically oriented professionals, the psychometric criteria, including normative data, reliability, and validity, represent the standards on the basis of which more clinically based procedures are often criticized.

For the assessment of abilities in the developmentally disabled population, however, there are several counts on which a purely classical test-theory approach may result in a limited perspective. First, adherence to rigorous psychometric standards is frequently difficult to meet, given the practical limitations often presented by this population. Whereas tests of abilities such as intelligence can be reasonably standardized in terms of test materials and conditions within the normal population, such standardization can be extremely difficult to achieve among handicapped individuals, especially the multiply handicapped. Other problems include the tendency for disabled individuals to show greater variability than the nondisabled in day-to-day performance, thereby threatening reliability of measurement. Psychometric standards can be held as ideal criteria; however, failure to be cognizant of and adaptive to the practical limitations of the individual client can result in data that are highly spurious. These factors may account in part for the less than desirable data for the instruments currently used with a handicapped population (Buros, 1978; Sattler, 1982).

Second, a classical test-theory approach to the selection of assessment instruments does not necessarily attend to questions of the purpose of the assessment, decisions that face the clinician on the basis of the assessment, and the implications that these issues present in the selection of the instruments. A classical test-theory approach emphasizes the evaluation of instruments *per se,* rather than the evaluation of the assessment process within the context of its *purpose* or the *required decisions.*

The third point is related to, but is more specific than, the second. That is, a limited perspective results from an assessment approach that does not consider the *specific utility needs* of the target population. Clinical assessment can serve multiple and varied purposes that require specification (e.g., screening, diagnosis, and prediction), and populations vary in their needs for assessment procedures to meet these purposes. Developmentally disabled children typically face a significant and chronic disorder that requires repeated assessment and for which repeated decisions, related specifically to program planning, are critical. Thus, an assessment approach that attends to issues of utility specifically related to the development of remedial programs is of utmost importance to this population. Assessment strategies without such a utilitarian function will prove grossly limited.

These problems with the strict application of only psychometric criteria in the selection of instruments for the assessment of developmentally disabled children indicate a need for an alternative strategy. A consideration of the objectives for the assessment, emphasized in the points above, has a potential for suggesting an alternative strategy that combines these objectives with psychometric concerns.

CONSIDERATION OF ASSESSMENT OBJECTIVES

Assessment can serve various functions or objectives. Typically, these objectives relate to decisions that need to be made. One type of assessment objective is *diagnostic,* when, on the basis of test results, an individual's performance is evaluated with respect to a normative reference or to diagnostic criteria (norm-referenced testing). Diagnostic assessment is often conducted to facilitate decisions that may involve either in institutions. One such decision may be a *selection* decision, in which some are selected for a particular purpose and others are rejected. For example, the in assessment of an otherwise normal child may serve the objective of diagnosing ~. *arda*-tion, which may, in turn, aid in the decision of selecting that child for enrollment in a regional center for the developmentally disabled. A *classification* decision is another type of decision related to diagnostic assessment that involves specifying which of several possible category assignments is most appropriate for a given individual. Classifying a child as mildly or moderately mentally retarded is an example of this type of decision. A *placement* decision may be highly related to a classification decision, such as determining whether a program for educable or trainable mentally retarded children is most appropriate.

The second type of objective that assessment can serve is *descriptive,* in the sense that a child's performance is detailed with respect to some specified behavioral criteria (criterion-referenced testing). A child's strengths, weaknesses, and emerging abilities can thus be elucidated when a test is used descriptively. Description may provide multidimensional information and hence may address multiple objectives.

The point of considering the various assessment objectives is that assessment can be conducted for different purposes at different times. It is important, therefore, before selecting an instrument, to specify the purpose of the assessment and the type of decision that is required. A test that may be useful for one type of decision may not be helpful with another. For example, a test that adequately classifies a child as moderately mentally retarded may give few useful data regarding appropriate treatment which, for many purposes, may be more important. This emphasis on the selection of assessment procedures vis-à-vis the purpose of the assessment and subsequent decisions to be made reflects a perspective known as *decision theory.* A decision-theory perspective is generally not inconsistent with a psychometric approach; rather, it modifies the traditional criteria to incorporate the context within which instruments are applied. Although in some instances such an approach may have the apparent effect of "loosening" the criteria for the acceptable use of instruments, when responsibly taken a decision theory perspective does not disband empirically based standards. In the following sections, the basic concepts of decision theory are outlined, followed by a discussion of the application of a decision theory model to the assessment of developmentally disabled children.

Basic Concepts

A decision-theory model of test construction and use emphasizes issues related to how tests can best serve in making specific decisions. The value of a test depends on many qualiities in addition to its accuracy, in particular on the relevance of the measurement to the particular decision being made and the loss that would result from an erroneous decision. According to decision theory, recommendations regarding the design, selection, and interpretation of a test must consider characteristics of the decisions for which the test will be used, as the test that may be most effective for one decision may not necessarily be most effective for other decisions (Cronbach & Gleser, 1965).

Decision theory represents an alternative model to traditional test theory. Cronbach and Gleser (1965) contrasted a decision model to classical test theory, which views a test as a measuring instrument intended to assign accurate numerical values to some quantitative attribute of the individual. Test or measurement theory, rooted in the physical sciences, stresses *precision*, or reliability of measurement, as the prime value. Cronbach and Gleser argued, however, that, in practical testing, a quantitative estimate is not necessarily the ultimate goal; rather, the goal may be a decision regarding the individual that may involve, for example, program or treatment planning. Accuracy of measurement is valuable, therefore, only insofar as it facilitates this type of qualitative decision. Additional contrasting features include the fact that, in traditional test theory, attention is focused on a particular measuring instrument that is applied in the same manner to all persons. In this context, the instrument is viewed with respect to the reliability and validity of the test itself. When testing is viewed as an aid in decision making, it is recognized that different information may be required for different individuals for different decisions; therefore, the focus is on the efficiency of the entire decision-making process.

Clearly, a decision theory perspective places a premium on the utility of measuring procedures for specific purposes. A test is rarely viewed outside the context of its purpose in a specific situation. Rather than raising the question "Is this test valid?" a decision theorist is likely to ask "How valid is this test for the decision I wish to make?" With this introduction, specific decision theory concepts as elucidated by Cronbach (Cronbach, 1970; Cronbach & Gleser, 1965) are discussed below.

Types of Decisions

Psychological tests can facilitate many types of decisions, involving both individuals and institutions. Reference has already been made to several types of decisions as they relate to assessment objectives (e.g., selection, classification, and placement decision). In a later section, these decisions and objectives will be discussed in greater detail as they relate specifically to developmentally disabled children. Suffice it to note at this point that the specifications of decision types represents a critical feature of decision theory.

Sequential versus Nonsequential Decision Strategies

In contrast to classical test theory in which a final decision is often made on the basis of a battery of tests administered to individuals, decision theory recognizes several decision strategies. The single-stage procedure described above is referred to as a *nonsequential* decision strategy. In contrast, in practical application, it is probably more common and reasonable to approach decisions *sequentially*; that is, according to a procedure that permits information at one point to determine what information will be obtained next that may or may not modify the ultimate decision. In decision theory, testing procedures are extended to include such sequential strategies.

Reliability

As a utilitarian perspective characterizes the decision theory model, so is this perspective applied to the concept of reliability. In classical test theory, estimations of instrument reliability are of primary importance, as they reveal the degree of accuracy in test scores, and therefore theoretically determine the upper limits of validity. Although decision theorists agree that an inaccurate test cannot be a good predictor, evaluation of accuracy is viewed in light of the particular decision to be made on the basis of test scores. Cronbach (1970) stated:

> To be sure, accuracy is less important than relevance. A highly accurate test does us no good if what it measures is irrelevant to the intended decision or conclusion. But if two tests are equally relevant, the more accurate test will yield more valuable reports. (p. 152)

Errors of measurement are viewed as most troublesome when individuals who differ only moderately are compared. A test that may be accurate enough to discriminate abnormality within a group representing a wide range of abilities (a selection decision) may not adequately classify individuals *within* the abnormal group. As is the case for validity, a decision theorist would replace the more typical question "Is this test reliable?" with "Is this test reliable enough for the intended purpose or decision?"

Several of Cronbach's points regarding the interpretation of findings on reliability further demonstrate an approach dependent on the specifications of test conditions. For example, he suggested that, although most test manuals report a single standard error of measurement, it is risky to assume that a test has the same accuracy for all types of persons to whom it may be applied. Along the same line, although tests are designed to measure a certain age range or level of ability, most tests assess within that range with varying levels of accuracy. For example, the Denver Developmental Screening Test (Frankenburg, Dodds, Fandal, Kazuk & Cohrs, 1975), which is designed to evaluate children 2 weeks to 6 years old is viewed as being most accurate at around 4 years of age and appears to be of questionable value under 30 months (Bagnato & Neisworth, 1981).

Validity

In decision theory, validity is defined in terms of the relationship between the information generated by a particular assessment procedure and a criterion variable. In this sense, it is quite comparable to criterion-related validity, discussed earlier. The unique aspect of the decision theory concept of validity is apparent, however, when validity is viewed vis-à-vis the decision process. That is, evidence for validity is generally obtained on the basis of empirical results pertaining to the *outcomes* or consequences of specific decisions. Validity is frequently evaluated by examining, for a given assessment or decision strategy, the "hit rate" (i.e., the proportion of cases in which accurate predictions were made) relative to the error rate (the rate of inaccurate predictions) or the base rate (the hit rate without the specific assessment or decision strategy). In this sense, validity is evaluated largely in terms of utility. As Cronbach and Gleser (1965) pointed out, however, validity coefficients and the relationships between validity and utility vary according to the specific type of decision (selection or classification) and the decision strategy used (single-stage versus sequential stage), as well as whether treatments for classification placement decisions are fixed (i.e., not modifiable) or adaptable. The notion of *incremental validity* is introduced when the value or benefit of a test is evaluated in terms of improvement over base-rate predictions, that is, in terms of predictive information *gained* beyond what would have been known without the test results. The predictive value of a test procedure can be compared to the known validity coefficient of the best strategy *not* using the test (i.e., the "best *a priori* strategy"); thus, any incremental validity or gain associated with the procedure is demonstrated.

The Bandwidth–Fidelity Dilemma

The bandwidth–fidelity dilemma refers to the trade-off between obtaining a single score of abilities with relatively high accuracy or "fidelity" and obtaining multiple scores that are less accurate but that describe a wide "bandwidth" of abilities. The relationship between fidelity and bandwidth results from the fact that scores based on a relatively large number of items or observations tend to be more reliable than those based on fewer observations. This phenomenon is accentuated as observations become more homogeneous. Whereas procedures with high fidelity are inherently appealing, a narrow-bandwidth approach has the effect of limiting the scope of the information provided. A familiar example is found in the Wechsler Intelligence Scale for Children—Revised (WISC-R; Wechsler, 1974) where a Full Scale score based on 10 subtests of abilities is more reliable than any one of the individual subtest scores. However, interpretation of a Full Scale score alone clearly restricts the range of information that may be available, although at a lower level of accuracy. A parallel phenomenon is found in the analysis of multiscore profile patterns, which describes the position of scaled scores relative to one another, when such profile patterns are found to be less dependable than total scores (e.g., Conger, 1974; Conger & Lipshitz, 1973).

As might be expected, a decision model approach to the bandwidth–fidelity dilemma is expressed in terms of ultimate utility:

> It is the purpose to be served and the way tests will be interpreted that determines whether limited bandwidth or low fidelity is more acceptable. There are tests with intermediate bandwidths, and a particular technique may be used as a narrowband method by some testers and as a wideband method by others. (Cronbach, 1970, p. 181)

Cronbach described the problem as philosophical as well as practical when he posed the questions: Is it better to take some risk, making use of information that may be sound? Or is it better to shun all such information, and to stop with scores that present an incomplete and featureless picture? An attempt will be made shortly to give some answers to these questions.

Application to Developmental Disabilities

Decision theory offers an empirically based, utilitarian model that can be of prime value in the assessment of handicapped children or, for that matter, of any clinical population. Instrument selection represents one part of the assessment process to which decisions regarding the selection of assessment instruments for developmentally disabled children is proposed. This model, based on decision-theory concepts, is summarized in stepwise fashion in Table 1. It represents the authors' integration of practical considerations, psychometric considerations, and consideration of assessment objectives. It should be noted that the exact order of the steps is less critical than the integration of the material.

Specify the Assessment Objectives

The most fundamental decision-theory concept is the one that urges the assessor to specify the purpose of the assessment and hence the decisions that must be made on the

Table 1. Instrument Selection Model Based on Decision Theory

Step 1. Specify the assessment objectives
  A. Screening: selection decision in which normal individuals are "rejected" and potentially abnormal individuals are "selected" for further evaluation
  B. Diagnostic: classification decision in which the type and degree of dysfunction are specified
  C. Descriptive: documentation of patterns of behavior and abilities, such as relative strengths and weaknesses and emerging abilities
  D. Treatment planning and assessment: description of abilities as related to potential intervention strategies (or in terms of progress)

Step 2. Specify the secondary decisions to be based on the assessment objectives
  A. Acceptable level of reliability: high reliability required for diagnostic and screening objectives
  B. Cost of error: high cost for diagnostic objective; generally high cost for false negative errors (misses) in screening; relatively low cost for description and treatment-planning objectives
  C. Importance of normative reference: normative reference essential for diagnostic and screening objectives; helpful for description and treatment planning
  D. Bandwidth versus fidelity: narrow bandwidth and high fidelity are required for diagnostic and screening objectives; wide bandwidth and reduced fidelity for description and treatment planning

Step 3. Specify the limitations of the child
  A. Handicap (e.g., motoric, visual, or auditory)
  B. Age
  C. Developmental level
  D. Behavior (e.g., attention span and frustration tolerance)

Step 4. Identify potentially useful instruments based on the assessment objectives, the secondary decisions, and the limitations of the child

Step 5. Select the best available instrument(s)

Step 6. Select further instruments when possible, based on appeal, cost, etc

basis of the assessment. Operationalizing the assessment task in this way provides a criterion and a utility focus for the assessment, as well as a context within which the secondary decisions related to instrument selection (such as those pertaining to acceptable levels of reliability, tolerable error, and bandwidth versus accuracy) can be made. For ease of discussion, these secondary decisions are introduced with the definition of the assessment objectives.

Assessment with respect to developmental disabilities can have a range of objectives and any given assessment can be conducted for the purpose of meeting one or more of these. One such objective is *screening* for disabilities within some sample of the general population. This might pertain particularly to disabilities such as retardation, when the physical characteristics of the child may not immediately indicate abnormality. The task of screening evaluation is less relevant to the content of this book which is specifically focused on identified disabled populations. However, it is worth noting because screening exemplifies a type of selection decision. That is, certain individuals are "selected out" among those evaluated, whereas others are "rejected" as they are identified as being within normal limits. For example, a commonly used instrument for screening preschool children across several functional areas is the Denver Developmental Screening Test, which designates children's performances as normal, abnormal, questionable, or untestable. When selecting an instrument for screening purposes, one must consider established validity for this purpose and must give particular attention to what will be considered acceptable levels of erroneous decisions, a topic discussed in a later section.

A second and common purpose of the assessment of handicapped children is *diagnostic*. For example, assessment of abilities is sought to determine if and to what degree the child suffers impairment in cognitive functioning. This represents a classification decision. Because this type of decision is highly significant for the individuals involved, a high degree of accuracy is required. Instruments with clear reference to a normative sample and established reliability are needed, as the cost of erroneous decisions can be very high. The instruments most frequently used to diagnose intellectual impairment in preschool children are the Bayley Scales of Infant Development (Bayley, 1969), the Stanford-Binet Intelligence Test (Terman & Merrill, 1960), and the Wechsler Preschool and Primary Scale of Intelligence (Wechsler, 1967). Their preponderant use, even with handicapped population, attests to the high value placed on their reliability and their normative data.

Another use for assessment instruments may be to *describe* a child's current abilities and behavior with a particular interest in identifying areas of relative strength and weakness. In this case, a multiscore approach is the primary objective, with emphasis given to bandwidth, or breadth of assessment. This approach typically has the effect of sacrificing fidelity or accuracy in the scores of specific areas compared with overall ability; however, this effect may be tolerable in light of the identified objective. The profiles generated by the Wechsler Scales and the McCarthy Scales of Children's Abilities exemplify the use of a multiscore approach. The preference of these multiscore measures over, for example, the Stanford-Binet, which yields only a total score, demonstrates at least the perceived utility of a multiscore approach for purposes of description. A descriptive approach is similarly taken when one wishes to identify emerging abilities, as indicated, for example, when a child passes a repeated item only a portion of the time. Although a focus on such a limited number of responses can be viewed as being comparable to a test with very few items and therefore limited reliability, this approach may be acceptable for purposes such as generating hypotheses about the child's current areas of learning and for testing limits in order to identify conditions that may facilitate learning for that child. These concepts underlying the notion of emerging abilities are often "built into" the administration and scoring of measures intended for prescriptive purposes, as is the case, for example, in the Psychoeducational Profile (Schopler & Reichler, 1979) for autistic children.

The last assessment objective that will be considered here is *treatment planning*, or delineating an individualized remedial program on the basis of an assessment. In contrast to instruments selected for diagnostic purposes, which demand high reliability as a priority, those selected for the purpose of programming should have strength in their ability to assess skills in a developmental progression, such as might characterize a resulting remedial program. The Learning Accomplishment Profile (Sanford, 1974) exemplifies such an instrument, as it describes curent abilities and is also designed to provide specific intervention or treatment guidelines. A prime example of the contrast between assessment for diagnostic and treatment-planning purposes is evident in the use of the WISC-R for older retarded children. No doubt, this measure can be extremely valuable in the identification of retardation. However, it is of questionable utility for the development of a *specific* program intended to facilitate the classroom education or the daily adaptation of the same child. Suffice it to note that instruments used for the purpose of program development are also frequently useful in the evaluation of an individual's progress with respect to that program.

In summary, specification of the purpose(s) of the assessment and of the subsequent decisions to be made sets the stage for instrument selection, in that the priorities of such parameters as reliability of measurement, cost of error, specificity of information, and utility for treatment can be defined. These parameters (outlined in Step 2) are discussed in greater detail below.

Specify the Secondary Decisions To Be Based on the Assessment Objectives

Acceptable levels of reliability should be specified within the context of the assessment and ensuing decisions. An instrument or procedure that may reliably *screen* individuals for a disability may not *classify* or *diagnose* individuals with adequate accuracy. For example, although the Denver Developmental Screening Test is regarded by many as an adequate screening measure, it is not sufficiently normed or reliable to justify its use diagnostically. For handicapped children, the selection of assessment instuments with high reliability is most crucial when decisions involving diagnosis are made. It is at this point that children are objectively classified for their parents and their community as abnormal, a decision that must be made with certainty. It is also at this point that children are identified as being in need of treatment, and it is often on the basis of such an assessment that a justification of further services is made. In contrast, less reliability is necessary for the purposes of a detailed description of abilities and for program planning. That is, once a child enters treatment, there is a greater opportunity for observation of the child's behavior across varying setting and time-related conditions. Thus, sources of unreliability can be more easily identified and taken into account.

Different types of instrument reliability (e.g., test–retest and internal consistency) should also be considered differentially, vis-à-vis the purpose of the assessment. To refer again to diagnostic assessment, which often determines the availability of treatment sources, one would seek an instrument with at least adequate *test–retest* reliability so as to reduce the chances of fluctuation in test results due to day-to-day variance in performance. On the other hand, for ongoing treatment planning, greater emphasis may be given to instrument *sampling* characteristics, which might pertain to the instrument's ability to yield information relevant to "real-world" events for the child. An example of the latter measure, cited by Bagnato and Neisworth (1981), is found in the Assessment Programming Guide for Infants and Preschoolers. This measure is intended to provide guidelines for individual program planning. Its test-retest reliability characteristics are unknown and perhaps irrelevant to its authors, as items in the motor, language, self-help, personal-social, and academic areas are planned for spontaneous exhibition rather than structured administration. (Complete evaluation may take several weeks.) Despite its gross limitations for diagnostic purposes, this measure is regarded as very useful for its intended purpose of treatment guidance (Bagnato & Neisworth, 1981).

For any assessment objective, it is critical to evaluate the reliability of the *assessment decision* rather than to focus solely on instrument reliability. During any assessment procedure, factors such as attention, motivation, and fatigue may operate to reduce the overall reliability of the decision-making process despite the use of a "reliable instrument." At the very least, the consistency of the decisions resulting from our assessments needs to be evaluated (Swaminathan, Hambleton, & Algina, 1974).

The *cost of error* involved in erroneous decisions is related to the level of reliability and must also be considered in determining an assessment procedure. Again, specifying the purpose of the assessment is critical to defining the tolerable error cost. For diagnostic purposes, the cost of error is generally high, as diagnostic decisions tend to have a significant impact on the lives of those involved. Although diagnosing a child as retarded or autistic can open the door to treatment services, it is not without tremendous emotional cost to the family. Conversely, failure to identify handicapped individuals, such as learning-disabled children, is costly in that their further development and adjustment promises to be difficult. In contrast, error tends to be less costly (though not insignificant) when description and treatment planning are the objectives of a specific assessment procedure. As already discussed, repeated observations of a child, once diagnosed and committed to ongoing treatment, can essentially prolong the assessment process and, in effect, "correct" previous errors.

A tolerable cost of error for screening assessment can be variable, although generally the cost of failing to identify abnormal individuals (often termed *false negatives*) is regarded as higher, at least to the individual, than the cost of incorrectly identifying normal individuals as abnormal (*false positives*). Presumably, normal individuals who are screened as "abnormal" will be reliably "diagnosed" as normal subsequently, though with some cost to the institution. However, deviant individuals who are not identified in screening do not have a chance to be diagnosed, which is a very costly error to these individuals. This trade-off can affect both instrument selection and the establishment of cut-off scores (i.e., scores that define normal and abnormal individuals) for making screening decisions.

The importance of *normative referencing* also varies with the assessment objective. Screening and diagnosis represent attempts to identify abnormal individuals and thus, by definition, require data regarding normal versus abnormal behavior. Norm referencing is therefore central to these assessment objectives, and it is only in the face of great opposition that accessors are dissuaded from using well-normed measures for diagnostic purposes. Assessment for description and treatment planning is more enlightening when behavior is norm-referenced; however, for these purposes, the focus is generally one of documenting relative strengths and weaknesses (i.e., relative to the client rather than to the norm) and/or designing a corresponding remedial program. Although the Wechsler Scales are most valuable in their norm-referencing capability, "intelligent testing" with these scales clearly involves a statistically based interpretation of *relative* strengths and weaknesses independent of normative data (Kaufman, 1979).

Decisions regarding *bandwidth versus accuracy* are similarly made in light of assessment objectives. When maximum reliability is sought, such as in screening and diagnosis, a single-score, or narrow, bandwidth is emphasized. When seeking information about multiple areas of ability, and particularly one area compared with another, a multiscore approach is taken. The reliability of individual scores in a multiscore profile is diminished; however, the information obtained can be quite useful for descriptive and treatment-planning objectives. The Wechsler instruments are again cited to exemplify this contrast. Although Full Scale IQ scores clearly represent the most reliable indicators of overall intellectual functioning, subscale scores provide less reliable though potentially useful information for understanding patterns of abilities.

Specify the Limitations of the Child

Consideration of the physical, developmental, and behavioral limitations of developmentally disabled children plays a large role in determining the type of evaluation instrument needed. Children's *physical limitations*, involving both sensory and response capabilities, were discussed at the beginning of this chapter in terms of the implication of practical considerations for instrument selection. In brief, assessment materials and procedures must meet the sensory capabilities of the child in order to have any expectation of a valid assessment. Modification in assessment is usually indicated for sensory-impaired populations. This is exemplified by the development of the Hayes-Binet Test of Intelligence for the Blind (Hayes, 1950), modified from the Stanford-Binet by substituting larger test materials presented tactually rather than visually. The Maxfield-Buchholz Social Maturity Scale for Blind Preschool Children (Maxfield & Buchholz, 1957) similarly represents an adaptation of the Vineland Social Maturity Scale (Doll, 1953) for blind children ages birth to 6 years. Assessments of deaf children must avoid verbal presentation of the material, as is the case with the Leiter International Performance Scale (Arthur, 1949; Leiter, 1948), or when only the Perfomance Scale subtests of the WISC-R (Anderson & Sisco, 1977) are used. Equal weight should be given to the response limitations of the child, particularly the motorically impaired such as children with cerebral palsy. The French Pictorial Test of Intelligence (French, 1964), which requires the child to point or otherwise indicate a selection response to one of an array of pictures, can be most useful with severely motorically impaired children.

A child's *age and developmental level* can quickly limit the selection of the assessment instruments. Although the WISC-R has been referred to frequently to exemplify assessment concepts, its use is obviously not appropriate for preschool children, as it was not developed and normed for this population. With retarded children, developmental level is also important to consider, as this can influence the selection of measures. For example, a severely retarded 3-year-old may not demonstrate abilities that would allow for a basal score on the Stanford-Binet, even thought in terms of chronological age this would apear to be the most appropriate instrument. In this case, use of the Bayley Scales of Infant Development may best document the child's abilities.

The *behavioral characteristics* of the child are important to note in any assessment procedure and, at times, can be central to the selection of measures. Tests that are relatively short or have colorful and interestng materials, such as the McCarthy Scales of Children's Abilities (McCarthy, 1972), may be sought for children known to have a short attention span or a low frustation tolerance. On the other hand, some autistic children who display these problems, as well as sensory sensitivities may be overstimulated by bright colors or intricate materials, and they may become overactive, distracted, or fixated on one object. These children may work better with plainer materials (Baker, 1983). In any event, individual and sometimes transient behavior characteristics of the child need to be considered in the selection of assessment procedures.

Identify Potentially Useful Instruments

Step 4 of the instrument selection model advises the assessor to take information from the prior three steps to arrive at some preliminary pool of plausible instruments. The previous sections discuss how secondary decisions are made (Step 2) on the basis of the assessment objectives (Step 1). Similarly, consideration of the child's limitations in Step 3 must be integrated with the assessment objectives if one is to arrive at a set of potentially useful measures. For example, if the objective is to assess the behavioral capability of a physically handicapped toddler relative to his or her normal peer group in order to aid in a decision about his or her placement in a normal peer-group situation, the unadapted Bayley may best meet this objective. On the other hand, if the objective is to describe the child's cognitive abilities, then a modified version of the Bayley (e.g., Hoffman, 1974), in which equipment allows the child to demonstrate understanding of the required task, may be more useful.

To this point, the discussion of the steps to be taken in instrument selection has been, in large part, theoretical. One can specify assessment objectives, secondary decisions, and limitations of the child but not yet be faced with the real task of identifying instruments that can potentially meet these demands. It is fully recognized by the authors that for many disabled children, identifying appropriate instruments *in practice* is no easy task. A well-thought-out decision-theory strategy may specifically indicate the need for a highly reliable instrument for diagnosing cognitive impairment in an 18-month-old blind child. Yet such an instrument may not currently exist. This state of reality forces the integration of a fourth, but no less important, consideration in the selection process, consideration of the current alternatives.

Select the Best Available Instrument

Assuming that one has several potentially useful instruments from which to choose, at least a preliminary decision (e.g., prior to meeting the child) must be made. At this point, the advantages and limitations of each instrument should be evaluated vis-à-vis the assessment task at hand, along with the inevitable trade-offs involved; for example, one may be forced to "trade" reliability for breadth of assessment. The clinician left with multiple adequate instruments to choose from can proceed to Step 6 and can leisurely enjoy selection on the basis of appeal or other finer variables. Unfortunately, as is more often the case, the clinician is forced ever more vigorously to increase her or his awareness of the assessment issues and to make intelligent choices on the basis of the best possible solution to the assessment problem at hand.

To help summarize and reify the selection model and assessment issues, the reader is referred to Table 2, in which a hypothetical case is presented to illustrate the clinical application of the selection model. The case is presented stepwise and corresponds to the model outlined in Table 1 and discussed throughout the text.

CONCLUSION

The assessment of developmentally disabled children is a challenging task that requires clinical skill and theoretical understanding of multiple assessment issues. The use

Table 2. Application of Instrument Selection Model: Illustrative Example

Step 1. Specify the assessment objectives
   A. Diagnostic evaluation of cognitive-intellectual functioning

Step 2. Specify the secondary decisions to be based on the assessment objectives
   A. High reliability required for diagnosis
   B. High cost of error in incorrect diagnosis
   C. Normative reference essential for diagnosis
   D. Narrow bandwidth and high fidelity preferred for diagnosis

Step 3. Specify the limitations of the child
   A. Handicap: moderate hearing loss; severe receptive and expressive communication disorder
   B. Age: 3 years, 8 months
   C. Developmental level: estimated one-year delay in overall cognitive functioning
   D. Behavior: active; short attention span

Step 4. Identify potentially useful instruments based on the previous steps
   A. Merrill-Palmer Scale of Mental Tests (Stutsman, 1948): primarily nonverbal test for preschool children, interesting materials and flexible scoring procedures; but limited standardization and outdated norms, inadequate reliability; yields crude measure of nonverbal skills
   B. Hiskey-Nebraska Test of Learning Aptitude (Hiskey, 1966): nonverbal measure for children age 3 and older; standardized on deaf and normal children with separate norms, high reliability, moderate validity; includes range of skill areas; but normative data are relatively weak under age 5, and basal may not be obtained for delayed 3-year-olds
   C. Leiter International Performance Scale (Leiter, 1948): nonverbal measure for ages 2 years to adult; satisfactory reliability and validity; but inadequate standardization, outdated norms, and limited range of skill areas

Step 5. Select the best available instrument(s)
   A. Hiskey-Nebraska Test of Learning Aptitude: selected as prime diagnostic measure of cognitive-intellectual functioning with Merrill-Palmer Scale of Mental Tests to be used if needed to obtain basal scores

Step 6. Further instrument selection
   (not applicable)

of psychometric properties as the sole criteria for instrument selection proves grossly limiting with this or, for that matter, any population. Alternatively, a decision theory perspective offers an empirically based and conceptually sound strategy for instrument selection when psychometric properties, practical limitations, and assessment objectives are considered and integrated. The systematic application of a decision theory model to instrument selection for developmentally disabled children, as discussed, should prove beneficial. Its ultimate value will be understood in the outcome results, particularly in its ability to help the clinician address assessment questions and to guide decisions for these children.

REFERENCES

Allen, M. G., & Yen, W.M. (1979). *Introduction to measurement theory*. Monterey, CA: Brooks/Cole
American Psychological Association. (1974). *Standards for educational and psychological tests*. Washington, DC: American Psychological Association.

Anderson, R. J., & Sisco, F. H. (1977). *Standardization of the WISC-R performance scale for deaf children.* Washington, DC: Gallaudet College Office of Demographic Studies.

Arthur, G. (1949). The Arthur adaptation of the Leiter International Performance Scale. *Journal of Clinical Psychology, 5,* 345–349.

Bagnato, S., & Neisworth, J. (1981). *Linking developmental assessment and curricula.* Rockville, MD: Aspen.

Baker, A. (1983). Psychological assessment of autistic children. *Clinical Psychology Review, 3,* 41–59.

Bayley, N. (1969). *Bayley Scales of Infant Development: Birth to two years.* New York: Psychological Corporation.

Buros, O. K. (Ed.). (1978). *The Eighth Mental Measurement Yearbook.* Highland Park, NJ: Gryphon.

Campbell, D. T., & Fiske, D. W. (1959). Convergent and discriminant validation by the multitrait–multimethod matrix. *Psychological Bulletin, 56,* 81–105.

Conger, A. J. (1974). Estimating profile reliability and maximally reliable composites. *Multivariate Behavioral Research, 9,* 85–104.

Conger, A. J., & Lipshitz, R. (1973). Measures of reliability for profiles and test batteries. *Psychometrike, 38,* 411–427.

Cronbach, L. J. (1970). *Essentials of psychological testing.* New York: Harper & Row.

Cronbach, L. J., & Glaser, G. C. (1965). *Psychological tests and personnel decisions.* Urbana: University of Illinois Press.

Doll, E. A. (1953). *Vineland Social Maturity Scale.* In A. Weider (Ed.), *Contributions toward medical psychology: Theory and psychodiagnostics method* (Vol. 2.). New York: Ronald Press.

Frankenburg, W. K., Dobbs, J. B., Fandal, A.W., Kazuka, E. & Cohrs, M. (1975). The Denver Developmental Screening Test. *Journal of Pediatrics, 71,* 181–191.

French, J. L. (1964). *Manual: Pictorial test of intelligence.* Boston: Houghton Mifflin.

Green, B.F. (1981). The primer of testing. *American Psychologist, 35,* 1012–1027.

Hayes, S. P. (1950). Measuring the intelligence of the blind. In P. A. Zahl (Ed.), *Blindness, modern approaches to the unseen environment.* Princeton: Princeton University Press.

Hiskey, M. (1966). *Hiskey-Nebraska Test of Learning Aptitude.* Lincoln, NE: Union College Press.

Hoffman, H. (1974). *The Bayley Scales of Infant development: Modifications for youngsters with handicapping conditions.* Commack, NY: Suffolk Rehabilitation Center.

Kaufman, A. S. (1979). *Intelligent testing with the WISC-R.* New York: Wiley-Interscience.

Leiter, R. G. (1948). *Leiter International Performance Scale.* Chicago: Stoelting.

Maxfield, K. E., & Buchholz, S. (1957). *A Social Maturity Scale for Blind Preschool Children: A guide to its use.* New York: American Foundation for the Blind.

McCarthy, D. (1972). *McCarthy Scales of Children's Abilities.* New York: Psychological Corporation.

Reynell, J. (1979). *Reynell-Zinkin Scales: Developmental scales for young visually handicapped children Part 1: Mental development.* Windsor, Berkshire, Great Britain: NSER Publishing.

Sanford, A. R. (1974). *Learning Accomplishment Profile.* Chapel Hill, NC: Chapel Hill Training Outreach Project.

Sattler, J. M. (1982). *Assessment of children's intelligence and special abilities.* Boston: Allyn & Bacon.

Schopler, E., & Reichler, R. J. (1979). *Individualized assessment and treatment for autistic and developmentally disabled children. Vol. 1: Psychoeducation profile.* Baltimore: University Park Press.

Stutsman, R. (1948). *Merrill-Palmer Scale of Mental Tests.* Los Angeles: Western Psychological Services.

Swaminathan, H., Hambleton, R. K., & Algina, J. (1974). Reliability of criterion-referenced tests: A decision-theoretic formulation. *Journal of Educational Measurement, 11,* 263–267.

Terman, L. M., & Merrill, M. A. (1960). *Stanford-Binet Intelligence Scale.* Boston: Houghton Mifflin.

Ulrey, G., & Rogers, S. J. (1982). *Psychological assessment of handicapped infants and young children.* New York: Thieme-Stratton.

Wechsler, D. (1967). *Wechsler Preschool and Primary Scale of Intelligence.* New York: Psychological Corporation.

Wechsler, D. (1974). *Wechsler Intelligence Scale for Children—Revised.* New York: Psychological Corporation.

4

Clinical Considerations in the Assessment of Young Handicapped Children

Vaughan Stagg

Early in my professional development, I worked in a special education cooperative that provided a variety of services, including psychoeducational assessment services, to an 11-county area in rural southeastern Texas. One day, my supervisor handed me the assignment of evaluating a young handicapped girl in a town 1½ half hours from the center. She was enrolled in a small community-supported program for developmentally delayed children. I was to provide her teacher with some practical information to assist in planning educational activities for the young girl.

I had very little background information on the child other than her age (5 years), her sex, and the fact that she was apparently developmentally delayed. I arrived at the child's school with my Standford-Binet kit and was faced with a blind, severely retarded child who displayed a number of self-injurious behaviors. I was utterly useless to that child and her teacher. Not only was my instrumentation inappropriate, but my training and knowledge base had provided me with few skills for working with low-incidence populations.

ASSESSMENT DILEMMAS

Assessment of handicapped infants and preschool children poses a number of dilemmas for the diagnostician. Aside from the fact that most front-line practitioners (e.g., school psychologists) have little training with or exposure to low-incidence populations (Barnett, 1983; Dubose, 1981; Ulrey & Schnell, 1982), instrumentation for children with significant handicapping conditions is lacking. Professionals have, in general, relied on a limited number of solutions to the diagnostic dilemmas posed by young handicapped children (Chase, 1975). One solution has been the development of a limited number of assessment instruments that are normed and validated for specific handicapping conditions, such as the Hiskey-Nebraska Test of Learning Ability (Hiskey, 1966). A second

VAUGHAN STAGG ● Department of Psychology, Louisiana State University in Shreveport, Shreveport, Louisiana 71115.

alternative has been the adaptation of an existing instrument for use with a particular population and the creation of new norms for a particular handicapping condition (Davis, 1970; Maxfield & Buckholz, 1957). A third solution, advocated by Anastasi (1976), has been the administration of the instrument as it was originally intended.

These three solutions all involve group comparisons. The comparisons to be made are either with normally developing children or with children of similar handicapping conditions.

Underlying group comparisons are several important assumptions (Hamilton, 1979). One assumption is that the children being compared have equivalent experiential or cultural backgrounds. Another is that the child is equally motivated to exert herself or himself in a test situation. The first assumption is not necessarily tenable when comparing many handicapped children to their nonhandicapped peers. Even comparisons within handicapping conditions may also fail to meet this assumption. For instance, the age of onset of blindness, its etiology, the degree of functional vision, the presence of other handicapping conditions, and educational experience vary widely in blind populations (Warren, 1977, 1981).

The second assumption is also questionable when referring to handicapping populations. Studies of mastery motivation (Jennings & Connors, 1984; Jennings, Connors, Sankaranarayan, & Katz, 1982) have indicated preference for novel tasks and lower persistence in physically handicapped preschoolers (with normal upper-limb functioning), as compared to a sample of nonhandicapped peers.

A third and frequently overlooked assumption includes the presence of a skilled or competent assessor in terms of establishing rapport, administering items, scoring, and interpreting. Several surveys have indicated problems in terms of training and instrument usage with handicapped populations, such as the deaf (Levine, 1974), the motorically impaired (Lewko, 1976), or others with severely handicapping conditions (Irons, Irons, & Maddux, 1984).

Given the likelihood that these and other assumptions (Salvia & Ysseldyke, 1981) are apt to be violated in assessing handicapped children, why not rely solely on an idiographic approach to the study of young handicapped children? The answer to this question, of course, depends on the purpose(s) for which assessment data are collected. When answers are sought for such questions as "What unique pattern of development is this child displaying at this time or across time?" or "What intervention areas should be targeted for this child?" (a descriptive-prescriptive concern), then idiographic data are to be emphasized. Criterion-referenced instruments have been recommended as one feasible means of gathering idiographic information. However, this approach is not without its pitfalls, as is illustrated in the overview of this book.

A nomothetic approach is to be emphasized for other questions, such as "How do numbers of children behave with respect to certain criteria?" Classification or screening questions and program-evaluation questions important to policymakers and administrators require the collection of group-type data. Research, which guides the development of practice, also requires normative benchmarks.

It is also true that these questions are not mutually exclusive. Normative benchmarks are often needed when planning for the future of handicapped children. Chess's comment that "it is necessary to assess physically damaged youngsters in accordance with normative yardsticks since a critical question is the time and degree to which they can be

brought into nonstressful integrated activity with normal children'' (1975, p. 152) is
pertinent to this point.

APPROACHES TO ASSESSMENT

The purposes of the assessment process are, of necessity, related to the referent of
comparison to be used. Hamilton and Swan (1981) noted a number of possible referents
for a child's performance during an assessment. The meaning of the child's performance
is determined by the source of reference. Three major sources for reference are other
normal or handicapped children's performance (norm-referenced); the test itself (criterion-referenced); and the child's own performance (child-referenced). Hamilton and
Swan (1981) argued that child-referenced comparisons (i.e., comparisons of a child's
own performance across time and settings) are generally ignored by practitioners in favor
of norm- or criterion-referenced approaches. This lack of attention occurs even though
child-referenced data are particularly pertinent to instructional decision-making.

As mentioned earlier, diagnosticians in clinical settings are faced with a number of
dilemmas in selecting the appropriate referent for comparison. Included among those
dilemmas is the balance between technical and normed adequacy necessary for group
comparisons and the need for accurate and useful information for diagnostic and prescriptive purposes. One solution to this dilemma is presented below. This child-referenced
approach, when used in conjunction with the testing-the-limits guidelines suggested by
Sattler (1982), affords the diagnostician the opportunity to collect both group-referenced
and child-referenced information simultaneously. Sattler (1982) recommended the administration and scoring of a test under standard procedures followed by modifications. A
comparison of the information gathered under both conditions can supply a much fuller
picture of the child under consideration.

A Child-Referenced Approach

Several authors have advocated the use of process-oriented, child-referenced approaches (Brinker & Lewis, 1982; Dubose, Langley, & Stagg, 1979; Haussermann,
1959). Brinker and Lewis (1982) outlined four key elements common to the process-
oriented approaches. *First*, the assessment process involves an ongoing interaction between the diagnostician and the child. This interaction involves a continual modification
in the task demands that depend on a child's responses. In other words, the examiner
becomes a hypothesis tester who investigates probable links between impairments and
child performance. This hypothesis testing involves sequential probing, a comparison of
skills, and the process of elimination to determine the link between the child's characteristics and the child's performance.

Dubose *et al.* (1979) provided an example of this dynamic process in evaluating a
child's failure to string beads. Motoric involvement as a contributing factor in the failure
to string beads can be eliminated if previous performance indicated appropriate eye–hand
coordination and grasp skills. Inefficient or inappropriate cognitive skills would be the
next hypothesis to be investigated. The child lacking cognition of object permanence

would not realize that the string is still present inside the bead and is shielded from view. Evidence to confirm this hypothesis can also be obtained from other tasks, such as the child's failure to retrieve objects hidden under a cup or difficulty in buttoning (i.e., the button is shielded during part of the buttoning task).

The *second* major element involves the goal of describing the child's problem-solving *approaches*, in addition to the child's *ability* to solve a particular problem. Carrow's sequence (1972) of increasingly difficult child responses provides a guideline for assessing the response patterns of young children. Similarly, Dubose *et al.* (1979) called attention to the need to ascertain the typical response modes of the child. If a child responds to a problem by banging an object, this minimal level of response should be noted. Likewise, if a child approaches a task through a trial-and-error mode, the child may be on the threshold of making generalizations to new concepts. If one observes a child self-correcting, this demonstration implies that the child has the ability to compare and contrast his or her own performance with the problem-solving task at hand. By observing the various response modes (e.g., mouthing or banging, perseverating, trial-and-error, and self-correction), one can more clearly determine a functional picture of the child.

The *third* key element involves a characterization of the range of the child's abilities, including optimal performance and performance under familiar conditions. An example was presented elsewhere (Dubose *et al.*, 1979) in the child who failed to accomplish the cube-nesting item on the Merrill-Palmer scale (Stutsman, 1948). Failure to accomplish this item does not lead to the assumption that a child lacks an awareness of serial and spatial relationships. What is required of the examiner is to establish where in the hierarchy of the development of these concepts the child functions. The administration of a downward progression of tasks is needed to tap these concepts. Failure of the child to correctly nest the cubes through visual comparison should be followed by observation of whether the child can accomplish the task via a trial-and-error approach. Failure with this approach might lead to an investigation of whether the child can match box lids to the correct boxes. Further down the hierarchy, the child who is able to pick up and return an inverted cup to its proper position is demonstrating a recognition of the cup despite its unusual spatial orientation. As one can see, the examiner's knowledge of developmental sequences and how to tap them through a creative adaptation of materials is essential to perform this process.

The *fourth* (common) element cited by Brinker and Lewis (1982) involves the lack of distinction between assessment and intervention, as the construction of a profile of the handicapped child is an ongoing interactive process. Others have characterized this as a test–teach–test model for assessment (Burns, 1984; Feuerstein, Rand, & Hoffman, 1979; Haywood, 1979; Vye, Burns, Delcos, & Bransford, 1987).

EXAMINER, INSTRUMENT, AND PROCEDURAL ADAPTATIONS

Critical components of the process model include an examiner skilled in the creative adaptation of materials and assessment procedures and the use of both formal and informal instruments. Dubose (1979, pp. 163–164) outlined a number of examiner characteristics that are desirable in the assessment of handicapped infants and children:

1. Knowledge of the precise sequences by which children acquire skills.
2. Knowledge of the impact certain impairments have on the development of skills.
3. Ability to determine the most appropriate procedure for presenting the tasks to the particular child.
4. Ability to establish a satisfactory communication system with the child.
5. Ability to select the most appropriate tests/tasks, administer them, or adapt them as needed.
6. Ability to select the most appropriate environments for testing.
7. Ability to time testing periods so as to evoke maximum responses.
8. Ability to manipulate testing conditions to enhance correct responses.
9. Ability to translate findings into functional program plans.
10. Ability to present data in a positive manner.

Types of Modifications

In general, there are a number of types of modifications that can be made when using instruments typically designed for nonhandicapped populations: (a) modifications in test stimuli; (b) modifications in the response required of the child; and (c) modifications in test procedures.

Modifications in test stimuli can include changes in the mode of communication on the part of the examiner (e.g., sign language versus the oral presentation of directions) or changes in the stimuli used (e.g., the substitution of high-contrast material).

Alteration in the response required of the child can take a number of forms, including the mode of response (e.g., the use of a motor response in place of a verbal one) or the rate of response (e.g., the elimination of time limits).

Procedural modifications include such aspects as changes in the positioning of the child (e.g., placing the child on the floor or using supportive sitting in adaptive equipment versus traditional table-top administration). The use of behavior management procedures is another type of procedural modification, as such techniques are often necessary with children who display a number of behaviors that interfere with the child's display of optimum performance. The Fox and Wise (1981) survey validated an inventory of social, tangible, and activity reinforcers for children below 6 years of age. The use of this survey can provide the clinician with potential reinforcers for use within diagnostic or intervention settings. The administration of selected items is another type of procedural modification. A prime example is the administration of only the verbal sections of the Wechsler Preschool and Primary Scale of Intelligence (WPPSI—(Wechsler, 1967) to blind children.

Unfortunately, very few commercially available instruments provide clinicians with guidelines for choosing the type of adaptation to be used. The Developmental Activities Screening Inventory (Dubose & Langley, 1977), the Developmental Activities Screening Inventory II (Fewell & Langley, 1984), and the Adaptative Performance Inventory (Gentry, 1980) represent instruments that were designed with adaptations for special handicapping conditions. For example, on the Adaptative Performance Instrument (API), each target item is accompanied by a listing of handicapping conditions (i.e., deaf or blind, hearing-impaired, visually impaired, and motorically impaired) for which standard adaptations can be used. These standard adaptations are cross-referenced to each of the four handicapping conditions, along with the type of adaptation (procedural or child response) to be made.

An example of a procedural adaptation for a motorically impaired child would be the use of a spoon with a built-up handle on one of the utensil-use items. An example of a response type of adaptation on the API for the visually impaired child is the substitution of the target item "makes a postural orientation to an adult" for the target item "makes eye contact with an adult." Each standard item is accompanied by a written rationale as well. All target items do not have adaptations for every handicapping condition, but provision for the use of novel adaptations is made if the intent of the target item is not changed.

Gentry (1980) offered some general guidelines for adaptations for a variety of handicapping conditions. With visually impaired children, a determination of the child's functional vision is essential before the selection of tests and procedures. Each stimulus should be placed within the child's field of vision (established before the administration of the items). At times, it may be necessary to move stimuli closer to the child, although care must be taken not to place an object so close that it fills the visual field and obscures important features of the object. Background–foreground contrast should be attended to as well. Light-colored stimuli should be used if one is working at a dark table. If possible, objects with high visual contrast (i.e., black and white) should be chosen.

Physical contact with the stimulus material is also recommended as an aid. As many visually impaired children may not be aware of the response requirements because of a lack of experience, physical guidance of the child may provide a model for the desired behavior.

With hearing-impaired children, the examiner must also have some notion of the child's functional auditory skills. This knowledge will influence the selection of communication modes and the choice of procedure. For the optimal use of visual information, the positioning of the hearing-impaired child is critical. The child should face the speaker properly in order to read signs or speech movements.

For orthopedically or neurologically impaired children, modifications in the child's positioning may be necessary. For instance, most instruments for young children include a large number of objects requiring the child to grasp and manipulate them while seated in a chair or in the mother's lap. Young cerebral-palsied children often have abnormal patterns of posture when sitting and, therefore, cannot interact with the materials appropriately. The use of adaptive positioning equipment, such as wedges, can often enable the child to perform the task correctly. Because most diagnosticians are quite unfamiliar with physically handicapped populations, consultation with a physical or occupational therapist is essential when selecting test-taking positions or using adaptative equipment. Finnie's review (1974) provides practical information with regard to handling techniques. (Also see Robinson & Fieber, Chapter 8 in this book).

Theoretical Issues Guiding Modifications

An important factor that should be considered in procedural adaptations is the theoretical base from which an assessment device was constructed. Stagg (1979) reviewed a potpourri of instruments appropriate for individual functioning below the 72-month level.

The instruments in this review were grouped according to the degree to which they were drawn from one of three ideologies (Dunst, 1977) underlying the theoretical models defining common early-childhood curricula. These theoretical models, as outlined by Dunst (1977), are maturational, cognitive-developmental, and environmental. Examples of instruments that parallel these models are the Gesell Developmental Schedules (Knobloch & Pasamanick, 1974), which was developed from a maturational perspective; the Infant Scales of Psychological Development (Uzgiris & Hunt, 1975), which was developed from a cognitive-developmental theoretical base; and the Cattel Infant Intelligence Scales (Cattel, 1940), which was developed from an implicit environmental or additive model of child development.

Knowledge of the theoretical notion on which an assessment instrument is based and of the theoretical base of the intervention setting is crucial in selecting an appropriate modification and interpretation of the child's response. For instance, the adequacy of the Gesell Developmental Schedules (Knobloch & Pasamanick, 1974) has been the subject of a running debate between psychologists and physicians for a number of reasons. Wilson (1963) viewed the reasons for disagreement as being rooted in the entirely different assumptions and aims held by the two professions. As Stott and Ball (1965) noted, many of the criticisms voiced by psychologists are based on the assumption that the Gesell is a test of intelligence, despite Gesell's (1940) and Knobloch and Pasaminick's (1960) contention that the Gesell is primarily a maturational-neurological tool. Modifications in the Gesell and subsequent use of the information gained from the modification should be made in the context of the theoretical notion behind the interventions planned for the child.

CLINICAL IMPLICATIONS

Stagg's review (1979) of the instrumentation suitable for the assessment of cognition in severely and profoundly handicapped populations presented a format for judging the relative technical merits of instruments suitable for young children. A similar framework could be used in judging the merits of instruments suitable for other areas (i.e., motor, language, and self-care and adaptative behavior). This review focused on seven instruments which were selected because (a) they were generally available to the practitioner; (b) they had been developed from a variety of theoretical perspectives; (c) they appeared to have utility with a variety of populations at various age levels; and (d) research, although limited, offered some information base from which to make educated judgments about their use.

This review (Stagg, 1979) did not include criterion-referenced instruments, although Bagnato (1979) noted that some of the scales (i.e., the Gesell Developmental Schedules) may be used as such. Neonatal instruments were also not included in this review. St. Clair (1978) provided an excellent review of neonatal assessment procedures that highlights the most widely used instrument for this age range, the Brazelton Neonatal Assessment Schedules (Brazelton, 1973). Summaries of research on the use of the instruments most widely employed with young handicapped children—the Binet (Terman & Merrill, 1973) and the Wechsler Scales (1967, 1974)—are found in Sattler (1982).

The review by Stagg (1979) noted the relative strength of seven instruments in a number of their technical and utilitarian characteristics for both handicapped and nonhandicapped children. Table 1 (pp. 70–71) contains conclusions from the 1979 review regarding the acceptability of four test characteristics with handicapped and nonhandicapped populations. Those characteristics are (a) test–retest reliability and internal consistency; (b) concurrent and predictive validity; (c) standardization samples; and (d) utility with special populations. The last category refers to the degree of appropriateness and flexibility that the instrument appears to offer the examiner working with particular handicapping conditions. For the convenience of the reader, the developmental ranges spanned by the measures are included in the table.

First, instruments were rated on the degree to which they were reliable, valid, and standardized. Ratings of "high acceptability" were given to assessment devices if the literature indicated that their test characteristics met conventionally accepted standards for test construction.

The same three ratings were used for the characteristic of "utility with special populations." Although these ratings were somewhat more subjective, they represented judgments based on the available studies, reviewers' comments, and the writer's own experience.

These judgments represent relative comparisons, not absolute ones. As evidenced by comments in this chapter and others in this book, the field clearly precludes adherence to rigid guidelines.

Impact of Modifications

The use of modifications cited above has direct relevance to issues of reliability and validity discussed in Chapter 3 of this book. Advocates of classical test-theory concepts correctly contend that norm-referenced interpretations are difficult when using either standardized or developmentally based instruments with young handicapped children (Salvia & Ysseldyke, 1981). The impact of modifications on presentation mode, child response, or other procedural alterations on the reliability and validity of most instruments currently in use with preschool handicapped populations is unknown, as suggested in Chapter 3. The issue of comparability between young handicapped and nonhandicapped children's performance on identical instruments or comparability under modified conditions may be a false one, depending on the decisions one wishes to base on the data obtained from the assessment process.

Comments by Bruening, Barrett, and Kerr (1983) on the impact of procedural alterations (i.e., positive reinforcement) in testing mentally retarded children are pertinent to this point: "The use of reinforcement during testing conditions is a debated issue and no clear guidelines are available. This issue is largely whether an examiner is content to know which items a client will respond to, or which items a client can respond to" (p. 233).

Of at least equal, if not predominant, concern in judging the reliability of the assessment process is the aptitude and ability of the examiner to make appropriate modifications, as well as his or her familiarity with the type of child under consideration. For example, Field's investigation (1981) of a number of clinical testing variables suggests that young handicapped children's scores on the Bayley Mental Scales (Bayley, 1969) and the Stanford-Binet (Terman & Merrill, 1973) may be inflated or deflated. The examiner's experience in testing handicapped children and the examiner's familiarity with the child were included in Field's investigation of clinical variables.

A good, but unfortunate, example of inappropriate modification that affected the content validity (the domain sampled) of an instrument was recently called to my attention at a diagnostic conference for a nonverbal multiply impaired child. The results of a modified administration of the Peabody Individual Achievement Test (Dunn & Markwardt, 1970) indicated a wide discrepancy between reading recognition and other measures of achievement. The reading recognition measure was significantly above what one would expect, based on the other test data and observations.

The format of the reading-recognition subtest of the Peabody Individual Achievement (PIAT) requires an oral response to visually presented stimuli, whereas PIAT measures of arithmetic achievement, spelling, and reading comprehension use a multiple-choice format, in which a one-word or a pointing response is required of the child. The diagnostician had modified both the mode of presentation and the response required of the child. The examiner pronounced the list of words contained in the PIAT stimulus reading-recognition subtest and asked the child to point out on the PIAT stimulus page the same word pronounced by the examiner. Needless to say, the increased number of cues available greatly inflated the child's performance, and the modification shifted the domain tapped by this subtest from reading recognition to spelling or letter recognition. This example suggests the need to carefully document modifications that are made, to make modifications in an objective manner, and to ensure that the essential nature of the test will be maintained.

SUMMARY

Any meaningful child-referenced assessment requires a dynamic approach from the diagnostician. This dynamic approach involves the judicious selection and use of a number of instruments, as well as creative alterations in materials and procedures if one is to obtain a functional picture of a child's skills. This approach must also be based on a careful *a priori* articulation of the purpose(s) of any particular child's assessment. Such an approach helps to prevent the far too frequent classification of children as "untestable." The use of this term as a descriptor of a young handicapped child is "more a comment on the techniques used by the examiner than a statement about the intelligence of the child" (Woodward, 1970, p. 708).

ACKNOWLEDGMENTS

I gratefully acknowledge the support, assistance, and helpful comments I received from Georgia D. Wills and Margaret G. Shemwell in drafting this chapter.

Table I.

| | Reliability | | | | Validity | | | |
| | Test-retest | | Internal consistency | | Concurrent | | Predictive | |
Measure	Hd	NHd	Hd	NHd	Hd	NHd	Hd	NHd
Environmental								
Infant Intelligence Scales	M	L	NA	M	H	M–H	M–H	L
Columbia Mental Maturity Scale	H	M–H	NA	H	M	L–M	NA	NA
Hiskey-Nebraska Test of Learning Aptitude	NA	NA	H	H	L–M	M–H	NA	NA
Pictorial Test of Intelligence	H	M–H	H	H	M	M	L–M	NA
Merrill-Palmer Scales	H	M–L	NA	NA	M[b]	L–M	NA	L–M
Maturational								
Maturial Gesell Developmental Schedules	M–M	L	NA	M	H[b]	M	L–M	L
Cognitive-Developmental								
Infant Psychological Developmental Scales	M–H	M–L	M–H	NA	M–H[b]	—	NA	L–M

[a]Key: Hd = handicapped; NHd = nonhandicapped; H = high acceptability; M = moderate acceptability; L = low acceptability; NA = not available
[b]Judgement based on one or two studies

Ratings of Test Characteristics[a]

Standardization sample/norms		Utility with special populations					Developmental range (months)			
Hd	NHd	Deaf	Blind	Motor/Ortho	MR	Non-verbal	0–12	12–24	24–36	36+
NA	M	M	M	M–L	H	M	X	X	X	—
NA	H	M	L	H	M	H	—	—	—	X
H	H	H	L	L	H	H	—	—	—	X
NA	H	H	L	H	H	H	—	—	—	X
NA	M	M–H	L	L	H	H	—	—	—	X
NA	L	M	M	M	M–H	M	X	X	X	—
NA	L	H	H	H	H	H	X	X	—	

REFERENCES

Anastasi, A. (1976). *Psychological testing* (4th ed.). New York: Macmillan.

Bagnato, S. J. (1979). Developmental scales and developmental curricula: Forgoing the linkage for early intervention. *Topics in Early Childhood Special Education, 1*(2), 1–8.

Barnett, D. W. (1983). *Nondiscriminatory multi-factored assessment: A sourcebook.* New York: Human Sciences Press.

Bayley, N. (1969). *Bayley Scales of Infant Development.* New York: Psychological Corporation.

Brazelton, T. (1973). *The Neonatal Behavior Assessment Scale.* Philadelphia: Lippincott.

Brinker, R. P., & Lewis, M. L. (1982). Discovering the competent handicapped infant: A process approach to assessment and intervention. *Topics in Early Childhood Special Education, 2*(2), 1–16.

Bruening, S. E., Barrett, R. P., & Kerr, M. M. (1983). Psychoeducational assessment of mentally retarded, psychiatrically disturbed individuals. In S. Ray, M. J. O'Nell, & N. T. Morris (Eds.), *Low incidence children: A guide to psychoeducational assessment.* Natchitoches, LA: Steven Ray Publishing.

Burns, S. M. (1984). *A comparison of graduated prompt and mediated dynamic assessment and static assessment with young children.* Paper presented at the America Educational Research Association, New Orleans.

Carrow, E. (1972). Assessment of speech and language in children. In J. E. McLean, D. E. Yoder, & R. L. Shiefelbusch (Eds.), *Language intervention with the retarded.* Baltimore: University Park Press.

Cattel, P. (1940). *The measurement of intelligence of infants and young children.* New York: Psychological Corporation.

Chase, J. B. (1975). Developmental assessment of handicapped infants and young children: With special attention to the visually impaired. *New Outlook for the Blind, 69*, 341–364.

Chess, S. (1975). Influence of defect on development in children with congenital rubella. In S. Chess & A. Thomas (Eds.), *Annual progress in child psychiatry and child development.* New York: Brunner/Mazel.

Davis, C. J. (1970). New developments in the intelligence testing of blind children. *Proceedings of the conference of New Approaches to the Evaluation of Blind Persons.* New York: American Foundation for the Blind.

Dubose, R. F. (1979). Assessment of visually impaired infants. In B. L. Darby & M. J. May (Eds.), *Infant assessment: Issues and applications.* Seattle: Western States Technical Assistance Resource Center.

Dubose, R. F. (1981). Assessment of severely impaired young children: problems and recommendations. *Topics in Early Childhood Special Education, 1*(2), 9–12.

Dubose, R. F., & Langley, M. B. (1977). *The developmental activities screening inventory.* Hingham, MA: Teaching Resources.

Dubose, R. F., Langley, M. B., & Stagg, V. (1979). Assessing severely handicapped children. In E. Myen, G. Vergason, & R. Whelan (Eds.), *Instructional planning for exceptional children.* Denver: Love Publishing.

Dunn, L. M., & Markwardt, F. C. (1970). *Peabody Individual Achievement Test.* Circle Pines, MN: American Guidance Service.

Dunst, C. J. (1977). An early cognitive-linguistic strategy. *Western Carolina Center Papers and Reports* (Vol. 8[1]). Morgantown, NC.

Feuerstein, R., Rand, Y., & Hoffman, M. B. (1979). *The dynamic assessment of retarded performers: The Learning Potential Assessment Device, theory, instruments and techniques.* Baltimore: University Park Press.

Fewell, R. F., & Langley, M. B. (1984). *The developmental activities screening inventory II (DASI II).* Austin, TX: Pro Ed Publishing.

Field, T. (1981). Ecological variables and examiner biases in assessing handicapped preschool children. *Journal of Pediatric Psychology, 6*(3), 155–163.

Finnie, N. R. (1974). *Handling the young cerebral palsied child at home.* New York: E. P. Dutton.

Fox, R., & Wise, P. S. (1981). Infant and preschool reinforcement survey. *Psychology in the Schools, 18*(1), 87–92.

Gentry, D. (1980). *The adaptative performance instrument-experimental edition.* Moscow, ID: Consortium on Adaptative Performance Evaluation.

Gesell, A. (1940). *The first five years of life: A guide to the study of the preschool child.* New York: Harper & Row.

Hamilton, J. L. (1979). Assessment in mental retardation: Toward instructional relevance. In R. B. Kearsley & I. E. Siegel (Eds.), *Infants at risk: Assessment of cognitive functioning.* Hillsdale, NJ: Erlbaum.

Hamilton, J. L., & Swan, W. W. (1981). Measurement references in the assessment of preschool handicapped children. *Topics in Early Childhood Special Education, 1*(2), 41–48.

Hausserman, E. (1959). *Developmental potential of preschool children.* New York: Grune & Stratton.

Haywood, H. C. (1979). Alternatives to normative assessment. In P. Mittler (Ed.). *Research to practice in mental retardation* (Vol. 2). Baltimore: University Park Press.

Hiskey, M. S. (1966). *The Hiskey-Nebraska Test of Learning Aptitude.* Lincoln, NE: Union College Press.

Irons, D., Irons, T., & Maddux, C. D. (1984). A survey of perceived competence among psychologists who evaluate students with severe handicaps. *The Association for the Severely Handicapped Journal, 9,* 55–60

Jennings, K. D., & Connors, R. E. (1984). *The effect of a physical handicap on the development of mastery motivation.* Paper presented at the Conference on Mastery Motivation, National Institute of Mental Health, Washington, DC.

Jennings, K. D., Connors, R. E., Sankaranaryan, A., & Katz, E. (1982). *Mastery motivation in physically handicapped and nonhandicapped preschool children.* Paper presented at the Annual Meeting of the American Academy of Child Psychiatry, Washington, DC.

Knobloch, H., & Pasamanick, B. (1960). An evaluation of the consistency and predictive value of the forty week Gesell Developmental Schedule. In D. Shagass & B. Pasamanick (Eds.), *Child development and the child psychiatry: Psychiatric research report of the American Psychiatric Association* (Vol. 13). Washington, DC: American Psychiatric Association.

Knobloch, H., & Pasamanick, B. (1974). *Gesell and Armatruda's developmental diagnoses* (3rd ed.). Hagerstown, MD: Harper & Row.

Levine, E. (1974). Psychological tests and practices with the deaf: A survey of the state of the art. *Volta Review, 76,* 298–319.

Lewko, J. H. (1976). Current practice in evaluating motor behavior in disabled children. *American Journal of Occupational Therapy, 30*(7), 413–414.

Maxfield, K. E., & Buckholz, S. (1957). *A social maturity scale for blind preschool children: A guide to its use.* New York: American Foundation for the Blind.

St. Clair, K. L. (1978). Neonatal assessment procedures: A historical review. *Child Development, 49,* 280–292.

Salvia, J., & Ysseldyke, J. E. (1981). *Assessment in special and remedial education* (2nd ed.). Boston: Houghton-Mifflin.

Sattler, J. (1982). *Assessment of children's intelligence* (2nd ed.). Boston: Allyn & Bacon.

Stagg, V. (1979). *A review of cognitive assessment instruments employed with severely handicapped children and youth.* Unpublished major area paper, George Peabody College for Teachers of Vanderbilt University, Nashville.

Stott, L., & Ball, R. S. (1965). Infant and preschool mental tests: Review and evaluation. *Monographs of the Society for Research in Child Development, 30*(3), 1–151.

Stutsman, R. (1948). *The Merrill-Palmer Scale of Mental Tests.* Chicago: Stoelting.

Terman, L. & Merrill, M. (1973). *Stanford-Binet Intelligence Scale, 1972 norms edition.* Boston: Houghton Mifflin.

Ulrey, G. I., & Schnell, R. R. (1982). Introduction to assessing young children. In S. Ulrey & S. J. Rogers (Eds.), *Psychological assessment of handicapped infants and young children.* New York: Thieme-Stratton.

Uzgiris, I., & Hunt, J. M. (1975). *Assessment in infancy: Ordinal scale of psychological development.* Urbana, IL: University of Illinois Press.

Vye, N. J., Burns, S. M., Delcos, V. R., & Bransford, J. D. (1987). Dynamic assessment of intellecutally handicapped children. In C. S. Lidz (Ed.), *Dynamic assessment: Foundations and fundamentals.* New York: Guilford.

Warren, D. (1977). *Blindness and early childhood development.* New York: American Foundation for the Blind.

Warren, D. H. (1981). Visual Impairments. In J. M. Kauffman & D. P. Hallahan (Eds.), *Handbook of special education.* Englewood Cliffs, NJ: Prentice-Hall.

Wechsler, D. (1967). *Manual for the Wechsler Preschool and Primary Scale of Intelligence.* New York: Psychological Corporation.

Wechsler, D. (1974). *Manual for the Wechsler Intelligence Scale for Children—Revised.* New York: Psychological Corporation.

Wilson, M. (1963). Gesell developmental testing. *Journal of Pediatrics, 62,* 162–164.

Woodward, W. M. (1970). The assessment of cognitive processes: Piaget's approach. In P. Mittler (Ed.), *The psychological assessment of mental and physical handicaps.* London: Metheum.

5

Involvement of Parents in Early Childhood Assessment

Robert Sheehan

The involvement of parents in the assessment of their infants and preschoolers is a topic that generates much heated discussion among professionals in early childhood special education. Many professionals, especially those trained in the rigors of psychological measurement and test construction argue vehemently that parents lack the necessary objectivity and training to provide accurate assessment data on their children. Some clinicians also argue that parents should not be encouraged to assess their children, as such activity only provides the impetus for a pressure-cooker relationship between parents and children.

In contrast, clinicians who are well aware of the benefits of home–school collaboration argue that assessment is one area in which such collaboration can provide useful insights (Blacher-Dixon & Simeonsson, 1981). The escalating costs of early intervention and prevention and the corresponding increases in the cost of assessment provide yet another impetus for a consideration of assessment strategies that involve fewer (and less costly) professional hours of involvement. Parent participation in assessment may provide that less costly alternative.

Despite the rhetoric surrounding this issue, listeners rarely hear reference to empirical support for either side of the argument. This absence of empirical reference is surprising in light of the fact that a relatively large number of empirical studies have been conducted on the congruence of parental and professional opinion in the assessment of children. The weight of these studies is further increased by the consistency of their findings, consistency that is certainly rare in the early-intervention and prevention literature.

This chapter reviews the most frequently cited reasons for and against parental involvement in early childhood assessment. Twenty-four empirical studies of parental and professional agreement in early childhood assessment are also reviewed, and the possible reasons for their findings are discussed. Finally, a model of parental involvement in early

ROBERT SHEEHAN ● Department of Foundation and Curriculum, College of Education, Cleveland State University, Cleveland, Ohio 44115.

childhood assessment is introduced as a potential tool for responding to the complexities of families and children encountered in early intervention and prevention efforts.

REASONS AGAINST PARENTAL INVOLVEMENT IN ASSESSMENT

Assessment of children has typically been the domain of psychologists. For example, the Bayley Scales of Infant Development (Bayley, 1969), a measure sold by the Psychological Corporation, cannot be purchased by parents or other lay individuals. Similarly, the administration and interpretation of intelligence tests is frequently limited by ordinances and/or professional organizations.

A major reason that nonprofessionals (and sometimes more specifically, non-psychologists) have been excluded from assessment is the belief that assessments must be administered in a "standard fashion" in order to be considered reliable and valid. Only those with requisite training can give tests in the correct way. A second, related reason is the fear that untrained personnel can do no good and can possibly do harm by interpreting intelligence or personality tests. This fear is based on the assumption that untrained persons do not know the meaning of scores or will overgeneralize the results of scores.

Even when assessment tools are based on naturalistic observation rather than on standard testing, parental involvement has been minimized because of the belief that observational skills are learned only with extensive training. This distrust of the subjectivity of an observer provides a strong foundation for resistance to the involvement of parents in the assessment of their infants and preschoolers.

Yet another reason that parents are excluded from involvement in assessment is to be found in the educational community. In a recent study, Joffe (1979) conducted a series of extensive interviews with staff and parents in several day-care settings. She also observed the interactions of parents and staff in the day-care centers. She identified the difficulty that early childhood clinicians experience in maintaining their role of professionals in light of extensive parent involvement in programs as follows: If parent involvement is encouraged in all areas of an educational program, how is a clinician to maintain a personal sense and a recognized sense of being a highly trained professional? The training received by a clinician cannot be lightly dismissed, so parents who are involved are frequently delegated to the role of aide or assistant to the teacher. The domain of educational assessment is not casually made available to parents, as it represents to a clinician an area of specialized training and professional identification.

A final reason that parents are excluded from assessment is that there is a lack of clarity in the purposes of assessment. For example, many clinicians use instruments for educational planning that require specialized training (e.g., the Bayley scales), without questioning whether such instruments are necessary.

In contrast, other instruments (e.g., the Developmental Profile) were designed to be used by "an evaluator who need not be a trained developmental expert" (Alpern & Shearer, 1980). The purpose of such instruments is more applied and immediate, providing information for purposes of developing educatonal programs for individual children. Educators unaware of the intended purpose of such measures or ambiguous in their own purposes in assessment might be more inclined to restrict parents from involvement in assessment.

REASONS FOR PARENTAL INVOLVEMENT IN ASSESSMENT

One major impetus for the involvement of parents in early childhood assessment is to be found in subparts of Public Law 94-142, the Education for All Handicapped Children Act. This law mandates parental involvement in the individualized educational planning (IEP) process. Obviously a critical part of educational planning is the assessment of the current functioning of a child or infant.

PL 94-142 also mandates parental involvement in any change in a child's status in an educational program, and it further guarantees parental access to all records. Once parents have access to children's developmental test results and protocols, and once parents have a formal place in the decision making about a child's educational program, parental involvement in the gathering of a child's assessment data seems a logical consequence.

A second reason would be the cost effectiveness of parental assessment. Early childhood assessment can be a process that is costly in dollars and in person hours. For example, an educational diagnostician may charge $300 to administer a battery of measures to a child. A program providing service to 30 chldren can obviously not afford to repeat such testings during the school year.

In contrast, Bricker and Littman (1983) noted that developmental screening is one area in which parental involvement might decrease the cost of assessment. They discussed the use of the Prescreening Developmental Questionnaire (PDQ) proposed by Frankenburg, Van Doornick, Liddell, and Dick (1976): "Based on the child's age, parents answer 10 items form the PDQ. Children who are suspect are rescreened 1–2 weeks later. Using the PDQ this way requires one minute of professonal time and costs 3 to 5 cents for the printed questionnaire" (Bricker & Littman, 1983, p. 6).

The time devoted by teachers and assistants to assessment is a hidden cost of assessment. Many programs beginning in September are involved in assessment through mid-October. In some cases, this time spent on assessment by the professionals is also time that is not spent on intervention with children. Parental involvement in such instances might mean a more cost-beneficial educational environment for children.

A third reason that parental involvement in early childhood assessment is warranted is to be found in the changing purpose of many assessment instruments. The last decade has witnessed a dramatic increase in the use of assessment instruments for instructional purposes (Sheehan, 1982). Assessment directed at instructional planning is assessment directed at educationally relevant developmental items that are (or should be) stable across a variety of settings. Said differently, if an item is a target for instructional intervention, then it should elicit performance that is observable to most individuals with a minimum of training, and it should elicit a behavior that generalizes to a variety of settings (at home and school).

This increased interest in assessment for instructional planning is now being supported by the availability of instructional planning-assessment measures requiring little or no training. One example that has already been mentioned is the Developmental Profile (Alpern & Shearer, 1980). This instrument assesses children (newborn–6 years) in five areas, including physical development, self-help skills, social development, academic development, and communication skills.

A second instrument that is used by clinicians for instructional planning is the Learning Accomplishment Profile (and it's infant version: the Infant Learning Accomplishment Profile). This instrument is used to assess children's development in six areas, including gross motor, fine motor, social, self-help, cognitive skills, and language.

A point that must be noted in this discussion of the reasons for parental involvement in assessment is that the purpose(s) of assessment must be clarified and consistent with parental involvement. Many of the arguments that have been cited against parental involvement, especially those pertaining to the specialized training needed to administer and interpret intelligence and personality measures, do not oppose parental involvement in assessment for educational planning.

A REVIEW OF EMPIRICAL STUDIES

The reasons that have just been cited for and against parental involvement in early childhood assessment have been based on psychometric theory, cost, and the changing purposes of assessment. These are reasons based on logic or pragmatics. A conspicuous absence in these rationales is reasoning based on empirical support. In preparation for this chapter, 24 studies were located investigating parental congruency with professionals' assessment ratings. The 24 studies represent an extremely large portion of the entire population of the available studies on this topic. Many, though not all, of the studies were referenced in a technical report prepared by Valencia and Cruz (1981) as part of a research project funded by the Administration for Children, Youth, and Families.

The sources for the 24 studies are to be found in Table 1. As Table 1 indicates, the studies were located in a variety of sources with a maximum frequency of three for any source. Of the studies, 75% (18/24) were located in the published literature, the rest being located in unpublished sources. One study (Johnson & Capobianco, 1957) could not be located in its primary citation but was mentioned as a secondary source in Capobianco and Knox (1964).

Excluded from this review are studies specifically investigating children's temperament or behavior disorders. The present chapter deals with the involvement of parents in the use of "developmental scales," measures that present a sequence of items of increasing developmental difficulty. Measures of temperament and behavior disorder are very different from this concept of a developmental measure (see Chapters 10 and 13 by Zental and McDevitt (respectively) for discussions of these types of measures).

The 24 studies reviewed in this chapter are relatively recent, as is indicated in Table 2. Of these studies, 75% (18/24) have been published since 1970, with almost half of the studies having been published since 1976.

The common denominator of all these studies is that they involved a comparison of parental assessments of children's functioning with some alternative professional assessment, that of either a trained diagnostician or a teacher (and sometimes both).

In locating these studies, an attempt was made to locate all studies of parental congruency that included children aged 7 years and younger. This was accomplished with the exception that one study (Tew, Laurence, & Samuel, 1974) included children aged 9 years, 3 months to 15 years, 8 months. Twelve studies (50%) included infants in their

Table 1. Sources of Empirical Studies on
Parental-Professional Congruency

Source	Frequency
American Journal of Mental Deficiency	3
Psychology in the Schools	2
Developmental Medicine and Child Neurology	2
Exceptional Children	2
Genetic Psychology Monographs	1
Language, Speech, Hearing Services in the Schools	1
Journal of Mental Deficiency Research	1
American Educational Research Journal	1
Pediatrics	1
Topics in Early Childhood Special Education	1
Journal Division of Early Childhood	1
Mental Retardation	1
Journal of Genetic Psychology	1
Dissertation	2
Paper presented at national conference	1
Unpublished paper	3

sample (in most cases, older children were also included in these studies), and the remaining studies (50%) were of children 3 yeas old or older.

Fourteen of the studies (58%) included handicapped children, with the most frequent classification being moderate to severe retardation. One study (Donnelly, 1983) involved a direct comparison of normal and handicapped populations (infants). The remaining studies were conducted either with a normal population of children or with a population of children whose developmental status was unknown (as in a screening effort; cf. Frankenburg et al., 1976).

Table 2. Citation Dates of Studies

Year	Frequency
1957	2
1959	1
1964	1
1969	2
1970	1
1971	1
1972	1
1974	1
1975	1
1976	3
1979	2
1980	2
1981	3
1983	3

Twenty-one of the studies (87%) were conducted with a group of primarily Caucasian American children. One study included a Greek population (Hunt & Paraskevopolous, 1980), one study a British population (Gould, 1975), and one study a Mexican-American population (Valencia & Cruz, 1981).

Table 3 contains a listing of the measures used in the 24 studies and their frequency of use. As Table 3 indicates, the three instruments most used in the programs were the Binet, the Bayley Scales, and the Vineland Social Maturity Scale. Each of these three measures requires professional training. Numerous measures that did not require such training were also used, including the Developmental Profile, the Carolina Record of Infant Behavior, and the Prescreening Developmental Questionnaire (PDQ).

Table 4 (pp. 82–83) contains a description of the findings of the 24 studies, including information (when available) regarding the magnitude of the obtained differences and the direction of the obtained differences. As Table 4 indicates, the overwhelming majority of the studies revealed that parents (usually mothers) overestimated their children's progress. This pattern was found in 18 of 24 studies (75%). Four studies (17%) found parental agreement with the diagnostic or teaching testing of Children (Blacher-Dixon & Simeonsson, 1981; Hanson, Vail, & Irvin, 1979; Schulman & Stein, 1959; Dopheide & Dallinger, 1976). One study (6%) found parents to underestimate the tested performance of their children (Donnelly, 1983), and one study found parents agreeing with the diagnostic testing at 8 months and underestimating infant's diagnostic testing at 4 months (Bricker & Littman, 1983).

The correlation between parental estimates of child performance and diagnostic or teacher testings of child performance was occasionally reported in the studies that have been discussed. These correlations were typically quite high. For example, Gradel,

Table 3. Instruments Used in Studies

Instrument	Frequency
Binet	5
Gesell	2
Bayley Scales	5
Vineland	5
Preschool Attainment Record	3
McCarthy Scales	2
Developmental Profile	2
Cattell	1
WISC	2
Prescreening Developmental Questionaire (PDQ)	1
Denver Articulation Screening Test	1
Illinois Test of Psycholinguistic Abilities	1
Peabody Picture Vocabulary Test	1
Carolina Record of Infant Behavior	1
Minnesota Child Development Inventory	1
Age Independence Scale	1
Learning Accomplishment Profile—Diagnostic	1
Valentine	1
Questionnaires	1

Thompson, and Sheehan (1981) reported maternal and diagnostic correlations of .69 and .67 for infants on the Bayley Scale Mental Index and Motor Index, respectively. Correlations were even higher for preschoolers, ranging from a low of .73 for parental and diagnostic ratings on the McCarthy Scales Quantitative Scale and a high of .95 for the McCarthy Scales Perceptual Scale. The parent–diagnostician correlation for the General Cognitive Index of the McCarthy scales was .88 for that sample of preschoolers.

The correlation statistic is not a particularly useful measure of association between parental estimates of children's development and teachers' or diagnosticians' testings, as the two groups of scores could, in fact, be quite far apart on the average and yet highly correlated—because of similar rankings of individuals in both groups. As stated earlier, the typical pattern across 75% of the studies was for the parents to rate their child's performance more highly than the children's test scores warranted. Thus, the correlations that have just been stated must be interpreted simply as a measure of similar rankings of individuals from parents and actual developmental testings.

Before proceeding to a discussion of the meaning of the results that have just been given, the two findings of parents' underestimating children's performance must be discussed. The first of these was the study by Bricker and Littman (1983), which was a report of a parent's estimating their 4-month-old infants' performance. The infants in this case were infants who had been born handicapped or at risk and had spent three days or more after birth in a neonatal intensive-care unit (NICU). At 4 months of age, these infants' parents underestimated their developmental ability, whereas the parents and diagnosticians agreed on the children's status at 8 months. The select nature of this population (NICU babies), the participation of these babies in an NCIU monitoring program, and the timing of the assessment (4 months from birth) certainly suggest a uniqueness about the study that would justify its findings' being discrepant from those of the many other studies mentioned. Also, the childen's time spent in the NICU very likely resulted in their parents' having less contact with the babies during the first four months of life, with the possible result of lower, less informed estimations.

The other study yielding such results was done by Donnelly (1983). In this study, mothers and fathers estimated their infant's development an average of two months less than the children tested (by diagnosticians). There is little in the procedures or population of this study that would indicate a qualitative difference from the other studies that have been cited. The study was conducted with a handicapped sample of infants ($n = 15$) and a nonhandicapped sample ($n = 15$). The handicapped children were all multiply handicapped exhibiting a wide range of disorders (Down syndrome, cerebral palsy, seizures, brain damage, and others). One possible difference between this sample and the samples in the other studies is that the educational level of the mothers was quite high (15 years' education) compared to the levels in a number of the other studies (e.g., the mothers of the infants in the Gradel *et al.* study, 1981, had an average of 9.8 years' education). Hunt & Paraskevopolous (1980) reported a negative, though moderate, correlation between mothers' educational levels and agreement between mothers and diagnosticians. Unfortunately, the issue of maternal education received so little reference in the remaining studies that its relevance to Donnelly's discrepant findings (1983) is still largely untested.

In summary, the 24 studies that have been cited yielded a fairly systematic pattern of parental estimates' being higher than the test performance determined by teachers or

Table 4. Summary of Findings of the Studies

Citation	Summary of finding	Magnitude of differences
Ewart *et al.*, 1976	Mothers estimated higher than children tested.	Average IQ from mothers=58; tested=44.1.
Johnson *et al.*, 1957	Parents estimated higher than children tested.	Reported average IQ point difference of 4 points (mothers reported higher-secondary citation).
Schulman *et al.*, 1959	General agreement between parents and staff (some estimations higher by parents, some lower).	Average IQ from parents=57.2; tested=55.5
Capobianco *et al.,1964*	Mothers estimated higher than children tested. Fathers estimated same as children tested.	Average IQ from mothers=67.7; fathers=61.7; tested=61.1.
Keith *et al.*, 1969	Parents estimated higher than children tested by staff.	Mothers estimated children would pass 33% tasks; fathers=30%; staff=27.93%
Stedman *et al.*, 1969	Mothers estimated higher than teachers tested.	Average PAR score from mothers=105; tested by teachers=98.7.
Blair, 1970	Mothers estimated higher than children tested.	No means reported.
Wolfsenberger *et al.*, 1971	Parents estimated higher than children tested.	Average developmental quotient from parents=67; tested=60.
Lederman *et al.*, 1972	Mothers estimated higher than children tested by teachers.	Average PAR score from mothers=110.72; tested by teachers=107.5.
Tew *et al.*, 1974	Parents estimated higher than children tested.	Reported average IQ difference of 9 points.
Gould, 1975	Parents estimated higher than children tested by teachers.	Average social quotient (Vineland) from mothers=*34.6; tested by teachers=32.3.*
Dopheide, 1976	Parental agreement with speech and hearing clinician when reporting ''no artic. problems''; some parental underestimation when reporting problems.	Could not derive means.
Frankenburg *et al.*, 1976	Parents estimated higher than children tested.	No means reported.
Adelman, *et al.*, 1979	Mothers and students themselves estimated higher than teachers.	Frequency reports of behavior problems more frequent by teachers.
Hanson *et al.*, 1979	General agreement on number of items estimated between mothers, parent adviser, and children tested.	No means reported.
Hunt *et al.*, 1980	Mothers estimated higher than children tested.	68.7% of items predicted by mothers. 52.2% of items children passed.

Table 4. (Continued)

Citation	Summary of finding	Magnitude of differences
Noble, 1980	Mothers estimated higher than children tested.	Average mental and motor scores (Bayley) of 111 and 111 from mothers; tested=103 and 102.
Blacher-Dixon et al., 1981	General agreement between mothers and teachers.	No means reported.
Gradel et al., 1981	Parents estimated higher than children tested.	Average motor (Bayley) score from mothers=89.5; tested=73.8; mental (Bayley) scale from mothers=94.3; tested=79.6.
Valencia et al., 1981	Mothers estimated higher than children tested.	Average general cognitive index from mothers=112; tested=95.
Bricker et al., 1983	At 4 months, parents more likely to estimate lower than children tested; at 8 months, general agreement between parents and children tested.	Could not derive means.
Donnelly, 1983	Mothers estimated lower than children tested. Fathers estimated lower than children tested.	Average developmental age from mothers=12.63 months; fathers=12.62 months; tested=14.74 months.
Sexton et al., 1983	Mothers estimated higher than children tested.	No means reported.

diagnosticians. When deviations from this pattern did occur, they were most likely to be in the form of agreement between parents and traditional test reports. Such systematic patterns of research findings are rare in the behavioral sciences.

EXPLAINING PARENTAL ESTIMATIONS OF CHILDREN'S DEVELOPMENT

Given the pattern of findings, the question of their implications is still unresolved. Much of the research in this area has been conducted for pragmatic reasons (i.e., developing cost-efficient screening) rather than for the purpose of explaining why these discrepancies exist. There are several notable exceptions however. Valencia & Cruz (1981) suggested that a reason for mothers' estimating higher than professionals' testings is that mothers think of test items in more of a "macro" sense than a "micro" sense. To explain further,

> For example, in the Block Building subtest, perhaps the mother was not responding in the minute, micro level cognitive demands of each item, but rather the mother was relying on a macro level assessment of the overall brightness of her child plus her assessment of how her child functions in tasks related to "block building." (Valencia and Cruz, 1981, p. 170)

If such is the case, one can easily see why a child would perform in a testing situation on a large number of items less successfully than a mother would predict. The macroperspective of a mother would apply in most, but not all, specific instances of a test situation. One could also argue that certain types of testing (i.e., testing for educational planning) might be directed at understanding children's greatest potential in a variety of situations on a variety of tasks. If so, the macroperspective of a parent might be more revealing than the microperspective of a diagnostician or a tester.

A subtly different perspective was offered by Gradel *et al.* (1981), who suggested that a child's test performance might, in fact, be an underestimation because of the limited perspective that a tester brings to a test situation. A child would have less likelihood of demonstrating a skill in a time-limited testing situation than at home. Viewed in this light, mothers' higher estimations are likely more accurate than the results of a diagnostician's or a teacher's test.

Item analyses by Gradel *et al.* (1981) revealed that the items of diagreement between mothers and professionals were the most difficult items clustered around a child's ceiling (the highest, most difficult item passed). Though other studies did not report conducting such analyses, the ordinal nature of developmental tests, the tests most frequently used in the studies discussed in this chapter, increases the likelihood of findings such as these. The items close to a child's ceiling are also the skills that are emergent, and not yet stabilized. They might be observed at home and not yet stabilized in the school or the testing situtation.

Boice (1983) provided some additional support for this possibility of mothers' being the more accurate observers by noting that "Except where the observational task is markedly simple [Gladding, 1978], females are better observers than males. The demonstation of female superiority is one of the oldest findings in this area [e.g., McGeoch, 1928] and probably the most general" (p. 14). Obviously, many diagnosticians and testers are females, but certainly with less frequency than mothers!

The hypothesis of diagnostician "underestimation" is not a problem as long as a standardized test is given (in a standard fashion) to identify or confirm a handicapping condition. In this situation, the purpose of the test is to identify children who perform differently from the norm (rather than to test the full capabilities of a child). Children so identified become likely targets for educational intervention. The only risk encountered with such a hypothesis is when professional and parental information is mixed in such a testing effort. The result would be a high Type II error rate—overlooking children in need of intervention—as parental estimates might be higher than would be expected from a diagnostician's more standard assessment.

As mentioned earlier, few of the cited studies were concerned with the implications of parental reports' being higher. One notable exception is the discussion that Hunt & Paraskevopolous (1980) presented with their reports of maternal overestimation in a sample of Greek preschoolers:

> It would appear to indicate that mothers who, for whatever reasons, hold false information about what their child can and cannot do also fail to provide development-fostering experience of as high a quality as mothers who hold accurate information about their children's developmental achievements. (p. 290)

Hunt & Paraskevopolous (1980) based this concern on a reported correlation of

—.80 between the number of false predictions and the children's tested performance. Hunt *et al.* argued further that errors in the form of overestimations correlated more highly (and negatively) with child performance than did errors in the form of maternal underestimations. The findings of Hunt *et al.* in this regard have not been tested in other studies.

Hunt & Paraskevopolous argued that overestimation might disrupt the caring, loving bond between a mother and an infant (though the data reflect only preschoolers). Interestingly enough, though reference is made several times to Hunt's well-known concept of "the match" and the benefits of mild disequilibrium in child development, the study presents a very gloomy picture for mothers who overestimate their children's development. Also of note is the fact that a correlation study has a weak link to causal theory.

An additional point of interest is that Hunt *et al.* did not cite a single empirical investigation of the congruency of maternal and professional assessment information. Perhaps the knowledge that "maternal overestimation" was the outcome of 75% of the studies conducted to date tempered the dire forecasting of the effects of maternal reports' being higher than those of teachers or diagnosticians.

A MODEL FOR PARENTAL INVOLVEMENT IN ASSESSMENT

If this chapter were being written 10 years ago or even 5 years ago, it would now discuss the universal benefits of parental involvement in assessment—just as studies of the early 1970s emphasized the benefits for all parents of being involved in their children's education. A model would be suggested, making use of the previously cited studies, that would ensure complete parental involvement in assessment, compensating for the systematic differences in assessment results yielded by parents and professionals.

Since the early 1980s, a different perspective has been developing with regard to parental involvement. This different perspective is an awareness that parental involvement is not a universal good for all parents, for all children, or for all schools. Rather, it is an activity that has benefits for some parents, many children, and most schools. The recent writings of Turnbull (Turnbull & Turnbull, 1982; Winton & Turnbull, 1981) provide a clear indication of this changing perspective. In critiquing Karnes and Teska's model (1980) of parent involvment and Shearer and Shearer's similar model (1977), Turnbull and Turnbull (1982) made the point that "To be a good parent [in these models], one must have skills comparable to a master's level special educator, and still have time for IEP participation, self fulfillment, individual and system advocacy, employment, and other family responsibilities" (p. 119). In short, one must be a master teacher, a superparent, and a heroic individual!

The comments above indicate an awareness that involvement in educational decision-making is not for all parents. Unfortunately we have, as yet, few specific guidelines for determining what parents might best be involved in assessing their child's developmental progress. The following interrelated factors must be included in a model of parental involvement in assessment:

1. The extent of parent involvement in early childhood assessment must be supported by the interest level and the skill level of the parents.

2. The purpose(s) for assessment must be consistent with involvement of the parents in the assessment.
3. The instruments used for assessment must be appropriate for parental involvement in the assessment.

Interest and Skill Level of Parents

Although there has been little research on the topic of parental interest in assessment, there is ample anecdotal evidence to indicate that parents vary greatly in their interest in such involvement. The professional training of clinicians provides a measure of relief for many parents. As an example:

> "You've got to have a staff that is smarter than you....I'm no genius, I mean, my background is giving enemas...but you've got to know that the people who are teaching your child know their stuff. Now I leave him off in the morning and I feel like—phew—people more competent than me are taking him and that's a great feeling." (Winton & Turnbull, 1981, p.15; cited in Turnbull & Turnbull, 1982, p. 118)

In contrast, other parents are intensely interested in becoming involved in their children's program. Winton and Turnbull (1981) presented data from 31 mothers of mild and moderately handicapped children in 15 different preschools. These data indicate that 84% of the parents desired parent-training opportunities. The type of parental involvement desired by the fewest parents (58%) was volunteering inside the classroom. Only 19% of the parents indicated a preference for no role. Winton and Turnbull also provided numerous parental quotes indicating that interest in parental involvement changes with time for many parents. Cross and Sheehan (1983) also presented a description of one parent's progression through a series of reactions to parental involvement in early childhood assessment.

The skill level of parents must also be considered in any attempt to involve them in assessment. Several of the studies mentioned (Gradel et al., 1981; Hunt & Paraskevopolous, 1980) suggested that the educational level of the mothers influences their agreement with the assessment perceptions of diagnosticians and teachers. In the absence of more specific data regarding the necessary skill levels of parents involved in assessment, we might speculate that parents who can express specific developmental goals for their children, parents who show an interest in the activity of their children, and parents who can describe their children's free-play behavior in discrete terms might be more effective in assessment than parents who are unable to exhibit any of these behaviors.

Purpose of Assessment

As stated earlier, many clinicians are unaware of or are unclear in their purposes for assessment. Possible purposes include screening, the diagnosis and categorization of children, educational planning, program evaluation, or basic or applied research. A model of parental involvement in assessment must balance the possible consequences of parental error (or disagreement with professionals) with the possible benefits.

As example, an assessment that is directed at diagnosing and categorizing children as developmentally disabled could not (and should not) be based entirely on parental report. The consequence of this decision's accuracy are certainly significant, as children needing intervention are likely to be overlooked because of parental overestimations.

Based on the studies cited, parents certainly have a role to play in screening most populations of infants and children. The likelihood of parents' developmental estimations' being higher than professional data must, however, be compensated for in the screening process. If a parent indicates that a child is not performing consistently with his or her age-mates, the implication is that the child is very likely in need of services and/or additional testing. If a parent indicates that a child is not in need of services, some additional external referent appears to be warranted.

Parents could also play an important (and cost-efficient) role in providing assessment data for program planning and/or research, as long as parental and professional reports are *not* inadvertently mixed. One example of such a mistake in assessment procedures would be if parental reports are used heavily at the beginning of the year, whereas professional reports on the same measure are used at the end of the year. Such practices would be likely to yield an underestimation of program effect, as the parental reports would be likely to be higher to begin with than professional reports would have been.

Instruments Used for Assessment

There do not seem to be any systematic patterns of differences in the studies cited based on the type of instruments used to assess children and to obtain parental estimates. The Binet, a test ordinarily used by psychologists, yields parental estimates higher than professional estimates, as does the Developmental Profile, a measure designed for non-professional use. The only study yielding highly divergent findings used the Bayley scales, an instrument that also yielded the more consistent finding of parental estimation's being higher than professional assessment.

One possible explanation for this absence of instrumentation effect is that the researchers had already modified the more specialized measures (measures requiring training) for parental use. This was the case for Gradel *et al.* (1981), Sexton, Hall, and Pally (1983), Noble (1980), and many others. As an example:

> The Bayley and McCarthy were both modified into interview instruments by simplifying their vocabularies, converting them into question format, and incorporating a demonstration into the presentation of each item. (Gradel *et al.*, 1981, p. 33)

Obviously, such a modification of the measures damages their reliability and validity for purposes of norm group comparison. As no child development measures have yet been standardized with parents, the reliability and validity of parental reports for norm group comparisons is also questionable. (Two exceptions to this statement are the extensive study already cited by Frankenburg *et al.*, 1976, and one part of a standardization effort on the Developmental Profile by Alpern and Shearer, 1980).

The implication of the studies cited is clear. Any model of parental involvement in assessment would have either to use instruments appropriate for parents (instruments designed to be used with no training or minimal training) or to revise the measures as stated above to ensure the clarity of each item.

DECISION RULES FOR INVOLVEMENT OF PARENTS IN ASSESSMENT

The decision rules or guidelines that are shown in Table 5 are suggested for the involvement of parents in the process of assessing their infants and preschoolers. These decision rules make use of the research studies that have been cited. They are also an attempt to incorporate most of the concerns that were expressed in the rationale for and against the involvement of parents in the assessment process.

SUMMARY

Parents are increasingly becoming involved in the assessment of their young children and infants. Public laws, inflationary times, and a changing spirit about assessment all contribute to such involvement. The available empirical literature indicates a remarkably high degree of consistency when comparing parental and professional assessment data, a consistency that also yields parental estimations that are somewhat higher than professional estimations in developmental assessment.

Traditional concerns that parents lack the rigor and training to contribute to assessment data are felt primarily in the area of diagnostic assessment, that is, assessment directed at confirming or disconfirming developmental disability. As the purposes for assessment are broadened, to include assessment for program planning, a place is being established for parents in the assessment process.

Table 5. Decision Rules

Population of parents	Type of information
1. Assessment information that can be expected from all parents.	General questions reporting children's prenatal and perinatal history. Children's immunization history and history of illnesses. Identification of related family or sibling problems.
2. Information that can be expected from many parents (general population) willing to commit about 15 minutes to the process.	A set of specific (relatively few) screening items regarding the children's development.
3. Information that can be expected from many parents of handicapped or at-risk children, those with a willingness to commit about 2 hours per assessment.	A set of specific developmental items (modified for parental report if necessary) at regular intervals for IEP planning and/or monitoring of high-risk children, under the guidance of professionals.
4. Information that can be expected from some parents of handicapped or at-risk children, those with maximum interest in assisting in the educational program of their child.	Completion of appropriate developmental measures at regular intervals for research purposes and/or program evaluation, under the guidance of trained professionals.
5. Information that can be expected from a few parents of handicapped or at-risk children, those with maximum interest and professional training in assessment.	Take complete charge of initiating and conducting assessment at regular intervals.

REFERENCES

Adelman, H., Taylor, L., Fuller, W., & Nelson, P. (1979). Discrepancies among student, parent, and teacher ratings of the severity of a student's problems. *American Educational Research Journal, 16*, 38–41.

Alpern, G., & Shearer, M. (1980). *Developmental profile*. Aspen, CO: Psychological Development Publications.

Bayley, N. (1969). *Manual for the Bayley Scales of Infant Development*. New York: Psychological Corporation.

Blacher-Dixon, J., & Simeonsson, R. (1981). Consistency and correspondence of mother's and teacher's assessments of young handicapped children. *Journal of the Division of Early Childhood, 3* (June), 64–71.

Blair, J. (1970). A comparison of mother and teacher ratings on the Preschool Attainment Record of four year old children. *Exceptional Children, 37*, 299–300.

Boice, R. (1983) Observational skills. *Psychological Bulletin, 93(1)*, 3–29.

Bricker, D., & Littman, D. (1983). *Parental monitoring of infant development*. Paper presented at the Banff International Conference, Banff, Canada, March.

Capobianco, R. J., & Knox, S. (1964). IQ estimates and the index of marital integration. *American Journal of Mental Deficiency, 68*, 718–721.

Cross, C., & Sheehan, R. (1983). A personal evaluation of parent education: Lessons for parents, educators, and evaluators. *Family Life Education, 2(1)*, 17–19.

Donnelly, B. (1983). *A comparison of maternal, paternal, and diagnostic evaluation of typical and atypical infants*. Unpublished doctoral dissertation, Purdue University.

Dopheide, W. R., & Dallinger, J. R. (1976). Preschool articulation screening by parents. *Language, Speech, and Hearing Services in the Schools, 7*, 124–127.

Ewert, J. C., & Green, M. W. (1957). Conditions associated with the mother's estimate of her retarded child. *American Journal of Mental Deficiency, 62*, 521–533.

Frankenburg, W. K., Van Doornick, W. J., Liddell, T. N., & Dick, N. P. (1976). The Denver Prescreening Developmental Questionnaire. *Pediatrics, 57*, 744–753.

Gladding, S. T. (1978). Empathy, gender, and training as factors in the identification of normal infant cry signals. *Perceptual and Motor Skills, 47*, 267–270.

Gould, J. (1975). The use of the Vineland Social Maturity Scale, the Merrill-Palmer Scale of Mental Tests (Non-Verbal Items) and the Reynell Developmental Language Scales with children in contact with the services for severe mental retardation. *Journal of Mental Deficiency Research, 21*, 213–226.

Gradel, K., Thompson, M., & Sheehan, R. (1981). Parental and professional agreement in early childhood assessment. *Topics in Early Childhood Education, 1(2)*, 31–40.

Hanson, M., Vail, M., & Irvin, L. (1979). Parent and parent advisory observation measures as indicators of early intervention program effects. *Mental Retardation, 17(1)*, 43–44.

Hunt, J., & Paraskevopolous, J. (1980). Children's psychological development as a function of the inaccuracy of their mothers' knowledge of their abilities. *Journal of Genetic Psychology, 136*, 285–298.

Joffe, C. (1979). *Friendly intruders*. Berkeley: University of California Press.

Johnson, G. O., & Capobianco, R. J. (1957). *Research project on severely retarded children*. Albany: New York State, Interdepartmental Health Resources Board.

Kaplan, H. E., & Alitashe, M. (1976). Comparison of ratings by mothers and teachers on preschool children using the Vineland Social Maturity Scale. *Psychology in the Schools, 13*, 27–28.

Karnes, M. B., & Teska, J. A. (1980). Toward successful parent involvement in programs for handicapped children. In J. J. Gallagher (Ed.), *New directions for exceptional children: Parents and families of handicapped children* (Vol. 4). San Francisco: Jossey-Bass.

Keith, R. A., & Markie,G. S. (1969). Parental and professional assessment of functioning in cerebral palsy. *Developmental Medicine and Child Neurology, 11*, 735–742.

Lederman, E., & Blair, J. R. (1972). Comparison of the level and predictive validity of preschool record ratings obtained from teachers and mothers. *Psychology in the Schools, 9*, 392–395.

Noble, L. (1980). *The impact of infant sex and birth order on the magnitude and direction of maternal expectation*. Unpublished doctoral dissertation, University of Virginia.

Schulman, J. L., & Stern, S. (1959). Parents' estimate of the intelligence of retarded children. *American Journal of Mental Deficiency, 63*, 696–698.

Sexton, D., Hall, J., & Pally, T. (1984). Multisource assessment of young handicapped children: A comparison of diagnosticians, teachers, mothers, and fathers. *Exceptional Children, 50*(6), 556–558.

Shearer, M. S., & Shearer, D. E. (1977). Parent involvement. In J. B. Jordan (Ed.), *Early childhood education for exceptional children*. Reston, VA: Council for Exceptional Children.

Sheehan, R. (1982). Infant assessment: A review and identification of emergent trends. In D. Bricker (Ed.), *Intervention with at-risk and handicapped infants: From research to application*. Baltimore: University Park Press.

Stedman, D. J., Clifford, M., & Spitznagel, A. (1969). A comparison of ratings by mothers and teachers on the Preschool Attainment Record of 17 5-year old children. *Exceptional Children, 35*, 488–489.

Tew, B., Laurence, K. M., & Samuel, P. (1974). Parental estimates of the intelligence of their physically handicapped children. *Developmental Medicine and Child Neurology, 16*, 494–500.

Turnbull, A., & Turnbull, H. R. (1982). Parent involvement in the education of handicapped children. *Mental Retardation, 20*(3), 115–122.

Valencia, R., & Cruz, J. (1981). *Mexican American mothers' estimations of their preschool children's cognitive performance*. Final technical report (contract 90-C-1777) submitted to Administration for Children, Youth, and Families, Office of Human Development Services, U.S. Department of Health, Education, and Welfare, July.

Winton, P., & Turnbull, A. (1981). Parent involvement as viewed by parents of preschool handicapped children. *Topics in Early Childhood Special Education. 1*(3), 11–19.

Wolfsenberger, W., & Kurtz, R. A. (1971). Measurement of parents' perceptions of their childen's development. *Genetic Psychology Monographs, 83*, 3–92.

Cognitive Assessment

As editors and authors, we are very clear in our belief that the cognitive development of handicapped infants and preschoolers is of great concern in intervention. In light of this concern, we have developed Part II of the text, which is devoted entirely to issues of cognitive development for six groups of children.

Orlansky begins the section (Chapter 6) with a caution that blindness is best viewed as a diverse phenomenon rather than a homogeneous grouping of children. He argues that assessment directed at progam planning should minimize comparisons with sighted children. Such comparisons describe visually impaired children's perfomance as difficult, inadequate, and lacking. Rather, a multi-instrument, multi-examiner approach emphasizing current functioning is advocated.

Hoffmeister (Chapter 7) sounds a call similar to Orlansky's when he advocates that the cognitive assessment of hearing-impaired children should be functional and should involve comparisons within the hearing-impaired population (i.e., less emphasis should be placed on comparisons with the hearing population). Hoffmeister argues strongly for the possibility of differing developmental pathways for hearing-impaired populations, and he highlights the existence of mulitple subgroupings of hearing-impaired children, depending on the etiology of a child's hearing loss and the environmental, cultural, and physical status of each child.

Robinson and Fieber (Chapter 8) return to the notion proposed by Stagg (Chapter 4), that assessors perceive themselves as hypothesis testers when working with motorically impaired infants and preschoolers. These authors describe an idiographic model of assessment that involves trial, notation of performance, trial of a different strategy, notation of performance, and so on until an examiner is satisfied that a child's best possible performance has been obtained. This use of a process approach is at marked variance with classical test theory, yet is one much more likely to reveal a child's capabilities.

Kahn (Chapter 9) provides support for the argument that clarification of the purposes of assessment is an important first step in assessing the cognitive performance of mentally retarded infants and preschoolers. He is more supportive of existing standardized instruments for assessing mentally retarded youngsters than are many of the other authors for the populations that they discuss in this text. Kahn does argue that the use of visual discrimination indices, and of measures of early recognition memory, may yield powerful alternative perspectives to the assessment process.

Zental undertakes a difficult task as she addresses, in Chapter 10, the cognitive

assessment of infants and preschoolers with severe behavioral disorders. The heterogeneity of this population is quite possibly the greatest of all the groups of handicapped
children addressed in this book. Zentall's chapter offers support to Kahn's perspective
(Chapter 9) that traditional assessment approaches provide useful information, but she
cautions about the examiner factors that can bias performance on tests. Zentall also
stresses the value of observational data in many situations when assessing infants and
preschoolers with severe behavior disorders.

Dunst and McWilliam (Chapter 11) return to a more pessimistic view of traditional
methods of assessing cognitive development in young children. They argue that such
approaches have restricted rather than advanced our intervention efforts with multiply
handicapped infants and preschoolers. These authors propose a multidimensional model,
emphasizing the interactive competencies that these children bring to a learning situation.
They further argue that social and nonsocial contexts affect the behavior of these children
and must become an intentional part of any valid assessment effort. Once again they
suggest an idiographic approach to assessment, one with successive variations in eliciting
procedures.

Part II of this book challenges assessors to articulate their purposes of assessment
(this challenge is consistent with that of the authors in Part I). Authors in Part II provide
very specific suggestions for assessment, especially in the area of assessment for instructional planning. To understand how a handicapped infant or preschooler will respond to
intervention, we are challenged to assess in a teaching (or hypothesis-testing) mode. We
are encouraged to carefully vary stimuli, and we are asked to consider as acceptable
nontraditional responses from our children. We are also being challenged to consider the
implications of such idiographic methods for the evaluation of intervention programs.
Has a program had an oveall impact? A statement leading to traditional outcome measures is now replaced with a much more sophisticated, individually focused approach.
The corresponding assessment must also be highly individualized.

6

Assessment of Visually Impaired Infants and Preschool Children

Michael D. Orlansky

Vision plays a massive and critical role in children's early cognitive development. Vision provides information that is far more extensive, more specific, and more rapid than any other sense; Padula (1983) maintained that some 80% of a child's ability to discern relationships, and to establish the perceptual experience necessary for normal development, occurs through the visual sense. Indeed, vision is frequently considered the mediator of all other sensory information, the principal avenue of incidental learning, and even the factor that stabilizes a child's interaction with his or her world (Barraga, 1983).

The absence or severe impairment of vision, particularly when present from birth, has far-reaching effects on virtually every area of a child's develoment and learning. Before considering these effects, however, it is important to point out that the population of visually impaired infants and preschool children, though relatively few in number, is extremely heterogeneous in character (Warren, 1981, 1984). As Kastein, Spaulding, and Scharf (1980) observed, blind preschool children tend to find their own individualistic ways of circumventing lack of vision, especially by developing a preference for using a certain area of the body to obtain information. One child, for example, might use her mouth to find out about objects in the environment, and another might find the forehead, the cheek, or even the entire body to be a more reliable source of information. These spontaneous attempts at exploration are gradually curtailed as the child learns more sophisticated means of gaining information, especially through language, which for the blind child "will remain the major source of acquiring knowledge, of 'seeing' the world, of communicating with others as well as with himself" (Kastein et al., 1980, p. 25).

TERMINOLOGY

Several authors (Barraga, 1983; Conant & Budoff, 1982; Orlansky, 1984) have described the proliferation of terms and descriptive labels that are applied to people with impaired vision, as well as the semantic ambiguity that ensues. A useful overview of current terminology was provided by Scholl (1983), from whom the following definitions are adapted:

MICHAEL D. ORLANSKY • College of Education, Ohio State University, Columbus, Ohio 43210.

Blind. This term is most appropriately applied to persons who are unable to see or whose vision is so severely impaired that they must rely on senses other than vision in testing and teaching situations. Such an "educational" definition does not coincide with the frequently cited "legal" definition of blindness (i.e., best corrected visual acuity in the better eye of less than $20/200$, or a field of vision restricted to a diameter no greater than 20°). Many legally blind children, in fact, have a degree of residual vision sufficient to be quite useful in their education and development.

Partially sighted or *partially seeing*. These terms refer to persons whose best corrected visual acuity in the better eye falls between $20/70$ and $20/200$. Although such measurements are sometimes used to establish eligibility for special educational services, the use of these terms is becoming less frequent.

Low vision. This term is increasingly used to describe persons who have significant limitations in their visual functioning; for example, children who need to get very close to objects in order to see them clearly. Although some tactual and auditory approaches to education may be called for, children with low vision are capable of learning effectively through the visual channel, particularly if given special training in the use of vision. The term *limited vision* is also used with similar connotations.

Visually impaired or *visually handicapped*. These terms are generally used interchangeably, to describe persons with either blindness or low vision. Typically, some modifications in assessment and education are required because of the visual impairment.

An extensive discussion of vision-related terminology has been provided by Barraga (1983), with particular emphasis on assessing and developing children's residual vision. Barraga wisely cautioned against treating low-vision children as though they were blind and promoted the concept of *visual efficiency* as "the most inclusive of all terms relating to vision" (p. 24). This attribute, considered unique to each child, incorporates such componenets as control of eye movements, accommodative capacity, speed and quality of the processing ability of the brain, and the familiar near and distant visual-acuity measures.

Alonso, Moor, Raynor, von Hippel, and Baer (1978) set forth several categorical and functional definitions of visual impairment, as used in the Project Head Start programs for preschool children. Like many other authors, they pointed out that visual acuity measurements do not indicate how well a person uses vision for everyday purposes, and they stated that most children who are considered visually handicapped have some residual vision, which they should be encouraged to use: "The eyes, especially in early childhood, benefit from use" (p. 14).

SOURCES OF INTERINDIVIDUAL AND INTRAINDIVIDUAL DIFFERENCES

In seeking to account for the heterogeneity of the visually impaired population, and in interpreting the results of any psychoeducational assessment, several objective and subjective factors must be considered as potential sources of interindividual and intraindividual differences. In his comprehensive review of the effects of visual impairment on child development, Warren (1981), identified three general categories of variables that influence learning and behavior in this population. The first category consists of the effects of other disabilities, ranging from mild to severe (e.g., mental retardation, hearing impairment, and neuromotor disabilities), that may coexist and interact with visual impairment. Second, there are several "important status variables related to the visual impairment itself" (p. 197), such as the degree of residual vision (if any), the child's age at the onset of visual impairment, the type of onset of visual impairment (e.g., sudden or gradually progressive), and present eye condition. Generally, noted Warren, these variables are more or less fixed and are not subject to change by the child, the parents, or the interveners. The third category of variables consists of the environmental circumstances in which visually impaired children are raised, including not only the physical setting, but also

> the variety and complexity of the sensory environment, the characteristics of the learning environment, including reinforcement patterns and the like, the linguistic environment, and in particular the social setting, including patterns of interpersonal interaction, family size, and characteristics and behavioral modes of significant others. (Warren, 1981, p. 198)

In contrast to the second set of variables, Warren observed, these environmental factors *are* under potential control and are believed to account for much of the variation among visually impaired children.

Causes of Visual Impairment

The visual system is complex, and there are many different conditions that can impair a child's visual acuity, visual field, color vision, or the ability of both eyes to function together effectively. The most common causes of congenital blindness and severe visual impairment are prenatal viral infections (e.g., meningitis and rubella), eye malformations, trauma, congenital cataracts, and exposure of the fetus to harmful substances (Batshaw & Perret, 1986; Garwood, 1983; Ward, 1986). Perhaps the most frequent postnatal cause of blindness and severe visual impairment among infants is retinopathy of prematurity (ROP), formerly known as retrolental fibroplasia (RLF). This condition occurs almost exclusively in premature or low-birth-weight infants who have received oxygen to treat respiratory distress syndrome. Throughout the 1940s and the early 1950s, when oxygen treatment was not recognized as the cause of ROP, this was a very frequent etiology of blindness. Although the incidence of ROP has markedly decreased with the lower concentrations of oxygen now used to treat respiratory distress syndrome (Silverman, 1980), it is still a significant cause of blindness among infants who are considered at risk. The number of American infants affected by RLF in a recent year was placed at approximately 546 (Phelps, 1981).

Few studies have investigated the differential effects of specific causes of visual impairment on children's cognitive development. This is probably attributable to the heterogeneity and the relatively low incidence of the young visually impaired population, as well as to the tendency of psychologists and educators to consider "the whole child" on an individual basis. Two "special cases," in which the etiology of visual handicap may influence intelligence, were reviewed and discussed at some length by Warren

(1984). One case is that of retinoblastoma, a malignant tumor that may impinge on the retina in one or both eyes. At least two studies, cited by Warren, have found children with retinoblastoma to have significantly higher IQs than children whose blindness is due to other causes. Possible explanations for these findings include a retention of early visual memory, environmental factors, a genetic link of retinoblastoma with intelligence, and the effects of therapeutic radiation treatments, A second case concerns children affected by retrolental fibroplasia. Although it is difficult to separate the effects of RLF from those of prematurity and of the additional impairments often found in this population, the available studies suggest that RLF children, as a group, tend to score somewhat lower than blind non-RLF children, as well as lower than prematurely born infants without RLF. As Warren suggested, further research is needed in both of these "special cases," and caution should be exercised in interpreting the available studies.

Further information on the types and causes of visual impairment can be obtained from a variety of sources. Of particular interest to psychologists and educators working with visually impaired children are two concise and relatively nontechnical texts written by ophthalmologists (Eden, 1980; Miller, 1979), two comprehensive guides to the assessment and treatment of low vision (Faye, 1984; Jose, 1983), and the educationally oriented text of Harley and Lawrence (1977).

PREVALENCE AND NATURE OF VISUAL IMPAIRMENT IN CHILDREN

Figures on the prevalence of blindness and visual impairment vary considerably and have changed somewhat in recent years. The incidence of certain causes of blindness has declined because of improved medical care, and many children who once would have been considered severely visually handicapped are now able to benefit from surgical procedures and/or optical correction. Despite this variability, there is general agreement on the following three characteristics of the visually impaired population:

1. Visual impairment and blindness are far more prevalent among adults than among children. About half of the legally blind persons in the United States are over age 65. Many significant causes of impaired vision (e.g., cataracts, diabetes, glaucoma, and macular degeneration) are clearly correlated with advancing age (Jose, 1983; National Society to Prevent Blindness, 1980).

2. Visual impairment and blindness occur infrequently in infants and children, even in comparison to other handicapping conditions. Batshaw and Perret (1986) cited an incidence figure for visual impairment in children of .4 per 1,000 children. Scholl (1983) reported that only about 1 school-aged child in every 10,000 is considered so severely visually impaired as to require the use of tactual materials. The low incidence of visual impairment means that relatively few clinical and educational personnel have had direct experience with young blind and visually impaired children. Concurrently, however, the number of visually handicapped children served in preschool programs appears to be increasing as a result of improved child-find programs, higher survival rates for premature and at-risk infants, and the general expansion of early-childhood special-education services. Ferrell (1984) predicted that the population of visually handicapped infants and preschool children is likely to reach 19,000 by 1990. This figure would be equivalent to

nearly two-thirds of the population of school-aged visually handicapped children that was served during the 1983–1984 school year.

3. Visually handicapped children with some degree of potentially useful vision substantially outnumber those who are blind. According to Bryan and Jeffrey (1982), some 75%–80% of school-aged visually impaired children have useful residual vision. Daugherty and Moran (1980) estimated that "over 70% of the children being served in programs for the visually handicapped in the United States are sighted children, with only 11% classified as braille readers" (p. 2). The assessment of residual vision in infants and preschool children is problematic; it is not unusual for children to demonstrate the ability to see after having been diagnosed earlier as totally blind because of apparent lack of response to visual stimuli.

Visually Impaired Children with Multiple Impairments

Those who assess visually impaired infants and preschool children should be aware of the high prevalence of multiple impairments in this population. Silberman (1981) reported that over 60% of the children enrolled in educational programs for the visually handicapped have additional impairments that cause developmental delays. Fewell and Carlson (1983) offered a good overview of issues related to the assessment and instruction of preschool multihandicapped children with sensory impairments, citing several studies that attest to the "multiplicative effect of additional impairments" (p. 266) in causing and compounding delays in cognitive, communicative, motor, and social development.

Infants and preschool children who are visually impaired and multihandicapped present formidable challenges in the assessment process; indeed, they were frequently regarded as "untestable" in the non-too-distant past. As Langley (1979) observed, "few psychologists are trained to assess normal infants, and even fewer are trained to assess individuals who may function as infants and also manifest some severe form of visual impairment or other sensory or physical deficit" (p. 97). Increasingly, however, the assessment of multihandicapped visually impaired children is being recognized as a complex process that calls for the involvement of professionals with various areas of expertise and experience, a process in which parents and teachers can rightfully play an active and important role, in view of their extended contact with the child. Useful references that specifically address the assessment of multihandicapped visually impaired children include the comprehensive sourcebooks of Langley (1978), Ray, O'Neill, and Morris (1983), and Reynolds and Clark (1983); several annotated guides to assessment instruments (e.g., Kansas State Department of Education, 1981; Langley, 1979; Yarnall & Carlton, 1981), and procedures for testing the functional vision of young multihandicapped children (Cote & Smith, 1983; Cress, Spellman, & Benson, 1984; Efron & DuBoff, 1975; Goetz & Gee, 1987; Kennedy, 1983).

EFFECTS OF IMPAIRED VISION ON DEVELOPMENT AND LEARNING

Many psychologists and educators have written of the blind child's inherent disadvantages in acquiring knowledge and concepts. Particularly when visual impairment is severe (or total) and congenital, the blind child must rely heavily on the deliberate presentation of information, and on the verbal descriptions and explanations typically offered to varying degrees by parents, siblings, teachers, peers, and others. The child's remaining senses—primarily hearing and touch—may develop into useful avenues of sensory input but can never fully compensate for the loss of vision, nor can they usually provide information that is as exact, complete, spontaneous, and continuous as that normally gained by children who are constantly able to see their environment. Chapman (1978) pointed to the difficulties encountered by young visually impaired children in integrating and generalizing information, and in grasping the "total context" of a situation. As an example of the "misconceptions which can arise from fragmented and unrelated discoveries," Chapman offered the question posed by a blind child on hearing a cow bellow: "Which horn did she blow?" (pp. 20–21).

Perhaps the best known and most widely accepted explanation of the effects of blindness on children's cognitive development is that of Lowenfeld (1948/1981):

> Blindness imposes three basic limitations on the individual:
> 1. In the range and variety of experiences.
> 2. In the ability to get about [mobility].
> 3. In the control of the environment and the self in relation to it. (p. 68)

Lowenfeld maintained that a thorough understanding of these basic cognitive restrictions is imperative for persons who work with blind children. A "detachment from the physical and, to a lesser degree, from the social world" (Lowenfeld, 1948/1981, p. 75) is viewed as an important disadvantage of blindness, particularly in infancy. Several investigators, notably Fraiberg (1977), Adelson and Fraiberg (1974), and Burlingham (1961, 1972), have documented the blind infant's delays in motor development and have attributed them principally to a lack of incentive and ability of the blind infant to reach out, to crawl toward objects, to explore the extended environment, and to acquire behavioral patterns through visual imitation. Such factors typically prolong the visually impaired infant's stage of dependency and diminish the stimulation provided by the parents or caregivers (e.g., observed parental approval to encourage the child to repeat his or her accomplishments). As Burlingham (1961) reported, "Retardation and restriction of muscular achievement are the order of the day.... the blind baby although not intentionally restricted yet behaves in many respects like a restricted sighted child" (p. 123).

Although a detailed discussion of the effects of visual impairment on cognition and development in early childhood is beyond the scope of this chapter, several sources of further information are recommended to professionals involved in the assessment of blind and visually impaired children. In particular, these sources describe many variables that may influence children's responses in testing situations, and they offer background knowledge pertinent to the counseling of parents.

Patterns of motor development in blind infants, as well as their implications for corresponding cognitive, language, and social development, have been explored by Fraiberg and colleagues (Adelson & Fraiberg, 1974, 1976; Fraiberg, 1977; Fraiberg, Smith, & Adelson, 1969), by Burlingham (1961, 1972), by Hill, Rosen, Correa, and Langley (1984), and by Griffin (1981). Language acquisition in blind and visually impaired children has been the subject of reports by Adelson (1983), by Mills (1983), by Mulford (1987), and by Urwin (1978, 1983). Psychosocial and emotional aspects of visual impairment are emphasized in the works of Hull (1983), Kirtley (1975), Lowenfeld (1980), Tuttle (1984), and Wills (1970). Stephens and colleagues (Stephens & Simpkins, 1974; Stephens, Grube, & Fitzgerald, 1977) have investigated the reasoning abilities of congenitally blind children. The particular characteristics and needs of children with low vision have been well discussed by Barraga (1983), and McInnes and Treffry (1982) addressed themselves to the needs of young children with both visual and auditory impairments. Practical information and strategies for parents and teachers of visually impaired preschool children have been offered by Brennan (1982), Chess and Fernandez (1981), Davidson, Fletcher, Howard, Joeck, Santin, Simmons, and Weaver (1976), Scott, Jan, and Freeman (1977), and Willoughby (1979). Finally, Warren (1981, 1984) has critically reviewed and synthesized a wide range of research and theoretical literature relevant to the effects of visual impairment on early child development.

GENERAL PRINCIPLES IN ASSESSMENT OF VISUALLY IMPAIRED CHILDREN

As Sheehan (1982) pointed out, most measures of infant development have been mainly descriptive in purpose; that is, they have typically been used to illustrate and document the course of early development in normal and/or atypical populations. This observation is clearly applicable to assessment procedures for visually impaired children. Frequently, tests have served as the basis for purported comparisons between blind children and sighted children in intelligence, achievement, language, perception, motor and social development, and other areas; not until fairly recently have assessment techniques been widely used to generate specific instructional and intervention procedures for visually impaired children.

There are many implicit problems in using tests to compare blind and sighted children. The most thorough consideration of the "blind-versus-sighted comparison" and its attendant philosophical and methodological concerns has probably been that of Warren (1981, 1984). According to Warren, it is faulty to surmise that *any* set of common measures applied to visually impaired and sighted children can yield information that is equally meaningful for both groups, even if such tests are modified or adapted for lack of vision. Warren (1981) contended that visually impaired children should be viewed as following a course of development that is *different* from that of normally sighted children, and not necessarily *slower*:

> It is certainly difficult, if not impossible, to design a single assessment device that taps the comparable characteristics of visually impaired and sighted children. More important, though, even if comparable characteristics could be assessed, it would not follow that those characteristics are equivalently important for visually impaired and sighted children when taken in the context of their overall develoment and capacity....a standardized task may tap a common ability, but that ability may serve a very different ecological function for visually impaired children than it does for sighted children. (p. 216)

The assessment of visually impaired preschool children, then, should minimize comparisons with sighted children. As Silverman and Davidson (1984) observed, early identification practices should shift from their traditional emphasis on "difficulty, weakness, inadequacy, lack-of-something, in the child" (p. 41). Rather, those who assess visually impaired children would do well to describe their subjects as fully and precisely as possible with reference to their functioning on specific tasks or skills considered important to present and future performance. A review of assessment procedures currently in use with visually impaired preschool children indicates that this recommendation is gradually finding acceptance.

Specific Concerns in the Assessment Process

Several professionals in the field of visual impairment have sought to address the concerns of psychologists, teachers, and others who may be called on to assess blind and visually impaired children—presumably with little or no previous experience in testing this relatively limited population. Swallow (1981), for example, described four areas of concern that are frequently raised:

1. Visual loss compounds the assessment process because of the known interrelationships of sensory, motor, cognitive, and emotional factors.
2. The multiplicity of physical and environmental conditions may contribute systematically to the functional delay of the child.
3. The performance of the student on a standardized assessment instrument may not be a valid indication of skills and abilities.
4. Modifications of formal testing procedures generally are considered to generate unreliable results. (p. 65)

Assessment procedures, intended primarily for use with normal infants, tend to rely heavily on the evaluation of motor development. This may limit their applicability and predictability with young visually impaired children, particularly those who are blind from birth. Blind infants' lags in the onset of such motor behaviors as head lifting, sitting, reaching, grasping, and crawling have been discussed by Adelson and Fraiberg (1976), Chess and Fernandez (1981), and Hart (1983b), among others. Similarly, many language-based items, widely used in preschool assessments, are based largely on visual concepts and carry the potential for misuse with visually impaired children. Hart (1983a) offered the example of a blind child who, when asked what the eyes were for, responded, "to put your hands in" (p. 204). Although the answer was reasonable in terms of this blind child's experience, it was scored as wrong on the test.

TESTS USED WITH VISUALLY IMPAIRED INFANTS AND PRESCHOOL CHILDREN

Verbal Intelligence Tests

Verbal intelligence tests, in spite of their pitfalls, remain the most prevalent means of assessing the intelligence of visually impaired school-aged children. According to reviews by Bauman (1973), Coveny (1976), and Warren (1984), adapted versions of the Binet tests, such as the current Perkins-Binet (Davis, 1980) and the verbal scales of the Wechsler Intelligence Scale for Children (WISC), are the instruments most frequently used with visually impaired students. Bauman (1973) stated that the verbal scales of the

WISC can generally be administered to blind students without modifications; in Bauman's experience, items such as "What should you do if you see a train approaching a broken track?" do not present the problems sometimes imputed to them; as blind children "are quite aware that the question is hypothetical . . . there seems to be no blocking on the fact that the child could not himself see the train approaching" (p. 99). Others view such items as less appropriate. Limited data exist on the suitability of the Wechsler Preschool and Primary Scale of Intelligence (WPPSI) for use with visually impaired children. Vander Kolk (1981) considered it less adequate than other Wechsler instruments, as many items call for visual learning, and the printed arithmetic items cannot be used by most visually impaired children.

The Perkins-Binet Tests of Intelligence for the Blind (Davis, 1980) are available in two forms, one for children with no useful vision (aged 4–18), the other for children with useful vision (aged 3–18). Caution is recommended in interpreting test results for children under age 6, however, as that population was underrepresented in the standardization sample. A critique of the current Perkins-Binet, with specific suggestions for test administration, has been offered by Ward and Genshaft (1983).

Performance Tests

As Warren (1984) observed, the history of performance IQ testing is less extensive than that of verbal IQ testing with visually impaired children. Numerous problems exist in devising a performance scale for visually impaired children that might be comparable to those commonly used with sighted children. Indeed, Barraga (1983) concluded that such efforts have failed mainly because of the difficulty and expense of obtaining sufficient numbers of children for standardization samples. Performance-based measures of intelligence that have been developed or adapted for use with blind children include the Blind Learning Aptitude Test (Newland, 1979), the Haptic Intelligence Scale for the Blind (Shurrager & Shurrager, 1964), the Stanford-Kohs Block Design Test for the Blind (Suinn & Dauterman, 1966), and a tactual adaptation of the Boehm Test of Basic Concepts (Caton, 1977). The use of these tests with children below about 10 years of age is generally not recommended.

Social Development

A specialized measure of social competency that has, for some years, found fairly wide use for both educational and research purposes is the Maxfield-Buchholz, Social Maturity Scale for Blind Preschool Children (Maxfield & Buchholz, 1957). An adaptation of the Vineland Social Maturity Scale, the Maxfield-Buchholz relies principally on information obtained from an interview with the child's parent or other caregiver, which may be supplemented by a direct observation of behavior. It is intended for use with visually impaired children from birth to age 6. Daugherty and Moran (1980) noted that the majority of the 484 "blind" children who served as a normative sample for the Maxfield-Buchholz apparently had usable vision; caution should certainly be used in inferring any relationship between a child's degree of vision and his or her social abilities.

Comprehensive Assessment Procedures

Current investigators and practitioners generally agree that the assessment of visually impaired infants and preschool children should be a process calling on the observations and recommendations of various professional disciplines (e.g., pediatrics, ophthalmology, audiology, psychology, education, physical therapy, language, and social work), with the continuing involvement of the child's parents or other caregivers. As Hart (1983a) observed, there is no specific test or "battery of tests that is recognized as optimal.... assessment information must come from many individuals, with some material of greater use than others" (p. 201).

Designed for Visually Impaired Children

Few broadly based measures of early development have been developed specifically for visually impaired preschool children. The two most comprehensive instruments in current use are (a) Growing Up: A Developmental Curriculum (Croft & Robinson, 1984), a refinement of the earlier Project Vision-Up, and (b) The Oregon Project for Visually Impaired and Blind Preschool Children (Brown, Simmons, & Methvin, 1979). Both these programs, developed for visually impaired children from birth to age 6, consist of extensive inventories of skills and behaviors grouped into several general areas, such as language, cognitive, fine motor, social, and self-help. There are guidelines for use with blind, low-vision, and multihandicapped children. Both programs emphasize parent involvement in assessing a child's repertoire of skills, and in selecting instructional objectives that are considered appropriate. The popularity of the Growing Up and Oregon assessments derives largely from their associated function as curriculum guides. Specific goals and suggested activities are provided for teachers and parents; those assessment items that the child fails to perform at age level may be translated into instructional objectives of high priority.

Another comprehensive and noteworthy program designed for the assessment and instruction of visually impaired preschool children is known as Alive...Aware...A Person (O'Brien, 1976). Subtitled "A Developmental Model for Early Childhood Services with Special Definition for Visually Impaired Children and Their Parents," this well-documented resource for diagnostic personnel and teachers includes extensive assessment and intervention strategies, numerous developmental checklists, and supportive reviews of related literature.

Use of General Assessment Instruments

Although the foregoing specialized assessment and instructional instruments are finding use in many early-childhood intervention programs, it is probably more usual for visually impaired infants and preschool children to be assessed through the administration of one or more instruments generally used in early childhood screenings. Several practitioners (e.g., Barraga, 1983; Genshaft, Dare, & O'Malley, 1980; Scholl, 1983) consider the Uzgiris and Hunt (1975) Ordinal Scales of Psychological Development a useful device for determining the effects of impaired vision on early cognitive and sensorimotor development. Use of the Bayley Scales for Infant Development (Bayley, 1969) with visually impaired children from birth to age 30 months has been advocated by Barraga

(1983), Genshaft *et al.* (1980), Sokolow (1983), and others. Langley (1979) cautioned that items throughout the first four months of the Bayley scales require performance that is heavily dependent on vision (e.g., "visually recognizes mother" and "eye–hand coordination in reaching"); test results are likely to be depressed and should be carefully interpreted with the visual impairment in mind. Genshaft *et al.* (1980), on the other hand, found the behavior scale of the Bayley "an excellent resource because it objectifies areas such as attention span and goal-directedness" (p. 347). A third instrument that has won qualified endorsement for use with visually impaired children from birth to age 6 is the Denver Developmental Screening Test (Frankenberg, Dodds, & Fandal, 1975). Swallow (1981) noted that the Denver has been successfully used with visually impaired children to indicate developmental progress but does not recommend the instrument for use with totally blind children. Genshaft *et al.* (1980) and Raynor (1978), among others, consider the Denver suitable if used as one of a battery of several measures with young visually impaired children. Als and colleagues (Als, 1983; Als, Tronick, & Brazelton, 1980) described the use of the Neonatal Behavioral Assessment Scale (Brazelton, 1973) in studying blind infants' responsivity, particularly in parent–infant interactions.

FURTHER RESOURCES

Several additional resources are recommended to the professional who may be called on to assess infants and preschool children with impaired vision. Hart (1983a) presented a thorough discussion of the specific areas of functioning that should be included in a multidisciplinary assessment, emphasizing a general information-gathering process rather than recommending specific instruments. Scholl and Schnur (1976) prepared a comprehensive annotated directory of psychological, educational, and other tests that have been developed for, adapted to, or used with blind and visually impaired subjects; some of these tests are applicable to young children. A briefer directory of assessment instruments is that of Swallow (1981), which contains short descriptions of 50 commonly used tests. Swallow, Mangold, and Mangold (1978) compiled a useful book consisting of informal checklists and developmental scales used by teachers of visually impaired children. About half of these scales may be suitable for use at the preschool level. Morse (1975), in a practical paper, addressed 15 of the "most common questions asked by the psychologist who is faced for the first time with assessing a visually handicapped child" (p. 350). Ferrell (1985) prepared a correspondence course for parents and teachers that includes instructional techniques and methods of evaluating the quality of early education programs for visually impaired children. Finally, Jastrzembska (1984) has offered an extensive annotated bibliography of resource materials for parents and professionals who work with visually impaired preschool children.

REFERENCES

Adelson, E. (1983). Precursors of early language development in children blind from birth. In A. E. Mills (Ed.), *Language acquisition in the blind child: Normal and deficient.* London: Croom Helm.

Adelson, E., & Fraiberg, S. (1974). Gross motor development in infants blind from birth. *Child Development,*

45, 114–126.

Adelson, E., & Fraiberg, S. (1976). Sensory deficit and motor development in infants blind from birth. In Z. S. Jastrzembska (Ed.), *The effects of blindness and other impairments on early development*. New York: American Foundation for the Blind.

Alonso, L., Moor, P. M., Raynor, S., von Hippel, C. S., & Baer, S. (1978). *Mainstreaming preschoolers: Children with visual handicaps* (DHEW Publication No. OHDS 78-31112). Washington: U.S. Government Printing Office.

Als, H. (1983). Assessment, intervention, and remediation: The study of the development of a blind infant in interaction with her mother. In M. E. Mulholland & M. V. Wurster (Eds.), *Help me become everything I can be*. New York: American Foundation for the Blind.

Als, H., Tronick, E., & Brazelton, T. B. (1980). Affective reciprocity and the development of autonomy: The study of a blind infant. *Journal of the American Academy of Child Psychiatry, 19*, 22–40.

Barraga, N. C. (1983). *Visual handicaps and learning* (rev. ed). Austin, TX: Pro-Ed.

Batshaw, M. L., & Perret, Y. M. (1986). *Children with handicaps: A medical primer* (2nd ed.). Baltimore: Paul H. Brookes.

Bauman, M. K. (1973). Psychological and educational assessment. In B. Lowenfeld (Ed.), *The visually handicapped child in school*. New York: John Day.

Bayley, N. (1969). *Bayley scales for infant development*. New York: Psychological Corporation.

Brazelton, T. B. (1973). *Neonatal Behavior Assessment Scale*. Philadelphia: Lippincott.

Brennan, M. (1982). *Show me how: A manual for parents of preschool visually impaired and blind children*. New York: American Foundation for the Blind.

Brown, D. E., Simmons, V., & Methvin, J. (1979). *The Oregon project for visually impaired and blind preschool children* (rev. ed.). Medford, OR: Jackson County Education Service District.

Bryan, W. H., & Jeffrey, D. L. (1982). Education of visually handicapped students in the regular classroom. *Texas Tech Journal of Education, 9*, 125–131.

Burlingham, D. T. (1961). Some notes on the development of the blind. *Psychoanalytic Study of the Child, 16*, 121–145.

Burlingham, D. T. (1972). *Psychoanalytic studies of the sighted and the blind*. New York: International Universities Press.

Caton, H. (1977). The develpoment and evaluation of a tactile analog to the Boehm Test of Basic Concepts, Form A. *Journal of Visual Impairment and Blindness, 71*, 382–386.

Chapman, E. K. (1978). *Visually handicapped children and young people*. London: Routledge & Kegan Paul.

Chess, S., & Fernandez, P. (1981). *The handicapped child in school: Behavior and management*. New York: Brunner/Mazel.

Conant, S., & Budoff, M. (1982). The development of sighted people's understanding of blindness. *Journal of Visual Impairment and Blindness, 76*, 86–90.

Cote, K. S., & Smith, A. (1983). Assessment of the multiply handicapped. In R. T. Jose (Ed.), *Understanding low vision*. New York: American Foundation for the Blind.

Coveny, T. E. (1976). Standardized tests for visually handicapped children: A review of research. *New Outlook for the Blind, 70*, 232–236.

Cress, P., Spellman, C. R., & Benson, H. (1984). Vision care for the preschool child with handicaps. *Topics in Early Childhood Special Education, 3*(4), 41–51.

Croft, N. B., & Robinson, L. W. (1984). *Growing up: A developmental curriculum*. Austin, TX: Parent Consultants.

Daugherty, K. M., & Moran, M. F. (1980). *Neuropsychological, learning and developmental characteristics of the sighted, visually impaired child*. Pittsburgh: Pittsburgh Public Schools.

Davidson, I., Fletcher, J., Howard, M., Joeck, I., Santin, S., Simmons, J. N., & Weaver, D. (1976). *Handbook for parents of preschool blind children*. Toronto: Ontario Institute for Studies in Education.

Davis, C. J. (1980). *Perkins-Binet Tests of Intelligence for the Blind*. Watertown, MA: Perkins School for the Blind.

Eden, J. (1980). *The eye book*. New York: Viking Press.

Efron, M., & DuBoff, B. R. (1975). *A vision guide for teachers of deaf-blind children*. Raleigh: North Carolina Department of Public Instruction, Division for Exceptional Children.

Faye, E. E. (1984). *Clinical low vision* (2nd ed.). Boston: Little, Brown.

Ferrell, K. A. (1984). The editors talk. *Education of the Visually Handicapped, 16*, 43–46.

Ferrell, K. A. (1985). *Reach out and teach* (parent's handbook, workbook, and teacher's manual). New York: American Foundation for the Blind.

Fewell, R. R., & Carlson, B. (1983). Young multihandicapped sensory impaired children: Making educational decisions. In C. R. Reynolds & J. H. Clark (Eds.), *Assessment and programming for young children with low-incidence handicaps*. New York: Plenum Press.

Fraiberg, S. (1977). *Insights from the blind: Comparative studies of blind and sighted infants*. New York: Meridian.

Fraiberg, S., Smith, M., & Adelson, E. (1969). An education program for blind infants. *Journal of Special Education, 3*, 121–139.

Frankenburg, W. F., Dodds, J. B., & Fandal, A. W. (1975). *Denver Developmental Screening Test* (rev. ed.). Denver: Ladoca Project and Publishing Foundation.

Garwood, S. G. (1983). Physical development in infancy. In S. G. Garwood & R. R. Fewell (Eds.), *Educating handicapped infants: Issues in development and intervention*. Rockville, MD: Aspen.

Genshaft, J. L., Dare, N. L., & O'Malley, P. L. (1980). Assessing the visually impaired child: A school psychology view. *Journal of Visual Impairment and Blindness, 74*, 344–349.

Goetz, L., & Gee, K. (1987). Functional vision programming: A model for teaching visual behaviors in natural contexts. In L. Goetz, D. Guess, & K. Stremel-Campbell (Eds.), *Innovative program design for individuals with dual sensory impairments*. Baltimore: Paul H. Brookes.

Griffin, H. C. (1981). Motor development in congenitally blind children. *Education of the Visually Handicapped, 12*, 106–111.

Hall, A., Scholl, G. T., & Swallow, R. M. (1986). Psychoeducational assessment. In G. T. Scholl (Ed.), *Foundations of education for blind and visually handicapped children and youth: Theory and practice*. New York: American Foundation for the Blind.

Harley, R. K., & Lawrence, G. A. (1977). *Visual impairment in the schools*. Springfield, IL: Charles C Thomas.

Hart, V. (1983a). Assessment of visually handicapped preschoolers. In C. R. Reynolds & J. H. Clark (Eds.), *Assessment and programming for young children with low-incidence handicaps*. New York: Plenum Press.

Hart, V. (1983b). *Characteristics of young blind children*. Paper presented at the Second International Symposium on Visually Handicapped Infants and Young Children: Birth to Seven, Aruba, Dutch West Indies.

Hill, E. W., Rosen, S., Correa, V. I., & Langley, M. B. (1984). Preschool orientation and mobility: An expanded definition. *Education of the Visually Handicapped, 16*, 58–72.

Hull, W. (1983). Social development of preschool visually handicapped children. In M. E. Mulholland & M. V. Wurster (Eds.), *Help me become everything I can be*. New York: American Foundation for the Blind.

Jastrzembska, Z. (1984). Resources for parents and professionals working with visually handicapped preschoolers. *Education of the Visually Handicapped, 16*, 115–134.

Jose, R. T. (Ed.). (1983). *Understanding low vision*. New York: American Foundation for the Blind.

Kansas State Department of Education. (1981). *Assessment tools for use with the severely multiply handicapped-deaf/blind*. Topeka: Author.

Kastein, S., Spaulding, I., & Scharf, B. (1980). *Raising the young blind child: A guide for parents and educators*. New York: Human Sciences Press.

Kennedy, V. (Ed.). (1983). *Vision and hearing screening of the severely handicapped: A resource guide*. Phoenix: Arizona Department of Education.

Kirtley, D. D. (1975). *The psychology of blindness*. Chicago: Nelson Hall.

Langley, M. B. (1978). *Assessment of multihandicapped visually impaired children*. Nashville, TN: George Peabody College of Vanderbilt University.

Langley, M. B. (1979). Psychoeducational assessment of the multiply handicapped blind child: Issues and methods. *Education of the Visually Handicapped, 10*, 97–115.

Lowenfeld, B. (1980). Psychological problems of children with impaired vision. In W. M. Cruickshank (Ed.), *Psychology of exceptional children and youth* (4th ed.). Englewood Cliffs, NJ: Prentice-Hall.

Lowenfeld, B. (1981). Effects of blindness on the cognitive functions of children. In B. Lowenfeld (Ed.), *Berthold Lowenfeld on blindness and blind people*. New York: American Foundation for the Blind. (Reprinted from *Nervous Child*, 1948, *7*, 45–54)

Maxfield, K. E., & Buchholz, S. (1957). *A social maturity scale for blind preschool children: A guide to its use*. New York: American Foundation for the Blind.

McInnes, J. M., & Treffry, J. A. (1982). *Deaf-blind infants and children: A developmental guide*. Toronto:

University of Toronto Press.

Miller, D. (1979). *Ophthalmology: The essentials*. Boston: Houghton Mifflin.

Mills, A. E. (Ed.). (1983). *Language acquisition in the blind child: Normal and deficient*. London: Croom Helm.

Morse, J. L. (1975). Answering the questions of the psychologist assessing the visually handicapped child. *New Outlook for the Blind, 69*, 350–353.

Mulford, R. (1987). First words of the blind child. In M. D. Smith & J. L. Locke (Eds.), *The emergent lexicon: The child's development of a linguistic vocabulary*. Orlando, FL: Academic.

National Society to Prevent Blindness. (1980). *Vision problems in the U.S.: Facts and figures*. New York: Author.

Newland, T. E. (1979). The Blind Learning Aptitude Test. *Journal of Visual Impairment and Blindness, 73*, 134–139.

O'Brien, R. (1976). *Alive...Aware...A Person: A developmental model for early childhood services with special definition for visually impaired children and their parents*. Rockville, MD: Montgomery County Public Schools.

Orlansky, M. D. (1984). Public perceptions of terms relating to blindness and visual impairment. *Journal of Rehabilitation, 50*(3), 46–49.

Padula, W. V. (1983). Vision and its influence on development of the visually impaired child. In M. E. Mulholland & M. V. Wurster (Eds.), *Help me become everything I can be*. New York: American Foundation for the Blind.

Phelps, D. L. (1981). Retinopathy of prematurity: An estimate of vision loss in the United States—1979. *Pediatrics, 67*, 924–925.

Ray, S., O'Neill, M. J., & Morris, N. T. (Eds.). (1983). *Low incidence children: A guide to psychoeducational assessment*. Natchitoches, LA: Steven Ray Publishing.

Raynor, S. (1978). *Curriculum development through the use of assessments*. Mason, MI: Ingham Intermediate School District.

Reynolds, C. R., & Clark, J. H. (Eds.). (1983). *Assessment and programming for young children with low-incidence handicaps*. New York: Plenum Press.

Scholl, G. T. (1983). Assessing the visually impaired child. In S. Ray, M. J. O'Neill, & N. T. Morris (Eds.), *Low incidence children: A guide to psychoeducational assessment*. Natchitoches, LA: Steven Ray Publishing.

Scholl, G. T., & Schnur, R. (1976). *Measures of psychological, vocational, and educational functioning in the blind and visually handicapped*. New York: American Foundation for the Blind.

Scott, E. P., Jan, J. E., & Freeman, R. D. (1977). *Can't your child see?* Baltimore: University Park Press.

Sheehan, R. (1982). Infant assessment: A review and identification of emergent trends. In D. D. Bricker (Ed.), *Intervention with at-risk and handicapped infants: From research to application*. Baltimore: University Park Press.

Shurrager, H. C., & Shurrager, P. S. (1964). *Manual for the Haptic Intelligence Scale for the Blind*. Chicago: Illinois Institute of Technology, Psychology Research Technology Center.

Silberman, R. K. (1981). Assessment and evaluation of visually handicapped students. *Journal of Visual Impairment and Blindness, 75*, 109–114.

Silverman, H., & Davidson, I. (1984). Early identification: An approach to reformulation. *Teacher Education, 24*, 40–54.

Silverman, W. A. (1980). *Retrolental fibroplasia: A modern parable*. New York: Grune & Stratton.

Sokolow, A. (1983). Differences in play and language development in a pair of blind and sighted twin infants. In M. E. Mulholland & M. V. Wurster (Eds.), *Help me become everything I can be*. New York: American Foundation for the Blind.

Stephens, B., & Simpkins, K. (1974). The reasoning, moral judgment, and moral conduct of the congenitally blind (Final Report, Project No. OEG-0-72-5464). Washington, DC: Bureau of Education for the Handicapped.

Stephens, B., Grube, C., & Fitzgerald, J. (1977). *Cognitive remediation of blind students* (Final Report, Project No. 443CH50410). Washingotn, DC: Bureau of Education for the Handicapped.

Suinn, R. M., & Dauterman, W. L. (1966). *A manual for the Stanford-Kohs Block Design Test for the Blind*. Washington, DC: Vocational Rehabilitation Administration.

Swallow, R. (1981). Fifty assessment instruments commonly used with blind and partially seeing individuals.

Journal of Visual Impairment and Blindness, 75, 65–72.

Swallow, R., Mangold, S., & Mangold, P. (1978). *Informal assessment of developmental skills for visually handicapped students.* New York: American Foundation for the Blind.

Tuttle, D. W. (1984). *Self-esteem and adjusting with blindness.* Springfield, IL: Charles C Thomas.

Urwin C. (1978). The development of communication between blind infants and their parents. In A. Lock (Ed.), *Action, gesture, and symbol: The emergence of language.* London: Academic Press.

Urwin, C. (1983). Dialogue and cognitive functioning in the early language development of three blind children. In A. E. Mills (Ed.), *Language acquisition in the blind child: Normal and deficient.* London: Croom Helm.

Uzgiris, I. C., & Hunt, J. McV. (1974). *Assessment in infancy: Ordinal scales of psychological development.* Urbana: University of Illinois Press.

Vander Kolk, C. J. (1981). *Assessment and planning with the visually impaired.* Baltimore: University Park Press.

Vander Kolk, C. J. (1987). Psychosocial assessment of visually impaired persons. In B. Heller, L. Flohr, & L. S. Zegans (Eds.), *Psychosocial interventions with sensorially disabled persons.* Orlando, FL: Grune & Stratton.

Ward, M. E. (1986). The visual system. In G. T. Scholl (Ed.), *Foundations of education for blind and visually handicapped children and youth: Theory and practice.* New York: American Foundation for the Blind.

Ward, M. E., & Genshaft, J. (1983). The Perkins-Binet tests: A critique and recommendations for administration. *Exceptional Children, 49,* 450–452.

Warren, D. H. (1981). Visual impairments. In J. M. Kauffman & D. P. Hallahan (Eds.), *Handbook of special education.* Englewood Cliffs, NJ: Prentice-Hall.

Warren, D. H. (1984). *Blindness and early childhood development* (2nd ed.). New York: American Foundation for the Blind.

Willoughby, D. M. (1979). *A resource guide for parents and educators of blind children.* Baltimore: National Federation of the Blind.

Wills, D. M. (1970). Vulnerable periods in the early development of blind children. *Psychoanalytic study of the child, 25,* 461–480.

Yarnall, G. D., & Carlton, G. R. (1981). *Guidelines and manual of tests for educators interested in the assessment of handicapped children.* Austin, TX: International Research Institute.

7

Cognitive Assessment in Deaf Preschoolers

Robert J. Hoffmeister

The question of whether cognitive development precedes language acquisition in infants is a continuing theoretical discussion. Clearly, cognitive development is a complex inter-relationship of mental processes and strategies that relate the development of internal mechanisms to external stimuli. This interrelationship then permits new knowledge to build on old knowledge, which, in turn, creates changes in mental structures and permits their development. Because of the profound role of language in human development, the exact influence of language on cognitive abilities has yet to be determined. Language itself consists of a set of mental structures that interface with cognitive structure (Menyuk, 1975).

Studies investigating the cognitive abilities of deaf children have typically focused on the role of language in cognition and thinking. Traditionally, deaf children are compared to their hearing "peers" on a variety of tasks that have been "controlled" for necessary and sufficient use of language. Language is commonly defined by hearing investigators as that spoken or acoustically represented by the hearing population of the world (Furth, 1966a). However, cognitive development in deaf children is difficult, if not often impossible, to assess because the deafness plus accompanying environmental situations results in a breakdown in the usual language–cognition relationship. Tasks that assess cognitive abilities in deaf infants are difficult to develop and apply. It is in the assessment of cognitive skills that language becomes confounded with cognitive abilities.

The major goal of this chapter is to present information that is pertinent to the assessment of cognitive abilities in young deaf children. As will be shown, the accurate assessment of cognitive abilities in young deaf children depends on a number of noncognitive factors. The major noncognitive factors influencing performance on the tasks developed to examine the cognitive abilities of deaf children have been identified as

1. The perspective of deafness held by the examiner.
2. The language capabilities of the child.
3. The language capabilities of the examiner.
4. The level of cognitive skill versus language skill necessary to complete the task.
5. Testing procedures and instruments.

ROBERT J. HOFFMEISTER ● Center for the Study of Communication and Deafness, School of Education, Boston University, Boston, Massachusetts 02215.

Each of these factors will be discussed in turn, and the implications of these factors for instrument selection will be considered.

DEFINITION OF MAJOR TERMS

For a proper understanding of the preschool deaf child's cognitive skills the following definitions of commonly used terms are necessary.

Language must be defined from the psycholinguistic viewpoint as consisting of many levels (Chomsky, 1965). One level, close to the surface, has to do with what particular language sounds or units are necessary for the delivery or receipt of the message. That is, the same underlying message (content) can be delivered through French, Spanish, Swahili, English, or American Sign Language (ASL). The inability or ability to process information using the sounds of English should not be the measure of everyone's knowledge of language, unless that person is a native speaker of English with no physical or mental problems that affect his or her speech production or reception. If there is a problem in the production or reception of speech sounds, then some compensatory means must be devised to actually measure ''language'' knowledge.

The term *deaf* has more to do with attitude than with level of hearing loss. The term *deaf* with a small *d* refers to the physically caused hearing loss experienced by people. There is no agreed-upon criterion for those who are deaf, and the range of hearing losses experienced among deaf people is great. This range may extend from the moderate to the profound levels. The term *Deaf* with a capital *D* refers to those persons who culturally and linguistically identify themselves as Deaf. Therefore, a person who is Deaf is one who has a hearing loss sufficient to interfere with the average spoken-communication situation, and who considers herself or himself Deaf. In this definition, *Deaf* refers to a cultural group, whereas *deaf* refers to a physical impairment. Given that audiological advancements and technical measures do not recognize *deaf* as a term relating to a specific hearing loss, the use of *deaf* becomes a cover term for those who have a hearing problem that interferes with typical communication by the general public. The term *Deaf* has become an identification element within the Deaf community (Padden, 1980).

Hearing impaired is the term used to identify and group all persons who have a problem hearing. This is a generic term and covers all levels of hearing loss.

Hard-of-hearing is a traditional term, not used a great deal currently. It is used to identify those persons who experience a hearing problem but who feel capable of interacting in the average spoken communication situation and do not consider themselves Deaf. As with the term *deaf*, hard-of-hearing may also cover an extended range of hearing loss. Both terms have more to do with functioning in spoken-communication settings than with the actual delineation of the level of hearing.

TWO PERSPECTIVES ON DEAFNESS

It is generally accepted that our view of the world or the paradigms that we hold as scientists and professionals tend to constrain the interpretations that are obtained (Kuhn, 1970). The way in which we view children who have disabilities influences what we expect of them (Rosenthal & Jacobson, 1968). When working with the deaf child, it is especially crucial to have an understanding not only of the background of the deaf child but also of one's view of deafness, to have appropriate professional training, and to have knowledge of the adult deaf community, as these can have a profound influence on expected levels of capability.

In the overview and Chapter 2 of this book, a discussion of normative versus criterion-referenced testing is presented. This distinction is directly relevant to the following discussion regarding perspectives on the deaf. The perspectives on deafness can be distinguished by the "norms" that are chosen as the standards. In the assessment of young deaf children, the professional's perspective on deafness will influence which "scales" will be used to judge the abilities of the child.

The first perspective on deafness is the *medical-audiological view*. The medical view sees the hearing problem as disease-based and focuses on the functioning of the ears. The goal of the medical model is attaining a "cure" or using a corrective procedure that will enable the individual to function in the "healthy" range. Concentration is on testing and developing procedures for the "improvement of hearing." Like the medical view from which it is derived, the audiological perspective is an extension of deafness as a pathology. The audiological perspective focuses on questions concerning both the degree and the level of hearing loss or impaired hearing, as compared with that group whose level of hearing falls within the "normal" range. The "normal" range is defined as the lowest level that 50% of the general population is capable of hearing; this is "0" level, or normal hearing. From this central standard, there is a normal range of hearing from 0 to 30 decibels[1] (Newby, 1979). The audiological view of handling dysfunction of the hearing mechanism is one of compensation through the introduction of highly sophisticated technical devices, such as hearing aids or cochlear implants in order to bring hearing within the "normal" range.

For a speech "pathologist" who shares the audiological view, the norms are those of the speaking population. Deafness, or hearing dysfunction, automatically influences speech production. The earlier the hearing loss occurs in a child and the greater that loss is, the larger is the impact on speech capabilities; in fact, the relationship is exponentially related (Moores, 1982). The most significant impact occurs in younger children and when the loss is over 70 dB. This loss is directly related to the reception of conversational speech (Moores, 1982).

These pathological perspectives on deafness significantly influence how the person with a hearing loss is viewed. All data or all achievements are viewed in comparison to the hearing norm (keep in mind that standards in cognitive tasks are also tied to the "normal" range—a "hearing norm" that is established by those whose facilities, physical or mental, are completely intact). Within this framework, there are no adjusted norms to compensate for any physical or mental problem. Therefore, these norms, which continue to indicate that the deaf child or adult is delayed or inferior, become impossible for the deaf child or adult to meet because the deaf person will never function identically to a hearing person.

The second perspective, one that attempts to depathologize deafness, is the *functional view* (Hoffmeister, 1985). Woodward (1982) was among the first to advocate the depathologizing of the deaf adult by suggesting that the Deaf be seen as a bicultural and bilingual group, that is, as a minority group within the hearing socieites of the world.

---

[1]A decibel (dB) is a unit of measure for level of hearing.

According to the functional view, the Deaf, as a bilingual and bicultural group, must be assessed within group norms and not between group norms. It is apparent in much of the literature on deafness, that the Deaf as adults appear to function appropriately and successfully in all areas of life except academic areas. The Deaf marry, successfully raise children, pay taxes, have appropriate socialization skills within the Deaf Community, hold adequate jobs (although their salary is less than that of the hearing overall), and function successfully as members of our society, meaning all of the world (Benderly, 1980; Higgins, 1980; Neisser, 1983).

This successful functioning is seen when the comparative measures are appropriate. The consequence of this view suggests that, for measuring performance on various scales, either

1. The scales need to be adjusted for in-group norms, or
2. The scales need to be adjusted for the "handicapping" condition that makes the population different or delayed.

The condition that creates a "handicap" for the deaf is clearly communication. However, I must caution the reader that "communication" has both narrow and extended definitions. In the narrow view, communication is simply the ability to send information to another and to receive information from another. The extended view suggests that adjusting for communicative differences involves far more than making "English" available and includes positive attitudes and an adjustment of the different cultural values held by the Deaf and the Hearing.

How Perspectives Influence Outcomes

In assessing the cognitive development of the deaf child, the particular perspective from which the evaluation is approached will have a major influence on the choice of the normative group used for assessment. It will also influence the level of expectations of the child by the examiner. For example, the examiner may not believe that a preschool deaf child is capable of performing at age level or above. This belief will influence the level of skills needed by the examiner. If the examiner assumes that the preschool deaf child is not capable of higher level skills, such as fluency in a Signed Language, the examiner may not have or use the skills necessary to assess these skills in the children. The selection of tests and their underlying assumptions will interact with all of the above. Vaughan Stagg (Chapter 4) presents similar issues dealing with adjustments needed in the measurement of cognitive skills in handicapped children. However, because of the unique situation of the deaf child, more elaborate adjustments are necessary.

The major influence of the medical perspective is on the definition of language in the deaf child. Myklebust (1964) is representative of the medical profession in its perspective that the deafness itself limits development. According to Myklebust, the hearing loss is organic in basis and constrains the level of thinking, prohibiting the deaf child from learning to read English and attaining a level of abstract thinking.

In his attempt to demonstrate the influence of language on thinking, Furth (1966a,b) has conducted a series of experiments that suggest that the deaf child is capable of reasoning without language. He is one of the few investigators who has attempted to move to a functional perspective. Unfortunately, he has failed to achieve a functional perspective in his very definition of what language constitutes. Blank (1965) aptly challenged Furth's definition of language when he (Furth) described deaf children as being without language because they lack the fluency and conversational skills of English.

This view of language as an auditorily based phenomenon has also been challenged by Signed-Language researchers (Bellugi & Klima, 1980; Wilbur, 1979a,b), who maintain that language can be thought of as an underlying system of symbolic representation that can be delivered through the air by at least two modalities, acoustic waves or visual signals.

Although the use of signs may suggest a strategy of maintaining hearing children as the normative group and then attempting to compensate by adjusting the definition of language, this approach ignores some of the fundamental issues in assessing deaf children's cognitive skills. In examining the intellectual skills of deaf children in Israel, Zwibel and Mertens (1985) suggested that cognitive skills should be seen from an intragroup perspective rather than an intergroup perspective. By examining the deaf children both by age level and over time, they found that deaf children rely on *different strategies at different developmental ages in order to perform the tasks expected of them.* As they become older, deaf children depend more on abstract thinking strategies with a strong visual perceptual basis. Hearing children, on the other hand, use abstract thinking based on auditory strategies.

The above findings suggest that there may be support for a functional view that the deaf child is different, but not deficient in the development of cognitive, linguistic, and social skills. In contrast, for professionals who abide by the medical-audiological perspectives, the deaf child is usually viewed as deficient. Interpretation of evidence obtained from testing and research is then dependent on the examiner's perspective. Table 1 is an example of how evidence from various studies may be viewed in terms of the defined outcomes.

Implications of Differing Perspectives for Assessment

One major implication derived from Table 1 is that, although the functional view presents the deaf child as a member of a bilingual-bicultural group who, as an adult, will be able to function appropriately and will be able to develop a positive sense of self, these outcomes depend on test and examiner factors. These specifically include (a) which tests are selected to measure the deaf child's performance and (b) the view or set of expectations held by the examiner. Instruments such as the Bayley scales, the McCarthy scales, and the Brigance will be incorrectly scored unless the examiner is aware of the linguistic structures in a Signed Language. The use of particular instruments will be only as reliable as the knowledge of the examiner in interpreting the results. For example, examiners who are knowledgeable about the underlying subject–object marking system in the linguistics of ASL will score a child as performing higher on categories of relating symbols to environmental actions versus just naming objects or will score a child higher on knowledge of spatial relationships and the functions of objects in space. Examiners who view gestures as nonlinguistic or nonproductive (the medical-audiological view) will not see the child as performing at levels equivalent to age or to hearing children of the same level.

Table I. How Views Influence Outcomes in Assessment of Deaf Children

Evidence	Deficient	Different
1.0 Late diagnosis	1.1 Delay in cognitive and linguistic development	1.2 Variation in communication and interaction strategies (Goldin-Meadow, 1975; 1980; 1982)
2.0 Lack of language	2.1 Delay in language development because slow in learning to speak	2.2 Language viewed as including a Signed Language, any other means of communicating with the child
3.0 Developing language and cognition dependent on interaction with environment	3.1 Parents must take a much stronger "teaching" role to create "natural" interaction episodes	3.2 Parents using a Signed Language may "naturally" interact with their deaf child
4.0 Developmental studies indicate lag when deaf children are compared to hearing children	4.1 Deaf children experience developmental delay due to hearing disorder	4.2 Deaf children are using different strategies in interaction and studies are based on "hearing" measures of success
5.0 Child sees self as others see him or her development of social identity	5.1 Parents must participate in interaction primarily as "teachers"; parents' role is second, deaf child is viewed as person for whom compensation is necessary to meet expectations of hearing children	5.2 Deaf child is viewed as part of family, interaction is natural, expectations and caretaking are similar across siblings or when compared to hearing children
6.0 Overprotection, lack of social skills	6.1 Child is not able to participate fully in family and adult matters. Child must learn to cope with the hearing world.	6.2 Child is a full participant in family and eventually will become a participant in the Deaf Community

As presented above, how the deaf child is viewed will have a significant impact on the determination of the causal relationship between the test results and the suggested corrections and adaptations. Cognitive development interacts with language development. This single fact is the crucial factor in viewing how well deaf children perform cognitively. Linguistic and social behavior are outcome measures of intellectual performance. If the view that Furth and associates have offered in their approach to the assessment of cognitive performance is true (i.e., that the deaf child is without language), then Myklebust and others are supported in their views that the deaf have an inherent organic deficiency. Current evidence and a reexamination of many of the studies suggest that cognitive development and language do interact and that the deaf child is not without language. Goldin-Meadow (1975, 1979, 1982) succinctly presented a strong argument that even the young orally trained deaf child who is not exposed to a Signed Language appears to develop a consistent system of gestures, which appear to have underlying structures similar to the underlying linguistic structures found for children in general. In addition, it is important to note that, because all deaf children in English-speaking communities are exposed to English (spoken and written) and because a basic belief is that deaf children are capable of learning, English at some level is learned. However, English may not be the "language" in which the deaf child is competent.

Those currently practicing in the field bring with them attitudes, communication power, and prior training. In a review of expectations of what deaf children are capable of achieving, Rittenhouse, Morreau, and Iran-Nejal (1981) suggested that expectations result in adjustment downward in work with deaf children. Examiners bring to the assessment the belief that the child is not able to perform at higher levels. Again, this problem stems from inadequate knowledge of what deaf children are capable of and from the view that deafness, as a pathology, somehow limits performance. This view is further supported by a study in which deaf children who wore hearing aids were rated more negatively than deaf children who did not (Blood & Blood, 1982). The pathological perspective of the deaf child as a handicapped person is fed not only by prior training but by physical appearance as well.

Labov (1973) poignantly pointed out the examiner–examinee problem in explaining that, through language, the experimenter brings not only communication power but cultural power as well. For a white middle-class examiner to assess black ghetto children, crossing linguistic and cultural barriers is almost impossible. Labov demonstrated that conclusions drawn by white and black examiners for the same black children were significantly different. Currently, studies are suggesting that the deaf child is similar to children who are culturally different and disadvantaged (Schlesinger, 1984). Therefore, the examiner or assessor must be trained in both linguistic and cultural frameworks when working with deaf children.

To change the above practices, exposure to competent and fully functioning deaf adults within the Deaf Community is also necessary. Professionals who do not know the intricacies, the values, and the subcultural influences and how these relate the Deaf Community to the hearing community will always continue to hold lower expectations of deaf children's cognitive performance.

CHILD LANGUAGE CAPABILITIES AND TASK PERFORMANCE

Typically, Deaf children fail in tasks that require English as a means of communication. Deaf children have problems either in understanding what the experimenter wants them to do or in actually performing the task. The outcomes are then interpreted, and in the usual circumstances, the deaf child is reported as lagging behind the hearing child in cognitive development.

Nature of Communication Skills in the Deaf Population

In the case of the deaf child, professionals in the field have, in the majority of circumstances, moved to using some form of a Signed Language (Jordan, Gustafson, & Rosen, 1976, 1979). This move to a Signed Language has affected hearing parents and their young deaf children. More and more deaf children 3 years old and younger are being exposed to some form of a Signed Language. Sign language acquisition has not been extensively studied for its learnability in young deaf children (Goodhart, 1984; Hoffmeister, 1987). Assumptions are being made by professionals that may not be entirely valid.

Currently, within the total communication movement[2], a number of signed systems are in use (see Wilbur, 1979a, for details). This variation in the visual presentation of a language (English) can be extensive; there is, without doubt, wide variation between schools, programs, and even classrooms (Marmor & Pettito, 1979).

These signed systems (commonly referred to as *Signed English*) are visual systems that borrow "signs" from ASL and create entirely new "signs" for a large number of morphemes. The major purpose of these systems is to visually present a one-to-one match to English word order and morphological structure. The major problem is the inability to achieve a one-to-one transfer from the visual-spatial, morphologically based ASL to the spoken, linear, morphosyntactically based English.

Professionals who are using these signed systems are following assumptions not yet empirically proven to be sound. For example, there has been no empirical research done to prove that Signed English is a viable and efficient means of language use by deaf children, as has been done on ASL (Klima & Bellugi, 1979; Wilbur, 1979a,b).

Historically, the conditions under which deaf children have been educated have created a situation in which ASL is passed on from child to child at school, and not from parent to child (except in the case of children with deaf parents). Sign language acquisition in deaf children is just beginning to be described empirically (Bellugi, 1984; Hoffmeister, 1978, 1982, 1987; Newport, 1982). The reports to date indicate that young deaf children, no matter what they are exposed to, appear to operate on their Signed Language and make it more efficient. In other words, these children move toward certain principles of operation in ASL. In addition, they appear to acquire language in the same underlying schemata as hearing children who are acquiring a spoken language. These results have important consequences for the interactiion between examiner and deaf child.

If the results of the initial studies are upheld, the young deaf child exposed to some form of a Signed Language will be able to communicate at a much higher level than is now generally expected. Deaf children whose parents are able to communicate rapidly with them will be able to relate much more of their knowledge about the world. Professionals who are assessing these children will need to be prepared for this level of communication; that is, they will need to have a detailed understanding of what the children are capable of producing, and of how it relates to the cognitive skills expected of children at these ages.

Very few, if any, studies have actually controlled for the variable of language used to complete tasks when the tasks involved deaf children. In almost all studies, only spoken language (English) has been the language used as the control language. Only recently have investigators recognized the need to obtain a measure of the level of Signed Language in young deaf children (Blank, 1974). In studies where language (i.e., spoken language) was carefully controlled, deaf children were found to perform equally to hearing children (Blank & Bridges, 1966). In a review of studies measuring cognitive performance in deaf children, Moores (1982) concluded that

---

[2]*Total communication* is the key term for describing the new genre of educating deaf children. It is typically practiced by presenting the spoken and signed form of English simultaneously. It is defined as the right of every deaf child to use whatever communication is necessary to receive and produce language, including messages spoken, signed, written, pantomimed, mimed, and so on.

the available evidence suggests that the condition of deafness imposes no limitations on the cognitive abilities of individuals. In addition, no evidence suggests that deaf persons think in more "concrete" ways than the hearing or that their intellectual functioning is in any way less sophisticated. (p. 162)

LANGUAGE CAPABILITIES OF THE EXAMINER

Moores (1982) suggested that tasks that indicate deficits in the deaf child can be related to the inability of the examiner to communicate with the child. Measures of intellectual capabilities rely on whether the examiner is able to explain the task to the child. Performance often involves success in understanding directions, as well as in dealing with the actual task itself. Adapting the task through some form of Signed English may be appropriate; however, an in-depth knowledge of Signed Languages by the examiner is required. Matching this knowledge to the child's communicative abilities becomes crucial. When this communication match is undertaken, deaf children appear to perform at levels more indicative of their abilities (Brunich, 1981).

The examiner's choice of a particular signed system may have a significant effect on the outcome of the assessment. Because the signed systems purport to be English on the hands, the assumption that the young deaf child is capable of learning and using this English-like system is not necessarily well founded. The examiner may, in fact, be using a communication system beyond the capabilities of the child. Now that total communication is prevalent and many hearing professionals have learned to "sign," the real problem is that there is no control over

1. How fluent the hearing professional is in producing any of the signed systems: Signed English (à la Bornstein), PSE,[3] or ASL.
2. How capable the hearing professional is in receiving any of the signed systems: Signed English, PSE, and ASL.
3. Whether the hearing professionals adjust their sign behavior to children's signing (especially when assessing 2- and 3-year-olds). There are no descriptions of "baby signs" in the signed systems or any of the signed languages except ASL (McIntire, 1974).
4. The attitudes that the hearing professionals bring to the assessment situation. Attitudes play a crucial role in how a child may be viewed within the testing situation (Woodward, 1982). For example, does the hearing professional recognize and value the deaf community and the role it plays in the socialization of the deaf child?

Stagg (Chapter 4) discusses adapatations of measures for various disabling conditions. For the deaf child, it is common practice to adapt the mode of presentation from a spoken language to a signed system. The assumption is that presenting a "signed" message to a deaf child solves the inadequate communication problem. This assumption has a number of pitfalls. Currently in practice are signed systems that vary from using the

---

[3]PSE (Pidgin Sign English) is the contact Signed Language used between deaf and hearing persons before the advent of the signed systems. It is still prevalent today.

principles of ASL to using many forms recently created and arbitrarily developed. In addition, if the examiner moves to using a "signed system," an assumption is made that this is the same signed system that the child is aware of. In many cases, there can be a great mismatch between the signing knowledge of the examiner and the knowledge of the system by the child. Professionals who have been exposed to only "signed systems" and are not conversant with the principles of ASL are in danger of not recognizing the mismatch between the examiner and the deaf child. Just because one is able to "carry on" a conversation with a young deaf child, one should not assume full comprehension by the child.

Finally, the skills of the examiner in using a signed system have recently become an issue in cognitive, social and linguistic assessment (Luetke-Stahlman, 1982, 1984). The assumption that "signing" English is the equivalent to spoken English is false. In addition, the amount of time needed to be a "good" signer may vary individually from one year to four years after the instruction period (Kluwin, 1984). Learning to sign in English order (i.e., Signed English) and learning to use ASL also vary considerably. The fact that there are no agreed-upon standards across the country creates monumental problems in determining who is a "fluent" sign communicator and who needs more practice. Errors in the adult productions of signed systems are numerous (Marmor & Pettito, 1979), though, over time, errors diminish and signers become more fluent (Kluwin, 1984). However, fluent signers are not necessarily fluent in ASL. Goodhart (1984) suggested that preschool deaf children are operating on the Signed-English input they receive and make it more efficient (more ASL-like). If the examiner is not aware of ASL principles, some information may be lost. This loss creates an interpretation gap. In complicated cognitive tasks, the deaf child may ask for clarification or may produce a result using a Signed Language. The experimenter may then be in danger of misinterpreting what the child means or needs. Professionals who have not had ASL and signed systems training for a minimum of two years are equivalent to those who learn Spanish in one or two semesters and proceed to assess Hispanic children in a bilingual setting.

Unfortunately, for the most part, the professionals who assess cognitive skills in deaf children vary in background and experience, in terms of being trained in deafness and/or trained in psychometrics. Clinical school psychologists and researchers seldom have the necessary background in deafness because this information is lacking in their preparation program. Very few programs have instituted the appropriate bicultural and cross-linguistic preparation necessary for training in assessment procedures for deaf children. The major implication of this fact is that great caution must be exercised in accepting the results of cognitive testing with the deaf from professionals who have not had these appropriate training experiences.

LEVEL OF COGNITIVE VERSUS LANGUAGE SKILLS NECESSARY TO COMPLETE THE TASK

In addition to the language of instruction, the language necessary to solve the task becomes critical. Tasks that are considered non-language-based or "nonverbal" may, in fact, be so complicated that some language is necessary to solve the tasks. Blank (1974) presented a strong case for reexamining tasks that were considered nonverbal or non-language, when a task that called for imagery or gesture could, in fact, be solved only through the power of language. Furth and his associates (1964, 1966a) conducted a long series of measuring and comparing the deaf child's performance on cognitive tasks. On many tasks, the deaf children performed as well as the hearing children. In those tasks in which the deaf children lagged behind, the issue of language was used to explain the deficit. However, when "language" is held constant in tasks between hearing and the deaf children, performance on all tasks appears to be equal (Best & Roberts, 1973; Blank & Bridges, 1966). Measures of intellectual functioning or cognitive functioning in the deaf child must, at some point, interact with language. Brunich (1981) demonstrated the high correlation between communication ability and IQ testing in deaf children. In testing the same deaf children over time, when the children were initially "oral" and later learned a Signed Language, there was a significant difference in the scores achieved by these deaf chilren.

Liben (1979) provided support for examining tasks that deaf children are capable of solving but do not solve because they may not draw on the correct strategies to solve the task. For the deaf child, it is a question not of knowing which strategies to use, but of not using the appropriate strategy. For example deaf children have the ability to categorize objects and to use category clustering to increase recall. However, they do not always use this strategy, and the result is a deficit in recall tasks. After training, deaf children were found to be able to redirect their strategies to enhance their recall ability. That is, deaf children trained to cluster items semantically and to use the semantic category for recall are able to recall significantly more information than their untrained peers, both hearing and deaf (Liben, 1979).

BACKGROUND INFLUENCES ON THE DEAF CHILD

The etiology of the hearing problem in a child may also influence test performance or behavior. External or postnatal causes of hearing problems should be kept in mind when evaluating a young deaf child. External causes, such as a high fever, problems at birth, or prematurity, all have the probability of affecting hearing (Moores, 1982; Vernon, 1968). Trauma- or disease-based causes of hearing loss may affect more than just the functioning of the ears. Prenatal causes of hearing loss such as rubella or drugs ingested during pregnancy are more than likely to create additional dysfunction and to result in more disturbance in performance by the child. It is therefore necessary to understand the child in terms of his or her current and past physical condition.

Cultural conflicts may also become a problem. In some cultures, eye gaze or pointing is viewed as socially negative, and therefore, they are not encouraged in the child. Using the amount of eye contact or the amount of pointing as a developmental rating in the home with a deaf child may have negative implications outside the home.

The most critical background factor for evaluators of cognitive skills in the deaf child is the fact that 95% of deaf children are born to hearing parents. The situation of these children is unique, in that the incidental and deliberate transmission of information regarding the world is hampered because the hearing loss blocks the usual spoken signals. The deaf child who is not exposed to a signed language during the early years will not be able to fully interact with his or her environment.

Two major influences in the growth and development of the deaf child are the attitudes of the parents and their use of language with their deaf child. Parents who have positive attitudes and are able to interact comfortably with their child will create an environment in which the deaf child will feel capable (Greenberg, 1980, 1983). This positive feeling will enhance play and exploration, which increase the child's interaction level with the environment, thereby permitting the normal development of cognitive skills. However, when language influences cognitive development, a much more complicated situation occurs. Etiologial factors and the amount of spoken-language input that can be processed begin to take on a much greater role in development. No matter how well the spoken language is received by the deaf child, there will always be some level of interference. For those children for whom the interference is minimal (deaf children whose hearing loss is such that it does not interfere with the reception of spoken language), a visual language may not be necessary. For children with more severe hearing losses, the learning and use of a Signed Language have currently been accepted as the way to compensate for the interference created by the hearing loss (Jordan, et al., 1979). However, parental attitudes toward the use of Signed Language also have an effect on how both parent and child deal with the issue of deafness (Hoffmeister, 1985). Parents who look favorably on a Signed Language, who learn and use it with their child, and who are knowledgeable about the adult Deaf community will be more comfortable during interaction episodes with their deaf child. Although the use of a Signed Language by parents can result in positive outcomes, it does not solve all the environmental interaction problems created by the hearing loss. Communication becomes restricted to the parents who know the Signed Language and to those few others who choose to learn it.

Most of those outside the family who choose to learn a Signed Language will be connected to a school or a program serving deaf children. It is at this point that the interaction and measurement of skills in deaf children directly become affected by the language used during interaction episodes.

TESTING PROCEDURES WITH THE YOUNG DEAF CHILD

Cognitive Testing

Cognitive achievement in deaf preschoolers has traditionally been measured by intelligence tests (Moores, 1982). As Wachs and Sheehan (Chapter 1) indicate, cognitive data on deaf preschool children are clearly lacking. Intelligence tests such as the Stanford-Binet and the Wechsler Intelligence Scale for Children (WISC) must be modified for their use with deaf children. This modification usually eliminates the verbal (vocal) subtests and uses the scores on the performance subtests as the overall score for the deaf child (Brunich, 1981; Moores, 1982; Vernon, 1968).

These modifications are usually adjusting the level of communication between examiner and child and eliminating those items that appear to require "verbal" skills. This adjustment assumes that the deaf child is not capable of performing these tasks. Fortunately, studies now suggest that "even when special care is taken to minimize such interference (level of communication ability), the children's communicative competence significantly correlated with their I.Q. score" (Brunich, 1981, p. 433).

Examples of Instruments

The following are instruments commonly used to assess cognitive development in young deaf children:

A. Intellectual performance measures (performance scales only)
   1. Wechsler Preschool and Primary Scale of Intelligence (Wechsler, 1967) — 4.0–6.5 years
   2. Hiskey-Nebraska Test of Learning Aptitude (Hiskey, 1966) — 2.0–18.0 years
   3. Stanford-Binet Test of Intelligence (Terman & Merrill, 1973)
   4. Leiter International Performance Scale (Leiter, 1948) — 2.0–18.0 years
      Arthur Adaptation of Leiter (1950)
   5. McCarthy Scales of Children's Abilities (McCarthy, 1972) — 2.5–8.5 years
   6. Catell Infant Intelligence Scale (Catell, 1950) — 0–30 months

B. Behavioral inventories of cognitive development
   1. Bayley Scales of Infant Development (Bayley, 1969) — 0–2.5 years
   2. Brigance Diagnostic Inventory of Early Development (Brigance, 1978) — 0–6.0 years
   3. Uzgiris-Hunt Ordinal Scales of Psychological Development (Uzgiris-Hunt, 1975) — 0–2.0 years
   4. Meadow-Kendall Scale of Emotional Adjustment (Meadow, 1984) — 0–18.0 years
   5. Learning Accomplishment Profile (LAP) (Sanford, 1974) — 3.0–5.0 years
   6. Early LAP (Sanford, 1974) — 0–3.0 years

Factors Influencing Choice of Instrument

For hearing children, scores on intelligence tests are totals of the verbal and performance scales. For the deaf child, only the performance scale is commonly used. This has become accepted practice because of the bias toward knowledge of English on the "verbal" scale. Only two measures of intellectual performance have norms for the deaf: the Hiskey-Nebraska and the Leiter International Performance Scale. This bias toward spoken language by previous investigators has resulted in a debate on the relevance of language to the measurement of cognitive capabilities in deaf children versus hearing children (see Vernon, 1968, for a review).

Throughout history, the role that language plays in the thinking process has been discussed and investigated. In a review of 33 research studies that were viewed as studies of the cognitive performance of deaf children, 11 studies found the deaf children to be inferior to hearing children, 7 studes found no significant difference, and 13 found the deaf child to be superior. Significantly, Vernon (1968) stated that "the research done by people who are most experienced in working with the deaf and who have achieved highest scholarship in the area yielded results unanimously showing the deaf and hearing function equally well" (p. 6). Experience with the deaf child and knowledge of the testing instruments appear to be crucial to the outcome of the assessment situation.

The choice of the tests used to assess deaf children's ability may be influenced by the perspective that one holds on deafness. In a survey of school administrators and programs, Anderson and Stevens (1970) found that the preferred tests of intellectual performance are the WISC performance scale, the Hiskey-Nebraska Test of Learning Aptitude (HNLA), and the Leiter-International Performance Scale (LIPS). The "nonverbal" nature of these instruments can be questioned, especially as the level of child's communication and the ability of the examiner to communicate with the child significantly affect performance on such tests (Brunich, 1981, Musgrove & Counts, 1975; Sisco & Anderson, 1980).

Currently, there are no adequate testing instruments for young deaf children. Evaluators must be especially aware that "language," which should be read as "English," must be carefully controlled for. The instrument using the least amount of English is the Leiter scale. However, evaluators who are not experienced with deaf children may record results that are not reliable. The "language" used in explaining what the child must do to complete the task can have a significant effect on the outcome. Hence, no test is "language-free."

Behavior Rating Scales

It appears that very little evidence exists supporting the proposition that assessment tools that are used to determine cognitive skills in older deaf children are valid and reliable for preschoolers (Hurley, Hirshosen, Hunt, & Kavale, 1979; Hurley, Kavale, Hirshosen, & Hunt, 1978; Musgrove, 1975). Recently, a number of behavioral observation measures have been produced. These scales are usually scored by parents and professionals who rate the behavior of a deaf child according to developmental criteria. Typically, the behavioral rating scales are divided into motor and self-help skills, cognitive or academic readiness, language, and social-emotional development. The only behavioral-observational measurement tool specifically created for and normed on deaf children is the Meadow-Kendall Scale of Emotional Adjustment (1984).

Observation scales based on parental or professional ratings, which classify various behaviors in children as belonging to some predetermined developmental level, can be informative but must also be viewed with extreme caution, as perspectives on deafness will again influence how behavior is rated. Specifically, because behavioral rating scales are a rating of observable behavior, the expectations of the performance capabilities of the deaf child will influence what the observer sees (Kushe, & Greenberg, 1983). The fact that the rater knows the child is deaf will influence the score on the observational tool. As noted earlier, the perspective that the rater holds will determine if the influence will be negative (medical-audiological) or positive (functional). Children viewed negatively, or as incapable of performing tasks, will be rated that way.

The significance of communication and its effect on rating the behavior of the deaf child also cannot be underestimated (Greenberg & Mervin, 1979). Deaf children who are viewed as poor communicators will receive very low rating scores. Communication affects interaction, play, attachment, and one's ability to control a situation. The influence of communication is so pervasive that, if the deaf child is viewed as deficient in communicative behavior, all other ratings are also affected (Meadow, 1967, 1976). In using scales that depend on interactions for positive assessment scores, those who view the deaf child as being noncapable, passive, and less competent will always score the deaf child in this negative way (Schlesinger & Meadow, 1972; Schlesinger, 1984; Wendell-Monig & Tumley, 1980).

Along these lines, it is interesting to note that a negative cycle of interaction may exist between the deaf child and those who interact with her or him. As interaction becomes more and more based on communicative competence, the interactions between the deaf child and others decrease substantially (Schlesinger & Meadow, 1972; Vandell & George, 1981). This interaction disruption directly influences how the child will be rated on behavioral scales. For example, in rating social-emotional development, the amount of time in interaction between parent and child at a particular age may indicate positive or negative social adjustment. In the deaf child's case, the amount of interaction may not depend on the child's ability to interact with the mother and may depend more on the mother's ability to interact with the child.

This point is nicely illustrated in a studying comparing the Alpern-Boll ratings of parents who received training in Signed Language (communicative focus) and had contact with deaf adults (attitude focus) and a control group that received minimal intervention other than typical medical-audiological services for their deaf children (Greenberg, 1980, 1983). These parents did not rate motoric or self-care abilities of their child as different in either group; these ratings do not depend on communication skill. However, significant differences were found in social, academic, and communicative abilities (Greenberg, 1980, 1983). Of importance is the fact that there were no differences in intellectual functioning between the two groups. *The major differences appeared to be in how the deaf children were viewed in their functioning*; that is, the children and parents who communicated more easily fared better. This interpretation is also supported by the positive change in parental views of deaf children in a project that increased parental contact with deaf adults at the time of identification of the child's hearing loss. The parents and the professionals who were in contact with the project altered their views of how a deaf child could behave. The parents viewed their deaf children more positively, were less control-oriented (i.e., less overprotective), recognized that their children would become a Deaf adult, and were able to perceive the positive aspects of what the Deaf Community had to offer (Hoffmeister, 1978; Hoffmeister & Shettle, 1980).

SUMMARY

Cognitive functioning in deaf children is still a major issue in the field of education of the deaf. The role of language and how it influences cognition is a major issue in the field of psychology. These facts make the assessment of the deaf child's cognitive function depend more on

1. The expectations of the examiner about the level of functioning that a deaf child is capable of reaching.
2. The knowledge of how influential language (not only English) can be during the assessment and diagnosis of the deaf child's performance in cognitive tasks.
3. The cultural, environmental, and physical status of the child.

REFERENCES

Anderson, R., & Stevens, G. (1970). Policies and procedures for admission of mentally retarded deaf children to residential schools for the deaf. *American Annal of the Deaf, 115*(1), 30–36.

Arthur, G. (1950). *The Arthur adaptation of the Leiter international performance scale.* Chicago, Ill: C. H. Stoetling.

Bayley, N. (1969). *Bayley Scales of Infant Development.* New York: Psychological Corporation.

Best, B., & Roberts, G. (1973). *Cognitive development and deaf children research report.* Research and Development Center in Education of Handicapped Children, University of Minnesota, Minneapolis.

Bellugi, U. (1984). *The acquisition of three morphological systems in a deaf child.* Unpublished Manuscripts. Salk Institution of Biological Studies, La Jolla, CA.

Bellugi, U., & Klima, E. (1980). The signs of language. Cambridge: Harvard University Press.

Benderly, R. (1980). *Dancing without music: Deafness in America.* New York: Anchor Press.

Blank, M. (1965) Use of the deaf in language studies: A reply to Furth. *Psychological Bulletin, 63,* 442–444.

Blank, M. (1974). Cognitive functions of language in the preschool years. *Developmental Psychology, 10,* 224–229.

Blank, M., & Bridger, W. H. (1966). Conceptual cross-modal transfer in deaf and hearing children. *Child Development, 37,* 29–38.

Blood, & Blood, (1982). Classrooms teachers' impressions of hearing impaired and deaf children. *Perceptual and Motor Skills, 54,* 877–878.

Brigance, A. (1978). *Brigance diagnostic inventory of basic skills.* Woburn, MA: Curriculum Associates.

Brunich, P. (1981). Relationship between intellectual functioning and communicative competence in deaf children. *Journal of Communication Disorders, 14,* 429–434.

Chomsky, N. (1965). *Aspects of a theory of syntax.* Cambridge: MIT Press.

Furth, H. (1966b). A comparison of reading test norms for deaf and hearing children. *American Annals of the Deaf, 111*(5), 461–462.

Furth H. (1966c). *Development of thinking in the deaf: Implications for the relation of thinking and language.* International Congress of Psychology.

Furth, H. G. (1964) Research with the deaf: Implications for language and cognition. *Psychological Bulletin, 62,* 145–164.

Furth, H. (1966a). *Thinking without language.* New York: Free Press.

Furth, H. (1974). The role of language in the child's development. *Proceedings of the 1973 Convention of American Instructors of the Deaf.* Washington, DC: U.S. Government Printing Office.

Goldin-Meadow, S. (1975). *The representation of semantic relations in a manual language created by deaf children of hearing parents: A language you can't dismiss out of hand.* Unpublished doctoral dissertation, University of Pennsylvania, Philadelphia.

Goldin-Meadow, S. (1979). Structure in a manual communication system developed without a convention model: Language without a helping hand. In H. Whitacker, & H. A. Whitacker (Eds.), *Studies in neurolinguistics* (Vol. 4). New York: Academic Press.

Goldin-Meadow, S. (1982). The resilience of recursion: A study of a communication system developed without a conventional language model. In E. Wanner, & L. Gleitman (Eds.), *Language acquisition: The state of the art.* Cambridge: Cambridge University Press.

Goodhart, W. (1984). *Morphological complexity, ASL, and the acquisition of signed languages in deaf children.* Unpublished doctoral dissertation, Boston University, Boston.

Greenberg, J. (1983). Family stress and child competence: The effects of early intervention for families with deaf infants. *American Annals of the Deaf, 128,* 407–417.

Greenberg, M. (1980), Social interaction between deaf pre-schoolers and their mothers: The effects of communication method and communication competence. *Developmental Psychology, 16,* 465–474.

Greenberg, M., & Mervin, R. (1979). Attachment patterns in profoundly deaf preschool children. *Merril-Palmer Quarterly, 25*(4).

Higgins, P. (1980). *Outsiders in a hearing world.* Beverly Hills, CA: Sage Publications.

Hiskey, M. (1966). *Hiskey–Nebraska test of learning aptitude.* Lincoln, NE: Author.

Hoffmeister, R. (1978). *The development of demonstrative pronouns, locatives, and personal pronouns in the acquisition of American Sign Language in deaf children of deaf parents.* Unpublished doctoral dissertation, University of Minnesota, Minneapolis.

Hoffmeister, R. (1982). The acquisition of language by deaf children. In H. Hoeman and R. Wilbur, (Eds.), *Communication in two societies: Monographs in social aspects of deafness.* Washington, D C: Gallaudet University Press.

Hoffmeister, R. J. (1985). Families with deaf parents: A functional perspective. *Handicapped Families: Functional Perspectives.* New York: Academic Press.

Hoffmeister, R. (1987). The acquisition of pronominal anaphora in ASL by deaf children. In B. Lust (Ed.), *Studies in the acquisition of anaphora: Defining the constraints* (Vol. 2). Boston: Reidel Publishing.

Hoffmeister, R. & Shettle, (1980). The results of a family sign language program. In H. Kopp, & F. Solano, (Eds.), *Focus on infusion* (Vol. 2). Washington, D C: Convention of American Instructors of the Deaf.

Hurley, O., Kavale, K., Hirshosen, A., & Hunt, J. (1978). Intercorrellations among tests of general mental ability and achievement for black and white deaf children. *Perceptual and Motor Skills, 46,* 1107–1113.

Hurley, O., Hirshosen, A., Hunt, J., & Kavale, K. (1979). Predictive validity of two mental ability tests with black deaf children. *The Journal of Negro Education,* 14–19.

Jordan, I., Gustason, G., and Rosen, R. (1976). Current communication trends at programs for the deaf. *American Annals of the Deaf, 121*(5), 527–531.

Jordan, I., Gustason, G., & Rosen, R. (1979). An update on communication trends in programs for the deaf. *American Annals of the Deaf, 125*(3), 350–357.

Kluwin, T. (1984). Keeping secondary school hearing impaired students on task. *Journal of Educational Research, 78*(1), 45–50.

Kuhn, T. (1970). *The structure of scientific revolutions.* Chicago: University of Chicago Press.

Kushe, C., & Greenberg, M. (1983). Evaluative understanding and role taking ability: A comparison of deaf and hearing children. *Child Development, 54,* 141–147.

Labov, W. (1973). The logic of nonstandard English. *Language in the Inner City,* University of Pennsylvania Press, Philadelphia, PA.

Leiter, R. (1948). *Leiter international performance scale.* Chicago, Ill: C. H. Stoelting.

Luetke-Stahlman, B. (1982). A philosophy for assessing the language proficiency of hearing impaired students to promote English literacy skills. *American Annals of the Deaf, 127,* 844–851.

Luetke-Stahlman, B. (1984). Replicating single-subject assessment of language in deaf elementary-age children. *American Annals of the Deaf, 129*(1), 40–44.

Marmor, G., & Pettito, L. (1979). Simultaneous communication in the classroom: How well is English grammar represented? *Sign Language Studies, 23,* 99–130.

McCarthy, D. (1972). *McCarthy scales of children's abilities.* New York: Psychological Corporation.

Meadow, K. (1976). The development of deaf children. In E. Hetherington, J. Hagen, R. Kroon, & A. Stein (Eds.), *Review of Child Development Research* (Vol. 5) Chicago, Ill: University of Chicago Press, 429–506.

Meadow, K. (1967). *The effect of early manual communication and family climate in the deaf child's environment.* Unpublished doctoral dissertation, University of California, Berkeley.

Meadow, K. (1980). *Deafness and child development.* Berkeley: University of California Press.

Meadow, K. (1984). *Meadow–Kendall scales of social and emotional adjustment.* Washington, D C: Gallaudet University Press.

Menyuk, P. (1975). The language impaired child: Linguistic or cognitive impairment? *Annals of the New York Academy of Sciences, 263,* 59–69.

Moores, D. (1982). *Educating the deaf: Psychology, principles, and practice.* Boston: Houghton-Mifflin.

Musgrove, W., & Counts, L. (1975). Leiter and Ravens Performance and Teacher Ranking: A correlational study with deaf children. *American Annals of the Deaf, 8,* 19–23.

Myklebust, H. (1964). *The psychology of deafness.* New York: Grune & Stratton.

Neisser, A. (1983). *The other side of silence: Sign language and the deaf community in America.* New York: Grune & Stratton.

Newby, H. (1979). *Audiology.* New York: Appleton-Century.

Newport, E. (1982). Task specificity in language learning. In E. Wanner & L. Gleitman (Eds.), *Language acquisition: The state of the art.* Cambridge: Cambridge University Press.

Padden, C. (1980). The deaf community and the culture of deaf people. In C. Baker & R. Battison (Eds.), *Sign language and the deaf community.* Silver Spring, MD: National Association of the Deaf.

Rittenhouse, R., Morreau, L., & Iran-Nejad, A. (1981). Metaphor and conservation in deaf and hard-of-hearing children. *American Annals of the Deaf, 126,*450–453.

Rosenthal, R., & Jacobsen, L. (1968). *Pygmalion in the classroom.* New York: Holt, Rinehart, & Winston.

Sanford, A. 1974. *Learning Accomplishment Profile.* Winston-Salem, NC: Kaplan School Supply.

Schlesinger, H. (1984). *Outline for panel on "early deficits."* Paper presented at the Spring 1983 meeting of the American Psychoanalytical Association.

Schlesinger, H. & Meadow, K. *Sound and sign: Childhood deafness and mental health.* Berkeley, CA: University of California Press.

Sisco, F., & Anderson, R. (1980). Deaf children's performance on the WISC-R relative to hearing status of parents and childrearing experiences. *American Annals of the Deaf, 125,* 923–930.

Terman, L. & Merrill, M. (1973). *Stanford-Binet intelligence scale, 1972 norms edition.* Boston: Houghton-Mifflin.

Uzgiris, I. & Hunt, J. McV. (1975). *Assessment in infancy.* Urbana, IL: University of Illinois Press.

Vandell, D., & George, L. (1981). Social interaction in hearing and deaf preschoolers; Successes and failures in initiation. *Child Development, 52,* 627–635.

Vernon, M. (1967a). Relationship of language to the thinking process. *Archives of Genetic Psychiatry, 16*(3), 325–333.

Vernon, M. (1967b). Rh factor and deafness: The problem, its psychological, physical, and educational manifestations. *Exceptional Children, 34,* 5–12.

Vernon, M. (1968). Fifty years of research on the intelligence of deaf and hard of hearing children: A review of literature and discussion of implications. *Journal of Rehabilitation of the Deaf, 1,* 1–12.

Wechsler, D. (1967). *Wechsler preschool and primary scale of intelligence (WPPSI).* New York: Psychological Corporation.

Wedell-Monig, S., & Lumbley, J. (1980). Child deafness and mother–child interaction. *Child Development, 55,* 766–774.

Wilbur, R. (1979a). *American Sign Language and sign systems.* Baltimore: University Park Press.

Woodward, J. (1982). *How you gonna get to heaven if you can't talk to Jesus: On depathologizing deafness.* Silver Spring, MD: T. J. Publishers.

Zwibel, A., & Merthens, D. (1985). A comparison of intellectual structure in deaf and hearing children. *American Annals of Deaf, 130*(1), 27–31.

8

Cognitive Assessment of Motorically Impaired Infants and Preschoolers

Cordelia Robinson and Nancy Fieber

INTRODUCTION

This chapter considers issues involved in and procedures available for the assessment of infants and preschoolers who have impairments in motor ability, within the context of the framework for assessment offered earlier in this book (see Chapters 1–5). Within this framework, the specific issues that will be examined include the implications of the assumptions underlying the use of assessment procedures and the purposes for which assessments are done on this population. Alternative strategies that have been used with motorically impaired young children are considered within the context of the application of the decision-making framework proposed by Hubert and Wallander (Chapter 3).

GOALS

A recurrent theme in the first several chapters of this book is the necessity for clarification of the purpose (questions to be answered) for which any assessment of a child is done. This theme is particularly relevant to several topics: the relationships among assumptions underlying an assessment process, the development of an assessment tool, and the use to which a given instance of assessment is put. In our discussion of the assessment of infants and preschoolers with significant motor disabilities involving their use of their upper extremities, we will argue that the current knowledge about assessment instruments and developmental patterns and pathways restricts us primarily to the use of an individual-case-descriptive approach (see Vaughan Stagg, Chapter 4), and that such a strategy is best used in the context of a process approach to assessment (Brinker & Lewis, 1982; Dubose, Langley, & Stagg, 1988; Hauessermann, 1958; Robinson, 1987; Simeonsson, 1977). We will first examine our rationale for insisting that the state of our knowledge is so restricted for motorically impaired children. Next we will describe the rationale for the design of a hypothesis-testing-process approach to the assessment of cognitive development in such children. The viewpoint central to the organization of this approach is a

CORDELIA ROBINSON and NANCY FIEBER ● Meyer Children's Rehabilitation Institute, University of Nebraska Medical Center, Omaha, Nebraska 68105.

stage theory of development, in which the emphasis is on the nature and the organization of the processes central to each stage (Piaget, 1952) or the organizational level of development (Uzgiris, 1976). An assumption being made, which is central to this viewpoint, is that development is integrated and organized across developmental domains (Sroufe, 1979).

APPROACHES TO ASSESSMENT

Traditional Approaches to Assessment

The traditional approach to the assessment of a population with a specific disability is basically comparable to the approach taken in the development of any assessment instrument. The purposes of the assessment instrument need to be defined, and these purposes, in turn, guide the development of the instrument. Attempts to develop appropriate instruments for persons with specific disabilities have involved several strategies. One strategy would be the administration of the standard instrument to a population of persons with the specific disability. Comparisons to the normative population are then made and interpreted accordingly. The implicit assumption made in this strategy is that a disability may result in delays in the acquisition of specific behaviors, but that the disability does not result in any substantive alteration in the eventual form of a behavior. A second strategy would be to administer only those test items that are deemed appropriate to administer to the disabled person. An example of the strategy would be the administration of the performance portion but not the verbal portion of the Wechsler Intelligence Scale for Children (WISC) to a deaf child. The use of such a strategy implies the reasoning that a valid assessment may be obtained by assessing only a portion of the total domain under consideration. The third strategy involves the development of an instrument designed and evaluated for reliability and validity on a specific disabled population. Generally, instruments representing each of these strategies have been used clinically for years, singly and in combination. Singly or in combination, they are not fully satisfactory. The validity of specific illustrations of such uses must be considered in the context and the purposes for which they were used. Limitations in the utility of these approaches—especially for the motorically disabled child who also has sensory disabilities, generally of a central nervous system (CNS) disorder in origin—form part of the basis of our assertion that we are not ready for instrument construction for this population of children.

Problems with Traditional Approaches

Lack of Background on Developmental Pathways

An examination of the developmental literature on infants reveals our dependency on motoric responses, as opposed to verbal responses on the part of an infant, to infer a specific level of cognitive development (Jens & Johnson, 1982; Kopp, 1974; Zelazo, 1979). We have pointed out elsewhere (Robinson, Fieber, & Rose, 1983) that the experience of the actual manipulation of objects and the experience of voluntary movement and exploration of the environment are apparently not necessary experiences for some children to accomplish the developmental tasks of the sensorimotor period. This issue has been addressed by Decarie (1969) in her studies of thalidomide children and by Kopp and Shapermann (1973) in a clinical study of a child with congenital amputation of both upper extremities. In both studies, children with impaired means for manipulating the objects or for self-determined exploration of their environments demonstrated the development of object permanence.

At least two qualifications of the interpretation of the above results should be considered. In a Piagetian framework, the observation of events and the mental consideration of alternative responses to these events can constitute action and are a legitimate domain of inquiry. Further, the children in these examples had disabilities that were not of a CNS disorder in origin. Therefore, there are two points to consider in regard to the impact of motor development on children's learning. The first point is that it is a potential error to assume incompetence when we limit our view of an infant's abilities by looking at performance only on cognitive tasks that require age-appropriate, fine motor skills for responding. Second, it is also a problem to assume that all motorically impaired children will be able to compensate for their lack of motor skills in the manner in which the children in Decarie's and in Kopp and Shaperman's descriptions were able to compensate.

Kagan (1970) offered a view of infant cognitive development that aids in interpreting the findings of Decarie (1969) and of Kopp and Shapermann (1973). Kagan suggested that children can develop perceptual and conceptual structures through observation, in the absence of the actual manipulation of material. Although Kagan agreed that motor actions are important aids in certain kinds of learning, they are not essential, *at least for some children*, for the development of sensorimotor accomplishments such as object concept and causality. Kopp (1974) argued that Kagan's data (1970) as well as other data on learning abilities of the infant during the first several months have implications for techniques of appraisal and the treatment of atypical children. In her paper, Kopp (1974) pointed out that "too many professionals, for too long a period, have conceptualized intelligence, particularly for the young, mainly in terms of voluntary controlled motor movements" (p. 7.). In discussing the issue of motor performance Zelazo (1979) proposed that infants are capable of receiving sensory information, and of storing and integrating this information at a central level without the necessity of physical participation in the event or overt motoric manipulation. The application of the expectancy or familiarization–novelty models to the assessment of cognitive processes in handicapped children, as described by Zelazo (1979), McDonough (1984), and Brooks-Gunn (1984), offers promise of new approaches to the problem of less biased assessment of such children.

In a discussion of the role that action (self-initiated active manipulation and exploration) plays in the pathways of development, Campos, Svejda, Campos, and Bertenthal (1982) asserted, "For both theoretical and empirical reasons, then, recent psychology has discarded serious consideration of motoric development as a significant factor in psychological growth" (p. 210). Campos *et al.* then went on to develop an argument, with which we concur, that such a dismissal of the impact of motoric development is inappropriate and will, in fact, limit our understanding of the development of children with significant motor handicaps. Their case is built on relating "specific motor skills" to "discrete psychological processes," and they cited relationships noted between the onset of self-produced locomotion and spatial, perceptual, and cognitive abilities. In their review regarding the emergence of self-produced locomotion, Campos, *et al.* (1982) pointed out that they had limited their consideration to the "role of self-produced loco-motion for the induction of new psychological skills" (p. 210). Several other questions should be considered as we concern ourselves with the implications of developmental pathways in development, and thus with looking at process and not simply product. What is the role of the acquisition of a specific milestone (in any domain of development) in maintaining skills, and as a facility influence? What are the influences of varying de-grees of ease of performance when one skill serves as a building block for the develop-ment of another skill? Within the developmental literature, there are ever-increasing illustrations of the integrated nature of development and the interactions among the do-mains and pathways of development.

The implications of this literature for assessment and intervention with children with specific disabilities are many. We are emphasizing two points that may seem contradic-tory. The first point is that, with the prelinguistic child, we should not look strictly at motor responses as the indices of intelligence. The second issue, which was raised by Campos *et al.* is that we should not assume that motor development, as a domain, is any less an integrated component of the fabric of development than are other domains. The first implication of these issues in the assessment of physically disabled children is that we must look for procedures that do not require physically impossible responses. The second implication is that, concurrently, we must avoid the risk of missing the informa-tion that is contributed by physical manipulation of the environment and observation of the consequences of this physical manipulation. Thus, at least initially, we must consider the limitation that a missing pathway of information places on the interpretations that are possible about future expectations for a given child's level of development. This issue is considered in more detail in the discussion regarding violations of the assumptions in assessment.

Violation of Assumptions in Traditional Assessment

A primary limitation in the assessment of children with motor impairments involves the assumptions that underlie the use of an assessment tool. Specifically, the assumptions that are at issue are (a) the representation of persons similar to the person being assessed within the standardization sample, (b) comparable opportunities for acculturation with persons on whom the instrument was standardized, and (c) the validity of the use of the instrument for predictive purposes. The extent to which the first two assumptions are met will affect the validity of the interpretation of assessment results for predictive purposes.

Representation within the Norm Population

The first assumption that must be met in order for assessment results to be valid for purposes of comparison or prediction is that persons who are comparable to the person being assessed were included in the standardization sample. The use of any standardized instrument with a significantly motorically disabled child, whose use of his or her hands and arms is limited, is going to be in violation of the first assumption, as children with significant motor and sensory impairments are typically excluded when populations are recruited for the standardization of instruments. A consideration of the population of children for whom a process approach to assessment is necessary is pertinent here.

The infants and preschoolers under consideration in this chapter have significant impairments in motor ability, often, but not always, due to a CNS deficit. As Wachs and Sheehan point out in Chapter 1 of this book, much of what is known regarding the development of young motorically handicapped children is based on reports of samples that are heterogeneous with respect to the etiology of the motor impairment. For example, some reports contrast children who have cerebral palsy with children whose etiologies include dystrophies, spina bifida, and congenital amputations of limbs. There can be vast differences among persons whose motor impairments have different etiologies. These differences make a meaningful comparison of the groupings (cerebral palsy versus mixed etiology) very difficult. Moreover, the extreme heterogeneity within individual diagnostic groups makes these comparisons still less trustworthy. For cerebral palsy, for example, there is not a universally acceptable classification system. When one can find some agreement across studies about the classification system used, there are still likely to be a high percentage of cases that cannot be classified by the system (O'Reiley & Walentynowicz, 1981).

Another dimension on which there is considerable variability within the population of individuals who carry the diagnosis of cerebral palsy is the severity of the degree of impairment in function. Again, reliable guidelines for describing the degree of severity of impairments are not universally accepted. The children selected to illustrate the assessment strategy that we are advocating also illustrates this diversity in etiology. A common feature of these children, despite the different etiologies of their motor disabilities (i.e., cerebral palsy, Guillain-Barré syndrome, and spina bifida), is the fact that their motor impairments were of such a degree that there was significant impairment in both the motor systems and the coordination of the motor systems, especially the coordination of the visual and upper-extremity systems. However, the degree of motor impairment clearly has implications for the selection of assessment strategies. In addition, the impact of the severely restricted and different learning histories of these children, based upon their motor impairments as well as on other associated impairments (e.g., impaired vision), must also be taken into consideration in assessing their performance and interpreting the meaning of that performance (Fishman & Palkes, 1974; Illingworth, 1971; Nielson, 1971; Tew, Lawrence, & Samuel, 1974).

Comparable Opportunities for Acculturation

A second assumption that is typically made in the interpretation of assessment results, and that is probably violated with every administration of a standardized assessment to a significantly physically handicapped infant or preschooler, is the comparability of opportunities for acculteration. This assumption means that a person's opportunities for experience with the content and tasks of an assessment instrument should be comparable to that of the persons who comprised the standardization sample. Examples of violations of this assumption of comparability of acculturation are typically thought of with respect to minority groups. Typically, the content of assessments represents the experience and mores of the majority culture and thus presents a bias when administered to persons whose experience is not that of the majority culture. Lack of equal opportunities for acculturation may be a consequence of sensory or motor impairment as well as consequence of cultural differences. This issue, which is not as frequently cited as a problem in the assessment of physically impaired children, is one with profound implications for interpreting an individual's behavior. Drawing on the discussion of the impact of developmental pathways and the integration of development across domains, we are emphasizing the point here that experiential deficits of the motorically impaired child can be pervasive, cumulative, and synergistic.

In making the case that the motorically impaired child may have experiential deficits, we are taking the perspective that development is integrated across developmental domains (Sroufe, 1979). Thus, limitations on development in one area not only affect potential and progress in the domain of the specific disability but may also influence opportunities for learning in other areas as well. For example, limited opportunities for movement can be expected to affect the understanding of spatial relationships (Campos *et al.*, 1982). To the extent that semantic development is enhanced by direct experience of meaning, especially of verb forms, limited range of movement may affect language acquisition. Thus, the ways in which motor disabilities affect opportunities for acculturation can be extensive and complex. In addition, these effects are not predictable, in that there may be children with extensive motor disabilities who show development consistent with normally developing chronological-age peers.

Validity for Predictive Purposes

Studies of the predictive validity of early assessments (up to 2 years of age) of children with developmental disabilities (VanderVeer & Schweid, 1974), and specifically with motor impairments (Fishman & Palkes, 1974; Illingworth, 1971; Nielson, 1971; Tew, Lawrence, & Samuel, 1974), tend to cite the relatively good predictive validity of infant assessments for children with significant IQ deficits, as compared to similar studies of children whose developmental quotients as infants were in the average range. What is generally not discussed in these reports of the predictive validity of early assessments of handicapped infants is the possibility that the use of standardized assessments may have been inappropriate, at least for children with significant motor impairments.

Assessments with standardized tools are frequently done with the justification that the assessment is being done in order to plan a program for the child and to have a standard for examining that child's progress over time. The experienced and conscientious clinician will counsel that the assessment results are not valid for predictive purposes. A risk in the use of standardized assessments on this population, even with strong caveats regarding the interpretations that are possible, is the fact that, in many educational systems, placement decisions for special-education services are made on the basis of the psychological assessment. Frequently, implicit within a placement decision is a prediction regarding future status.

In summary, then, our concerns regarding the use of standardized assessments, when the purposes of assessments are either program planning and program evaluation or diagnosis or prognosis, rest on the violation of the underlying assumption that "acculturation is comparable." Violation of the standard of lack of representation within the standardization sample compromises the meaning of assessment results, primarily in relation to questions regarding an individual's standing with respect to the norm. Violation of the standard of comparability of opportunity for acculturation is a standard that has significant implications regarding the interpretation that is possible of any traditional assessment approach with this population of children.

AN ALTERNATIVE APPROACH TO ASSESSMENT

Rationale for the Process Approach

One of the most obvious strategies available to us for the evaluation of a handicapped child is to select specially normed testing procedures so as to try to minimize the effect that the specific handicap(s) will have on a child's performance. Stagg (Chapter 4) cites instruments such as the Hiskey Assessment for deaf persons, the Maxfield-Buchholz adaptation and standardization of the Vineland, and the Perkins-Binet for blind persons as examples of such an assessment approach. Adding to the utility of such instruments for blind or deaf persons is a fairly rich and growing body of literature on the development of deaf and blind children. This is literature that has gone beyond the "They-can-do-this-but-they-can't-do-that" stage. Rather, the emphasis is on possible alternative developmental pathways and processes to end states that are potentially equivalent in function, if not in form, to the performance of the person who does not have the specific impairment (see Chapter 11 by Dunst & McWilliam and Chapters 1 and 19 by Wachs & Sheehan for a review of these literatures).

When we look for normed instruments and developmental literature to use as guidelines in the assessment of the infant or preschooler who is motorically impaired, we find much less guidance. When we looked for instruments for this population, what we found were advocates of strategies (Dubose et al., 1977; Haeussermann, 1958; Jens & Johnson, 1982; Robinson, 1987; Robinson & Fieber, 1974; Robinson et al., 1983). These "strategy" approaches involve a number of different techniques, generally relying on the assumption that underlying cognitive processes are tapped in the performance of the tasks (Haeussermann, 1958; Robinson & Fieber, 1974; Robinson & Robinson, 1978, 1983). Thus, rather than developing test, "strategy" approaches involve efforts to modify tasks, materials, or responses in order to allow for responses that are logically feasible for the individual and that appear to validly reveal basic cognitive processes.

The objection that is raised by many psychologists to the use of such strategies in the assessment of the motorically impaired child is that adaptation of procedures violates the test standardization. This objection may be legitimate if the purpose of the assessment is a comparison of the individual to the standardized norm for predictive purposes. However, such a purpose has already been noted as being of questionable value for infants, toddlers, and preschoolers whose handicaps are moderate to severe in degree. Adaptation is legitimate when one is exploring, for example, the circumstances under which a given person can do specific tasks. Such information can be invaluable to program planning for and documentation of the progress of individual children.

The dependency on motoric responses and the concomitant limitations on assessment approaches, especially with the preverbal child, have been cited earlier in this chapter. Indeed, it is this recognition that has resulted in the proposal that assessment procedures be adapted. A point less often cited, but one that is receiving an increased amount of attention from the growing number of developmentalists who argue that development cannot be separated neatly into independent domains (Brinker & Lewis, 1982; Chess, 1983; Fisher, 1980; Robinson, 1982; Sroufe, 1979), is the limitation that lack of motoric input and output may have on typical developmental pathways. What this means in practice is that our task in assessment and intervention with infants and toddlers with significant motoric impairment is to identify situations or tasks that permit adequate insight into such children's underlying competence, and also to appreciate more fully the limitations that significant motoric impairments place on the acquisition of the information and schemes that underlie the successful performance of cognitive tasks. Robinson (1982) summarized her position regarding the impact that a specific disability may have on development in this way:

> It may not be simply limited data which affects [sic] the handicapped child's performance. Limited opportunities to integrate information from various sources is [sic] also a likely consequence of a specific disability. We must consider that not only will the child's information base differ, his experience with processing information will also differ in form from the nonhandicapped child's experience. (p. 244)

The effects of variations of visual and manipulative experiences and response strategies in cognitive tasks have been demonstrated in studies on normal infants and preschool children. In studying error responses on an object permanence task in which the infant searches for an object hidden under one or two screens, Landers (1971), compared manual-search and direction-of-gaze responses. More error perseveration was found among those children who used manual search, a finding suggesting that different cognitive strategies may be involved in the two tasks. Ruff (1982) found that haptic manipulation enhanced attention to different invariants (form vs. texture or pattern) from visual familiarization alone, in a concept task using a familiarization–novelty paradigm. Consistency of mode in familiarization and response phases was found to affect performance in a study by McKay-Soroka, Trehub, Bull, and Corter, (1982). In a study with preschool-aged children, Gelman (1980) found that the opportunity to touch materials seemed to facilitate counting performance, as compared with a condition in which the children could see, but not touch. The fact that such performance differences can be found under different conditions of motor experience not only calls assessment tools into question but also suggests that the paths to concept formation may be different for a child who cannot manipulate and who thus relies on other sources of information.

Brinker and Lewis (1982) noted a number of mechanisms by which the infant with motor impairment is likely to be limited in his or her experience:

1. Medical involvement decreases the opportunity for social interaction (Klaus & Kennel, 1976; Vietze, Falsey, O'Connor, Sandler, Sherrod, & Altemeier, 1980).
2. Parental attitudes and feelings may reduce the number of co-occurrences that the parents provide (Bell, 1980; Broussard & Hartner, 1970).
3. The limited response repertoire of some handicapped infants makes both social and object co-occurrences less likely (Brooks-Gunn & Lewis, 1979).
4. The ability to detect and remember co-occurrences may be limited for some handicapped children (Detterman, 1979).
5. A complex process of infant–environment transactions progressively reduces the frequency of social co-occurrences (Brinker & Lewis, 1982, p. 7).

The Process Approach

Consistent with the assessment framework offered earlier in this book, and in concurrence with those who have argued for and defined process-oriented approaches to assessment, we are proposing the following guidelines for a process approach to the assessment of cognitive development in children with significant motor impairment(s).

Simeonsson (1977) discussed assessment as a process distinct from testing, a process that can be used to evaluate strengths and deficits in order to provide a basis for intervention. Whether normed or criterion-referenced tools are used, additional products of this assessment process include (a) evaluation of the skills already mastered by the individual; (b) response to interventions designed to teach specific skills or tasks; and (c) the child's ability to perform given tasks in different settings and with different persons (Bourgeault, Harley, DuBose, & Langley, 1977; Dubose *et al.*, 1977; Langley, 1978; Simeonsson, Huntington, & Parse, 1980).

Dubose *et al.* (1977) identified the assumptions made in a process-oriented approach to assessment. Those assumptions include:

1. A view of the child as an "active agent" who operates on his or her own development;
2. that the learning processes used by the individual child can be measured and modified within the context of a process oriented assessment;
3. that the child's learning potential is best assessed by observing performance in a task where corrective feedback is provided, i.e., a learning task. (p. 3)

Developmental Framework for the Process Assessment

Based on our work with children with significant motor handicaps, we feel that this process-oriented approach is the only meaningful approach to the assessment of such individuals. In addition, we feel that a developmental, conceptual framework is certainly helpful and, to our mind, essential in approaching this task.

For the infant and preschool-aged child, for our conceptual framework, we draw on the writings of those who have interpreted Piaget (Hunt, 1961; Uzgiris, 1976; Uzgiris & Hunt, 1975). Adding to those basic interpretations, we also draw guidance from the developmental literature for information regarding relationships among sensorimotor, communication, and social development (Fisher, 1980; Golinkoff, 1981; Sroufe, 1979; Zelazo, 1979). In our opinion, information about normal developmental pathways contributes to interpretations of performance by children with significant motoric disabilities. In addition, this literature also offers guidance regarding the impact that task modifications may have on expected performance and, therefore, again facilitates the interpretability of that performance. Specifics of how we use the conceptual framework offered by the Uzgiris-Hunt Ordinal Scales (1975) are described elsewhere (Fieber, 1977a, 1978; Robinson, 1982, 1987; Robinson & Robinson, 1978, 1983) and will not be detailed here. However, our use of the scales over the past 10 years with motorically disabled children, as well as with other developmentally disabled children, has resulted in our strong belief that a great deal of the utility of the scales does not necessarily derive from the specific landmarks or eliciting situations or even the schematic themes (object permanence, means ends, casuality etc.). Rather, utility is found within the overall stage organization, as a framework for interpreting child behavior. In this regard, we have found the organizational levels described by Uzgiris (1976) especially helpful. Wachs and Sheehan (Chapter 1) point out that one of the potential dangers in accepting scale items at face value is that many items "may be highly teachable but irrelevant... and may be neither the precursors nor critical mediators of important developmental processes." By placing our emphasis in this process-oriented assessment approach on the *underlying organization* of the sensorimotor or preoperational stages, we feel that we receive guidance in both our assessment strategies and our interpretation of assessment results for the design of intervention strategies. These advantages of a process-oriented approach are illustrated in the case reports presented in a following section of this chapter.

When assessing children who are functioning at the early sensorimotor levels, an overriding concern is how they respond to the *means–end* and *causality* landmarks, as we feel that these areas are the basis for designing intervention strategies for the child's use of alternative communication strategies and forms (Carlson, 1981; Chapman & Miller, 1980; Musselwhite & St. Louis, 1982; Robinson, 1976, 1982, 1987; Snyder, 1978). Without minimizing the content deprivations and deficits that are reality for most severely physically handicapped children, once an alternative form of communication is established the tasks of assessing competencies and designing intervention strategies becomes relatively easier for professionals to conceptualize.

Strategies for Adaptation of Tasks

Although the guidance for the content of our assessment is conceptual, the actual strategies used reflect an empirical approach. One tries a strategy and notes performance, tries another strategy and notes performance, and this cycle continues until the examiner is satisfied that the best possible performance has been obtained. This process typically takes repeated sessions of trying a strategy, observing, modifying, and trying again.

Implicit within any presentation of a task or eliciting situation, as well as subsequent modifications of such presentations, are hypotheses. The entire process approach can be characterized within a hypothesis-testing framework, drawing on a number of sources of information. These sources of information include:

1. The documented organization and content of cognitive development and concomitant typical responses for the hypothesized developmental level.
2. The patterns of responses, especially across cognitive, communication, and affective domains, from which is derived the assumption that development is integrated and organized.
3. The predictable motor patterns evidenced by children whose motor development is atypical but consistent within type for some diagnostic categories.
4. The effects of modifications in task presentations (modifying or substituting material, greater time delays) on performance among nonhandicapped children.
5. The behavioral manifestations of the impact of multiple physical and sensory impairments, especially visual impairments in both acuity and eye–head coordination.
6. Parents' reports of the meaning of the child's facial expressions and movements and their descriptions of how they have responded to those behaviors.

In Table 1 (p. 138), strategies for adapting assessment tasks are presented. Understanding the relations between cognitive stage, prelinguistic communication, and affective development is essential in modifying tasks, in eliciting situations, and in intepreting responses (see the tables presented with child examples). Interpretation requires reliability checks. These may include interrrater observations within a session or observations across assessments by different disciplines, multiple examples of a behavior with different materials, and congruence between several items reflecting the same stage of development. Although some scatter is expected, wide differences in subscales of the Uzgiris-Hunt might suggest that one has underestimated or overinterpreted abilities because of the difficulties of assessment.

In Robinson (1987) and Robinson *et al.* (1983), the interrractions between appropriate assessment strategies and a child's cognitive level are discussed and presented. Tables 2 and 3 (pp. 140 and 141), modified slightly from the original presentation in Robinson (1987), are reproduced here to illustrate the interaction between organizational or sensorimotor level and the relative appropriateness of various strategies. In Robinson (1987), each of Uzgiris's proposed organizational levels (1976) is discussed, as are examples of the performance of motorically impaired children. For example, for sensorimotor Stage 4 (organizational Level 2), the child's insistence on trying to do things himself or herself is noted; consequently, the strategy of modifying task requirements to facilitate active responding is emphasized.

Appropriate strategies for the Stage 4 child are provided in Table 2. At sensorimotor Stage 5 (or organizational Level 3), we find that, with greater receptive language and intentional communication, although it may be gestural in form, the child now understands assisted movement strategies and the cause-and-effect concept involved. Strategies appropriate for a Stage 5 child are presented in Table 3. It should be noted that, with respect to the strategies outlined in Table 1, the least intrusive strategy should always be tested, for two reasons. The first is consistent with the rehabilitation dictum never to do for people what they can do for themselves. The second reason is so as to not set an artificial ceiling on the individual performance level by providing more assistance than the person needs.

CLINICAL EXAMPLES OF THE PROCESS APPROACH

In the following pages, we present vignettes of several significantly motorically disabled children. These vignettes illustrate the proposed strategy of process-oriented assessment, using Piagetian sensorimotor and preoperational tasks.

Sensorimotor-Stage Examples

The first two children, Roger and Amy, both appeared to be developing cognitive abilities characteristic of sensorimotor Stage 4. The issues involved in whether the child has motor disability due to CNS involvement or motor disability due to other causes are illustrated, both in the nature of their handicaps and in the assumptions about risks for mental retardation. Both children showed such severe motor impairment that alternative strategies of task presentation and response forms were indicated. In Table 4, communi-

Table 1. Adapted Assessment Strategies

Adapted task presentations

Positioning of the child. The child with inadequate head control or sitting balance requires support and stability for optimal visual control, hand use, and attention. Positioning and seating equipment needs will vary with the child's individual motor patterns and oculomotor problems. Consult a pediatric physical or occupational therapist.

Positioning of the material. Materials should be placed where the child can move his or her hand(s). For example, a child with a stiffly extended arm that he or she can move only in a horizontal arc to one side needs materials placed within the intersection of that arc, and a switch may need to be responsive to the horizontal movement, not to downward pressure. If a child has a significant asymmetric tonic neck reflex (ATNR), effort to bring the flexed arm and hand to an object at the midline may require the child to turn his or her head away, thus losing visual contact and also contributing to trunk asymmetry. Such a child will be better able to monitor his or her hand movement with the object placed to one side. If head or eye control is lost with downward gaze, objects or pictures presented as choices might be placed on a tipped-up rack at a comfortable focal distance. Whether the rack is centered or to one side will depend on the child's oculomotor status and the movement response requested.

Modification or substitution of the material. Materials may be modified to facilitate responding. Examples include a bead on the end of the string to be pulled or cutting up an array of pictures and placing them on a special display rack. Materials may be substituted: a larger stimulus may make uncoordinated hand-pointing or eye-pointing responses clearer, or a larger toy may be used in functional use or representational play.

It should not be assumed that modifications necessarily change the conceptual level of difficulty of a response. The task may be equivalent, may actually be more difficult because of the greater motor effort and reaction time involved, or may reflect a less mature level. For example, Largo and Howard (1979), in studying representational play, found that miniature toys become meaningful at about 18 months. Does the bigger cup change the level of difficulty, or are the structure of the play and language demands equivalent?

Adapted response forms and stage-equivalent structures

Eye-pointing. The best known alternative response is eye pointing or looking at earlier levels of communicative intent. Unfortunately, many children with severe cerebral palsy also have oculomotor problems limiting the usefulness of this strategy.

Movement approximations. Movement responses that are approximations of the standard response and appear to demonstrate intent, though unsuccessful in completion of the intent, should be acknowledged and verified. These approximations may take an atypical form because of the child's abnormal tone and movements and may be difficult to read by someone unfamiliar with the movement configurations of cerebral palsy.

Assisted movements. In assisted movements, the adult follows the child's movement attempts, assisting only as necessary. Assistance may vary in degree. The child may require assistance only in the completion of an obvious intent, such as in a task requiring a precise placement of an object. Other children with cerebral palsy may need only partial assistance at the shoulder or cradling the elbow to prevent extraneous movement or abnormal tone to facilitate a movement response. If the child has difficulty maintaining grasp during a movement, a light hand-over-hand assistance will enable the child to respond. The adult reads the feeling of the movement direction, the direction of gaze, and pauses at each phase of the movement sequence. Sometimes, a response can be checked by deliberately diverting the child's movement or placement and observing affective responses. For children with essentially no voluntary movement, guided movements can be used with rhythmic on-off cycles, giving the child the opportunity on the pauses to control the activity through some level of signaling, such as eye contacts, smiles, vocalizations, very slight movements, or tension that can be felt. These responses may vary from the "procedure" level at earlier stages to more aware communicative intent and cooperative effort at the Stage 5 level. When a child insists on doing the task herself or himself, "bargain" for an eye-point first (a clear response), then assist the child in the manipulation, which serves as a positive reinforcement. This strategy allows the child to evaluate how her or his messages are being received and to adjust her or his strategies accordingly, an important step for a child with some speech approximations and a supplementary augmentative communication system.

Affective responses. Affective responses have been useful as indicators of cognitive processes and are associated with cognitive stage (Sroufe, 1979). Surprise at violation of expectancy, a "yes" smile to confirm the examiner's interpretation of a response, and humor may provide supportive information. In use of affect in assessment, consideration of this population's varied experiences and atypical facial expression configurations is important. For example, a child who has been fed by nasogastric tube may not find mommy drinking from a bottle funny. A child with cerebral palsy may begin to smile, and the smile may overflow into marked jaw thrust.

Stage equivalent behaviors. Performance on a task may not be possible in standard or adapted form. The underlying process in the task should be considered and other behaviors noted that may reflect similar structures. For example, if the child is not able to uncover objects and eye pointing is not clear, the separation protest when the child's mother is out of contact should be noted as also related to emerging representation (Fisher, 1980; Sroufe, 1979; Uzgiris-Hunt, 1975).

Learning as an assessment strategy. If the child's disabilities have severely limited experience, rapid learning through an adapted strategy within the assessment session may be an indication of the child's level of cognitive structures. For example, a child with severely involved hands may never have played with string, nor pulled it and incidentally obtained the attached object. If the child quickly learns with the string looped around the wrist and the object placed for the movement available, one might infer Stage 4 capacities. Zelazo (1979) described studies demonstrating the acquisition of functional use play and other tasks after brief training and viewed this rapid assimilation as implying capacity for generating specific associations or structures at that level. Rosenberg and Robinson (1984) found significant relationship between rate and pattern of performance on a "switch task" and sensorimotor stage.

Familiarization and novelty or violation-of-expectancy paradigms

Habituation–dishabituation paradigms and familiarization–paired-choice paradigms have been recently applied to the assessment of handicapped children for prediction (Fagan, 1984), for assessment of processing capacities (Zelazo, 1979), and for understanding concept acquisition (Brooks-Gunn, 1984; McDonough, 1984). In the habituation–dishabituation paradigms, a stimulus is presented to the child for repeated trials until a response decrement (i.e., decreased duration of fixation) is noted. A novel stimulus is then introduced, and renewed interest (increased duration of fixation) is noted. This paradigm has been useful with children functioning at an early sensorimotor stage, both in informally exploring visual differentiation and in the inferences that can be made about recognition memory. The familiarization–paired-comparison paradigm involves a familiarization phase in which visual stimuli are presented for repeated trials or the child is able to manipulate or touch the materials. This phase may be carried to habituation or an arbitrarily defined duration. During the paired-comparison phase, the familiar varies with cognitive level and situational variables such as consistency of mode across phases, interruption of the flow of a child's play, and change of spatial location (Hunter, Ross, & Ames, 1982; MacKay-Soroka, Trehub, Bull, & Corter, 1982; Ross, 1980; Ruff, 1982). We have used this paradigm to explore visual differentiation and recognition, and as a basis for intervention strategies in which the child is given opportunities to compare and to communicate wants through preferential looking, intentional eye-pointing, or attempted reaching. These strategies are important in preparation for alternative communication systems.

cation and affective responses typical of Stage 4 children, which may assist in designing task presentations and interpreting responses, are identified. The information about typical responses for the Stage 4 child and the relationships between cognitive communicative and affective response were used in the design of the assessment process for these two children.

Case Example 1: Roger

History and Referral

Roger, chronological age 14 months, 28 days, was referred by his public school program for standardized psychological assessment to satisfy state regulations and for

Table 2. Sensorimotor Stage 4

Concept	Sensorimotor accomplishments	Strategies with motorically impaired children
General	Uses schemes together intentionally, but their use depends on a familiar context.	Modify task requirements to facilitate active responding.
Object permanence	Searches for object hidden under one screen.	Place child in position that favors active responding. Use easily removed cover. Place cover over a well so object doesn't move if cover is pulled away quickly or with uneven motion. Begin to teach game by interpreting his or her looking at the location of the object or movement attempts as evidence child remembers location. Child is not yet aware that looking responses communicate intent.
	Searches for object hidden under one of two screens.	Same strategies as in previous example. The two screens may be placed to each side of center for clear looking, or movement attempts to either side are possible, or to one side if child uses only one hand.
Means ends	Uses tool, such as string or cloth, to obtain an object. Locomotes to obtain objects if able.	Facilitate responding by using something that will serve as a handle to end of string; or loop string around hand.
Causality	Indicates with object or person directed scheme that he wants something to happen again, or replicates action of toy directly	Accept child's schemes as communicating want. Child may show replication of action by turning ferris wheel, or arrow of See-'N'-Say.
Schemes	Brief recognition schemes that represent functional use.	Observe attempts at functional use schemes and assist to complete intents. For more severely involved child demonstrate through guided movement and note if child attempts to repeat with assistance.
	Combines familiar schemes and engages in dropping and throwing games.	Throwing games may be accomplished by swiping.
Gestural imitation	Begins to approximate or imitate novel visible movements	Guide to demonstrate and assist participation responses. Credit approximations.
Spatial relationships	Takes objects out of container; may put single object in.	Easier material and position important. Assist to complete any movement components to carry out intents.

Table 3. Sensorimotor Stage 5

Concept	Sensorimotor accomplishments	Strategies with motorically impaired children
General	Discovers new means to ends by new combination of familiar schemes and modification of schemes during the problem-solving process.	Position materials, use easier materials, or assist movements as necessary.
Object permanence	Searches for object when exact location is unknown (i.e., invisible displacements).	Point with hands or eyes as child is more aware of communication at this level. Respond to any movement attempt.
Means ends	Uses unattached tool to obtain object. Uses an attached tool to obtain object.	Stage situation in which tool is needed and demonstrate tool use. Use assisted movements to see if child attempts to use tool.
Causality	Gives or pushes to adult to activate or "fix" or guides adult's hand to toy. Attempts to activate mechanical toy after demonstration.	Demonstrate action of mechanical toy and observe attempts to push toy to adult or imitate use of winder, lever, and so on. For more involved child, have child hold your hand as you activate; child may try to bring your hand to toy to repeat.
Schemes	Shows aware pretense as represents functional use of objects first in self-directed schemes, then in play with another person.	Assist attempts at self-directed pretense with objects. For more involved child guide in demonstration and assist attempts to repeat action. Ask child to give you a taste with thought to position and feasible movements. Assist if necessary. Establish a ritualized "give-and-take game," tugging or holding object as child pulls off grasp or releases, observing attempts to imitate giving by dropping toward you. Child may substitute exchanged glances as a way of pointing or commenting.
Gestural imitation	Imitates novel visible object schemes and gestures and begins to imitate invisible facial movements.	Same as previously.
Spatial relationships	Sequences objects in and out of containers. Begins to stack and to experiment with gravity. Moves to get object that is behind barriers.	Assist components as necessary, pausing to let child show intents. Position materials carefully, and use materials that are easy to manipulate and place. May use "gimmee" reach or look/fuss toward wanted objects.

Table 4. Affective and Communication Responses Characteristic of Stage 4 Infants

Affective responses[a]	Communication abilities[b]
Makes meaning of event responsible for affect, and affect becomes determinant of behavior.	Shows emergence of the illocutionary-conventional.
Is aware of own emotions with capacity to evaluate an event.	Signifiers represent associated events (with adequate vision and hearing). Ex.: Mother putting coat on means bye-bye.
Shows joy in being an active agent, in recognition, and in mastery.	Recognizes intonations, names, game words and songs, and some requests with context cues that have been ritualized.
Laughs in anticipation of social games rather than in response to completed sequence.	Initiates social interactions and familiar games.
May cry in anticipation of event. Anger at interruption or blocking of intended act.	Begins to share pleasure in object or activity by exchanging glance with adult or holding object toward adult as if to show or share.
Is wary toward strangers or strange object events. May protest if stranger is too intrusive. May assimilate stranger or activity into existing negative scheme.	Signals for more of enjoyed events with complex schemes, either person-or object-directed, depending on context.
Protests on separation from mother.	Indicates "not wants" by protesting, turning the head, pushing away or clinging to toy.
Shows surprise reactions to violation of expectancy. May smile or laugh at moderate novelty, such as mother drinking from infant's bottle or funny sound. May show fear or anger at too much violation of expectancy or novelty—the same sound at another time.	Emergent "gimmee reach" or reach/fuss, not yet fully aware of communicative aspect and not planfully combined with getting adult attention. "Eye-points" are pre-intentional.
	Gives responsively to verbal-gestural request or tug cue.

[a]Sroufe (1979).
[b]Bates et al., (1975, 1977); Bayley (1969); Bruner (1975); Snyder (1978); Sugarman, Bell, (1978).

educational and communication assessment to assist in intervention planning. Requests at this time were to ascertain his cognitive level, to suggest ways to adapt his environment to facilitate active responding, and to address additional possibilities for communication techniques, given his cognitive level and his handicaps.

Roger had a history of being the firstborn of twins with a birth weight of 5 pounds, 2 ounces. He suffered perinatal asphyxia, a subarachnoid hermorrhage, and hypoglycemia. He had severe neuromotor sequelae with spastic quadriplegic cerebral palsy. He had a seizure disorder that had been fairly well controlled recently, with some small seizures occurring several times a day. Because of major oral motor problems and poor weight gain, a gastrostomy was being considered, but had thus far been deferred.

Roger also had visual and auditory system problems. Ophthalmological and neuro-ophthalmological evaluations suggested central visual system problems, manifested by an inability to fixate and follow in the first few months, and his ultimate potential vision was still unknown. Audiological testing at 4 months with brain-stem evoked-response audiometry suggested a hearing loss, in at least the higher frequencies, at a moderate level for the left ear and at a mild level for the right ear. Testing at 14 months had shown some improvement, with mild impairment on the left and borderline impairment on the right. The findings suggested a cochlear level loss and neuromaturational delays in the auditory brain-stem pathways. Middle-ear involvement had been ruled out.

Previous Educational Assessment

Roger had originally been seen at age 5 months, 9 days. His severe motor and visual difficulties had limited his response modes; however, he had tried to repeat movements producing a visual-auditory spectacle. Strong total extension and interfering conjugate eye movements had limited visual contact. When positioned in flexion in supine tilt with his head centered, he had briefly fixated and followed shiny or wiggly objects. He had inconsistently achieved eye-to-eye contact and had showed some preferential responses to two-dimensional patterned stimuli.

Current Assessment

Assessment with the Bayley Mental Scale was performed by a psychologist and was observed by the infant educator and the speech pathologist, who then worked together in a further assessment of Roger's cognition and communication. With standardized administration, Roger's performance on the Bayley ranged from first failures at 1 month to highest success at 4½ months, with an age equivalent of 2½ months. It was agreed that Roger appeared to show intents suggesting higher abilities, and that his motor and sensory deficits interfered with his reception of and his responses to stimuli.

Roger's parents and teacher accompanied him and participated in the administration and interpretation of the educational and communication assessments. Situations derived from the Uzgiris-Hunt Ordinal Scales were presented, and observations of functional vision, hearing, and some communicative behavior were noted.

Positioning

During the assessment, Roger's position was varied to permit observation both of how he organized information and of his response capabilities in several situations. When he was supine on the floor, his face was turned to the right, and he was unable to turn his head. A centering cushion facilitated midline posture and better looking responses. He was noticeably less extended than when seen previously; however, his hypertonus was strong, and his spontaneous limb movements were very limited in arc and frequency. Activities were also tried in a Tumble-form seat, which has an abductor post and can be adjusted for tilt, and in this position, he could center his head. In supported sitting on his mother's lap, he tended to drop his head forward unless he was tilted back.

Sensory Organization

Roger continued to have problems achieving visual contact, but in an optimal position, supine or tilted back, with his head centered, he was able to fixate, to follow a few degrees, and to shift his gaze between objects. He continued to have abnormal conjugate movements of his eyes associated with abnormal muscle tone or head movement, which interfered with his looking responses. Assessment demonstrated that he was differentiating people's faces, as well as familiar and novel objects and patterns, but his eye-to-eye contact was inconsistent in interactions. His visual localization of sound sources was inconsistent or delayed with objects or persons within his visual field. If the sound source was lateral and out of view, he might turn his head slowly but often did not achieve a visual fixation or identification of the source. He appeared to recognize family members' voices, and in the context of auditory-motor games, he appeared to be aware of marked changes in vocal pitch. He may have been responding to some elements of intonation messages, but he did not appear to recognize words. He showed awareness of on-off changes in musical toys and he showed surprise when one musical toy was substituted for another in an on-off expectancy-cycle context.

In Table 5, examples of Roger's sensorimotor cognitive assessment is described. Although Roger was unable to perform the motor responses typical of children of Substage 4, he appeared to demonstrate some cognitive characteristics of that level through the use of strategies such as assisted movements and the sensitive reading of his affective and movement cues. Roger's experiences continued to be limited by motor, visual, and auditory deficits, and he was dependent on contrived experiences for learning opportunities. Touch and handling cues were important as signifiers of familiar handling events and were assessed in detail, with recommendations for intervention. The possibility of aiding hearing was not yet resolved.

Case Example 2: Amy

History and Referral

Amy, chronological age 9 months, 24 days, was referred to the infant program by her physician after hospital discharge. At 6 months of age, she suffered a paralytic condition diagnosed as Guillain-Barré syndrome, which involved a progressive paralysis of extremities and trunk and severe respiratory paralysis. This syndrome, which affects the lower motor neurons, has not been associated with intellectual deficit. Recovery of muscle function occurs in many cases, but some patients are left with residual paralysis. Amy's potential for recovery was still unknown. In addition to physical therapy and occupational therapy needs, referral was made to assist her parents in providing a facilitating environment for cognitive and communication development in view of her paralysis.

Procedures Used

Amy was seen at home with her parents and her home teacher. Select items of the Bayley Mental Scale were scorable, and situations were also adapted from the Uzgiris-Hunt scales.

Motor Status and Responses

Side-lying was a better position for Amy than supine because of her secretions. She had been placed for short periods in an adapted car-seat at a 45-degree tilt but had shown respiratory and cardiovascular distress in this situation.

Table 5. Roger: 14-Month-Old Child with Severe Cerebral Palsy, Example of Stage 4

Standard tasks: Presentations and responses	Adapted strategies: Presentation and responses	Suggestions for intervention
Object permanence	**Object permanence**	**Object permanence**
Adult places object under single screen with placement visible to child. Child follows, reaches, removes cover, and picks up object. The two-screen problem is also presented at this level.	As Roger was unable to reach and grasp, directed gaze was explored but proved impractical because of his oculomotor difficulties. Separation protest is an alternative response indicative of representational abilities at the same level (Jackson et al., 1978; Fox et al., 1979). At the beginning of the session, Roger showed wariness of strangers. He fussed several times when he was out of eye, voice, and touch contact with his parents and tried to turn his head toward where he had previously contacted them.	Roger's responses to strangers and separation were explained, and suggestions were made for therapists to guide his parents in physical handling techinques until he was comfortable with them. Peek-a-boo games with different levels of complexity were described. Hiding of objects was demonstrated as probes interspersed with play, taking care that he saw the object's location. It was suggested that the adult remove the cover when he looked or made a slight movement, and that he would not yet understand looking as a "point" in this context. If he could not use looking responses, general expressions of expectancy or slight movements should be interpreted as memory of the object.
Means of obtaining desired environmental events	**Means of obtaining desired environmental events**	**Means of obtaining desired environmental events**
Visually directed reach and grasp would typically be achieved by 4–5 months. Anticipatory differentiation of means and ends and anticipatory adaptation of means are assessed by observing the following: whether child sets down one object in order to pick up another; pulls a support to obtain a toy out of reach; uses alternative strategy, such as reaching toward object held above a support; uses locomotion to obtain an object or goal. Anticipatory construction of alternate means to a given end is implied in tasks such as pulling a string to obtain an object.	Roger was unable to reach, grasp or locomote. His arms were stiffly held in front, and his hands were fisted. He could not open his hand to receive a contacted toy. Strategies were used to explore his cognitive intents, given his motor inabilities. He was assisted to open his hand and to play with a Slinky placed in his grasp. It was then offered again near his right hand, and he responded by moving his arm and hand up and backward, which opened his hand partially, and he then moved his hand forward again toward the toy. This is a strategy some children with cerebral palsy come to understand and to use	We encouraged further development of Roger's intent in his reach–grasp approximation in offering toys, giving him time to execute the sequence and responding even when he got stuck. Some physical-therapy strategies to reduce fisting before play were also demonstrated. Because of Roger's motor difficulties, communicative aspects of means–ends development were emphasized rather than tool use strategies. These included the "give-and-take" game, using a tug cue with the verbal request to give and watching for him to try to pull his hand off, and the adult's taking a turn and offering the toy

(continued)

Table 5. (Continued)

Standard tasks: Presentations and responses	Adapted strategies: Presentation and responses	Suggestions for intervention
		back to elicit his responsive "reach." Violation of expectancy by holding the toy or setting it down could be introduced to elicit generated "gimme's" which might take the form of arm movement, a look, or a look-fuss. Such behaviors should be treated as requests, "Oh, do you want it?" and Roger might begin to give confirmatory "yes" smiles. A paired-choice strategy was also demonstrated in which a toy just played with was offered with another and Roger was asked which he wanted. We wanted to see him practice shift of gaze and comparisons and come to understand that his look or arm movement was being interpreted as communication.
	deliberately to try to open their hands to grasp, and it involves extra steps in the plan. He sometimes got stuck in the backward movement and could not complete the forward component. This response occurred when he was supine or tilted back in the Tumbleform seat. In a more upright position with his shoulders forward, his arms were more stiffly extended, and he was unable to move. During the session, he used a similar strategy in other contexts, such as a ritualized "give and take" game, whenever the toy was offered back to him, and in anticipation of his turn when the examiner "forgot" to offer the toy back. This response was treated as an emerging "gimme" along with unreliable looks toward objects. We proposed that the level of intent and planning to carry out this maneuver might be higher than the easy reach of the Stage 4 child and thus might be consistent with anticipatory adaptations and constructions of means.	
	Operational causality	Operational causality
Operational causality	A musical toy was activated near Roger's hand, but not in contact. He showed expectancy in the pauses and moved his arm slightly but could not reach it. To test the hypothesis that his movement might have implied intent and understanding of causality outside himself, and not the earlier "procedures" when causality was understood as being within himself, the following strategies were used. The toy was placed in contact with his hand and was activated and	We encouraged provision of many opportunities for Roger to indicate that he wanted repetition of enjoyed events in several types of contexts, e.g., interpersonal movement games, adult activation of toys and feeding. As activities were repeated and paused, he should have the opportunity to *generate* signals or actions toward objects or persons, rather than always asking and eliciting responsive behaviors. The strategy of "distancing" one's attention by procrastina-
Appreciation of causality outside self: Adult creates object spectacle (winds music box, moves Slinky, etc.) and pauses with hand and object both *within reach*. Child touches object or hand. Adult activates mechanical toy, which performs an action, and child may try to move toy or activate part directly. In a familiar game situation, when the adult pauses a child may attempt a movement that is part of the activity to renew the game. At this stage,		

the child also often uses eye contact and smiles as a request. In familiar contexts, the child may initiate a familiar game.

Ability to activate switch-activated toys was also explored because of the belief that opportunities for independent play would be important for self-concept, and for preparing for a possible augmentative communication system in the future.

paused, and on the pauses, he moved his hand on the toy and vocalized softly. He smiled as if pleased with himself. The examiner then had Roger hold her finger as she activated several toys, for example, pulling the ring of a See 'N' Say. He signaled for more by trying to move the examiner's hand again in the motion. When the examiner violated expectancy, Roger looked surprised, then looked at her face, then repeated the movement.

Roger's father demonstrated a "song-and-dance" game, moving Roger's legs and holding them still on the pauses. Roger tried to repeat the leg movement, and his father could feel this and responded. Roger's attempt was also visible to observers. Roger showed surprise and smiled when his father added a new component to the game. Roger could not give eye contact, as the movement interfered with his oculomotor control, causing loss of eye contact.

During the session, Roger learned through successive approximations to use his backward arm—hand movements to activate a "leaf switch" connected to a cassette player for direct contingency activation. He appeared more interested in experimenting with turning the music on and off than in the music itself. With an adapter set for a specific duration, his dad sang when the music was on, and Roger laughed and repeated turning it on. When his dad "forgot" to sing, Roger tried to turn toward him. It was our impression that Roger understood causality outside himself and was beginning to understand agency and the communicative aspect of his behaviors.

tion, after several cycles in which one responded to his signals, was explained to see what he would do to solve the problem. It was suggested that adults should respond to whatever he used as control behaviors and that these would vary with the context, his tone, and his understanding. With mechanical toys, it was suggested that, after responding to his behavior, one might invite him to help and have him hold a finger, giving him a chance to learn more about how the toy was activated. He might begin to move one's hand toward the toy, combining person- and object-directed schemes. At the beginning of familiar activities, one might violate expectancy and watch for the first generated signals to initiate the event. This might take the form of a movement to initiate a game also.

We also suggested assisting Roger in object play, exploring action properties of objects, inspecting them from different perspectives, and engaging in early pretense with his feeding objects. By using the on-off cycles, Roger could control the activity by signals and could try participatory movements.

Use of switch-operated toys was discussed, and we stressed the need for him to feel and handle the object activated as well as the need to design communication games involving turn taking, commanding adults, and participatory movements in imitative action songs. The speech pathologist discussed risks for future speech in view of his oral-motor problems and demonstrated augmentative systems used by older children with similar problems.

She showed some spontaneous small movements of her right fingers and wrist and of her left foot. Trace contractions of larger muscle groups were evident in standard manual muscle testing (Worthingham & Daniels, 1972) by the physical therapist. With assisted movements in planes with gravity reduced, she was able to move through partial ranges. Suspended overhead slings were constructed to support her limbs for exercise and for play. Assisted movements, looking behaviors, and facial expressions were also clues to her intent or understanding, although her facial expressions were still affected by paresis. Her vocalization was infrequent and very soft because of respiratory muscle involvement.

Sensory Organization

Within the limits of her head position, Amy could fixate, follow, and shift gaze between objects. She appeared to recognize people and some objects, and she showed preferential interest when paired stimuli were presented. Amy's hearing appeared to be consistent with her chronological age and her cognitive responses. She showed selective attention and specific recognition of some familiar words. When asked, "Where's daddy?" she looked toward her dad. She appeared to recognize the intonation patterns of common communication functions, but she had not really experienced the "No-no!" intonation yet.

In Table 6 (p. 152) are described the way in which task presentations were modified, along with Amy's responses to these adapted tasks. Amy appeared to have some cognitive abilities characteristic of a sensorimotor Stage 4 infant. Typically, this substage occurs between 8 and 12 months in nonhandicapped infants. Bayley items that could have been credited included participation in games (7.6 months), listening selectively to familiar words (7.9 months), and looking for the contents of a box (9.5 months). Our assumption was that she was functioning at age level, although she might lack some experiences leading to specific knowledge or skills. Experiences needed to be designed to compensate for those she could not get into by herself, and to be geared to chronological age expectations. A facilitative language environment and feedback to her signals were stressed. At this point, the need of a future augmentative communication system was still unknown.

Preoperational-Stage Examples

The following two children, Robert and Terri, were developing cognitive abilities characteristic of the preoperational period. Robert represented a transitional or early preoperational level, and Terri, at 3½ years, was functioning close to her age level. Both had CNS involvement, and Robert also had flaccid paralysis. They both had demonstrated receptive language but were unable to speak because of severe oral-motor problems and were being assessed for augmentative communication systems. Their preschool programs were anxious for information about appropriate program content level and task presentations and response strategies. At the preoperational level, the ability of both children to understand the use of eye pointing and affective responses as communication was helpful; however, they both had their own ideas about how they wanted to communicate. Positioning was of major importance for both, and they had specially prescribed chairs with trays; however, adequate support for a functional head position remained a problem.

Case Example 3: Robert

History

Robert, chronological age 2 years, 11 months, had a meningomyelocele with lumbar-level defect and high-thoracic–low-cervical neurological level. He had hydrocephalus, which had been shunted. He had flaccid paralysis of the lower extemities, mixed paresis, and spasm of the upper extremities, and he had multiple orthopedic problems, including a dislocated right hip. He had a neurogenic bladder and a history of urinary tract infections.

Procedures Used

Robert was accompanied by his parents and was seen for joint problem-solving by physical and occupational therapists, a speech pathologist, and an educator before individual assessments and again following the assessments to determine program planning and equipment needs. The educational assessment included selected items from the Bayley Mental Scale, which were adapted; the Hauessermann psychoeducational evaluation; and a representational play scale derived from the work of Nicolich (1977) and Westby (1980).

Findings

The first thing noticed about Robert was how interested and socially responsive he was. He showed some initial wariness and turned to his mother to seek reassurance. He was able to work for 1½ hours with short breaks.

Positioning and Movement Repertoire

Initial activities were presented while he was seated in his travel chair with its attached tray. His head tended to be laterally tilted to the right, and it was difficult for him to turn his head and eyes to the left. Several head-support options were explored by the physical therapist, and a special scoop-out unit enabled him to center and turn his head and to scan and eye-point effectively. Robert had some functional shoulder muscles and raised his arm from the shoulder and flexed his elbows, but he could not extend his elbows except by flinging his arms out. He had only slight finger movements.

Sensory Organization

Once Robert's head was stable, he had adequate oculomotor control. He descriminated line-drawing pictures and, according to the ophthalmologist, had no significant refractive error or acuity problems. His audiological evaluations were within normal limits, and he demonstrated receptive language. Because of his motor problems, he was not always able to get a good look at what people were talking about or to see what was making sounds.

Cognition

Robert demonstrated several cognitive abilities characteristic of an early preoperational level, about 2½ years, with capacity to learn some 3-year-level tasks during the assessment session. These findings were supported by the speech pathologist's assessment of his receptive language. Examples of task presentations and response strategies are shown in Table 7 (p. 154). Immediate and future plans for augmentative communication are described briefly as they related to his cognitive level and motor abilities.

Case Example 4: Terri

History

Terri, chronological age 3 years, 7 months, had severe cerebral palsy with athetosis. She attended a preschool program for handicapped children. She had been difficult to test with standardized measures or with eye-pointing alternative strategies. She was referred at this time for assistance in exploring her cognitive level, for identifying strategies for task presentations and responses, and for the planning of an augmentative communication system.

Procedures Used

Terri was seen for joint problem-solving by physical and occupational therapists, a speech pathologist, and an educator, as well as for individual assessments. She was accompanied by her parents, her teacher, and the school psychologist. The Hauessermann psychoeducational evaluation and a representational play scale derived from the work of Nicolich (1977) and Westby (1980) were used.

Findings

Terri was seated in her travel chair with its attached tray. The head supports on the chair kept her head fairly well aligned until she tried to look down at things on her tray, which caused her to lose head control and efficient eye contact. A tilted-up rack with shelves was used to present objects and representational materials to facilitate scanning and eye-pointing responses. Terri's arms tended to posture back in retraction–flexion–external-rotation, or forward in stiff-extension–internal-rotation, or in the asymmetric tonic neck reflex pattern with change of head position. She moved between these arm postures and could also move in horizontal arcs with either arm in the forward extended position. When she attempted moving her hand toward an object at her midline, she turned her head to the opposite side (a way of managing the movement with the tonic reflex), but she then lost eye contact with her hand and materials. When the rack was placed to one side, she was able to indicate her choice of two objects with her hand. She was inconsistently able to open her hand to grasp, and once grasped, objects were inadvertently released as she tried to move her arm.

Sensory Organization

Terri had been found to have a slight hyperopic refractive error and had an occasional variable strabismus for selected tasks. To facilitate scanning and clarity, materials were presented against a black background rather than a transparent tray or rack. Terri had normal hearing.

Cognition

According to the Hauessermann psychoeducational evaluation, Terri demonstrated a number of concepts at 3- to 3½ year level. The assessment of receptive language by the speech pathologist was consistent with these findings. Examples of task presentations and responses for several cognitive tasks are described in Table 8 (p. 156). Plans for Terri's augmentative communication system are described briefly. Interesting toys, books, and use of representational play as a context for presenting concepts were demonstrating, as Terri had not responded well to the formal massed-trial directive approach that her teacher had been using. None of the children in her class were verbal, and possible ways of introducing contacts with verbal peers were discussed.

CONCLUSION

In this chapter, we have argued for the use of a process approach assessment as the one that will yield the most useful descriptive and programmatic information for children with significant motor impairment. We have based this argument on several points, including the problems in the use of traditional approaches to assessment, particularly the violation of underlying assumptions.

In describing a process approach to assessment for use with motorically handicapped infants and preschoolers, we have advocated the use of a developmental-conceptual framework. The sources for this framework are Piagetian theory and current developmental research on infant and preschool-aged children, research that reflects investigations of all domains of development and the integration of these domains. An assumption that is critical to the approach that we propose is that alternative developmental pathways must be explored as a basis for both assessment and intervention for such children.

An interdisciplinary approach is an important feature of the assessment strategies we describe. The effective use of these strategies requires a knowledge of content and developmental pathways in the motor, cognitive, language, and affective domains of development. This information must then be integrated across the domains of development, a process that we have found works best when an interdisciplinary team has ample opportunity to observe and assess a child, both in individual and in combined situations. Such a process is obviously very costly in time. In our opinion, such an investment of time in assessment is necessary if programmatically useful information is to be obtained.

Table 6. Amy: 9-Month, 24-Day-Old Infant with Paralysis Due to Guillain-Barre Syndrome: Example of Stage 4

Standard tasks: Presentations and responses	Adapted strategies: Presentation and responses	Suggestions for intervention
	Object permanence	
Adult places object under single screen with placement visible to child. Child follows, reaches, removes cover, and picks up object. The two-screen problem is also presented at this level (Uzgiris-Hunt, 1975).	Amy's initial response to the "strangers" was wariness as they entered the room. She fussed on approach, as Sroufe (1979) described assimilation of strangers into negative categories—possibly related to her hospitalization and her continued need for intrusive procedures. She fussed when her mother left the room. Later in the session, her mother played a peek-a-boo game, and Amy smiled before recovering. When a toy was covered, she maintained her gaze, and after several times when the adult uncovered the toy, her looks became more systematic. When an object was substituted, she showed surprise when it was uncovered.	Professionals should not move too quickly into interaction with Amy. The teacher might bring out a toy and play with it or pause it and wait for Amy to signal that she wanted play. Physical therapy procedures were to be presented as games, with opportunities for Amy to signal positively and negatively. Peek-a-boo and hiding games were to be interspersed with play with toys. Amy's look or slight movements were accepted as responses and the cloth was lifted for her. In view of fatigue, effort was conserved for actions on toys.
	Means of achieving desired environmental events	
Visually directed reach and grasp would be typically achieved by 4–5 months. Anticipatory differentiation of means and ends and anticipatory adaptation of means would be assessed by observing whether child sets down	Amy was positioned in side-lying to reduce problems with secretions. She seemed to show an intent to reach and grasp objects with slight finger movements and participation in assisted movements but could not move her arm on her	A set of slings was designed to be suspended from a rack that could be used for exercises and for play. A cuff was designed to help Amy hold a toy. She had some practice with "pulling strings" and innovations such as pulley-creating

one object to pick up another; pulls a support to obtain toy out of reach; uses an alternative strategy such as reaching toward object held above a support; uses locomotion to obtain an object or goal.

Anticipatory construction of alternate means for a given end is implied in tasks such as pulling a string to obtain an object (Uzgiris-Hunt, 1975).

own. Suspended slings to support upper arm, forearm, and wrist were improvised (similar to those used for exercise), and objects were placed so she could contact them. With the effect of gravity and surface resistant reduced, she achieved partial movement arcs. With a string looped around her wrist and an object placed on an incline, she quickly learned to pull a toy close enough to finger it and smiled as she mastered this. When toys were offered with the slings, she attempted movement. In a "give-and-take" game ritual without the slings, she responded to the offered toy by eye-to-eye contact and mouth movements as if trying to vocalize, and the toy was given for assisted play. When expectancy was violated, she sequenced looking toward the toy and the person several times, then smiled as the toy was offered again.

variations in spectacles; however, communication as a way to get things was emphasized. The "give-and-take" game involved offering toys to elicit either responsive movement in the slings or a look or vocalization leading to more aware communicative intent. Violation of expectancy (to elicit an initiated behavior) and spatial distancing (to see if she might look or look-fuss toward the toy) were suggested. Choices between toys were also offered to allow her to practice comparisons and to develop instrumental eye-pointing.

Operational causality

Appreciation of causality outside self. Adult creates object spectacle and pauses with hand and object both within reach.

Child touches object or hand or tries to move toy or part directly.

Amy signaled for more of the musical ferris wheel and animal See-'N'-Say by trying to touch them when wearing the slings. Without the slings, she looked toward the object or the person's hand. When assisted to pull the ring, she tried to repeat the movement. Amy appeared to understand causality outside herself, and communicative understanding was emerging.

We wanted to see Amy generalize her object- or person-directed schemes to the repetition of a number of events, giving her a chance to generate. At this time, someone usually asked if she wanted more. Switch-activated toys were also investigated. Other play could be assisted with her control signals.

Table 7. Robert: Age 2 Years, 11 Months Old Boy with Paralysis Due to Meningomyelocele at High-Thoracic–Low-Cervical level

Standard tasks: Presentation and responses	Adapted strategies: Presentation and responses	Suggestions for intervention
	Identification of labeled objects and responses	
Adult presents doll and asks child to show named body parts. Child touches or points to parts. Adult presents three objects—cup, plate, and box—and asks child to give named object. Child reaches for, picks up, and gives object to adult. Adult shows child line-drawing pictures arranged in collection of four to six on a page and asks child to name and/or point to named picture. Adult presents two cups, one inverted, and child is asked to place cube "in" and "on" cup. Child requests wants by gesture or speech and uses phrases and sentences (Bayley, 1969).	Robert was unable to speak and was inconsistently able to voice. He could not point. His paralysis was such that he had some control of his shoulders and elbow flexors and had slight finger movements. If two objects were placed to each side of his tray, he attempted a point by using a trick shoulder movement to fling his arm toward his choice. His accuracy was poor and was limited to the two choices. With his head adequately supported in the midline, he could eye-point to choices of four objects or pictures presented on a tilted-up rack with shelves at the rim of his tray. He wanted to touch and a bargain was made: "You look, then I'll help you do it." He indicated the objects and pictures when named, and two cups with a cube "in" and one "on." With the small Bayley doll, his	Robert was a candidate for a communication board and was to work with a speech pathologist specializing in this area. At his age and cognitive level, direct selection was planned to start with collections of pictures and "Pic-Syms" (Carlson, 1985) appropriate for different contexts to be mounted on a portable carrier. Yes and no responses by affect were to be acknowledged, and he would be taught to clarify these responses by looking toward red and green sweatbands on his wrists (independent of other equipment). A pressure switch was arranged at one side, which he activated by moving his elbow laterally; this switch turned on a cassette recorder to call someone. As he became familiar with the symbols and their uses in several communicative functions, he progressed to a

speaking device with a direct selection method. Scanning or hierarchical coded devices were not yet appropriate at his cognitive level but would be future options, as would access to computers.

eye points were unclear, so a larger doll was used, and parts were named in an order to assist clarity: eyes, feet, hair, etc. Robert correctly indicated all and was assisted to touch the parts after he looked. He was also introduced to using eye points to pictures to indicate which toy he wanted—the toy in view, then out of view—and quickly caught on.

Classification

Robert eye-pointed immediately to a correct match when three socks were presented on the rack, but he wanted to participate motorically (as demonstrated by arm movement and his "fuss face"), so he was assisted to put the sock on. Socks were also matched for his teddy bear, and he picked matching tennis shoes for each. When asked, "Is this the one you want?" he responded with a confirmatory smile but could not nod. When his choice was deliberately misread and the wrong one was put on the doll, Robert laughed. He then chose the wrong one, laughing with a teasing expression at the big joke—a typical response at this age.

Robert's emerging concepts of classification were encouraged in the context of play and daily care by calling comparisons of color, form, and size to his attention. He was invited to choose on the basis of wants—which shirt he wanted to wear, the red or the white, and so on. Matching activities were incorporated in representational play, in assisted construction with blocks, etc. He was given a chance to note and correct incorrect choices. Other early preoperational concepts to be introduced included modeling of counting and beginning one-to-one correspondence, as in passing out a plate or a cookie to each person at snack time.

Adult presents doll with one sock on and two or three socks on table and asks child to "find the other sock like this," etc. Child picks up sock and brings it to doll's foot or hands it to adult, usually requiring help to put it on. Children of this age may think only of giving the sock or putting it on the doll, but with corrective feedback ("Oh, oh, this isn't the same color" and point cues), they begin to catch on and select the matching sock. The adult labels colors. Several trials are interspersed with doll play to confirm the concept (Haussermann, 1958).

Table 8. Terri: 3½-Year-Old Girl with Cerebral Palsy Tension Athetoid Type)

Standard tasks: Presentations and responses	Adapted strategies Presentations and responses	Suggestions for intervention
	Classification (color)	
Adult presents doll with one sock on and two or three socks on table and asks child to "Find the other sock like this," etc. Child picks up sock and brings it to doll's foot or gives it to adult. Adult asks child to show named colors, and child responds to several color names correctly by giving or pointing (Haussermann, 1958).	As Terri lost head control and eye contact when she tried to look down at things on her tray, three socks were presented on a tilted-up rack with shelves. She correctly used eye pointing to indicate matching colors and was assisted to put the socks on and off the doll. When her responses were unclear, yes-no responses were used to verify, asking, "Is this the one you want?" A yes consisted of a nod (losing head control), vocalizations when she could phonate, or eye-contact–smile. A no was turning her eyes to the side or a slight frown. As reception for color names was checked, she correctly indicated red, yellow and blue by eye points.	Terri was encouraged to generalize classification concepts about color across a variety of concrete materials. Materials should at first be alike except for the one attribute, gradually introducing color when form or size were not constant. She was encouraged to acquire more color-name associations through modeling and comments. Drill tasks were discouraged, and examples of play and daily living experiences were discussed as contexts. Although Terri was too young for a hierarchical coding system with a communication device, the speech pathologist decided to use color for structural groupings of "Pic-Syms" (Carlson, 1985) on a direct-selection communication device.

Classification (form)

Geometric forms on cards are arranged on the table in a row of five, and child is shown a stimulus card and asked, "Where does it go?" Variations of verbal requests are explored as children may respond to one form and not another; examples: "Here's mine, where's yours?" and "Which one is the same?" Child may respond by pointing or by picking up card and placing it on or by its match, or by giving it to adult, and variations are checked (Hausser-mann, 1958).

Geometric forms on white cards were presented on the tilted rack in an array of three choices. By the time placement of the stimulus card on the shelf immediately above, its match was demonstrated for the first two forms, Terri understood the task and eye-pointed to the third location. The task was then repeated by showing her the stimulus, asking, "Where does it go?" and placing the card in the location she indicated. She matched the solid circle, square, and triangle with line drawings of circle, square, triangle, and cross. She was able to indicate a named circle and square. The array size was increased, and Terri was unable to organize scanning of a larger array and tended to make errors between square and triangle.

We suggested that Terri needed experiences with concrete materials through assisted movements, including form boxes, form boards, and simple puzzles; however, these were likely not to be as interesting for Terri as for children who could manipulate them. With both concrete and representational materials, we would introduce other forms and work toward increasing the array size and the systematic scanning of comparisons in a left-to-right and top-to-bottom sequence. To prepare for an eventual scanning communication-device, she would also practice signaling when the adult stopped sequential pointing.

Representational play contexts

Terri needed a great deal of experience with representational play through assisted movement. A play board was also desinged on which toys could be moved along slots, as well as a tray with wells that prevented things from scattering around. Concepts around color, form, size, amounts, or spatial relationships were incorporated.

(continued)

Table 8. (Continued)

Standard tasks: Presentations and responses	Adapted strategies Presentations and responses	Suggestions for intervention
	Classification (size)	
Miniature toys consisting of a doll family and furniture are presented on the table, and the child's spontaneous representational play is observed as well as responses to verbal requests. A tiny crib and a bigger adult bed are included, and one observes whether the child places the dolls in the appropriate-size and -formed bed. The child is asked to give or point to the "big" and "little" dolls and beds (Haussermann, 1958).	Terri was not satisfied with eye pointing and wanted to manipulate the materials. It was necessary to manually support her head in a forward tilt and at the same time to assist and follow her movement intents with a light hand-over-hand to her right hand. Terri then placed dolls in appropriate beds spontaneously, sat them on chairs, tried to stand them up, etc. She tried to place the mother doll in the crib, which was too small, and was allowed trial and error, making her own decision to release it and picking up the baby for the crib. On verbal request, she correctly indicated "big" and "little" dolls and beds by eye pointing.	

REFERENCES

Bates, E., Camaioni, L. & Volterra, V. (1975). The acquisition of performatives prior to speech. *Merrill-Palmer Quarterly of Behavior and Development, 21*, 205–225.

Bates, E., Benigni, L., Bretheston, I., Camaioni, L., & Volterra, V. (1977). From gesture to the first word: On cognitive and social prerequisites. In M. Lewis & L, Rosenblum (Eds.), *Interaction, conversation and the development of language*. New York: Wiley.

Bayley, N. (1969). *Bayley scales of infant development*. New York: Psychological Corporation.

Bell, P. B. (1980). *Characteristics of handicapped infants: A study of the relationship between child characteristics and stress as reported by mothers*. Unpublished doctoral dissertation. Chapel Hill, NC: University of North Carolina.

Bell, S. M. (1970). The development of the concept of object as related to infant-mother attachment. *Child Development, 41*, 291–311.

Bourgeault, S., Harley, R., Dubose, R., & Langley, M. (1977). Assessment and programming for blind children with severely handicapped conditions. *Journal of Visual Impairment and Blindness, 71*, 49–53.

Brinker, R., & Lewis, M. (1982). Discovering the competent handicapped infant: A process approach to assessment and intervention. *Topics in Early Childhood Special Education, 2*, 1–16.

Brooks-Gunn, J. (1984). *Visual attention in handicapped infants: The effects of chronological age, mental age and disability*. Paper presented at International Conference on Infant Studies, New York.

Brooks-Gunn, J., & Lewis, M. (1982). Affective exchanges between normal infants and handicapped infants and their mothers. In T. Field & A. Fogel. (Eds.), *Emotion and early interaction*. Hillsdale, NJ: Erlbaum.

Broussard E. R., & Hartner, M. S. S. (1970). Maternal perception of the neonate as related to development. *Child Psychology and Human Development, 1*, 16–25.

Bruner, J. (1975). The ontogenesis of speech acts. *Journal of Child Language, 2*, 1–19.

Campos, J., Svejda, M., Campos, R., & Bertenthal, B. (1982). The emergence of self-produced locomotion: Its importance for psychological development in infancy. In D. Bricker (Ed.), *Intervention with at-risk and handicapped infants: From research to application*. Baltimore: University Park Press.

Carlson, F. (1981). *Alternate methods of communication*. Danville, IL: Interstate Printers and Publishers.

Carlson, F. (1985) *Picsyms: Categorical dictionary*. Lawrence, KS: Baggeboda Press.

Chapman, R. S., & Miller, J. F. (1980). Analyzing language and communication in the child. In R. L. Schiefelbusch (Ed.), *Nonspeech language and communication*. Baltimore: University Park Press.

Chess, S. (1983). *Temperament, handicap and the vulnerable child*, Mary Elaine Meyer O'Neal Award Lectureship in Developmental Pediatrics, University of Nebraska Medical Center, Omaha.

Decarie, T. (1969). A study of the mental and emotional development of the Thalidomide child. In B. Foss (Ed.), *Determinants of infant behavior* (Vol. 4). London: Methuen.

Detterman, D. K. (1979). Memory in the mentally retarded. In N. R. Ellis (Ed.), *Handbook of mental deficiency, psychological theory and research*. Hillsdale, NJ: Erlbaum.

Dubose, R., Langley, M., & Stagg, V. (1977). Assessing severely handicapped children. *Focus on Exceptional Children, 9*, 1–13.

Fagan, J. F. (1984). *Infants attention to visual novelty and the prediction of later intellectual deficit*. *Symposium: Early information processing and later cognitive functioning in delayed and normal infants*. Paper presented to the International Conference on Infant Studies, New York.

Fieber, N. (1977a). Cognitive skills, In N. G. Haring (Ed.), *Developing effective individualized education programs for severely handicapped children and youth*. Washington, DC: Department of Health, Education and Welfare, Office of Education, Bureau of Education for the Handicapped.

Fieber, N. (1977b). *Sensorimotor cognitive assessment and curriculum for the multihandicapped child*. Paper in proceedings of workshop on sensorimotor assessment, Austin, Texas Education Agency.

Fieber, N. (1978). The profoundly handicapped child: Assessing sensorimotor and communication abilities. In D. H. Clark (Ed.), *The deaf-blind/severely-profoundly handicapped*. Proceedings of Nebraska Statewide Conference, Cozad, 1978. Lincoln: Nebraska Department of Education.

Fisher, K. W. (1980). A theory of cognitive development: The control and construction of hierarchies of skills, *Psychological Review, 87*, 477–531.

Fishman, M. & Palkes, H. (1974). The validity of psychometric testing in children with congenital malformations of the central nervous system. *Developmental Medicine and Child Neurology, 16*, 180–185.

Fox, N., Kagan, J., & Weiskopf, P. (1979). The growth of memory during infancy. *Genetic Psychology Monographs, 99*, 91–130.

Gelman, R. (1980). What young children know about numbers. *Educational Psychologists, 15*, 54–68.

Golinkoff, R. M. (1981). The influence of Piagetian theory on the study of the development of communication. In D. E. Sigel, D. M. Brodzinsky, & R. M. Golinkoff (Eds.), *New directions in Piagetian theory and practice*. Hillsdale, NJ: Erlbaum.

Hauessermann, E. (1958). *Developmental potential of preschool children*, New York: Grune & Stratton.

Hunt, J. McV. (1961). *Intelligence and experience*. New York: Ronald.

Hunter, M. A., Ross, H. S., & Ames, E. W. (1982) Preferences for familiar or novel toys: Effects of familiarization time in 1 year olds. *Developmental Psychology, 18*, 519–529.

Illingworth, R. S. (1971). The predictive value and developmental assessment in infancy. *Developmental Medicine and Child Neurology, 13*, 721–725.

Jackson, E., Campos, J. J., & Fischer, K. W. (1978). The question of decalage between object permanence and person permanence. *Developmental Psychology, 14*, 1–10.

Jens, K. G., & Johnson, N. M. (1982). Affective development: A window to cognition in young handicapped children. *Topics in Early Childhood Special Education, 2*, 17–24.

Kagan, J. (1970). Attention and psychological change in the young child. *Science, 170*, 826–832.

Klaus, M., & Kennel, J. (1976). *Maternal-infant bonding*. St. Louis: Mosby.

Kopp, C. (1974). *Development of fine motor behaviors: Issues and research*. Paper presented at Synposium on Aberrant Development in Infancy, Gatlinberg, Tennessee, March.

Kopp, C. & Shapermann, J. (1973). Cognitive development in the absence of object manipulation during infancy. *Developmental Psychology, 9*, 430.

Landers, W. F. (1971). Effects of differential experience on infant's performance in a Piagetian Stage IV object-concept task. *Developmental Psychology, 5*, 48–54.

Langley, M. (1978). Psychoeducational assessment of the multiply handicapped blind child: Issues and methods. *Education of the Visually Handicapped, 10*, 97–115.

Largo, R. H., & Howard, J. A. (1979). Developmental progression in play behavior of children between nine and thirty months: 1. spontaneous play and language development. *Developmental Medicine and Child Neurology, 21*, 299–310.

MacKay-Soroka, S., Trehub, S., Bull, D., & Corter, C. (1982). Effects of encoding and retrieval conditions on infants' recognition memory. *Child Development, 53*, 815–818.

McDonough, S. (1984). *Concept formation in motorically impaired infants*. Paper presented at the International Conference on Infant Studies, New York.

Musselwhite, C., & St. Louis, K. (1982). *Communication in programming for the severely handicapped: Vocal and non-verbal strategies*. Houston: College-Hill Press.

Nicholich, L. M. (1977). Beyond sensorimotor intelligence: Assessment of symbolic maturity through analysis of pretend play. *Merrill-Palmer Quarterly, 23*, 88–99.

Nielson, H. (1971). Psychological appraisal of children with cerebral palsy. *Developmental Medicine and Child Neurology, 13*, 707–720.

O'Reiley, D. E., & Walentynowicz, J. E. (1981). Etiological factors in cerebral palsy: A historical review. *Developmental Medicine and Child Neurology, 23*, 633–642.

Piaget, J. (1952). *The origins of intelligence in children*. New York: International Universities Press.

Robinson, C. (1982). Questions regarding the effects of neuromotor problems on sensorimotor development. In D. Bricker (Ed.), *Intervention with at-risk and handicapped infants: From research to application*. Baltimore: University Park Press.

Robinson, C. (1987). A strategy for assessing motorically impaired infants. In I. Uzgiris & J. McV. Hunt (Eds.), *Research with scales of psychological development in infancy*. Urbana: University of Illinois Press.

Robinson, C., & Fieber, N. (1974). *Development and modification of Piagetian sensorimotor assessment and curriculum for developmentally handicapped infants*. Paper presented at American Academy for Cerebral Palsy, Denver.

Robinson, C., & Robinson, J. (1978). Sensorimotor functions and cognitive development. In M. Snell (Ed.), *Systematic instruction of the moderately and severely handicapped*. Columbus: Charles E. Merrill.

Robinson, C., & Robinson, J. (1983). Sensorimotor functions and cognitive development. In M. Snell (Ed.), *Systematic instruction of the moderately and severely handicapped*. (2nd ed.). Columbus: Charles E. Merrill.

Robinson, C., Fieber, N., & Rose, J. (1983). *Cognitive assessment of infants with cerebral palsy: Motor or mental?* Instructional course presented at American Academy for Cerebral Palsy and Developmental Medicine, Chicago.

Ross, G. (1980). Categorization in 1-to-2 years old. *Developmental Psychology, 16*, 391–396.

Ruff, H. (1982). Role of manipulation in infants' responses to invariant properties of objects. *Developmental Psychology, 18*, 682–691.

Simeonsson, R. (1977). Infant assessment. In B. Caldwell, D. Stedman, & K Goin (Eds.), *Infant education: A guide for helping handicapped children in the first three years*. New York: Walker.

Simeonsson, R., Huntington, G., & Parse, S. (1980). Assessment of children with severe handicaps: Multiple problems-multivariate goals. *Journal of the Association for the Severely Handicapped, 5*, 55–72.

Snyder, L. (1978). Communicative and cognitive abilities and disabilities in the sensorimotor period. *Merrill-Palmer Quarterly, 24*, 161–181.

Sroufe, L. A. (1979). Socioemotional development. In J. Osofsky (Ed.), *Handbook of infant development*. New York: Wiley.

Sugarman-Bell, S. (1978). Some organizational aspects of preverbal communication. In I. Markova (Ed.), *The social context of language*. New York: Wiley.

Tew, B., Laurence, K. M., & Samuel, P. (1974). Parental estimates of the intelligence of their physically handicapped children. *Developmental Medicine and Child Neurology, 16*, 494–500.

Uzgiris, I. (1976). Organization of sensorimotor intelligence. In M. Lewis (Ed.), *Origins of intelligence: Infancy and early childhood*. New York: Plenum Press.

Uzgiris, I., & Hunt, J. McV. (1975). *Assessment in infancy: Ordinal Scales of Psychological Development*. Urbana: University of Illinois Press.

Vietze, P. M., Falsey, S., O'Connor, S., Sandler, H., Sherrod, K., & Altemeier, A. (1980). Newborn behavioral and interactional characteristics of nonorganic failure-to-thrive infants. In T. M. Field (Ed.), *High-risk infants and children*. New York: Academic Press.

Westby, C. E. (1980). Language abilities through play. *Language, Speech, and Hearing Services in Schools, 11*, 154–168.

Worthingham, C., & Daniels, L. (1972). *Muscle testing: Technique of manual examination*. Philadelphia: W. B. Saunders.

Zelazo, P. R. (1979). Reactivity to perceptual-cognitive events: Application for infant assessment. In R. B. Kearsley & I. E. Sigel (Eds.), *Infants at risk: Assessment of cognitive functioning*. Hillsdale, NJ: Erlbaum.

Cognitive Assessment of Mentally Retarded Infants and Preschoolers

James V. Kahn

All definitions of mental retardation that have been proposed over the years have included one central feature: deficits in the intellectual (or cognitive) capacity of the mentally retarded person. Professionals working in the field of mental retardation have disagreed on almost every other possible aspect of the definition (e.g., age of onset or diagnosis, etiology, degree of cognitive deficit, other concomitant deficits, and permanence), but all agree that, in order for a person to be considered mentally retarded, he or she must be shown to have a deficit in cognitive functioning. Thic characteristic of mentally retarded persons is so basic that reliable and valid instruments must be available for determining whether cognitive deficits exist.

Since the mid-1960s, a great deal of progress has been made in the education of mentally retarded persons. During this time, it has become apparent that the earlier the educational process begins, the greater is its impact. This is true both of children who are at a high risk of mental retardation because of environmental and gestational factors and of children who have neurological abnormalities that result in cognitive impairment. The earlier these children are identified and programs are established for them, the better is their prognosis (e.g., Ramey & Hakins, 1981). Thus, it is crucial that instruments for the assessment of cognitive functioning in infants and preschool children be accessible for purposes of diagnosis and program planning.

This chapter reviews the methods of measuring the cognitive functioning of infants and preschoolers that are currently available, as well as some that may become available in the near future. These methods include formal intelligence tests that result in an IQ or an analogous standard score, other standardized tests that do not result in an IQ equivalent, nonstandardized assessment methods, and a method that is experimental and is not yet appropriate for clinical use. Each instrument described is discussed in terms of its possible uses. Hubert and Wallander (Chapter 3) discuss the selection of an instrument in relation to its intended use. They point out that an instrument could be used for one or more of the following purposes: screening persons for possible problems; diagnosing and

JAMES V. KAHN • Department of Special Education, University of Illinois at Chicago, Chicago, Illinois 60680.

classifying a person; describing a person's present status in terms of capabilities and deficits (severity of problems); and designing a remedial program for an individual. This approach will be used in this chapter to describe the use or uses of each instrument.

It is not possible to cover in a single chapter all cognitive assessment methods that are used with infants and preschoolers who are, or are suspected of being, mentally retarded. This chapter attempts to describe and discuss those methods that are most commonly used, that are of most interest with this population, or that are most promising.

INFANT TESTS

A large number of tests have been designed to measure the intellectual functioning of infants. Some of these instruments are fairly standard intelligence tests and others are more useful for screening or for program planning. Although many of the tests go beyond the age of 2 years, (for instance, the Gesell schedules go up to 6 years), each test described in this section is used mostly as an infant test.

The instruments are divided into three types of tests, based on how they are most commonly used: screening tests to identify infants with potential problems, intelligence tests for diagnostic purposes, and tests that can be useful for program planning. In addition, one method that must still be considered experimental, but that promises to have a major impact in the future, will be described. Assignment to these categories was determined by the way the test is most frequently used. In some cases, this chapter suggests other, more appropriate uses for these measures.

Screening Tests

The Denver Developmental Screening Test (DDST) (Frankenburg & Dodd, 1970) consists of 105 items taken from a number of existing infant and preschool instruments. The items are ordered according to chronological age and are divided into four areas: gross motor, fine-motor–adaptive (includes imitation), language, and personal-social. The child's performance on each item is scored as normal, questionable, or abnormal, based on a standardized sample. The test authors advise against using the DDST to diagnose mental retardation or to derive an IQ equivalent. Their purpose was to develop a screening device to find children between 2 weeks and 6 years of age who should be referred for a more complete assessment.

The standardization sample consisted of 1,036 healthy children between 2 weeks and 6.4 years of age. The sample reflected the occupational and ethnic characteristics of the Denver area's population according to the 1960 U.S. census. The standardization sample is considered by some (e.g., Moriarty, 1972) a major problem in the DDST, particularly in its use with minority children outside the Denver area. Reliability and validity data are provided through a series of studies by the authors and their colleagues. Test–retest and interexaminer reliability are reasonably high. Validity, determined by comparing DDST results with the Stanford-Binet or the Bayley scales, is acceptable. Although some children who are found to be in the abnormal range on the Bayley or the Binet are not identified as abnormal on the DDST, the number of such underrefferals is relatively small when the DDST is administered properly (Hunt, 1975).

The Developmental Screening Inventory (DSI) (Knobloch, Pasamanick, & Sherard, 1966) consists of items selected from the Gesell Developmental Schedules that are from each of five areas: adaptive, gross motor, fine motor, language, and personal-social skills. The items are at 4-week intervals from 4- to 56-week-old infants and at 3-month intervals until 18 months. The examiner scores the infant as abnormal, questionable, or normal for his or her age in each of the areas. The DSI was designed for use by physicians and nurses familiar with the Gesell, but no restrictions are placed on its use. Childcare and development specialists who are well trained in infant assessment may find the DSI useful.

No standardization of the DSI is reported. The authors apparently relied on the Gesell test standardization, as the items came from there. Reliability and validity are minimal but adequate. In one study, the DSI was compared to later complete examination results and was found to predict later abnormality quite well ($r = .81$). However, its lack of a standardization sample of its own, the rather widely spaced items, and the training needed to administer it, make the DSI less useful in most situations than the DDST. The DSI is most useful in the medical setting for which it was designed.

The Kent Infant Development (KID) Scale (Katoff, Reuter, & Dunn, 1980) is designed to be completed by a caretaker (e.g., teacher, parent, or child-care worker). It is proposed that the KID can replace a professionally administered test such as the Bayley scales (Stancin, Reuter, Dunn, & Bickett, 1984). However, the KID is discussed here, under the heading of "screening tests," because I do not believe that there are adequate data to support its use as a final diagnostic test.

The KID scale consists of 252 sentence stems "that describe behaviors characteristic of the first year of an infant's life" (Katoff et al, 1980, p. 7). The items were selected, through a lengthy process, from an initial group of 2,000 derived for 70 existing tests. The items are written in "readable, behavioral language and divided into five domains (cognitive, motor, language, social, and self-help) common to other infant tests and stimulation curriculums" (p. 7). The caregiver is asked to read and respond to each sentence stem (e.g., "Immediately notices an object placed in front of him or her") by checking one of four possible responses: "Yes"; "Used to do it, but outgrew it"; "Is no longer able to do it"; or "No, cannot do it yet" (p. 11). An estimated developmental age is derived for each domain, as well as for the full scale.

The standardization sample consisted of 357 presumably healthy infants. Developmental ages for each item were then estimated. Test–retest and interrater reliability coefficients for the individual domains and full-scale ages were quite high (all reported to be above .85) for the normative sample. Concurrent validity was also high for 38 of the subjects from the normative sample; the KID scale correlations with the Bayley scales were above .84. In a recent report, Stancin et al. (1984) studied the reliability and validity of the KID scale with a sample of severely and profoundly retarded children between the chronological ages of 18 months and 9 years, whose developmental ages were below 12 months. Their findings indicated high reliability and high correlations between the KID and the Bayley scales. However, mothers scored their children higher in every domain of the KID scale than did the children's teachers. This finding, the lack of data on more borderline cases (e.g., mild to moderately retarded children and high-risk infants), and the lack of predictive data lead me to conclude that this test should be used with parents as a screening device. Children found to be below the norms should then be professionally tested with the Bayley or some other age-appropriate test. I should also note that the KID scale may be useful for program planning. Stancin *et al*. reported that a survey of the psychologists involved in testing the children in their studies indicated that the psychologists believed "that 65% of the time the Kent Infant Development Scale results yielded enough information to design an individual habilitation plan" (p. 390). Although this might be an overstatement on the psychologists' part, it does indicate that the five domains and the individual items do provide useful information for the development of an individual program.

Diagnostic Measures

A number of tests have been designed to measure the intellectual functioning of infants and preschool-age children. Most of these tests have been used diagnostically to classify children as mentally retarded and, more important, to determine the infants' current status (severity of the problem). Some have also been useful in determining the strengths and weaknesses of an individual, a determination that is useful in designing an individual program.

Infants below 2 years of age are probably the most difficult group to test. Such young subjects often are inattentive and fatigue easily. These problems are compounded with infants who are mentally retarded or at risk for mental retardation. Despite the additional problems of testing mentally retarded infants, infant intelligence tests are better predictors of later childhood IQs for mentally retarded infants than for nonhandicapped infants (McCall, 1982). The three tests to be discussed here are the Gesell Developmental Schedules (Gesell & Amatruda, 1947), the Catell Infant Intelligence Scale (Cattell, 1940, 1960), and the Bayley Scales of Infant Development (Bayley, 1933, 1969).

Before the work of Arnold Gesell and his colleagues (e.g., Gesell, 1925, 1940; Gesell & Amatruda, 1947; Gesell & Thompson, 1938), the field of infant assessment did not exist. In fact, most later attempts to develop infant intelligence tests borrowed from Gesell's earlier work and items. It should be noted that, although Gesell and his colleagues were continually engaged in collecting normative data and restandardizing the schedules, he did not conceive of his schedules as being an intelligence test useful for the prediction of later performance. Rather, he viewed his schedules as being appropriate for determining an infant's present condition and for making decisions regarding services needed by that infant (Yang, 1979). Nevertheless, most psychologists have used the schedules as an itelligence test, interpreting the developmental quotient (DQ) as being synonymous with IQ.

The Gesell Developmental Schedules (Gesell & Amatruda, 1947) contain a large number of items for children ranging in age form 1 month to 6 years. Items are ordered by age and consist of behaviors normally observed in children. They are grouped into four major categories of functioning; motor behaviors such as locomotion, reaching, and balance; adaptive behaviors such as finding an object and building a tower; language, including gestures (pointing) and verbalizations; and personal and social behaviors, such as eating and playing with others. The child's responses to standard situations and stimuli, when supplemented with parental information, can be used to determine an overall developmental quotient (DQ), although, as mentioned earlier, this was not Gesell's stated primary purpose.

Yang (1979) reviewed some of the research on the predicitve validity of the Gesell Developmental Schedules. He concluded that "the results have not been encouraging" (p. 168). This is particularly true when the subjects have been normally developing infants. However, research studies that have included clinical samples of neurologically and/or mentally retarded subjects have typically found higher correlations between infant DQs on the Gesell schedule and childhood IQs on the Stanford-Binet or other tests (e.g., Knobloch & Pasamanick, 1963, 1967). Thus, the Gesell Developmental Schedules appear to be more useful in predicting childhood IQs in the range of mental retardation (below 70) than those in the average or superior ranges.

It is important to remember that the primary purpose of the Gesell schedules was never to predict later IQ. The negative view of the Gesell schedules held by many psychologists is probably due to the schedules' questionable psychometric qualitities. It may be that the more positive view of these schedules held by pediatricians and neurologists is due to the greater concern of these medical practitioners about describing the child's present state than about predicting the child's future IQ. Educators may also be able to use the Gesell schedules as a criterion-based measure of curriculum effectiveness. Bagnato (1981) suggested the use of the developmental age (DA) rather than the DQ for this purpose.

The Gesell schedules have been revised, (Knobloch & Pasamanick, 1974). The revisions, which are minor and include new normative data, have improved the schedules. The schedules are still not intended as an intelligence test, and clinical judgment is still of major importance.

Whereas Gesell was concerned in developing a broad clinical assessment, Cattell (1940, 1960) was primarily concerned in the development of a standardized infant-intelligence test. Her test was conceived of as a downward extension of the Stanford-Binet. Cattell used items from the Gesell scales that she did not think were unduly influenced by home training or gross muscular control. Other items filled the gaps created by discarding many Gesell items.

The Cattell Infant Intelligence Scale has five items at each age level, with one or two alternatives. The scale is used with infants from 2 to 30 months old, with norms every month from 2 to 12 months, every 2 months from 12 to 24 months, and every 3 months from there on. As the Cattell scale was designed to be a downward extension of the Stanford-Binet, it is not very good at predicting later Stanford-Binet scores. The correlations between Binet scores at 3 years and Cattell scores at 3 months, 6 months, 9 months, 12 months, 18 months, and 24 months were reported as .10, .34, .18, .56, .67, and .71, respectively.

Given that Cattell meant her scale to be a downward extension of the Stanford-Binet and to be more objective than other infant assessments, it is surprising that she recommended that test users pay close attention to their subjective, clinical impressions of the infant. These observations could be useful in revealing dysfunctions that may have affected or distorted test performance.

Relatively little research has been done on the utility of the Cattell scale with mentally retarded infants. One study, conducted by Werner, Honzik, and Smith (1968), is of particular interest. They correlated Cattell scores at 20 months with Primary Mental Ability (Thurston & Thurston, 1954) scores at 10 years. The correlation for a normal group of children was .49, but for children who scored below 80 on the Cattell, the correlation with the 10-year Primary Mental Ability scores was .71. Thus, as with the Gesell schedules, there is evidence that the Cattell has more predictive utility when the scores are low, indicating at least the potential for mental retardation.

The Bayley Scales of Infant Development (Bayley, 1969), formerly known as the California Mental Scales (Bayley, 1933), are probably the most widely used infant intelligence test. The scales consist of three parts; the mental scale, the motor scale, and the infant behavior record. The mental scale is of most interest here and consists of 163 items that are "designed to assess sensory-perceptual acuities, discriminations, and the ability to respond to these; the early acquisition of 'object constancy' and memory, learning, and problem-solving ability; vocalizations and the ability to form generalizations and classifications which is the basis of abstract thinking" (Bayley, 1969, p. 3). This scale is normed at half-month intervals, from 2 to 5 months and at 1-month intervals from 6 to 30 months. The motor scale includes gross-motor and fine-motor abilities, and the infant behavior record measures aspects of personality. All three scales are designed for use with 2- to 30-month old children. Many of the items originally came from Gesell's early work. However, Bayley continued to work on and improve her scales for over 40 years. Thus, the current product is the result of a lengthy clinical and research process.

The Bayley mental scale allows for two different measures, a mental development index (MDI), which is a standard score similar in nature to the IQ, and a mental age equivalent. Bayley (1969) pointed out that the MDI has limited use as a predictor of later intellectual ability because the rate of growth in the first 24 months of life is extremely variable. "The primary value of the development indexes is that they provide the basis for establishing a child's current status, and thus the extent of any deviation from normal expectancy" (p. 4). She suggested that integrating the MDI with the mental age "might provide a basis for instituting early corrective measures when the child shows evidence of retarded mental...development" (p. 4). This is important because, to be most effective, an intervention program should be designed to fit with the child's developmental age.

A good deal of research has been done on the usefulness of the Bayley scales with mentally retarded children. However, it should be noted that the lowest MDI for Bayley's normative sample is 50. Thus, only by using extrapolated MDIs (Naglieri, 1981) can MDIs below 50 be found. The problem with using these extrapolated scores is that they come from regression equations rather than from a normative sample and may not be highly accurate. Thus, they should be considered only estimates.

Hunt and Bayley (1971) reviewed some of the research on the predictability of the Bayley scales. They found that the scales do differentiate between normal and neurologically abnormal infants. Lasky, Tyson, Rosenfeld, Priest, Krasinski, Heartwell, and Gant (1983) reported that there is a good deal of similarity between the factor-analytic structure of the Bayley scales for full-term infants and high-risk infants. Ramey and Brownlee (1981) found that the Bayley MDI is useful as one of a group of predictors of risk for mental retardation at 6 months of age. It is clear from these and other studies (e.g., Ireton, Thwing, & Gravem, 1970) that the Bayley mental scale is useful in identifying children who are likely to have cognitive deficiencies in later childhood. In fact, VanderVeer and Schweid (1974) reported that, of 22 children found to be mentally retarded (from borderline to profound) by use of the Bayley scales between 18 and 30 months, all were still classified as mentally retarded 1–3 years later on the Stanford-Binet.

Ramey and his colleagues (e.g., Haskins, Ramey, Stedman, Blacher-Dixon, &

Pierce, 1978; Ramey & Haskins, 1981; Ramey & Smith, 1976) have used the Bayley scales to evaluate the effectiveness of early intervention projects with high-risk infants. They have found the Bayley to be useful both as a predictor (Ramey & Brownlee, 1981) and as a measure of program effectiveness. Haskins et al. (1978) found that repeated administrations of the Bayley did not bias the test scores. Thus, children's performance on the Bayley is not affected by prior knowledge of the test.

Finally, I should mention that the Bayley scales have also frequently been used with older severely and profoundly retarded children. The scales are particularly useful in finding mental and motor age-equivalents. Haskins and Bell (1978) found that "the Bayley Mental Scale appears capable of serving both descriptive and theoretical functions, and thus of assisting in the organization of new approaches to intervention with profoundly retarded and organically impaired individuals" (p. 327).

Several conclusions can be drawn from this review of these three infant intelligence tests. First, it is clear that each of these tests can be used to classify infants who are mentally retarded and to indicate the severity of their problem. These tests are not highly predictive of childhood IQs in the average and those who are above range, but they are reasonable predictors of childhood IQs in the mental retardation (<70) range. Although care must be taken to avoid classifying nonretarded infants as retarded, as McCall and his colleagues (McCall, Hogarty, & Hulbert, 1972; 1982) warned, those children with low standard scores and low mental ages on any of the scales, who also have additional clinical symptoms, can reasonably be classified as mentally retarded or as being at risk for mental retardation.

This review has also shown that the three tests have similarities and differences. Erickson, Johnson, and Campbell (1970) demonstrated that the Cattell scores and the Bayley MDIs for retarded infants are almost identical. Thus, as the Cattell takes less time to administer, it is probably a better screening instrument. However, the Bayley scales and the Gesell schedules give far more information regarding the particular strengths and weaknesses of an individaul infant. So the Bayley and the Gesell are more useful in describing an individual infant's current status so that recommendations can be made regarding remediation and intervention plans.

The Bayley scales have additional advantages over the Cattell scale and the Gesell schedules, particularly because of their extensive use in clinical and research settings. The Bayley scales have been shown to be useful in program evaluation with high risk infants. They can be administered repeatedly without affecting the infant's subsequent performance (Haskin et al., 1978). They have also been shown to be equally useful when administered in the home or in a clinic setting (Horner, 1980). Thus, they are flexible in the setting required for their administration. Finally, research has shown that, if mothers are given a simplified questionaire of Bayley items, their scores will be highly correlated ($r=.686$ for the MDI and $r=.845$ for mental age) with the scores obtained by trained diagnosticians (Gradel, Thompson, & Sheehan, 1981). It should be noted, however, that the scores from the mothers are significantly higher than those found by the diagnosticians. The Bayley questionnaire does seem to have the potential to be useful as a screening device when administered by untrained mothers. As mothers' scores are higher, those infants who are found by their mothers to have low MDIs are likely to need specialized services. An advantage of having mothers administer the Bayley as a questionnaire is the enormous savings in professional time and expense.

Program Planning

Attention has focused in recent years on the use of assessment devices for program planning. The scales discussed in this section are of two types: those based on Piagetian theory and those using behavioral approaches. Both types of assessments have implications for assessing an individual's cognitive competence in such a way as to lead to program initiatives.

A number of infant tests based on Piaget's sensorimotor period have been developed since the mid-1960s (Casati & Lezine, 1968; Decarie, 1965, 1972; Escalona & Corman, undated; Uzgiris & Hunt, 1966, 1972, 1975). Two of these have received the most attention: Escalona and Corman's Albert Einstein Scales of Sensorimotor Development and Uzgiris and Hunt's Scales of Psychological Development in Infancy. Both of these instruments were constructed for use with normally developing infants, but they have also been used with mentally retarded persons from infancy through adulthood.

The Albert Einstein scales measure three areas of sensorimotor functioning: prehension (early behaviors including primary and secondary circular reactions), object permanence, and space. The prehension scale contains 16 items and is scored by assigning the child to either Stage 2 or Stage 3. The object permanence scale has 18 items spanning Stages 3, 4, 5, and 6. The space scale has 21 items and also spans Stages 3–6. The scales are available in mimiograph form, but like the other unpublished scales, have been used less frequently since the publication of Uzgris and Hunt's scales (1975).

Uzgiris and Hunt constructed an instrument containing seven moderately related scales: visual pursuit and permanence of objects (object permanence), means of obtaining desired environmental events (means–end), vocal imitation, gestural imitation, operational causality, construction of object relations in space (spatial relations), and schemes for relating to objects. The scales are scored in terms of the highest step passed (ranging from 7 steps to 14 steps on the different scales) rather than according to stages like the Albert Einstein scales. The scales are administered one at a time, and the items are ordered according to their developmental progression.

A good deal of research has been conducted using the Uzgiris and Hunt Scales with normally developing infants, as well as with handicapped infants and children. Much of this research is reviewed in a book edited by Uzgiris & Hunt (1987). One of the chapters in their book (Kahn, 1987) deals specifically with the literature on using these scales with mentally retarded persons. In general, the research has shown that these scales are reliable over time and across testers with severely and profoundly retarded children (e.g., Kahn, 1976; Karlan, 1980). However, as Kahn (1987) pointed out:

> The validity of the scales with this population . . . is not firmly established. There is evidence that the scales' scores are moderately correlated with each other and with mental age as Piaget's theory would predict. However, only the object permanence scale has been repeatedly shown to be ordinal. [Once an item is not passed, all subsequent items should also not be passed if the scale is ordinal.] Since there is some question as to the ordinality of all but the object permanence scale with this population, the scales should be used cautiously; that is, failure on one item should not terminate the testing on that scale since a profoundly retarded person may still succeed on a higher item (p. 263).

It should be noted that much of the research reviewed in reaching this conclusion was conducted with older retarded children and even adults. It is possible that the ordinality problem may be a function of the chronological ages of the subjects and that the use of the scales with mentally retarded infants and young preschool children may not present a serious problem. Further research is needed to clarify this potential problem. In the meantime, the scales can be used, with appropriate care, to provide the needed assessment data.

Many of the items on the various Uzgiris and Hunt scales appear to be similar to those in other developmentally based assessment devices, including the Bayley scales. Yet the Uzgiris and Hunt scales are still useful in addition to having Bayley scale scores. First, the Uzgiris and Hunt scales have many items that are different from any of the Bayley items. In addition, the Uzgiris and Hunt items are organized into seven separate, though related, scales. Thus, the items and the individual scales are more useful for program plannning.

A number of studies (e.g., Kahn, 1975, 1983; Mahoney, Glover & Finger, 1981; Mundy, Seibert, & Hogan, 1984; Wachs & DeRemer, 1978) have found significant relationships between retarded infants' and children's sensorimotor scores and a variety of communicative and other adaptive behaviors. Other research has demonstrated that sensorimotor period development can be accelelerated through rather direct training of the concept. In particular, object permanence has been successfully trained (Brassell & Dunst, 1976; Henry, 1977; Kahn, 1978)). Kahn (1984) demonstrated that the training of object permanence and means–end concepts may make it easier for young mentally retarded children to learn to use verbalizations. These training programs are still rather experimental. However, the Uzgiris and Hunt scales are currently useful in programs planning for mentally retarded individuals. Specifically, these scales can be useful in ascertaining the type of materials and the level of programming that are most appropriate for an individual. The scales also provide more useful information about mentally retarded infants and preschoolers than standardized intelligence tests and should be used to supplement IQ tests.

There are also a number of behaviorally based criterion-referenced measures and curricula that include cognitive scales or scattered items of a cognitive nature. These measures are not standardized and generally do not include reliability and validity data. However, they give information about what an individual infant or child can do and what he or she can't do. This information is, obviously, highly useful to teachers and parents in designing the child's curriculum. Only four measures are mentioned here because of limitations of space. These four are representative of the many others available and were designed for use with both mentally retarded infants and mentally retarded preschoolers.

The Wabash Center's Guide to Early Developmental Training (1977) includes five areas: motor; cognition; language; self-care; and number concepts and skills. Each area includes a specific procedure for determining the child's appropriate level for training. The cognitive assessment is based on Piagetian scales.

The Behavioral Characteristics Progression (BCP)—(1973) is a continuum of behaviors in chart form. In it, 2,400 observable traits are grouped into 59 strands. It was designed as "the major assessment, instructional and communication tool" for a federally funded project of Santa Cruz County's Special Education Department. It is designed for special educators to use as a method of determining a child's appropriate program.

Somerton and Turner (undated) developed an assessment guide for the Pennsylvania Department of Education for use with severely and profoundly retarded children. The guide includes 475 items that are grouped into 14 checklists, which can be grouped into six general categories: discrimination; motor; self-help and hygiene; communications; perceptual-cognitive; and social interaction. This criterion-referenced assessment leads directly into "individual prescriptive planning." Thus, this assessment guide is designed to be used in planning for a severely and profoundly retarded child's educational-training program.

Popovich (1977) constructed behavioral checklists for use with severely and profoundly retarded children. A number of the items in the checklists in the language development area are cognitive and may be useful in developing cognitive training programs. Popovich listed objectives, behaviors, task analyses of behaviors, and methods of implementation for a number of skills. Thus, this criterion-referenced instrument is used directly in program planning for severely and profoundly retarded infants and children.

An Experimental Approach

Since the mid-1960s, a number of developmental psychologists have studied the attending behaviors of infants. Much of this research has examined the process by which infants' responsiveness to novel visual stimuli develops. Recently, research has been directed at the implications of individual differences among infants (see for reviews, Fagan, 1984a; Fagan & Shepherd, 1982). The research in this area may lead to clinical tools that are more useful for diagnosis and placement decisions, and possibly for intervention, than the current infant intelligence tests.

It has become apparent that infants are capable from birth, of some degree of visual perception. By observing the length of time that an infant fixates on alternative stimuli presented simultaneously, investigators have been able to determine the aspects of stimuli that infants prefer at different ages. Evidence exists that these preferences develop in a constant pattern. Preschool children's visual perception continues this ordered development and is also measurable by the use of visual-recognition memory-tasks.

Recent reseach has demonstrated that later intelligence can be predicted by infant visual-perception tasks. One such study by Fagan and McGrath (1981) found statistically significant and moderate correlations between infant recognition memory at 4–7 months and scores on the Peabody Picture Vocabulary Test (PPVT) at 4 and 7 years. Fagan (1984b) found a high concurrent correlation among 5-year-olds on recognition memory and the PPVT ($r = .70$). The children in this study had IQs (on the PPVT) ranging from 40 to 136 with a mean of 98.1. It seems clear from the studies cited here, as well as from a good deal of other research (e.g., Lewis, 1982; Miranda, Hack, Fantz, Fanaroff, & Klaus, 1977; Zelazo, 1982), that early visual-recognition memory is related to current and later measures of intelligence.

A number of studies on the early recognition memory of mentally retarded infants and preschoolers have also been reported. Miranda and Fantz (1974) compared two samples of infants, Down syndrome and normal, on their recognition of familiar visual patterns in the first 8 months of life. As predicted, Down syndrome infants showed significantly poorer visual recognition than nonimpaired infants (though Shepherd & Fagan, 1980, found that even profoundly retarded children can exhibit visual recognition memory). Thus, these memory-recognition techniques are useful with all levels of mentally retarded children.

Fagan (1984b) suggested that an instrument can be developed based on infants' visual preferences for novelty, which can be used "in predicting later mental retardation for individual children when applied to groups of infants 'at risk' for later cognitive deficits" (p. 6). He also stated that such an instrument would be useful in indicating the effectiveness of intervention programs. Similarly, Switzky, Woolsey-Hill, and Quoss (1979) found that nonverbal profoundly retarded children show appropriate habituation and dishabituation to visual stimuli. They suggested that information derived from a visual preference assessment can be useful in designing an educational program: "If the child does show the habituation recovery effect, that child can discriminate between the stimulus events and does possess a memorial representation, schemata [sic], or concept of the stimulus events; and the teacher can work on teaching the child other discriminations and concepts" (p. 145).

More research is needed before these measures can be put into general practice. In particular, a detailed standardized instrument must be constructed and researched. Such an instrument is likely to be highly useful in the screening diagnosis, and suggestion of intervention approaches for mentally retarded infants and preschoolers. In the meantime, individual researchers and practitioners may be able to use these techinques in particular settings and circumstances.

PRESCHOOL TESTS

Screening Tests

There are a number of short, relatively easily administered intelligence tests that can be given to children as young as 2 years old. The three to be described here are the Peabody Picture Vocabulary Test (Dunn, 1965), the Slosson Intelligence Test (Slosson, 1963), and the Columbia Mental Maturity Scale (Burgmeister & Blum, 1972). Each of these tests can be administered relatively quickly by professionals other than psychologists and can be used to screen young children for possible cognitive deficits.

The Peabody Picture Vocabulary Test (PPVT), designed for use with those as young as 2½ through adulthood, consists of 150 plates, each with four pictures, presented in their order of difficulty. The person taking the test points to the picture that illustrates the stimulus word presented by the examiner. Two forms of the test, A and B, are available. The same plates are used, but the spoken stimulus and, therefore, the correct response are different for the two forms. Although a mental age and a deviation IQ can be derived from the PPVT, and despite the author's claim that the test measures verbal intelligence, the PPVT is actually a test of recognition vocabulary, which is only one aspect of verbal intelligence.

The PPVT has reasonably good reliability and some predictive validity. However, it was standardized entirely on white children and youth in the Nashville, Tennessee, area. This standardization procedure might account for the findings of Sattler (1974), that minority-group children receive lower IQs on the PPVT than on the Stanford-Binet. Despite the standardization sample and the concern about the test's accuracy with minority children, the PPVT is still usable. Its ease and speed of administration make it a fairly inexpensive and un-time-consuming test whose primary purpose should be its use as a screening device from which children can be selected for a more intensive and broader diagnostic battery. It is particularly useful to screen young children who may be mentally retarded, as they frequently have problems and delays in speech.

The Slosson Intelligence Test (SIT) is a brief test that can be administered relatively easily even by not highly trained examiners. The SIT was developed as a short version of the Stanford-Binet, but it also adapted items from the Gesell schedules for children below 2 years of age. The author does not claim validity for the infant portion (under 2 years) of the test. In addition, because of its language skills emphasis, there is some question about the usefulness of the SIT with children from 2 to 4 who have delayed speech or "whose environments do not include middle class language patterns" (Hunt, 1972, p. 766). In defense of the SIT, correlations of SIT IQs with Stanford-Binet IQs are generally quite high. In addition, one of the more pervasive criticisms of the SIT, its use of ratio IQs, is no longer pertinent, as deviation IQs are now available (Armstong & Jensen, 1981). Considering its ease of administration and its high concurrent validity with the Stanford-Binet, the SIT is recommended as a screening test of intelligence, at least for children aged 4 and above. It should not, however, be considered a replacement for the Binet or Weschler scales (discussed in the next section).

The Columbia Mental Maturity Scale is divided into eight overlapping levels for ages ranging from 3½ to 9 years, 11 months. Each level consists of 51–65 items that ask the child to indicate one of three to five dawings that do not belong with the others. This test is useful with children of limited verbal skills and/or poor fine-motor abilities, as it does not require a verbal response or fine-motor coordination. Thus, this test is useful with mentally retarded children as well as with physically and auditorily impaired children. However, research using the Columbia with mentally retarded persons has not been highly supportive of its use with this population. Riviere (1973) found good reliability of the Columbia but only moderate concurrent validity with the Stanford-Binet on a sample of mentally retarded children. Johnson and Shinedling (1974) also used a sample of mentally retarded children to compare the Solsson, the Peabody, and the Columbia. They concluded that the Slosson and the Peabody were superior to the Columbia. It should be noted, however, that both of these studies used mentally retarded persons well above the chronological ages suggested by the Columbia. Thus, although the Columbia may be useful with mentally retarded children below 10 years of age, further research is needed.

Diagnostic Measures

A large number of intelligence tests have been designed for use with children over 2 years old. Some of these are primarily for use with preschool-age children, but most include age ranges well beyond the preschool years. Most tests of intelligence for children over 2 years old have as their primary goal determining an IQ that can be used to diagnose children who have, or who are likely to have, cognitive deficits. This section describes some of the more commonly used tests and evaluates their relative usefulness.

The Stanford-Binet Intelligence Scale (Terman & Merrill, 1960, 1973) and the Weschler scales are preeminent in the field of intelligence testing. Both are individually administered by a trained psychologist. Whereas Weschler developed three scales for different ages, the Binet is used with persons 2 years old through adulthood. Because of this wide age range, the Binet includes items of widely varying difficulty and scope.

There are six items, each really more like a subtest, at each age level (every half year from 2 to 5 and every year from then on). The Binet is reasonably well related both to future scholastic achievement (predictive validity) and to current performance (concurrent validity). Cronbach (1970) reported a high internal-consistency reliability-coefficient for the Binet.

The Binet is used primarily for diagnosis and classification. However, as it is based on a view of intelligence as a general factor, a view that is rejected by the majority of psychologists today, it has limited utility. Friedes (1972) suggested that the Binet is most useful in filling in the gap between the ceiling of the Bayley scales (30 months) and the beginning of the Wechsler Preschool and Primary Scale of Intelligence (WPPSI) (48 months). For this age range (30–48 months), the Binet is most appropriate for diagnosing young children who may be mentally retarded. Despite its excellent psychometric features, it serves little other significant function.

The WPPSI (Wechsler, 1967) is designed for use with children from 4 to 6½ years. The reason for this relatively small age range is that the WISC-R starts with 6-year-olds, and Wechsler did not believe that a global measure of intelligence was possible for children under 4 (Bayley, 1970). This test includes 11 subtests that are downward extensions or analogous to the Wechsler Intelligence Scale for Children—Revised (WISC-R) subtests. The administration of the WPPSI is also similar to that of the WISC-R. In addition to scale scores for each of the subtests, a verbal IQ, a performance IQ, and a full-scale IQ are ascertained.

Eichorn's review (1972) of the WPPSI details many of the positive and negative traits of the test. She pointed out that many of the psychometric characteristics of the WPPSI, particularly its reliability are quite good. However, the WPPSI provides limited validity data. Eichorn's review of studies on the WPPSI indicates that the mean scores on the WPPSI are lower than those on the Binet for culturally disadvantaged, advantaged, and gifted groups; the two test correlate moderately. In addition, the WPPSI is a better predictor of later academic achievement than the Binet or the Peabody (discussed earlier). The studies cited by Eichorn also "contraindicate pattern analysis of subtest scores" (p. 806). That is, the individual scale scores are not reliable for profiling a person's strengths and weaknesses. However, more recent research (Carlson & Reynolds, 1981; Ramanaiah & Adams, 1979) does support Wechsler's contention that the scales do represent two major factors; verbal and performance. Thus, these two scores can be useful, in addition to the full-scale IQ. It is interesting that, despite her critical review of the WPPSI, Eichorn (1972) concluded by stating, "For the age and ability range covered, the WPPSI is the best standardized and most up-to-date individual test available" (p. 807), although it should be noted that this statement preceded the introduction of the McCarthy scales. In general, it appears that the WPPSI can be used as a diagnostic tool, to identify and classify children with cognitive deficits, to make placement decisions, and to develop long-range educational goals.

Three other comprehensive intelligence tests for preschool-aged and older children are the Detroit Tests of Learning Aptitude (Baker & Leland, 1967), the Hiskey-Nebraska Test of Learning Aptitude (Hiskey, 1966), and the McCarthy Scales of Children's Abilities (McCarthy, 1972). These three tests were selected for consideration here for a variety of reasons: the Detroit is a comprehensive measure with a large number of subtests; the Hiskey-Nebraska can be administered via pantomime instructions and does not require verbal responses; and the McCarthy has been used frequently with mentally retarded children and is frequently cited in the literature.

The Detroit tests consist of 19 tests covering a wide range of content. However, the tests' authors recommend that only 9–13 of the tests be administered to any given child. The selection of tests to be used depends on the child's approximate mental age, ranging from 3 to 19 years. The tests are to be administered individually by a trained diagnostician. An individual's mental age is determined for each test administered, and the median of these mental ages is considered a measure of general ability that can be used to determine a ratio IQ.

The information given in the Detroit's manual regarding its standardization is minimal. In fact, as this test was first published in 1935, it is amazing how few data exist. Test–retest reliability is reasonable, including data from mentally retarded subjects. However, the intercorrelations among 16 of the tests were found to mostly be between .20 and .40. Thus, it is questionable if the Detroit is useful as a measue of general ability. Its usefulness is in the breadth of its tests' contents. The individual-test mental ages permit the examiner and the educator to analyze a profile of strengths and weaknesses. This profile can be helpful in developing short-term and long-range goals for the individual and in program planning.

The Hiskey-Nebraska was developed as a test of learning aptitude for deaf persons between 3 and 17 years of age. It is described here because, in testing young mentally retarded children, a test such as the Hiskey-Nebraska that does not require verbal responses can be very important. This is a performance test that can be administered verbally or entirely through pantomimed gestures. No verbal response is required from the subject. Thus, in addition to its usefulness with deaf children, this test is extremely useful with subjects who have limited speech skills, as do many young mentally retarded children.

The Hiskey-Nebraska consists of 12 subscales, all requiring motor responses. The median of the age levels on each subscale is known as the learning age, which can be converted to a ratio learning quotient. The learning age and the learning quotient are analogous and are nearly identical to the mental age and the intelligence quotient of other tests. Bolton (1978) cited evidence of high correlations between the Hiskey-Nebraska and other IQ tests with various samples, including mentally retarded children. He also stated that there is evidence of "an underlying performance dimension, supporting the use of a total score" (p. 217). There is, however, no evidence supporting the use of the individual subscales for differential diagnosis. Thus, this test is most appropriate for use with mentally retarded children who have speech problems that make the use of the WPPSI, the Binet, or the McCarthy impractical.

The McCarthy scales may not replace the WPPSI and the Binet as the major tests used to identify and classify children as mentally retarded, but it has some featuers that make it a very attractive test for persons working with young retarded children. The test, consisting of 18 subtests grouped into six scales, is designed for use with children between the ages of 2½ and 8½. Three of the six scales—verbal, perceptual-performance, and quantitative—include 15 of the 18 subtests and are combined to determine the fourth scale, known as the general cognitive index (GCI), a score analogus to an IQ. The motor scale combines the remaining three subtests with two already used, and the memory scale is derived from four subtests used in determining the GCI. Hunt (1978) and Sattler (1978) have both indicated that the psychometric qualities of the test and its standardization are quite good. The GCI is a highly reliable and valid measure. It correlates well with Binet, WPPSI, and achievement scores. The other five scales are not as reliable but can be useful in diagnosing the relative strengths and weaknesses of an individual.

As is necessary with the MDI of the Bayley scales, it is necessary to extrapolate to get GCI scores below 50 (Harrison & Naglieri, 1978). Recent reseach has indicated that with mentally retarded subjects, although scores on the McCarthy GCI correlate significantly with Stanford-Binet IQs, the mean GCI is significantly lower than the IQ. Levenson and Zino (1979a,b) found a mean Binet IQ of 64.46 and a mean McCarthy GCI of 44.26 with 15 retarded children. These findings are very similar to those of Naglieri and Harrison (1979), who found a mean IQ of 64.0 and a mean GCI of 45.8 with their 15 retarded subjects. Thus, it appears that the McCarthy GCI may underestimate Binet IQ, particularly of retarded children. Conversely, it is also possible that the Binet overestimates IQ in this population. However, the Stanford-Binet and the WPPSI are still considered the standards when classification and placement decisions are involved, whereas the McCarthy scales' primary utility is in providing information regarding an individual's strengths and weaknesses. This information can be useful in long-range planning and, possibly, in establishing short-term goals for individuals.

Program Planning

A number of behavioral approaches that include cognitive sections or items were discussed in the section for infants. These methods are also useful with preschool mentally retarded children and could also have been presented in this section. One other method of evaluating the psychoeducational competence of preschool children is discussed in this section. Else Haeussermann (1958) became interested in assessing the educational abilities of cerebral-palsied children between the two world wars. After World War II, she began to organize and formalize the test items that she had developed earlier. Her book *Developmental Potential of Preschool Children* (1958) has long been useful in developing educational programs for the motorically handicapped. So the publication of a manual for the "Haeussermann approach" (Jedrysek, Klapper, Pope, & Wortis, 1972), which can be used with all preschool-aged children in combination with her earlier text, was quite welcome,

The Haeussermann approach, as detailed in the two publications mentioned above, is a "systematic method for determining the psychoeducational standing of each child in a preschool program. With this kind of psychoeducational assessment at hand, the teacher-evaluator can set his or her immediate training goals and develop the appropriate curriculum for the individual child" (Jedrysek *et al.*, 1972, p. 1). This instrument includes five areas of functioning considered important for learning (physical functioning and sensory status, perceptual functioning, competence in learning for short-term retention, language competence, and cognitive functioning). The instrument consists of 41 main test items, in the presumed order of difficulty, many of which are followed by additional probes. The test is not standardized, and no reliability or validity data are provided. It is still a useful instrument.

The primary purpose and function of the Haeussermann approach are to assist in the development of an individual educational program for preschoolchildren. As Jedrysek *et al.* (1972) stated, "the educational diagnosis deriving from the child's performance [in the Haeussermann approach] should at the same time serve as an individualized curriculum guide or teaching plan for that child" (p. 3). When a child has difficulty with a main test item, probes are used to determine what aspect(s) of the item is causing the difficulty. For example, if a child has difficulty naming colors, a series of probes follow that are aimed at determining possible reasons for the difficulty, including such things as too many items are presented at once (reduce the number), naming (ask the child to point to the named color), or the objects lack meaning (use more meaningful objects, such as socks). The purpose is to determine the child's strengths and weaknesses, that is, what he or she knows or doesn't know. This process results in knowledge about what the child should be taught and the best method of teaching it. Thus, despite its lack of psychometric credentials, the Haeussermann approach can be a useful tool for teachers.

CONCLUSIONS

I have attempted, in this chapter, to review the major cognitive assessment procedures that are used with, and/or that are appropriate for, mentally retarded infants and preschoolers. The results of this review indicate that some assessments are most useful as screening devices (e.g., the Denver Developmental Screening Test, the Kent Infant Development Scale, the Peabody Picture Vocabulary Test and the Slosson Intelligence Test); other assessments are most useful as diagnostic or placement instruments and in describing a person's present status in terms of the severity of the problem (e.g., the Bayley Scales of Infant Development, the Stanford-Binet, and the Wechsler Preschool and Primary Scale of Intelligence). Finally, other assessments are most useful in program development and planning for individual mentally retarded infants and preschoolers (e.g., behaviorally based criterion-referenced measures, the Detroit Tests of Learning Aptitude, the Gesell Developmental Schedules, Haeussermann's approach, the McCarthy Scales of Children's Abilities, and Uzgiris and Hunt's Piagetian-based scales of sensorimotor period functioning).

Although the uses of the instruments do overlap somewhat (e.g., the Bayley scales can be useful for program planning as well as diagnosis), this division of the various assessment devices into these categories is worthwhile. It is important to be aware of which instrument is most useful for a particular purpose or situation. In addition, except for instances when a screening test excludes a person from further consideration as mentally retarded, a number of tests would normally be administered. The selection of an appropriate battery should be based on having the tests that are most useful for assisting in both diagnosis (including placement and severity determinations) and the designing of the individual's educational program. The child's chronological and mental ages, as well as other pertinent factors such as additional disabilities (e.g., speech delay may indicate use of the Hiskey-Nebraska Test of Learning Aptitude) or home environment (see Chapter 16 by Wachs), are also used to select the appropriate battery of tests. This chapter has attempted to point out a few tests that are useful, for each purpose, with children of different ages and in different circumstances.

Finally, this chapter has included a brief discussion of the use of visual-discrimination and early-recognition memory as an early predictor and indicator of intelligence. As was noted, these procedures are still experimental. However, I expect to see them in general use by the mid-1990s. Their uses will include diagnostic–placement–severity decisions and, hopefully, educational programming. Ultimately, this will depend on the creativeness of psychologists and educators in finding the appropriate uses. Researchers in this field have, however, given us reason to be very hopeful that these procedures will lead to more valid diagnostic decisions and to better educational approaches.

ACKNOWLEDGMENTS

The author thanks Chris Pellikan for his research assistance and Penny Witte for her patience in typing the manuscript.

REFERENCES

Armstrong, R. J., & Jensen J. A., (1981). *Slosson intelligence test: 1981 norms tables application and development*. East Aurora, NY: Slosson Educational Publications.

Bagnato, S. J. (1981). Developmental scales and developmental curricula: Forging a linkage for early intervention. *Topics in Early Childhood Special Education, 1*, 1-8.

Baker, H. J., & Leland, B. (1967) *Detroit tests of learning aptitude*. Indianapolis: Bobbs-Merrill.

Bayley, N. (1933). Mental growth during the first three years. *Genetic Psychology Monographs, 14*, 1–92.

Bayley, N. (1969). *Bayley scales of infant development*. New York: Psychological Corporation.

Bayley, N. (1970). Development of mental abilities. In P. H. Mussen (Ed.), *Carmichael's manual of child psychology (3rd ed.)*. New York: Wiley.

BCP Observation Booklet. (1973). Palo Alto, CA: VORT Corporation.

Bolton; B. F., (1973). Review of the Hiskey-Nebraska test of learning aptitude. In O. K. Buros (Ed.), *The eighth mental measurements yearbook*. Highland Park, NJ: Gryphon Press.

Brassell, W. R., & Dunst, C. J. (1976). Fostering the object construct: Large-scale intervention with handicapped infants. *American Journal of Mental Deficiency, 82*, 507–510.

Burgmeister, B., & Blum, L. (1972). *The Columbia mental maturity scale: 1972 revision*. New York: Psychological Corporation.

Carlson, L., & Reynolds, C. R. (1981). Factor structure and specific variance of the WPPSI subtests at six age levels. *Psychology in the Schools, 18*, 48–54.

Casati, I., & Lezine, I. (1968). *Les étapes de l'intelligence sensorimortice*. Paris: Les Éditionds du Centre de Psychologie Appliquée.

Cattell, P. (1940, 1960). *The measurement of intelligence of infants and young children*. New York: Psychological Corporation.

Cronbach, L. J. (1970). *Essentials of psychological testing (3rd ed.)*. New York: Harper & Row.

Decarie, Th. G. (1965). *Intelligence and affectivity in early childhood*. New York: International Universities Press.

Decarie, Th. G. (1972). *La réaction du jeune enfant à la personne étrangère*. Montreal: Les Presses de l'Université de Montreal.

Dunn, L. M. (1965). *Peabody Picture Vocabulary Test: Manual*. Circle Pines, MN: American Guidance Service.

Eichorn, D. H. (1972). Review of the Weschler preschool and primary scale of intelligence. In O. K. Buros (Ed.). *The seventh mental measurement yearbook*. Highland Park, NJ: Gryphon Press, 806–807.

Erickson, M. T., Johnson, N. M., & Campbell, F. A. (1970). Relationships among scores on infant tests for children with developmental problems. *American Journal of Mental Deficiency, 75*, 102–104.

Escalona, S., & Corman, H. (no date). *Albert Einstein Scales of Sensorimotor Development*. Unpublished manuscript, Department of Psychiatry, Albert Einstein College of Medicine, New York.

Fagan, J. F. (1984a). The intelligent infant: Theoretical implications. *Intelligence, 8*, 1–9.

Fagan, J. F. (1984b). Recognition memory and intelligence. *Intelligence, 8,* 31–36.

Fagan, J. F., & McGrath, S. K. (1981). Infant recognition memory and later intelligence. *Intelligence, 5,* 121–130.

Fagan, J. F., & Shepherd, P. A. (1982). Theoretical issues in the early development of visual perception. In M. Lewis & L. T. Taft (Eds.), *Developmental disabilities: Theory, assessment, and intervention.* New York: SP Medical & Scientific Books.

Frankenburg, W. K., & Dodds, J. B. (1979). *Denver developmental screening test.* Denver: LADOCA Foundation.

Friedes, D. (1972). Review of the Stanford-Binet. In O. K. Buros (Ed.), *The seventh mental measurement yearbook.* Highland Park, NJ: Gryphon Press.

Gesell, A. (1925). *The mental growth of the preschool child.* New York: Macmillan.

Gesell, A. (1940). *The first five years of life.* New York: Harper.

Gesell, A., & Amatruda, C. S. (1947). *Developmental diagnosis* (2nd ed.). New York: Hoeber.

Gesell, A., & Thompson, H. (1938). *The psychology of early growth.* New York: Macmillan.

Gradel, K., Thompson, M. S., & Sheehan, R. (1981). Parental and professional agreement in early childhood assessment. *Topics in Early Childhood Special Education; 1,* 31–39.

Haeussermann, E. (1958). *Developmental potential of preschool children.* New York: Grune & Stratton.

Harrison, P. L., & Naglieri, J. A. (1978). Extrapolated general cognitive indexes on the McCarthy scales for gifted and mentally retarded children. *Psychological Reports, 43,* 1291–1296.

Haskin, J., & Bell, J. (1978). Profound developmental retardation: Descriptive and theoretical utility of the Bayley mental scale. In C. E. Meyers (Ed.), *Quality of life in severely and profoundly mentally retarded people: Research foundations for improvement.* Washington, DC: American Association on Mental Deficiency.

Haskins, R., Ramey, C. T., Stedman, D. J., Blacher-Dixon, J., & Pierce, J. E. (1978). Effects of repeated assessment on standardized test performance by infants. *American Journal of Mental Deficiency, 83,* 233–239.

Henry, J. C. (1977). *The effect of parent assessment and parent training of preschool mentally retarded children on Piagetian tasks of object permanence and imitation.* Unpublished dissertation, Temple University, Philadelphia.

Hiskey, M. S. (1966). *Hiskey-Nebraska test of learning aptitude.* Lincoln: The Hiskey-Nebraska Test.

Horner, T. M. (1980). Test-retest and home-clinic characteristics of the Bayley scales of infant development in nine- and fifteen-month old infants. *Child Development, 51,* 751–758.

Hunt, J. V. (1972). Review of the Slosson intelligence test. In O. K. Buros (Ed.), *The seventh mental measurement yearbook.* Highland Park, NJ: Gryphon Press.

Hunt, J. V. (1975). Review of the Denver developmental screening test. In W. K. Frankenburg & B. W. Camp (Eds.), *Pediatric screening test.* Springfield, IL: Charles C Thomas.

Hunt, J. V. (1978). Review of the McCarthy scales of children's abilities. In O. K. Buros (Ed.), *The eighth mental measurement yearbook.* Highland Park, NJ: Gryphon Press.

Hunt, J. V., & Bayley, N. (1971). Explorations into patterns of mental development and prediction from the Bayley Scales of Infant Development. In J. P., Hill (Ed.), *Minnesota Symposia on Child Psychology* (Vol. 5). Minneapolis: University of Minnesota Press.

Ireton, H., Thwing, E., & Gravem, H. (1970). Infant mental development and neurological status, family socioeconomic status, and intelligence at age four. *Child Development, 41,* 937, 946.

Jedrysek, E., Klapper, Z., Pope, L. & Wortis, J. (1972). *Psychoeducational evaluation of the preschool child: A manual for utilizing the Haeussermann approach.* New York: Grune & Stratton.

Johnson, D. L., & Shinedling, M. M. (1974). Comparison of Columbia mental maturity scale, Peabody picture vocabulary test, and Slosson intelligence test with mentally retarded children. *Psychological Reports, 34,* 367–370.

Kahn, J. V. (1975). Relationship of Piaget's sensorimotor period to language acquisition of profoundly retarded children. *American Journal of Mental Deficiency, 79,* 640–643.

Kahn, J. V. (1976). Utility of the Uzgiris and Hunt scales of sensorimotor development with severely and profoundly retarded children. *American Journal of Mental Deficiency, 80,* 663–664.

Kahn, J. V. (1978). Acceleration of object permanence with severely and profoundly retarded children. *AAESPH Review, 3,* 15–22.

Kahn, J. V. (1983). Sensorimotor period and adaptive behavior development of severely and profoundly retarded children. *American Journal of Mental Deficiency, 88,* 69–75.

Kahn, J. V. (1984). Cognitive training and its relationship to the language of profoundly retarded children. In J. M. Berg (Ed.), *Perspectives and progress in mental retardation*. Baltimore: University Park Press.

Kahn, J. V. (1987). Uses of the scales of psychological development with mentally retarded populations. In I. C. Uzgiris & J. McV. Hunt (Eds.), *Infant performance and experience: New findings with the ordinal scales*. Champaign: University of Illinois Press.

Karlan, G. R. (1980). The effects of preference for objects and repeated measures upon the assessed level of object permanence and means/end ability in severely handicapped students. *Journal of the Association for the Severely Handicapped, 5,* 174–193.

Katoff, L., Reuter, J., & Dunn, V. (1980). *The Kent infant development scale manual*. Kent, OH: Kent State University.

Knobloch, H., & Pasamanick, B. (1963). Predicting intellectual potential in infancy: Some variables affecting the validity of developmental diagnosis. *American Journal of Diseases of Children, 106,* 43–51.

Knobloch, H., & Pasamanick, B. (1967). Prediction from the assessment of neuromotor and intellectual status in infancy. In J. Zubin & G. A. Jervis (Eds.), *Psychopathology of mental development*. New York: Grune & Stratton.

Knobloch, H., & Pasamanick, B. (1974). *Gesell and Amatruda's developmental diagnosis* (3rd rev.). New York: Harper & Row.

Knobloch, H., Pasamanick, B., & Sheard, E. I. (1966). A developmental screening inventory for infants. *Pediatrics, 38,* 1095–1109.

Lasky, R. E., Tyson, J. E., Rosenfeld, C. R., Priest, M., Krasinski, D., Heartwell, S., & Gant, N. F. (1983). Principal component analysis of the Bayley Scales of Infant Development for a sample of high-risk infants and their controls. *Merrill-Palmer Quarterly, 29,* 25–31.

Levenson, R. L., & Zino, T. C. (1979a). Assessment of cognitive deficiency with the McCarthy scales and Stanford-Binet: A correlation analysis. *Perceptual and Motor Skills, 48,* 291–295.

Levenson, R. L., & Zino, T. C. (1979b). Using McCarthy scales extrapolated general cognitive indexes below 50: Some words of caution. *Psychological Reports, 45,* 350.

Lewis, M. (1982). Attention as a measure of cognitive integrity. In M. Lewis & L. T. Taft (Eds.), *Developmental disabilities: Theory, assessment, and intervention*. New York: SP Medical & Scientific Books.

Mahoney, G., Glover, A., & Finger, I. (1981). Relationship between language and sensorimotor development of Down syndrome and nonretarded children. *American Journal of Mental Deficiency, 86,* 21–27.

McCall, R. B. (1982). A conceptual approach to early mental development. In M. Lewis (Ed.), *Origins of intelligence* (2nd ed.) New Yok: Plenum Press.

McCall, R. B., Hogarty, P. S., & Hurlburt, N. (1972). Transition in infant sensorimotor development and the predictor of childhood IQ. *American Psychologist, 27,* 728–748.

McCarthy, D. (1972). *Manual for the McCarthy scales of children's abilities*. New York: Psychological Corporation.

Miranda, S., & Fantz, R. (1974). Recognition memory in Down's syndrome and normal infants. *Child Development, 45,* 651–660.

Miranda, S., Hack, M., Fantz, R., Fanaroff, A., & Klaus, M. (1977). Neonatal pattern vision: A predictor of future mental performance? *Pediatrics, 91,* 642–647.

Moriarity, A. E. (1972). Review of the Denver developmental screening test. In O. K. Buros (Ed.), *The seventh mental measurement yearbook*. Highland Park, NJ: Gryphon, Press.

Mundy, P., Seibert, J. M., & Hogan, A. E. (1984). Relationship between sensorimotor and early communication abilities in developmentally delayed children. *Merrill-Palmer Quarterly, 30,* 33–48.

Naglieri, J. A. (1981). Extrapolated developmental indices for the Bayley Scales of Infant Development. *American Journal of Mental Deficiency, 85,* 548–550.

Naglieri, J. A., & Harrison, P. L. (1979). Comparison of McCarthy general cognitive indexes and Stanford-Binet IQs for educable mentally retarded children. *Perceptual and Motor Skills, 48,* 1251–1254.

Popovich, D. (1977). *A prescriptive behavioral checklist for the severely and profoundly retarded*. Baltimore: University Park Press.

Ramanaiah, N. V., & Adams, M. L. (1979). Confirmatory factor analysis of the WAIS and the WPPSI. *Psychological Reports, 45,* 351–355.

Ramey, C. T., Brownlee, J. R. (1981). Improving the identification of high-risk infants. *American Journal of Mental Deficiency, 85,* 504–511.

Ramey, C. T., & Haskins, R. (1981). The modification of intelligence through early experience. *Intelligence, 5,* 5–19.

Ramey, C. T., & Smith, B. J. (1976). Assessing the intellectual consequences of early intervention with high-risk infants. *American Journal of Mental Deficiency, 81,* 318–324.

Riviere, M. S. (1973). The use of the Columbia mental maturity scale with institutionalized mentally retarded children. *Educational and Psychological Measurement, 33,* 993–995.

Sattler, J. M. (1974). *Assessment of children's intelligence.* Philadelphia: Saunders.

Sattler, J. M. (1978). Review of the McCarthy scales of children's abilities. In O. K. Buros (Ed.), *The eighth mental measurements yearbook.* Highland Park, NJ: Gryphon Press.

Shepherd, P. A., & Fagan, J. F. (1980, March). *Visual recognition memory in the profoundly retarded child.* Paper presented at the Gatlinburg Conference on Research in Mental Retardation, Gatlinburg, TN.

Slosson, R. L. (1963). *Slosson intelligence test for children and adults.* East Aurora, NY: Slosson Educational Publications.

Stancin, T., Reuter, J., Dunn, V., & Bickett, L. (1984). Validity of caregiver information on the developmental status of severely brain-damaged young children. *American Journal of Mental Deficiency, 88,* 388–395.

Switzky, H. N., Woolsey-Hill, J., & Quoss, T. (1979). Habituation of visual fixation responses. *AAESPH Review, 4,* 136–147.

Terman, L. M., & Merrill, M. A. (1960). *Measuring intelligence.* Boston: Houghton Mifflin.

Terman, L. M., & Merrill, M. A. (1973). *Stanford-Binet intelligence scale: 1972 norms edition.* Boston: Houghton Mifflin.

Thurstone, L., & Thurstone, T. (1954). *SRA primary mental abilities* (elementary form) (rev. ed.). Chicago: Science Research Associates.

Uzgiris, I. C., & Hunt, J McV. (1966). *An instrument for assessing infant psychological development.* Unpublished manuscript, University of Illinois, Urbana.

Uzgiris, I. C., & Hunt, J. McV. (1972). *Toward ordinal scales of infant psychological development.* Unpublished manuscript, University of Illinois, Urbana.

Uzgiris, I. C., & Hunt, J McV. (1975). *Assessment in infancy.* Urbana: University of Illinois Press.

Uzgiris, I. C., & Hunt, J. McV. (Eds.) (1987). *Infant performance and experience: New findings with the ordinal scales.* Urbana: University of Illinois Press.

VanderVeer, B., & Schweid, E. (1974). Infant assessment: Stability of mental functioning in young retarded children. *American Journal of Mental Deficiency, 79,* 1–4.

Wabash Center for the Mentally Retarded. (1977). *Guide to early developmental training.* Boston: Allyn & Bacon.

Wachs, T. D., & DeRemer, P. (1978). Adaptive behavior and Uzgiris-Hunt scale performance of young developmentally disabled children. *American Journal of Mental Deficiency, 83,* 171–176.

Wechsler, D. (1967). *Wechsler preschool and primary scale of intelligence: Manual.* New York: Psychological Corporation.

Werner, E. E., Honzik,, M. P., & Smith, R. S. (1968). Prediction of intelligence and achievement at 10 years from 20 months pediatric and psychologic examinations. *Child Development, 39,* 1063–1075.

Yang, R. K. (1979). Early infant assessment: An overview. In J. D. Osofsky (Ed.), *Handbook of infant development.* New York: Wiley.

Zelazo, P. R. (1982). An information processing approach to infant cognitive assessment. In M. Lewis & L. T. Taft (Eds.), *Developmental disabilities: Theory, assessment, and intervention.* New York: SP Medical & Scientific Books.

10

Cognitive Assessment of Infants and Preschoolers with Severe Behavioral Disabilities

Sydney S. Zentall

The area of behavioral disabilities is broad because of the range of disorders that have been identified. Therefore, differentiating among these disorders and identifying disordered children as being different from normals require a more extensive description of characteristics than would be necessary in other disability areas. The characteristics reviewed in this chapter include cognitive abilities as well as those related to cognitive and behavioral style. It is these latter characteristics that provide a basis for the identification of disordered children and of target behavior, whereas cognitive ability assessment provides some indication of prognosis and the framework for instructional programming.

School-aged children are labeled seriously disordered by the provisions of Public Law 94-142 (*Federal Register*, 1977, p. 42478). However, the definition in this law is not suitable for infants and young children who have not yet demonstrated the adverse effects of behavioral disorder on their educational progress. A definition has been selected that is more appropriately ecological in orientation for young behaviorally disordered (BD) children: "Behavioral disabilities are defined as a variety of excessive, chronic, deviant behaviors ranging from impulsive and aggressive acts to depression and withdrawal acts: (a) which violate the perceiver's expectations of appropriateness, and (b) which the perceiver wishes to see stopped" (Graubard, 1973, p. 246). Although this definition is not specific enough to be diagnostic, it can be used to identify disordered child behavior through an examination of the social consequences of that behavior.

The most widely accepted diagnostic nomenclature is found in the American Psychiatric Association's Diagnostic and Statistical Manual of Mental Disorders (DSM). In 1980, this manual was revised to become the DSM-III, which includes the following diagnostic categories: attention disorder with and without hyperactivity, conduct disorders, anxiety disorders, eating disorders, disorders with physical manifestations such as enuresis, pervasive developmental disorders such as infantile autism, and other disorders of infancy or childhood such as elective mutism.

The classification system proposed by the DSM-III does provide objective criteria as guidelines for making diagnostic decisions; yet categorization systems of this type also

SYDNEY S. ZENTALL ● Department of Special Education, Purdue University, West Lafayette, Indiana 47907.

give the impression that behavior-disordered children are qualitatively different from normal children. Many of us (e.g., Davison & Neale, 1974; Zentall, 1979) would argue that there is a continuum between normal and abnormal behavior. This continuum is reflected by Achenbach and Edelbrock (1978), who classified behavior-disordered children as either "overcontrolled" or "undercontrolled" (see Chapter 1 of this book). Achenbach and Edelbrock's approach differs from the designation of qualitatively different types of disordered behavior, as seen in the DSM-III, in that it is a dimensional approach that is statistically derived from behavioral covariation. Specifically, multivariate procedures employing factor and cluster analyses were used to identify two broad patterns of childhood disorder, labeled *undercontrolled* (e.g., hyperactive, aggressive, and conduct disorders) and *overcontrolled* (e.g., withdrawn, schizoid, anxious, and depressed). These two deviate patterns are relatively stable across time and rater (Achenbach & Edelbrock, 1978); at middle ranges between these patterns of inhibition and exhibition are "normal" individual differences, often attributed to differences in temperament.

Exemplary of the overcontrolled pattern of behavior is autism, which has been selected for cognitive assessment analysis in this chapter. Autistic children display a more pervasive and extreme form of disorder than the associated milder disorders of withdrawal, anxious, or phobic reactions. Similarly, an examination of hyperactivity, as an example of the undercontrolled pattern of behavior, provides a framework in which to understand the related disorders of conduct disorders, aggression, and impulsivity. Each disorder, in turn, will be defined by typical procedures of identification, and will be further differentiated from normal behavior and other related disorders on the basis of cognitive abilities and cognitive and behavioral style.

ASSESSMENT OF COGNITIVE ABILITIES

Ability Differences in Autism

In a review of studies examining the characteristic behavior of infantile or childhood autism, in which onset of the symptoms occurred before 30 months of age, Rutter (1978) concluded that three broad groupings of symptoms were found in most autistic children. The symptom clusters that differentiate autistic children from other populations are (a) failure to develop social relationships (failure to bond with parents, to form other human attachments, or to imitate interactions); (b) language disorder (delayed and deviant patterns of development); and (c) an insistence on sameness (ritualistic or compulsive play patterns, repetitive acts or stereotypies, and resistance to change in the immediate environment). Rutter's criteria closely resemble the DSM-III criteria and best summarize current empirical knowledge about differentiating symptomatology (Newsom & Rincover, 1982). Autistic children share many behaviors with other categories of disorders in children, such as mental retardation, childhood schizophrenia, deafness, and aphasia. However, mentally retarded children, nonpsychotic deaf children, and aphasic children demonstrate more appropriate social behavior, and deaf and aphasic children use more communicative gesturing than autistic children (Newsom & Rincover, 1982).

The Diagnostic Checklist (DCL) for Disturbed Children (Form E-2) (Rimland, 1971), based on Kanner's original definition of autism (1943), has been demonstrated to differentiate autistic children from other psychotic groups (Davids, 1975; DeMyer, Churchill, Pontius, & Gilkey, 1971; Douglas & Sanders, 1968). The DCL is a parent checklist of the behavior and experiences of a child from birth to 5 years, designed to provide detailed information on a child's language and motor development. It yields considerable agreement with Kanner's diagnosis (Rimland, 1971), and with the results of a biochemical study of high blood levels of serotonin, a neurotransmitter (Boullin, Coleman, O'Brien, & Rimland, 1971).

Other checklists have also been developed to identify autistic children. A relatively new instrument for the identification of autism is the Autism Screening Instrument for Educational Planning (ASIEP). It includes the Autism Behavior Checklist (ABC)— (Krug, Arick, & Almond, 1980). The ABC incorporates behavioral characteristics taken from other checklists grouped into symptom areas. Preliminary findings indicate that the ABC is successful in diagnosing autism.

Although a number of behavioral symptoms are useful in the diagnosis of autism, there is some speculation in the field that it is the cognitive deficits that are primary in the pathogenesis of the disorder.

Cognitive Abilities

Cognition, as defined by Neisser (1967), includes all the processes by which sensory input is transformed, reduced, elaborated, stored, recovered, and used. These processes have been delineated below as perception, memory, and reasoning. Additional differences between autistic and comparison children in motor and language functioning are also described.

Perceptual-Memory Differences. A perceptual-memory explanation for the occurrence of autistic behavior (Ornitz, 1974) has been derived from such characteristics as fascination with and abnormal responding to sensory stimuli (see Koegel & Egel, 1979). According to this view, withdrawal from social and nonsocial stimulation is due to the child's difficulty in forming stable perceptual models of events (i.e., the world is continuously experienced as novel).

DeMyer (1976) reported that the perceptual-motor skills of most autistic children are retarded, but that they can be enhanced when the stimuli remain visible at all times. Prior (1979), in her review, similarly reported that perceptual discrimination is aided by haptic cues for autistic children. Thus, there is some indication that the perceptual problems of autistic children reflect developmental differences that can be reduced by means of concrete visual stimuli. In addition to delayed perceptual-motor abilities, other differences in processing have been reported. For instance, autistic children demonstrate a preference for processing information spatially rather than temporally. Evidence reported by Shah and Frith (1983) indicates that autistic children performed better than normals matched on chronological age (CA) and retarded comparison children matched on mental age (MA) on the Children's Embedded Figures Test (CEFT). On this test of spatial abilities and attention to detail, autistic children performed at CA level or above.

Memory abilities also appear to be relatively intact for autistic children–with some indication that their memory for auditory stimuli is better than their memory for visual stimuli (Prior, 1979). Some autistic children are able to memorize large numbers of simple facts and details, even though their understanding of the relationships among those stimuli may be impoverished. When autistic children are presented with a number of items to be recalled that exceeds their visual memory span, they fail because they do not extract a rule by noting redundancies or similarities that would allow the reduction of the information load (Wing, 1976). In testing contexts, this is demonstrated by the fact that autistic children do not offer answers approximate to those that cannot be recalled from memory storage. Instead of using approximations or feature extraction, they rely on rote memory. Reliance on rote memory was further indicated by Hermelin and O'Connor (1970), who reported that autistic children were equally able to recall anomalous ungrammatical sentences and meaningful grammatical sentences. In contrast, retarded and normal children were always able to do better in the recall of meaningful visual and auditory information. Research reviewed by Prior (1979), however, suggests that these differences may be interpretable in developmental terms. That is, lower functioning autistic children were less effective in using semantic or syntactic cues in the recall of sentences; high-functioning autistic children did not differ from controls.

Because of ''splinter'' skills in memory ability, the term *idiot savant* has been used to describe some of these children. However, we would not expect autistic children to perform better overall than mental-age controls on memory tasks, because these special memory abilities, when they occur, are due to an extremely narrow focus of attention and compulsive activity in areas of interest (see Prior, 1979).

Motor Differences. Autistic children demonstrate some motor delay. DeMyer (1976) reported that retarded autistic children performed more poorly than comparison groups of retarded children on most motor tasks, with the exception of tasks involving the lower limbs (e.g., stair climbing, running, skipping, jumping, and hopping). Retarded autistic children also performed worse in imitating body movements and playing ball than retarded nonautistic children.

Cognitive-Reasoning Differences. An alternate but related view of autism is that autistic children perceive and recall the elements of their environment accurately. However, they experience their interactions as unrelated and meaningless and thus respond with irrelevant repetitive behavior (Schopler, 1965). Similarly, Rutter and Bartak (1971) proposed that cognitive deficit is the primary disorder, and that social, language, and behavior differences appear as consequences of this deficit. According to this view, organisms may repeat experiences that are not understood and may selectively attend to simple nonsocial stimuli in the absence of the ability to cognitively integrate complex stimuli. Thus, repetitive noncommunicative verbal behavior (i.e., echolalia) and nonfunctional motor behavioral (e.g., spinning a toy) reflect poor comprehension of verbal or nonverbal symbols.

Whether repetitive behavior does, in fact, indicate poor comprehension will be addressed in a subsequent section. At this point, it is sufficient to indicate that a majority of autistic children are retarded and that cognitive assessment is important.

Language Differences. One of the three broad symptoms of autism is language dysfunction. For this reason, it has also been hypothesized that some of the defining characteristics of autism, such as social aloofness and insistence on sameness, may be secondary to a more basic deviance in language development (Rutter, 1968). Those autistic children who are not mute (i.e., 50%; Rutter, 1978) have speech that typically is not spontaneous, that tends to be repetitive (i.e., immediate or delayed echolalia), and that generally does not function to communicate with or to contact the environment. Words are learned passively or in an operant fashion and are not stored or related to other experience.

The developmental pattern and usage of language by autistic children differ from those of normal children. Whereas normal infants develop babbling that approximates the tonal and rhythm qualities of speech, autistic children often do not. They also lack pre-language skills (imitative play such as waving) and inner language (e.g., the appropriate fantasy use of toys). This is seen specifically in their extremely poor ability on the manual expression subtest of the Illinois Test of Psycholinguistic Abilities (ITPA), which requires the child to demonstrate the use of familiar objects such as a toothbrush (Prior, 1979).

Bartak, Rutter, and Cox (1977) compared autistic boys with receptive dysphasic children and concluded that the autistic boys demonstrated not only a delayed but a deviant use of both language and gesture. Deviant patterns were indicated by quantitatively less spontaneous language produced by the autistic children than by the dysphasics and by repetitive speech, a lack of reciprocity in the use of language, and by lack of responsivity to verbal stimuli. There is some indication, however, that autistic adolescents outgrow much of the echolalia (Rutter, Greenfield, & Lockyer, 1967). In summary, the phonological and syntactical development of autistic children is delayed but essentially normal in form, whereas the pragmatic or social use of speech in context is deviant (Fein, Humes, Kaplan, Lucci, & Waterhouse, 1984).

Ability Differences in Hyperactivity

Primary characteristics of hyperactivity are excessive activity and impulsivity, as well as an inability to sustain attention on an activity or task. These broad symptom classes are represented in the DSM-III classification system, subsuming hyperactivity within the category of "Attention Deficit Disorder with Hyperactivity" (ADD-H).

A clinical description of hyperactive infants up through the preschool years, reported by Ross and Ross (1982, pp. 28–38), indicates that these infants are typically active, restless, difficult to feed and settle down to sleep, and, in just one word, *difficult*. In the preschool years, they still appear more active but are now more talkative, more prone to accidents, and less compliant than normal children. They are seen as aggressive and inattentive, often evoking negative reactions from preschool teachers and peers.

The diagnosis of hyperactivity has been operationalized through teacher rating scales (e.g., the Abbreviated Teacher Questionnaire, or ATQ–Conners, 1973; Rating Scales for Hyperkinesis—Davids, 1971). These scales are reliable across raters who have had equivalent exposure to the same child in similar contexts (Zentall & Barack, 1979). Teacher ratings of 3- to 7-year-old children show substantial predictive validity (Zentall, Gohs, & Culatta, 1983). Hyperactive youngsters identified by rating scales were significantly more active and talkative, as assessed by objective measures, than were comparison children during the performance of a task requiring response delay (behavioral inhibition). To diagnose ADD-H, clinicians and researchers are using additional scales derived specifically from the DSM-III criteria (e.g., the SNAP checklist—Pelham &

Bender, 1982). However, there is some evidence of a 92% overlap between judgments on the more comprehensive ADD-H–rated criteria (e.g., the SNAP) and the hyperactivity rating scales, which includes only one or two items on attentional and impulsivity problems (i.e., the ATQ) (Pelham & Bender, 1982, p. 370).

Like, autism, which is typically accompanied by mental retardation, hyperactivity also overlaps with other childhood disorders (i.e., most frequently with learning disabilities). Possibly for this reason, a theory of hyperactivity based on cognitive ability differences has also been proposed.

Cognitive Abilities

A cognitive-deficit theory attributes hyperactivity to antecedent learning difficulties and failure experiences, which cause the affected children to avoid continued exposure to failure contexts through the use of inattentive, impulsive, and active responses (Cunningham & Barkley, 1978b). Evidence for this position is based on the 70%–80% of hyperactive children who have at least one specific learning disability (Safer & Allen, 1976, p. 11), and to the fact that 70% of even those hyperactive children who remain in regular classes fail at least one grade level by age 12 (Minde, Lewin, Weiss, Lavigueur, Douglas, & Sykes, 1971). Furthermore, learning problems have been observed to correlate with activity problems. For example, hyperactive children responded initially with higher rates of activity in the presence of visually complex stimuli than did normal comparison samples (Zentall, Zentall, & Booth, 1978b). Similarly, differences between groups in activity or distractibility were reduced by practice on difficult perceptual-memory tasks (Conners, 1975; Zentall et al., 1978b), or by easy task requirements (e.g., art tasks, Zentall & Leib, 1985). The validity of this position is further suggested by the range of cognitive disabilities that these children present, as described below.

Perceptual-Memory Differences. Hyperactive children have been reported to consistently perform worse than equivalent-IQ normal children on a variety of perceptual-motor tasks (e.g., the Goodenough Harris Draw-a-Person Test and the Berry Visual-Motor Integration Test) (Douglas, 1972, p. 263; Zentall, Zentall, & Barack, 1978a). According to a review by Safer and Allen (1976, p. 18), 75% of hyperactive children score one year or below on the Bender, whereas only 20%–40% of nonhyperactive children do this poorly. In contrast, on other individually administered tests of such different abilities as auditory discrimination and short-term memory, hyperactive children as a group performed equivalently to normal children (Douglas, 1972). There is some evidence, however, that the free recall of arbitrary pairs of words through the use of rehearsal or mnemonic techniques and of semantically related (but not acoustically related) word pairs may be poorer in hyperactive than in control children (see Douglas, 1980; Weingartner, et al. 1980).

Motor Differences. Comparisons of hyperactive children and controls on the Lincoln-Oseretsky Schedule of Motor Development indicate that hyperactive children also perform worse than controls in the fine-motor area (Douglas, 1972). However, hyperactive children do perform as well in gym and art as their peers (Minde et al., 1971).

Cognitive-Reasoning Differences. Typically hyperactive and control children do not perform differently on individually administered IQ tests (see Cohen & Minde, 1983; Douglas & Peters, 1979; Zentall & Barack, 1979; Zentall *et al.*, 1983; Zentall *et al.*, 1978a). However, Loney (1974) found reduced intellectual functioning in fifth-grade boys but not in second-grade boys. She concluded that the deficits in the older children were motivational differences that had accumulated over time. Alternatively, hyperactive children may score lower than nonhyperactive children on those individual IQ tests that have a multiple-choice format (Cunningham & Barkley, 1979; Whalen, Henker, Collins, McAuliffe, & Vaux, 1979). These differences are similar to the poorer performance of hyperactive children observed on tasks that involve a response choice from among five items, relative to their performance on tasks with only two choices (Hoy, Weiss, Minde, & Cohen, 1978).

In contrast, on group-administered IQ tests, hyperactive children more consistently have been reported to perform worse than controls (Safer & Allen, 1976, p. 19; Zentall & Barack, 1979; Zentall, Falkenberg, & Smith, 1985), although equivalent performance on group IQ tests has also been documented (Zentall, 1980; Zentall & Shaw, 1980).

The generally better performance of hyperactive children on individual than on group tests has not been established by direct performance comparisons using comparable test stimuli. That such comparisons would produce differences is suggested by evidence that hyperactive, minimally brain-dysfunctioned children maintain attention to a difficult arithmetic task when an adult examiner is present, but not when the examiner is absent (Steinkamp, 1980). There is further evidence, using concept identification tasks, that procedural differences attributable to attention and feedback can moderate test-talking performance (Freirbergs & Douglas, 1969; Zentall, 1986). In these studies, hyperactive children were shown two pictures at a time and were told to discover which of the two was the "correct" concept. One of the pictures was an examplar of a concept (e.g., "flower") or of a number concept (e.g., "two"), and the other was a nonexemplar. Hyperactive children performed as well as controls when they were given continuous reinforcement but worse than controls when they were given a 50% fixed-ratio schedule of reinforcement. In sum, it may be concluded that young hyperactive children perform statistically as well as controls on cognitive tasks and IQ tests that are presented individually, with an adult present, or with continuous reinforcement, and poorer on group-administered tests and those with multiple-choice formatting.

Language Differences. Hyperactive children also perform worse than controls on receptive language tasks. Using referential communication tasks designed to determine problems that hyperactive children would encounter as receivers and senders of information, Whalen *et al.* (1979) reported that hyperactive boys experienced difficulty only as receivers of information. Conclusions from this study were not altogether interpretable, however, because the hyperactive children verbally requested less of the information necessary to confirm appropriate task responses and also differed from controls in IQ. Other research has similarly demonstrated that hyperactive children use less efficient questioning strategies in solving problems than normal or reading-disabled groups (Tant & Douglas, 1982). Therefore, these studies indicate only that hyperactive children do not ask for critical information, and not that they could not analyze the information if it were provided. In a subsequent study on 3- to 7-year-old hyperactive children, which controlled for the amount of information received as well as the intellectual ability to process that information, Zentall and Gohs (1984) reported that hyperactive children made more decision errors than controls in a receptive communication task only when the information was detailed, and not when it was global. Detailed information required a narrow focusing of attention on the parts of a whole.

Expressive language differences have also been documented and indicate that hyperactive children spontaneously talk more than comparison children in home contexts (Zentall, 1984) and in individual test-type contexts with adults (Zentall et al., 1983). We found that nursery through first-grade hyperactive children used more exclamatory, commanding, and interrupting statements, as well as questions and comments that were unrelated to the task (Zentall et al., 1983). We have recently analyzed data that suggest that the excessive verbalizations of hyperactive children occur only when the children are not asked to talk. When they are asked to tell stories, they demonstrate a language production deficiency (Zentall, 1987).

Preschool hyperactive children have also been observed to perform worse on the Grammatical Closure subtest of the ITPA (Weithorn & Kagen, 1978), and to have more dysfluencies than controls in their spontaneous language (incomplete statements, starters, fillers, and revisions; Zentall et al., 1983).

Conclusions

From this review of the cognitive abilities of behavior-disordered children, it is apparent that both under- and overcontrolling types of children experience specific problems in the visual-perceptual and fine-motor areas of functioning. For autistic children, selecting test procedures that involve minimal instructions, imitation, or need to visualize and analyze stimulus properties may offset some of their perceptual problems (Prior, 1979).

Stable differences in the quantity and quality of language have also been documented for both autistic and hyperactive children. Hyperactive children demonstrate problems in listening, especially when the information is detailed. They also spontaneously talk more than normal children but give fewer elicited verbal responses. On the other hand, autistic children display less spontaneous language then aphasic and normal comparison groups, and they demonstrate considerable difficulty in the social use of expressive language.

Neither hyperactive nor autistic children have been reported to evidence general problems in short-term memory, as long as sustained attention and spontaneous use of memory strategies are not required for hyperactive children, and use of semantic or syntactic cues is not required in memory tasks for low-functioning autistic children.

Cognition differences are frequently found in autistic children. Differences may also be demonstrated for hyperactive children in multiple-choice tests, in group tests that require independent progress, or in problem-solving tasks that require efficient questioning. When test items and child responses are tied together by frequent examiner directions or reinforcements, group differences are reduced.

Although differences in cognitive abilities are found in both types of behavior-disordered populations, a profile of abilities does not differentiate behavioral disabilities from other profiles (i.e., it is not diagnostic); nor are ability differences primary in the pathogenesis of these disorders. Autistic children do have inconsistent perceptual responses, as well as language, and cognitive deficits that contribute to a number of their associated problems. Furthermore, most of these children are retarded. However, a cognitive-language deficit account of their behavior does not explain the fact that autism is identified early, often within the first few days to the first year of life. It is improbable that the characteristic body rigidity, lack of startle reflex, disturbance in early sleeping and motility patterns, or the abnormalities in visual-evoked potentials, brainstem-evoked potentials, and autonomic responsivity of autistic infants are responses to cognitive or language demands (for a review, see Fein *et al.*, 1984).

To determine what behavior is preeminent in defining autism, direct comparisons of autistic children with comparison groups of retarded children are used. From a review of such evidence, we concluded that learning deficits do not play a determining role in autistic behavior, because these learning deficits are also observed in retarded children who do not display autistic behavior (Zentall & Zentall, 1983). Comparisons of normal-IQ autistic children with matched (chronological-age) low-IQ autistic children have yielded more behavioral similarities than differences in spite of the cognitive differences between the groups. Both groups demonstrated seriously impaired social relationships and the absence of friendships or group play behavior, even though the retarded groups also had more language delay and other social-skill deficits. Both low- and high-IQ groups demonstrated repetitive behavior, although the normal-IQ group had more rituals, whereas the retarded group had more stereotypies. Thus, the behavioral differences between retarded children and retarded autistic children, as well as the similarities between retarded autistic children and nonretarded autistic children, suggest that, although there may be some overlap, autism and retardation can be differentiated.

Similarly, the task failure hypothesis may explain specific task precipitants of hyperactive behavior, but there is much that contraindicates this account as a full explanation of this behavior. It does explain behavior that is an initial response to an ambiguous or delayed-response task, but it does not explain why only some children with learning problems resort to increased activity. More important, it does not explain hyperactivity identified in infancy nor that observed in the absence of a task, during easy tasks, or in the absence of external physical or social stimuli (see Zentall & Zentall, 1983).

MEASUREMENT OF ABILITY DIFFERENCES

Regardless of the extent to which specific cognitive disabilities reflect primary or secondary problems, the cognitive assessment of behaviorally disordered children appears warranted. Assessment appears to be most appropriate when conducted from a development perspective, using norm-referenced measures that allow for comparisons to normal and other handicapped populations.

In testing very young or low-functioning autistic children, a choice can be made among infant developmental scales such as the Bayley Scales of Infant Development, the Merrill-Palmer Scale, or the Gesell Developmental Schedules. These are often used to determine if there is retardation. Alpern and Kimberlin's Catell-Binet short form (1970) has the widest range of applicability with retarded autistic examinees because it is a combination of both scales that thus creates an IQ test with items extending down to 2 months of age. Its additional advantages, according to Newsom and Rincover (1982, p. 418), include a brief 20-minute administration time and a derivation of scores similar to those from the Stanford-Binet. Its disadvantages include a high degree of judgment in scoring many of the infant items and a lack of population-specific reliability and validity data beyond those provided in the original article based on a small sample of retarded autistic children.

Traditional IQ testing can be appropriate for this population, depending on the range of IQ assessed and the amount of language comprehension and usage required. The Wechler Preschool and Primary Scale of Intelligence (WPPSI) and the revised Wechler Intelligence Scale for Children (WISC-R) have similar problems in not providing for IQs below 40. The Stanford-Binet derives scores that are highly related to a child's verbal skills (Freeman & Ritvo, 1976), but it is easier than the WPPSI for children in the age group 4–6 ½ years. For this reason, the Stanford-Binet is used more frequently with young autistic children (Newsom & Rincover, 1982, p. 417). Standardized tests such as the Peabody Picture Vocabulary Test (PPVT), the ITPA, and the Northwestern Syntax Screening Test (NSST) are of questionable value in assessing the abilities of autistic children because these tests were specifically designed to rely on language performance (Fay, 1980, p. 13).

Subscale differences in IQ tests may provide further information. A characteristic pattern for autistic children is manifested by deficits on subtests of comprehension, arithmetic, vocabulary, picture arrangement, and coding tasks, with improved performance on block design, object assembly, digit span, similarities, and picture completion tasks (Simmons & Tymchuk, 1973). Statistically, autistic children score lower on verbal scales because of language delay and deviance (Fein et al., 1984). However, an analysis of 30 individual profiles indicated that only 19 autistic children had a lower verbal IQ and that 11 did not (Lockyer & Rutter, 1970).

Milich and Loney (1979) suggested that hyperactive children's inattention and use of global rather than analytic strategies are the causes of their low verbal scores. Others have reported that the poor attentional skills of hyperactive children depress WISC subtest scores on arithmetic, coding, information, and digit span (the ACID factor) (Ackerman, Dykman, & Peters, 1977; Stevens, Boydstun, Dykman, Peters, & Stinton, 1967). Subtests that are not confounded by attentional requirements elicit improved performance from this group. These include similarities, picture completion, picture arrangement, block design, and object assembly (Milich & Loney, 1979). Individual IQ tests, although of little value in the diagnosis of hyperactivity, can be useful in an appraisal of learning disabilities (Safer & Allen, 1976, p. 20).

Perceptual and motor functioning may be assessed by traditional instruments such as Berry's Visual Motor Integration Test, which assesses children as young as 2 years old, and the Oseretsky for children of ages 4 ½ and older. Language delays can be assessed by standardized norm-referenced tests or developmental scales. However, standardized tests do not provide sufficient information on the child's use of language or on the quantitative (nondevelopmental) differences in language often demonstrated by behavior-disordered children. The ASIEP (Krug et al., 1980) includes an informal procedure for sampling language behavior with a variety of language-eliciting stimuli. Language can be coded into 50 response categories and can be compared with nonautistic handicapped norms.

In summary, the assessment of cognitive abilities typically involves the use of traditional measures. In this assessment, items that load on language or attention represent an assessment of deficit functioning as well as delay. Norm-referenced assessment of IQ, language, perceptual, and motor functioning provides a profile of abilities in areas demonstrated to be typically impaired in behavior-disordered children. For both autistic and hyperactive children, IQ assessment can also serve (a) in their traditional role as a rough predictor of scholastic aptitude and (b) as an indicator of outcome in a more general sense. For example, hyperactive adults' self-reported aggressive and antisocial outcomes are related to their earlier IQ scores assessed at referral (Loney, Whaley-Klahn, Kosier, & Conboy, 1981). Given that the referral and the assessment of IQ were made during childhood, Loney *et al.* concluded that stabilization of IQ occurred before the reported psychopathological behavior. Similarly, Prior (1979) concluded that the behavioral symptoms of autism and their severity are less influential in the outcome of this disorder than is IQ or language level before age 5. However, there is considerable evidence that IQ and overall clinical severity are correlated (e.g., Freeman & Ritvo, 1976). Overall, cognitive ability assessment not only provides an understanding of the child's level of functioning but may also be of prognostic value.

ASSESSMENT OF COGNITIVE AND BEHAVIORAL STYLE DIFFERENCES

The assessment of cognitive abilities is necessary but not sufficient for behavior-disordered children. Overall assessment should produce a fairly accurate understanding of the level of the child's abilities, but it also should describe how the child uses cognitive strategies and approaches environmental stimuli. These strategy and style variables that influence cognitive performance are functional characteristics of children that are unique in defining their disorder and that are relatively stable across time and context. Mash and Terdal (1982) indicated that consistency across time and age level is more likely to be found where broad response classes of behavior (e.g., aggression) are identified than where a specific behavior (e.g., hitting others) is defined. Stable behavior traits that are identified early, in addition to intellect, are problem-solving strategies, cognitive style, general activity, aggression, individual preferences for amount and type of stimulation, and general temperament (e.g., rate of adaptation to novel situations) (Mash & Terdal, 1982, p. 12).

Some of these behavior traits (i.e., response to novelty and need for stimulation) have also been identified as theoretically important to an understanding of disordered activity. The optimal stimulation theory (e.g., Berlyne, 1960) proposes that all organisms work to maintain optimal levels of central arousal through instrumental activity. When infants and children demonstrate deviations in activity, they may fall beyond the normal range of individual differences in need for stimulation (Zentall, 1975; Zentall & Zentall, 1983). For example, children with a preference for novel stimulation (hyperactive children) demonstrate a high rate of sensation-seeking activity that is approach-oriented toward novel stimulation and that is characterized by variability and minimal response delay. On the other hand, autistic children demonstrate a preference for familiar stimuli. The activity that is exhibited is avoidance-oriented, away from novel environmental and social stimuli, and is characterized by repetitiveness (nonvariability). Because these types of behavior can differentiate autistic children from mentally retarded children (e.g., in social approach versus avoidance) and hyperactive from learning-problem children (e.g., in activity level or attraction to novelty), and because these types of behavior influence cognitive performance, they have been selected for further review.

The attentional response of hyperactive and autistic children will be examined for type and range of stimuli preferred and for span (length). The motor response includes verbal and motor activity and is analyzed for frequency, repetitiveness, response delay, and direction (approach or avoidance). When task stimuli have been examined as elicitors of response, the response pattern is often labeled *cognitive style*. However, the generality of this pattern of response goes beyond specific responses to task stimuli.

Style Differences in Autism

Cognitive Style

Broadly defined, *cognitive style* refers to a child's characteristic manner of learning. This may be demonstrated for autistic children in their focus of attention on familiar objects, simple tasks, or self-produced repetitive activities (stereotypies), often for long periods of time (i.e., they show a narrow, sustained focus of attention). For example, autistic children were better able to sustain attention on a simple visual discrimination task in the presence of noise distraction than retarded children matched on MA (Nathanson, 1977).

Autistic children may also demonstrate a narrow focus by being selective in their attention to simple stimuli. Although minimal data suggest that selective attention specifically characterizes autistic children (Zentall & Zentall, 1983), a more recent study equated retarded and autistic retarded children on performance IQ and mental age and did find evidence of greater stimulus overselectivity in the autistic group (Frankel, Simmons, Fichter, & Freeman, 1984). Thus, overly selective attention to parts of a whole may be related to style as well as to developmental factors. Compared with both retarded and mental-age controls, autistic children also respond to learning tasks with overly selective responses (perseveration and position and pattern preferences) and with delayed responses to previous task stimuli (Boucher, 1977; Hermelin & Frith, 1971; Prior, 1977).

Autistic children also avoid focusing on complex, novel, or socially threatening stimuli (Hermelin & O'Connor, 1970; Hutt & Ounsted, 1968). For example, when autistic children were exposed to a number of pictures of faces that varied in complexity, blank faces and animal faces were preferred over complex faces and human faces (Hutt & Ounsted, 1968). Similarly, Langdell (1978) found that autistic children attend to different features of the human face in recognition tasks than do normal and retarded controls. In this study, young autistic children were significantly better at recognizing the lower half of faces than the upper half, in contrast to the recognition pattern of both comparison groups. O'Connor and Hermelin (1967) presented further evidence that autistic children do not attend to their environment in the same way that retarded and normal children do. When presented with photographs and cards of different colors, autistic children spent much of their time looking at the viewing box rather than at the display, in contrast to the attentional behavior of both comparison groups. Additionally, they shifted their focus from one display to another less frequently than the MA controls. The fact that autistic children demonstrate greater physiological responsiveness to novel stimuli and fail to habituate relative to normal and retarded children (individually matched for age, sex, and IQ) may explain their preference for familiar, nonthreatening stimuli (James & Barry, 1980; Hermelin & O'Connor, 1968; Palkovitz & Wiesenfeld, 1980).

Behavioral Style

Autistic children often demonstrate stereotyped behavior patterns of rocking, toy spinning, or hand flapping. As previously discussed, their verbal behavior also tends to be repetitive. Some of their delayed echolalia appears to be maintained by its sensory consequences. That is, when earphones and masking sounds reduced or eliminated echoic responses (e.g., the repetition of commercials), the frequency of responses that were unrelated to punishment were eliminated (Newsom & Rincover, 1982, p. 418). The sensory effects of this repetitive behavior appear to reduce physiological indices of arousal (Sroufe, Steucher, & Stutzer, 1973). Similar physiological effects of repetitive behavior on arousal have been observed in normal adults (Lipowski, 1975). The fact that these repetitive behaviors may be functional arousal-moderating responses of the organism is also suggested by the fact that some stereotypies are inversely correlated with others (i.e., so that reduction in one stereotypy may result in an increase in another) (Knoblock, 1983, p. 202).

The direction of the motor behavior of autistic children is avoidance-orientated. The withdrawal from social stimuli is demonstrated clinically in what is termed *gaze aversion* (i.e., poor maintenance of eye contact). Richer (1976) demonstrated that autistic children rarely start or continue interactions, compared with (nonautistic) retarded and language-delayed children, and that they avoid social encounters by staying on the periphery of an area, by moving away from others, and by nonaggressive "flight" kinds of behavior. Their avoidance behavior was demonstrated not only in response to possibly threatening approaches, similar to the responses of other children, but also to nonthreatening approaches.

Style Differences in Hyperactivity

Cognitive Style

In very young children, the span and breadth of the attentional field are demonstrated in task persistence and by the number of activity or toy changes. Although Schleifer, Weiss, Cohen, Elman, Cvejic, and Kruger (1975) reported no group differences in task persistence, other researchers have observed that 2- and 3-year-old behavior-problem toddlers engaged in more short-duration activities (20 seconds or less) and fewer long-duration activities (2 minutes or longer) during free play (Campbell, Szumowski, Ewing, Gluck, & Breaux, 1982). Young hyperactive children also changed their activities more than controls during teacher-directed play (Schleifer *et al.*, 1975) and during free play (Campbell *et al.*, 1982).

This wide field of attention or short span appears to be a stable trait. Elementary-level children are also attracted to peripheral or salient extratask stimuli (for a review, see Zentall & Gohs, 1984). Furthermore, hyperactive children have been observed to look away from their tasks more in stimulating than in nonstimulating environments (Shores & Haubrich, 1969), especially when they are performing boring or difficult tasks that allow for slow progress (Steinkamp, 1980). Although these children spend less time attending to their tasks, they typically perform as well as they do in stimulus-reduced environments or as well as controls do in stimulating environments (i.e., as long as the baseline performance is equivalent for both groups) (Zentall & Zentall, 1983). This finding suggests that the wide attentional focus of hyperactive children may provide temporary increases in stimulation that allow for more efficient performance. Performance measures of sustained attention indicate that elementary and adolescent hyperactive individuals continue to experience difficulty with attentional tasks (Weiss, Minde, Werry, Douglas, & Nemeth, 1971; Zentall, 1984a).

Hyperactive children also respond impulsively to learning tasks. Measures of impulsivity, such as performances on early childhood versions of the Matching Familiar Figures Test, the Draw a Line Slowly Test, the Cookie Delay Task, and various maze tasks, all require delay or inhibition of responses. These measures have, for the most part, been observed to differentiate hyperactive from nonhyperactive preschoolers (Campbell *et al.*, 1982; Cohen *et al.*, 1981; Schleifer *et al.*, 1975). Similar differences have been observed in elementary-aged children (Campbell, Douglas, & Morgenstern, 1971; Dwyer & Zentall, 1987), indicating the stability of the construct.

Behavioral Style

Young hyperactive children are more active during the performance of listen and response-delay tasks with an adult examiner (Zentall *et al.*, 1983). In classroom-type contexts, preschool children spend more time away from their seats than controls (Campbell *et al.*, 1982; Schleifer *et al.*, 1975), a finding that suggests differences in motor activity as well as inadequate attentional persistence. These activity differences appear to be stable throughout the elementary years in classroom contexts, in free play, and as rated by parents in home contexts (Zentall, 1983, 1984). Safer and Allen (1976, pp. 21–22) concluded from their review that by, mid-junior high, hyperactive students were better able to stay in their seats but were now characterized by restlessness. Hyperactive preschool children are also more talkative than comparison children (Zentall *et al.*, 1983). Talkativeness may be functional in the moderation of arousal as it produces higher levels of arousal than listening (Smith, Malmo, & Shagass, 1977).

The overall direction of the behavior may be characterized as approach-oriented (Childers, 1935), although it is often socially aggressive in quality. Preschool hyperactive children have been observed to be more disruptive and aggressive with their peers (Campbell & Cluss, 1982; Campbell, Endman, & Bernfield, 1977; Schleifer *et al.*, 1975) and more noncompliant with their teachers (Buchan, Swap, & Swap, 1977; Campbell & Cluss, 1982). The increased physical and social contacts and the often aggressive, disruptive nature of those contacts appear to be stable throughout the elementary years (Zentall, 1983).

Measurement of Style Differences

Autistic children attend to simple familiar stimuli for extended lengths of time. Their motor responses are invariant and typically involve an avoidance of social stimuli. Hyperactive children, on the other hand, are attracted to novel stimuli and thus attend to a familiar activity for a brief period of time. They exhibit high rates of nonrepetitive activity, have considerable difficulty in delaying responses, and demonstrate approach-oriented behavior that may be aggressive. These cognitive and behavioral style traits are stable, unique in defining the disorders, and observable across contexts.

The recommendation to assess style variables is based on the observation that quantitative differences in these parameters have been found to precede cognitive disabilities and disordered behavior. For example, activity level alone has predictive validity, in that preschool children who show high rates of activity were more likely to show poor cognitive abilities and poor social interaction at age 7½ (Halverson & Waldrop, 1976). In autistic children it may be that the attentional and activity deficiencies, such as lack of exploratory behavior, inattention to parents' voices or faces, and avoidance of most novel stimuli for the first few years of life, may result in perceptual experiences that are insufficient to form the basis of higher level cognitive abilities (Fein et al., 1984). The similarities often observed between sensory-deprived animals and autistic children may be attributable to lack of input in the former case and lack of attention to input in the latter (Fein et al., 1984). Thus, the attentional and behavioral style of both types of children are important precursors of cognitive functioning and should be assessed to determine long-term risk.

I have indicated that, in the assessment of cognitive abilities, norm-referenced testing is useful. Similarly, a normative approach would be appropriate for the style variables described as excesses or deficiencies in attention, activity, and aggressive behavior. However, developmental norms that describe age trends for normal child behavior are not documented in the literature, aside from descriptions of the prevalence of behavior problems at different ages (e.g., Jenkins, Owen, Bax, & Hart, 1984). For this reason, traditional norm-referenced assessment of behavioral and learning style is not possible.

Criterion-referenced approaches, on the other hand, are used only in areas in which identifiable absolute performance goals are possible (e.g., academic or athletic performance) (Mash & Terdal, 1982). In the areas of behavioral disabilities, it is less clear what behavior or what level of behavior is important for adjustment. For example, some work has been done on increasing the delay of response for hyperactive children (i.e., reduced impulsivity), but increased delay has not reduced errors (see Kauffman, 1981, p. 178). Similarly, increases in sitting still, decreased talking, and increased visual on-task behavior have not consistently improved task performance (Zentall & Zentall, 1983). Furthermore, the reduction in the quantity of spontaneous verbalizations and social initiations that were produced by stimulant drug therapy in hyperactive preschool children were not even desirable changes according to the parents of these young children (Cunningham & Barkley, 1978a, p. 639) and may, in fact, lead to poor psychological and social development (Winett & Winkler, 1972). Thus, many of the traits that have previously been targeted for intervention for hyperactive children (attention-to-task, talkativeness, and sitting still) and for autistic children (stereotypies and gaze avoidance) are resistent to change or, if changed, may not result in improved social development. We have presented evidence that these behaviors may be functional in the moderation of arousal, a function that may explain their resistance to change.

Because of the endogenous and possible functional nature of these behaviors, an initial approach to the child is not intervention but assessment through observation. The specific behaviors observed can include aspects of attention and activity. For example, getting up and down within the same activity (out-of-seat) or the number of activity changes differentiates hyperactive from control children in schools and in home contexts, possibly because it includes both attentional and motor activity factors. Because autistic children are characterized by persistence in a familiar activity, observation of this behavior would be valid for this group as well.

Autistic children are further characterized by their stance on the periphery of an area and by their failure to move toward the center (Richer, 1976). Locomotor activity for young children is often measured in playrooms that have been marked off with tape into quadrants (Routh, Schroeder, & O'Tuama, 1974). This technique could be adapted by designating the center area as a target area or by designating other children as social targets. In this manner, locomotor activity and the direction of that activity could be assessed for both types of behavior-disordered children.

Another bipolar characteristic of both hyperactive and autistic children is the quantity of their spontaneous verbalizations. The amount of spontaneous verbalization predicts outcome for autistic children, as previously discussed. For hyperactive children, excessive spontaneous, non-task-related verbalizations are characteristic behaviors observed in a number of contexts. A measure of language productivity that could be used with both hyperactive and autistic children and that takes into account the amount and repetitiveness of verbal content is "type-token." Type-token is the ratio of the number of different words, divided by the square root of twice the number of words in the sample (Carroll, 1964, p. 2).

Interpretation of Style Differences

For Risk Assessment. It is necessary to use normative comparisons to make decisions about levels of risk. Methods of comparison that can be used (in the absence of existing behavioral norms) are social judgments and variation with respect to an appropriate comparison child. Social judgments involve subjective comparisons among children. These judgments are typically made by teachers using behavioral checklists, or by peers using sociometric devices, and are reliable indicators of behavioral deviance and of change in behavior (Madan-Swain & Zentall, 1987; Zentall & Barack, 1979). Social judgments can also be validly made by parents, observers, and teachers using global ratings of noncompliance and quantity of verbalizations and activity (Madan-Swain &

Zentall, 1987). Such ratings have the advantage of overriding the behavioral variability that is so characteristic of infant and preschool behavior (Lidz, 1983, p. 18). The Werry-Weiss-Peters Activity Rating Scale (Werry, 1968) for hyperactive children has the additional advantage of rating specific behavior (e.g., "changing activities") within predefined settings (play, homework, social settings, mealtime, TV, and sleep). Thus, this scale accounts for some of the variance attributable to the setting. For example, the first three settings on this scale differentiated between hyperactive and nonhyperactive children, whereas the others were not differentiating for elementary-age children (Zentall, 1984).

Although these ratings are invaluable in the identification and monitoring of behavior disorders, they are not precise measures of specific behavior, and occasionally high ratings may reflect the expectations of parents or teachers (unless an observer has been trained). It is for this reason that additional normative information should be obtained. A cost-efficient method for obtaining (a) the frequency of activity-changes, (b) the quantity and repetitiveness of verbalizations, and (c) the frequency and direction of locomotor behavior for a target child, as well as for obtaining normative comparison data, can be adapted from time-sampling or event-recording methods (e.g., by Schleifer *et al.*, 1975; Zentall, 1980). These methods involve first recording the frequency of a behavior for a target child for 5 seconds to 5 minutes and then recording the same behaviors of a normal comparison child for the same amount of time within specific activity-settings.

The activity setting selected should be observable at a range of age levels at home and school. Activity settings could include independent activity (e.g., seatwork or play) or adult-directed activities (e.g., listening to a story, lecture, or presentation, or completing a task with an adult). The behavior of the normal comparison child matched for age or mental age with the target child provides the standard that controls for differences in the effects of age (i.e., activity decreases for all children across age levels), and for the effects of task, setting, and time. The normal comparison child should not be interacting with the target child at the time of the observation; we have recently demonstrated negative behavioral contagion effects from behavior-disordered children to normal peers in dyadic interactions (Madan-Swain & Zentall, 1987). Observations should be made in mainstream but not in segregated settings, because a child's skill level depends on the social responsivity of peers (Strain & Shores, 1983). In these settings, Harris, Vincent, and Williams (1977) found that stable classroom behavioral data can be recorded within a relatively short period of time.

In summary, certain primarily quantitative types of behavior were designated for observation in a determination of risk. Methodologically, these assessments can be made through social judgment ratings or through alternating observations of the behavioral frequency of the target and the normal comparison child. These primary behaviors have been found to presage, but not to determine, negative outcome and thus may not, in themselves, be valid targets for intervention.

For Intervention. The second area involves assessment for intervention. Assessment for intervention pinpoints current observable problem behavior within a specific setting. This behavioral approach requires the documentation of specific observable behaviors

(e.g., hitting), environmental supports (e.g., free play with blocks, environmental consequences), and the relationship of these behaviors to more stable outcome variables (e.g.,
activity or aggression). The methodology involves intraindividual baseline comparisons
using frequency and duration rates of behavior.

Targets for intervention are often those characteristics that are socially learned and
secondary to the primary characteristics of activity and attention. However, it is these
secondary characteristics that often determine whether the primary symptoms of hyperactivity will result in negative outcome for the child (Ross & Ross, 1982, p. 61). The
secondary dimensions of behavior that have been selected for intervention include approach and avoidance behavior, as well as the positive or negative valence of the behavior. These secondary characteristics (e.g., hitting) may be found in the presence of
primary quantitative differences (i.e., high rates of activity), but their interrelationship is
not determining. Although there is considerable evidence that the high level of activity
typically displayed by young hyperactive children is associated with later coercive peer
interactions, aggression, disruption,interruptions, and use of commands (Milich & Landau, 1982; Schliefer et al., 1975), there exists a subset of active and hyperactive children
who are well liked and who have good adjustment. Madan-Swain and Zentall (1987)
reported which behaviors differentiated accepted and rejected hyperactive children. The
non-task-relatedness of the verbal and nonverbal behavior, excessive physical aggression,
and lack of positive physical contact were all appropriate targets of interventions for
rejected hyperactive children. Intervention should focus on changing behaviors from negative to positive, and from unrelated to related, rather than simply on decreasing the
frequency of the inappropriate.

Where sufficient behavior exists, it is appropriate to alter the quality of the behavior.
In autistic children, however, where insufficient spontaneous behavior exists, the focus of
treatment should be on increasing the quantity and approach orientation of social behavior. Autistic children are characterized by their failure to initiate verbal interactions with
others or to move within 1 meter of others (Richer, 1976). Modifying this behavior
directly may be extremely difficult because it requires altering primary characteristics of
the quantity of interaction (i.e.,the need for stimulation). In support of this premise,
Lovaas, Koegel, Simmons, and Long (1970) concluded that behavior modification methodologies have been more effective with autistic children in eliminating specific behavior
than in establishing or increasing specific appropriate behavior. For this reason, it may be
advisable to change the behavior (a) by teaching the child to substitute task-relevant
motor rituals for stereotypies, or (b) by altering the environment (e.g., through sensory
restrictions). For example, Suedfeld and Schwartz (1983) demonstrated that 48 hours of
decreased levels of environmental stimulation resulted in improved social interaction and
improved discrimination learning for autistic children. Other situational factors relevant
to risk assessment and interventions are reviewed below.

SITUATIONAL VARIANCE IN ASSESSMENT

A number of situational factors influence behavior disordered children differently
from other comparisons groups. Although testing assumes standardized stimuli, these
stimuli refer only to instructions and test materials, and not to other external moderating

factors, such as time, the examiner, motivation and reinforcement, or other context variables that have been demonstrated to affect the cognitive performance of behaviorally disordered children.

Test Stimuli

The attentional deficits of hyperactive and autistic children would not be characterized by Skinner (1953) as a disorder, but as a disturbance in the relationship between the controlling task stimuli and the response. To understand the nature of the disturbance, it is important to identify those stimulus conditions that both exacerbate and modulate the attentional deficit. Some of these have already been discussed in this chapter. For example, hyperactive children perform worse on group-administered IQ tests and tests that are in a multiple-choice format. A sequential analysis of multiple stimuli or of detail that is not directed by an examiner is difficult for hyperactive children. Thus, their performance on measures with multiple stimuli may reflect a cognitive style (i.e., impulsivity) rather than cognitive disability.

Hyperactive children also demonstrate poorer performance with task stimuli that are overly familiar (Zentall, 1986). For this reason, repetitive exercises are especially tedious for hyperactive children, whose performance deteriorates more rapidly over time than does the performance of mental-age controls. Consistent with the optimal stimulation theory and with many of our empirical findings, Ross and Ross (1982) summarized those stimuli factors that result in optimal performance:

> If the attributes of the task are sufficiently powerful—for example, novel, exciting, visually focusing to mobilize the child's cognitive energy and he possesses the requisite task competencies, then he will perform at a level appropriate for his IQ score....He also attends closely to television programs, movies, and to the passing scene while riding in an automobile for relatively long periods. In these situations his cognitive energy is to a great extent being mobilized for him: in the first case by a compelling adult and in others by an attention directing presentation. (p. 220)

For autistic children, attentional performance is optimized by the presence of concrete visual stimuli that require spatial rather than temporal processing and by detailed, familiar, and simple nonsocial stimuli. In general, memory may be improved if the stimuli-to-be-recalled are auditory rather than visual. Individual preferences for specific stimuli may be identified from the stereotypical behavior of a particular child (e.g., tapping may produce auditory consequences and may indicate selective attention to familiar low-intensity auditory input).

In addition to selecting tests and test stimuli that will optimize the performance of behaviorally disordered children, modifications in response requirements and testing procedures may need to be made, especially for autistic children who have severe language impairments. Where verbalizations are required that are beyond the child's ability, the test can be restructured to allow the child to point or to use other indicators of yes-no, rather than to verbalize an answer. Questions, instructions, and commands should be short, concrete, and repeated to offset receptive language deficits. These modifications and others, such as not imposing time limits, may violate the standardization of norm-referenced tests. In such cases, the results should be reported in conjunction with the specific modifications necessary to elicit the optimal results.

Motivation and Reinforcement

Although standardized testing assumes adequate child motivation, it is especially difficult with disordered children to determine whether poor performance is produced by cognitive disability or poor motivation. Furthermore, the timing and type of reinforcement for eliciting and maintaining performance are not specified in test manuals. Examiners may decide to increase the frequency of reinforcement or the magnitude of social reward to reduce the probable motivational deficits in behaviorally disordered children, but such changes may be counterproductive.

Theoretically, positive reinforcement should be more effective with autistic children if the reinforcer consists of reduced levels of stimulation or a high degree of stimulus predictability. In support, there is evidence that suggests that repetitive stimulation (kaleidoscope, strobe light, vibration, or rocking) can be reinforcing (e.g., Fineman, 1968; Frankel, Freeman, Ritvo, Chikami, & Carr, 1976; Freeman, Frankel, & Ritvo, 1976). Repetitive stimulation offers considerable advantage over more typically used primary reinforcers (e.g., food) because satiation does not occur (Margolies, 1977).

Similarly, hyperactive children have unique responses to reinforcement (Barkley, 1985). For example, there is evidence that hyperactive children need higher density schedules of reinforcement than normal children to maintain adequate levels of performance. Physiological data further suggest that when reinforcement is administered to hyperactive children, it is accompanied by increased autonomic arousal (Zentall & Zentall, 1983). Therefore, it may be that an increased rate of reinforcement would be especially useful during later test performance, when task and context novelty decline. However, because hyperactive children are attracted to novelty, tangible reinforcers of high reward magnitude can shift their attention away from the task to the reinforcer or the reinforcing adult (Parry & Douglas, 1983).

Examiner and Context Familiarity

Mash and Terdal (1982) stated that the assessment of young children may be affected by wariness of strangers. The effect of the examiner on performance is particularly evident in children who are socially unskilled, perhaps because testing is a social situation and not just a standardized stimulus setting, as indicated by the evidence provided by Fuchs and Fuchs (1984). These researchers demonstrated that examiners who were unknown imposed a differential bias against handicapped children. Specifically, preschool language-disordered children performed better on language tests with familiar than with unfamiliar examiners, whereas controls did not differ in their response. A follow-up analysis revealed that the children spoke more and with greater complexity when tested by a familiar examiner (Fuchs, Zern, & Fuchs, 1983). The differences were attributed to the frequent and longer intervals of silence provided by familiar examiners, the use of eye contact to denote child-response time, and the use of examiner language that was primarily directive, rather than participatory.

Because behaviorally disordered children typically have language disorders, their verbal performance would be expected to be poorer with strangers than with familiar examiners. However, this language bias would exist only when normative comparisons are made to nonhandicapped peers who do not demonstrate negative verbal performance effects from unfamiliar examiners.

In addition, examiner novelty would be expected to alter the behavior and performance of hyperactive children differently from that of autistic children. As previously discussed, autistic children demonstrate an avoidance of novelty with such behaviors as gaze avoidance, overselective response, and stereotypical behavior, all of which reduce attention to the test and to the examiner's input. Hyperactive children, on the other hand, modulate activity in novel contexts to the extent that first visits to the doctor or the psychologist rarely confirm the diagnosis of hyperactivity (see Barkley, 1982). It thus appears that familiar testers and environmental conditions will elicit more typical kinds of behavior and performance from both types of disordered children. In contrast, assessment in novel contexts will provide some indication of potential for hyperactive children and of handicap for autistic children.

CONCLUSIONS

Cognitive differences were examined for two broad patterns of disorder. Hyperactivity was described as being an example of an undercontrolled pattern, whereas autism represents an overcontrolled pattern. These differences are summarized in Table 1.

Autistic children demonstrate perceptual motor delay. Performance in this area was found to be improved by the use of haptic cues, continuously visible stimuli, and the requirements for visual-spatial skills and attention to detail. Rote memory is intact for these children, their recall of auditory stimuli being better than their recall of visual stimuli. Because their reasoning and problem-solving abilities are typically retarded, autistic children rely on rote memory. Low-functioning autistic children, in particular, fail to (a) use semantic cues; (b) offer approximations of answers; or (c) use feature extraction when information input is excessive. Phonological and syntactical language delays are also characteristic of autistic children. Deviant language can be observed in social contexts when the pragmatic use of spontaneous language is required.

Hyperactive children typically demonstrate perceptual-motor problems. Rote memory abilities also appear to be relatively intact in this group, as long as rehearsal and the selection and spontaneous use of memory strategies are not necessary. Hyperactive children, especially young children, perform as well as normals on cognitive tasks, and on IQ tests that are presented individually or with continuous reinforcement. They may perform worse than comparison children on group-administered tests, tests with multiple-choice formatting, and tests that require the efficient use of questioning strategies. The poorer performance on these types of tests has been attributed to differences in cognitive style (i.e., impulsivity) and to language deviance. Hyperactive children demonstrate poorer receptive-language performance than matched controls when the input is detailed, but not when the information is global. Expressively, they produce more nonelicited verbalizations that are dysfluent and inappropriate, and they produce fewer elicited statements.

For both types of children, norm-referenced assessment was seen as useful for determining level of functioning in those perceptual-motor, IQ, and language areas that reflect developmental delay. However, in this assessment, items and instructions that load on attentional requirements may represent an assessment of deficit functioning as well as delay. Cognitive ability assessment provides some understanding of the child's level of functioning and degree of retardation or learning disability. This type of assessment also

Table 1. Differentiating Behaviorally Disordered Children from Normal Children

	Instrument	Publishers
Screening	Preschool Behavior Problem Checklist (Quay & Peterson, 1967) Dimensions: Conduct Disorders Personality Disorder Inadequacy, immaturity Socialized delinquency	Children's Research Center University of Illinois Champaign, IL 61820
	Behavior Rating Profile Behavior assessed at home, in school, and with peers.	Pro-Ed 33 Perry Books Bldg. Austin, TX 78701
	Devereau Elementary School Behavior Rating Scale (Spivak & Swift, 1967) 11 dimensions of overt behavior problems that are related to classroom achievment.	The Devereau Foundation 1208 Old Lancaster Road Devon, PA 19333
	Ottawa School Behavior Checklist 100 specific behaviors teachers report as inappropriate in a social setting.	Pimm Consultants Limited 85 Sparks Street Suite 211 Ottawa 6, Ontario Canada K1A 0B1
	The Class Play (Bower, 1969) Identification of accepted and rejected children.	Educational Testing Service Princeton, NJ 08540

	Identification of specific disorders and of differences	
	Undercontrolled (hyperactive)	Overcontrolled (autistic)
Specific instruments	ATQ (Conners, 1973)	ABC (Krug et al., 1980)
	Rating Scale for Hyperkinesis (Davids, 1971)	DCL (Rimland, 1971)
	SNAP (Pelham & Bender, 1982)	
Behavior style differences (deviance)	Frequent activity changes Excessive spontaneous verbalizations. Social approach locomotor activity Impulsive (short-latency) responses to environmental stimuli. Response variability.	Infrequent activity changes. Infrequent spontaneous verbalizations. Social-avoidance locomotor activity Delayed responses to environmental stimuli. Response invariance (repetition).
Cognitive or attentional style differences (deviance)	Short span of attention. Attraction to novel stimuli. Wide focus of attention to global stimuli (under-selective attention).	Long Attention span. Attraction to familiar stimuli and avoidance of complex social stimuli. Narrow focus of attention to detailed stimuli (over-selective attention).
Cognitive ability differences (delay) Perceptual	Perceptual-motor problems.	Perceptual problems in the absence of

Table 1 (Continued)

Identification of specific disorders and of differences *(cont.)*

	Undercontrolled (hyperactive)	Overcontrolled (autistic)
Motor	Fine-motor delay.	Delay in imitating motor actions and in social play.
Memory	Poorer than norm in free recall of word pairs, especially with requirements of sustained attention or spontaneous use of memory strategies.	Ability in recall of meaningful and non-meaningful material equivalent to that of CA comparisons.
Language	Delay in receptive communication during the performance of tasks with detailed stimuli.	Inconsistent and delayed responses to verbal stimuli.
	Expressively more verbal when talking is not elicited. Less able to generate questioning strategies to solve problems or to tell stories when these verbal responses are elicited.	Extreme language deficiencies, especially in communicative gesturing and the pragmatic social aspects of verbal communication. Phonological and syntactic language delay.
Reasoning	Poorer performance on group IQ tests and tests with multiple-choice formatting than on individual IQ tests.	Delayed reasoning abilities, especially on verbal scales of intelligence.
	Poorer performance on concept formation tasks requiring selective attention to multiple dimensions in the absence of continuous feedback.	Inability to note redundancies in information to form abstractions, as well as an overreliance on memory.
	Poorer performance on the ACID (attentional) factor of the WISC test.	

predicts scholastic aptitude and outcome in a more general sense for both types of children. However, cognitive ability differences are not diagnostic of behavioral disabilities and are not primary in the pathogenesis of the disorders.

Primary characteristics were identified and targeted for assessment through alternating observations of the disordered child and a normal comparison in a specific setting. Characteristics were selected if they were (a) stable over time from infancy through later childhood; (b) unique in defining the syndrome; (c) observable across a number of contexts (home, school, and clinic); and (d) typically identified before a determination of cognitive delay. Primary characteristics of hyperactive children are excesses in spontaneous verbal and motor activity that is approach-oriented and often aggressive. In contrast, autistic children are characterized by nonvariant verbal and motor activity that is avoidance-oriented. Autistic children demonstrate attentional persistence in familiar activities, whereas hyperactive children demonstrate relatively short attention to familiar rote tasks and activities.

Although these primary characteristics were reported as presaging negative outcome, they were not found to be determining, at least for hyperactive children. Therefore, targets for intervention were identified as secondary social characteristics (e.g., aggression) that are often found in the presence of primary characteristics (e.g., a high rate of activity). Intervention is designed to minimize the negative social consequences of deviant patterns of behavior.

When the goal is to minimize the cognitive deficits that also characterize these children, it is critical to understand those task and extratask factors that moderate the performance of disordered children. These factors were identified as task or test stimuli (novelty, complexity, number of choices, detail, and sensory modality), testing procedures (instructions, time limit, reinforcement, and examiner presence), and characteristics of the examiner (e.g., familiarity).

In sum, differential diagnosis calls for (a) norm-referenced assessment to determine ability levels (i.e., developmental delay), taking into account the situational and task factors that moderate cognitive performance, (b) assessment of the primary characteristics of the target child and a normal comparison child to determine behavioral and cognitive style (i.e., deviance), and (c) intraindividual baseline comparisons of a specific social behavior to be targeted for intervention.

REFERENCES

Achenbach, T. M., & Edelbrock, C. S. (1978). The child behavior profile: II. Boys aged 12–16 and girls aged 6–11 and 12–16. *Journal of Consulting and Clinical Psychology, 47*, 223–233.

Ackerman, P. T., Dykman, R. A., & Peters, J. E. (1977). Teenage status of hyperactive and nonhyperactive learning disabled boys. *American Journal of Orthopsychiatry, 47*, 577–596.

Alpern, G. D., & Kimberlin, C. C. (1970). Short intelligence test ranging from infancy levels through childhood levels for use with the retarded. *American Journal of Mental Deficiency, 75*, 65–71.

Barkley, R. A. (1982). Hyperactivity. In E. J. Mash & L. G. Terdal (Eds.), *Behavioral assessment of childhood disorders*. New York: Guilford Press.

Barkley, R. A. (1985). Do as we say, not as we do: The problem of stimulus control and rule-governed behavior in attention deficit disorder with hyperactivity. In J. Swanson & M. Bloomingdale (Eds.), *Emerging trends in research on attention deficit disorders*. New York: LEA Publications.

Bartak, L., Rutter, M., & Cox A. (1977). A comparative study of infantile autism and specific developmental receptive language disorder: III. Discriminant functions analysis. *Journal of Autism and Childhood Schizophrenia, 7*, 383–396.

Berlyne, D. E. (1960). *Conflict, arousal and curiosity*. New York: McGraw-Hill.

Boucher, J. (1977). Alternation and sequencing behavior and response to novelty in autistic children. *Journal of Child Psychology and Psychiatry, 18*, 67–72.

Boullin, D. J., Coleman, M., O'Brien, R. A., & Rimland, B. (1971). Laboratory prediction of infantile autism based on 5-hydroxytryptamine efflux from blood platelets and their correlation with Rimland E2 score. *Journal of Autism and Child Schizophrenia, 1*, 63–71.

Bower, E. (1969). *Early identification of emotionally handicapped children in school* (2nd ed.). Springfield, IL: Charles C Thomas.

Buchan, B., Swap, S., & Swap, W. (1977). Teacher identification of hyperactive children in preschool settings. *Exceptional Children, 43*, 314.

Campbell, S. B., & Cluss, P. (1982). Peer relationships of young children with behavior problems. In K. H. Rubin & H. S. Ross (Eds.), *Peer relationships and social skills in childhood*. New York: Springer Verlag.

Campbell, S. B., Douglas, V. I., & Morgenstern, G. (1971). Cognitive styles in hyperactive children and the effect of methylphenidate. *Journal of Child Psychology and Psychiatry, 12*, 55–67.

Campbell, S. B., Endman, M. W., & Bernfeld, G. (1977). A three-year follow-up of hyperactive preschoolers into elementary school. *Journal of Child Psychology and Psychiatry, 18*, 239–249.

Campbell, S. B., Szumowski, E. K., Ewing, L. J., Gluck, D. S., & Breaux, A. M. (1982). A multidimension assessment of parent-identified behavior problem toddlers. *Journal of Abnormal Child Psychology, 10*, 569–591.

Carroll, J. (1964). *Language and thought*. Englewood Cliffs, NJ: Prentice-Hall.

Childers, A. T. (1935). Hyperactivity in children having behavior disorders. *American Journal of Orthopsychiatry, 5*, 227–243.

Cohen, N. J., & Minde, K. (1983). The "hyperactive syndrome" in kindergarten children: Comparisons of children with pervasive and situational symptoms. *Journal of Child Psychology and Psychiatry, 24,* 443–455.

Cohen, N. J., Sullivan, J., Minde, K., Novak, C., & Helwig, C. (1981). Evaluation of the relative effectiveness of methylphenidate and cognitive behavior modification in the treatment of kindergarten hyperactive children. *Journal of Abnormal Child Psychology, 9,* 43–54.

Conners, C. K. (1973). Rating scales for use in drug studies with children (special issue). *Psychopharmacology Bulletin, 9,* 24–84.

Conners, C. K. (1975). Minimal brain dysfunction and psychopathology in children. In A. Davids (Ed.), *Child psychopathology and personality: Current topics.* New York: Wiley.

Cunningham, C. E., & Barkley, R. A. (1978a). The effects of methylphenidate on the mother-child interactions of hyperactive and identical twins. *Developmental Medicine and Child Neurology, 20,* 634–642.

Cunningham, C. E., & Barkley, R. A. (1978b). The role of academic failure in hyperactive behavior. *Journal of Learning Disabilities, 11,* 274–280.

Cunningham, C. E., & Barkley, R. A. (1979). The interactions of normal and hyperactive children with their mothers in free play and structured tasks. *Child Development, 50,* 217–224.

Davids, A. (1971). An objective instrument for assessing hyperkinesis in children. *Journal of Learning Disabilities, 4,* 35–37.

Davids, A. (1975). Childhood psychosis: The problem of differential diagnosis. *Journal of Autism and Childhood Schizophrenia, 5,* 130–138.

Davison, G. C., & Neale, J. M. (1974). *Abnormal psychology.* New York: Wiley.

DeMyer, M. K. (1976). The measured intelligence of autistic children. In E. Schopler & R. J. Reichler (Eds.), *Psychopathology and child development: Research and treatment.* New York: Plenum Press.

DeMyer, M. K., Churchill, D. W., Pontius, W., & Gilkey, K. M. (1971). A comparison of five diagnostic systems for childhood schizophrenia and infantile autism. *Journal of Autism and Child Schizophrenia, 1,* 175–189.

Douglas, V. I. (1972). Stop, look, and listen: The problem of sustained attention and impulse control. *Canadian Journal of Behavioral Science, 4,* 259–282.

Douglas, V. I. (1980). Higher mental processes in hyperactive children: Implications for training. In R. M. Knights & D. J. Bakker (Eds.), *Treatment of hyperactive and learning disabled children.* Baltimore: University Park Press.

Douglas, V. I., & Peters, K. G. (1979). Toward a clearer definition of the attentional deficit of hyperactive children. In G. A. Hale & M. Lewis (Eds.), *Attention and the development of cognitive skills.* New York: Plenum Press.

Douglas, V. I., & Sanders, F. A. (1968). A pilot study of Rimland's diagnostic checklist with autistic and mentally retarded children. *Journal of Child Psychology and Psychiatry, 9,* 105–109.

Dwyer, A. M., & Zentall, S. S. (1987). *Color stimulation and its effects on the impulsive errors and activity of hyperactive children.* Manuscript submitted for publication.

Fay, W. H. (1980). Aspects of language. In W. H. Fay, A. L. Schuler, & R. L. Schiefelbusch (Eds.), *Emerging language in autistic children.* Baltimore: University Park Press.

Fein, D., Humes, M., Kaplan, E., Lucci, D., & Waterhouse, L. (1984). The question of left hemisphere dysfunction in infantile autism. *Psychological Bulletin, 95,* 258–281.

Fineman, K. R. (1968). Visual-color reinforcement in establishment of speech by an autistic child. *Perceptual and Motor Skills, 26,* 761–762.

Frankel, F., Freeman, B. J., Ritvo, E., Chikami, B., & Carr, E. (1976). Effects of frequency of photic stimulation upon autistic and retarded children. *American Journal of Mental Deficiency, 81,* 32–40.

Frankel, F., Simmons, J. Q., III, Fichter, M., & Freeman, B. J. (1984). Stimulus overselectivity in autistic and mentally retarded children—A research note. *Journal of Child Psychology and Psychiatry, 25,* 147–155.

Freeman, B., & Ritvo, E. (1976). In E. Ritvo, B. Freeman, E. Ornitz, & P. Tanguay (Eds.), *Autism: Diagnosis, current research and management.* Holliswood, NY: Spectrum.

Freeman, B. J., Frankel, B. J., & Ritvo, E. J. (1976). The effects of response contingent vestibular stimulation on the behavior of autistic and retarded children. *Journal of Autism and Childhood Schizophrenia, 6,* 353–358.

Freibergs, V., & Douglas, V. I. (1969). Concept learning in hyperactive and normal children. *Journal of Abnormal Psychology, 74,* 338–395.

Fuchs, D., & Fuchs, L. S. (1984). *Systematic bias in the assessment of handicapped children.* Paper presented at the annual meeting of the American Educational Research Association, New Orleans, April.

Fuchs, D., Zern, D. S., & Fuchs, L. S. (1983). Participants' verbal and nonverbal behavior in familiar and unfamiliar test conditions: An exploratory analysis. *Diagnostique, 8,* 159–169.

Graubard, P. (1973). Children with behavioral disabilities. In L. M. Dunn (Ed.), *Exceptional children in the schools* (2nd ed.). New York: Holt, Rinehart, & Winston.

Halverson, C. F., & Waldrop, M. F. (1976). Relations between preschool activity and aspects of intellectual and social behavior at age 7½. *Developmental Psychology, 12,* 107–112.

Harris, G., Vincent, J., & Williams, B. (1977). *Temporal stability of behavior profiles and behaviors of hyperactive and control children.* Paper presented at the meeting of the American Psychological Association, San Francisco.

Hermelin, B., & Frith, V. (1971). Can autistic children make sense of what they see and hear? *Journal of Special Education, 5,* 107–117.

Hermelin, B., & O'Connor, N. (1968). Measures of the occipital alpha rhythm in normal, subnormal, and autistic children. *British Journal of Psychiatry, 114,* 603–610.

Hermelin, B., & O'Connor, W. (1970). *Psychological experiments with children.* Oxford: Pergamon.

Hoy, E., Weiss, G., Minde, K., & Cohen, N. (1978). The hyperactive child at adolescence: Cognitive, emotional and social functioning. *Journal of Abnormal Child Psychology, 6,* 311–324.

Hutt, C., & Ounsted, C. (1968). Gaze aversion and its significance in childhood autism. In S. J. Hutt & C. Hutt (Eds.), *Behavior studies in psychiatry.* New York: Pergamon Press.

James, A. L., & Barry, R. J. (1980). Respiratory and vascular responses to simple visual stimuli in autistics, retardates, and normals. *Psychophysiology, 17,* 541–547.

Jenkins, S., Owen, C., Bax, M., & Hart, H. (1984). Continuities of common behavior problems in preschool children. *Journal of Child Psychology and Psychiatry, 25,* 75–89.

Kanner, L. (1943). Autistic disturbances of affective contact. *Nervous Child, 2,* 217–250.

Kauffman, J. M. (1981). *Characteristics of children's behavior disorders (2nd ed.).* Columbus, OH: Charles E. Merrill.

Knoblock, P. (1983). *Teaching emotionally disturbed children.* Boston: Houghton Mifflin.

Koegel, R. L., & Egel, A. L. (1979). Motivating autistic children. *Journal of Abnormal Psychology, 88,* 418–426.

Krug, D. A., Arick, J., & Almond, P. (1980). Behavior checklist for identifying severely handicapped individuals with high levels of autistic behavior. *Journal of Child Psychology and Psychiatry, 9,* 105–109.

Langdell, T. (1978). Recognition of faces: An approach to the study of autism. *Journal of Child Psychology and Psychiatry, 19,* 255–268.

Lidz, C. S. (1983). Issues in assessing preschool children. In K. D. Paget & B. A. Braken (Eds.), *The psychoeducational assessment of preschool children.* New York: Grune & Stratton.

Lipowski, Z. J. (1975). Sensory and information inputs overload: Behavioral effects. *Comprehensive Psychiatry, 16,* 199–221.

Lockyer, L., & Rutter, M. (1970). A five-to fifteen-year follow-up study of infantile psychosis: IV. Patterns of cognitive ability. *British Journal of Social and Clinical Psychology, 9,* 152–163.

Loney, J. (1974). The intellectual functioning of hyperactive elementary school boys: A cross-sectional investigation. *American Journal of Orthopsychiatry, 44,* 754–762.

Loney, J., Whaley-Klahn, M. A., Kosier, T., & Conboy, T. (1981). *Hyperactive boys and their brothers at 21: Predictors of aggressive and antisocial outcomes.* Paper presented at the meeting of the Society for Life History Research, Monterey, California.

Lovaas, O. I., Koegel, R., Simmons, J. Q., & Long, J. S. (1970). *Strengths and weaknesses of operant conditioning techniques for the treatment of autism.* Proceeding of the Conference and Annual Meeting of the National Society for Autistic Children.

Madan-Swain, A., & Zentall, S. S. (1987). *Behavioral comparisons of accepted and rejected hyperactive children and their matched controls in social play contexts.* Manuscript submitted for publication.

Margolies, P. J. (1977). Behavioral approaches to the treatment of early infantile autism: A review. *Psychological Bulletin, 84,* 249–264.

Mash, E. J., & Terdal, L. G. (1982). Behavioral assessment of childhood disturbance. In E. J. Mash & L. G. Terdal (Eds.), *Behavioral assessment of childhood disturbance.* New York: Guilford Press.

Milich, R., & Landau, S. (1982). Socialization and peer relations in hyperactive children. In K. D. Gadow & I. Bialer (Eds.), *Advances in Learning and Behavior Disabilities* (Vol. 1). Greenwich, CT: JAI Press.

Milich, R. S., & Loney, J. (1979). The factor composition of the WISC for hyperkinetic/MBD males. *Journal of Abnormal Child Psychology, 9,* 55–64.

Minde, K., Lewin, D., Weiss, G., Lavigueur, H., Douglas, V. I., & Sykes, E. (1971). The hyperactive child in elementary school: A 5-year controlled follow-up. *Exceptional Children, 38,* 215–221.

Nathanson, L. W. (1977). *Autism versus retardation: Discrimination maintenance along a distracting visual continuum.* Paper presented at the Eighty-fifth Annual Convention of the American Psychological Association, San Francisco.

Neisser, U. (1967). *Cognitive psychology.* New York: Appleton-Century-Crofts.

Newsom, C., & Rincover, A. (1982). Autism. In E. J. Mash & L. G. Terdal (Eds.), *Behavioral assessment of childhood disorders.* New York: Guilford Press.

O'Connor, N., & Hermelin, B. (1967). The selective visual attention of psychotic children. *Journal of Child Psychology and Psychiatry, 8,* 167–179.

Ornitz, E. M. (1974). The modulation of sensory input and motor output in autistic children. *Journal of Autism and Childhood Schizophrenia, 4,* 197–214.

Palkovitz, R. J., & Wiesenfeld, A. R. (1980). Differential autonomic responses of autistic and normal children. *Journal of Autism and Developmental Disorders, 10,* 347–360.

Parry, P. A., & Douglas, V. I. (1983). Effects of reward on concept identification in hyperactive children. *Journal of Abnormal Child Psychology, 11,* 327–340.

Pelham, W. E., & Bender, M. E. (1982). Peer relationships in hyperactive children, Description and treatment. *Advances in Learning and Behavioral Disabilities, 1,* 365–436.

Prior, M. R. (1977). Conditional matching learning set performance in autistic children. *Journal of Child Psychology and Psychiatry, 18,* 183–189.

Prior, M. R. (1979). Cognitive abilities and disabilities in infantile autism: A review. *Journal of Abnormal Child Psychology, 7,* 357–380.

Richer, J. (1976). The social-avoidance behavior of autistic children. *Animal Behavior, 24,* 898–906.

Rimland, B. (1971). The differentiation of child psychosis: An analysis of checklists for 2,218 psychotic children. *Journal of Autism and Childhood Schizophrenia, 1,* 161–174.

Ross, D. M., & Ross, S. A. (1982). *Hyperactivity: Current issues, research, and theory* (2nd ed.). New York: Wiley.

Routh, D. K., Schroeder, C. S., & O'Tuama, L. (1974). Development of activity level in children. *Developmental Psychology, 10,* 163–168.

Rutter, M. (1968). Concepts of autism: A review of research. *Journal of Child Psychology and Psychiatry, 9,* 1–25.

Rutter, M. (1978). Diagnosis and definition of childhood autism. *Journal of Autism and Childhood Schizophrenia, 8,* 139–157.

Rutter, M., & Bartak, L. (1971). Causes of infantile autism: Some considerations from recent research. *Journal of Autism and Childhood Schizophrenia, 1,* 20–32.

Rutter, M., Greenfield, D., & Lockyer, L. (1967). A 5 to 15 year follow-up study of infantile psychosis: II. Social and behavioral outcome. *British Journal of Psychology, 113,* 1183–1199.

Safer, D. J., & Allen, R. P. (1976). *Hyperactive children: Diagnosis and management.* Baltimore: University Park Press.

Schleifer, M., Weiss, G., Cohen, N., Elman, M., Cvejic, H., & Kruger, E. (1975). Hyperactivity in preschoolers and the effect of methylphenidate. *American Journal of Orthopsychiatry, 45,* 38–50.

Schopler, E. (1965). Early infantile autism and receptor processes. *Archives of General Psychiatry, 13,* 327–355.

Shah, A., & Frith, U. (1983). An islet of ability in autistic children: A research note. *Journal of Child Psychology and Psychiatry, 24,* 613–620.

Shores, R. E., & Haubrich, P. A. (1969). Effect of cubicles in educating emotionally disturbed children. *Exceptional Children, 36,* 21–24.

Simmons, J., & Tymchuk, A. (1973). The learning deficits in childhood psychosis. *The Pediatric Clinics of North America, 20,* 665–679.

Skinner, B. F. (1953). *Science and human behavior.* New York: Macmillan.

Smith, A. A., Malmo, R. B., & Shagass, C. (1977). An electromyographic study of listening and talking. *Canadian Journal of Psychology, 8*, 219–227.

Spivak, G., & Swift, M. (1967). *Devereux elementary school behavior rating scale.* Devon, PA: Devereux Foundation Press.

Sroufe, L. A., Steucher, H. V., & Stutzer, W. (1973). The functional significance of autistic behaviors for the psychotic child. *Journal of Abnormal Child Psychology, 1*, 225–240.

Steinkamp, M. W. (1980). Relationships between environmental distraction and task performance of hyperactive and normal children. *Journal of Learning Disabilities, 13*, 209–214.

Stevens, D., Boydstun, J., Dykman, R., Peters, J., & Stinton, D. (1967). Presumed minimal brain dysfunction in children: Relationship to performance on selected behavioral tests. *Archives of General Psychiatry, 16*, 281–285.

Strain, P. S., & Shores, R. E. (1983). A reply to "misguided mainstreaming." *Exceptional Children, 50*, 271–273.

Suedfeld, P., & Schwartz, G. (1983). Restricted environmental stimulation therapy REST as a treatment for autistic children. *Developmental and Behavioral Pediatrics, 4*, 196–201.

Tant, J. L., & Douglas, V. I. (1982). Problem solving in hyperactive, normal, and reading-disabled boys. *Journal of Abnormal Child Psychology, 10*, 285–306.

Weingartner, H., Rapoport, J. L., Buchsbaum, M. S., Bunney, W. E., Ebert, M. H., Mikkelsen, E. J., & Caine, E. D. (1980). Cognitive processes in normal and hyperactive children and their response to amphetamine treatment. *Journal of Abnormal Psychology, 89*, 25–37.

Weiss, G., Minde, K., Werry, J., Douglas, V., & Nemeth, E. (1971). Studies of the hyperactive child: VII. Five-year follow up. *Archives of General Psychiatry, 24*, 409–414.

Weithorn, C. J., & Kagen, E. (1978). Interaction of language development and activity level among first-graders. *American Journal of Orthopsychiatry, 48*, 148–159.

Werry, J. S. (1968). Studies on the hyperactive child: IV. An empirical analysis of the minimal brain dysfunction syndrome. *Archives of General Psychiatry, 19*, 9–16.

Whalen, C. K., Henker, B., Collins, B. E., McAuliffe, S., & Vaux, A. (1979). Peer interaction in a structured communication task: Comparisons of normal and hyperactive boys and of methylphenidate (Ritalin) and placebo effects. *Child Development, 50*, 388–401.

Winett, R. A., & Winkler, R. C. (1972). Current behavior modification in the classroom: Be still, be quiet, be docile. *Journal of Applied Behavior Analysis, 5*, 499–504.

Wing, L. (1976). *Early childhood autism.* Oxford: Pergamon Press.

Zentall, S. S. (1975). Optimal stimulation as theoretical basis of hyperactivity. *American Journal of Orthopsychiatry, 45*, 549–563.

Zentall, S. S. (1979). Effects of environmental stimulation on behavior as a function of type of behavior disorder. *Behavior Disorders, 5*, 19–29.

Zentall, S. S. (1980). Behavioral comparisons of hyperactive and normally active children in natural settings. *Journal of Abnormal Child Psychology, 98*, 93–109.

Zentall, S. S. (1983). Effects of psychotropic drugs on the behavior of preacademic children: A review. *Topics in Early Childhood Special Education, 3*, 29–39.

Zentall, S. S. (1984). Context effects in the behavioral ratings of hyperactivity. *Journal of Abnormal Child Psychology, 12*, 345–352.

Zentall, S. S. (1986). Effects of color stimulation on performance and activity of hyperactive and nonhyperactive children. *Journal of Educational Psychology, 78*, 159–165.

Zentall, S. S. (1987) *Production deficiencies in elicited language but not in the spontaneous verbalizations of hyperactive children.* Manuscript submitted for publication.

Zentall, S. S., & Barack, R. S. (1979). Ratings scales for hyperactivity: Concurrent validity, reliability, and decisions to label for the Conners and Davids abbreviated scale. *Journal of Abnormal Child Psychology, 7*, 179–190.

Zentall, S. S., & Gohs, D. E. (1984). Responses of hyperactive and comparison children to global vs. detailed information. *Learning Disability Quarterly, 7*, 77–87.

Zentall, S. S., & Leib, S. (1985). Structured tasks: Effects on activity and performance of hyperactive and normal children. *Journal of Educational Research, 79*, 91–95.

Zentall, S. S., & Shaw, J. H. (1980). Effects of classroom noise on performance and activity of second grade hyperactive and control children. *Journal of Educational Psychology, 72*, 830–840.

Zentall, S. S., & Zentall, T. R. (1983). Optimal stimulation: A model of disordered activity and performance in normal and deviant children. *Psychological Bulletin, 94*, 446–471.

Zentall, S. S., Zentall, T. R., & Barack, R. S. (1978a). Distraction as a function of within-task stimulation for hyperactive and normal children. *Journal of Learning Disabilities, 11*, 540–548.

Zentall, S. S., Zentall, T. R., & Booth, M. E. (1978b). Within-task stimulation: Effects on activity and spelling performance in hyperactive and normal children. *Journal of Educational Research, 71*, 223–230.

Zentall, S. S., Gohs, D. E., & Culatta, B. (1983). Language and activity of hyperactive and comparison preschoolers in a listening task. *Exceptional Children, 50*, 255–266.

Zentall, S. S., Falkenberg, S. D., & Smith, L. B. (1985). Effects of stimulation on copying performance of attention problem adolescents. *Journal of Abnormal Child Psychology, 13*, 501–511.

11

Cognitive Asssessment of Multiply Handicapped Young Children

Carl J. Dunst and R. A. McWilliam

The basic premise of this chapter is that traditional methods of early cognitive assessment have restricted rather than advanced our ability to adequately assess and intervene with multiply handicapped young children. Support for this contention comes from a number of sources (Decarie, 1969; Fagan & Singer, 1983; Kopp & Shaperman, 1973; Lewis, 1982), but especially from the work of Zelazo and his colleagues (Kearsley, 1979; Zelazo, 1979, 1982a). These investigators found that handicapped infants, despite significant delays on traditional psychometric tests of intellectual performance, displayed age-appropriate information-processing capabilities when dependence on gross and fine motor skills were minimized. That is, the cognitive abilities of these children were often found to be intact when psychophysiological indices (e.g., heart rate), visual attentiveness, and social responsiveness, rather than gross and fine motor behaviors, were used as a basis for assessing mental processes. Zelazo (1979) contended that such disparities between results obtained from traditional and nontraditional assessment procedures call into question the assumption of the predominantly neuromotor and sensorimotor bases of infant intelligence. He noted the need for modification of both the conceptual nature of early cognitive development and methods for assessing cognitive capabilities.

In this chapter we use the *assessment* to refer to the systematic gathering of behavioral data for the purposes of (a) characterizing a child's topography[1] of cognitive interactive capabilities and (b) developing and implementing intervention procedures designed to facilitate acquisition of social-adaptive interactive competencies. This term includes essential components (data collection, description, and decision making) that Simeonsson and Bailey (Chapter 2) and Wachs and Sheehan (in the Preface) have identified as being fundamentally important in any assessment process. However, our use of the term diverges considerably from common usage. We do not distinguish, nor do we believe it is beneficial *for* intervention purposes to distinguish, between different types of assessment

---

[1]The term *topography* is used throughout this chapter to refer to the manner in which different behaviors bear a clear relationship to one another, thus constituting behavior classes, and where the behaviors are likely to be influenced by different situational and contextual settings.

CARL J. DUNST and R. A. MCWILLIAM ● Family, Infant, and Preschool Program, and the Human Development Research and Training Institute, Western Carolina Center, Morgantown, North Carolina 28655.

(screening, diagnosis, prognosis, and prescription). Our basic contention is that assessment for intervention purposes need focus only on those dimensions of behavior (type, form, and context) that permit the facilitation and elaboration of interactional competencies. We use the term assessment quite similarly to Simeonsson and Bailey (Chapter 2), who describe it as a "profile of functional capacities."

By far, the majority of approaches currently used for assessing early cognitive development (psychometric, Piagetian, and criterion-referenced) rely almost entirely on *a priori* selected motoric responses to infer mastery of progressively more complex forms of cognitive abilities. Behaviors indicative of different levels of cognitive performance are preselected as indices of mastery, and the child is tested for the extent to which he or she has acquired these behaviors. Test items are typically ordered according to either the average of the median age at which infants comprising a standardization sample "pass" the items (e.g., Bayley, 1969), or test items are rank-ordered by degree of difficulty (e.g., Uzgiris & Hunt, 1975). When these tests are used to assess handicapped children, administration procedures are often modified (see, e.g., Dubose, Langley, & Stagg, 1979; Stagg, Chapter 4), but the youngsters are still required to manifest the *a priori* selected motoric responses in order to be credited with a mastery of different levels of cognitive abilities.

These traditional approaches to cognitive assessment are based on a number of assumptions that we believe are not entirely tenable, and thus suggest a need for alternative procedures for discerning cognitive interactive capabilities. First, traditional approaches to cognitive assessment explicitly advance the position that cognition is primarily neuromotor and sensorimotor in origin, but as the work of Zelazo (1979, 1982a, b) has shown, this assumption is not entirely correct. Second, traditional approaches to assessment implicitly assume inherent significance with regard to the items on the tests (Uzgiris & Hunt, 1975). It is our contention that *all* items on infant and preschool cognitive tests are no more than a subset of overt indicators of cognitive mastery, and that we could (and can) discern a child's topography of cognitive abilities by using an entirely different subset of behaviors. Third, traditional approaches to assessment implicitly advance the notion that individual test items (and the scores derived from them) have explanatory and causative value, when, in fact, they provide a very limited perspective from which to describe competence, let alone to identify the factors associated with the acquisition of these behaviors (Dunst, Lesko, Holbert, Wilson, Sharpe, & Liles, 1987). Fourth, traditional approaches to assessment implicitly assume that there are certain sequences in development that all children must follow in order to attain cognitive competence. We argue, in line with Fischer (1980), that there are alternative pathways in development, and that children with developmental handicaps can and do traverse different routes toward the achievement of cognitive competence.[2]

[2]It is our contention that all children, regardless of their handicapping condition, acquire cognitive, interactive competencies in the stagelike sequence described below. We do not believe, however, that it is necessary for all children, and particularly multiply handicapped youngsters, to follow *a priori* behavior sequences as defined on developmental scales of cognitive development (e.g., object permanence). Nor do we believe that instances of failure to manifest lower level behaviors on these scales, while demonstrating higher level competencies, invalidates the applicability of cognitive-developmental theory to the assessment of handicapped youngsters. We would argue that mastery of cognitive competence has occurred and has manifested itself in alternative forms, and that, with the use of alternative assessment procedures, this stagelike mastery can be discerned.

In this chapter, we propose an alternative strategy for assessing the early cognitive interactive capabilities of multiply handicapped children. Although the proposed model has utility in the assessment of both nonhandicapped and handicapped youngsters, it is particularly useful with multiply handicapped children, inasmuch as the assessment model permits the use of a wide variety of behavior indicators for inferring the mastery of different types and forms of competence. The assessment strategy builds on and elaborates on the work of Chatelanat and Schoggen (1980) and Robinson (1987).

The chapter is divided into three major sections. The first includes a description of a developmental model of early cognitive growth on which the assessment strategy is based. The model focuses on the delineation of the *levels, types,* and *contexts* of the progressively more complex behavioral competencies that children use in interactions with their environments. The second section illustrates how the model can be used for assessment purposes. The third section describes how the assessment information can be applied to the design and implementation of interventions for fostering the acquisition of interactive competencies. Together, the information presented in the three sections represents a framework for linking theory, assessment, and intervention. The framework is designed as a systematic strategy for identifying the targets of intervention and for facilitating the acquisition of these targets (see Dunst *et. al.*, 1987).

A DEVELOPMENTAL MODEL OF INTERACTIVE COMPETENCIES

Our model includes three dimensions of behavioral abilities: levels, types, and context of cognitive interactive competencies. The *levels* dimension describes the progressively more complex kinds of interactions that infants have with their environment. The *types* dimension describes the different kinds of behaviors that constitute interactive competencies. The *context* dimension describes the settings and situations in which certain levels and types of interactions are most likely to occur.

Levels of Interactive Competence

The following represents a stage-level conceptualization of early cognitive growth that delineates the progressively more complex kinds of interactions that infants and young children have with their social and nonsocial environments. The model specifically focuses on the description of the types and forms of interactions that youngsters manifest in response to different environmental demands and challenges. The progressively more complex kind of interactions represent shifts in "balance of power" (Bronfenbrenner, 1979) that reflect the child's ability to exercise control over his or her environment in a social-adaptive manner, particularly in terms of the acquisition and use of conventionalized behavior (i.e., behavior that is both socially and culturally defined and valued).

Table 1 shows the five levels of interactions described by the model. The model integrates and synthesizes data from a number of sources, most notably McCall (1979), Piaget (1951, 1952, 1954), and Uzgiris (1983). The contributions of Uzgiris deserve

Table 1. A Developmental Model of Interactive Competencies

Level	Interactive type	Definition	Function	Examples
I	Attentional interactions	The capacity to attend to and discriminate between stimuli.	Provides a basis for establishing selective attention to salient and consequently reinforcing features of the environment.	1. Smiling on seeing a familiar person. 2. Anticipatory feeding response.
II	Contingency interactions	The use of simple, undifferentiated forms of behavior to initiate and sustain control over reinforcing consequences.	Provides a basis for the infant to learn about his or her own capabilities as well as the propensities of social and nonsocial objects.	1. Simple lap games (e.g., "so-big"). 2. Swiping at a mobile
III	Differentiated interactions	The coordination and regulation of behavior that reflects elaboration and progress toward conventionalization.	Provides the infant with a set of behaviors that permit adaptations to environmental demands and expectations, especially social standards.	1. Nonverbal gestures (point, give, etc.). 2. Independent cup drinking
IV	Encoded interactions	The use of conventionalized forms of behavior that are context-bound and that depend on referents as a basis for evoking the behaviors.	Provides the child with a set of "rule-governed" behaviors that permit increased "balance of power" (independence) favoring the developing child.	1. Verbal or nonverbal communication (e.g., sign language, communication board) 2. Helping "set" a table.
V	Symbolic interactions	The use of conventionalized forms of behavior (language, pretend play, sign language, drawings, etc.) to "capture, preserve, invent, and communicate information" (Wolf & Gardner, 1981, p. 209).	Provides the child with a set of behaviors that permit recollections of previous occurrences, requests for future occurrences, and construction of novel forms of "rule-governed" behavior.	1. Communicating "want drink" in the absence of reference-giving cues. 2. Role-taking (e.g., enacting part of a previously heard story).

special recognition as our model is, in large part, based substantially on her work.[3] Table 2 shows how the proposed levels of cognition correspond to Uzgiris's model, as well as to those of Piaget and McCall.

Attentional Interactions

Attentional interactions refer to the child's capacity to attend to and discriminate between stimuli. Operationally, attentional interactions are defined as behaviors that infants use to respond to and maintain stimulus inputs (e.g., orienting toward and maintaining attention to an adult's face). These behaviors provide a basis for ascertaining the infant's attention-getting and attention-holding capacities. Attentional behaviors allow one to discern (1) what the child is attending to; (2) which particular child behaviors reflect attentional capacities; (3) what elicits positive and negative responses; and (4) what maintains attention and thus functions as a reinforcer. To the extent that one can ascertain that an infant is responsive to environmental events and attempts to maintain stimulus inputs, attentional interactive competencies set the occasion for adults to reinforce the child for gaining and maintaining control over social and nonsocial stimuli.

Attentional behaviors may be manifested in response to different stimulus events and may be demonstrated in numerous ways. These include, but are not restricted to, *looking* at an object or person; *orienting* toward sounds; *tracking* an object moving across the child's visual field; *smiling* in response to seeing a familiar person; *laughing* in response to seeing an interesting event; *sucking* on a nipple placed in the child's mouth; *grasping* an object placed in the child's hand; *cessation* of body movement on hearing a familiar voice; and *crying* in response to a sudden noise. The attentional capacities of nonhandicapped infants are so well documented that there is no need to review in detail the evidence supporting infants' capabilities in this area (e.g., Cohen, DeLoache, & Strauss, 1979; Fagan & Singer, 1983; Lewis & Brooks-Gunn, 1981). Suffice it to say that the available data indicate that infants attend to, process, and store information about numerous aspects of their environment (shape, color, size, and temporal events).

Evidence concerning the attentional capacities of handicapped infants indicates that their attentiveness to different environmental events reflects similar abilities (e.g., Glenn & Cunningham, 1983; McDonough, 1982; Miranda & Fantz, 1973, 1974). Glenn and Cunningham (1983) found that the auditory processing capabilities of Down syndrome infants were similar to those of nonhandicapped infants. Likewise, Miranda and Fantz (1973, 1974) found the visual information-processing abilities of Down syndrome infants to be similar to those of nonhandicapped infants with regard to the acquisition, storage, and retrieval processes. In one of the few studies of the attentional behaviors of cerebral-palsied infants, McDonough (1982) found that although their attention-getting behavior lagged behind that of nonhandicapped babies, their attention-holding behaviors were identical. That is, it took longer to gain the attention of the handicapped infants, but once it was obtained, visual attention(-holding) to an eliciting stimulus was maintained in a manner similar to that of the nonhandicapped infants.

Although there is evidence that the quality of the attentional behaviors of hand-

---

[3]It should be noted, however, that we have taken a liberty in redefining and recasting Uzgiris's conceptual description of cognitive development in order to relate the model more directly to intervention. Any discrepancies between our descriptions and those of Uzgiris, and any resulting omissions, should be attributed to us.

Table 2. Contrasting Models of Early Cognitive Development

Proposed model	Piaget's model	Uzigiris's model	McCall's model
I Attentional interactions	I Use of reflexes	I Undifferentiated responsiveness	I Endogenous responsiveness
	II Primary circular reactions		
II Contingency Interactions	III Secondary circular reactions	I Simple unitary actions	II Complete subjectivity
III Differentiated interactions	IV Coordination of secondary circular reactions	I Differentiated actions	III Separation of means from ends
	V Tertiary circular reactions	III Regulation of behavior by differentiated feedback	IV Objectification of environmental entities
IV Encoded interactions	VI Representational actions and mental combinations	IV Anticipatory regulation of actions	V Symbolic reactions
V Symbolic interactions			

icapped infants differs from that of their nonimpaired counterparts (see, e.g., Dunst, 1985), the types and forms of attentional behaviors are much alike, and it is possible to map the topography of the attentional capacities of these infants. The extent to which handicapped infants "tell us" that they are attending to their environment is an important developmental step; and as we shall see, the extent to which we can discern attentional capacities becomes an important step in the assessment process of discerning cognitive competence.

Contingency Interactions

Contingency interactive behavior is the infant's capacity to initiate and sustain interactions with the environment in a simple but efficacious manner. Piaget (1952) labeled such behaviors "secondary circular reactions"; Watson (1972), "response-contingent" behavior; Uzgiris (1983), "simple unitary actions"; and learning theorists, "operants." These types of interactions are *instrumental* in producing reinforcing consequences as a result of the infant's actions on the social and nonsocial environment. Operationally, contingent interactions are defined as undifferentiated response-contingent behaviors that are used in a *repetitious manner* to maintain feedback produced by the child's own actions (e.g., repeatedly producing a reinforcing consequence by swiping at a roly-poly).

Contingency interactive behaviors include *batting* at a mobile to produce auditory feedback; *touching* an adults's mouth to get the person to repeat an interesting sound; *shaking* or *banging* a rattle to produce a sound; *vocalizing* to get someone's attention, *smiling* to get a person to repeat an interesting spectacle; and *rolling over* to reinstigate a social interaction (see Dunst, 1981, for a more complete compilation of infant response-contingent behavior). Developmentally, these behaviors represent an important transition toward cognitive competence. In contrast to the attention-getting and attention-holding behaviors characteristics of attentional interactions, contingency interactions represent a set of behaviors that allow a child to interact with the environment in a simple but nonetheless competent manner. Contingency behaviors are those that *elicit*, as opposed to ones that are *elicited by*, environmental stimuli.

Engagement in contingency interactions leads to the infant's acquisition of three very important developmental competencies: contingency awareness, predictability, and controllability (Friedman & Vietze, 1972; Lamb, 1981; Watson, 1966, 1972). Watson (1966, 1972) used the term *contingency awareness* to refer to the infant's capacity to understand and appreciate his or her own behavior capabilities; that is, the ability to "know" that he or she can produce interesting effects in the environment. *Predictability* refers to the infant's awareness that certain behaviors can repeatedly produce the same effects in interactions with the social and nonsocial environments (Lamb, 1981). *Controllability* refers to the infant's capacity to understand that certain aspects of the environment can be affected as a function of his or her attempts to produce environmental consequences (Friedman & Vietze, 1972; Lamb, 1981). It is well documented that different classes of behavior (sucking, smiling, vocalizations, visual responsiveness, head rotation, kicking, and manual behaviors) are used by infants to initiate and sustain interactions with their environment (e.g., Hulsebus, 1973; Lipsitt, 1969; Lipsitt & Werner, 1981; Millar, 1976; Sameroff & Cavanaugh, 1979). Evidence concerning the nonhandicapped infant's capacity to engage in contingency interactions is such that basic behavior competencies embodying contingency awareness, predictability, and controllability are acquired beginning around 2 months of age and increase rapidly over the next 4–6 months.

A number of studies of severely handicapped infants have found that these youngsters also engage in contingency interactions that lead to the acquisition of contingency awareness, predictability, and controllability (Cyrulik-Jacobs, Shapira, & Jones, 1975; Dunst, Cushing, & Vance, 1985; Friedlander, McCarthy, & Soforonko, 1967; Laub & Dunst, 1974; Utley, Duncan, Strain, & Scanlon, 1983). Cyrulik-Jacobs *et al.* (1975) found that cerebral-palsied infants were able to learn to manually activate PLAYTEST (Friedlander, 1975) switches (large nipplelike manipulanda) to choose auditory reinforcement varying in complexity. Friedlander *et al.* (1967), also using the PLAYTEST apparatus, found that two severely retarded infants, one of whom was multiply handicapped, were able to learn to activate manipulanda to produce differing auditory information when the reinforcement was contingent on operant responding. Dunst *et al.* (1985), in studying the learning capabilities of profoundly retarded, multiply handicapped infants, found that, despite very limited behavior repertoires, the infants were able to learn to rotate their heads from side to midline position to activate a visual display consisting of multicolored lights. Laub and Dunst (1974) successfully demonstrated that the rate of vocalizations of a severely handicapped, microcephalic, cerebral-palsied infant could be increased when adult imitation of the sounds was made contingent on the infant's vocalizations. Utley *et al.* (1983) found that four multiply handicapped infants and young children increased their visual attention to multicolored lights when the visual display was activated contingent on the fixation behavior of the infants.

Taken together, these studies provide encouraging (even convincing) evidence that multiply handicapped infants can acquire contingency-interactive behaviors that permit them to become more independent and adaptive in their interactions with their environment. By no means are the contingency-interactive behaviors of severely and multiply handicapped infants qualitatively equivalent to those of nonhandicapped children. Nonetheless, the available evidence clearly indicates that these infants, in their own way, manifest the ability to initiate and sustain interactions with their environment in a competent manner. Handicapped infants' learning control strategies in interacting with their social and nonsocial environment is an important developmental acquisition, and the extent to which we can discern the child's topography of contingency behaviors becomes an important part of the assessment process for discerning cognitive competencies.

Differentiated Interaction

The term differentiated interactions refers to the infant's capacity to both *coordinate* and *regulate* (e.g., modify and adjust) behavior that reflects elaboration and progress toward conventionalization.[4] Operationally, differentiated interactions are defined as nonrule-governed socially defined behavior that matches or approximates social standards and expectations (e.g., cup drinking, walking, and the use of appropriate modes of nonverbal communication). The child's acquisition of differentiated behaviors is, in part, affected by environmental demands and adaptations, and especially by adult expectations regarding the infant's use of conventionalization behavior. Differentiated, conventionalized behavior makes the child "social," so to speak, and provides the child with a set of behavior competencies that permit him or her to exercise greater control over social and nonsocial events by using culturally valued modes of interactions.

Uzgiris (1983) provided a review of the different forms of differentiated behaviors: *searching* for hidden or displaced objects; using *intermediaries* (e.g., strings, supports, and "tools") as means to secure desired objects; *imitating* novel sounds and gestures; and using *socially recognized* actions with objects. Other behaviors that represent differentiated interactions include *locomotion* (of any form) to attain a desired object, the use of a *cup or spoon* (as tools) to feed oneself, the use of *nonverbal gestures* to communicate needs and desires, and attempts to *take off and put on* clothes. Taken together, these various behaviors reflect differentiated elaborations and adaptations as well as increased conventionalization in response to interactions with the environment.

Research with a clear focus on the manner in which multiply handicapped children manifest differentiated interactions is relatively scarce, although converging evidence indicates that these youngsters engage in these kinds of behavior in ways that parallel those used by nonhandicapped children. For example, Robinson (1982; Robinson & Robinson, 1983) found that the use of *alternative* indicators of cognition (e.g., eye pointing) permit age-appropriate inferences to be made regarding the multiply handicapped child's understanding and mastery of relationships fundamental to differentiated interactions. Feters (1976), using Bower's method (1974) of assessing cognitive competence involving object permanence, found that cerebral-palsied youngsters, despite their inability to physically produce overt indicators of cognition, were able to display an understanding of the object construct at near-age-appropriate levels. This understanding was discerned in vi-

---

[4]We view conventionalization in behavior as representing cognitive, interactive competence *par excellence*. The term is used to mean socially and culturally defined and recognized behavior that permits an individual to become a progressively more competent and socially adaptive member of different cultural settings and contexts. Conventionalization is most notably manifested in behavior that meets socially accepted standards.

sual searching behavior in response to a violation of an expectation regarding the disappearance and reappearance of an object. Using other types of alternative indicators, researchers (Decarie, 1969; Kopp & Shaperman, 1973; Zelazo, 1982a,b) have also found that when dependence on gross and fine motor performance is minimized, handicapped infants can and often do demonstrate the ability to engage in differentiated interactions. Engagement by handicapped children in differentiated interactions—and therefore their recognition of their ability to construct and regulate behavior—is an important developmental attainment. This is particularly the case with regard to their ability to learn and perfect conventionalized behavior, and thus, the importance of the ability to assess mastery of differentiated behaviors becomes apparent.

Encoded Interactions

The term *encoded interactive behaviors* refers to a child's capacity to use conventionalized forms of behavior—either culturally (e.g., verbal language) or arbitrarily (e.g. rebus symbols) established—that are based on a set of rules that govern their construction. These include verbal language, sign language, pretend play, and helping to set a table for dinner. Encoded behaviors equip children with a range of competencies that they can use both to initiate and sustain interactions (e.g., signing "more play" to indicate a desire to continue a game) and to adapt and respond to requests and demands (e.g., answering questions using a communication board). Operationally, encoded interactions are defined as a conventionalized system of signals that reflect an underlying set of rules that govern their construction, but that depend on perceptually present stimuli in order to be manifested. According to Uzgiris (1983), these types of behaviors represent "sequence of actions [that] appear to be coordinated not through after-the-fact compensations, but by means of anticipatory compensations" (p. 177). Encoded behaviors are characterized by the preplanning of actions as opposed to the trial-and-error and groping actions dominant in differentiated interactions. Encoded interactions serve one very important function: they lead to *economy* in the infant's interactions with his or her environment through an increased conventionalization of behavior. That is, increases in the child's topography of behavior reflect not only progress toward the mastery of socially and culturally defined behavior, but also the ability to select and use the appropriate conventionalized actions in given contexts (e.g., selecting from all words in the child's repertoire the one that has the highest probability of resulting in the anticipated effect).

Unlike Uzgiris (1983) and others (e.g., Siebert, Hogan, & Mundy, 1982) who equate encoded behaviors with representational behaviors (à la Piaget, 1951), we make a fundamental distinction between the two types of cognitive capacities. This distinction is consistent with evidence that encoded behaviors are a transitional level of functioning between behaviors typifying differentiated actions and symbolic functioning (see especially McCune-Nicolich, 1981). In our model, encoded behaviors may take the form of signifiers for the signified, but their manifestation is apparently the result of reference-giving cues that evoke the behaviors. For example, Bloom (1970) described a situation in which a child used the words "mommy bounce" to request continuation of a game involving the mother's bouncing the child up and down on a bed, a game that the mother initiated. In this instance, the context-bound nature of the interaction played a fundamental role in the child's use of the words.

Encoded behaviors take a number of forms, including the paramount attainment of early cognitive competence: linguistic behaviors. Pretend and make-believe play are other forms of encoded behavior (McCune-Nicolich, 1981). Uzgiris (1983) provided examples of other anticipatory behaviors, most notably the ability to *conserve* an image of an object; *foresight* in solving problems; the *imitation of* novel, invisible gestures; the *imitation of* new words; and the *anticipatory construction* of spatial solutions to problems. In addition, formal sign language (e.g., signed English, American Sign Language, and Amerind), symbol systems (e.g., rebus, Blissymbols), computerized voice-synthesized communication devices, finger spelling, and other forms of augmentative communication using prosthetic devices represent additional means that permit the manifestation of encoded behavior.

The extent and manner in which handicapped individuals display behaviors that may be taken as manifestations of encoded behaviors have been examined in a number of studies (Hulme & Lunzer, 1966; Wing, Gould, Yeates, & Brierley, 1977; Zelazo, 1982a,b; Zelazo & Kearsley, 1980). In a comparative study of retarded and nonretarded youngsters, Hulme and Lunzer (1966) found considerable similarities in the manner of play of the two groups, with increases in the level of play behavior becoming progressively more conventionalized with increasing mental age. Wing *et al.* (1977) found that conventionalization in the play of severely handicapped children was generally demonstrated in their sample of subjects, although symbolic play was manifested only among children with mental ages (MA) exceeding 20 months. Zelazo (1982b) reported that although handicapped and developmentally delayed infants often manifest undifferentiated forms of play with toys and other materials, play behaviors representing encoded forms of interactions are nonetheless manifested by these children. As is often the case, the qualitative aspects of the encoded behaviors of handicapped children would be expected to differ from those used by nonhandicapped children. Nonetheless, systematic observations reveal that handicapped youngsters do display encoded behaviors, although often in their own way and sometimes with the need of considerable environmental support. The extent to which we are able to discern how handicapped children display encoded behaviors is an important part of any assessment process. Knowledge of how the infant is able to convey and display conventionalized behavior permits inferences to be made regarding the child's level of cognitive interactive competence.

Symbolic Interactions

The term *symbolic interactions* refers to the child's capacity to use words, images, figures, memory, drawings, numbers, and so on as signifiers for the objects, persons, events, and so on that are symbolized. In contrast to encoded behaviors, which are manifested in response to the immediate demands of the environment in which the child is currently functioning, symbolic behaviors permit the recollection of previous events or evocations of future events (e.g., saying "member doggie" to communicate an encounter that happened several days ago). Operationally, symbolic interactions are defined as rule-governed, conventionalized behaviors that are used to describe, request, and enact (for example) persons, objects, or events in the *absence* of reference-giving cues.

Discussions and empirical tests of the characteristics of the *symbolic function* abound (Bates, Benigni, Bretherton, Camaioni, & Volterra, 1979; McCune-Nicolich, 1981; Wolf & Gardner, 1981). The major characteristics are *decontextualization* (a lessening of reliance on stimulus support for signifiers to be used to signify objects, persons, and events); *distancing* (the capacity to use signifiers that are both physically different and increasingly distant from the referent in time and space); and *sign–signifier differentiation* (the use of socially recognized and defined signs as signifiers). Symbolic interactions serve one important function: they provide the child with a set of rule-governed behaviors that permit the child to interact with the social and nonsocial environment adaptively by using almost entirely conventionalized behavior. In contrast to encoded behaviors, which are context-bound, symbolic interactions permit reflections on the past, requests for future events, and the construction of new forms of expression through combinations of different symbols and signs. Although the distinction between encoded and symbolic interactions is often easier to describe than to observe, particularly during transitions between levels, the distinction is fundamentally important with regard to the emergence of cognitive competencies. Symbolic interactions permit the child to master aspects of his or her environment without having to interact directly with it, as well as to convey this mastery by using conventionalized behavior.

Types and Forms of Interaction

The earliest manifestations of interactive competencies have traditionally been viewed as encompassing, primarily, the mastery of different aspects of the inanimate environment. Flavell (1977) noted, about a decade ago, that we lacked "solid research evidence on infant social cognition, and a really detailed understanding of its step-by-step development" (p. 49). Since Flavell made this statement, considerable advances in the study of social cognition have occurred (Lamb & Sherrod, 1981; Lewis & Rosenblum, 1978; McGurk, 1978). It is now recognized that the acquisition of social-cognitive competencies is extremely important, especially with regard to both conventionalization (see Golinkoff, 1983) and adaptations (Ambrose, 1978; Charlesworth, 1979) to environmental demands. Dunst (1984) summarized the recent work for which progressively more complex sequences of attainments had been proposed: affective development, communication, emotional development, imitation, person permanence, self-knowledge, social development, and social play. To the extent that the attainments of these various developmental progressions meet the criteria of the developmental model described above, the attainments may be taken as manifestations of cognitive interactive competencies.

As part of the assessment and enhancement of interactive competencies, we have found it useful to think of interactive competencies in terms of *behavior functions*. Figure 1 displays a diagram of two major types (engaging and modulating), four forms (initiating, sustaining, regulating, and adapting), and two categories (social and nonsocial) of interactive competencies.

The term *engaging* refers to behavior that a child uses to elicit or maintain input from either or both the social and the nonsocial environment. *Initiating* behaviors are those used by the child to begin an interaction (e.g., picking up a spoon to initiate a feeding episode). *Sustaining* behaviors are those used by the child to maintain or repeat interactive episodes (e.g., using a spoon and repeating the food-to-mouth sequence in order to alleviate hunger). Both initiating and sustaining interactive competencies function to establish and maintain, respectively, interactions with the social and the nonsocial environment.

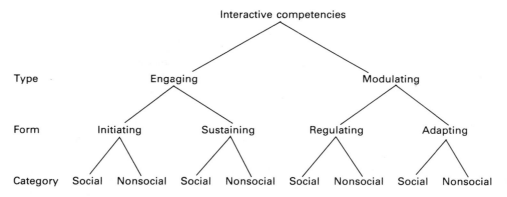

Figure 1. A graphic representation of the types, forms, and categories of interactive competencies.

The term *modulating* refers to behavior that a child uses to modify or accommodate to interactions with the social or the nonsocial environment, or both. *Regulating* behaviors are those used both to terminate input from the environment and to set the occasion for reinitiating interactions (e.g., using gaze aversion to terminate adult stimulation and then using fixation on adult's face to initiate adult responsiveness). *Adapting behaviors* are those used by the child to respond to others' efforts to establish interactions or to get the child to respond to adult requests or comments (e.g., handing an object to an adult in response to a hand-extended–palm-up gesture). Both regulating and adapting behaviors provide the child the opportunity to gain balance of power in interactions through the use of behaviors that function as modulators of adult behavior.

In addition to describing behaviors in terms of their types and forms, interactive competencies may be broadly classified into two categories: social and nonsocial. Social cognitive behaviors are interactions involving the animate environment. Nonsocial cognitive behaviors are interactions involving the inanimate environment. By no means are the two categories mutually exclusive. The reason for distinguishing between the two interactive competencies is to broaden our conceptualizations of what constitutes cognitive competence. Visually tracking an object is one type of attentional capacity, and so is recognition of a familiar person. Making a roly-poly produce an interesting sound is one type of contingency interaction, and so is playing the adult–child game of peek-a-boo. Using a spoon as a tool for eating is one type of differentiated behavior, and so is extending the arms to be picked up. Showing foresight in getting an object out of a container (e.g., pouring milk into a glass) is one type of encoded behavior, and so is the use of sign language to request help from an adult. Remembering the placement of an object across several hours is one type of symbolic behavior, and so is saying "go play" to request an adult to take the child to the park. Cognitive interactive competencies are manifested in many different ways and forms, and a proper framework from which to recognize these different kinds of interactions is crucial as a mnemonic for recognizing the broad-based cognitive components of *all* infant behavior.

Contexts of Interactions

Both social and nonsocial contexts have rather dramatic effects on the types and forms of behavior that infants are likely to manifest (Bronfenbrenner, 1979; Lamb, 1979). Behavior is rarely random; rather, it tends to be emitted in response to specific features of different settings. Moreover, behavior type and form are likely to differ as a function of the interpersonal context of interactions (Bronfenbrenner, 1979; Dunst, 1985; Goldberg, 1977). Thus, a parent's contention that he or she can get the child to perform a given behavior at home that the child will not manifest in a clinical test situation may have less to do with unreliability on the part of the parent and more to do with variations in behavior resulting from environmental and interpersonal contextual differences. Sheehan (Chapter 5) provides an excellent discussion of factors related to differences between the parental and professional assessments of children's behavior.

Contexts, or setting effects (Ekehammar, 1974; Endler & Magnusson, 1976), are the rules rather than the exceptions where human behavior is of concern. Person-by-setting interactions are, to paraphrase Bronfenbrenner (1979), the main effects in the ecology of human development. In a discussion of his own research as well as that of others, Lamb (1979) noted that the nature of *interpersonal context* significantly affects the behavior of infants. Likewise, Sroufe, Waters, and Matas (1974) found that context played an important role in affecting the social behaviors produced by infants. Behavior has also been found to vary dramatically in intrasetting comparisons (see Patterson, 1979, pp. 155–157). In reviewing the evidence regarding person-by-setting interactions, Bronfenbrenner (1979) noted that "different kinds of settings give rise to distinctive patterns of role, activity, and relation for persons who become participants in these settings" (p. 109). It is well known, for example, that attachment behavior, as well as stranger anxiety, is more likely to be manifested indoors than outdoors (Blurton-Jones, 1972). Likewise, stranger anxiety is likely to be less intense in the child's own home than in a laboratory (Lamb, 1979).

In our own work with mildly to severely handicapped infants and toddlers in preschool settings, we find rather dramatic differences in the children's behavior as a function of context. The independent variable in our work is the different learning zones that comprise typical preschool-classroom schedules (e.g., circle time and snack time). The dependent variable is the child's amount of engagement (interaction) with materials, peers, and adults in these different settings. Our research shows that the amount of engagement manifested by the children varies as a function of the context (i.e., the learning zone). That is, interactions with materials, peers, and adults differ as a function of the particular contexts in which the children are afforded learning opportunities. In another study (McWilliam, Trivette, & Dunst, 1985), we found that behavior also varies as a function of the organizational aspects of situations within settings. The independent variable in this study was the type of instruction within the classroom: isolated one-to-one instruction versus individualized instruction within the context of groups. The dependent variable was the number of children actively engaged in learning episodes. Comparisons between instructional types revealed that engagement levels were significantly greater in the classrooms that focused on individualized instruction within groups.

Because behavior varies as a function of context, the extent to which a child is likely to manifest certain types and forms of interactive competencies would be expected to differ according to the interpersonal and the intersetting context. It is our contention that the differential effects of settings on behavior are, in part, a result of the functional adaptations and expectations that the child must master in interactions with the environment. Moreover, we suspect that the reason children often do not manifest certain types and forms of behavior when attempts are specifically made to elicit them (as in a standardized test situation) is that the assessment is out of context and there is no adaptive reason for the child to manifest the behavior. Out-of-context assessment calls into question the ecological validity of this type of assessment procedure. If context has an important effect on behavior, the assessment of given types and forms of interactive behaviors is best performed within the particular context in which the probability of evoking the behavior is the highest.

ASSESSMENT OF INTERACTIVE COMPETENCIES

The assessment process derived from the above developmental model is designed to map the topography of the types and forms of interactive competencies for different ecological settings and contexts. In contrast to traditional approaches to cognitive assessment, which require children to match their behavior to the response demands of specific test items, the proposed strategy is designed to identify those indicators of interactive competencies that meet the criteria of the five levels of cognition defined by our model of development. Stated differently, the purpose of the assessment strategy is to discern the manner in which a particular child manifests interactive competencies at each level of performance. The focus is not on whether the child can produce certain preselected overt indicators of cognition but on how the child demonstrates interactive competencies. Thus, one child may be able to verbalize needs, another to use sign language to make needs known, and yet another to use a prosthetic device (e.g., a symbol board) to convey needs; nonetheless, all three children would have manifested identical levels and types of interactive competencies, but by using different modes of expression. To the extent that a child can manifest different types of interactive behaviors, regardless of the particular type and form, a child's topography of competencies can be discerned.

Methods of Eliciting Interactive Competencies

A child's topography of interactive competencies may be determined in a number of ways; however, these competencies are determined by observing the child's responsiveness to different environmental stimuli and events. In their description of the use of ordinal scales of infant psychological development, Uzgiris and Hunt (1975) made a distinction between the eliciting situations and the critical behaviors manifested in response to these situations, a distinction that has been useful in our own work. Eliciting situations are procedures that are designed to evoke a possible range of critical behaviors that represent different levels of cognitive functioning. Any stimulus event to which a child is exposed represents an eliciting situation (broadly conceived), and the child's range of responses provides a basis for discerning cognitive competence. Thus, a child's cognitive capacities can be discerned by noting which stimulus events (eliciting situations) evoke different types and forms of behavior. Such an approach will yield valuable information regarding a child's topography of interactive competencies.

Eliciting situations may be conceptualized in a number of different ways. At their simplest level, they may be thought of as naturally occurring events (e.g., feeding) that routinely take place in the child's life. The question posed at this level is "What types and forms of interactive competencies are manifested during routine events?" At a second level, we may vary a typical routine (e.g., by not responding to a communicative bid) and may ask the question, "How does the child adapt to the disconfirmation of an expectation?" We know, for example, that disconfirmations typically have the effect of evoking adaptations, and if the child has the capacity to manifest differentiated, encoded, or symbolic behaviors, the probability of the child producing any of these will be enhanced considerably. At a third level, we may introduce novelty into a routine (e.g., by introducing new materials) and may ask the question, "Do the types and forms of behavior reflect the child's capacity to master features of the demands posed by the novelty?" At a fourth level, we may vary the interpersonal context of the child's interactions with the environment (e.g., by introducing a second adult or a second child into a child–person play episode) and may ask the question, "What types and forms of behavior are manifested as a function of variations in interpersonal context?" At a fifth level, we may change the physical context for the child (e.g., by moving the child from one setting to another) and may ask the question, "Do the types and forms of behavior vary as a function of context, and in what way?" By no means are those five types of eliciting situations mutually exclusive or exhaustive. The point that we want to make is that each and every stimulus event with which the child is confronted represents a potential eliciting situation, and that the optimal use of these eliciting situations permits a determination of a child's cognitive competencies.

Modes of Interactions

The modes that the interactive competencies of multiply handicapped children take, in addition to varying in terms of type, form, and category, differ considerably as a function of the type, degree, and severity of their impairments. It is therefore difficult to provide an extensive taxonomy of the different modes that cognitive interactive behaviors may take. We reviewed a number of the alternative modes of expression as part of the description of the developmental model of cognition. These included, but were not restricted to, visual fixation, psychophysiological responses, social responsiveness, and the ability to demonstrate competencies by using a variety of prosthetic devices (e.g., PLAYTEST, walkers, and communication boards). The modes that interactive competencies take also differ by child as well as by environmental factors. Inasmuch as it is often easier to effect environmental changes (e.g., through the use of prosthetic devices), supportive opportunities can and should be afforded the child in order to optimize the probability of the child's demonstrating interactive competencies. As a rule of thumb, we should do whatever is necessary to discern the child's types and forms of competencies, and we should use whatever indicators are possible to permit the demonstration and/or inference of cognitive behaviors.

Context of Interactions

Depending on the level of analysis one wishes to use to define different contexts of interactions, an infinite number of situations are possible. It has been our experience, however, that macrolevel analyses are generally sufficient for at least an initial determination of a child's topography of interactive competencies. In the application of the assessment process, we operationally distinguish between three broad categories of settings: home, classroom, and community.

In the home settings, the specific child routines that we use as contexts of interactions are dressing, mealtimes, bathing, nap- and bedtime, toileting, leisure times, and independent-play times. The classroom routines used as the context of interactions are arrival and departure, naptime, mealtimes, group times, water and sand play, outdoor play, music time, table activities, and social play. The community routines used as the context of interactions are shopping, visits to the doctor or the hospital, eating at restaurants, recreational activities, church activities, and other social activities. (Typically, our assessment of the interactive competencies in the community routines are made by report via questioning the parents in order to determine the extent to which behaviors are displayed across settings.)

The Assessment Process

The appendix shows a prototypical form that can be used to conduct an assessment of a particular child. The assessment form is designed as a framework for mapping the types and forms of a child's topography of behavior according to level and context. The levels of cognitive performance are, of course, ordered hierarchically. The context section permits one to note the particular situations and settings in which the assessments occurred. Specific manifestations of the types, forms, and categories of interactive competencies are entered in the relevant cells. We have found it useful to note the manner in which the child was given credit for manifestation of the behavior types. We distinguish between three types of assessments (although one could easily develop a coding scheme that meets one's particular needs and requirements). Our coding scheme comprises assessments performed by *observation* (behavior actually observed during the course of the assessment); *knowledge of the child* (assessment based on the observer's knowledge of the child in different settings); and *report* (caregivers descriptions of the child's capabilities).

Case Example

Table 3 shows portions of an assessment conducted with a young severely impaired, multiply handicapped cerebral-palsied child as part of his participation in a classroom program. ''Jason'' was a 60-month-old child who was functioning as a 14-month level according to the Griffiths (1954) Mental Development Scale. Within our levels-of-interactive-competence framework, the results would have placed him at the differentiated level of development. However, as Table 3 clearly shows, Jason was capable of much more sophisticated types and forms of interactions when alternative indicators of cognitive functioning were used for mapping his topography of behavior. Specifically, he displayed a broad range of encoded interactions, although, as one can see, these varied as a function of the particular classroom routine in which the assessment was conducted. Nonetheless, the "mapping" process illustrates the utility of the approach for discerning the types and forms of interactive competencies displayed by a child, and how the results differ significantly from the findings obtained by a more traditional method of cognitive assessment.

FROM ASSESSMENT TO INTERVENTION

We conclude this chapter with a brief discussion of the implications of the assessment model for intervention. The reader is referred to Dunst *et al.* (1987) for a detailed description of the intervention procedures used with the assessment strategy. The assessment process itself yields a host of information about the child's topography of interactive competence: levels of functioning, types of behavior, forms of interactions, and the context (both interpersonal and intersetting) in which different types and forms of behavior are manifested. A completed assessment form (see Table 3 above) provides a summary of the modal level of functioning as well as information regarding transitions betwen levels. A large repertoire of behaviors within a given level across settings may be taken as an indication of the child's mastery of that level of functioning; a limited repertoire of behaviors may be taken as an indication of a transition into that level of functioning; and the manifestation of very few behaviors at a given level may be taken as an indication that limited mastery has occurred.

The mapping of a child's topography of interactive competencies permits one to isolate the types and forms of behaviors that the child used in interactions with the environment. Implicit in the model is the contention that cognitive growth represents both movement from lower to higher levels of functioning and increases in the topography of interactive competencies. Thus, the focus of intervention logically derived from this assertion is the facilitation of progressively more complex types and forms of behavior manifested in various forms in a variety of settings (see especially Dunst, 1981; Dunst *et al.*, 1987). The proposed assessment process permits the identification of the types, forms, and contexts that are targets of intervention.

The primary method of instruction that we use to facilitate targeted behavior is incidental teaching (Hart & Risley, 1978). *Incidental teaching*, as we use the term, begins with interactions that a child has with the social and nonsocial environment that arise either naturally or through afforded opportunities in which the child's responsiveness and interactions with the environment provide a basis for both sustaining and elaborating on the child's topography of behavior. The incidental teaching process simply formalizes adult responses during everyday interactions with the child, through a systematic series of steps designed to foster progressively more complex forms of social-adaptive competencies. Incidental teaching is not the same as incidental learning. There are specific targets for intervention, and incidental teaching episodes provide the structure for teaching targets each and every time the opportunities arise. In fact, an incidental teaching oppor-

Table 3. Selected Findings from Using the OBSERVE to Map a Child's Topography of Behavior[a]

Levels of development	Circle time	Free play	Group time	Meals	Outside play	Bathroom
			Context of assessment			
Attentional interactions	1. Looks at caregiver when she's talking or singing. 2. Orients toward different caregivers and children when they talk.	1. Attends to caregiver's actions 2. Laughs at funny events. 3. Tracks objects moving in and out of visual field.	1. Smiles when talked to. 2. Attends to other children. 3. Looks with interest at toys placed on his travel chair tray.	1. Watches other children at the table. 2. Searches for sources of sounds.	1. Orients toward voice when his name is called. 2. Pays attention to sights and sounds on the playground.	1. Tracks children and caregivers as they come and go.
Contingency interactions	1. Reaches for child to initiate interaction. 2. Vocalizes to get adult's attention.	1. Makes kite (suspended from ceiling) move using a string attached to his arm. 2. Swipes at wind chimes to make them move. 3. Rolls over to reinitiate social interaction.	1. Smiles or laughs to get adult to continue activity. 2. Picks up toys and "examines" them.	1. Finger-feeds self with some difficulty.	1. Vocalizes to have an adult continue activity (e.g., swinging).	
Differentiated interactions	1. Responds to "What do you want to sing now?" using arm movements to indicate which song he wants to hear (nonconventional gestures).	1. Moves toward play activity in walker. 2. Points to items on shelf. 3. Uses objects and toys to initiate play with caregiver.	1. Chooses "favorite" activity among several options. 2. Points to items he wants if out of reach. 3. Associates sound with action	1. Uses head shake or facial expression to indicate yes or no. 2. Reaches for or grasps spoon to help with feeding. 3. Uses spoon to	1. Moves toward children (in walker) to engage in play episodes. 2. Will imitate motor actions made by other children.	1. Indicates yes or no when asked if he has to go to the bathroom. 2. "Raises arms" to be taken out of walker or chair.

(continued)	2. Imitates actions of other children and caregivers. 3. Engages in reciprocal turn-taking during interactive episodes.	4. Demonstrates complex motor action with objects (rolls car). 5. "Talks" and holds pretend phone conversations.	(attempts car sounds). 4. Hands toys and objects to adults to have them activated. 5. Shows ability to feed doll using spoon and bottle.	eat with (although with considerable difficulty).	3. Plays cooperatively with other children (takes turns trying to throw ball).
Encoded interactions		1. Engages in pretend play (makes hotdogs, puts them in the oven to cook). 2. Pretends to "drive car"—vocalizations in attempt to make a motor sound. 3. Uses communication board to indicate desired activity. 4. Engages in pretend eating and drinking in doll corner.	1. Displays problem-solving abilities in getting to objects and activities he wants. 2. Puts dolls in appropriate situations when playing house (e.g., baby in bed in bedroom, car in garage, stove in kitchen).	1. Uses symbol board to select food item he wants.	1. Chooses from approximately 10 outside activities on communication board. 2. Follows series of two related commands.
Symbolic interactions				1. Uses symbol board to signal desire to go to kitchen and eat.	

[a]Many of the behaviors that Jason displayed were approximations of those described because of his physical impairment. In all instances, however, he conveyed his understanding and capabilities by using overt indicators that permitted the observer to infer a certain level of mastery and interactive capability.

tunity arises whenever the child is in the presence of another person and emits a behavior that can be used to *sustain* and *elaborate* the child's topography of behavior.

The steps in our incidental teaching process, together with a brief description of the major emphasis of each of the steps, are as follows:

1. *Ensure the child's responsiveness to the environment through the provision of opportunities that secure (attention-getting) and maintain the child's attention (attention-holding).* The purpose of this step is to engage the child in attentional interactions with the environment. This can generally be accomplished through arrangement of the environment in such a way that those stimulus events that evoked and sustained attentiveness during the assessment process are made available to the child.

2. *Focus attention on those aspects of the environment that maintain attention.* The purpose of this step is to discern what is maintaining attention-holding behavior. If the child is paying attention to certain stimulus features, the stimuli must be functioning as reinforcers. Note that this step in the teaching process differs from traditional methods of instruction inasmuch as the teacher focuses on the child rather than having the child attend to the adult, who *directs* the learning.

3. *Elicit and sustain the child's interactions with the environment.* The purpose of this step is to engage the child in contingency interactions in which the reinforcers identified in Step 2 are made contingent on the child producing an operant behavior. At this step, the focus is not to evoke some preselected contingency behavior (unless this is an appropriate target for the child's level of competence), but to initiate and sustain interactions that embody contingency awareness, predictability, and controllability. The child should simply be provided opportunities to demonstrate interactive competencies that permit his or her behavior to determine outcomes in a way that increases the probability of sustaining interactions.

4. *Work for and sustain elaboration in the child's topography of behavior.* According to Hart and Risley (1978), "This step is the focal point of the incidental teaching interaction" (p. 418). The purpose of this step is to produce variations in the child's behavior that successively approximate the particular type and form of behavior targeted to be taught for the context in which the incidental teaching episode is occurring. That is, the adult, through systematic efforts designed to evoke differentiated behavior, intervenes in a way (by prompting, modeling, or rearranging the environment) that increases the opportunity for the child to demonstrate the particular type and form of behavior targeted to be taught.

5. *Work for and sustain conventionalization as a part of response elaboration.* The purpose of this step is to evoke conventionalized behavior as part of response elaboration, where the conventionalized acts are used as equivalent, yet alternative ways of affecting a desired goal or goal state. Conventionalization in behavior brings the child closer to becoming an adaptive member of his or her particular culture or social group and thus represents cognitive interactive competence *par excellence*.

Figure 2 shows the relationship between the five steps in the incidental teaching process and the five levels of cognition. As can be seen, incidental teaching provides the basis for facilitating both stage-level progress and different types and forms of interactive competence. To the extent that different interactive competencies are targeted to be

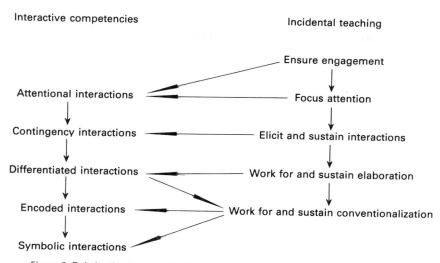

Figure 2. Relationship between the developmental model of interactive competencies and the incidental teaching process.

taught, incidental teaching provides an instructional method of effecting behavior change. The following description of an incidental teaching episode illustrates how the teaching process can be used to facilitate targeted behavior. This is an actual case study that arose within the context of a project designed to enhance the communicative competencies of young handicapped children:

Judy was a 27-month-old handicapped child. Her developmental age was about 12 months. The targeted behaviors for her in terms of communicative competence were the use of conventionalized nonverbal gestures to initiate interactions with adults and to make requests and demands. In this particular incidental teaching episode, the child was sitting on the floor in a preschool classroom (she did not yet walk or ambulate in any way) with several materials within her immediate visual field (e.g., a bucket filled with blocks, a toy truck, and several wind up toys). Judy focused on the bucket, which was out of her immediate reach (attentional interaction). The teacher noticed her attention-holding behavior to the bucket and moved it within Judy's reach (it was placed between her legs). Judy now noticed the blocks in the bucket and reached in to take one out. The teacher did the same and demonstrated for Judy, banging the block repeatedly on top of the truck, which was next to the child. This had the effect of getting Judy to do the same, which she seemed to enjoy (contingency interaction). The teacher and the child engaged in this "parallel play" for about 20 seconds, until Judy accidently dropped the block into the back of the truck, which elicited her visual attention to the effect she had produced. The teacher also dropped his block into the truck and immediately gave Judy another block, which she dropped into the truck (response elaboration). The teacher handed four blocks in a row to Judy. Each time the child dropped the blocks into the truck. The teacher than stopped handing the blocks to Judy as a means of evoking further response elaboration. Judy looked up to the teacher and then held her hand out to request a block (conventionalized response elaboration). The child then used the socially recognized nonverbal gesture three or four more times to have the teacher give her a block. The teacher than did not respond to elicit further requests and asked Judy what she wanted. The query had the effect of evoking yet another conventionalized nonverbal gesture: pointing toward the blocks. Several child requests later, the teacher waited until another attempt at elaboration occurred. This time the child pointed at the blocks, looked at the adult, and emitted a sound (''at'') that approximated the encoded conventionalized behavior of using a word to make a request.

In this particular incidental teaching episode, the teacher followed the child's lead (attentiveness to different features of the environment) and successively evoked different response elaborations from the child until she emitted an encoded behavior that approximated a conventionalized word. This entire teaching episode lasted less than 2 minutes, yet the child's ability to demonstrate cognitive interactive competencies was manifested in numerous ways. There is a growing body of evidence that nonhandicapped as well as handicapped children are more likely to display competent behavior if interactive episodes are child-initiated and caregivers are responsive to and encourage their children's ongoing behavior (Hanzlik, 1986; Mahoney, Powell, Finnegan, Fors, & Wood, 1986; Uzgiris, 1986; Wenar, 1972; White & Watts, 1973). Thus, in contrast to teaching techniques that emphasize bringing the learner under stimulus control, where behaviors are likely to be manifested only in the presence of certain discriminative stimuli, the use of ''responsive'' intervention techniques like incidental teaching are more likely to result in greater interactive competence, and consequently in a greater shift in balance of power toward the developing child.

SUMMARY

The purpose of this chapter was to propose an alternative framework for the cognitive assessment of multiply handicapped preschool children. The assessment strategy is based on a developmental model that describes cognitive competencies in terms of the levels, types, forms, and contexts of interactions with the social and the nonsocial environment. The model describes five levels of cognitive competencies (attentional interactions, contingency interactions, differentiated interactions, encoded interactions, and symbolic interactions); two types (engaging and modulating); four forms (initiating, sustaining, regulating, and adapting); and two categories (social and nonsocial) of competencies. It also describes three broad contexts in which competencies are assessed (home, school, and community). The goal of the assessment strategy is to discern how a child manifests interactive competencies by using whatever behavior indicators may be taken as examples of cognitive capabilities. To the extent that a child can manifest different types and forms of cognitive competencies, a child's topography of interactive competencies can be determined. The model of development, as well as the assessment process, is directly linked to the use of incidental teaching as an instructional method for fostering both elaborations and increased conventionalization of behavior.

Traditional methods of cognitive assessment, which focus on children's abilities to match their behavior to the response demands of test items, may be inappropriate and even discriminatory when used with multiply handicapped preschoolers. The method of assessment described in this chapter offers at least one alternative way of discerning the multiply handicapped child's cognitive interactive capabilities.

APPENDIX: The OBSERVE record form for mapping a child's topography of interactive competencies

OBSERVE

Observation of Behavior in Socially and Ecologically Relevant and Valid Environments

Child's Name _____ Date of Birth_____ Date of Observation_____ Age_____ Observer_____

LEVELS OF DEVELOPMENT	CONTEXT OF ASSESSMENT						NOTES
I Attentional Interactions							
II Contingency Interactions							
III Differentiated Interactions							
IV Encoded Interactions							
V Symbolic Interactions							

ACKNOWLEDGMENTS

Appreciation is extended to Pat Condrey for her assistance in the preparation of this manuscript and to Lynne Sharpe for conducting the assessments described in the chapter. This work was supported, in part, by grants from the North Carolina Department of Human Resources, Division of Mental Health, Mental Retardation and Substance Abuse, Research Section (#81A08 and #82A22), and the American Academy for Cerebral Palsy and Developmental Medicine (#1233).

REFERENCES

Ambrose, A. (1978). Human social development: An evolutionary-biological perspective. In H. McGurk (Ed.), *Issues in childhood social development*. London: Methuen.

Bates, E., Benigni, L., Bretheron, I., Camaioni, L., & Volterra, V. (1979). *The emergence of symbols*. New York: Academic Press.

Bayley, N. (1969). *The Bayley Scale of Infant Development*. New York: Psychological Corp.

Bloom, L. (1970). *Language development: Form and function of emerging grammars.* Cambridge: MIT Press.

Blurton-Jones, N. G. (1972). Nonverbal communication in children. In R. Hinde (ed.), *Nonverbal communication.* Cambridge: University Press.

Bower, T. G. R. (1974). *Development in infancy.* San Francisco: W. H. Freeman.

Bronfenbrenner, U. (1979). *The ecology of human development.* Cambridge: Harvard University Press.

Charlesworth, W. R. (1979). An ethological approach to studying intelligence. *Human Development, 22*, 212–216.

Chatelanat, G., & Schoggen, M. (1980). Issues encountered in devising an observation system to assss spontaneous infant behavior-environment interactions. In J. Hogg & P. Mittler (Eds.), *Advances in mental handicap research.* New York: Wiley.

Cohen, L., DeLoach, J., & Strauss, M. (1979). Infant visual perception. In J. Osofsky (Ed.), *Handbook of infant development.* New York: Wiley.

Cyrulik-Jacobs, A., Shapira, Y., Jones, M. (1975). Applications of an automatic operant response procedure to the study of auditory perception and processing ability of neurologically impaired infants. In B. Friedlander, G. Sterritt & B. Kirk (Eds.), *Exceptional Infant* (Vol. 3). New York: Brunner/Mazel.

Decarie, G. T. (1969). A study of the mental and emotional development of the thalidomide child. In B. Foss (Ed.), *Determinants of infant behavior* (Vol. 4). London: Methuen.

Dubose, R., Langley, M. B., & Stagg, V. (1979). Assessing severely handicapped children. *Focus on Exceptional Children, 9*, 1–13.

Dunst, C. J. (1981). *Infant learning.* Allen, TX: Teaching Resources/DLM.

Dunst, C. J. (1984). Toward a social-ecological perspective of sensorimotor development among the mentally retarded. In P. Brooks, R. Sperber, & C. McCauley (Eds.), *Learning and cognition in the mentally retarded.* Hillsdale, NJ: Erlbaum.

Dunst, C. J. (1985). Communicative competence and deficits. Effects on early social interaction. In E. McDonald & D. Gallagher (Eds.), *Facilitating social-emotional development in the young multiply handicapped child.* Philadelphia: HMS Press.

Dunst, C. J., Cushing, P. J., & Vance, S. D. (1985). Response-contingent learning in profoundly handicapped infants: A social systems perspective. *Analysis and Intervention in Developmental Disabilities, 5*, 33–47.

Dunst, C. J., Lesko, J. J., Holbert, K. A., Wilson, L. L., Sharpe, K. L., & Liles, R. F. (1987). A systemic approach to infant intervention. *Topics in Early Childhood Special Education, 7*(2), 19–37.

Ekehammar, B. (1974). Interactionism in personality from a historical perspective. *Psychological Bulletin, 81*, 1026–1048.

Endler, N., & Magnusson, D. (Eds.). (1976). *Interactional psychology and personality.* New York: Wiley.

Fagan, J., & Singer, L. (1983). Infant recognition memory as a measure of intelligence. In L. Lipsitt & C. Rovee-Collier (Eds.), *Advances in infancy research.* Norwood, NJ: ABLEX Publishing.

Feters, L. (1976). *The development of object permanence in infants with motor handicaps.* Paper presented at the Annual Conference of the American Physical Therapy Association, New Orleans.

Fischer, K. (1980). A theory of cognitive development: The control and construction of hierarchies of skills. *Psychological Review, 87*, 477–531.

Flavell, J. H. (1977). *Cognitive Development.* Englewood Cliffs, NJ: Prentice-Hall.

Friedlander, B. (1975). Automated evaluation of selective listening. In B. Friedlander, G. Sterritt, & G. Kirk (Eds.), *Exceptional infant* (Vol. 3). New York: Brunner/Mazel.

Friedlander, B., McCarthy, J., & Soforonko, A. (1967). Automated psychological evaluation with severely retarded institutionalized infants. *American Journal of Mental Deficiency, 71*, 909–919.

Friedman, S., & Vietze, P. (1972). The competent infant. *Peabody Journal of Education, 4*, 1–8.

Glenn, S., & Cunningham, C. (1983). What do babies listen to most? A developmental study of auditory preferences in nonhandicapped infants and infants with Down syndrome. *Developmental Psychology, 19*, 332–337.

Goldberg, S. (1977). Social competence in infancy: A model of parent-infant interaction. *Merrill Palmer Quarterly, 23*, 163–177.

Golinkoff, R. (Ed.). (1983). *The transition from prelinguistic to linguistic communication.* Hillsdale, NJ: Erlbaum.

Griffiths, R. (1954). *The abilities of babies.* London: University of London Press.

Hanzlik, J. R. (May, 1986). *Mother-developmentally disabled infant interaction and intervention.* Paper presented at the annual meeting of the American Association on Mental Deficiency, Denver, CO.

Hart, B., & Risley, T. (1978). Promoting productive language through incidental teaching. *Education and Urban Planning, 10,* 407–429.

Hulme, I., & Lunzer, E. (1966). Play, language, and reasoning in subnormal children. *Journal of Child Psychology and Psychiatry, 7,* 107–123.

Hulsebus, R. (1973). Operant conditioning of infant behavior: A review. In H. Reese (Ed.), *Advances in child development and behavior* (Vol. 8). New York: Academic Press.

Kopp, C., & Shaperman, J. (1973). Cognitive development in the absence of object manipulation during infancy. *Developmental Psychology, 9,* 430.

Kearsley, R. (1979). Iatrogenic retardation: A syndrome of learned incompetence. In R. Kearsley & I. Sigel (Eds.), *Infants at risk.* Hillsdale, NJ: Erlbaum.

Lamb, M. (1979). The effects of social context on dyadic social interaction. In M. Lamb, S. Suomi, & G. Stephenson (Eds.), *Social interaction analysis.* Madison: University of Wisconsin Press.

Lamb, M. (1981). The development of social expectations in the first year of life. In M. Lamb & L. Sherrod (Eds.), *Infant social cognition.* Hillsdale, NJ: Erlbaum.

Lamb, M., & Sherrod, S. (1981). *Infant social cognition.* Hillsdale, NJ: Erlbaum.

Laub, K., & Dunst, C. J. (1974). *The conditioning of vocalizations in an 8-month-old microcephalic infant.* Paper presented at the meeting of the North Carolina Speech and Hearing Association.

Lewis, M. (1982). Attention as a measure of cognitive integrity. In M. Lewis & L. Taft (Eds.), *Developmental disabilities: Theory, assessment, and intervention.* New York: SP Medical & Scientific Books.

Lewis, M., & Brooks-Gunn, J. (1981). Attention and intelligence. *Intelligence, 5,* 231–238.

Lewis, M., & Rosenblum, L. (Eds.). (1978). *The development of affect.* New York: Plenum Press.

Lipsitt, L. (1969). Learning capabilities of the human infant. In R. J. Robinson (Ed.), *Brain and early behavior.* New York: Academic Press.

Lipsitt, L., & Werner, J. (1981). The infancy of human learning processes. In E. Gollin (Ed.), *Developmental plasticity.* New York: Academic Press.

Mahoney, G., Powell, A., Finnegan, C., Fors, S., & Wood, S. (1986). *The transactional intervention program: Theory, procedures and evaluation.* Unpublished paper, Department of Special Education, School of Education, University of Michigan, Ann Arbor.

McCall, R. (1979). Qualitative transitions in behavioral development in the first two years of life. In M. Bornstein & W. Kessen (Eds.), *Psychological development from infancy.* Hillsdale, NJ: Erlbaum.

McCune-Nicolich, L. (1981). Toward symbolic functioning: Structure of early pretend games and potential parallels with language. *Child Development, 52,* 785–792

McDonough, S. (1982). Attention and memory in cerebral palsied infants. *Infant Behavior and Development, 5,* 347–353.

McGurk, H. (1978). *Issues in childhood social development.* London: Methuen.

McWilliam, R. A., Trivette, C. M., & Dunst, C. J., (1985). Behavior engagement as a measure of the efficacy of early intervention. *Analysis and Intervention in Developmental Disabilities, 5,* 59–71.

Millar, W. S. (1976). Operant acquisition of social behaviors in infancy: Basic problems and constraints. In H. Reese (Ed.), *Advances in child development and behavior* (Vol. 11). New York: Academic Press.

Miranda, S., & Fantz, R. (1973). Visual preferences of Down syndrome and normal infants. *Child Development, 44,* 555–561.

Miranda, S., & Fantz, R. (1974). Recognition memory in Down syndrome and normal infants. *Child Development, 45,* 657–660.

Patterson, G. (1979). A performance theory for coercive family interaction. In R. Cairns (Ed.), *The analysis of social interactions.* Hillsdale, NJ: Erlbaum.

Piaget, J. (1951). *Plays, dreams and imitation in childhood* (C. Gattegno & F. Hodgson, trans.). New York: Norton.

Piaget, J. (1952). *The origins of intelligence in children* (M. Cook, trans.). New York: International Universities Press.

Piaget, J. (1954). *The construction of reality in the child* (M. Cook, trans.). New York: Basic Books.

Robinson, C. (1982). Questions regarding the effects of neuromotor problems on sensorimotor development. In D. Bricker (Ed.), *Intervention with at risk and handicapped infants.* Baltimore: University Park Press.

Robinson, C. (1987). A strategy for assessing motorically-impaired infants. In I. Uzgiris & J. McV. Hunt

(Eds.), *Infant performance and experience*. Champaign: University of Illinois Press.

Robinson, C., & Robinson, J. (1983). Sensorimotor functions and cognitive development. In M. Snell (Ed.), *Systematic instruction of the moderately and severely handicapped* (2nd ed.). Columbus, OH: Charles E. Merrill.

Sameroff, A., & Cavanaugh, P. (1979). Learning in infancy: A developmental perspective. In J. Osofsky (Ed.), *Handbook of infant development*. New York: Wiley.

Siebert, J., Hogan, A., & Mundy, P. (1982). Assessing interactional competencies: The Early Social-Communication Scales. *Infant Mental Health Journal, 3*, 244–258.

Sroufe, L., Waters, E., & Matas, L. (1974). Contextual determinants of infant affective response. In M. Lewis & L. Rosenblum (Eds.), *The origins of fear*. New York: Wiley.

Utley, B., Duncan, D., Strain, P., & Scanlon, K. (1983). Effects of contingent and noncontingent visual stimulation on visual fixation in multiply handicapped children. *TASH Journal, 8*, 29–42.

Uzgiris, I. (1983). Organization of sensorimotor intelligence. In M. Lewis (Ed.), *Origins of intelligence* (2nd ed.). New York: Plenum Press.

Uzgiris, I. (1986, May). *Interaction as context for early intervention*. Paper presented at the Third Annual Eric Denhoff Memorial Symposium on Child Development, Brown University, Providence.

Uzgiris, I., & Hunt, J. McV. (1975). *Assessment in infancy*. Urbana: University of Illinois Press.

Watson, J. S. (1966). The development and generalization of contingency awareness in early infancy. *Merrill Palmer Quarterly, 12*, 123–136.

Watson, J. S. (1972). Smiling, cooing and the "game." *Merrill Palmer Quarterly, 18*, 323–339.

Wenar, C. (1972). Executive competence and spontaneous social behavior in one-year-olds. *Child Development, 43*, 256–260.

White, B., & Watts, J. C. (1973). *Experience and environment* (Vol. 1). Englewood Cliffs, NJ: Prentice-Hall.

Wing, L., Gould, J., Yeates, S., & Brierley, L. (1977). Symbolic play in severely mentally retarded and autistic children. *Journal of Child Psychology and Psychiatry, 18*, 167–178.

Wolf, D., & Gardner, H. (1981). On the structure of early symbolization. In R. Schiefelbusch & D. Bricker (Eds.), *Early language acquisition and intervention*. Baltimore: University Park Press.

Zelazo, P. (1979). Reactivity to perceptual-cognitive events: Application for infant assessment. In R. Kearsley & I. Sigel (Eds.), *Infants at risk*. Hillsdale, NJ: Erlbaum.

Zelazo, P. (1982a). Alternative assessment procedures for handicapped infants and toddlers. In D. Bricker (Ed.), *Intervention with at-risk and handicapped infants*. Baltimore: University Park Press.

Zelazo, P. (1982b). An information processing approach to infant cognitive assessment. In M. Lewis & L. Taft (Eds.), *Developmental disabilities: Theory, assessment, and intervention*. New York: SP Medical & Scientific Books.

Zelazo, P., & Kearslsy, R. (1980). The emergence of functional play in infants: Evidence for a major cognitive transition. *Journal of Applied Developmental Psychology, 1*, 95–117.

Noncognitive Assessment

An increasing emphasis is being placed on the noncognitive performance of infants and preschoolers in intervention settings. Gallagher and Cech (Chapter 12) stress that motor impairments reduce children's ability to interact with their environment, and they stress the need for an assessment of the underlying components of motor functioning (e.g., muscle tone and postural reactions). Gallagher and Cech also return to the now-familiar theme that the intended purpose of assessment should guide the selection of measures.

McDevitt (Chapter 13) moves the reader to consider the *how* of behavior rather than the *what* (content) or the *why* (motivation) in his chapter on temperament. He is candid in his perception that methods of assessing temperament by direct measurement have not yet been developed, yet he holds out great promise for the potential value of such data. He argues that temperament data may help us to understand how infants and preschoolers will react to intervention. Such an argument takes on even more significance as we watch assessment efforts themselves being directed toward more of an intervention (or hypothesis-testing) focus.

Chapter 14 represents an attempt by Brockman, Morgan, and Harmon to address the why of developmentally disabled infants' and preschoolers' behavior. These authors argue that the mastery motivation of youngsters provides an important window into a child's functioning. They suggest that observers focus on the amount (and type) of task-directed behavior as well as on the outcome of that behavior. Observers can address children's mastery motivation in structured and unstructured settings and can also make use of parental-report data.

Olswang and Bain (Chapter 15) reaffirm the argument that enormous variability of performance exists among the language-impaired children being served in early intervention programs. They argue strongly that such variability can be overcome only within an interdisciplinary or transdisciplinary team approach. These authors carefully describe the strengths and limitations of language assessment conducted at two extremes: standardized testing and naturalistic assessment. Once again, they emphasize the importance of the purpose of assessment's being the determining factor in the selection of instruments.

Few intervenors would argue that environments have no effect on the performance of developmentally disabled infants and preschoolers. Despite widespread support of environmental assessment, such an assessment is all too often rejected. Wachs (Chapter 16) suggests that assessors have rejected environmental assessment as unwieldy or too costly because they have not carefully considered the purpose(s) of such assessment.

Once again, we are presented with the strong arguments that a decision theory appoach should be applied to instrument selection, and that no one approach is sufficient for all purposes.

An important chapter in Part III completes the noncognitive assessment of developmentally disabled infants and preschoolers. This chapter, by Magyary, Barnard, and Brandt, represents an acknowledgment that children with developmental disabilities also often suffer from one or more biophysical disabilities. These authors argue that skilled health maintenance and assessment are essential to successful intervention for children with handicaps. The authors also identify the important perspective provided by parental report in determining children's health history and ongoing health status. Finally, the authors realistically assert that children's health status must be assessed, as it affects all areas of educational intervention.

The common themes of Parts I and II are also evident in Part III. We must carefully consider the purposes of assessment, and we must be flexible (and individualized) in our selection of assessment strategies. We must also realize the interrelatedness of environment, temperament, motivation, and biophysical factors in planning, implementing, and evaluating our early intervention program.

12

Motor Assessment

R. J. Gallagher and D. Cech

INTRODUCTION

The motor behavior of children is a basic substrate of a child's development, and thus, deviations in the acquisition of skills that are motor-dependent have the potential of drastically affecting a child's developmental outcome. From the newborn's general activity, to the infant's first attempts at crawling and walking through the toddler's climbing, motor activity makes available to the child an ever-expanding and ever-changing environment. Through motor activity, the youngster learns relationships among objects and their characteristics and finally develops an ability to adapt and control situations that effect environmental change.

Normal developmental processes can be dramatically altered by handicapping conditions. Critical to environmental adaptation is the process through which children learn the effect that behavior has on ongoing events. When compared with their normally developing peers, children with motor problems experience many differences when interacting with and attempting to assume control of their world. For example, if it is difficult for an infant to establish head control, the chances of the infant's interacting with the environment are greatly reduced. Delays in the integration of primitive motor patterns reduce the child's ability to develop greater volitional control over movement, thus diminishing his or her chances of affecting the environment. These and other examples have generalized effects on the child's development:

> Motor behavior provides the basis for the infant's interactions with the environment. The experience gained from such interaction is a foundation for cognitive advances in the sensorimotor period. Environments that provide different experiences to infants produce infants that advance through the sensorimotor period at different rates (Hunt, 1976). (Sameroff & McDonough, 1984, p. 184)

The degree to which a child is able to participate actively in environmental events, and to learn from those experiences, determines a child's developmental outcome. For example, a multiply handicapped child, when placed in a room with many objects may make no attempt to orient to the objects, to move toward them, or to interact with the objects in any other way. Because this child is not actively engaged in either the object or

R. J. GALLAGHER ● Department of Early Childhood Special Education, University of Cincinnati, Cincinnati, Ohio 45221. D. CECH ● Department of Physical Therapy, Chicago Medical School, North Chicago, Illinois 60664.

the social world, relationships between behavioral action and reaction are neither experienced nor learned. The child is deprived because of an inability to participate actively in environmental transactions, and if this deprivation proceeds unabated, some degree of developmental delay may ensue. To alter a child's developmental course, experiences must be provided that capitalize on the child's abilities. Critical to the success of this intervention process is to accurately determine the cognitive and motor skills of the child and the extent to which motor and/or cognitive impairment contributes to the child's delay.

With the rapid increase in the availability of intervention services for young developmentally delayed children, their parents and other advocates have demanded more complete assessment information. The resulting effect has been an emphasis on broadening the information base for each child, as well as a changing view of how assessment instruments and the information they provide might be used. Motor assessment information is called on to assist not only in planning an individual child's intervention program and evaluating its success or failure, but also to help evaluate a total program's effectiveness. However, most early-childhood special-education personnel have only limited training in the fundamentals of normal and abnormal motor development. In light of the large number of infants and preschoolers with motoric problems who are referred to early intervention programs, we find this lack of information distressing. Therefore, we feel a discussion of motor development is necessary to and understanding of, the issues that surround the assessment of motor disability.

To be successful, motor assessment devices must examine the underlying components that comprise movement. The assessment process addressed in this chapter is structured toward describing the components of movement necessary to adequately assess motor problems. It is intended not to examine specific instruments but to suggest how the assessment process can determine a child's level of motor performance. This is necessary for formulating any intervention plans and for evaluating the effectiveness of the intervention provided.

NORMAL MOTOR DEVELOPMENT

Some limited discussion of normal motor development is pertinent to this chapter. Motor learning is a sensorimotor process during which the child masters an upright position, overcoming the force of gravity. During this learning process, the child experiences sensations of movement and practices those movements that lead to interesting results. At birth, the child is transported from a relatively gravity-free environment to an environment where the force of gravity is a major influence that affects all movement. Normal motor development is the process of learning to control movement against gravity and of achieving an upright standing position.

Broadly viewed, the process of acquiring voluntary contol over movement is based on three general developmental principles. First, an infant's motor development progresses in a cephalocaudal orientation: control of the head, neck, and shoulder precedes contol of the trunk. The second principal is that development progresses proximodistally, or from the midline out. Skills with the arms precede skills with the hands. Finally, motor development that leads to the control of body movement occurs in the horizontal plane before it does in the vertical plane. For example, infants first gain a mastery of general body movement in supine and prone positions before they are able to establish control in positions that work against gravity, that is, sitting and standing (Scherzer & Tscharnuter, 1982). Each of these lines develops simultaneously, and the child's movement patterns are the outward products of this integrated development.

One result of this developmental process is that the child experiences a myriad of new movements, each bringing information from tactile and proprioceptive sensory receptors. The infant draws on this sensory information when attempting to replicate exploratory movements that culminate in interesting results. Consider for a moment the infant who flips over from stomach to back. This movement provides the child a different view of the world, and when the child is returned to the original position, sensorimotor memory is called on to replicate each new movement. With practice, the child perfects the movement pattern which becomes linked to more complex movement patterns that assist in the further exploration of the environment. This ever-enlarging motor repertoire of the child facilitates more efficient exploration, giving the child access to the rich and diverse experiences important to cognitive growth.

Movements in the first stage of an infant's motor development are dominated by primative reflexes. Present at birth, these motor responses are predictable responses to environmental stimulations and thus are important to the infant's early development. However, as important as they are, their persistence into the latter half of the first year can interfere with a child's acquisition of more advanced motor skills (Capute, Shapiro, Accardo, Wachtel, Ross, & Palmer, 1982). It is important to note that not only is motor skill acquisition hindered by continued premature reflexes, but the reduced environmental exploration can have an impact on the child's cognitive outcome. For example, the maintenance of these skills will hinder the acquisition of developmentally appropriate and adaptive skills, such as head control, rolling over, reaching, and grasping objects, as well as sitting and walking.

The integration of primitive reflexes coincides with the acquisition of the postural responses. These responses include righting reactions, equilibrium responses, and protective reactions. Although this developmental progression does not depend on the total integration of the primitive reflexes, their integration into postural reactions is necessary before normal postural control can be established (Illingworth, 1975). These automatic reactions in response to changes in posture allow a child to maintain proper balance and to assume an upright posture. This line of development proceeds sequentially, beginning with the child's first attempts to lift the head, to sitting and walking. During this process, the child develops a sense of the relationship among his or her body parts and the sense of space necessary to maintain balance and postural stability.

ABNORMAL DEVELOPMENT

Campbell (1979) classified motor impairments as having two basic origins: (a) lower motor-neuron lesions and (b) upper motor-neuron lesions. Lower motor-neuron problems arise from damage to the spinal cord or to nerves or muscles themselves, whereas damage to the brain is classified as an upper motor-neuron lesion. Either origin places limitations on a child's movements, which is manifested as lack of coordination, muscle tone impairment, and/or abnormal movement patterns of all or part of the body.

Central motor control can be altered by insults to the brain or the spinal cord. The net result is a breakdown of communication between the brain and the muscle groups. In the case of cerebral palsy, where the brain is damaged, an altered message may be initiated, resulting in abnormal movement patterns; and the integration of reflexes and coordination, normally the responsibility of higher brain centers may be lost (Bobath & Bobath, 1975). Postural muscle tone, the interaction of opposing muscle groups, and the acquisition of righting and equilibrium reactions are usually affected by this type of lesion (Bobath & Bobath, 1975). The location of the brain injury also dictates what parts of the body will be affected. For example, if the insult is on the right side of the brain, motor impairment will manifest itself on the child's left side.

In spinal cord injury or spinal cord disease, messages of motor control may originate normally in the brain, but their transmission is hindered or blocked from the point of the insult to the muscle. The result is often muscle weakness, altered muscle tone, changed interactions between opposing muscle groups, and/or altered ability to achieve postural control against gravity. Muscle disease, such as muscular dystrophy, changes muscle strength and leads to abnormal motor development.

Abnormal motor development, like normal motor development, is based on sensorimotor experience and progresses in orderly developmental sequences, that is, with a cephalocaudal-proximaldistal orientation (Scherzer & Tscharnuter, 1982). As in the normally developing infant, one would not expect to see motor control at the hips before control is established at the shoulders. Also a lack of control proximally at the shoulder or the hips can result in poor distal control in the form of poor manipulative or prehensile skills or poor knee–ankle control. As in normal motor development, abnormal motor skills allow the child to work against gravity, facilitating explorations and interaction with the environment. Like their normally developing peers, infants who have movement disabilities are involved in a process of perfecting postural control. However, without the appropriate interacting components of movement, the child must develop alternative methods of control. These alternative methods may include the prolonged use of primitive reactions; the use of excessive muscle tone in some muscle groups as a stabilizing force; and the use of the skeletal structure to stabilize mechanically:

> When muscle tone is abnormal, the body musculature may be prevented from producing the patterns of movement that automatically produce the righting and balancing functions. Balance may not be maintained because the response is blocked (or prevented) but because of abnormal muscle tone. Bricker & Campbell, 1980, (p. 14).

Long-term deviations result in abnormal movement patterns that increase the potential for deformities (Wetzel & Wetzel, 1984). The pervasiveness of muscle tone can be seen from its effect on the quantitive and qualitive aspects surrounding movement patterns. Both are drastically changed by abnormal muscle tone.

Muscle tone can range from hypertonicity to hypotonicity, as well as fluctuate between the two. Tone-based movement limitations reduce the ability of a child to respond to the environment. When hypotonicity is present, the reduced tension of the muscle allows excessive mobility around the joints (Drillien & Drummond, 1977; (Zelle & Coyner, 1983). These hypotonic children can achieve abnormal stability when prone, seated, or while assuming an upright posture by using the skeletal system for support. For example, head support can be maintained by propping the head on an elevated shoulder and using the vertebral column for additional support. By hyperextending their extremities and, in this way, locking their elbow and knee joints, low-tone children can achieve abnormal stability while prone, or when maintaining a hand-and-knees position, or while standing.

In compensating for muscle tone deviations, abnormal stability can be achieved by prolonged use of primitive movement patterns or responses. One example of a primitive movement pattern used to achieve stability is reflected by the use of the "frogleg" posture. In the sitting, supine, or prone position, the legs may be held in a widely abducted (draw away from the midline), flexed,and externally rotated (turned out from the midline) position to provide a wide base of support and added stability. This abnormal position replaces the normal active trunk control that occurs when the abdominal and back muscles work together to provide support. Other examples of the use of primitive reactions and reflexes include the use of the asymmetrical tonic neck reflex to initiative reaching, or the use of a toe to "grasp" the supporting surface in weight-bearing positions. For a child with diminished tone, the force of gravity has the effect of producing abnormal behavior patterns and of reducing that child's general activity level.

Excessive muscle tone can also be used as a stabilizing force. For example, to facilitate lifting his or her head when prone, an infant can use the abnormal motor ability of arching the back and straightening the legs; to facilitate standing, an infant stands on his or her toes and stiffly extends the legs. Increased muscle tone creates motor blocks, resulting in retardation of these children's ability to move. Variations in these deviations of mucle tone may also produce an altered interaction of the opposing muscle groups necessary for dynamic stability. For example, if all the muscles of the hip joint cannot work together with appropriate timing, the controls necessary to balance on one leg while taking a step with the other cannot be maintained.

The use of alternative methods of postural control against gravity allows some degree of interaction with and exploration of the environment. However, these atypical and inefficient motor patterns affect the quality of movement or the ability of the child to produce and organize coordinated components of movement (Bricker & Campbell, 1980). Although abnormal motor patterns are somewhat adaptive to the child, normal movement is significantly impaired. Moreover, the sensorimotor foundations from which is later motor control is built lacks the variety and refinement necessary for the development of efficient postural control (Zelle & Coyner, 1983).

Motor development, whether normal or abnormal, is established on a foundation of many interacting factors, for example, muscle and postural tone, righting and equilibrium reactions and sensorimotor experiences (Capute *et al.,* 1982). All motor learning is based on learning the sensation of movements, and thus, the acquisition of new motor skills is based on previously mastered skills. Abnormal motor patterns evolve when children base the acquisition of new motor skills on abnormal sensations of movement that do not include the normal prerequisite components necessary to developing normal righting and equilibrium movements (Bobath & Bobath, 1975).

IMPLICATIONS OF MOTOR IMPAIRMENT FOR DEVELOPMENT

There is a direct link between motor impairment and broader developmental problems in children. Berkson (1968) posited that the persistent stereotypical behaviors found among some groups of developmentally delayed children may be traced to atypical motor development. Animal research and research with mentally retarded children have shown that repetitive behavior may persist and may become sterotypical behavior patterns when opportunities for environmental interactions are reduced (Berkson, 1983). Stereotypical or repetitive movements are nonvarying, maladaptive movements and, in effect, become an end in themselves, producing nothing "new" for the individual. Such behavior in fact, reduces or eliminates opportunities for environmental interactions (Gallagher & Berkson, 1986).

Among children whose motor repertoire is limited, yet another hindrance surfaces. Their limited motor behavior decreases their ability to elaborate on their basic motor skills. These limited movements are not adaptive to varying situations and reduce these individuals' ability to adapt to demands in an ever-changing environment (Bricker & Campbell, 1980). Because of their limited motor repertoire, motor exploration is accomplished by means of identical or routinized schemes with no elaboration and no ability to adjust to new objects, individuals, or situations.

Normalizing muscle tone, using proper positioning techniques, and providing other specific intervention may enable children with a limited ability to move and explore to engage the environment, may enhance opportunities for object and social interaction and may thus decrease the frequency of stereotypical behaviors (Berkson, 1983; Gallagher & Berkson, 1986; Rincover, Cook, Peoples & Packard, 1979a; Rincover, Newsom, & Carr, 1979b):

> These behaviors (stereotypies) are essentially eliminated from the repertoire as complex interaction with the environment emerges; however, they may be retained if children are reared in an environment that deprives them of social and object experience appropriate for their developmental level. (Berkson, 1983, p. 245).

A child's ability to express normal affect can be dramatically affected by motor impairment (Gallagher, Jens & O'Donnell, 1983). Recent research has demonstrated the relationship between a child's increasing motor impairment and that child's reduced ability to express a normal range of positive affects; that is, physical disability diminishes a child's affective responsivity (Gallagher, 1986). Affective behavior aids the young child in controlling stimulation, by either encouraging or discouraging the continuance of a stimulus situation. A change in the intensity or the direction of affective responses signals an infant's state of being and thus a change in stimulus situations (Stroufe & Waters, 1976):

> Affective expression is clearly a function of the interaction between a child's motor status and cognitive ability. Both variables are necessary components to a young child's ability to express affect and the extent to which both variables merge determines the intensity of the affective response. (Gallagher, 1986; p. 72).

As the severity of the motor impairment increases, the child's ability to express affect in the expected manner decreases. This motor–affect relationship is critical within the context of the social responsiveness of the young child. The degree to which social responsiveness is dampened in the young child determines whether the child's opportunity for interaction with others in the environment will be reduced.

Because of its breadth of influence, the early detection of motor impairment is critically important if the motor competence of the child is to be normalized. Like cognitive assessment, motor assessment is restricted in providing specific information. Often, even the most rigorous testing situation leaves the interventionist with an incomplete picture of the source of the child's impairment. Because the typically used assessment instruments assess only the presence or absence of general motor skills (e.g., manipulating objects, rolling over, and crawling) rather then how a child performs the skill, an incomplete picture of the child's ability emerges. From these data, the clinician finds what the child can and cannot do motorically but not the reasons for the impairment. These tests are valuable for screening purposes because they can identify a general delay. However, the information that defines an underlying motor impairment is missing, and it is this type of information that is necessary to develop intervention strategies. It is from this level that the successful measurement of change in motor ability can proceed.

MOTOR ASSESSEMENT: ISSUES OF CONCERN

Motor assessment is one aspect of the total assessment process. Information on the motoric status of developmentally delayed children is vital for accuracy in screening, plans for intervention, and evaluation. Moreover, the content and the administrative criteria of various assessment instruments help to determine the effectiveness of the instrument in screening, evaluation, or program planning. In short, the purpose of the motor assessment dictates the choice of a motor assessment instrument.

Discontinuous development, rate variability, and the handicapped child's abnormal movement patterns make the assessment of current motor status difficult. Currently available assessment instruments may provide a method of screening children for developmental delays but may fall short in providing information concerning the child's impairment that is adequate for planning intervention.

Psychometric Properties

Traditional motor assessment of handicapped infants has an interest in the detailed assessment of functioning with attention paid to (a) where a child ranks relative to his or her peers and (b) the specific pattern of functioning in the domain being assessed. This information is necessary for referral to appropriate service agencies, and for the planning of individual programs (Hobbs, 1975). However, assessment procedures using traditional instruments fall short of expectations. Instruments like the Bayley Scales of Infant Development and the Gesell Developmental and Neurological Schedules which have a norm-referenced orientation, provide adequate information on a child's performance relative to a peer group and the level of the child's motor functioning relative to a broad range of motor skills. But this information is not adequate for planning intervention or for the evaluation of program effectiveness. Said differently, these motor instruments provide information on a child's functioning on broadly defined age-related skills (e.g., sitting, crawling, and walking). These data are important because they define, in broad terms, the extent of a child's motor delay, but little or no information is provided concerning the underlying causes of the delay. Information is lacking in many of these instruments concerning the specific components of movement that provide the foundations for more complex motor patterns and any accounting for the quality of the movement being assessed.

Content

Like cognitive development, the early motor development of children does not proceed at a uniform rate. Instead motor skills are acquired at varying rates across time, with rapid change in certain periods followed by periods of little change, when the consolidation of skills takes place. Although the sequence of acquiring motor skills appears to be invariant, the rate at which motor milestones are attained shows individual variation among children. In striving to meet the need for greater detail from motor assessment when assessing handicapped children, it is important to remember that one is working with behaviors that are fewer in number, slower to change, and abnormal in their expression. Slower motor development of handicapped populations ensures that the children will exhibit fewer skills in the motor domain. Therefore, assessment must be more focused, and must concentrate on a more limited range of content than among normally developing children. The result is that traditionally used instruments that make larger developmental leaps between test items are less useful for handicapped populations because of this lack of item specificity.

When assessing handicapped populations, the variability of skill within any individual child is a problem in that the more general an assessment device is, the lower is its ability to detect individual variability. Therefore, the specific strengths and weaknesses of an individual child are lost in these broad-based assessment scores. As delays in motor development among handicapped children increase in severity, a twofold problem emerges. The differences between the handicapped group and the normally developing reference group are magnified and at the same time, individual variations among the more severely handicapped children are substantially reduced.

It can be seen that motor instruments must tap into a broader repertoire of motor skills to provide useful information about the motor-impaired child. This additional information can have important benefits. Improved content will provide more specific information on the underlying makeup of the child's motor impairment. This specificity will yield information important to intevention planning, as well as evaluative information vital for measuring the child's changes across time. To accomplish this task, instruments must not simply be skill-oriented but must include items that tap components that make movement possible (e.g., strength, muscle tone and postural reactions).

Another content issue is the age range for which the instrument was designed. Many motor-assessment instruments are designed to give detailed information but cover very narrow developmental age ranges. For example, the Motor Assessment Instrument (Harris, Haley, Tada, & Swanson, 1984) uses items appropriate only for 4-month-olds in order to predict development at 12 months of age. Likewise, neonatal assessments apply only to children in the first few days or months of life. Even though these assessments yield information about the child at specific times, their use as anything other than screening devices is limited. In contrast, instruments such as the Bayley Scales of Infant Development or the Denver Developmental Screening Test (Frankenburg & Dodds, 1967) encompass wide age ranges and broader skills, but as a result they sacrifice item specific-ity in certain domains or across ages. The shortcomings of these broad-based instruments render them only marginally useful for diagnosis or evaluation. Instead, their utility is limited to broad-based screening.

Another problem among the currently used assessment instruments is the distribu-tion of items. Many instruments have an unequal distribution of test at items each age level. This disporportionate distribution of items presents poblems because, at certain age levels competency or developmental progress can be demonstrated by the passing of relatively few items whereas at other ages the opposite is true. When the scoring is based on the total number of items passed, this unequal item distribution is particularly impor-tant. At one age, several items must be passed before the child shows any progress, whereas at another age one or two items passed result in several months' gain in develop-ment.

Administrative Criteria of Motor Assessment

In order to satisfy the multiple purposes of motor assessment (e.g., screening, diag-nosis and evaluation), several administrative issues should be considered in the choice of instruments: (a) the scoring protocol; (b) the administration and training requirements; (c) the characteristics of the instrument; and (d) the function of the instrument.

Scoring Protocol

The methods of translating a child's performance into a score, a rating, or a level of development vary with different assessment instruments. When choosing a motor instru-ment, one should attend not only to the purpose for which the assessment is to be used, but also to the type of information that the assessment must generate. Two general criti-cisms of current motor instruments were defined by DeGangi, Berk, and Valvano (1983). First, the instruments often lack qualitative performance measures. The second criticism, and a more pervasive problem surrounding motor assessment, is that many instruments are not clinically sensitive enough to determine the extent to which abnormal motor development and neurological development interfere with normal developmental func-tions and development. Bagnato (1981) suggested that both qualitative and quantitative information should be included in assessments. This information, combined with more traditional developmental indices, could be useful in developing a more complete profile on the child's strengths and weaknesses.

Most standardized motor instruments such as the Bayley scales and the Gesell sched-ules, translate child performance into a developmental age or a developmental quotient. This quantitative measure of performance is useful in documenting a child's general developmental delay but does not offer any information concerning the quantitative as-pects of movement. Quantitative measures do not offer an acceptable measure of change over time, particularly for moderately to severely handicapped children whose rates of change can be slow and very subtle. Among these children, achieving gross motor mile-stones may not occur, but the underlying movement patterns already in the child's reper-toire may improve qualitatively.

Formats such as developmental checklists that use a dichotomous judgment assess only whether a skill is present or absent. The skills chosen are usually developmental markers and reflect the presence of mastered skills, readiness for the emergence of other skills, or an absence of motor abilities. Little attention is paid to the quality of the movement or to the degree of its occurrence (Plothier, Friedlander, Morrison, & Herman, 1983). The information gained from these instruments is often insufficient for the identification of specific movement problems, offers little help in program planning, and does not account for subtle differences or degrees of involvement. The impact of these oversights is amplified below.

Among normally developing children, the ability to prop themselves on their extended arms when prone is an important skill. It marks the degree of head control attained by an infant. It also marks the degree to which the shoulder girdle and the arms are developed. These are prerequisites that reflect readiness for more advanced skills, such as pushing into a hands-and-knees position or acquiring important prehensile skills.

When assessing this same skill in a developmentally delayed child, it is important to account for abnormal motor deviations. For example, babies who have hypotonicity or hypertonicity may be able to prop themselves on extended arms at an even earlier age that an infant with normal muscle tone. Their arms may be rigidly extended and locked at the elbow, or their shoulders may be elevated so that they can support the head. The ability to perform the task in these instances can still be scored as present. However, the quality of the performance does not reflect development of head control, shoulder strength, or stability. In fact, the developmental acquisitions that the assessment item is meant to mark may be entirely absent.

Another developmental marker—sitting with the hands free to play—is meant to reflect adequate postural control of the head and trunk. However, if the baby has abnormal muscle tone or a sensory impairment affecting balance and equilibrium she or he may be able to achieve the same sitting position (with the hands free for play) by keeping the legs widely abducted and/or the back arched. With either of these adaptations, the skill no longer marks head and trunk control or readiness for more advanced upright postures. As in the previous example, these abnormal motor deviations are overlooked when one adheres to the many administration protocols scoring the simple presence or absence of a particular skill. It is not enough simply to deal with a presence or absence scheme and to overlook the quality of movement and the components that comprise a particular motor skill. This oversight has implications that impact on the whole intervention process.

For many children who are more severely impaired, it may be more useful to use a scoring format that measures performance on a *continuum* from normal to severely impaired, as opposed to the simple presence or absence of a skill. Assessment having age-independent variables, such as muscle tone or strength and that make an effort to quantify performance may provide this kind of information. Some recent efforts in motor assessment have attempted to gauge motor skill and the underlying components of movement on a qualitative continuum (see the Chicago Infant Neuromotor Assessment—Cech, Josephs, Pearl, & Gallagher, 1983; the Motor Assessment Instrument—Chandler, Andrews, & Swanson, 1980).

Training Requirements

Another important area in motor assessment, and one determining the extent to which the assessment is usable, is the level of training and the ability of the examiner. Some instruments can be administered only by physical and/or occupational therapists;

and a great deal of training and specific knowledge is required before valid information can be obtained. However, at the program level, these highly trained personnel are not always available on a regular basis, and yet motor assessment is a necessary component of the intervention program. For these situations, motor instruments are available that require less training. Instruments at this level have some advantages in that they are usually not time-consuming to administer and can be very useful in the classroom for monitoring student progress. No matter what level of training is required of the examiner, it is important that the assessment information be valid and reliable: "Both medical and education professionals are frequently required to document motor development in children with multiple handicaps. It is important therefore, that their assessment tools provide valid information about the child's functional level" (Harris, Thompson, & McGren, 1983, p. 468). It is important for the professional to know his or her limitations before a particular instrument is chosen for a program. Also, the examiner must understand the strengths and weaknesses of the instrument to be used. In general, it is important that the examiner be qualified, and be familiar with the instrument and the type of information generated by the instrument.

Another factor in determining the quality of information generated by a motor instrument is the extent to which the examiner is familiar with young children in general and, more specifically with children who have developmental impairments. An examiner who has limited experience with young children and/or limited training in the motor development of young children will obtain information from the assessment that will be of limited value.

Characteristic of the Instrument

A final set of administrative concerns centers on the characteristics of the instrument: Does the instrument measure what it is supposed to measure (i.e., is it a valid measure of a child's motor skill)? Does the instrument reliably assess the motor skills of a child with a particular involvement? If it is used as a screening instrument, it is important to know whether the instrument tends to overidentify impairments (false positives) or to underidentify impairments (false negatives). Other characteristics of an assessment instrument to be investigated are (a) its appropriateness for the population being assessed, (b) the amount of time required for its administration, (c) its cost, and (d) the match between the assessment instrument and the instructional or therapy program.

Functions of the Instrument

In general how a motor instrument is to be used and for whom requires careful examination. Some instruments, because of their construction and the information they generate, are best used as screening devices (e.g., the Denver Developmental Screening Test, Frankenberg & Dodds, 1967). Instruments also have age limitations to which attention must be paid. Some instruments are appropriate for use only with newborns (e.g., Neurological Assessment of the Full-Term Newborn Infant, Neonatal Behavioral Assessment Scale, Brazelton, 1973); Neurological Assessment of the Preterm and Full-Term Infant, Dubowitz & Dubowitz, 1981; Prechtl & Beinterra, 1975) or at a particular age (e.g., Movement Assessment of Infants, Chandler, Andrews, & Swanson, 1980) whereas others maintain coverage over a broader age range but sacrifice quality of information for breadth (e.g., the Bayley Scales of Infant Development, Bayley, 1969). Although the aforementioned screening instruments function in placement decisions, they do not yield information that is useful in planning intervention strategies and/or evaluating program effectiveness. They do provide information on the child's current developmental status, but this information often bares little relationship to the child's subsequent treatment. This same information may result in inappropriate therapy programs that waste the time of both the child and the staff. Finally, a reliance on inaccurate information makes the evaluation of the changes in a child and program's effectiveness nearly impossible.

CONCLUSION

The range of assessment instruments for normal children is itself limited, and the choice of instruments for use with handicapped populations is even more restricted. As noted, serious problems are associated with using most motor assessment instruments with handicapped children. The general nature of these instruments is that they often have large steps in development between items, and that they lack component measures defining the quality of movement so that the interpretation of results is difficult.

To adequately assess a child's level of motor impairment and to, in turn, use that information as a basis for intervention, the assessment process must generate information pertinent to those ends. Fundamental to any braod-based motor assessment are certain neuromotor dimension that are basic to mobility and manipulation, and that therefore ought to be a part of motor assessment across all ages. These interactive movement dimensions are basic to movement and include:

1. The term *muscle tone* refers to the elasticity or tension of the muscle. Normally, it is sufficient to overcome the force of gravity (but not so strong that it interferes with movement and as such muscle tone is a primary substrate to movement.
2. The term *muscle strength* refers to the force-generating ability of the muscle. This is the capacity of the muscle to contract and the endurance with which it can maintain this countraction.
3. The *postural reactions* are equilibrium, righting, and protective responses that are automatic reactions to changes in posture and that allow us to maintain an upright position against gravity. Implied in this dimension is the concurrent integration of primitive reflexes.
4. *Structural mobility and integrity* are related to the construction of the skeletal system and provide optimal relationships among bones, joints, and muscles for fluid movement. Fixed muscles or orthopedic deformities such as contractures, scoliosis, or hip dislocations can interfere with the ability of the body to produce fluid, efficient movement.

An assessment device that quantifies the above dimensions can provide a basis for designing plans for motor intervention and the evaluation of the intervention's effects. In general, this assessment process examines the components of movement and their effects on muscle tone, as well as the development of postural reactions against gravity. How the interplay of each dimension affects the quality and quantity of movement should be addressed.

Variety and breadth of movement skill are as significant in establishing a functional level of motor performance as is the quality of those skills. To be complete, a motor assessment instrument's content should be sensitive to the multidimensional components of movement that define quality and should take a sampling of a broad range of tasks at several age levels over a broad age span.

REFERENCES

Bagnato, S. (1981). Developmental scales and developmental curricula: Forging a linkage for early intervention. *Topics in Early Childhood Special Education, 1,* 1–8.

Bayley, N. (1969). *Bayley scales of infant development.* New York: Psychological Corp.

Berkson, G. (1968). Development of abnormal stereotyped behaviors. *Developmental Psychobiology, 1,* 118–132.

Berkson, G. (1983). Repetitive stereotyped behaviors. *America Journal of Mental Deficiency, 88,* 239–246.

Bobath, B. & Bobath, K. (1975). *Motor development in different types of cerebral palsey.* London Heinemann.

Brazelton, T. B. (1973). *Neonatal Behavioral Assessment Scale.* Philadelphia, Lippincott.

Bricker, W. A., & Campell, P. H. (1980). Interdisciplinary assessment and programming for multihandicapped students. In W. Sailor, B. Wilcox, & L. Brown (Eds.), *Methods of instruction for severely handicapped students.* Baltimore, Brookes.

Bricker, W. A., & Filler J. (Eds.). *Serving the severely retarded: from research to practice.* Reston, VA: Council for Exceptional Children.

Brinker, R. P. (1984). Curricula without recipes: A challenge to teachers and a promise to severely retarded students. In D. Bricker, W. A., & Filler, J. (Eds.). *Serving the severely retarded: from research to practice.* Reston, VA: Council for Exceptional Children.

Campbell, P. H. (1979). *Basic considerations in programming for students with motor problems.* Paper presented at the meeting of the Southeastern Regional Training Coalition, Nashville, Peabody College.

Campbell, S. (1981). Movement assessment of infants: An evaluation. *Physical and Occupational Therapy in Pediatrics, 1,* 53–57.

Capute, A., Palmer, F., Shapiro, B., Wachtel, R., Ross, A., & Accardo, P. (1984). Primitive reflex profile: A quantification of primitive reflexes in infancy. *Developmental Medicine and Child Neurology, 26,* 375–383.

Capute, A., Shapiro, B., Accardo, P., Wachtel, R., Ross, A., & Palmer, F. (1982). Motor functions: Associated primitive reflex profiles. *Developmental Medicine and Child Neurology, 24,* 662–669.

Cech, D., Josephs, A., Pearl, O., & Gallagher, R. J. (1983). *Chicago Infant Neuromotor Assessment.* Unpublished assessment instrument, Institiute for the Study of Developmental Disabilities, University of Illinois at Chicago.

Chandler, L. Andrews, M. & Swanson, M. (1980). *Movement Assessment of Infants.* P.O. Box 4631, Rolling Bay, WA.

Degangi, G. A., Berk, R. A., Valvano, J. (1983). Test of motor and neurological functions in high-risk infants: Preliminary findings. *Developmental and Behavioral Pediatrics, 4,* 180–189.

Drillien, C. & Drummond, F. L. (1977) *Neurodevelopmental problems in early childhood.* Oxford: Blackwell Scientific.

Dubowitz, L. & Dubowitz, V. (1981). *The neurological assessment of the preterm and full-term infant.* Philadelphia: Lippincott.

Frankenburg, W. K., & Dodds, J. B. (1967). The Denver developmental Screening Test. *Journal of Pediatrics, 71,* 181–191.

Gallagher, R. J. (1986). Affective expression: Implications for the educator, clinician, and therapist. *Physical and Occupational Therapy in Pediatrics 6,* 65–74.

Gallagher, R. J., & Berkson, G. (1987). The effect of intervention techniques in reducing stereotypic handgazing in young children disabled children. *American Journal of Mental Deficiency, 91,* 170–177.

Gallagher, R. J., Jens, K. G., & O'Donnell, K. E. (1983). The effect of physical status on the affective expesion of handicapped infants. *Infant Behavior and Development, 6,* 73–77.

Hamilton, J., & Swan, W. (1981). Measurement references in the assessment of preschool handicapped children. *Topics in Early Childhood Special Education, 1*, 41–48.

Harris, S. R., Thompson, M., & Mcgrew, L. (1983). Motor assessment tools: Their concurrent validity in evaluating children with multiple handicaps. *Archives of Physical Medicine and Rehabilitation, 64*, 468–470.

Harris, S., Haley, S., Tada, W., & Swanson, M. (1984). Reliability of observational measures of the movement assessment of infants. *Physical Therapy, 64*, 471–477.

Hobbs, N. (1975). *The future of children: Categories, labels and their consequences: Report on the project on classification of exceptional childen.* San Franciso: Jossey-Bass.

Hunt, J. McV. (1976). Environmental programming to foster competence and prevent mental retardation in infancy. In R. N. Walsh & W. T. Greenough (Eds.), *Environments as therapy for brain dysfunction.* New York: Plenum Press.

Illingworth, R. S. (1975). *The development of the infant and young child: Normal and abnormal* (6th Ed.). New York: Churchill, Livingston.

Plothier, P. C., Friedlander, S., Morrison, D. C., & Herman, L. (1983). Procedure for assessment of neuro-developmental delay in young children: Preliminary report. *Child: Care, Health and Development, 9*, 73–83.

Rincover, A., Cook, R., Peoples, A., & Packard, D. (1979a). Sensory extinction and sensory reinforcement principles for programming multiple adaptive behavior change. *Journal of Applied Behavior Analysis, 12*, 221–233.

Rincover, A., Newsom, C. D., & Carr, E. G. (1979b). Using sensory extinction procedures in the treatment of compulsive like behavior of developmentally disabled children. *Journal Consulting and Clinical Psychology, 47*, 695–701.

Sameroff, A. J., & McDonugh, S. C. 1984). The role of motor activity in human cognitive and social development. In E. Possitt & P. Amante (Eds.), *Energy intake and activity.* New York: Liss.

Scherzer, A., & Tscharnuter, I. (1982). *Early diagnosis and therapy in cerebral palsy.* New York: Marcel Dekker.

Sroufe, L. A., & Waters, E. (1976). The ontogenesis of smiling and laughter: A perspective on the organization of development in infancy. *Psychological Review, 83*, 173–189.

Wetzel, A., & Wetzel, R. (1984). A review of the Ameil-Tison neurologic evaluation of the newborn and infant. *American Journal of Occupational Therapy, 38*, 585–593.

Zelle, R., & Coyner, A. (1983). *Developmentally disabled infants and toddlers: Assessment and intervention.* Philadelphia: F. A. Davis.

13

Assessment of Temperament in Developmentally Disabled Infants and Preschoolers

Sean C. McDevitt

Temperament, or behavioral style, refers to the *how* of behavior, as opposed to the what (content) or why (motivation). Temperament assessment captures the stylistic manner in which behavior is carried out by an individual and the way in which this affects interaction with the environment, including significant others (parents, teachers, and peers). There is good evidence that individual differences in behavioral style are present at birth, and methods of measuring temperamental individuality have been developed for infancy, childhood, adolescence, and adulthood. Although the study of temperamental differences extends back to the time of Hippocrates (Carey, 1981), the recent emphasis on the influence of stylistic aspects of behavior on growth and development dates back to the seminal work of Thomas, Chess, and associates (Thomas, Chess, Birch, Hertzig & Korn, 1963) about 25 years ago. Much remains to be learned about the role of behavioral style in person–environment interaction, particularly with special populations such as the developmentally disabled. At the same time, enough is known to recommend temperamental assessment as a clinically relevant dimension to those who accept the challenge of working with handicapped infants and children and their families.

This chapter has the following goals: (a) to briefly summarize concepts of temperament intended to be useful with clinical populations; (b) to indicate measurement techniques and problems in assessment; (c) to discuss the role of temperament in assessing young handicapped children and (d) to review strategies of intervention that may be useful in working with parents, teachers, and children.

CONCEPTS OF TEMPERAMENT

Although temperament as a domain of personality assessment has been increasingly accepted, there has also been a proliferation of dimensions of temperament proposed and defined by various investigators . Like the study of intelligence, these range from single-

SEAN C. MCDEVITT • Western Behavioral Associates, Inc. 367 N. 21st Ave., Phoenix, Arizona 85009.

dimension concepts of general difficulty of temperament (Bates, Freeland, & Lounsbury, 1979), to factorially derived and statistically independent constructs (Buss & Plomin, 1975, 1984; Rothbart, 1981), to dimensions derived from a clinical perspective (Thomas *et al.*, 1963). Each approach is associated with its own set of assumptions and theoretical underpinnings, consistent with an integrated view of what temperament is and how it may be useful in understanding growth and development. There is little agreement on which concepts or which dimenstions will ultimately be of most value in research and practice. Simeonsson and Bailey (in Chapter 2 of this book) have described the fundamental differences in approach between global and multiaxial classifications of child characteristics. The current research literature is not extensive enough to answer this question empirically, and if the analogy with the study of intelligence is valid, no consensus will be forthcoming. If, as Hubert and Wallender (Chapter 3) suggest, the issue of practical value is related to the ability to make decisions about a client in a specific situation, the weight of empirical evidence is unlikely to favor one system of temperament exclusively. What may evolve is an understanding of the strengths and limitations of specific temperament concepts in explaining or predicting certain clinical or developmental phenomena reliably. This alone would be helpful in guiding the practitioner.

The most widely recognized and used system of temperament in clinical research and practice derives from the work of Thomas, Chess, and their associates in the New York Longitudinal Study (NYLS)—(Thomas *et al.*, 1963; Thomas & Chess, 1977; Thomas, Chess, & Birch, 1968). Because of its widespread use, the Thomas and Chess model will be the focus of this chapter. Using a content analysis of behavioral descriptions derived in infancy, these researchers identified nine temperamental characteristics that were conceptually distinct and potentially important clinically. These characteristics are activity level, rhythmicity, approach–withdrawal, adaptability, intensity of reaction, mood, distractibility, sensory threshold, and persistence. Working from data gathered from semistructured interviews, the NYLS group followed a sample of over 100 individuals from infancy into adulthood. Along with an analysis of the longitudinal consistency of temperament, Thomas and Chess monitored the development of behavioral disorders, school and family adjustment, and other indices of development. Based on their findings, three clinical clusters of temperament characteristics were identified that seemed to predict the presence or absence of behavioral disorders later in life: The difficult child, defined as arhythmic, withdrawing, nonadaptable, intense, and negative, was much more likely to develop psychiatric symptomatology and was more difficult for the parent to rear. The slow-to-warm-up child, defined as inactive, withdrawing, nonadaptable, mild, and negative, seemed more likely to exhibit reactive disorders. And the easy child (regular, approaching, adaptable, mild, and positive) had little predisposition to behavioral problems. These clusters characterized about 65% of the total sample. Although there was overall predictability from temperament cluster to outcome, it was clear that there were exceptions in all categories.

Over and above the global easy–difficult dichotomy, certain specific temperamental predispositions may be particularly useful in predicting later outcome. High activity and negative mood in infancy, for example, are two characteristics associated with children who remain in the difficult temperament group through early childhood (Carey & McDevitt, 1978), whereas adaptability and persistence, in combination, are the characteristics found to correlate with school adjustment (Carey, Fox & McDevitt, 1977). As

Rutter (1982) noted, different groupings of characteristics may be more useful than others for predicting specific outcomes in various situations. Here again, the parallels with the decision-theory approach to assessment outlined by Hubert and Wallander and the mutiple classification model presented by Simeonsson and Bailey are noteworthy.

Most critically, Thomas and Chess noted that temperamental characteristics themselves were not the same as behavioral problems, nor would they lead inevitably to developing them. The "goodness-of-fit" model of these authors emphasized the process of interaction with the environment, with demands, expectancies, and supports being important parts of the interplay between temperament and overall adjustment. Thus, a "difficult" child in a supportive, nurturing environment may be well adjusted and may exhibit no signs of psychopathology. Another child with this same temperament profile who is confronted repeatedly with unrealistic expectations and demands may exhibit severe emotional or behavioral disturbance. Within the goodness-of-fit model, it is the relationship between temperament and environment that has implications for functioning rather than the nature of either one alone. This relative concept explains how a very temperamentally difficult baby can develop quite normally with no evidence of behavioral or social maladjustment, whereas an easy child may have a severe behavioral disorder. Though tendencies and predispositions are associated with certain patterns of temperament, as noted above, many exceptions exist. In fact, mothers often perceive their babies as average or even easy, when their ratings of the infant on a temperament questionnaire indicate that the child's actual behavioral style is quite difficult. Although in some cases this may be the result of denial or other defensiveness, clinical experience has shown that it often means that the mother is coping quite well (Carey, 1981). Intervention is not needed in these cases because there is a relative "match" between the child's characteristics and the parent's ability to present a functionally sound environment. In situations where there is clearly stress in the interaction between child and environment, intervention is warranted.

DEVELOPMENTAL ASPECTS OF TEMPERAMENT

The NYLS was concerned with investigating, in addition to psychopathology, the longitudinal stability of temperamental characteristics. Temperament was thought to be a relatively enduring characteristic that was biologically based and perhaps partially genetically determined. Data were generated showing longitudinal stability for most characteristics from one year to the next for the first 5 years of life. However, though the correlations were statistically significant, there was at least as much change as stability in early life, indicating that behavioral style is modified by the environment as the infant interacts with it (Thomas & Chess, 1977). Recent evidence has shown that individual differences in temperament become much more stable after 3 years of age (McDevitt, 1986) and predictions about the status of a particular child become firmer then. The stability and change in temperamental characteristics show a developmental pattern that may have implications for assessment and intervention. To the extent that temperament measures become more reliable as the preschool years begin, the clinician may consider more detailed assessment of the child's interactions and adjustment when the potential for a behavioral disorder is identified. Conversely, intervention designed to change established dysfuntional patterns of interaction may be less effective as the child grows older. More intensive effort may be required and concurrent change in behavior style may be less likely to follow changes in the interaction with the caregiver.

MEASUREMENT TECHNIQUES AND PROBLEMS

Methods for assessing temperament by direct environmental measurement of infant or child behavior have not yet been developed. Strategies for determining behavioral style have included either interview techniques or questionnaires rated by individuals who have ongoing experience with the child's day-to-day functioning. These are typically parents, teachers, and other caregivers. Standardized interview techniques have some advantages in determining precisely what the interviewee's experience with the youngster has been, as clarification and amplification of responses can be obtained directly from the subject. Further, ratings based on interview material can be directly scored by interviewers having sufficient training (see Stevenson-Hinde & Simpson, 1982, for additional discussion). However, in clinical practice, interviews are inordinately time-consuming, and most clinicians do not have training in the interview protocols or access to experts for scoring. Questionnaires are much more time-efficient and their scoring is very objective, typically involving only 20–30 minutes of professional time to complete and analyze (Carey & McDevitt, 1978).

Numerous attempts to develop temperament assessment techniques have been reported in the literature, and the potential user will need to choose from the array of available instruments the ones that would be most suitable to the situation at hand. A comprehensive critical review of the psychometric properties of temperament assessment instruments (Hubert, Wachs, Peters-Martin, & Gandour, 1982) summarizes evidence of the reliability and validity of many current methods of assessment and cautiously recommends specific instruments at various age levels.

The use of questionnaires to assess temperament is controversial because of disagreements regarding the accuracy of parents ratings of their own child's behavior. Some (Sameroff, Seifer, & Elias, 1982; Vaughn, Deinard, & Egeland, 1980), have argued that temperament questionnaires measure more about the parent than about the child, and others (Carey, 1983) decry the professional arrogance of those who fall into various pits of "maternal perception fallacies." Even proponents of using questionnaires caution against taking all ratings by all raters at face value and stress the importance of supplemental interviews with parents, plus observations of parent–child interactions, before making a clinical judgement regarding the role of temperament in any child's presenting problems (McDevitt & Carey, 1978). Sheehan's discussion of the level of parental involvement in the assessment process (Chapter 5) is therefore especially pertinent to the measurement of temperament. Parental overinvolvement or detachment may influence how the child's behavior is rated. For example, the parent who has learned to respond "objectively" to intensely negative expressions of feeling by a willful toddler may normalize ratings of the youngster's temperament, signifying a change in the parent's response to the emotion expressed rather than a change in behavior itself.

Finally, it is important to understand the role of the environment in determining how behavioral styles are expressed. Correlations reported between parent and teacher ratings of temperament, although significant, have tended to be moderate in magnitude (Billman

& McDevitt, 1980; Keogh & Pullis, 1980). Thus, it is not certain that assessment of temperament through parental ratings is directly generalizable to school or other intervention settings. Where assessment goals dictate the need for data regarding a particular context, the clinician would be well advised to assess temperament in that environment. This recommendation parallels Hubert and Wallender's discussion (Chapter 3) of the bandwidth–fidelity problem in assessment. The overall pattern of a child's interaction with his or her environment may not be captured adequately by a measure that limits the rater's direct experience to particular realms of observation.

Measuring the Temperament of the Developmentally Disabled

There are a number of considerations to be made in selecting an appropriate instrument for assessing the temperament of developmentally disabled clients, including the nature and severity of the handicapping condition, the purpose of the evaluation, and the contexts in which the data will be used. Many, but not all, temperament questionnaires use items that describe typical behaviors in home or school settings. Thus, the nature of the child's disability may make some items or dimensions of temperament inappropriate. For example, many items in activity-level scales refer to the child's running or jumping, and this dimension may not be applicable to a severely motorically impaired client. Similarly, items tapping distractibility by asking for ratings of response to sounds are not functional in assessing a deaf infant.

The extent of developmental delay may also present a key problem. A temperament questionnaire constructed and standardized for a 2 year old child will not be descriptive of the behavior of a youngster who uniformly functions at a 6-month-old level, even though chronologically the child is 2 years old. Although using a temperament questionnaire for a 6-month-old may solve the problem of appropriateness of context, it may also introduce other difficulties, as the norms and the reference group are not then consistent with the subjects' condition. Moreover, infant questionnaires may begin each item with "The infant..." and this may impair the acceptability of the questionnaire to the parent who recognizes that the child is no longer an infant. For an involved parent who is committed to the intervention process, this can be emotionally disastrous (Malone, 1979, personal communication). The practitioner, then, must carefully review the items to be presented to determine what value would accrue to the use contemplated and weigh this against potential problems. Instrument modification may be appropriate in deleting or rewording items, though the risk of introducing systematic measurement error or the loss of a normative reference group would increase with each change that is necessary. No specific guidelines can be given for how much modification is appropriate or what types of changes are reasonable for which measures. Consultation with the test author, or at least with another clinician, would be prudent when instrument modifications are made.

STUDIES OF THE TEMPERAMENT OF THE DEVELOPMENTALLY DISABLED

Comparatively little temperament research has been done on developmentally disabled infants and children. The sparsity of research may be due in part, to the difficulty of collecting a sample of appropriate children, while avoiding the problems of heterogeneity identified earlier in this book (Wachs & Sheehan, Chapter 1). The most extensive study of a handicapped group by the NYLS was conducted by Chess, Korn, and Fernandez (1971), using a clinical sample of youngsters with congenital rubella. These children were studied between 2½ and 4 years of age, and most presented visual, auditory, neurological, and cardiac defects, either singly or in combination. Data were obtained on both temperament status and behavioral disorders for the entire sample. Interestingly, the distribution of temperament characteristics for the rubella children was similar to that of NYLS longitudinal sample. However, of those with behavior disorders (about half of the sample), almost 50% had four or five signs of the difficult child, as opposed to 15% in the group without behavior disorders. The relationship between temperament and behavior disorders appears stronger in this group than in the NYLS study group. Similarly, a mentally handicapped sample studied by Chess and Korn (1970) showed that difficult temperament was strongly associated with behavioral disorder, and that the combination of difficult temperament and cognitive impairment posed a particularly high risk of behavioral disturbance.

More recently, a study by Greenberg and Field (1982) indicated that temperament ratings may vary as a function of the type of handicapping condition as well as the environmental context in which the ratings are done. In this study, infants with audiovisual handicaps (defined as deafness or blindness) and cerebral-palsied (CP) infants were rated as significantly more difficult temperamentally during a classroom play sequence than normal, developmentally delayed, or Downs syndrome subjects. Specifically, CP and sensory-handicapped infants were rated as having lower activity levels, being less approaching, being less persistent, having less positive mood scores and being less soothable (distractible) than the other groups. Interestingly, the Downs syndrome infants were rated as the most adaptable and most soothable of any group, including the normal infants. Although limited in generalizability by sample and measurement issues, the findings of this study raise the question of whether certain handicapping conditions predispose children to certain profiles of temperamental characteristics. Clinical folklore has sterotyped Downs syndrome individuals as sociable and easy-going. A previous study by Baron (1972) failed to find support for this stereotype in temperament ratings, and the Greenberg and Field study did note differences. Clearly, further exploration of this question will be needed to clarify matters. A secondary question is whether the sensory or motoric deficits associated with various handicapping conditions influence temperament ratings in some systematic way. Activity level, distractibility, persistence, and sensory threshold, in particular, seem to be intertwined with the infant's ability to perceive, process and react to information from the environment. With impaired ability to respond physically, infants with sensory or motor handicaps, as a a group, may differ from normals, *while at the same time exhibiting individual differences from one another*. Moreover, if the degree of developmental delay (independent of the associated handicapping condition) has a systematic effect on temperamental characteristics, the clinical picture becomes even more complex. Whether either or both of these factors influence outcome (e.g., long-term adjustment) for difficult individuals compared to easy ones would then be of interest.

Huntington and Simeonsson (1985) reported a comparative longitudinal study of handicapped infants (Downs syndrome, mentally retarded, and multiple handicapped) and a normal control group. Using 12- and 36-month assessments, these authors found that infants with multiple handicaps were initially more likely to be classified as "diffi-cult" (about one third compared to 10%–15% for other groups), but by 36 months, the percentage had decreased. Downs syndrome infants, on the other hand were more likely to be classified as slow to warm up at 12 months, but the percentage decreased by 36 months, as these same infants tended to be rated as either "easy" or "difficult." The percentages of infants in these temperamental groupings were essentially unchanged in the normal sample across the time period studied. These findings suggest that the temper-ament patterns of handicapped infants may follow a specific *course* of development over time, depending on the handicapping condition. If so, clinicians and researchers will want to know what patterns tend to be found across development, how these changes are related to environmental events, and whether the likelihood of a positive outcome can be increased by intervention. Even though the current literature on temperament and devel-opmentally disabled infants is not extensive, the available studies have raised some im-portant questions regarding the relationships between individual differences in temperament, developmental competencies, and the interaction of these factors with the environment over time.

THE ROLE OF TEMPERAMENT IN THE ASSESSMENT OF HANDICAPPED CHILDREN

As a measure of individual differences, temperamental characteristics do not play a part in the diagnosis of developmental disabilities themselves. It would be inappropriate to associate temperamental characteristics with either cause or effect in the etiology of developmental disorders. However, this statement does not imply that behavioral style has no influence on children with developmental disabilities. Rather, temperament may have significant value in the descriptive and prescriptive process of assessment. Descrip-tively, a temperament profile can delineate how the child's activity level, attentional features, emotional expression, and characteristic response to changes and routines is likely to interplay with her or his cognitive and sensorimotor strengths and deficits. Pre-scriptively, the likelihood that these factors will predispose a child to behavior disorder in addition to developmental disabilities has obvious implications for outcome. Clearly, the handicapped child's needs and his or her abilities to profit from intervention will depend upon how he or she interacts with people and objects in the environment. In specifying how the child is likely to respond to stimuli, to adapt to, and handle new situations, and to persist with objects, the nature of the environment that will be needed to promote optimal development becomes more apparent. A temperament profile can determine which of the child's individual characteristics will be most likely to effect learning and/or development.

At present, difficult temperament is considered a predisposing condition for the later development of behavior disorder, and there is good anterospective evidence for this relationship (Thomas, *et al.*, 1968). Clinicians know that a developmentally disabled youngster is much more difficult to raise, educate, and socialize when the child also presents behavioral problems that interfere with functioning. In this sense, the tempera-mentally difficult child has a higher probability of interacting in a dysfunctional way with environment. Diagnostically, then, a youngster at risk for behavioral disorder (whether developmentally disabled or not) may require more frequent monitoring or additonal supportive and preventive intervention than one whose risk is low. On the other hand, a developmentally disabled child who already has a behavior disorder may need immediate and intensive intervention, whether or not there are indicators of difficult temperament identified by the clinician. If the youngster needing intervention also shows indicators of temperamental difficulty, it is likely that clues regarding how to intervene effectively with parents and teachers will be apparent from the temperament profile, though this is by no means certain. The task of the assessing clinician, therefore, depends in part on what will be found in the data and is, of course, unknown when the assessment process begins.

The role of temperament discussed in these studies involves primarily a predisposition to a particular behavioral outcome. Clinical analyses of the problems and issues faced by individual families and children appear to clarify the role of temperament in terms of outcome. For example, deaf children with high distractibility may have great difficulty in interpersonal development, as communication for this population is so dependent on maintaining visual attention to pick up cues and signs and to read lips (Thomas & Chess, 1977). Given the documented difficulties in interpersonal development for deaf children as a group (Wachs & Sheehan, Chapter 1) temperamental distractibility may be a crucial part of the clinical assessment of deaf clients. Thus in temperament assessment, potential stress factors can be identified or anticipated in certain situations or environments. These can then be analyzed for possible methods of compensation or accommodation to the stressful interaction. Thomas, Chess, and associates (Thomas, et al., 1968; Thomas & Chess, 1977) present numerous case studies indicating how careful assessment by the clinician can be helpful in reducing the mismatch between the child and the environment.

Temperament and Intervention Strategies

The match–mismatch model of temperament–environment interaction presumes that there are no absolute "healthy" or "unhealthy" profiles of individual differences in behavioral style. Temperamental characteristics can be congruent with the demands and expectations of the environment or in conflict with the environment. In the former case, adequate personality adjustment and development are expected to follow, even though an individual child's temperament may be very difficult, compared with that of another child of similar age and circumstances. It is in the situation where a conflict or a mismatch occurs that the clinician may consider intervention. However, the goal of such an intervention is not to alter the temperamental characteristics themselves, but to change the nature of the interaction that is observed to be dysfunctional. At present, there are no known ways to directly change the temperamental characteristics of an individual. We do know that temperament profiles tend to change within certain limits over the course of time (see Carey & McDevitt, 1978), and that certain features of temperament (high activity level and negative mood) tend to be associated with continued difficult temperament during infancy and into early childhood. The individual or environmental factors that may be responsible for changes in temperament are not well understood, and more will need to be known before this kind of intervention will be feasible.

Clinicians who work with infants and children and their caregivers have thus focused on the changes in the environment that will tend to reduce the pattern of mismatch observed between child and environment. Carey (1979) delineated three ways in which a knowledge of temperament characteristics can be helpful clinically: (a) in increasing awareness of the existence of temperament characteristics; (b) in discussing the child's specific temperament profile with significant others; (c) providing guidance or suggestions regarding environmental modifications that will reduce dysfunctional interactions between the child and the environment. Each of these methods may have an impact on the nature of the interaction, and it is the clinican's role to carefully assess the situation at hand and to determine what course of action, if any, would be helpful to the client. Intervention may be accomplished through primary caregivers, teachers, professionals, or others who have a direct ongoing contact with the child.

The first type of intervention, awareness of individual differences in temperament, may be useful in reducing labeling or sterotyping of the child's behavior. Just as not every persistent child who is developmentally disabled can be considered "perseverative," not every one with a high activity level can be considered "hyperactive." An awareness of normal individual differences in temperament can alter how a caregiver thinks and feels about a child's behavioral characteristics, and this alteration will hopefully affect the caregiver's expectations and interactions with the youngster. This would seem particularly important for a developmentally impaired population, as the children have already been identified as abnormal and there would be a tendency to see other characteristics from this vantage point.

The second type of intervention, discussion of the child's individual profile, may be valuable in assisting the caregiver (or professional) to understand the specific features of the behavioral style of a particular client, and how this is being expressed in everyday situations. For the parent or teacher struggling to work effectively with a difficult child, acknowledging that the youngster's intense emotional reactions or negative moods are temperamental characteristics can allay the caregiver's anxieties and relieve feelings of frustration in handling these reactions. Correlating temperamental characteristics with ongoing behavior may also tend to reduce the tendency to interpret the child's behavior in ways that may be dysfunctional. For example, the nonadaptable child may be seen as defiant or disobedient, whereas it is really the child's ability to respond to limitations that is the major source of the problem. If the child is seen as slowly adaptable, however, caregivers will have assurance that success will come in time, and that no incipient behavior disorder is being observed.

The third method, changing the environment to reduce mismatch, involves developing strategies for making a child more successful by adapting parenting or teaching styles to the child's temperament. The highly distractible child, for example, compared to a less distractible one, may need short, more frequent instructional intervals in a preschool classroom, in order to acheive the same level of progress. Through a change in the teaching "environment," the method of instruction becomes compatible with the child's temperament, and the level of success is increased. Similarly, the child who is low in approach to new situations, such as having a new babysitter, may need to have the parents present for an hour before feeling comfortable about the parents' departure. If this special intervention is not provided, the result could easily be hours of tantrumming or crying while the parents are away. Clinicians providing consultation on intervention strategies to caregivers can become aware of potential problem areas, as well as more fully understand current areas of difficulty, by assessing the child's temperament. With careful interviewing and observation, in addition to the results of a temperament questionnaire, the clinical picture is usually clarified enough to warrant responsible intervention. For children who are otherwise handicapped, intervention may take various forms depending on the specifics of the overall treatment program. An understanding of behavioral style and its contribution to the child's patterns of behavior will give an additional dimension of insight to the repertoire of skills that the practitioner brings to working with developmentally disabled children and their families.

REFERENCES

Baron, J. (1972), Temperamental profile of children with Down's syndrome. *Developmental Medicine and Child Neurology, 14,* 640–643.

Bates, J. E., Freeland, C. A. B., & Lounsbury, M. L., (1979). Measurement of infant difficultness. *Child Development, 50,* 794–803.

Billman, J., & McDevitt, S. C., (1980). Convergence of parent and observer ratings of temperament with observations of peer interaction in nursery school. *Child Development, 51,* 395–400.

Buss, A. H., & Plomin, R., (1975). *A temperament theory of personality develpment.* New York: Wiley-Interscience.

Buss, A. H., & Plomin, R., (1984) *Temperament: Early developing personality traits.* Hillside, N.J.: Erlbaum.

Carey, W. B., (1979). *Clinical appraisal of temperament.* Paper presented at the symposium on Developmental Disabilities in the Preschool Child. Chicago.

Carey, W.B., (1981). The importance of temperament environment interaction for child health and development. In M. Lewis & L. Rosenblum (Eds.), *The uncommon child.* New York: Plenum Press.

Carey, W. B., (1983). Some pitfalls in infant temperament research. *Infant Behavior and Development, 6,* 247–254.

Carey, W. B., & McDevitt, S. C., (1978). Stability and change in individual temperament diagnosis from infancy to early childhood. *Journal of the American Academy of Child Psychiatry, 17,* 331–337.

Carey, W. B., Fox, M. M., & McDevitt, S. C., (1977). Temperament as a factor in early school adjustment. *Pediatrics, 60,* 621–624.

Chess, S., & Korn, S., (1970). Temperament and behavior disorders in mentally retarded children. *Archives of General Psychiartry, 23,* 122.

Chess, S., Korn, S., & Fernandez, P. (1971). *Psychiatric disorders of children with congenital rubella.* New York: Brunner/Mazel.

Greenberg, R., & Field, T., (1982). Temperament ratings of handicapped infants during classroom mother and teacher interactions. *Journal of Pediatric Psychology, 7,* 387–405.

Hubert, N. C., Wachs, T. D., Peters-Martin, P., & Gandour, M. J., (1982). The study of early temperament; Measurement and conceptual issues. *Child Development, 53,* 571–600.

Huntington, G., & Simeonsson, R., (1985). *Comparative and developmental analysis of temperament clusters in Downs syndrome infants.* Paper presented at the Biennial Meetings at the Society for Research in Child Development, Toronto.

Keogh, B. K., & Pullis, M. E., (1980). Temperament influences on the development of exceptional children. *Advances in Special Education. 1,* 239–276.

McDevitt, S.C., (1986) Continuity and discontinuity of temperament in infancy and early childhood: A psychometric perspective. In R. Plomin & J. Dunn (Eds.), *The study of temperament: Changes, continuities and challenges.* Hillside, NJ: Erlbaum.

McDevitt, S.C., & Carey, W. B., (1978). The measurement of temperament in 3-7 year old children. *Journal of Child Psychology and Psychiatry, 19,* 245–253.

Rothbart, M. K., (1981). Measurement of temperament in infancy. *Child Development. 52,* 569–578.

Rutter, M., (1982). Temperament: Concepts, issues and problems. In R. Porter & G. M. Collins (Eds.), *Temperament differences in infants and young children.* London: Pitman Books (Ciba Foundation Symposium 89).

Sameroff, A. J., Seifer, R., & Elias, P. K., (1982) Sociocultural variablility in infant temperament ratings. *Child Development, 53,* 164–173.

Stevenson-Hinde, J., & Simpson, A. E., (1982). Temperament and relationships. In R. Porter & G. M. Collins (Eds.), Temperamental differences in infants and young children. London: Pitman Book (Ciba Foundation Symposium 89).

Thomas, A., & Chess, S, (1977). *Temperament and development.* New York: Brunner/Mazel.

Thomas, A., Chess, S., Birch, H.G., Hertzig, M. E., & Korn, S., (1963). *Behavioral individuality in early childhood.* New York: New York University Press.

Thomas, A., Chess, S., & Birch, H. G., (1968). Temperament and behavior disorders in children. New York: New York University Press.

Vaughn, B., Deinard, A., & Egeland, B., (1980). Measuring temperament in pediatric practice. *Journal of Pediatrics, 96,* 510–514.

14

Mastery Motivation and Developmental Delay

Lois M. Brockman, George A. Morgan, and Robert J. Harmon

INTRODUCTION

Until recently, the assessment of children with developmental delay or disabilities has focused almost exclusively on cognitive abilities, perhaps, in large part because of the available tests which were originally designed to screen for academic potential and success. Though some of these tests have been adapted to more validly accommodate specific disabilities, such as visual and auditory impairments, the same ability areas are still measured. However, the academic success of children with developmental delay or disabilities is generally not the primary concern of parents, teachers, and clinicians. Rather, their first concern is that their children be competent, that is, that they interact effectively in their physical and social environment. Even for normally developing children, success is a function not merely of intellectual capacities but also of such noncognitive factors as motivation and social adjustment (Scarr, 1981).

The focus of the chapter is on mastery motivation, which is viewed as a necessary precursor of and condition for the continuing development of competence. The underlying assumption of mastery motivation assessment is that the child not only receives stimulation from the environment, but also initiates interactions that elicit stimulation from both the physical and the social environment. Thus, in contrast to the assessment of competence, which measures the outcome of what the child has already achieved developmentally, the assessment of mastery motivation focuses on what the child is currently working on mastering.

The concern is this chapter is to describe how clinicians can get a "window" on the characteristics of a child's developmental activity that can lead to the development of competencies, which then become the measurable outcomes in assessments of abilities. Recent research in the area of mastery motivation suggests ways in which such a window may be available and how it may be used in the process of assessment and in the planning

LOIS M. BROCKMAN • Department of Family Studies, University of Manitoba, Winnipeg, Manitoba, Canada R3T 2N2. GEORGE A. MORGAN • Human Development and Family Studies, Colorado State University, Fort Collins, Colorado 80523. ROBERT J. HARMON • Division of Child Psychiatry, University of Colorado School of Medicine, Denver, Colorado 80362.

of appropriate forms of intervention for a child. Specific attention is given to the concept of mastery motivation, its behavioral indicators, and approaches to its assessment and use in working with children who have developmental delay or disabilities. As part of a battery including assessments of abilities, adaptive behavior, temperament, and the environment of the child, mastery motivation assessment can provide information relevant to the design to effective intervention strategies for the individual child.

WHAT IS MASTERY MOTIVATION?

Though psychologists cannot agree on a definition of motivation (Kleinginna & Kleinginna, 1981), everyone recognizes its reality. Even the preschooler says that she or he "tries", and the toddler says, "Me do." These children recognize themselves as the initiators of effort toward the achievement of a goal. Yet, it was not until White (1959) challenged psychologists to reconsider their drive-reduction theories of motivation that play and exploration, motivated by curiosity and a need to control or master one's environment through self-initiated efforts, were considered relevant to effective interaction with the environment and the attainment of competence.

Generally, the term *motivation* refers to a psychological force that moves the individual in a direction either toward or away from a goal. Specific areas of motivation that have been studied are frequently characterized by distinctive goals (e.g, need achievement, need for power, need for affiliation). Mastery motivation also reflects a goal to be achieved, namely, competence in transactions with and control of one's physical and social environment. The motivation to master derives from the organism's need to interact within a physical and social environment and to continually adapt its mode of interaction as it develops and grows. It is maintained and fueled by feelings of efficacy following self-recognized achievement of mastery over one's own physical and/or social environment. Mastery motivation and these elements of self-recognized achievement and feelings of efficacy are internal to the organism. As a result, these motivations are observable only through behavior that White (1959) described as showing "a lasting focalization and that has the characteristics of exploration and experimentation...that is selective, directed, and persistent, and the instrumental acts will be learned for the sole reward of engaging in it" (p. 322).

It is important to point out that mastery motivation as we use the term, is not identical to Harter's effectance motivation (1978). This difference may derive from the ages of the children with whom the respective authors have worked, and possibly reflects the developmental characteristics of the motivational mechanism. Common to both constructs are the essential components of self-initiated activity directed toward the development of competence with recognition by the self of feelings of efficacy. However, the "self-reward system and system of standards or mastery goals" (p. 50) that Harter described as gradually internalized by the child are not yet present in the young infant. Yet, this same young infant is observed to selectively and persistently direct activity toward producing interesting effects such as kicking to produce movement of a crib mobile (Watson, 1972) or smiling and cooing to keep the mother responding (Brazelton, Kosolowski & Main, 1974). Although such activity may not be directed toward the solution of a problem in the strict sense, the infant is certainly exercising control over the environment. Thus, in contrast to effectance motivation, in which an achieved goal is recognized and compared with learned and internalized standards, the goal recognized by the child in mastery motivation is the added control that has been exercised over the environment.

Historical Background

Interest in the role and importance of mastery motivation arose with the concern expressed by some psychologists regarding the Head Start programs for disadvantaged preschoolers, in which the focus of the intervention was almost exclusively on intellectual and language development. Early results of the Follow-Through program indicated that, after 5 years, the cognitive gains of the children who had participated were no longer evident[1] What had gone wrong? Edward Zigler, then Director of the Office of Child Development, asked whether, with the narrow focus on the cognitive-learning domains, a more significant aspect of the child's development had been overlooked or even negated. For example, when a 4-year-old male child in one of these programs was asked his name and he answered "I don't know," the deficit would not appear to have been intellectual, but it could have been motivational. In a similar vein and reflecting the same concern, Yarrow, Klein, Lomonaco, and Morgan (1975a, pp. 491–492) commented "that an effectively functioning child is more than an intellectual paragon" for this child also has "a feeling that he can have an effect on his environment" and he has an urge to interact effectively with the environment.

With such concerns regarding the narrow focus of intervention programs on cognitive development, and with White's urging that motivation be considered a necessary component of competence, a new thrust of research centering on competence, effectance, and mastery motivation evolved. In 1978, Harter extended White's concept to a developmental model of effectance motivation. Meanwhile, Yarrow and his associates were investigating mastery motivation in normal and developmentally delayed children younger than 4 years old and were developing mastery motivation measures apropriate to these age levels.

At about the same time as research on effectance and mastery motivation was progressing, two closely related concepts were under study by developmentalists. In the area of ability testing, the naggingly low predictability of infant scales spurred a critical reexamination of the concept of constancy of IQ. Based on careful and thorough reanalysis of the infant test data from the Bayley and Fels Longitudinal Studies, McCall et al., (1973, 1977) pointed out that intelligence is not a single, linear, and cumulative entity that can be represented by a single score. Rather, some abilities measured as qualitative functions are better described as changing discontinuously, whereas quantitative functions are more likely to change continuously. That is, measures of ability domains in which development involves change in the characteristics of specific behaviors from stage to stage tend to be discontinuous (McCall, 1981). Thus, when examined individually, an infant's developmental profile relative to age indicates a pattern of spurts and lags within and across domains (McCall, 1979).

---

[1]However, a 15-year follow-up study (Lazar & Darlington, 1982) indicated significant long-term outcomes of these programs in school competence, developed abilities, children's attitudes and values, and impact on the family.

The second concept under reevaluation was that of "the child as a recipient of stimulation." Bell (1968) had earlier pointed out that, in the mother–child relationship, the child not only receives stimulation from the mother but is also an active partner who can influence the mother's behavior. Sameroff (1975) extended this concept to recognize children not only as active, but as initiators of interactions or transactions between themselves and both the physical and the social environment. Children are thus seen as an active agent in their own growth and development. Competence in ability areas that are observed and assessed in children are then, at least in part, the product or outcome of their own initiatives.

The concepts of overlapping domains of development and of the child as an initiator in transactions have both contributed to research in the area of mastery motivation. But what is more relevant to the present discussion is the impact that the theoretical and empirical advances have made on effecting major changes in the approach to and the interpretation of assessments. As Wachs and Sheehan point out in the Preface to this book, assessment approaches generally lack a link between what is assessed and what the child is taught.

We might add that, though ability assessments indicate what the child can do in the various developmental domains, these instruments do not indicate how the child is achieving those levels of competence. Similarly, curricula for children with handicapping conditions are generally designed around the content of development rather than the process of development (Brinkler & Lewis, 1982). The critical link between ability testing, which yields an estimate of the level of content a child can achieve, and program planning possibly lies in the assessing of mastery motivation. An assessment of abilities tells us how far a child has come in developing competencies. An assessment of mastery motivation can indicate how the child got there. What is more important for program planning, mastery motivation delineates the developmental domains on which the child is focusing energies, as well as the persistence and effectiveness with which the child is working on each of these domains. Such information may be particularly critical to effective program planning for children with varying types of handicapping conditions.

MASTERY MOTIVATION ASSESSMENT

From the early 1970s onward, there has been continuing research directed toward the selection and development of suitable tasks and procedures for the measurement of effectance or mastery motivation, principally by Harter (1975, 1977), Yarrow and his associates at the National Institute of Child Health and Human Development (Yarrow, McQuiston, MacTurk, McCarthy, Klein & Vietze, 1983), and more recently by Morgan and Harmon (1984) in Colorado and Jennings in Pittsburgh (Jennings, Connors, Stegman, Sankaranarayan, & Mendelsohn, 1985). Though the mastery tasks (test items) and procedures are not yet standardized and norms are not yet available, consistencies in mastery motivation behaviors have become evident both within and across ages and in several types of children who are at risk. In their 1984 paper, Morgan and Harmon summarized the development of mastery motivation tasks, current procedures, and evidence on the reliability and validity of these procedures. Furthermore, as is described in later sections of this chapter, the use of the mastery motivation assessment in conjunction with standardized tests and observations of free play has been found to be particularly valuable in clinical interpretation and program planning for developmentally delayed children.

A number of forms of mastery motivation assessment have been developed and are currently used in research and clinical settings. To illustrate the breadth of application and the varied situations in which mastery motivation may be measured, an example of each of four types is presented: (a) a structured situation with selected mastery tasks; (b) a parental report questionnaire; (c) a global rating of goal-directedness adapted from the Bayley Infant Behavior Record; and (d) systematic observations during a free-play situation. Because the approach and measures of mastery motivation assessment are most explicit in the structured situation, the basic characteristics of the tasks, procedures, and measures used during this form of assessment are first described in some detail. The interpretation of assessment results and their application to program planning are presented in later sections.

The Structured Mastery-Task Situation

The primary objective of mastery motivation testing is to elicit and to observe systematically the child's attempts to master challenging tasks. Although the child's competence at the tasks is also elicited, the focus of the observations is on the amount of task-directed behavior, not on the child's successful completion of the task. The mastery motivation tasks are selected to be interesting, to take some time to complete, and to be optimally challenging relative to a child's own developmental level; that is, a task should be easy enough so that a child can demonstrate some competence but sufficiently difficult so that it is not completed in a short period of time.

There are two basic measures of mastery motivation: mastery pleasure and persistence. *Mastery pleasure* is defined as instances of positive affect during task-directed behavior or immediately following a solution. *Persistence* is defined as the amount of time a child works at or plays with toys in a task-directed manner. Behaviors considered indicative of task-directedness are characterized by trying on one's own to complete part of the task, whether or not one is successful. Simply looking at the toy or the task materials, making a bid to an adult for help, attention, or comfort, or manipulating to explore the sensory qualities of the materials are not considered task-directed behaviors.

Mastery Motivation Tasks

Table 1 provides a conceptual model for several types of mastery motivation tasks that have been used for different ages by different investigators. Before approximately 9 months of age, exploration and curiosity are identified as the best indicators of mastery motivation. Although persistence tasks, like those described in Part 2 of Table 1, have been given to 6-month-old infants, the infants' limited manipulative skills make it difficult to distinguish simple exploration from task-directed behavior. Morgan and Harmon (1984, pp. 280ff.) presented a more detailed discussion of the empirical reasons for separating exploration and curiosity assessments from the persistence tasks. Of course, it is possible to measure curiosity and exploration at any age, and they may be indicative of one aspect of mastery motivation throughout infancy and early childhood.

Table 1. Developmental Hierarchy of Mastery Motivation Tasks[a]

---

1. *Exploration and curiosity* (5 months and older)

   Because this type of item should assess the child's interest in actively using the object, it should not pose a major cognitive or fine-motor challenge for the child to do. The question is whether the child is motivated to explore all parts of the object and will maintain interest until he or she has completed the exploration. Measures of both the duration or persistence and the variety of behavior should be recorded. The object should be complex enough to promote sustained exploration. With appropriate objects, this type of item could be used with children of almost any age.

2. *Persistence tasks*

   a. *Practicing an emerging skill* (9 months and older)

      This type of task can usually be completed or solved rather quickly by the child, but it elicits, at least in children about 1 year of age, practicing or repeating of the maneuver that led to success. Three somewhat overlapping categories of persistence in emerging skills tasks have been used.

      (1) *Effect production tasks* (e.g., simple cause-and-effect toys such as a busy box or an activity center).

      (2) *Combinatorial tasks* (e.g., putting pegs or balls in holes).

      (3) *Means–end tasks* (e.g., getting a toy from behind a barrier).

   b. *Completing a multipart task* (15 months and older)

      This type of task is sufficiently difficult or complex so that it usually takes some time (i.e., at least 90 seconds) to complete. Two somewhat overlapping categories of persistence in completing a task item have been used.

      (1) *Combinatorial tasks* (e.g., completing a shape sorter, a peg board with different-size holes, or a complex formboard).

      (2) *Means–end tasks* (e.g., appropriately using all parts of a surprise box, a cash register, or a lock board).

3. *Preference for challenging tasks* (3 years and older)

   In this type of task, the child is presented with a choice of a relatively hard and an easy task (e.g., build a six-block tower or a two block tower) and is asked which one he or she wants to work at.

---

[a]Adapted from Morgan and Harmon (1984).

The tasks commonly used with children about 1 year of age involve persistence in practicing emerging skills. These tasks have included (a) those that give the child an opportunity to produce visual and/or auditory feedback (effect production tasks), (b) those on which children are expected to combine or take apart objects in an appropriate way (combinatorial tasks), and (c) those that require the child to circumvent a barrier or an obstacle to reach a goal object (problem-solving tasks). The details of specific tasks can be found in Yarrow, Morgan, Jennings, Harmon, and Gaiter (1982) and in Yarrow, McQuiston, MacTurk, McCarthy, Klein, and Vietze (1983).

In our recent research with toddlers (Brockman, 1984; Morgan, Maslin, & Harmon 1987), we have developed tasks that have a number of parts to put together or figure out. These elicit "persistence in completing multipart tasks" and are divided into two types: (a) those that require completing a puzzle or a formboard (combinatorial tasks and (b) those that elicit using all parts of a complex toy to make things happen (means-end tasks). Of course, the distinction between practicing emerging skills and completing multipart tasks is relative. For example, putting a set of round pegs into round holes involves repeating the same schema, but it also involves completing a task.

With 3½- and 4½-year-olds, Jennings, *et al.,* (1985) used not only curiosity and persistence but also preference for challenging tasks to assess mastery motivation in normally developing and physically handicapped children. They concluded, however, that preference for challenge may be too difficult for some 3½-year-olds.

From the examples of mastery task toys described in Table 1, it is evident that these materials are not unique; many are the types of toys available from commercial outlets or are similar to items included in infant tests. The criterion essential in the selection of any mastery task is that the toy challenges and entices the child to continue to work at the leading edge of competence, and to persist in trying to succeed at the task.

Administration Procedure

Among groups of researchers, there have been several overlapping but somewhat different procedures for administering the mastery motivation tasks in a structured situation. In all instances, the primary procedural objectives are to ensure (a) that the tasks presented will be optimally challenging to the child, (b) that the child will be enabled to engage in task-directed behavior without interference for as long he or she desires, and (c) that the total amount of time the child is involved in task-directed behavior will be recorded. To illustrate such procedures, an example of administering mastery tasks to toddlers is described based on the mastery task manual by Morgan, Maslin, and Harmon (1987).

Mastery motivation tasks are generally given to the child while seated at a low table or on the floor with the examiner at his or her side. The mother, if present, is seated a few feet behind and off to the side of her child. In the testing of younger infants, the mother may hold the child on her lap at a table. Social interaction between the examiner and the child is minimized so that play initiated by the child on his or her own can be observed. Limited interaction with the child allows the examiner to score the child's behaviors as they occur and, in turn, discourages bids for attention from a "busy" examiner. Similarly, if the mother is involved in an activity such as answering questions about the child's experience with toys, the frequency of seeking her attention or assistance is also reduced.

Tasks for toddlers come in sets or sequences of similar tasks (e.g., sets of puzzles or shape boxes) that have several levels of difficulty, from easy to hard. The procedure for administering these tasks involves selecting the task from each set that is judged to be appropriately challenging at the child's own developmental level. This task should be sufficiently interesting to get the child started working at it, not so easy that it is completed in less than 60 seconds, and not so hard that the child cannot do at least part of the solution in 60 seconds. The toys in a set are presented one at a time, beginning with tasks estimated to be moderately challenging for the child. Using prescribed rules, the tester determines whether a given task meets the requirements of being appropriately difficult and continues to present the tasks until one in each set meets the criteria. This task is then continued for a maximum of 4 minutes, but it may be terminated earlier under certain prescribed conditions.

Behavioral Codes

During each mastery motivation task, the modal or most common motivational behavior shown by the child during a 15-second period is coded. A principal category is task-directed behavior (T), which includes trying successfully or unsuccessfully to solve the problem or to master the task. A second behavioral category (+) is expression of positive affect (smiling, excited vocalization or movements) during task-directed behavior or immediately after successfully completing part of the task.

Other behaviors that assist in administration and interpretation are also noted. These include (O) own task behaviors, which is play interpretable as task-directed from the child's point of view but not the experimenter's; (P) practicing or repeating the same or very similar behaviors in consecutive intervals; (L) looking intently at the toy; (A) active manipulative exploration of task materials, such as touching, mouthing, and throwing the toy; (N) non-toy-directed behaviors, such as moving around the room; (M) seeking attention from the mother, or (E) bids for attention from the examiner.

These behaviors may be coded either live or from videotaped recordings. A recording of behavioral codes is illustrated in the sample score sheet in Figure 1. Reading through the shapes task of this record, we note that the session started with Level 3; the child tried to put a shape into the hole (T = task-directed behavior) during most of the first 15-second interval. She then put the shape into the hole (1 = solution of the task) and smiled (+ = positive affect) during the second interval. After shaking the form several times (A), the child spent most of the next 3 minutes working at the task. Finally, the child got all the shapes into the holes, completing the task with a smile (C +) during the 16th interval. The difficulty level of the task was judged to be appropriate because it met the criteria specified earlier.

Scoring

The scoring of the tasks, illustrated in the lower portion of the score sheet, is relatively simple. The number of 15-second intervals characterized by each of codes (e.g., T, +) is counted and recorded for the "appropriate-level" task of each set. There are two basic measures of mastery motivation: persistence and mastery pleasure. *Persistence* is the number of intervals scored as T; *mastery pleasure* is the number of intervals with a + , that is, positive affect during task-directed behavior or immediately following a solution.

The other codes are supplementary and may assist in the interpretation of the child's performance. For example, the number of Ps represents repetitive behavior and may be an indicator of perseveration if it occurs successively for a number of intervals. We have not seen many instances that were judged perseverative, but in certain developmentally disabled children, perseveration may be more common. Likewise, we see very little idiosyncratic or own-task (O) behavior, but it could be more common in certain special populations.

Note that the mastery motivation tasks as described are confined to tasks with objects and to what can be called combinatorial and means–end problems. Thus, the resulting measures may well be limited to the motivation to master these kinds of tasks. Because persistence seems to be fairly task-specific, we have given some thought to broadening the types of tasks to include, for example, gross-motor, symbolic-pretend, and social tasks. However, except for the attempt by Wachs and Combs (in press) to measure social mastery motivation, little research has been done on broadening the tasks in this manner.

Parental Reports of Observed Mastery Behavior

Differences among children in their drive to master and to have an effect on their environment have not only been reported by a number of investigators (e.g., Yarrow, Rubenstein, & Pedersen, 1975b) but are also observed by parents and teachers. There-

SCORE SHEET FOR MASTERY MOTIVATION TASKS

CHILD'S # 99 NAME JANE DOE   BIRTHDATE 12/01/82 AGE 24 Mos
SCORER GAM   LIVE X   TAPE_____   SESSION DATE 12/10/84

15-sec. interval	TASK: SHAPES Level 3 Mot.	S/+	Level Mot.	S/+	TASK: CAUSE + EFFECT Level 3 Mot.	S/+	Level 2 Mot.	S/+	TASK: PUZZLES Level 3 Mot.	S/+	Level 4 Mot.	S/+
1	T				A		T	I	L		T	I
30" 2	T	I+			T		T	I+	A		T	I
3	A				N		E		T	III	N	
1 min. 4	T				N		T		T	IC	T	II
5	T						T	I			T	I
6	T				TOO		P		TOO		T	II
7	T				HARD		P		EASY		T	
2 min. 8	A						M				T	C
9	N						M				T	
10	A										T	I
11	T										A	
3 min. 12	M										T	I
13	T										T	
14	T										T	I
15	T										O	
4 min. 16	T	C+									O	
# of Ts	11						4				12	
# of Ps	0						2				0	
# of Os	0						0				7	
Affect +								I				O
# of different solutions	0 1̸ 2 3 4 5 6 7 8 9 ⑩ 11		0 1 2 3 4 5 6 7 8 9 10 11		0 1 2 3 4 5 6 7 8 9 10 11		0 1̸ 2̸ 3̸ 4 5 6 7 8 9 10 11		0 1 2 3 4 5 6 7 8 9 10 11		0 1̸ 2̸ 3̸ 4̸ 5̸ 6 7̸ 8̸ 9 10 11	

Figure 1. A coded sample of a structured mastery-task session.

fore, as another source of mastery motivation assessment, we have developed a questionnaire, now called the Dimensions of Mastery Questionnaire (DMQ), for parents or observers to use to rate a child's behaviors with toys from "not at all typical" to "very typical," in respect to dimensions that are similar to those assessed by means of the structured mastery tasks described above.

A revised version of this instrument (Morgan, Maslin, Jennings & Busch-Rossnagel, in press) was designed to measure four general aspects of adults' perceptions of a child's mastery behavior: (a) general persistence; (b) mastery pleasure; (c) independent mastery during challenging play; and (d) competence. In addition, the DMQ also contains items that elicit ratings of a child's persistence at five specific types of play: (a) gross motor; (b) combinatorial; (c) means-end; (d) symbolic; and (e) social.

Each of these scales has good internal consistency (alphas = .72 to .81), and the items produced factors generally consistent with the hypothesized scales. The questionnaire also appears to provide valid measures of young children's mastery behaviors because these are predictable relationships between the scales of the questionnaire and behaviors during structured mastery tasks (Fung, 1984; Morgan, Harmon Pipp, Maslin, & Brockman, 1984; Morgan et al., in press), and because there are predictable differences between risk and nonrisk groups (Morgans, Harmon, Pipp & Jennings, 1983).

A Global Rating of Goal-Directedness

Mastery motivation can also be assessed in other structured settings, such as during competence evaluations. For this purpose, Maslin and Morgan (1984) adapted one of the ratings from the Bayley Infant Behavior Record (IBR) so that aspects of behavior that correspond closely to persistence at the structured mastery tasks could be assessed. This rating, along with nine others from the IBR, has been used to rate children's behavior during the structured mastery tasks, developmental tests, and free play (see Table 2).

Free-Play Situation

Mastery behavior is also observed in nonstructured settings. Free-play scoring-systems have been developed for this purpose (Glicken, Couchman, Harmon, 1981; Harmon, Glicken, & Couchman, 1981, Maslin, Bretherton, & Morgan, 1986; Morgan, Harmon, & Bennett, 1976); These systems focus on obtaining detailed descriptions of what infants do with objects, especially their attempts to produce feedback, to use toys appropriately, to combine them, and to use them symbolically (Harmon, Glicken, & Gaensbauer, 1982; Harmon & Glicken, 1982). Gross-motor, affective, and social behaviors, including interactions with the mother, are also recorded. Thus, mastery and contextually associated behaviors are coded and can be scored. We have found this system useful for distinguishing task-directed behaviors from general exploratory behavior, especially among 12-to 18-month-old infants. This distinction has been particularly relevant in the assessment of a number of at-risk populations, including abused and/or neglected infants and very-low birthweight preterm infants (weighing less than 1,500 grams).

For example, in a study described in Gaensbauer, Mrazek, and Harmon (1981), the play of abused, neglected, and age-matched normal infants was compared. Both the abused and the neglected infants persisted in play less than the normal infants. In addition, the nonpersistent behavior of the abused infants differed markedly from that of the neglected ones. Infants who had been abused actively explored the room and the toys, but in a disorganized manner characterized by moving quickly from one toy to another, scattering toys throughout the room, and in some instances, damaging the toys. In contrast, those infants who had been neglected were more likely to show motor retardation and lack of interest in the toys. Thus, whereas abused infants were quite active and at times seemed angry and destructive, neglected infants were more likely to show low levels of interaction and seemed depressed. Though the measures of persistence were

Table 2. Global Rating of Goal-Directedness

This scale assesses purposeful activity, with an emphasis on persistence in trying to achieve a goal. The rating should be based on the child's independent attempts to achieve a goal or to engage in purposeful activity, rather than on attempts that have been spurred by adult direction or coaxing.

Goal-directedness is not necessarily tied to a child's level of competence. For example, a child who achieves a goal after only one try and then refrains from repeating or practicing that behavior or tackling a new goal would receive a low score on this scale. Alternately, a child may try for some time to accomplish one task (solving it or not solving it) and would thus obtain a high score on this scale.

1. No evidence of directed effort or purposeful activity.
2. Makes an occasional attempt at goal-directed action but does not repeat attempts.
3. Makes some attempts to attain a goal with some repetition but does not show interest in carrying attempts to completion.
4. Attempts at goals are more frequent but generally lack sustained persistence; does not continue if initial attempt fails.
5. Usually makes an initial attempt to attain a goal and shows some repetition of efforts; however, quits fairly soon if not successful.
6. Makes initial attempts to attain goals with moderate persistence; however, gives up if task requires repeated efforts. Usually does not repeat solutions of tasks.
7. Initial attempts are followed by moderate to high persistence, even if task is somewhat difficult. Repeats solutions of some tasks.
8. Persistence in attaining goals is high, even when task is challenging, but without the marked absorption that characterizes a score of 9. Often repeats solutions of tasks.
9. Very high absorption in task; willingly repeats solutions of tasks, stays with tasks until they are solved even if they are very difficult; practices tasks until they are thoroughly mastered.

equally low for both of these groups of children, qualitative differences in their behavior became apparent and were distinguishable from the contextual codes.

The use of this scoring system has also been of value in research on preterm infants. In a study of 30 preterm infants, who at 12 months of postconceptual age were matched with 12-month old full-term infants, Harmon and Culp (1981) observed the child's persistence at tasks during free play and the interaction of the infants and their mothers. In general, preterm infants were less active and less motivated to explore their environment than full-terms. Here again, a tentative explanation and a clue to intervention became apparent from the contextual codes. Even though all the mothers had been instructed not to interact with their children unless the child made a bid to them, the mothers of the preterm infants were more likely to initiate interaction with them during free play. Thus, the difference between preterm and full-term infants in persistence and exploratory behavior may be associated with differences in their mothers' initiation of interaction.

In summary, measures of mastery motivation may be obtained in a variety of situations, ranging from the highly structured to free play, and from several sources, including direct observation of a child's behavior and parental, caregiver, or teacher ratings. Which situation is most appropriate, what source is most valid, or which combination of these is best needs to be determined by the researcher or the clinician relative to the purpose and the circumstances of the assessment. Some forms are obviously less involved and expensive (e.g., the Global Rating of Goal Directedness obtained during the regular administration of the Bayley Infant Scales of Development). Other approaches may provide corroborative or explanatory data from additional situations (e.g., free play), or sources (e.g., the Dimensions of Mastery Questionnaire). Whatever form or combination of forms is selected as most suitable to the purpose, the objective is to observe a child's behavior when she or he is optimally challenged. Of one thing we are certain; a developing child constantly encounters challenging tasks and continually strives to become competent in interactions with the physical and social environment. Whether there are factors in respect to either the child or the child's environment that may be interfering with the child's achievement of mastery and competence is a challenge for the clinician to discern and to assist in alleviating for the individual child, and for the researcher to investigate and explain for children in general.

INTERPRETATION AND USE OF MASTERY MOTIVATION INDICATORS IN THE ASSESSMENT OF CHILDREN WITH DEVELOPMENTAL DELAY

The assessment of and program planning for children with handicaps presents special challenges. Given the variability in etiology, type, and degree of primary handicaps, as well as the variety and extent of secondary involvement among children with developmental delay, the validity of standards of comparison becomes questionable and decisions about appropriate forms of intervention become weighty. (see Wachs & Sheehan, Chapter 1). As pointed out earlier in this chapter, the link between competence assessment and effective intervention is not well articulated. However, the inclusion of mastery motivation in an assessment battery may provide some tie between competence assessment and program planning, and it may also serve as an additional means of monitoring the effectiveness of intervention. Though basic research and instrument development in the area of mastery motivation has taken place only relatively recently, the research reviewed by Yarrow and Messer (1983) and by Morgan and Harmon (1984) indicates lower persistence in tasks among preterm, neglected, abused, and mentally retarded children, and suggests that persistence at one age provides a relatively good indication of a child's competence at a later age.

Given the basic assumptions that children have an urge to become competent (Yarrow et al., 1975b) and that they work longer at tasks that are optimally challenging, an assessment of mastery motivation systematically focuses an assessor's attention on *what* the child is currently doing to increase competence and on *how* the child is trying to achieve greater competence. Persistence is a measure of how long a child plays in a task-directed manner, and the contextual measures indicate how the child is trying to master, (e.g., with pleasure, in an exploratory way, or in a repetitive and possibly nonproductive manner). In contrast, competence assessment asks only what a child can do in each developmental domain, (i.e., what the child has already achieved). The resulting profile may indicate specific areas of delay, but it will yield little information about how the child is trying to become competent in a specific domain or even whether the child is trying or persisting in becoming competent in any domain.

For effective program planning, we need to know on what developmental domain(s) a child is focusing his or her energy, whether this developmental energy is being used effectively, and whether inherent deficits, environmental factors, or a combination of these is interfering with the child's development. A mastery motivation assessment may indicate which factor or set of factors is hindering or diverting a child from striving to become competent. Some ways in which mastery motivation measures and assessment may be used in the initial detection of a disability and in conjunction with competence assessment to link its findings to program planning are described relative to developmental delay, developmental disabilities, dysfunctional behavior, and interfering environmental factors.

Developmental Delay

In infancy and early childhood, *developmental delay* is a label that encompasses all children who perform below the levels expected for their chronological age, whatever the etiology of the delay may be. This group, therefore, includes children whose general rate of development is slower, but whose pattern of development in the various domains is otherwise similar to that found in normally developing children. In respect to mastery motivation, MacTurk, *et al.* (1985) observed that the persistence of 12-month-old Down syndrome infants is similar to that of normal 6-month-old infants. Thus, if the competence measures indicate an overall slower rate of development in a child, the mastery motivation behavior shown by the child could be expected to be comparable to those of a normally developing child at the same development level.

If a child is advancing through the developmental landmarks at a slower rate than is expected of children on the average, then program planning may require a finer breakdown of task elements to enable the delayed child to proceed step-by-step. During competence assessment, the optimal extent of such a task breakdown can be easily explored. After the child's level of achievement on an item has been ascertained, an assessor can simplify the task and then incrementally increase its complexity. *Noting the child's persistence at each step can indicate the level of difficulty at which the child perceives the task as challengeable.* Activities can then be programmed to reflect this level of task difficulty.

Developmental Disability

Delayed development in some children is associated with a deficit in a specific aspect of development (e.g., visual, auditory, or motor impairments). Sometimes such a deficit is difficult to discern, in part, because the child learns ways to compensate for it. If a compensatory behavior is unsuitable or inadequate, the primary deficit may also constrain development in other domains that are, in themselves, intact. Systematic observation of the task or materials with which a child becomes actively involved, together with the way the child is engaged and for how long, may indicate the presence of deficits in specific domains.

From the way in which the child copes, an examiner can observe whether the child's approach to mastering tasks is functional or whether continuing in this way could lead to the development of a dysfunctional pattern of behavior. In instances of specific disabilities, such as a simple motor or visual impairment, an examiner can observe what other domains are being constrained by the disability and whether the child shows mastery behavior relative to intact areas. *Involvement in and persistence at challenging tasks may suggest functional ways for the child to use intact capacities and ways in which the deficits may be circumvented.* These approaches can then be more effectively incorporated into the intervention program.

For example, it is not uncommon for a hearing impairment to be unnoticed in a child until there is a delay in language development. Because infants with hearing impairment readily learn cues from their home environment that enable them to interact quite normally, delayed speech development may be the first sign noted by the parents. Earlier detection may be possible through observations of persistence relative to the auditory components of a task. In such observations, it is especially important to note the stimulus aspects of the toys toward which the child is responding during task-directed play. Jackson (1979) reported that hearing-impaired children play with sound-producing toys just as long as children with normal hearing; however, in their play, they do not explore the sound-producing qualities of the toys.

In other instances, advanced development in some domains may obscure a deficit in another domain. For example, a child who was described by his caregiver as showing exceptional verbal abilities was at the same time seen as hyperactive and as roving about the play area a great deal. Observations during free play indicated that the child engaged in dramatic play and construction activities with large blocks and Lego but never chose picture puzzles, painting, or paper-and-pencil activities. On the basis of this pattern of persistence across varying types of activities, a referral was made. The formal assessment indicated a perceptual deficit.

Similarly, systematic observations of a child's pattern of persistence during free play suggested a possible incorrect diagnosis. The child's play was characterized by continuity, constructiveness, and persistence, particularly in cognitive tasks. However, these characteristics were not consistent with a diagnosis of "brain damage." A subsequent reassessment by a clinical team including a child psychologist, a pediatrician, and a speech and hearing specialist indicated that the child was almost totally deaf. Obviously, with this new information, the focus of the programming for this child changed dramatically.

Thus, in the assessment of children with a developmental delay related to a disability, the manner in which children play with materials may indicate both how they are attempting to master the environment in an area that involves their disability and how they attempt to circumvent it. From the way in which a child copes, an examiner can observe whether the approach to task mastery is functional, or whether continuing in such a course could lead to the development of a dysfunctional pattern of behavior.

Dysfunctional Behavior

A pattern of behavior that interferes with the achievement of competence is dysfunctional. It is obvious when behavior is not task-directed, but in some forms of task involvement interference is less apparent although it may be more pervasive and may have longer lasting consequences. For example, if the means of trying to achieve a goal are inappropriate or if the reason for working at a task is not related to its accomplishment, the development of competence may be impeded, and ineffective behavioral patterns may become habitual. Observation of persistence during free play and during performance on standardized infant tests or the structured mastery motivation tasks may indicate how a behavior is dysfunctional and may suggest a suitable approach to intervention.

For example, observation of a retarded toddler indicated that, when he was not lying on the floor kicking and headbanging, he consistently showed a single and persistent response to toys: he picked up a toy or object, held it up to examine it visually, and then threw it away. This behavior of visually examining each object appeared purposeful, but there was no other exploration of the object and its disposal was completely random. The initial approach taken in working with this toddler was to find a way to make the throwing response one that was appropriately goal-directed. The first step was to intercept the trajectory of the thrown object so that it would land in a large metal container. The sound of the object hitting the container attracted the child's attention. Gradually, his aimless throwing became directed toward the container and the production of the sound. From this point he was guided to put objects into various kinds of containers, and then to retrieve objects from containers. In time, he explored objects in various ways: he strung hoops onto his arm, put rings onto pegs, and even used the drumstick to produce sounds. Learning to explore objects in a variety of functional ways allowed this toddler to develop competence in interactions with his physical and social environment.

A child's behavior may be task-directed, but if the way in which the goal is achieved is not suitable to the task, the child will either stop trying or continue to try in a non-productive way. For example, a child who holds a crayon as though it were a stirring stick will experience difficulties in coloring and in following a pathway. Thus, though a child may be challenged by a task and may persist in working at it, such efforts may remain nonproductive. If nonadaptive behavior is associated with a handicap, the means of achieving the goal need to be adapted. Intervention may then consist in helping the child to find alternative approaches to develop the competence in the involved domain.

Nonproductive persistence may also be associated with the inappropriate reinforce-ment of an activity or with a response by a person who is significant to the child. Such a person may be reinforcing the child with good intention and may not recognize that the child may learn that pleasing the adult is more important than initiating activity. The child is then diverted from and deprived of opportunities for developing competence.

Parents' Responses to the Child's Play and Mastery Motivation

Observation of parents' responses to their child's performance on mastery tasks can be particularly helpful in planning the intervention program and in advising parents. It has been observed (Fung, 1984) that children perform more competently on mastery motivation tasks when the mother watches attentively while allowing them to work on their own, and when the mother responds appropriately to their initiations. In contrast, when the mothers indicate a desire to interact while their children are involved in master-ing a task, the children show less persistence and perform less competently. For example, mothers of preterm infants seem to initiate interaction. In the Harmon *et al.* (1984) study, this type of interaction style, when compared with that of normal infants and their mothers, resulted in less initiation, lowered persistence, and less mastery pleasure. If this is a characteristic response of the parent to the child's performance, the parent may be counseled to watch the child at play and to respond with encouragement and support following the child's initiation.

Generally, the objective of an adult, whether parent or caregiver, is to support and encourage a child in developing potential. Unwittingly, an adult can easily support a child in becoming a better responder and a less effective initiator of action. As Brinker and Lewis (1982) pointed out, a child can become progressively more passive than active when the adult's interaction is directive, for then the child is usually "placed into the role of a respondent...and infrequently in the role of initiator in which the infant can define the topic of interaction'' (pp. 8–9). As a consequence, the child becomes an efficient responder rather than an effective initiator, passive rather than active.

Multiple and Sequential Assessment

The type of interpretation of mastery motivation measures and program planning discussed suggests a need for repeated assessment. It is through observing shifts in persistence across developmental domains and noting whether there is increased competence in areas where the child previously persisted longer that the effectiveness of a program plan may be monitored. If no advance in competence is observed, then special note should be made of *how* the child approaches and works at a task relative to the developmental domains is needed. Thus, multiple and sequential assessments of children with developmental delay are critical, particularly if, as Sameroff (1975) pointed out, "the plastic character of both environment and the organism as it actively participates in its own growth" (p. 281) means that the child's "own competence in initiating transactions" is the key to development. Through sequential testing a child's developmental progress can be evaluated over time with the possibility of examining the continuities and discontinuities in developing functions.

In conclusion, recognition of persistence in tasks as a relevant indicator of the continuing development of competence may provide significant linkages between the child's behavior in usual settings (home or center) and competence assessment and, subsequently, between assessment and effective program planning. A measure of persistence may indicate a child's developmental progress or lack of progress. Deficits that may be hindering or interfering with the child's progress may come into focus, and factors operating in the child's physical or social environment that may be suppressing, diverting, or hindering initiatives in developing competence may be observed. For a child to develop competence, the freedom to initiate interactions needs to be available, as well as opportunities to carry these actions through to the point where they can be perceived as having been accomplished.

Acknowledgments

The authors wish to express appreciation for support in writing this chapter that was received from the John D. and Catherine C. MacArthur Foundation Network on the Transition from Infancy to Early Childhood; the Grant Foundation Endowment Fund of the Developmental Psychobiology Research Group; the Department of Psychiatry, University of Colorado School of Medicine; and the Travel Fund, University of Manitoba.

Dr. Harmon was supported by a Research Scientist Development Award 5 KO1 MHOO281 from the National Institute of Mental Health. Drs. Morgan and Harmon are members of the MacArthur Foundation Network of investigators studying the transition from infancy to early childhood and of the Developmental Psychobiology Research Group, University of Colorado School of Medicine.

REFERENCES

Bell, R. Q. (1968). A reinterpretation of the direction of effects in studies of socialization. *Psychological Review, 75,* 81–95.

Brazelton, T. B., Koslowski, B., & Main, M. (1974). The origins of reciprocity: The early mother-infant interaction. In M. Lewis & L. A. Rosenblum (Eds.), *The effect of the infant on its caregiver.* New York: Wiley.

Brinker, R. P., & Lewis, M. (1982). Discovering the competent handicapped infant: A process approach to assessment and intervention. *Topics in Early Childhood Special Education, 2* (2), 1–16.

Brockman, L. M. (1984, May). *Old issues and new methods.* Paper presented at the NIH Workshop on Mastery Motivation, Bethesda, Maryland.

Fung, A. Y. (1984). *The relationship of mother's perception to the child's competence and mastery motivation.* Department of Family Studies, University of Manitoba, Winnipeg, Canada.

Gaensbauer, T. J., Mrazek, D., & Harmon, R. J. (1981). Behavioral observations of abused and/or neglected infants. In N. Frude (Ed.), *Psychological approaches to the understanding and prevention of child abuse.* London: Batsford.

Glicken, A. D., Couchman, G., & Harmon, R. J. (1981). *Free Play Social Scale.* Denver: University of Colorado School of Medicine, Infant Development Laboratory.

Harmon, R. J., & Culp, A. M. (1981). The effects of premature birth on family functioning and infant development. In I. Berlin (Ed.), *Children and our future.* Albuquerque: University of New Mexico Press.

Harmon, R. J., & Glicken, A. D. (1981). *Mastery motivation scoring manual for 12 month old infants.* Denver: University of Colorado School of Medicine, Infant Development Laboratory.

Harmon, R. J., & Glicken, A. D. (1982). Development of free play in infancy. In R. Pelz (Ed.), *Developmental and clinical aspects of children's play.* WESTAR Series Paper #16.

Harmon, R. J., Glicken, A. D., & Couchman, G. M. (1981). *Free Play Scoring Manual.* Denver: University of Colorado School of Medicine, Infant Behavior Laboratory.

Harmon, R. J., Glicken, A. D., & Gaensbauer, T. J. (1982). The relationship between infant play with inanimate objects and social interest in mother. *Journal of the American Academy of Child Psychiatry, 21,* 549–554.

Harmon, R. J., Morgan, G. A., & Glicken, A. D. (1984). Continuities and discontinuities in affective and cognitive-motivational development. *International Journal of Child Abuse and Neglect, 8,* 157–167.

Harter, S. (1975). Developmental differences in the manifestation of mastery motivation on problem-solving tasks. *Child Development, 46,* 370–378.

Harter, S. (1977). The effects of social reinforcement and task difficulty level on the pleasure derived by normal and retarded children from cognitive challenge and mastery. *Journal of Experimental Child Psychology, 24,* 476–494.

Harter, S. (1978). Effectance motivation reconsidered. *Human Development, 21,* 34–64.

Jackson, G. (1979). *Play behaviours of hearing impaired and normal hearing preschool children with selected toy materials.* Department of Family Studies, University of Manitoba Winnipeg, Manitoba, Canada.

Jennings, K. D., Connors, R. E., Stegman, C. E., Sankaranarayan, P., & Mendelsohn, S. (1985). Mastery motivation in young preschoolers: Effect of a handicap and implications for educational programming. *Journal of the Division of Early Childhood,* 162–169.

Kleinginna, P. R., Jr., & Kleinginna, A. M. (1981). A categorized list of motivation definitions, with a suggestion for a consensual definition. *Motivation and Emotion, 5* (3), 263–278.

Lazer, I. & Darlington, R. (1982). Lasting effects of early education: A report from the consortium for longitudinal studies. *Monographs of the Society for Research in Child Development, 47,* No. 195.

MacTurk, R. H., Vietze, P. M., McCarthy, M. E., McQuiston, S., & Yarrow, L. J. (1985). The organization of exploratory behavior in Down syndrome and nondelayed infants. *Child Development, 56,* 573–581.

Maslin, C., & Morgan, G. (1984). *Manual for rating scales of child characteristics (Modified IBR).* Fort Collins: Department of Human Development and Family Studies, Colorado State University.

Maslin, C. A., Bretherton, I., & Morgan, G. A. (1986, April). *The influence of attachment security and maternal scaffolding on toddler mastery motivation.* Paper presented at the Fifth International Conference on Infant Studies, Los Angeles.

McCall, R. B. (1979). The development of intellectual functioning in infancy and the prediction of later IQ. In J. D. Osofsky (Ed.), *Handbook of infant development.* New York: Wiley.

McCall, R. B. (1981). Nature-nurture and the two realms of development: A proposed integration in respect to mental development. *Child Development, 52,* 1–12.

McCall, R. B., Appelbaum, M. I., & Hogarty, P. S. (1973). Developmental changes in mental performance. *Monographs of the Society for Research in Child Development, 38,* No. 150.

McCall, R. B., Eichorn, D. H., & Hogarty, P. S. (1977). Transitions in early mental development. *Mono-

graphs of the Society for Research in Child Development, 42, No. 171.

Morgan, G. A., & Harmon, R. A. (1984). Development transformations in mastery motivation: Measurement and validation. In R. N. Emde & R. J. Harmon (Eds.), *Continuities and discontinuities in development.* New York: Plenum Publishing Corporation.

Morgan, G. A., Harmon, R. J., & Bennett, C. A. (1976). A system for coding and scoring infants' spontaneous play with objects. *JSAS Catalog of Selected documents in Psychology, 10* (Ms. 1355).

Morgan, G. A., Harmon, R. J., Pipp, S., & Jennings, K. D., (1983). *Assessing mothers' perceptions of mastery motivation: The utility of the MOMM questionnaire.* Fort Collins: Department of Human Development and Family Studies, Colorado State University.

Morgan, G. A., Harmon, R. J., Pipp, S., Maslin, C. A., & Brockman, L. M. (1984, May). *Assessing mothers' perceptions of mastery motivation: The utility of the MOMM questionnaire.* Paper presented at the Biennial Conference of the Developmental Psychobiology Research Group Retreat, Estes Park, Colorado.

Morgan, G. A., Maslin, C. A., & Harmon, R. J. (1987b). *Mastery motivation tasks: Manual for 15- to 36-month-old children.* Fort Collins: Department of Human Development and Family Studies, Colorado State University.

Morgan, G. A., Maslin, C. A., Jennings, K. D., Busch-Rossnagel, N. (In press). Assessing mothers' perceptions of mastery motivations: Development and utility of the Dimensions of Mastery Questionnaire. In P. M. Vietze & R. H. MacTurk (Eds.), *Perspectives on mastery motivation in infancy and childhood.* Norwood, NJ: Ablex.

Sameroff, A. J. (1975). Early influences on development. Fact or fancy? *Merrill-Palmer Quarterly, 18,* 65–79.

Scarr, S. (1981). Testing for children: Assessment and the many determinants of intellectual competence. *American Psychologist, 36* (10), 1159–1166.

Wachs, T. D. & Combs, T. (In press). Mastery motivation as a potential individual differences parametric. In P. M. Vietze & R. H. MacTurk (Eds.), *Perspectives on mastery motivation in infancy and childhood.* Norwood, NJ: Ablex.

Watson, J. S. (1972). Smiling, cooing, and "the game." *Merrill-Palmer Quarterly, 18,* 323–329.

White, R. W., (1959). Motivation reconsidered: The concept of competence. *Psychological Review, 66,* 297–323.

Yarrow, L. J., & Messer, D. J. (1983). Motivation and cognition in infancy. In M. Lewis (Ed.), *Origins of intelligence* (2nd ed.). Hillside , NJ: Erlbaum.

Yarrow, L. J., Klein, R., Lomonaco, S., & Morgan, G. (1975a). Cognition and motivational development in early childhood. In B. Z. Friedlander, G. M. Sterritt, & G. E. Kirk (Eds.). *Exceptional infant: Assessment and intervention.* New York: Brunner/Mazel.

Yarrow, L. J., Rubenstein, J. L., & Pedersen, F. A., (1975b). *Infant and environment: Early cognitive and motivational development.* Washington, DC: Hemisphere, Halsted, Wiley.

Yarrow, L. J., Morgan, G. A., Jennings, K. D., Harmon, R. J., & Gaiter, J. L. (1982). Infant's persistence at tasks: Relationships to cognitive functioning and early experience. *Infant Behavior and Development, 5,* 131–142.

Yarrow, L. J., McQuiston, S., MacTurk, R. H., McCarthy, M. E., Klein, R. P., & Vietze, P. M. (1983). Assessment of mastery motivation during the first year of life: Contemporaneous and cross-age relationships. *Developmental Psychology, 19,* 159–171.

15

Assessment of Language in Developmentally Disabled Infants and Preschoolers

Lesley B. Olswang and Barbara A. Bain

INTRODUCTION

Assumptions

The language assessment of infants and developmentally delayed preschoolers requires a usable definition of language and a comprehensive understanding of language development. Language is a complex skill that has traditionally been viewed as consisting of four basic parts: phonology, semantics, syntax, and pragmatics. *Phonology* refers to the sound system of our language; *semantics*, to the meaning of words and word relations; *syntax*, to the grammatical rules for ordering words; and *pragmatics*, to communication, or the use of language in social contexts. Although language must always be viewed as an interactive system in which the whole is greater than the sum of the parts, the assessment process requires that the major components be examined separately. This approach is necessary for evaluating language development and for identifying specific deficit areas.

The focus of this chapter is on the diagnostic and descriptive assessment of infant and young preschool children who may not be developing language normally. By definition, this population includes preverbal and early verbal children, including those who should be demonstrating emerging prerequisite skills for language development, single-word productions, word combinations, and early developing grammatical structures. The traditional approach of classifying children according to disabilities (e.g., motorically impaired, mentally retarded, and hearing-impared, will not be used in this chapter.) Although considerable research regarding language disorders has focused on disability categories (see McCormick, 1984, pp.91–102, for a review), the results have generally failed to identify significant correlations between specific language skills and disability categories. Rather, the research has indicated that children within the same category often exhibit different language characteristics. The approach taken in this chapter will be to

LESLEY B. OLSWANG • Department of Speech and Hearing Sciences, University of Washington, Seattle, Washington 98195.   *BARBARA A. BAIN* • Department of Communication Sciences and Disorders, University of Montana, Missoula, Montana 59812.

describe the language system and its components, and to use this description as a foundation for identifying basic skill deficits in infants' and preschoolers' language development. A model that allows for the description of strengths and weaknesses in individual children, regardless of etiology, is most useful in making informed decisions regarding the nature and severity of the language impairment and the need for recommending treatment (Fey, 1986). Although a discussion of assessment might focus additionally on procedures or techniques for planning intervention and monitoring progress, such information will not be included in this chapter. A broader view of language assessment, such as that, would include a number of issues about language learning and measurement that would extend beyond the scope of a single chapter. Thus, using Hubert and Wallander's terms (see Chapter 3), the assessment objectives referred to in this chapter will be *diagnostic* and *descriptive*.

Research examining linguistic development in the 0- to 4-year-old age range has provided the foundation for the creation of theoretically sound language assessment procedures (Richardson, 1982). Further, the early identification of children who are at risk developmentally has provided an incentive to examine the skills specifically related to the diagnosis of prelanguage and early language disorders. Although there has been considerable research yielding promising diagnostic procedures for assessing infants and preschoolers, there are no clear clinical indices for differentiating the "genuinely" impaired child from the slow normal child. As a result "identification and assessment must incorporate a probablistic perspective" (Liebergott, Bashir, & Schultz, 1984, p.45). With this in mind, this chapter attempts to identify important variables in assessing the infant and the young child to highlight the behavioral milestones that may serve as gross indices for evaluating the occurrence of normal versus pathological language development.

An important assumption of this chapter is that an effective and efficient comprehensive evaluation of this population cannot be completed by an isolated discipline or profession. An interdisciplinary or transdisciplinary team approach always yields more thorough results and more definitive conclusions. Although the authors believe that this approach is critical in the ultimate evaluation of young children at risk for language impairments, the orientation of this chapter is somewhat more circumscribed. The focus is on specific language-assessment issues and procedures, rather than on an interdisciplinary assessment protocol.

Purpose

The general goal of this chapter is to specify what aspects of language should be assessed in infants and preschoolers (through 4 years of age). This goal will be accomplished by describing (a) issues pertinent to the accurate assessment of language development, (b) child behaviors that typify normal language development and procedures for collecting data on such behaviors, and (c) tools for organizing and interpreting these data to determine normal versus pathological performances. Further, some information will be provided to describe how normal and language-impaired children may differ in their developmental abilities. All of this information will highlight areas of interest and procedures for assessing the language development of infants and preschoolers as typically conducted by speech and language clinicians. In addition, this information should suggest to specialists in other disciplines when children should be referred for a speech and language evaluation.

DATA COLLECTION

General Issues: Testing Variables

Regardless of the population being tested, clinical assessment requires that the data collection procedures be valid and reliable. As discussed in Chapter 3 of this book, valid procedures ensure that the methods of observation will measure what the clinician truly intends to measure, and reliable procedures ensure that the methods of observation will be replicable in different settings with different examiners and, of course, with corresponding stability in the client's performance. In language assessment, this means ensuring that the procedures will optimize the child's performance, without overestimating it, so that the usual, habitual language performance will be sampled. The assessment goal is to identify the regularities in the child's preverbal and early verbal behaviors so that true deficits can be documented. Such a goal relies on valid information that is obtained in a reliable fashion, which is difficult to insure because of the tremendous variability in young children's performances. Variability in performance can arise from several different sources: the nature of what is being tested, the testing situation, and the individual being tested.

The *nature of what is being tested* refers to the complexities of language and the difficulties in assessing all aspects of the system equally. Recall that language is a complex phenomenon comprised of many components, all of which need to be assessed: comprehension and production; phonology; syntax; semantics; and pragmatics. All components are always present, and yet, at any point, one component may be dominant, more frequently occurring, or more observable in the child's repertoire. During assessment, the speech or language clinician must be cautious about focusing on the dominant behaviors and failing to sample the less dominant behaviors. The variablilty in performance may reflect the true nature of the developing language system, but it may also reflect what the clinician has sampled in his or her testing. Some child behaviors occur infrequently during typical testing situations, for example, pointing (Olswang, 1983), verbally coding possession (Scott, Palin & Davidson, 1979), and requesting information (Wilkinson, Clevenger, & Dollaghan, 1981). The naturally low incidence of many behaviors, such as these, makes a comprehensive sampling of language difficult and thus influences the validity of the assessment procedures. The solution is to use multiple measures of language, which sample all of the components, and to structure the assessment to ensure the sampling of infrequently occurring behavior. This solution will increase the likelihood of obtaining a truly representative sample of the child's communication skills.

A second source of performance variablity in young children is *the testing situation*, more specifically the examiner and the context (Gallagher, 1983). Several studies have documented that the communicative partner (e.g., whether examiner, parent, or peer) can inflence the language output of young children. Children producing primarily two- and three-word utterances appear to produce more language with their mothers than with clinicians (Olswang & Carpenter, 1978), whereas more linguistically advanced children have been found to produce more language with clinicians (Prutting, Gallagher & Mulac, 1975). Linguistic variablity has also been observed in young children's interactions with their fathers and their peers (Cooper, 1979; Rondal, 1980; Wellman & Lempers, 1977). The physical context can also influence young children's language. For example, language collected in the home is different from language collected in the clinic (Scott & Taylor, 1978). Different toys have been found to elicit different types of communicative behavior (Cook-Gumperz & Corsaro, 1977; Smith & Daglish, 1977), and a structured environment seems to affect variablility in the quantity and quality of verbal output (Bloom & Lahey, 1978; Coggins, Olswang & Guthrie, 1987). The performance variability introduced by features of the testing situation needs to be addressed when one is considereing validity and reliability. One solution is to sample behaviors in more than one situation and to use information provided by the parent about what situations are most apt to yield optimal, representative performance (Gallagher, 1983).

A final source of variability comes from the *person being tested*. A critical distinction that must be made is between the behavior a child exhibits and the knowledge that is ascribed to the child (Lund & Duchan, 1983). Very often young children exhibit behaviors that are not really part of their rule-governed linguistic system. Rather, these behaviors are learned stimulus–response routines, or memorized sterotypical behaviors. For example, a 2-year-old child may say ''I don't know'' along with his or her more typical two-word combinations. Such an utterance illustrates rather complex linguistic forms: the *I* indicates the first-person-singular pronoun, and the structure *don't* represents the obligatory *do* plus the contracted negative form *not*. For the 2-year old child, the utterance ''I don't know'' may be a sterotyped ''single-word'' phrase, of which the grammatical components are not part of his or her linguistic rule system. If this were true, there would seem to be variability, or inconsistency, in the child's verbal output. Specifically, the child would be using simple two-word utterances of the noun + noun, noun + verb, adjective + noun type, with the exception of this more sophisticated utterance. Such variability in the performance of young children is extremely common (Clark, 1974, 1978; Peters, 1977). Children often produce linguistic structures of more advanced complexity because they memorize them as part of a social routine. Although the clinician is interested in the child's complete repertoire, including memorized, sterotyped utterences, he or she is more interested in the language behaviors that are rule-governed and that are a part of the child's true linguistic system. These rule-governed behaviors reflect the child's linguistic competence and are ultimately used to determine whether a language disorder is present.

These sources of variability make the language assessment of young children a difficult task. Validity and reliability can be measured by adequately sampling a variety of behaviors, in a variety of contexts, and with a variety of communication partners. But efforts to improve the validity and reliability of assessment procedures result in increased time demands. The clinician must consider the variables affecting performance and wisely select or construct the testing procedure that will best account for them.

General Assessment Procedures

The assessment of young children's language skills usually involves obtaining two primary types of information: data that are historical and data that are based on direct client examination (Meitus & Weinberg, 1983). Parents can serve as important team members for both. When the clinician is obtaining historical information, the parents can provide background information and describe their child's current level of functioning. In fact, much of the parents' information may guide the clinician's direct client-examination procedures. When a clinician implements the direct examination, the parent may continue to participate. Parents are sometimes more capable than the clinician in eliciting particular behaviors from the child during the assessment session. Parents can also evaluate the representativeness of the child's behavior as the child interacts with the clinician. Although, as Sheehan points out (see Chapter 5), parents often have a tendency to overestimate their children's performance, clinicians need to be aware of a parent's potential as a valuable resource in conducting an efficient, thorough language assessment.

There are a number of procedural options for the direct examination of young children's language skills. Each option has its advantages and disadvantages in yielding the information necessary for determining if a child is acquiring language normally. Miller (1978) discussed four basic categories of assessment procedures:

1. Standardized tests
2. Developmental scales
3. Nonstandardized tests (elicited production and imitation tasks)
4. Behavioral observation (typically conducted in the natural environment)

These four categories may best be described as corresponding to a continuum from highly structured (standardized tests) to low structured (behavioral observation in the natural environment). When selecting procedures for assessing infants and young children, this continuum offers a useful framework.

On the highly structured end are standardized tests, which are defined by structured administration guidelines, data for comparing an individual's performance with a group norm, and information on validity and reliability. Although standardized tests must meet these criteria, some do so far better than others. The main advantage of a standardized procedure is that it allows for some precision in comparing a particular child with other children of the same age. Another advantage is that a standardized test allows for repeated measures of the specific behaviors of one child at different times. Repeated measures are useful in monitoring and measuring normal growth and development. The main disadvantage of standardized tests is that they often provide a fairly limited view of language. As so few tests are available, only limited aspects of language are assessed under this testing option. And indeed, many tests that are available are outdated in their stimulus materials and in the linguistic theory on which they were based. Another disadvantage in using standardized tests is the amount of structure built into the testing procedures. This structure, needed to improve reliability, is often a problem in work with young children who are handicapped or otherwise difficult to test. Many authors have suggested selecting particular items or modifying the tasks to meet the individual needs of each child; thus begins the unstructuring of the most structured procedures. Although standardized tests have their limitations, they serve a useful function by providing normative data and by providing direction for further testing. As long as examiners never rely on one test instrument nor one type of assessment tool in assessing a young child, standardized tests should be considered a very useful part of the assessment protocol.

Developmental scales are related to standardized tests and may be considered a type of standardized procedure. These structured assessment procedures are used to locate a child's performance on a developmental sequence of language behaviors. The assumption is that language development can be described in terms of predictable emerging behavioral milestones. Some developmental scales are highly structured in test form, such as the Preschool Language Scale (Zimmerman, Steiner, & Evatt, 1969) and the Environmental Prelanguage Battery (Horstmeier & MacDonald, 1978). Others are more informal and have emerged from the results of research, as Piaget's Sensorimotor Skills (Uzgiris & Hunt, 1975), the acquistion of the 14 grammatical morphemes (Brown, 1973; deVilliers & deVilliers, 1973), or the acquisition of English sounds (Poole, 1934; Prather, Hedrick, & Kern, 1975; Sander, 1972; Templin, 1957; Wellman, Case, Mengurt, & Bradbury, 1931). Developmental scales are useful in describing children's level of language functioning, but like any formal tool, they are useful only if the right behaviors are being (pp. 314–317) sampled. The appendix provides a list a standardized tests and developmental scales appropriate for assessing the language development of infants and preschoolers.

Behavioral observation of the child in his or her natural environment is at the other end of the continuum. At its extreme, no restrictions are placed on the child or his or her environment; the child is free to play and perform in his or her own way. The clinician is an unobtrusive observer whose task it is to take data in whatever way is appropriate, from informal notations to highly structured, systematic data-collection procedures (see Schiefelbusch & McCormick, 1984, for a review of data collection procedures). The main advantage of observation in a natural environment is that the many components of the language system can be evaluated, including the child's sound system, vocabulary, syntactic forms, and functional and communicative uses of language (e.g., requesting, commenting, labeling, and protesting). Natural observation is also more likely to evoke the child's habitual, usual language skills, rather than an atypical performance that might result from standardizing testing. The main limitation of this assessment option is the possibility of sampling error. As discussed in the previous section, performance variability is a major problem in assessing young children. Performance variability increases the likelihood that a single natural observation will not sample adequately the child's behaviors and thus may result in an invalid measure of language performance. The clinician can recognize this potential problem and correct it by sampling on numerous occasions, in a variety of settings, and with a variety of people. The younger the child, or the more difficult she or he is to test, the greater the advantages of a natural observation, for a great deal of relevant information can be obtained in a reasonable amount of time.

Various options exist between the two extremes of the continuum. Structure can be added to the natural observation to ensure the sampling of particular behaviors, especially infrequently occurring behaviors. Elicited production activities are useful for evoking specific behaviors from a child by altering the environment in ways that create opportunities for the child to produce particular behaviors (Miller, 1978, has placed these procedures in his ''Nonstandardized tests'' category). For example, in eliciting a request behavior from a young child, the clinician might put a toy of high appeal within the child's sight but out of reach. These opportunities can be more highly structured by including verbal instruction to the child (e.g., ''Tell me what you want'' or ''Show me''). If desired, imitation can be included to structure the task even more, for example ''Tell me 'get the baby.''' These nonstandardized tasks allow the clinician to have more control of the situation and the behaviors that occur. The tasks can be highly contrived, structured, and prepared in advance of the assessment, or more naturalistic and altered within the session according to the child's performance.

Each type of procedure, from high to low structure, provides useful information in assessing the young child. When a performance needs to be compared to normative data, standardized tests are of value. When more detail is desired about the natue of a particular performance, the nonstandardized procedures and behavioral observations would be preferred. Selecting the proper procedure for obtaining the most valuable information about a particular child is of critical importance. Probably the most useful assessment protocol is one that uses a variety of procedures. The nature of the information desired, in combination with the child's level of functioning, determines which procedures will work best (Coggins, Olswang, & Guthrie, 1987). To select the most useful procedure, the clinician must know exactly what information needs to be obtained. In the section that follows, the focus is on the type of information needed to determine whether a child is developing language normally.

Specific Assessment Procedures

The focus of this chapter thus far has been on general issues and procedures for assessing the young child. In this section, specific preverbal and early verbal behaviors and procedures for assessing these behaviors are discussed. For obvious reasons, only the highlights of early prelanguage and language behaviors can be provided, but this information should enable specialists in other disciplines to understand the initial speech and language assessment process and to provide a direction for their making an appropriate referral.

The organization of this discussion is based on a commonly agreed-upon definition of language provided by Bloom and Lahey (1978), who defined language as a code by which ideas about the world are represented through a system of symbols for communication (p. 4). According to Bloom and Lahey, this definition describes three major components of language: *form, content* and *use.*[1] The value of this definition is that it can be used to describe preverbal development (i.e., form, content, and use behaviors occurring before first words), as well as verbal development. *Form* refers to the system of symbols in Bloom and Lahey's definition. During the preverbal period of development, form includes gestures and vocalizations. During the verbal period, the symbols become more conventional, in that the child uses recognizable verbalizations (speech sounds) to code words, word combinations, and grammatical structures. *Content* refers to ideas about the world (i.e., knowledge about objects and events in the environment). Content is often thought to reflect cognitive development and, therefore, the basis for language acquisition. Sensorimotor skills (as described by Piaget) provide the means by which a child acquires knowledge about objects, events, and object–event relations during the preverbal period of development. Early verbal development appears to reflect many of the concepts learned preverbally. As the child matures linguistically, content becomes increasingly more complex and abstract, reflecting the child's cognitive development. *Use*

---

[1]The more traditional components of phonology, syntax, semantics, and pragmatics have been incorporated into Bloom's and Lahey's taxonomy as follows: *form* refers to phonology and syntax; *content*, to semantics; and *use*, to pragmatics. The Bloom and Lahey orientation has been selected for this chapter because of its suitability to a discussion of the infant and preschool population.

refers to the communicative aspect of language, particularly pragmatic (i.e., interpersonal) communication. This is the social, affective basis of language acquisition. During the preverbal period of development, the child's earliest social interaction behaviors may not be intentional (e.g., crying, smiling, and fussing), but are interpreted as communication attempts by adults. These behaviors are followed by intentional communicative interactions, but ones that are not yet in conventional word form (e.g., pointing and vocalizing to signal a request). With the onset of words and word combinations, a child begins communicating with conventional verbal forms (e.g., "Mama help" to signal a request).

Each of the three components of form, content, and use also involves two processing domains: comprehension and production. Comprehension refers to discriminating and understanding the symbolic code of the language (i.e., decoding the system of symbols). Production refers to the way in which the code is produced, or articulated, by the individual (i.e., encoding the system of symbols). The preverbal and early verbal behaviors indicating a child's development of *form*, *content*, and *use* provide an assessment focus to determine whether he or she is acquiring language normally. Each language component will be discussed separately, including descriptions of specific comprehension and production behaviors that the clinician should attempt to observe, and suggestions will be provided for ways in which these observations can be made. The reader should be aware that although ages have been provided to indicate the acquisition of many language milestones, these are approximate ages. The order of development for these milestones has been well documented in the literature, but ages for the mastery of behaviors are highly variable. The data provided in the following pages and tables are meant to serve as general guidelines for assessment.

Form: Preverbal Development

The preverbal form of language includes the production and comprehension of both motor behaviors, (signs and gestures) and oral behaviors (vocalizations). During approximately the first 6 months of life, a normal child moves from reflexive motor and oral productions to intentional productions. For example, reflexive arm movements gradually become more purposeful reaching and grasping, and cries and coos gradually become streams of vowel-like productions, squeals, and yells (Oller, 1980). The child also demonstrates a variety of auditory discrimination skills during this period, from a general responsiveness and attentiveness to speech sounds, to the localization and discrimination of specific speech sounds, such as /d/ and /t/, /ba/ and /ga/, vowels, and various intonation patterns (Eilers, Wilson, & Moore, 1977); Eimas, Siqueland, Jusczyk, & Vigorito, 1971). These discrimination abilities enable the child to comprehend and learn language. During the second half of the first year, a child increases his or her production of communicative gestures to include showing, giving, and pointing. At first, these behaviors occur infrequently and in isolation, but they gradually become a large part of the child's repertoire. During the 6- to 12- month age period the child's sound repertoire and syllable structure increase. Most children produce a variety of consonants (e.g., h, b, p, d, t, g, k, m, n, f, s, z), and the entire range of vowels. They also demonstrate the adult-like rise–fall intonation contour when they produce strings of vocalizations. For approximately 3–4 months during this 6- to 12-month age period, the child's babbling is characterized by a reduplication of syllables, such as /ba-ba-ba-/, /da-da-da/, or /ma-ma-ma/. Infants can be heard repeating consonant–vowel productions for long time periods. As the child produces her or his first conventional words at approximately 12–15 months of age, gestures have been combined to form rather sophisticated messages, and babbling continues, but with more variety in the sounds comprising the consonant–vowel (or vowel–consonant) strings and in the prosodic features of pitch, stress, and intensity. During this period of development, a child's understanding of language may appear to be quite sophisticated, especially in familiar contexts. Chapman (1978) suggested that children around 12–15 months of age comprehend primarily single words, but they appear to understand much more because they use "comprehension strategies," or nonlinguistic cues, to respond to the language they hear. For example, if a child complies to an adult's request to "Give the doll a big hug," the child may appear to comprehend the entire sentence, whereas, in fact, he or she is merely using the following strategies (Chapman, 1978):

1. Look at the object the adult looks at.
2. Act on the object that is noticed.
3. Perform as usual in routine games.

The basic rule the child follows is to pick out single words that are comprehended and then to perform as he or she usually does in the situation.

Although preverbal production behaviors can be observed in the natural environment, (i.e., the low-structured testing situation), it is possible to evoke them from the child through more structured imitation tasks. According to Piaget's work, a child will imitate gestures and speech sounds that are in her or his vocal repertoire at around 4–8 months. Between 8 and 12 months, the child will vocalize a familiar sound on hearing novel ones. After a year, novel gestures and vocalizations can be imitated by most normally developing children. These findings have resulted in the use of nonstandardized elicitation procedures for sampling preverbal production behaviors.

Form: Verbal Development

The verbal development of language form refers to the emergence of verbalizations, including single-word utterances, word combinations, and grammatical structures of noun-and-verb phrase elaborations. The acquisition of first words at approximately 12–15 months of age does not result in a corresponding reduction of gestures (Carpenter, Mastergeorge, & Coggins, 1983; Olswang & Carpenter, 1982). Rather, children use gestures to accompany their verbalizations well into their second year of life. First words are highly variable in their sound production and yet are fairly predictable, given the speech sounds in the child's repertoire. Several studies have examined speech acquisition in preschooler's early language (Poole, 1934; Prather, Hedrick & Kern, 1975; Stoel-Gammon, 1985; Templin, 1957; Wellman et al., 1931) and have suggested a fairly invariant sequence of sound and feature emergence. When children produce approximately 50 different single words, they begin to combine words. These two-word productions, which occur at approximately 24–30 months of age, are simple constructions, consisting of this, that, more, and no, plus another word (e.g., "more cookie"). Gradually adjectives, nouns, and verbs are produced together (e.g., "big boy," "run home," "baby home"), and then noun phrases and verb phrases become expanded (e.g., "my big ball," "running to store," "Bobby's blocks"), primarily by the acquisition of particular grammatical structures called *grammatical morphemes:*

Early emerging grammatical morpheme		Example
-ing	present progressive	"running"
in, on	prepositions	"in box," "on table"
-s, -es	plurals	"cats," "dogs," "glasses"
's	possessives	"Mom's coat"

Children around 30 months of age are capable of asking simple questions (e.g., "What doing?" "Where Daddy going?"), of grammatically negating a statement (e.g., "No go home," "Boy not hitting girl," "I don't know"), and of using some pronouns (e.g., "I wanna play," "You get my candy"). Vocabulary growth is quite rapid. By age 36 months, the child comprehends and produces a large number of grammatical structures. And by 48 months, he or she begins to comprehend and produce complex sentences (e.g., "Watch me hit the ball"). Comprehensive summaries of the acquisition of noun-phrase and verb-phrase constituents and of simple to complex sentence types have been provided by Miller (1981, pp. 57–73) and by Coggins and Carpenter (1978, pp. 28–41).

Numerous standardized tests exist to screen and assess sound acquisition, simple word combinations, and more complex grammar (some of these tests are listed in Appendix A). However, a more reasonable place to start an assessment is by sampling the child's spontaneous language. One can determine fairly efficiently whether a child is producing appropriate language milestones given her or his chronological (or developmental) age by computing the child's mean length of utterance (MLU) for a given sample of spontaneous language. The MLU is a metric that is obtained by counting the total number of morphemes (the smallest meaningful linguistic units) in a language sample (typically consisting of 50 consecutive utterances) and dividing this number by the total number of utterances (in this example, 50). Given a particular MLU range, distinct linguistic achievements can be predicted. The MLU is a rather gross index of language performance, but it allows a determination of the syntactic forms appropriate for a given age (CA or MA) (Miller, 1981, pp. 25–27). The MLU is most useful for children of age 5 and younger as a general indicator of grammatical development. Table I highlights the emergence of particular verbal behaviors according to the MLU and chronological age.

Content: Preverbal Development

The preverbal development of content is best described by the use of a Piagetian framework. During the sensorimotor period of development, children learn about objects and events by acting on their environment. Active exploration and manipulation of objects help the child learn that objects have distinct shapes, sizes, and textures, and that they can be located in different ways in time and space. This becomes the knowledge necessary for eventually labeling and describing objects. The concepts that a child learns preverbally, such as mean–ends, object permanence, spatial and locational relationships, and symbolic play, become the foundation for the content of first words and word combinations. Piaget (1952,1954) identified emerging behaviors that reflect a child's acquisi-

Table 1. Comprehension and Production of Verbal Behaviors According to Chronological Age and Mean Length of Utterance (MLU)

Age and MLU	Comprehension	Production
18–24 months MLU=1.0–1.5	Responds to labels of familiar objects. Follows simple two-step commands.	Production of 50 words. Consonant production includes *p, m, h, n, ng* (Prather, Hedrick, & Kern, 1975). Early word combination.
2–2½ years MLU=1.5–2.5	Understands variety of two-word combinations. Answers simple questions: "Do you want ___X___ ? What? Where?"	Beginning use of *f, y, k, d* in words. Frequent omission of consonants at the ends of words and simplication of consonant blends (*top* for *stop*). Use of simple noun phrase ("big boy"). Use of simple verb phrase; no inflections ("run home"). Asks questions with rising intonation ("Baby home?").
2½–3 years MLU=2.5–3.0	More specific understanding of grammatical components of a sentence; plurals, negatives, modifiers. Answers: What (what's that)? What doing? Where (direction)?	Use of *w, b, t, g*. Produces most endings on words. Main verb showing movement with *-ing* (*running*). Beginning use of plurals, preposition *in-on*. Indicates negation with *no* and *not*. Asks what, where questions.
3–3½ years MLU=3.0–4.0	More specific understanding of grammatical components of a sentence; prepositions (*beside, between, under*); higher level negatives (*doesn't*), pronouns (*he, she, they*). Answers: Who? Whose? Why? How many?	Use of *s, r, l*. Further expands the noun phrase ("the big boy"). More consistent use of inflections: plurals possessives. Some verb phrase elaboration ("That's a big dog"; "I want to play"). Asks more "Wh" questions. Makes negatives with *can't, don't*. Uses irregular past tense. Increase in pronouns: *I, me, you, my, mine*.
3½–4 years MLU=4.0–5.0	Mastery of grammatical structures of simple affirmative or negative, size and color modifiers, derivational suffixes (*smaller, smallest*). Answers: How? How much? How long? How far? When?	Uses *ch, sh, th, zh*, and later *j, v, z*. More use of blends /bl,kl/. Speech almost 100% intelligible, although errors still exist. Expands noun phrase to include prepositional phrases. Interchanges auxiliary with subject noun phrase to form questions ("The boy is home"="Is the boy home"; "Mommy is pretty"="Isn't mommy pretty"). Uses past tense, but errors noted (*eated*). Combines noun phrases and verb phrases; uses conjunctions (*and*). Asks *how, when, why* questions.

tion of these concepts. These behaviors change from reflexive activities to purposeful actions on other people and objects. During the first 2 years of life, the child becomes more aware of self, and of his or her ability to achieve different effects on the environment, such as making interesting sights last, finding hidden objects, using tools to reach a goal, placing objects in a variety of spatial relationships, and playing with groups of objects in meaningful ways. The concepts uderlying these behaviors have been described as *cognitive prerequisites* for language development, for they reflect the child's knowledge of the world, which becomes the content for the production of first words and word combinations.

The assessment of preverbal content involves examining the presence or absence of behaviors that reflect underlying cognitive concepts, particularly object permanence, means–ends, spatial and locational relationships, and symbolic play. Such preverbal behaviors have been sampled traditionally through nonstandardized elicitation procedures or developmental scales. These procedures involve the creation of tasks that would have a high probability of eliciting particular behaviors. Such tasks have been descibed by Bates (1979), Miller, Chapman, Branston, and Reichle (1980), and Uzgiris and Hunt (1975) for sampling object permanence, means–ends, and play behaviors. Assessment procedures and performance scales have been constructed for means–ends, space–location, and play behaviors by Olswang (1983) and Carpenter (1983).

Content: Verbal

The development of content during the verbal period is best described by examining the meaning of single-word utterances and multi-word combinations. Children's first words develop around 12 months and have been described by Bloom as having a high mortality rate (existing one day and not another) and being used only in the immediate presence of their environmental referent. A better index of a child's first spoken words is his or her first 10 different words(Nelson, 1973). Although considerable individual variation exists in the meaning of the first words that children begin using (e.g., some children produce object names; others, more social terms, such as "hi," "bye-bye"), the majority of first words are called *substantive words* and are nouns referring to specific objects and people (e.g., "Mommy," "Daddy"); modifiers or action words are used less frequently (Nelson, 1973). The other commonly used single words are *functional words* which apply to many objects (e.g., *this, that, more, want*). The emergence of a child's first 10 productive words appears to occur after the child has acquired a firm comprehension of an average of 50–60 words (Benedict, 1979). Approximately 4–6 months may pass before a child produces 50 different single words, but thereafter, growth in the lexicon is quite rapid (Benedict, 1979).

The content of the first 50 words reflects the concepts learned during the preverbal period of development. Children talk primarily about the existence and the nonexistence of objects. As children develop, the meaning of single words becomes more complex. For example, at first *mama* may indicate the existence of a particular person and may reflect a referential meaning. Later *mama* may mean that person as a possessor of an object; thus the term is used in a relational sense. Single words used in a relational sense herald the onset of successive single-word utterances (strings of a single words separated by brief pauses) and next, early two-word combinations. These productions milestones occur at about the same time that a child is demonstrating the ability to comprehend noun + verb combinations; at first, these occur in predictable commands (e.g., "Kiss baby," "throw ball"), and later, in unpredictable, semantically anomalous commands (e.g., "Kiss plant") (Sachs & Truswell, 1976). Two-word combinations, which appear at approximately 24–30 months of age, but may appear as early as 18 months, are linguistic encodings of concepts developed during the sensorimotor period of development. The most common meanings of two-word utterances have been described by Brown (1973) and Schlesinger (1971) and are described in Table 2. As single-word utterances provide the basis for two-word combinations, two-word combinations provide the basis for three- and four-word combinations. New meanings are not typically coded in a child's three- and four-word utterances. For example, a child typically moves from saying, "Baby eat," to "Eat cookie," and finally to "Baby eat cookie." Sometime after the child has become prolific in her or his production of two-term relations, the emergence of grammatical morphemes can be observed, as the production of plurals, possessives, and tense markers. The content coded by these early grammatical structures reflects concepts that the child has used for some time. The later developing linguistic structures, such as pronouns, subject-verb agreement, and other forms of sentence clarification, reflect more abstract, cognitive concepts.

The assessment of the content of children's one-, two-, and three-term utterances can be accomplished by collecting a representative sample of conversational language and comparing utterances to developmental milestones in lexical production, as discussed above (see Coggins & Carpenter, 1978, for a complete listing of such milestones with the approximate ages of their acquisition). A more formal assessment of two- and three-term relations has been provided by MacDonald (1978). This nonstandardized test uses spontaneous language, elicited production, and elicited imitation procedures to assess children's productions.

Use: Preverbal Development

The preverbal development of language use is observed in the young child's gestures and vocalizations. Reciprocal gaze patterns and vocal play routines with adults, which have been observed during the first month of life, have been suggested as the earliest behaviors indicating the development of communication, or use of language (Bloom & Lahey, 1978). These have characteristics of turn taking that parallel the later emerging dialogue. These early behaviors, as well as others, such as squealing, yelling, and reaching, are probably not intentional attempts to communicate, but they are interpreted as such by adults. Bates, Camaioni, and Volterra (1975) called this stage of communication development, which occurs between zero and 8 months, "perlocutionary"; the child's *un*intentional behaviors are reacted to by the adult as if they were *in*tentional. Gradually, the child's behaviors appear to become increasingly more intentional, probably as shaped through the adult's reactions. The child demonstrates increased awareness of his or her ability to act on the environment and to effect change. The child realizes that, through an increased repertoire of vocalizations and gestures, he or she can produce changes in the immediate environment, particularly through other people.

At around 8 months, vocalizations and gestures begin to be used for intentional communication; Bates *et al.*(1975) referred to this stage as the "illocutionary" stage of communication development. During this stage, the child between 8 and 12 months (i.e., before first words) can be observed showing, giving, and pointing, with accompanying

Table 2. Common Meanings of Two-Word Utterances

Meaning category	Definition and example
Existence or nomination	Naming word or notice word + an object[a] name ("this ball," "hi mama").
Negation (nonexistence, rejection, denial)	A negative word + object name—indicating nonexistence or absence of object, rejection of object, or denial of existence of object ("no cookie"; "allgone boat"; "bye-bye daddy").
Recurrence	Refers to recurrence of object ("more cookie," "another book").
Agent + action	Initiator of an action + action word (noun/pronoun + verb) ("boy run," "girl eat").
Action + object	Action + recipient object of action (verb + noun/pronoun) ("eat cookie," "throw ball").
Agent + object	Initiator of action + recipient of action (noun/pronoun + noun/pronoun) ("girl cookie", *eat* is omitted).
Possession (possessor + possession)	Indication of property or territoriality (noun/pronoun + noun) ("my doll," "daddy car").
Attribution (entity + attribute)	An attribute or modifier + object name (adjective + noun) ("big ball," "blue car").
Location (static-entity + locative; action-action + locative)	Reference to a static location relationship (noun/pronoun + noun; preposition + noun) ("on table," "there car") or Action location relationship (verb + noun) ("run home," "go grocery").

[a]Objects include persons.

variations in vocalizations to indicate a variety of communicative intentions, such as requesting, commenting, protesting, and greeting. Several taxonomies exist for describing children's communicative intentions, the most well known of which were created by Halliday (1975) and Dore (1974). Such taxonomies, though originally created to describe verbal communicative intentions, have been found useful in describing preverbal (i.e., gestural and gestural + vocal) communicative intentions. For example, Coggins and Carpenter (1981) developed an inventory for coding children's gestural and vocal behaviors according to the communicative intentions adapted from Dore (1974). In such a coding scheme, a child might demonstrate *requesting* by bringing to an adult a box that is difficult to open. The child's behaviors might consist of giving the box to the adult, pointing to the latch, and vocalizing a grunting sound several times in succession until the adult performs the desired task of opening the box. By using a variety of gestures and vocalizations, children can become quite sophisticated communicators before their use of first words. Table 3 summarizes preverbal behaviors that indicate children's communicative intentions.

Assessing preverbal communication can be achieved by interacting with a child in a relatively low-structured activity and by creating oppurtunities for the occurence of a variety of communication behaviors. The combination of low-structured observation and more highly structured elicitation tasks appears to provide the best protocol for sampling communicative intentions (Coggins et al., 1987). A coding system, like the one developed by Coggins and Carpenter (1981), is frequently used to indicate which gestural and vocal behaviors represent the various communicative intention categories that can be observed during this period of development.

Use: Verbal Development

The verbal development of use refers to verbalizations (i.e., conventional speech forms) to communicate a variety of intentions. At approximately 12–15 months, as the child moves into one-word productions, he or she now uses conventional forms to indicate a variety of communicative intentions. Bates *et al.* (1975) referred to this as the "locutionary" stage of development. The child uses words to communicate intentions more clearly. During this phase of development, an increase in dialogue (i.e., turn taking) occurs. Both the speaker and the listener are participants in verbal communication, and so the child is more apt to participate in dialogue with an increased use of different communicative intents. Of course, as the child's language form becomes more complex, his communicative intentions become the more obvious. For example, a child might at first produce a request for information with a rising intonation (e.g., "Dog?"). Later, he can produce "What that?" and eventually "Is that a dog?" Table 3 also presents a taxonomy based on the works of Coggins and Carpenter (1981) and Dore (1974, 1975) for categorizing children's one- and two-word utterances according to their communicative intent. As the child's language becomes more sophisticated, the categorization of communicative intent becomes less difficult. The 2- and 3-year-old child communicates about objects and events not immediately present and asks an increasing number of questions to request information. She or he also builds on topics in a conversation, participating in increasingly more complex dialogues. As the child reaches 4 or 5 years of age, he or she begins to produce more subtle and indirect uses of language, such as the utterance

Table 3. Preverbal and Verbal Communicative Intentions[a]

Communicative intention category	Preverbal-illocutionary stage; intentional communicative gestures and vocalizations	Verbal-locutionary stage; intentional communicative verbalizations
Labeling or commenting	Looks at adult and object; and/or shows object to adult; may vocalize.	Uses a word while attending to an object; doesn't await an adult response.
Answering	Responds to adult's query with head nod or other gesture; may vocalize.	Attends to adult; uses a word or words to answer adult's query.
Requesting action or object	Looks at adult and object of desire; points to object and/or gives object to adult; may fuss or whine or may vocalize repeatedly.	Addresses adult; uses a word or words to direct adult's attention to event or object of desire; awaits a response.
Requesting information	Looks at adult and object; points to object, movement, or location and/or manipulates object; vocalizes (often with rising intonation).	Addresses adult; asks a question; awaits adult's response.
Repeating	Repeats adult's gesture or vocalization (repetition may not be entirely accurate).	Repeats all or part of adult's previous utterance.
Calling	Vocalizes with increased intensity; responds positively on obtaining adult's attention.	Addresses adult by producing adult's name; awaits adult response.
Greeting	Uses gesture or vocalization to greet object or adult on appearance.	Uses word to greet object or adult on appearance.
Protesting	Turns away from adult or pushes adult's hands or shakes head; may scream or vocalize loudly.	Uses a word or words to resist, reject, or deny adult action.
Practicing	Vocalizes with different prosodic patterns; no apparent attention to adult or object in the environment.	Uses word or words with no apparent attention to adult or object in the environment; doesn't await adult response.

[a]Coggins and Carpenter (1981); Dore (1974,1975).

"I sure love ice cream" used *not* to state an opinion but as a request for ice cream. The production of these more abstract uses increases with age. Children are more aware of the listener's background and needs in a conversation. They increasingly use language as a tool for learning.

No standardized tests yet exist for assessing young children's communicative intentions, probably because communication can best be examined in a naturalistic context. In a beginning assessment of language use, clinicians typically engage verbal children in conversations about a variety of topics and attempt to identify different communicative intentions, as described in Table 3. Conversational language should be sampled in a variety of contexts with different communication partners to ensure a valid estimate of communication behaviors. To increase the efficiency of testing, the clinician can create contrived situations to evoke particular communicative intentions, but breadth of sampling must not be sacrificed.

General Differences in Development between Normal and Developmentally Disabled Children

Although in general, the language acquisition of children with specific language disabilities does not differ markedly from that of normal children who are at an equivalent mental age, some differences have been observed. The results of studies examining normal and impaired children at the one-word stage of language production have revealed that language-impaired children produced fewer verbal and more gestural responses than did MLU-matched normals (Snyder, 1975, 1978). Several studies have isolated weaknesses in young language-impaired children's ability to sustain communicative interactions. These children seem to initiate conversation less (e.g., being less prone to label spontaneously), and to produce more irrelevant utterances (i.e., they verbally encode less relevant, less informative elements in the environment) (Leonard, Camarata, Rowan, & Chapman, 1982; Snyder, 1975, 1978). Their conversations are characterized by apparently adequate responses to others, but a large number of off-topic utterances as well. Language impaired children often take longer to acquire the consistent, correct production of linguistic structures than normal children at the same language level, but both groups of children appear to follow the same developmental progression in their acquisition of language (Johnston & Schery, 1976; Leonard, Bolders, & Miller, 1976). A slower mastery of linguistic structures results in grammatical errors being present in the children's language longer than would normally be expected. For example, all children go through a period in development in which they produce grammatically inaccurate utterances, such as *runned* or *mens*. Language-impaired children produce such errors longer than normally developing children. Regarding phonologicl development, there is indeed some evidence to suggest that language-impaired children often exhibit limited sound repertoires at a young age, or that they exhibit complete sound repertoires that are misused according to the adult model (Stoel-Gammon & Dunn, 1984). Although these few differences can be used for a preliminary screening to identify language-impaired children, it is important to recognize that, generally, children with specific language impairments look very similar to normal children of the same mental age.

To some extent, the etiology associated with a developmental disability can influence language acquisition; however, children with the same etiology very often demonstrate different patterns in language development. The recommendation suggested in this chapter for examining the language of children with any type of developmental disability is to conduct detailed, in-depth assessments that cover all components of the language system. Data reflecting a child's form, content, and use behaviors are necessary for judging normal language development. The data organization and data interpretation approach described below provides the clinician with a means of analyzing a child's language achievements in order to determine normal versus pathological development and to recommend management options.

DATA ORGANIZATION

After the clinician has completed the assessment, all available data must be organized into a usable format which will enable the clinician to synthesize the information and subsequently to make informed clinical decisions. Data organization involves several general issues that the clinician must consider and that lay the groundwork for profiling, or describing, a child's language performance.

General Issues

A clinician faces three general issues during data organization: (a) deciding on an organizational framework for the data; (b) evaluating the adequacy of the data base; and (c) specifying a measurement unit to represent language development. In the previous sections of this chapter, language functioning was defined as consisting of the components of form, content, and use for both the production and the comprehension domains. A developmental form, content, and use framework is useful for analyzing the results obtained from a variety of assessment procedures. For example, a standardized test such as the Peabody Picture Vocabulary Test—Revised (PPVT-R)—(Dunn & Dunn, 1980) provides data on content in the comprehension domain, and the MLU provides data on form in the production domain. Thus, this framework helps to ensure a comprehensive assessment of language functioning by providing the clinician with the specific components that need to be evaluated. Although other frameworks are available for data organization (Denes & Pinson, 1963; Minifie, Hixon, & Williams, 1973; Nation & Aram, 1984; Newman, Low, Haws, & Bone, 1973; Stevens & House, 1972) they will not be discussed in this chapter.

The clinician must also evaluate the adequacy of the data representing the child's performance in each of the components and domains. As language assessment involves the sampling of performance, the clinician will ideally obtain more than one sample for each component and each domain to ensure a representative view of the child's language behaviors. The clinician may find that the different samples provide conflicting information. For example, a child may perform at a more advanced level on one measure than on another, such as performance on a standardized test versus in a natural observation. Consequently, the clinician must assess whether this apparent conflict of information can be resolved and must decide if one of the procedures represent the typical productive-language functioning of the child. In addition, the clinician must determine whether each language component in both domains has been assessed or whether specific components or domains have been omitted from the data base. To summarize, clinicians must be sure that data have been obtained on all components and domains, must consider the strengths and weaknesses of the obtained information, and must recognize that some of the evaluative procedures may not have provided a representative sample of the child's behavior. (Arkes, 1981; Nation & Aram, 1984).

The third general issue is the choice of a unit of measurement to be used during data organization and interpretation. Performance on various procedures expressed in standard deviation units from the mean would be an ideal measurement for data organization and interpretation. It would account for the variance that exists within each assessment procedure. Unfortunately, many procedures used by speech or language clinicians have not established standard deviation information. A developmental approach can express language functioning in terms of years and months and is commonly used by speech or language clinicians as an alternative to standard deviation units. Other options include language quotients, standardized scores, and percentiles. As stated earlier, a variety of procedures should be used during the assessment. The results of most procedures can be converted to a language level represented in years and months. Thus, this measure has been found to be useful because the clinician is not tied to particular assessment procedures that yield particular numerical scores.

Once the clinician has specified the framework for data organization, has evaluated the adequacy of the data base, and has established the measurement unit, the data are arranged in the format that best describes or profiles the child's performance.

Profiling

Profiling consists of charting an individual child's level of functioning in various language components and domains, and in other relevant achievement areas. The intent of profiling is to compare a child's abiltities in one area to those in another (Sattler, 1982). Figure 1 contains the organization schema used in profiling a child's performance. The ordinate (y axis) represents the developmental level of functioning in months. The abscissa (x axis) represents the various achievement areas that have been assessed for both comprehension and production. These include locations for (a) chronological age (CA); (b) nonverbal cognitive abilities, which may be reported as mental age (MA) or performance IQ; (c) comprehension of form; (d) comprehension of content; (e) comprehension of use; (f) production of form; (g) production of content; and (h) production of use. Under each of these is a place to specify the tests and/or procedures that were administered, along with a place to note the standard error of measurement (S.E.M.), and the standard deviation (SD) for each procedure, when known.

The first step in profiling is for the clinician to enter on the profile format the results of the various procedures used in the language assessment, the standard error of measurement, and the standard deviation of each, if known. The second step is to determine a developmental level for the child's performance in each achievement area, that is, nonverbal cognitive area and each language component. Thus, the clinician must decide the developmental level at which a child is functioning in the nonverbal cognitive area (i.e., mental age); in comprehension of form, content, and use; and in production of form, content, and use. Often, a clinician is faced with the task of summarizing data that are somewhat contradictory, and of weighing the strengths and weaknesses of each procedure

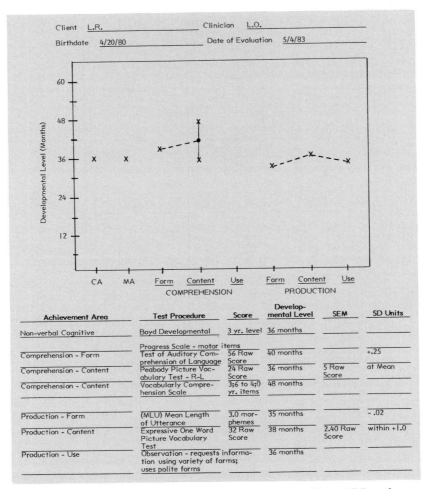

Client   L.R.   Clinician   L.O.

Birthdate   4/20/80   Date of Evaluation   5/4/83

Achievement Area	Test Procedure	Score	Develop-mental Level	SEM	SD Units
Non-verbal Cognitive	Boyd Developmental Progress Scale - motor items	3 yr. level	36 months		
Comprehension - Form	Test of Auditory Comprehension of Language	56 Raw Score	40 months		+.25
Comprehension - Content	Peabody Picture Vocabulary Test - R-L	24 Raw Score	36 months	5 Raw Score	at Mean
Comprehension - Content	Vocabularly Comprehension Scale	3;6 to 4;0 yr. items	48 months		
Production - Form	(MLU) Mean Length of Utterance	3.0 morphemes	35 months		- .02
Production - Content	Expressive One Word Picture Vocabulary Test	32 Raw Score	38 months	2.40 Raw Score	within +1.0
Production - Use	Observation - requests information using variety of forms; uses polite forms		36 months		

Figure 1. A completed profile demonstrating an organization schema for profiling a child's performance; results obtained during a language assessment. CA = chronological age; MA = non-verbal cognitive abilities reported as mental age; SEM = standard error of measurement; SD units = standard deviation units above (+) or below (−) the mean median.

to determine which procedure best represents the client's ability. For some children, a specific level of functioning summarizing the ability may be inappropriate, and the clinician may note a range of functioning for a specifiic component. For example, in the area of comprehension of content, if a child received a score on the PPVT-R (Dunn & Dunn, 1980) indicating a level of functioning of 3 years and received a score on the Vocabulary Comprehension Scale (Bangs, 1975) of 4 years, the clinician may indicate that the child's functioning in comprehension of content is between the 3- to 4-year level. The level or range of functioning for each achievement area is then indicated at the intersection of the appropriate area with the appropriate month (see Figure 1). The resulting profile is a graph summarizing performance on a variety of tasks in the various cognitive and language achievement areas (see Figure 1). The intent of a profile analysis is to determine whether the child is more adept in specific abilities in one area than in another. Based on profiled data, the clinician can interpret the assessment performance by evaluating a child's strengths and weaknesses and then can make appropriate recommendations. To illustrate the interpretation of assessment data, various profile configurations will be described.

DATA INTERPRETATION

Discrepancy

Profile analysis helps to identify the presence or absence of statistically or clinically significant differences between the child's abilities in the various cognitive and language achievement areas (Fey, 1986; Lyman, 1978; Sattler, 1982). Unfortunately, many of the assessment procedures and tests used in language assessment do not have statistics available, such as standard error of measurement and standard deviation, to aid in the judgment of statistical significance. The lack of this information makes the interpretation of significant variability difficult for the clinician. Even with these limitations, however, profile analysis can assist in determining whether a given child is more adept in one component or area than in another. Profile analysis involves determining the degree of performance discrepancy that a child exhibits across achievement areas. To determine this, the clinician needs a reference: "Words such as average, typical, or normal only have meaning when we can answer with respect to what" (Darley, 1978, p.20). Various references have been proposed and often reflect a clinician's philosophical orientation to language. Two general references frequently used are interindividual (between-person) comparison and intraindividual (within-an-individual) comparison (Fey, 1986; Lyman, 1978; Sattler, 1982). Each of these references and possible discrepancies in performance will be described, and various clinical decisions and implications will be considered.

Interindividual Comparisons

Interindividual comparisons entail the clinician's comparing the performance of the child being evaluated with the performance of children who are either the same chronological age (CA) or the same mental age (MA) (Fey, 1986; Kemp, 1983). The clinician has already charted the performance levels of the child who received the language assessment. For the purposes of interindividual comparison, the clinician notes on the profile the expected performance level for children who are the same CA or who have a similar MA. This information is usually based on normative data or developmental scale data. A profile that indicates no discrepancy between the performance of the child evaluated and the performance of other children with the same CA or MA indicates comparable functioning on the various language components. A profile that shows interindividual discrepancy indicates that the child's performance in the language components is below or above that of other children who are the same CA and/or MA. Figure 2 provides an example of a child who demonstrates no interindividual discrepancy, and Figure 3 provides an example of a child who demonstrates interindividual discrepancy. Note that, in Figure 3 the child's language abilities are below the performance expected for the children of the same CA.

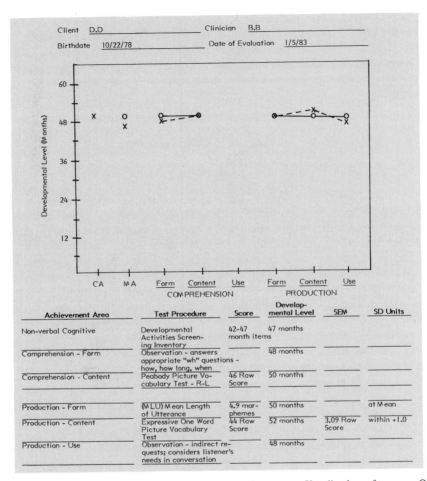

Client D.D   Clinician B.B

Birthdate 10/22/78   Date of Evaluation 1/5/83

Achievement Area	Test Procedure	Score	Developmental Level	SEM	SD Units
Non-verbal Cognitive	Developmental Activities Screening Inventory	42-47 month items	47 months		
Comprehension - Form	Observation - answers appropriate "wh" questions - how, how long, when		48 months		
Comprehension - Content	Peabody Picture Vocabulary Test - R-L	46 Raw Score	50 months		
Production - Form	(MLU) Mean Length of Utterance	4.9 morphemes	50 months		at Mean
Production - Content	Expressive One Word Picture Vocabulary Test	44 Raw Score	52 months	3.09 Raw Score	within +1.0
Production - Use	Observation - indirect requests; considers listener's needs in conversation		48 months		

Figure 2. Profile representing interindividual comparison; no discrepancy. X = client's performance; O = expected performance for children of same age; CA = chonological age; MA = nonverbal cognitive abilities, mental age; SEM = standard error of measurement; SD units = standard deviation units above (+) or below (−) the mean or median.

Two clinical decisions may be made on the basis of interindividual comparisons: (a) who should receive direct intervention and (b) what is the appropriate educational placement. "Who to treat" is based on whether a given child is judged to have a language disorder. The decision of whether a child has a language disorder can be based on two different references. One reference is other children of this child's chronological age, and the second is other children who have similar handicapping conditions and mental ages. Thus, a severely retarded Downs syndrome child would have a language problem when compared to other children of his or her chronological age. On the other hand, when compared to other severely involved Downs syndrome children of the same MA, the child may indeed be judged not to have a language problem if the child's language

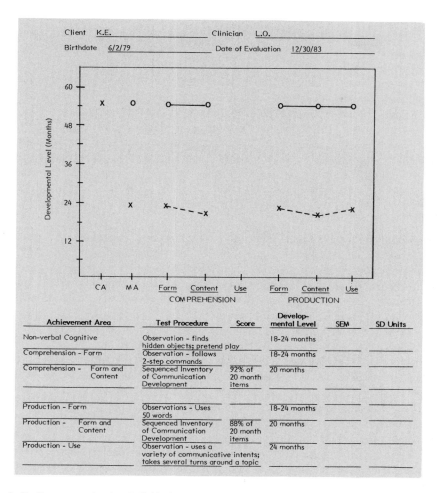

Client K.E.   Clinician L.O.

Birthdate 6/2/79   Date of Evaluation 12/30/83

Achievement Area	Test Procedure	Score	Developmental Level	SEM	SD Units
Non-verbal Cognitive	Observation - finds hidden objects; pretend play		18-24 months		
Comprehension - Form	Observation - follows 2-step commands		18-24 months		
Comprehension - Form and Content	Sequenced Inventory of Communication Development	92% of 20 month items	20 months		
Production - Form	Observations - Uses 50 words		18-24 months		
Production - Form and Content	Sequenced Inventory of Communication Development	88% of 20 month items	20 months		
Production - Use	Observation - uses a variety of communicative intents; takes several turns around a topic		24 months		

Figure 3. Profile representing interindividual comparison; discrepancy as language abilities are poorer than those of children of the same chronological age. X = client's performance; O = expected performance for children of same age; CA = chronological age; MA = nonverbal cognitive abilities, mental age; SEM = standard error measurement; SD units = standard deviation units above (+) or below (−) the mean or median.

abilities are comparable to these peers. Thus, determining who has a language problem is a relative judgement. Using chronological age may imply a more restrictive range of development than exists, and indeed, average functioning becomes the expected standard for all children. Also, if one extends the logic or consequence of this type of thinking, the clinical implications may become unrealistic. If chronological age is always used as the reference for determining the presence or absence of a language problem, the implication is that all children have the potential to be normal in language functioning. We know that this is not the case, especially in some of the more severely involved handicapping conditions. In adddition, if a clinician uses only an interindividual comparison to determine treatment eligibility, treatment would be indicated for any child who does not have language abilities commensurate with his or her chronological age. Whether these children with a flat profile would benefit from therapy any more than they would from general stimulation in an educational classroom or from maturation factors has not been documented empirically.

A second clinical decision based on interindividual comparisons concerns the appropriate educational placement for a child. If a child demonstrates language abilities significantly below chrononlogical age, he or she may have difficulty with regular education or preschool placement. If the mental functioning of peers is used as the reference, the clinician then has information that may be useful regarding special-education placement for the child being evaluated. Thus, interindividual comparisons are probably most useful in determining the most appropriate educational setting for a given child.

Intraindividual Comparisons

Intraindividual comparisons contrast various abilities within a given individual. During an intraindividual comparison, the clinician determines how performance in the various language components compares directly with the child's nonverbal cognitive skills (Miller, 1981) and how the language components compare with one another (intralinguistic referencing) (Fey, 1986; Kemp, 1983). These comparisons will be described, and the clinical relevance of each will be discussed.

In the first type of intraindividual comparison, nonverbal cognitive abilities are used as the primary reference. When this reference is used, the clinician is usually subscribing to some form of cognitive hypothesis (strong, weak, or correlational) (Cromer, 1976). The assumption is that a child's language abilities should be commensurate with his or her nonverbal cognitive abilities, regardless of the child's chronological age. Thus, in a profile that indicates no discrepancy, a child's language abilities are similar to his or her nonverbal cognitive functioning. Figure 4 contains an example of such a profile. On the other hand, various types of discrepancies can occur when nonverbal cognitive abilities are used as the primary reference. For example, a child may perform relatively poorly in all production components and yet demonstrate comprehension abilities commensurate to his or her nonverbal cognitive abilities. This profile appears in Figure 5. In some other instances, a child may demonstrate a very specific language component deficit. For example, a child may show a significant deficit in the production of language form, whereas her or his content production abilities are similar to his or her nonverbal cognitive skills and comprehension abilities. This case is illustrated in Figure 6. Thus, various types of discrepancies may occur, but all are characterized by poorer performance in any one or all language components than in nonverbal cognitive abilities. In intralinguistic referencing, the language components are compared with one another, and CA and nonverbal cognitive comparisons are omitted. A discrepancy is judged to exist in this type of referencing if performance in any one language component or language process is poorer than in the others.

Both forms of discrepancy, those with reference to noverbal cognitive level and those with reference to other language abilities, can influence clinical decisions. If there is a significant deficit in a child's language abilities and nonverbal cognitive abilities, the clinician would diagnose the child as exhibiting a language disorder and would probably recommend therapy. Similarly, if a child has a significant discrepancy within the linguis-

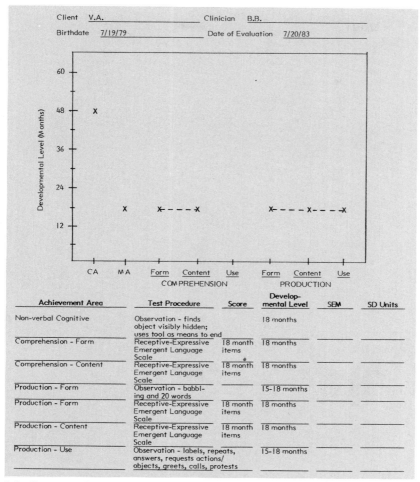

Figure 4. Profile representing intraindividual comparison; no discrepancy between child's nonverbal cognitive and language functioning. CA = chronological age, MA = nonverbal cognitive abilities, mental age; SEM- = standard error of measurement; SD units = standard deviation units above (+) or below (−) the mean or median.

tic areas, regardless of his or her cognitive functioning, this child would also be diagnosed as having a language disorder and would be likely to receive direct intervention. On the other hand, if a child's language abilities are commensurate with his or her nonverbal cognitive abilities, the clinician would conclude that the child does not have a language disorder and would probably not recommend direct therapy. When using intralinguistic referencing, a clinician would probably decide that a child whose language functioning was similar across components did not demonstrate a language disorder. Consequently, direct remediation might not be recommended.

Using intraindividual comparisons to make clinical decisions has some limitations. The amount of within-person variation that is acceptable or common across the language

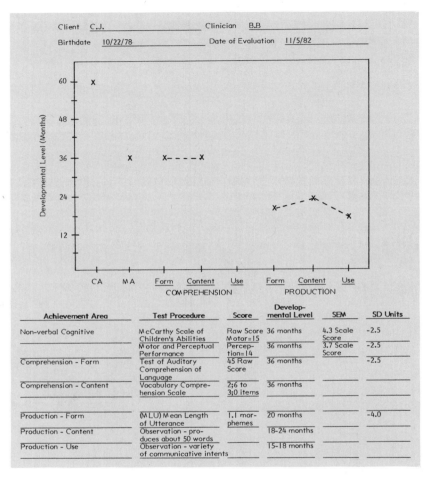

Figure 5. Profile representing intraindividual comparison; discrepancy between both production abilities, and comprehension abilities, and between production abilities and nonverbal cognitive abilities; nonverbal cognitive abilities commensurate with comprehension abilities. CA = chronological age; MA = nonverbal cognitive abilities, mental age; SEM = standard error of measurement; SD units = standard deviation units above (+) or below (−) the mean or median.

components has not been documented, although some work is in progress (Olswang, Stoel-Gammon, Coggins, & Carpenter, 1987). Frequently, a 6-month discrepancy in functioning between the language abilities or between language and non-verbal cognitive abilities is considered a significant discrepancy that warrants intervention (Crystal, Fletcher, & Garman, 1976). The logic of using a ± 6-month criterion across all age ranges is questionable (Kemp, 1983) in light of the lack of information on normal intra-ability variation. In addition, although profiling and determining the degree of discrepency have been advocated and have been commonly used by many speech or language clinicians (Fey, 1986; Kemp, 1983; Miller, 1981) to determine eligibility for direct intervention, this view is not universally held. For example, Leonard (1983) suggested that a

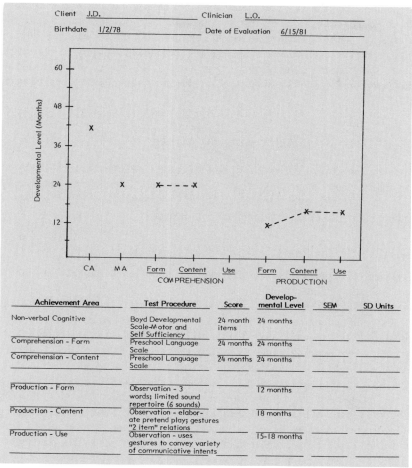

Client J.D.   Clinician L.O.

Birthdate 1/2/78   Date of Evaluation 6/15/81

Achievement Area	Test Procedure	Score	Developmental Level	SEM	SD Units
Non-verbal Cognitive	Boyd Developmental Scale-Motor and Self Sufficiency	24 month items	24 months		
Comprehension - Form	Preschool Language Scale	24 months	24 months		
Comprehension - Content	Preschool Language Scale	24 months	24 months		
Production - Form	Observation - 3 words; limited sound repertoire (6 sounds)		12 months		
Production - Content	Observation - elaborate pretend play; gestures "2 item" relations		18 months		
Production - Use	Observation - uses gestures to convey variety of communicative intents		15-18 months		

Figure 6. Profile representing intraindividual comparison; intralinguistic discrepancy with production form abilities being poorer than other language and nonverbal cognitive abilities. CA = Chronological age; MA = nonverbal cognitive abilities, mental age; SEM = standard error of measurement; SD units = standard deviation units above (+) or below (−) the mean or median.

discrepancy need not exist between nonverbal cognitive and communication abilities in order to indicate that therapy is necessary. He did caution, however, that children with this type of profile may indeed benefit from a general educational setting more than specific language intervention. Thus, the framework used to determine who needs therapy depends on the clinician's philosophy as well as the clinician's definition of intervention.

Summary

Both inter- and intraindividual referencing examine the degree of discrepancy present in a person's abilities, which, in turn, may influence clinical decisions. Interindividual referencing provides a clinician with useful information in deciding about the appropriate educational placement for a child, whereas intraindividual referencing provides a clinician with information to use in determining a child's need for direct speech and language therapy. Research is needed to ascertain the validity of the discrepancy model used in determining the presence or absence of a language disorder, and whether individuals demonstrating discrepant performance in various abilities benefit from intervention.

Implications for Management

Once a clinician has evaluated a child's language abilities and has determined the need for intervention, other clinical decisions are made. A clinician must decide who would be the most effective agent for changing (improving) a child's language abilities and whether referal to other professionals is indicated.

Agent for Change: The Role of the Speech or Language Clinician

A speech or language clinician provides various professional services. One service involves evaluating or assessing language abilities to determine whether a child has a language problem. Another service is implementating direct intervention. In many instances, a speech or language clinician consults with parents and/or teachers. The agent selected to work with the child may depend on factors such as the assessment profile, the therapy goal, or the learning stage. According to the discrepancy model, children can be identified who would be eligible for direct initial intervention by the speech or language clinician. As a child acquires a skill, the speech or language clinician may also include parents and teachers in the therapy process to foster generalization. If a child performs relatively consistently at the same development level for the various abilities, the parents and/or the teachers may be likely candidates to become the primary initial agents for change. In this case, the speech or language clinician may serve as a consultant to the parents and/or the teachers and may provide techniques and suggestions to facilitate the child's language behaviors.

Much research has been conducted on the effectiveness of various agents for change. Some of these studies have been conducted in a more stringent manner than others, but in general, all document that parents, teachers, and clinicians can induce an improvement in the child's language functioning (Bricker & Bricker, 1976; Bronfenbrenner, 1975a,b; Ramey, Sparling, & Waslik, 1981; Robinson & Robinson, 1971; Shearer & Shearer, 1976). For example, Ramney and colleagues (1981) investigated three groups of at-risk children in different training modes: home visitation, home and day care, and a no-training control group. Both of the training groups demonstrated more advanced language functioning than did the control group. Bricker and Bricker (1976) also indicated that children's language abilities advanced when parents were included in conjunction with classroom programs. Thus, evidence indicates that teachers, parents, and clinicians can all act as effective agents for change.

One issue that remains unresolved is whether certain agents are more effective at certain ages for certain behaviors. A second issue is whether certain agents are more effective at certain learning stages within an individual. For example, a speech or language clinician may be more effective in establishing a behavior change, and parents and teachers may be more effective in transferring and maintaining a new behavior (Olswang, Bain, Rosendahl, Oblak, & Smith, 1986). Obviously these issues need to be addressed empirically.

Referrals

Developmentally disabled children often have educational, medical and management needs that extend beyond the scope of a single discipline. Therefore, the speech or language clinician needs to view the "whole child" rather than just the child's language abilities. The clinician is responsible for knowing what professionals should be involved with any particular child and must refer the child to other professionals as appropriate. With the increased emphasis on multidisciplinary teams, and child study teams, hopefully more needs of a child are being identified and met. However, in some remote parts of the country, the "team approach" may not be possible. In those situations, appropriate referrals to other disciplines must be made.

SUMMARY

This chapter attempts to outline procedures for assessing infants and preschoolers for whom language development is a concern. A major focus of the chapter is on describing preverbal and early verbal form, content, and use behaviors. In addition, the chapter provides a framework for interpreting children's behaviors to determine normal versus pathological development and for recommending management options. The probablistic perspective described by Liebergott *et al.* (1984) alerts the clinician to the difficulty of the assessment and identification task because there are, as yet, no clear indices for recognizing clinically significant differences in performance between children who are developing normally and children who are not. The discrepancy models described in this chapter provide a practical tool for reaching informed decisions in the absence of such definitive criteria.

Assessment is a dynamic and ongoing process. When a child is initially evaluated and management decisions are made, the clinician must be aware that these decisions or conclusions should be considered tentative. At a later time, they may change naturally or may be found to be inaccurate. Therefore, clinicians need to regard assessment as an ongoing process and need to be sensitive to involving as many relevant others in the process as appropriate. If other disciplines are involved on an ongoing basis with a particular child, changes in performance and management needs are easier to monitor. If, on the other hand, a child is mainstreamed and her or his parents and teachers are selected to be the primary agents of change, the clinician has the responsibility to monitor the child's progress to determine if the original decisions regarding management needs are continually appropriate. Viewing language assessment as an ongoing process allows the clinician to more accurately describe a child, interpret his or her performance, and make relevant, appropriate clinical decisions that change as the child changes.

APPENDIX: LANGUAGE ASSESSMENT PROCEDURES

I. STANDARDIZED TESTS

A. Screening Tests

The Communication Screen
Authors: Nancy Stiffler and Sharon Willig
Age range: 2;10–5;9; comprehension and production. Specific areas tested—
Form: syntax, speech intelligibility; Content: comprehension of action pictures,
prepositions, questions; Use: answering questions.
Publisher: Communication Skill Builders, Tucson, Arizona, 1981.

Del Rio Language Screening Test
Authors: Allen S. Toronto, D. Leverman, Cornelia Hanna, Peggy Rosenzweig,
and Antoneta Maldonado.
Age range: 3;0–6,11; comprehension and production. Specific areas tested—Content: receptive single word vocabulary subtest; Form: syntax, production of a
variety of sentence types.
Publisher: National Educational Laboratory Publishers, Austin, Texas, 1975.

The Denver Articulation Screening Examination
Author: Amelia F. Drumwright
Age range: 2;5–6;0; production. Specific area tested—Form: phonology, sounds
in words.
Publisher: Ladoca Project and Publishing Foundation, Inc., Denver, Colorado,
1971.

Fluharty Preschool Speech and Language Screening Test
Author: Buono Fluharty
Age range: 2;0–6;0; comprehension and production. Specific areas tested—Form:
phonology, syntax; Content: vocabulary.
Publisher: DLM Teaching Resources, Allen, Texas, 1978.

Northwestern Syntax Screening Test
Author: Laura L. Lee
Age range: 3;0–7;11; comprehension and production. Specific grammatical struc-
tures tested—Form: syntax, personal pronouns, possessives, *wh-* questions, plu-
rals, verb tenses, negation, yes-no questions, and passives.
Publisher: Northwestern University Press, Evanston, Illinois, 1969/71.

Screening Kit of Language Development
Authors: Lynn S. Bliss and Doris V. Allen.
Age range: 30–48 months; comprehension and production. Form: syntax, sen-
tence repetition, following commands; Content: vocabulary comprehension.
Publisher: University Park Press, Baltimore, Maryland, 1983.

B. Specific Component Tests

Arizona Articulation Proficiency Scale
Author: Janet Barker Fudala

Age range: 3;0–11;11; production. Specific area tested—Form: phonology, sounds in the context of words.

Publisher: Western Psychological Services, Los Angeles, California, 1970.

Carrow Elicited Language Inventory

Author: Elizabeth Carrow

Age range: 3;0–7;11; production. Specific areas tested—Form: syntax, articles, pronouns, negatives, prepositions, plurals, and all components of the verb phase.

Publisher: Learning Concepts, Austin, Texas, 1974.

Expressive One Word Picture Vocabulary Test

Author: Morrison F. Gardner

Age range: 2;0–11;11; production. Specific area tested—Content: identification of single-word vocabulary.

Publisher: Academic Therapy Publications, San Rafael, California, 1979.

Peabody Picture Vocabulary Test (PPVT-R)

Authors: Lloyd M. Dunn and Leota M. Dunn

Age range: 2;6–40;0; comprehension. Specific area tested—Content: single-word vocabulary items.

Publisher: American Guidance Service, Circle Pines, Minnesota, 1980.

Photo Articulation Test

Authors: Kathleen Pendergast, Stanley E. Dickey, John W. Selmar, and Anton L. Soder.

Age range: 3;0–12;0; production. Specific area tested—Form: phonology, sounds in words, and connected speech.

Publisher: Interstate Printers and Publishers, Danville, Illinois, 1969.

Rhode Island Test of Language Structure

Authors: Elizabeth Engen and Trygg Engen

Age range: 3;0–6;0; comprehension. Specific area tested—Form: syntax, comprehension of simple and complex sentence types.

Publisher: University Park Press, Baltimore, Marland, 1983.

Sequenced Inventory of Communication Development

Authors: Dona Lea Hedrick, Elizabeth M. Prather, and Annette R. Tobin

Age range: 4–48 months; comprehension and production. Parent interview and child-administered format. Specific areas tested—Form: response to and production of gestural, vocal, and verbal, behaviors; syntax is assessed through connected speech sample; Content: response to and production of gestural, vocal, and verbal behaviors, and connected speech sample.

Publisher: University of Washington Press, Seattle Washington, 1984.

Test of Early Language Development

Authors: Wayne P. Hresko, D. Kim Reid, and Donald D. Hammill

Age range: 3;0–7;11; comprehension and production. Specific areas tested— Form: syntax; Content: semantics.

Publisher: Publishers Test Service, Monterey, California, 1981.

II. DEVELOPMENTAL SCALES: NORM- AND CRITERION-REFERENCED

Birth to Three Developmental Scale
Authors: Tina E. Bangs and Susan Dodson
Age range: Birth–3 years; comprehension and production. Parent interview and child-administered format. Specific areas tested—Form: motor (gestural), vocal, and verbal, syntax: Content: cognitive prerequisites (e.g., means–end, causality); Use.
Publisher: DLM Teaching Resources, Allen, Texas, 1979.

Bowen-Chalfant Receptive Language Inventory
Authors: Mack L. Bowen and James Chalfant
Age range: 2;6–9;6; comprehension. Specific areas tested—preverbal content.
Publisher: C. C. Publications, Inc., Tigard, Oregon, 1981.

Preschool Language Scale
Authors: Irla Lee Zimmerman, Violette G. Steiner, and Roberta Evatt Pond
Age range: 1;6–7;0; comprehension and production. Child-administered. Specific areas tested—Form: syntax, phonology, grammatical morphemes; Content: vocabulary.
Publisher: Charles E. Merrill Publishing Company, Columbus, Ohio, revised 1979.

Receptive-Expressive Emergent Language Scale
Authors: Kenneth R. Bzoch and Richard League
Age range: Birth–36 months; comprehension and production. Parent interview and child-administered format. Form; content; use.
Publisher: Tree of Life Press. Gainsville, Florida, 1971.

The Early Language Milestone Scale
Authors: James Coplan
Age range: Birth–36 months; comprehension and production. Parental report and child-administered format. Specific areas tested—Form, content, use.
Publisher: Modern Education Corporation, Tulsa, Oklahoma, 1984.

Test for Auditory Comprehension of Language—Revised
Author: Elizabeth Carrow-Woolfolk
Age range: 3;0–9;11; comprehension: Specific areas tested—Form: grammatical morphemes, word order; Content: substantive and functional vocabulary.
Publisher: DLM Teaching Resources, Allen, Texas, 1985.

Test for Examining Expressive Morphology
Authors: Kenneth G. Shipley, Ph.D., Terry A. Stone, and Marlene B. Sue
Age range: 3;0–8;0; production. Specific area tested—Form: syntax, grammatical structures including present progressives, plurals, possessives, past tenses, third-person singular, and adjectives.
Publisher: Communication Skill Builders, Tucson, Arizona, 1983.

The Templin-Darley Test of Articulation, 2nd Ed.

Authors: Mildred C. Templin and Frederic L. Darley

Age range: 3;0–8;0; production. Specific area tested—Form: phonology, sounds in words or sentences.

Publisher: Bureau of Educational Research and Service, University of Iowa, Iowa City, Iowa, 1969.

The Token Test for Children

Author: Frank Disimoni

Age range: 3;0–12;6; comprehension. Specific areas tested—Form: and content: receptive language skills.

Publisher: DLM Teaching Resources, Allen, Texas, 1978.

Vocabulary Comprehension Scale

Author: Tina E. Bangs

Age range: 2;0–6;0; comprehension. Specific areas tested—Form: syntax, grammatical structures including pronouns, adjectives; Content: vocabulary comprehension of pronouns, prepositions, and adjectives (quality, quantity, and size).

Publisher: DLM Teaching Resources Corporation, Allen, Texas, 1975.

The Initial Communication Process

Authors: T. Schery and A. Glover

Age range: Birth–3 years; comprehension and production. Observational scales format. Specific areas tested—Form: auditory skills, vocal, verbal, and oral motor skills; Content: manipulative and symbolic play skills; Use: social and pragmatic development.

Publisher: Publishers Test Service, Monterey, California, 1982.

REFERENCES

Arkes, H. (1981). Impediments to accurate clinical judgment and possible ways to minimize their impact. *Journal of Consulting and Clinical Psychology, 49,* 323–330.

Bangs, T. E. (1975). *Vocabulary comprehension scale.* Allen, TX: Learning Concepts.

Bangs, T. E., & Dodson, S. (1979). *Birth to three developmental scale.* Allen, TX: DLM Teaching Resources.

Bates, E., (1979). *The emergency of symbols* New York: Academic Press.

Bates, E., Camaioni, L., & Volterra, V. (1975). The acquisition of performatives prior to speech. *Merrill-Palmer Quarterly, 21* 205–206.

Benedict, H., (1979). Early lexical development: Comprehension and production. *Journal of Child Language, 6,* 183–200.

Bloom, L., & Lahey, M. (1978). *Language development and language disorders.* New York: Wiley.

Bowen, M. L., & Chalfant, J. C. (1981). *Receptive language inventory.* Tigard, OR: C. C. Publications.

Bricker, W. A., & Bricker, D. D. (1976). The infant, toddler, and preschool research and intervention project. In T. Tjossem (Ed.), *Intervention strategies for high-risk infants and young children.* Baltimore: University Park Press.

Bronfenbrenner, U. (1975a). Is early intervention effective? In M. Gutlentag & E. Struening (Eds.), *Handbook of evaluation research* (Vol. 2). Beverly Hills, CA: Sage.

Bronfenbrenner, U. (1975b). Is early intervention effective? In B. Z. Friedlander, G. M. Sterritt, & G. E. Kirk (Eds.), *Exceptional infant assessment and intervention* (Vol. 3). New York: Brunner/Mazel.

Brown, R., (1973). *A first language.* Cambridge,: Harvard University Press.

Bzoch, K. R., & League, R. (1971). *Receptive-expressive emergent language scale.* Gainsville. FL: The Tree of Life Press.

Carpenter, R. (1983, November). *Assessing prelinguistic and early linguistic behaviors in developmentally young children: Play scale.* Paper presented at the Annual Convention of the American Speech-Language-Hearing Association, Cincinnati.

Carpenter, R., Mastergeorge, A., & Coggins, T. (1983b). The acquisition of communicative intentions in infants eight to eighteen months of age. *Language and Speech, 26,* 101–116.

Chapman, R. (1978). Comprehension strategies in children. In J. F. Kavanagh & W. Strange (Eds.), *Speech and language in the laboratory, school and clinic.* Cambridge: The MIT Press.

Chapman, R. (1983). Deciding when to intervene. In J. Miller, D. Yoder, & R. Schiefelbusch (Eds.) *Contemporary issues in language intervention* (Asha Reports 12, pp. 221-225). Rockville, MD: The American Speech-Language-Hearing Association.

Clark, R. (1974). Performing without competence. *Journal of Child Language, 1,* 1–10.

Clark, R. (1978). Some even simpler ways to learn to talk. In N. Waterson & C. Snow (Eds.), *The development of communication.* New York: Wiley.

Coggins, T., & Carpenter, R. (1978). Introduction to the area of language development. In M. Cohen & P. Gross (Eds.), *The developmental resource: Behavioral sequences for assessment and program* (Vol. 2). New York: Grune & Stratton.

Coggins, T., & Carpenter, R. (1981). The communicative intention inventory: A system for observing and coding children's early intentional communication. *Applied Psycholinguistics, 2,* 235–251.

Coggins, T., Olswang, L. & Guthrie, J. (1987) Assessing communicative intents in young children: Low structured observation or elicitation tasks? *Journal of Speech and Hearing Disorders, 52,* 44–49.

Cook-Gumperz, J., & Corsaro, W. (1977). Social-ecological constraints on children's communication strategies. *Sociology, 11,*411–434.

Cooper, M. (1979). Verbal interactions in nursery school. *British Journal of Educational Psychology, 49,* 214–225.

Cromer, R. F. (1976). The cognitive hypothesis of language acquisition and its implications for child language deficiencies. In D. M. Morehead & A. E. Morehead (Eds.), *Normal and deficient child language.* Balitimore: University Park Press.

Crystal, D., Fletcher, P., & Garman, M. (1976). *The grammatical analysis of language disability.* London: Edward Arnold.

Darley, F.L. (1978). A philosophy of appraisal and diagnosis. In F. L. Darley & D. C. Spriestersbach (Eds.), *Diagnostic methods in speech pathology* (2nd ed.), New York: Harper & Row.

Denes, P. B., & Pinson, E. N.(1963). *The speech chain: The physics and biology of spoken language.* Garden City, NY: Anchor Press.

deVilliers, J., & deVilliers, P. (1973). A cross-sectional study of the acquisition of grammatical morephemes in child speech. *Journal of Psycholinguistic Research, 2,* 267–278.

Dore, J. (1974). A pragmatic description of early language development. *Journal of Psycholinguistic Research, 4,* 343–350.

Dore, J. (1975). Holophrases, speech acts and language universals. *Journal of Child Language, 2,*21–39.

Dunn, L. M., & Dunn, L. M (1980). *Peabody picture vocabulary test (PPVT-R).* Circle Pines, MN: American Guidance Service.

Eilers, R., Wison, W., & Moore, J. (1977). Developmental changes in speech discrimination in infants. *Journal of Speech and Hearing Research, 20,* 766-779.

Eimas, P., Siqueland, E., Jusczyk, P., & Vigorito, J. (1971). Speech perception in infants. *Science, 171,* 303–306.

Fey, M. (1986). *Language intervention with young children.* San Diego: College-Hill Press.

Gallagher, T. (1983). Pre-assessment: A procedure for accommodating language use variability. In T. Gallagher & C. Prutting (Eds.), *Pragmatic assessment and intevention issues in language* (pp.1-28). San Diego: College Hill Press.

Halliday, M. A. K. (1975). *Learning how to mean: Explorations in the development of language.* London: Edward Arnold.

Hayden, A. H., & Haring, N. G. (1976). Early intervention for high risk infants and young children: Programs for Down's syndrome children. In T. Tjossem (Ed.), *Intervention strategies for high-risk infants and young children.* Baltimore: University Park Press.

Horstmeier, D., & MacDonald, J. (1978) *Environmental pre-language battery.* Columbus, OH: Charles E. Merrill.

Johnston, J., & Schery, T. (1976). The use of grammatical morphemes by children with comunication disorders. In D. Morehead & A. Morehead (Eds.) *Normal and deficient child language*. Baltimore: University Park Press.

Kemp, J. C. (1983). The timing of language intervention for the pediatric population. In J. Miller, D. Yoder, & R. Schiefelbusch (Eds.), *Contemporary issues in language intervention* (Asha Reports 12, pp.183-195). Rockville, MD: The American Speech-Language-Hearing Association.

Leonard, L. (1983). Defining the boudaries of language disorders in children. In J. Miller, D. Yoder, & R. Schiefelbusch (Eds.), *Contemporary issues in language intervention* (Asha Reports 12, pp. 107-112). Rockville, MD: The American Speech-Language-Hearing Association.

Leonard, L., Bolders, J., & Miller, J. (1976). An examination of the semantic relations reflected in the language usage of normal and language disordered children. *Journal of Speech and Hearing Research, 19,* 371–392.

Leonard, L., Camarata, S., Rowan, L., & Chapman, K. (1982). The communicative functions of lexical usage by language-impaired children. *Applied Psycholinguistics, 3,* 109–126.

Liebergott, J., Bashir, A., & Schultz, M. (1984). Dancing around and making strange noises: Children at risk. In A. Holland (Ed.), *Language disorders in children*. San Diego: College-Hill Press.

Lund, N., & Duchan, J. (1983). *Assessing children's language in naturalistic contexts*. Englewood Cliffs, N.J.: Prentice-Hall.

Lyman, H. B. (1978) *Test scores and what they mean* (3rd ed.) Englewood Cliffs, NJ: Prentice-Hall.

MacDonald, J. (1978). *Environmental language inventory*. Columbus, OH: Charles E. Merrill.

McCormick, L. (1984). Perspectives on categorization and intervention. In L. McCormick & R. Schiefelbusch (Eds.), *Early language intervention*. Columbus, OH: Charles E. Merrill.

Meitus, I., & Weinberg, B. (Eds.). (1983). *Diagnosis in speech-language pathology*. Baltimore: University Park Press.

Miller, J. (1978). Assessing children's language behavior: A developmental process approach. In R. L. Schiefelbusch (Ed.), *Bases of language intervention*. Baltimore: University Park Press.

Miller, J. (1981). Assessing language production in children. Baltimore: University Park Press.

Miller, J., Chapman, R., Branston, M., & Reichle, J. (1980). Comprehension development in sensorimotor stages 5 and 6. *Journal of Speech and Hearing Research, 23,* 284–311.

Minifie, F. D., Hixon, T. J., & Williams, F. (1973). *Normal aspects of speech, hearing and language*. Englewood Cliffs, NJ: Prentice-Hall.

Nation, J. E., & Aram, D. M. (1984). *Diagnosis of speech and language disorders* (2nd ed.). San Diego: College Hill Press.

Nelson, K. (1973). Structure and strategy in learning to talk. *Monographs of the Society for Research in Child Development, 38*(1–2, Serial No. 149).

Newman, P. W., Low, G. M., Haws, R. J., & Bone, J. W. (1973). Communication, its disorders and professional implications. *Asha, 15,* 290–293.

Oller, D. K. (1980). The emergence of the sounds of speech in infancy. In G. Yeni-Komshian, J. Kavanagh, & C. Ferguson (Eds.), *Child phonology: Vol. 1. Production*. New York: Academic Press.

Olswang, L. (1983, November). *Assessing prelinguistic and early linguistic behaviors in developmentally young children: Cognitive antecedents to word meaning scale*. Paper presented at the annual convention of the American Speech-Language-Hearing Association, Cincinnati.

Olswang, L., & Carpenter, R. (1978). Elicitor effects on the language obtained from young language-impaired children. *Journal of Speech and Hearing Disorders, 43,* 76–88.

Olswang, L., Bain, B., Rosendahl, P., Oblak, S. & Smith, A. (1986). Language learning: moving performance from a context dependent to independent state. *Child Language Teaching and Therapy, 2,* 180–210.

Olswang, L., & Carpenter, R. (1982). Ontogenesis of agent: Linguistic expression. *Journal of Speech and Hearing Research, 25,* 306–313.

Olswang, L., Stoel-Gammon, C., Coggins, T., & Carpenter, R. (1987). *Assessing prelinguistic and early linguistic behaviors in developmentally young children*. Seattle, WA: University of Washington Press.

Peters, A. (1977). Language learning strategies: Does the whole equal the sum of the parts? *Language, 53,* 560–573.

Piaget, J. (1952). *Origins of intelligence in children*. New York: International Universities.

Piaget, J. (1954). *The construction of reality in the child*. New York: Basic Books.

Poole, E. (1934). Genetic development of articulation of consonant sounds in speech. *Elementary English Review, 11,* 159–161.

Prather, E., Hedrick, D., & Kern, C. (1975). Articulation development in children aged two to four years. *Journal of Speech and Hearing Disorders, 40,* 179–191.

Prutting, C., Gallagher, T., & Mulac, A. (1975). The expressive portion of the NSST compared to a spontaneous language sample. *Journal of Speech and Hearing Disorders, 40,* 40–48.

Ramey, C. T., Sparling, J. J., & Waslik, B. H. (1981) Creating social environments to facilitate language development, In R. L. Schiefelbusch & D. D. Bricker (Eds.), *Early language: Acquisition and intervention* (pp. 447–476). Baltimore: University Park.

Richardson, S. (1982). Historical perspectives. In D. McClowry, A. Guilford, & S. Richardson (Eds.), *Infant communication* (pp. 1–8). New York: Grune and Stratton.

Robinson, H. B., & Robinson, N. M. (1971). Longitudinal development of very young children in a comprehensive day care program: The first two years. *Child Development, 42,* 1673–1683.

Rondal, J. (1980) Father's and mother's speech in early language development. *Journal of Child Language, 7,* 353–371.

Sachs, J., & Truswell, L. (1976). Comparison of two-word instructions by children in the one-word stage. *Papers and Reports on Child Language Development, 12,* 212–220.

Sanders, E., (1972). When are speech sounds learned? *Journal of Speech and Hearing Disorders, 37,* 55–63.

Sattler, J. M. (1982). *Assessment of children's intelligence and special abilities* (2nd ed.). Boston: Allyn and Bacon.

Schiefelbusch, R., & McCormick, L. (1984). Initial and ongoing assessment. In L. McCormick & R. Schiefelbusch (Eds.), *Early language intervention* (pp. 117–156). Columbus, OH: Charles E. Merrill.

Schlesinger, I. (1971). Production of utterances and language acquisition. In D. Slobin (Ed.), *The ontogenesis of grammar* (pp. 63–101). New York: Academic.

Scott, C., & Taylor, A. (1978). A comparison of home and clinic gathered language samples. *Journal of Speech and Hearing Disorders, 43,* 482–495.

Scott, C., Palin, S., & Davidson, A. (1979, November). *Semantic and pragmatic coding of early child language: Methodological and sampling issues.* Paper presented at the Annual Convention of the American Speech-Language-Hearing Association, Atlanta.

Shearer, D. E., & Shearer, M. S. (1976). The portage project: A model for early childhood intervention. In T. Tjossem (Ed.), *Intervention strategies for high-risk infants and children.* Baltimore: University Park Press.

Smith, P., & Daglish, L. (1977). Sex differences in parent and infant behavior in the home. *Child Development, 48,* 1250–1254.

Snyder, L. (1975). *Pragmatics in language disordered children: Their prelinguistic and early verbal performatives and presuppositions.* Unpublished doctoral dissertation, University of Colorado.

Snyder, L. (1978). Communicative and cognitive abilities and disabilities in the sensorimotor period. *Merrill-Palmer Quarterly, 24,* 161–180.

Stevens, K. N., & House, A. S., (1972). Speech preparation. In J. V.. Tobias (Ed.), *Foundations of modern auditory theory* (Vol. 2). New York: Academic Press.

Stoel-Gammon, C. (1985). Phonetic inventories, 15-24 months: A longitudinal study. *Journal of Speech and Hearing Research, 28,* 505–512.

Stoel-Gammon, C., & Dunn, C. (1984). *Normal and disordered phonology in children.* Baltimore: University Park Press.

Templin, M., (1957). Certain language skills in children: Their development and interrelationships. *Institute of Child Welfare* (Monograph 26). Minneapolis: University of Minnesota Press.

Uzgiris, I., & Hunt, J. McV. (1975). *Assessment in infancy.* Urbana: University of Illinois Press.

Wellman, B., Case, I., Mengurt, I., & Bradbury, D. (1931). Speech sounds of young children. *University of Iowa Studies in Child Welfare, 5.*

Wellman, H., & Lempers, J. (1977). The naturalistic communication abilities of two year olds. *Child Development, 48,* 1052–1057.

Wilkinson, L., Clevenger, M., & Dollaghan, C. (1981). Communication in small instructional groups: A sociolinguistic approach. In W. P. Dickson (Ed.), *Children's oral communication skills.* New York: Academic Press.

Zimmerman, I., Steiner, V., & Evatt, R. (1969). *Preschool language scale.* Columbus, OH: Charles E. Merrill.

16

Environmental Assessment of Developmentally Disabled Infants and Preschoolers

Theodore D. Wachs

In recent years there has been an increasing realization that not all of the dysfunctional behavior of the developmentally disabled can be attributed solely to biomedical factors. Although primary sensory or motor deficits have a biomedical etiology, many of the cognitive-social-emotional problems of the developmentally disabled, as described in Chapter 1, may have an environmental as well as a biological basis (Green & Durocher, 1965). The relevance of psychosocial environmental factors[1] to cognitive, social, or emotional development has been noted for the *hearing impaired* (Altshuler, 1974; Cheskin, 1981; Galenson, Miller, Kaplan & Rothstein, 1979; Sanders, 1980), the *visually impaired* (Willis, 1979), the *mentally retarded* (Poznanski, 1973), and the *motorically impaired* (Battle, 1977; Cruickshank, Hallahan & Bice, 1976; Lewandowski & Cruickshank, 1980; Shere & Kastenbaum, 1966; also see review in Chapter 1 by Wachs & Sheehan). Particularly for the hearing-impaired and the motorically impaired, most theorists hypothesize an interactive process, in which an initially less responsive handicapped child does not elicit the types of parental interactions necessary for optimal cognitive- social-emotional development (Greenberg & Marvin, 1979; Henggler & Cooper, 1983; Kogan, 1980; Richardson, 1969; Wedell-Monnig & Lumley, 1980).

If differences in the psychosocial environment are related to developmental outcomes for the young disabled child, the necessity of obtaining measures of the child's environment seems obvious. Environmental measurement may have its greatest utility in four areas: assessment, program planning, feedback to parents, and program evaluation.

---

[1]For this chapter, with a few exceptions (e.g., social support networks), psychosocial environment is defined primarily on the basis of parent–child interactions. We recognize that the child's environment consists of more than just parent–child interactions, involving not only different layers (ecological aspects of the environment and social systems) but also interactions among individuals not directly involving the child (second-order effects, such as those of marital relationships). However, for the developmentally disabled, consideration of these other aspects of the environment has rarely gone beyond the theoretical stage (Crnic, Friedrich, & Greenberg, 1983). Hence, by necessity, our discussion must be restricted primarily to that aspect of the child's psychosocial environment where the data are most available (parent–child interactions).

THEODORE D. WACHS • Department of Psychological Sciences, Purdue University, West Lafayette, Indiana 47905.

In terms of *assessment*, environmental measurement may be used to identify aspects of the child's psychosocial environment that are likely to inhibit the child's social or cognitive development, or to interfere with intervention attempts (Novak, Olley, & Kearney, 1980). Examples of this approach with the mentally retarded are seen in the work of Brassell (1977; Brassell & Dunst, 1978). Alternatively, environmental information can be used to *program* remedial approaches. A clinical example of this process is seen in case studies by Curson (1979), illustrating how observation of blind preschoolers' reactions to new situations were used by teachers to help them decide how best to work with individual children.

Environmental measurement can also be used to provide *feedback* to parents of developmentally disabled children. This feedback is most often provided through the videotaping of observations of parent–child interactions. These videotapes are then used to illustrate developmental principles or inappropriate behaviors to the parents. Examples of these approaches are seen in Fraiberg's work (1971) with blind infants and their caregivers, in the work of Mash and Terdal (1973) with parents of profoundly retarded children, and in the work of Kogan (1980) with parents of physically handicapped children.

A final use of environmental measurement is in *program evaluation*. Environmental measurement is traditionally used to determine if interventions have influenced the patterns of parent–child interactions in the desired direction. An excellent description of this procedure is seen in a chapter by Johnson, Breckenridge, and McGowan (1984), using the Caldwell HOME Scale (Elardo & Bradley, 1981) as a measure of the impact of multidimensional intervention on the parents of young, disadvantaged Mexican-American infants. A similar approach, for the developmentally disabled, is shown in the work of Greenberg (1983) with young deaf children receiving early intervention. An alternative use of environmental measurement is seen in studies observing children's social interactions, to determine the impact of mainstreaming on the social development of disabled children (White, 1980).

Of even more interest may be environmental measurements that are conducted during the course of intervention. For example, Green and Durocher (1965) noted that the parents of disabled children may not be treating their children in the ways that intervention specialists have recommended. Similarly, Schlesinger and Meadow (1972) reported that, in spite of training to get parents to treat their hearing-impaired children as "normal," observations indicated that many of these children were still being overcontrolled by their parents. Even more subtly, environmental measurement may be useful in detecting unwanted negative by-products of intervention programs. An example is seen in data by Kogan, Tyler, and Turner (1974), who reported a decline in positive affect toward physically handicapped children—not only by their mothers, who were involved in training, but also by the children's physical therapist. These authors suggested that a lack of progress by the child in motor development may lead to frustration on the part of parents and therapists, causing the decline in positive affect.

Given the importance of measuring the young disabled child's psychosocial environment, the major question is how to best attempt this assessment. Historically, the approach to measuring environment has involved obtaining demographic measures, such as parental socioeconomic status or parental educational level. However, recent methodological reviews have pointed out the general inadequacy of using demographic measures to assess environment (Wachs & Gruen, 1982). The variability of the psychosocial environments encountered by children within a given SES level means that these measures can tell us little about the *specific experiences* of a particular child. The fact that social class and educational level *per se* account for significantly less variability in predicting subsequent functioning than do more detailed measures of the child's environment (Gottfried, 1984) only confirms the point that these demographic indices are poor substitutes for more precise environmental measures.

Given the inadequacy of demographic indices as measurements of the child's psychosocial environment, what procedures can be used? Here, we are faced with an embarrassment of riches. The clinician faced with the problem of measuring the child's psychosocial environment can choose between clinical interviews with the parents, questionnaires, attitude scales, and direct observation of parent–child interactions. The purpose of this chapter is to suggest procedures for choosing among these various alternatives. *The basic point to be made is that the choice of the approach to be used to measure the environment is not to be made arbitrarily.* Rather, choices must be based on how well the available instruments fit four specific criteria. *First*, there are standard psychometric criteria, such as reliability and validity. *Second*, the chosen instrument must be consistent with the purpose for which the environmental measurement is done and with the available resources (decision theory criteria). *Third*, there is the question of how representative of the child's environment the environmental measure is. The *final* criterion involves specification of how well measurements assess the environmental parameters relevant to the population under study.

A detailed discussion of each of these criteria is found in the next section.

CRITERIA FOR CHOICE OF PROCEDURES

Psychometric Considerations

In discussing criteria, a critical concern is to determine if evidence is available on the psychometric properties of our measures. Specifically, as in the case of direct observation procedures or in the case of clinical interviews, what are the interjudge reliabilities for these procedures? When scales or questionnaires are used, evidence on predictive or construct validity should be available.

These requirements may seem obvious, but all too often, environmental assessment procedures are used for which there are either no psychometric data available, or the clinician assumes reliability or validity when factors exist that negate this assumption. Reliabilities or validities established under one set of conditions may not generalize when measures are used in different situations or with different populations. In this situation, it may be necessary to reconfirm the adequacy of psychometric characteristics *before* using an instrument, so as to prevent the discovery of psychometric inadequacies only after measures have been taken. As an example, Brinick (1980) reported inadequate reliabilities for a high percentage of behavioral categories used in a study of mothers' interactions with their young deaf children. This lack of reliability occurred as a result of the low level of occurrence of these interaction categories. Interaction categories that rarely occur are more likely to be missed by one of the observers and hence are less likely to be reliable than more frequently occurring categories.

Instruments that do not have adequate reliability or validity are less likely to prove useful as measurements of the child's environment, regardless of what other desirable qualities they have (e.g., ease of examiner use and good communication value to intervention specialists).[2]

Decision Theory and the Environmental Assessment Process

Earlier in this book, both Simeonsson and Bailey (Chapter 2) and Hubert and Wallander (Chapter 3) discussed the relevance of a decision theory approach to test selection. A similar orientation can be used in the selection of environmental assessment procedures as well. In selecting tests, Hubert and Simeonsson stressed the importance of delineating the purpose for which the test is to be used, both as a means of evaluating the adequacy of test reliability and validity and as a means of aiding in test selection. Similarly, for environmental assessment, it is important to ask what the purpose of the assessment is. For example, we may wish to determine if the environment of the child is so inadequate as to make the environment one more risk factor that must be considered when designing an intervention procedure, or our purpose may be to determine which specific aspect of the child's environment should become the focus of intervention. Similarly, our purpose may be to assess mother–infant interactions in terms of how the mother feels about her disabled infant, or our purpose may be to determine what the mother does with her disabled infant. Each of these questions will call for a different level of sensitivity. For example, the level of sensitivity required to detect whether the child's environment will inhibit intervention attempts is lower than the sensitivity needed to provide information to parents about which specific child–parent interactions need to be modified.

Relevant to the above discussion is the sensitivity–cost ratio of available procedures. In traditional test theory, *sensitivity* refers to the accuracy with which a measure assesses a phenomenon (e.g., how accurate a measure of the child's home environment Measure X is). *Cost* refers not only to the cost of testing materials, but also to variables like the time involved in giving the procedure. In general, for environmental assessments, the more detailed or direct the assessment, the more costly it will be in terms of personnel qualification, personnel time, and personnel training. Thus, interview procedures and questionnaires tend to be *less costly* but also *less sensitive* than direct observation procedures. This does not automatically make direct observation the method of choice. Observations may be justified as a procedure when we need assessments of great sensitivity, regardless of cost. In this case, the use of questionnaires and interviews would not be warranted, as these procedures would not provide us with sensitive enough information to fulfill our purpose. However, if our goal is environmental screening, the less costly, less detailed questionnaires or interviews may be more useful. In this second case, direct observational procedures would be unwarranted, as the cost would not in any way justify the use to which this information would be put (see Chapter 3, Hubert & Wallander, for a more detailed discussion of this point).

Viewing the selection of environmental assessment procedures in terms of a decision-theory model involves a three-stage process. The first stage is formulating the *pur-*

---

[2]In discussing psychometrics, we must keep in mind that adequacy of reliability and validity for a specific measure is not an absolute; rather it is determined by the purposes for which the measure is to be used (Cronbach & Glaser, 1965). For a detailed discussion of this point, see Chapter 3, by Hubert and Wallander.

pose of the assessment. The second stage is determining both the degree of *assessment sensitivity* necessary to accomplish the stated purposes and the *resources* available in terms of time, funds, and personnel. The third stage is to survey the available environmental-assessment procedures in terms of psychometric adequacy (more reliable and valid measures are also likely to be more sensitive), cost, and sensitivity, and to determine which assessment procedure best *matches* the purpose and the resources specified in the second stage. In the third, compromise may often be necessary, as when the most sensitive or adequate procedure is beyond the resources of the clinic. In making these compromises, selection should not be done randomly, or on the basis of picking the cheapest procedure. Rather, the procedure chosen must be the most adequate, sensitive, and appropriate for the purpose intended, given the available resources.

What this means in practice is that there is no recommended single procedure for measuring the young disabled child's psychosocial environment. The choice of an instrument becomes a function of the clinician's balancing the strengths, weaknesses, and costs of the available instruments with the types of data that must be obtained. When trade-offs between sensitivity and cost must be made, it is critical to specify how the instruments will be used, so as to make the best choice.

Representativeness of Environmental Assessments

In addition to psychometric and decision theory considerations, a third major criterion of the adequacy of environmental assessment involves representativeness. Specifically, with how much confidence can we assert that the information we obtain about the nature of the child's psychosocial environment is *truly representative* of the experiences that the child normally encounters? There are *three aspects* of this question that must be considered.

The first aspect has to do with the *number of measurements* made before drawing conclusions about the nature of the child's psychosocial environment. As a general principle, the smaller the data base, in terms of the number of measurements, the less likely it is that our information will be representative of the child's actual environment (Rushton, Brainerd, & Pressley, 1983). Thus, a single short-duration observation of the child's environment tends to show little stability across time (Wachs, 1985). What this means in practice is that, just as the quality of the decisions based on very short tests will be quite low (Traub & Rawley, 1980), so the quality of the decisions based on a single environmental measurement are also likely to be low.

It is possible to overcome this problem by using repeated measurements. However, repeated measurements are very costly in terms of effort. It is also possible to use a more intensive single assessment. Comparing stability coefficients across studies, we find little difference in stability between repeated short-duration observations (45 minutes per observation) (Wachs, 1985) and a single long-duration observation (3 hours of observation) (Lytton, 1980). Although somewhat less costly than repeated measurement, intensive measurement also requires a considerable investment of staff time. The least costly approach is to use data sources such as parental reports, based either on interview or on questionnaires. Empirically, these sources can be viewed as representing summaries of the parents' repeated interactions with their child (Epstein, 1980). However, parental reports have their own set of problems, which will be discussed below (also see Chapter 5 by Sheehan, on parental involvement).

A second aspect of representativeness has to do with the influence of differing *situations* on the types of information being obtained. A number of studies using young handicapped populations have pointed to strong situational influences. In one of the earliest studies looking at this phenomenon, Kogan *et al.* (1974) reported that observers rated much higher negative affect between physically handicapped preschoolers and their mothers when the mother was involved in physical therapy with the child than when the mother and child were involved in free play. Obviously, conclusions drawn about parent–child interactions based on only one of these situations would be highly misleading.

More recent research has looked at situational influences on peer interactions with handicapped children. These data indicate clear differences in interaction patterns as a function of whether the interaction occurs in a setting conducive to gross-motor activities or whether it occurs in settings involving less active free-play (Guralnick, 1981; Novak *et al.*, 1980), as a function of the degree of adult interaction with the children (Novak *et al.*, 1980; Shores, Hester, & Strain, 1976) and as a function of the degree of structure provided by adults (Shores *et al.*, 1976).

Given the above, if clinicians wish to generalize their conclusions or recommendations beyond a narrow class of settings or situations, interactions should be sampled across a variety of situations. Again, however, such an approach may be quite costly.

A third aspect of representativeness encompasses parents responding or behaving in ways that are not characteristic of the normal interactions that they have with their child.[3] Most evidence of *parental bias* has involved either clinical interviews or parents questionnaires, though evidence also exists for nonrepresentative parent behavior during directly observed parent–child interactions (Cheskin, 1981). Biased reporting is most likely to occur when the parents of developmentally disabled children (or the parents of nondisabled children) feel that they are "on display" when observed or questioned. In this situation, the parents may act to convince the clinician that they are adequate parents, rather than to show how they characteristically behave toward their child. The use of "lie scales" in questionnaires or of repeated direct observations appears to be the most effective means of avoiding this particular problem (Wachs, 1985).

Applicability to the Population

As a general rule, randomly selected environmental parameters will be of little use to the clinician. Rather, environmental parameters should be selected that are of *particular relevance* to specific aspects of development for children with specific disabilities. Even in the early 1970s, it is unlikely that such a statement would have been made. At that time, we were operating under the assumption of a global model of environmental action, so that we thought only two relevant aspects of the environment needed to be considered: positive environmental stimulation and negative environmental stimulation. Under the assumptions of a global model, positive environmental stimulation was thought to facilitate all aspects of development for all individuals. Negative environmental stimuli were thought to inhibit all aspects of development for all individuals.

More recent theoretical formulations have rejected this global model in favor of models emphasizing more specific patterns of environment–development relationships

---

[3] A variant of this problem is seen in Chapter 5, where Sheehan discusses why the parents of handicapped children overestimate or underestimate their child's level of functioning.

(Wachs & Gruen, 1982). Specifically, the available evidence now suggests that different aspects of the environment are relevant to different aspects of developmental for different individuals at different ages. Thus, the same patterns of stimulation that facilitate cognitive growth may be irrelevant to social-emotional development. The patterns of stimulation relevant to the development of normal infants may be irrelevant or even detrimental to the development of risk infants. Said differently, we have come to recognize that there is no longer such a thing as a totally "good" or "bad" environment. Rather, we must ask, "Good (or bad) for what and for whom?"

What are the implications of this shift in our understanding of the nature of the environment? Although these assumptions are often not explicitly stated, the majority of clinicians working with the developmentally disabled apparently assume that the same environmental parameters relevant to the development of younger nondisabled infants and toddlers are also relevant to the development of older handicapped children (Wachs & Gruen, 1984). However, there is virtually no empirical evidence to support the validity of this assumption. Quite the contrary, evidence from a variety of sources, including *reviews of development in the handicapped* (Battle, 1977; Tjossem, 1976), *intervention projects used with the motorically impaired* (Kogan, 1980), *observational studies of mother–child interactions in handicapped infants and preschoolers* (Fraiberg, 1968; Greenberg & Field, 1982; Smith & Hagen, in press), *survey studies on the relevance of maternal achievement attitudes to the development of the deaf* (Gordon, 1959), and *experimental studies on the relationship of maternal language to development in the retarded* (Cheseldine & McConkey, 1979; Petersen & Sherrod, 1982)—all point to the opposite conclusion: *Different aspects of the environment may be relevant to the development of the normal and the developmentally disabled.* Even within a given diagnostic group, different aspects of the environment may have to be considered, based on different functional characteristics, such as the level of communication in the deaf (Greenberg & Marvin, 1979) and the level of cognitive functioning in the retarded (Cunningham, Reuler, Blackwell, & Deck, 1981).

The principle that different aspects of the environment may be relevant to development in different diagnostic groups (or subgroups within a diagnostic group) implies that an identical set of environmental dimensions should not be assessed across all groups of the developmentally disabled. Rather, assessment dimensions should be tailored to the specific groups under consideration. However, tailoring environmental dimensions to groups implies that we have a solid knowledge of what aspects of the environment are *uniquely* related to development, for each type of developmental disability. Unfortunately, such direct knowledge is lacking at present. However, some tentative conclusions can be drawn from existing clinical and intervention studies, plus the few available studies on the disabled and environment–development relationships. With this information, we can make some recommendations about which environmental dimensions may be of particular salience when we assess the environments of specific groups of developmentally disabled children. These data are summarized in Table 1. The first group of cited studies compares the disabled and the nondisabled and indicates environmental parameters that may be of specific salience for the disabled. The latter group of studies refers only to parameters that have been identified as relevant to the development of disabled infants and preschoolers, with no implication of their relevance to the nondisabled.

Table 1. Environmental Dimensions That Have Been Shown to Be Relevant to the Functioning of the Young Developmentally Disabled Child

Group	Dimensions	Reference
All developmentally disabled versus nondisabled	Developmentally disabled infants and pre-schoolers appear to have higher stimulation thresholds then nondisabled infants and pre-schoolers (i.e., stimulation levels that would be optimal for the nondisabled could be functionally understimulating for the developmentally disabled).	Greenberg & Field (1982)
Mentally retarded versus nonretarded	Availability of object in the environment appears to have special alience for the cognitive development of older retarded infants as compared to normals.	Smith & Hagen (1984)
Mentally retarded	Availability of objects in the environment facilates cognitive development.	Piper & Ramsey (1980)
	Variety of available stimulus material, organization of the environment, and maternal involvement with the child facilitates cognitive development.	Smith & Hagen (1987); Piper & Ramsey (1980)
	Maternal referencing of objects for the child facilitates cognitive developments.	Smith & Hagen (1984)
	Combination of high maternal directiveness and high maternal sensitivity to the child facilitates cognitive development.	Crawley & Spicker (1983)
Hearing-impaired	Excessive maternal control may inhibit language development.	Cunningham *et al.*, (1981)
	Excessive maternal control or intrusiveness may inhibit social and language development.	Brinick (1980); Cheskin (1981, 1982); Schlesinger & Meadow (1972)
Severely behaviorally disordered	Quality of family communication may inhibit or promote behavior disorder in predisposed individuals.	Doane (1978)
	Parental availability and responsivity may inhibit development of severe behavioir disorders in risk populations.	Baldwin, Cole & Baldwin (1982)
Motorically impaired	Availability of objects in the environment has lowered salience for development of motorically impaired.	Shere & Kastenbaum (1966)
Visually impaired	Few empirical data available.	

Given the data in Table 1, several conclusions can be drawn about the applicability of environmental measures to different populations of disabled children. First, with our limited knowledge base, the most appropriate environmental measures would be broad-scale, assessing a variety of different aspects of the child's environment. Second, in interpreting and using the data from broad-scale measures, the clinician must be prepared to disregard certain environmental dimensions and to emphasize others for each specific population. Decisions about which dimensions to disregard or emphasize should be based on empirical evidence and clinical judgement, as in Table 1.

Summary

Thus far, we have identified the following principles to be used in guiding the selection of environmental measurement procedures for use with the young developmentally disabled child:

1. Determine the level of reliability and of construct validity.
2. Assess the degree to which the procedures are concordant with the purpose of the assessment, in terms of cost, psychometric considerations, and sensitivity.
3. Assess the degree to which the procedures yield representative measures of the child's environment.
4. Assess the degree to which the procedures, used for specific developmentally disabled populations, encompass the components of environment that are most salient for those aspects of development being studied.

Within this framework, we can now look at various environmental assessment procedures that either have been used with the young developmentally disabled child or are potentially useful with this population.

PROCEDURES FOR ENVIRONMENTAL ASSESSMENT

Clinical Interviews

Interview methods typically involve questioning the parent about the types of experiences provided to the child, about parent–child interactions, or about parent attitudes toward the child. Interviews may concern themselves either with events that occurred in the child's past (retrospective interviews) or events currently occurring (concurrent interviews). Interviews have been combined with direct observation, as in the case of the Caldwell HOME scales (Elardo & Bradley, 1981, see section on direct observations), but the present section is concerned primarily with interview methods *per se*.

The use of interview procedures to obtain information about the developmentally disabled child appears to be a common clinical practice. Reports on the use of specific interview formats, as a means of assessing the environment of developmentally disabled children, have appeared for a variety of groups including the *motorically impaired* (Shere & Kastenbaum, 1966), the *blind* (Wills, 1979), and the *hearing-impaired* (Greenberg, 1983; Schlesinger & Meadow, 1972).

The major virtue of interview procedures is clearly economy. Large amounts of information across a variety of areas can be gathered in a short time period (typically 1– 1½ hours). Interviews are also useful for obtaining information about events that rarely occur (e.g., out-of-town travel), which would be missed if the clinician relied solely on direct observation. Further, when a *knowledge base is available*, interview procedures can be revised to incorporate questions about those aspects of the environment that are of unique relevance to the particular disability being considered.

Although interview procedures have the virtues of economy and flexibility, there are also a number of problems in using interview procedures as an environmental assessment. One of the most obvious is the lack of psychometric data about interview procedures, particularly in terms of interjudge reliability on the *interpretation of the information* gathered during the interview. This problem can be partially overcome through the use of semistructured interviews, which encompass specific questions on specific areas. An example of the use of this type of procedure with normal infants, where reliability data are available, is seen in the use of the interview-based Satisfaction with Family Scale, which taps maternal feelings about her child and about her parental role (Ragozin, Basham, Crnic, Greenberg, & Robinson, 1982). Alternatively, interviewers can rate parents on specific areas following the interview. For example, Greenberg (1983) used interview data to rate the environments of young deaf children across four areas: parental overprotectiveness, quality of environment, and child adaptation and attachment. Interjudge reliabilities ranged from .84 to .93 across the four areas. A similar approach has also been used by Nihara, Mink, and Meyers (1985) to derive five environmental-quality scores from interviews with parents of older retarded children.

Even when satisfactory psychometric information is obtained about interview procedures, other difficulties with interviews must be noted. The validity of retrospective data concerning previously occurring parent–child interactions has become increasingly tenuous, given the large amount of evidence available indicating a lack of accuracy of retrospective parental reports (i.e., Yarrow, Campbell, & Burton, 1970). This problem can be overcome by focusing solely on current events within the interview.

Even with concurrent interviews, the problem remains of obtaining representative information. Reviews on the use of concurrent interview procedures with parents of nondisabled infants (Wachs & Gruen, 1982) note that, all too often, parent reports are based not on what the parents are doing with or feeling toward the child, but on what the parents feel they *ought* to be doing or feeling. The parents' conception about what they ought to be doing or feeling is very often based on social stereotypes about what a "good" parent is, or on what child guidance experts say parents should be doing. Although most evidence on this problem is based on research with nondisabled populations, a similar concern has been expressed when interviews are used as an assessment technique with parents of the handicapped (Kogan, Wineberger, & Bobitt, 1969). An example of this problem is seen in data from Shere and Kastenbaum (1966), who reported a clear discrepancy between what mothers say their physically handicapped infant does when left alone and what observers report the child is actually doing. These data suggest that great care must be taken in accepting parent reports as being representative of the child's actual environment.

One approach to dealing with this problem of nonrepresentative reporting by parents would be to use the child as the informant, particularly as events characterized in one way by the parent may not be construed in the same way by the child (Kagan, 1967). The major problem with this strategy is that the reports of children tend not to be reliable (stable) until around age 10 (Edelbrook, Costello, Dulcan, Kalas, & Conover, 1985). Obviously, this instability makes it difficult to interpret interview data obtained from children in the age range covered by this chapter.

The above discussion suggests that interview methods, though commonly used, are not likely to be a very accurate source of information about the environment of the young developmentally disabled child. Thus, these procedures can be recommended *only* in conjunction with more sensitive measures, or when cost factors are such as to rule out other, more sensitive approaches.

Parent Questionnaires

Parent questionnaires typically assess one of three things: (a) parent attitudes toward the child, (b) parent perceptions about the nature of the family environment, and (c) parent perceptions about the extent and value of nonfamily environmental factors, such as social support networks. In terms of parent attitudes, adequate measures *specifically* designed to be useful with young developmentally disabled populations are rarely found in the literature. The instrument most commonly used with parents of the developmentally disabled is the Parent Attitude Research Instrument (PARI) developed by Schaefer and Bell (1958). The PARI consists of 115 items measuring parental attitudes toward children and child rearing across 23 separate categories (e.g., fostering dependency, suppression of aggression, and approval of child activities). These categories can be collapsed into two bipolar dimensions: authoritarianism and warmth. Several studies have used the PARI with heterogeneous groups of disabled children of varying ages and have reported differences in child-rearing attitudes between parents whose children have different types of disabilities (Cook, 1963; Ricci, 1970). Although concern has been expressed that these differences in attitude may be a function of differences in parental educational level rather than of differences in the child's disability (Dingman, Eyman, & Windle, 1963), at least some of these differences do remain even after educational level has been statistically controlled (Cook, 1963).

Questionnaires rating perceptions of the parents of handicapped children about their family environments are somewhat more available. Some questionnaires have been used for highly specific purposes, like the instrument by Fox and Wise (1981), which is designed to elicit parents' perceptions about their retarded child's reinforcement preferences. Other instruments, such as Holroyd's Questionnaire on Resources and Stress (QRS), are more wide-ranging in scope. Specifically, the QRS consists of 285 true–false items, which are combined into 15 scales assessing various dimensions of the family environment and parents' problems with their children. The QRS is applicable to various handicapped groups, including the retarded (Holroyd & McArthur, 1976), the motorically impaired (Friedrich & Friedrich, 1981), the deaf (Greenberg, 1983), and the behaviorally disturbed (Holroyd & Guthrie, 1979). Data are available indicating a certain degree of construct validity for the QRS (Beckman, 1983; Holroyd & McArthur, 1976). The size of the original QRS, in terms of the number of questions, may offer some practical difficulties. However, a recent factor analysis of the QRS (Crnic, Friedrich, & Greenberg, 1983) has reduced the number of questions to a more manageable 52 items.

An alternative questionnaire, which has better psychometric properties, is the Family Environment Scale (FES—Moos & Moos, 1981). The FES is a 90-item true–false scale that assesses the social climate of the family across 10 dimensions, including family cohesion, family conflict, and family achievement orientation. Both reliability and validity data are available for the FES. This scale has been successfully used with families of older mentally retarded children (Mink, Nihara, & Meyers, 1983; Nihara, Meyers, & Mink, 1983; Nihara *et al.*, 1985).

The relevance of social support networks (defined as individuals within or outside the family who are available to offer physical or emotional support to the primary caregiver) to children's development and to adequate family functioning has been stressed both for nonhandicapped populations (Cochran & Brassard, 1979) and for the developmentally disabled (Crnic *et al.*, 1983; Lewandowski & Cruickshank, 1980). Of particular interest are data indicating that caregiver participation in intervention programs with at-risk infants may be minimal, *unless adequate social support is available* (Bee, Barnard, Eyres, Gray, Hammond, Spietz, Snyder, & Clark, 1982). Thus, in any intervention setting where mothers participate in the treatment, the relevance of assessing the degree of social support available to the mother seems critical. Of the instruments available for this purpose that have been used with developmentally disabled populations, the measure devised by Suelzel and Keenan (1981) has sparse psychometric data, and its extreme length (57 pages) makes its utility dubious. The Nuckols Social Support Inventory, as revised by Friedrich (1979) for use with the parents of developmentally disabled children, appears to have satisfactory internal consistency but poor concurrent validity. A more satisfactory measure may be the Social Networks Form (SNF), designed by Weinraub and Wolf (1983). This 23-item instrument assesses the availability of social support across five dimensions, including emotional support, practical help, and satisfaction with support. Data are available on both stability of maternal perceptions and construct validity. Although the use of this scale with developmentally disabled populations has not yet been reported, the SNF has been used with populations that are at environmental risk.

How well do questionnaire procedures for environmental assessment with the developmentally disabled fit the criteria delineated earlier? Like interview methods, questionnaires provide an economical and varied data source. Unlike interviews, data on the psychometric properties of questionnaires are often available.[4] Questionnaires have been used successfully with parents of children with a variety of developmental disabilities. Unfortunately, with one exception, questionnaires have the same problem of representativeness of data as do interview procedures. Although questionnaires may not be as vulnerable as interviews to parental distortion or nonrepresentative responding, there is ample opportunity in the questionnaire format for parents to respond in ways that do not reflect the reality of the child's environment (Wachs & Gruen, 1982). This is particularly true of questionnaires assessing parental attitudes and parental perceptions about the nature of the family environment. For attitudinal and family environment measures, this problem suggests caution in the use of these procedures as the *sole* measure of the child's psychosocial environment.[5]

For questionnaires measuring social support networks, an argument can be made that what is critical is the caregiver's perception of the existence of these networks. If the

---

[4]For example, Freese and Thoman (1978) reviewed the psychometric adequacy of five instruments assessing mothers' perceptions of their experiences with their infants in the first month of life. Although some of these instruments clearly have adequate psychometric properties, the restrictive age range for these procedures makes their use with handicapped populations questionable, at least for clinical work.

[5]One possible approach to dealing with this problem is through the use of sib questionnaires (e.g., Daniels & Plomin, 1985). These may be useful as a cross-check, in terms of comparing parents' responses about the environment provided to their handicapped child with sib perceptions about the environment provided.

caregiver feels that social support is available, the caregiver may well behave as if this support is available, whether it is or not. Hence, by assessing maternal perceptions about the existence of social support networks, instruments like the SNF may avoid the whole question of the representativeness of information. Social network questionnaires appear to avoid many existing problems and may be useful as an efficient, low-cost approach to measuring this aspect of the environment.

Direct Observation

Direct observation encompasses the recording of naturally occurring child–caregiver interactions. Observations may be done either in the child's home or in some neutral setting, such as a laboratory playroom. Direct observation may involve no constraints on either parent or child (free play), or it may involve structuring the observational setting in specific ways, either by providing specific toys or by providing specific tasks for the parent to do with the child (structured play). Observations may be either recorded directly (direct coding) or videotaped. The scoring of observational information may involve either counting the frequency of specific behaviors as they occur, or the rating of parent–child interactions on predetermined codes.

In comparing observation to other forms of environmental assessment, both advantages and disadvantages are associated with this approach. In terms of our criteria given earlier, reliability data are commonly obtained with observational procedures. Construct validity is assumed, as there are few inferences to be made when directly measuring caregiver–child interactions. In terms of representativeness, with *repeated observations*, the available evidence clearly indicates that parents revert to normal interaction patterns with their children, thus ensuring the representativeness of the information (Wachs, 1985; Wachs & Gruen, 1982). Unless previously established codes are used (as in the HOME scale–Elardo & Bradley, 1981), environmental observations have the flexibility to incorporate a variety of interaction dimesions, which may be unique to particular populations. When high sensitivity is needed (as when feedback must be provided to parents about specific interactions that may be detrimental to the development of their child), there appears to be no substitute for direct observation, *regardless of cost.*

Balanced against these positive aspects of observational assessments are several critical negatives. The main one is that observations are the most costly of the environmental assessment techniques. Among other things, cost involves time. Short-term single observations may be done, but these are less likely to provide us with representative information about naturally occurring parent–child interactions (Wachs, 1985). In good part, this is due to the increased probability of parents' reacting to the presence of an observer during the initial phases of observation (Wachs & Gruen, 1982). Cost can also involve personnel. Unless trained personnel are available, the staff must be trained to do observations. Training takes a good deal of time, but without training and the establishment of satisfactory interjudge reliability, observational data will be of little value. All of these factors must be considered in choosing whether or not to use direct observation.

In terms of observational assessment procedures used with the developmentally disabled, given the number and variety of observational approaches that are available, we have organized studies using these procedures in Table 2. Three sources of information are omitted from this table. The first are descriptions of observational procedures that,

Table 2. Studies Using Observational Procedures with the Young Developmentally Disabled Child

Reference	Setting	Observational type	Recording procedure	Codes	Comments
				IA. Mentally retarded infants	
Crawley & Spicker (1983)	Home	Free play with specific toys provided	20-min video-taping	Ratings of 10 mothers, 10 children, and 1 dyadic interaction. Maternal variables include directiveness, sensitivity, stimulation value and mood.	
Farran et al. (1984)	Home or clinic	Free play	20-min video-taping	Rating of amount, quality, and appropriateness of mother–child interaction in 11 areas (e.g., verbal and physical involvement, responsiveness, teaching).	Better data obtained on home ratings than in ratings done in clinic. Assumes that areas rated are those most relevant to development.
Piper & Ramsey (1980)	Home	Free play with questioning of mothers	direct coding	Caldwell HOME scale (Elardo & Bradley, 1981): rating of mother–child interactions across six areas (e.g., of environment, responsivity of caregiver, avoidance of punishment).	Approximately 90-min observation time required to get HOME codes.
Smith & Hagen (1984)	Home	Free play	1½–2 hr of observation with direct coding	At 6½-months codes used are those devised by Yarrow, Rubenstein, & Pedersen (1975). These rate the occurrence of specific behaviors across seven interaction categories (vocal stimulation, social stimulation, tactual stimulation) plus three categories coding the inanimate environment. At 17 months, codes devised by Clarke-Stewart (1973)	

used. These rate occurrences of 17 interaction categories (physical stimulation, vocalization, directs).

IB. Mentally retarded preschoolers

	Setting	Task	Method	Measures	Comments
Buckhalt et al. (1978)	Preschool waiting-room	Free play	5-min videotaping	Time sampling of occurrence of maternal vocalization, looking, and touching.	For waiting-room procedure mother is told that she will have to wait while equipment is being set up. Child is placed in chair, and mother is seated near child next to table with magazines. Two observers needed to code.
Cunningham et al. (1981)	Playroom	Both free and structured play	15-min direct coding for both free and structured situations	Behavior ratings across seven months–child interaction categories (e.g., questions, responds, encourages, play, rewards compliance).	
Filler & Bricker (1976)	Laboratory	Structured and teaching task	Videotape of 18 min across each of 3 days	Rating of mother–infant interaction during teaching task across 12 categories (e.g., verbal direction, cueing, demonstrating, use of feedback).	
Kogan et al. (1974)	Playroom	Structured play	Auditory recording of vocalization plus direct coding of nonverbal interaction for 36 min each on two occasions	Occurrence of 43 behavioral codes (e.g., visual contact, expressive behavior) plus three summary ratings (e.g., involvement).	

(continued)

Table 2. (Continued)

Reference	Setting	Observational type	Recording procedure	Codes	Comments
Marshall, Hegrenes, & Goldstein (1973)	Laboratory	Free play	Auditory recording of vocalizations for 15 min	Vocalization categorized into four codes derived from Skinner's verbal operant model (e.g., mand, tact).	Two observers needed.
Novak et al. (1980)	Preschool	Freeplay	3 min of direct coding over 4-day cycle for 8–12 weeks.	Frequency of occurrence of 20 peer-interaction social codes (e.g., passive play, aggressiveness).	
Terdal, Jackson, & Garner (1976)	Playroom	Both free and structured play	15-min direct coding for both free and structured play	Frequency of occurrence of specific mother–child interactions (e.g., commands, praises).	
White ((1980)	Preschool	Both free and structured play	Direct coding for 20 min across four occasions.	Frequency of occurrence of specific social behaviors during peer interactions (e.g., inappropriate behavior, alone time) plus observers' ratings of quality of play.	
Wulbert et al. (1975)	Home	Free play with questioning of mother	Direct coding	Caldwell HOME (see Piper & Ramsey under IA).	

IIA. *Hearing-impaired infants*

No procedures reported in available literature

IIB. *Hearing-impaired Preschoolers*

Brinick (1980)	Laboratory	Both free and structured play	Videotaping of 12 min free play and 8 min structured play	8 behavior codes of mother–child interaction (e.g., attention getting, control, instructs).
Cheskin (1982)	Home	Free play	Direct coding of 15-min observation	10 rating codes based on functions of maternal language to child (e.g., controlling, describing).
Greenberg (1980)	Playroom	Structured	15-min videotaping observations.	Ratings of communication competence and social interaction between mother and child plus a rating of functional language systems used in the interactions.
Henggler & Cooper (1983)	Home	Free play and mother teaching situation	Videotaping of 15-min free play and 7-min teaching interaction	Number of times behavior occurs across 10 maternal interaction codes (e.g., responsivity, control) plus child's response to control. Includes a section during observation when mother leaves child alone in room.
Novak et al. (1980); see also reference by this author IB.				

(*continued*)

Table 2. (Continued)

Reference	Setting	Observational type	Recording procedure	Codes	Comments
Schlesinger & Meadow (1972)	Playroom	Free and structured play	20-min of videotaping	Interactions rated across 10 maternal dimensions (e.g., control, intrusiveness) plus 10 child dimensions and 10 interactive dimensions.	

IIIA. Motor-Impaired Infants

Farran et al. (1984); also see reference by these authors under IA.					
Kogan et al. (1974)	Clinic	Free play and child interaction while child getting physical therapy	Either videotaping or direct observation can be used 12 min per observation	Rating of caregive control, affection, and involvement.	

IIIB. Motor-Impaired Preschoolers

Kogan et al. (1974); see also reference by these authors under IIIA.					

Kogan (1980)	Clinic	Free play	Videotape of 30 min of interaction repeated once	Coded occurrence or nonoccurrence of seven categories (e.g., attention, acceptance of control).	Assumes a knowledge of how interactions will influence development.
Shere & Kastenbaum (1966)	Home	Free play	Direct recording for two observations, with each observation approximately 2–3 hr	Observational notes coded into whether interactions fostered, inhibited, or did not effect emotional and social development of child.	
White (1980); also see reference by this author under IB.					

IVA. Visually impaired infants

Fraiberg (1968)	Home	Free play	Direct recording and videotaping	Observational ratings coded into global interaction categories.	Not clear what categories were derived or how ratings translated into categories.

IVB. Visually impaired preschoolers

No procedures reported in available literature.

although potentially useful with developmentally disabled populations, have, as yet, not been reported as being used with these populations. These include (a) procedures for assessing the infant's physical environment, such as the Purdue Home Stimulation Inventory (Wachs, Francis, & McQuiston, 1979); (b) social interaction codes that have been used primarily with at-risk populations (Baldwin, Cole, & Baldwin, 1982; Beckwith, Cohen, Kopp, Parmelee, & Marcy, 1976; Bee *et al.*, 1982); and (c) variations in the Caldwell HOME scale that have not been used with the developmentally disabled (Carew, 1980).

The second omission involves observational studies using microanalytic procedures. These procedures involve the very detailed (often frame-by-frame) analysis of videotapes of caregiver–child interactions. Although microanalytic procedures have been used with developmentally disabled populations, including the *blind* (Als, Tronik & Brazelton, 1980), the *deaf*, (Wedell-Monnig & Lumley, 1980), and the *behaviorally disturbed* (Kubicek, 1980; Martini, 1980), the tremendous investment in equipment, trained personnel, and time makes these procedures useful primarily for research purposes. Finally, studies that use observational techniques in which the prime focus is not psychosocial interactions have also been omitted. An example of these is the study of language interactions between mothers and hearing-impaired children (e.g., Cheskin, 1981; McKirdy & Blank, 1982).

Within these constraints, Table 2 shows the observational procedures currently available for assessing the psychosocial environment of the young developmentally disabled child.

In deciding which of the above environmental observational procedures are most useful, two factors must be kept in mind at all times. First, there is the question of which procedure is most useful for the particular decision or problem faced by the clinician; second is how well the procedure fits the criteria described earlier in this chapter. Without a knowledge of the first factor, there is little that can be done in this chapter to help the clinician decide. However, in terms of the criteria factor, certain suggestions can be made.

In terms of psychometric factors, most of the techniques shown in Table 2 have at least moderate reliability. Some have yielded satisfactory evidence for predictive validity as well (i.e., Crawley & Spicker, 1983; Filler & Bricker, 1976; Piper & Ramsey, 1980; Smith & Hagen, 1984). Predictive validity is particularly critical in terms of deciding which specific codes are to be used, as codes that do predict later functioning may be more salient for decision making than codes that are nonpredictive.

For the criterion of representativeness, as a general rule, assessments done in unfamiliar surroundings are less valid than observations made in the home (Belsky, 1980; Novak *et al.*, 1980; Wachs & Gruen, 1982), particularly if the observations are highly overt (Field & Ignatoff, 1981). However, home observation techniques may be more costly, in terms of personnel time, than observations done in a clinical setting, particularly when repeated observations must be done to increase the representativeness of the information obtained. One possible compromise would be to use a waiting-room observation technique (e.g., Buckhalt, Rutherford, & Goldberg, 1978) within the clinic setting, in conjunction with home observations, to minimize the number of times clinical personnel must be sent to homes to do observations. In contrast, if the purpose of observation involves measuring interactions during times when the child is being *trained* on specific intervention techniques, it may be more appropriate and cost-effective to do these observations in the clinic during training sessions, as there we can get directly at the interactions that are of most interest to the clinician. An example is seen in Kogan *et al.* (1974).

One other aspect of representativeness noted earlier is the need for repeated observations to minimize nonrepresentative behavior by parents. Based on our own data using nondisabled infants (Wachs, 1985), at least *three separate observations* are needed to minimize nonrepresentative responding. If repeated observations are not possible, one compromise would be to use a single long-term observation across a period of at least 3 hours (Lytton, 1980). Combining the data obtained in a single long-term observation may not yield as representative a sample of parental behavior as data from repeated observations, but is is more likely to yield representative data than information obtained from a single brief observation. Alternatively, if observations are to be done in a central setting, such as a clinic or a preschool, a variation of the technique used by Novak *et al.* (1980), in which very short observations (3 minutes per observation) are done in weekly cycles over a period of several months, may also prove to be a cost-effective way of obtaining representative data. In this type of situation, the observer focuses first on one child, obtains data, and then moves to the next child in the setting.

In term of the criterion of appropriateness for a specific population, adapting appropriate codes to the population under study appears to be a more valid procedure than using a set of already-established codes lacking predictive validity for the population under study. The one exception to this rule would be situations in which a set of established observational codes does have predictive validity for the specific population, as in the case of the HOME scale with the mentally retarded (Piper & Ramsey, 1980; Wulbert, Inglis, Kriegsman & Mills, 1975).

In terms of decision theory considerations, obviously the cost of the procedure is a major consideration. In general, direct coding is less costly than videotaping. Although many of the studies cited in Table 2 used videotaping for short periods, the potentially reduced cost of this procedure is misleading for several reasons. First, short-duration videotaped interactions are less likely to yield representative data and may thus represent a case of being penny-wise and pound-foolish. Second, the above figures represent only observational time; they do not take into account the time required to code the videotaped interactions. This time commitment may amount to as much as 2–3 minutes of coding for each 1 minute of observation time. The one situation in which videotapes may be particularly cost-effective is where we do not know exactly which of a long list of environmental dimensions is most relevant to the population under study. In contrast to direct coding, which often allows observers to code only a limited number of dimensions, videotaping allows as to repeatedly review tapes to code a variety of different dimensions, thus maximizing the chances of identifying the appropriate observational categories. Videotaping may also be particularly cost-effective when we wish to inform parents about their use of interaction patterns that may be detrimental. However, as in the data by Kogan (1980), this may be done much more cost-effectively through direct coding, with immediate feedback to the parent via earphones worn by the parent.

A decision theory perspective can also be useful when decisions must be made between using behavior ratings or coding the frequency of occurrence of specific behaviors. In general, if our purpose is to characterize the nature of caregiver interactions, ratings are much more useful. However, if our goal is to point out specific behaviors to parents, then the use of behavior codes may be more appropriate (e.g., Mash & Terdal, 1973).

CONCLUSIONS

In this chapter, we have reviewed various environmental assessment procedures available for use with developmentally disabled infants and children. The utility of these procedures for assessment, intervention, and program evaluation has been noted. The choice of which approach to use should be based on specific criteria, including *psychometric adequacy, the representativeness* of the information obtained, and the *appropriateness* of information for the population and parameters under consideration. Also relevant are criteria from decision theory, including the *cost of the assessment* and the *purposes* for which the assessment is done. With these criteria in mind, clinicians can make the appropriate choice of which environmental assessment procedure is most useful in their particular program. It should be stressed that this choice must be based on all of the criteria and not on just one. For example, if a choice is made just on the basis of cost (the cheapest) or on the basis of sensitivity (the most sensitive), the results are less likely to be useful to the clinician than those obtained when all of these parameters are simultaneously considered.

ACKNOWLEDGMENTS

The author gratefully acknowledges the comments of Robert Bradley and Rob Sheehan on a preliminary version of this chapter.

REFERENCES

Als, H., Tronick, E., & Brazelton, T. (1980). Stages of early behavioral organization: The study of a sighted infant and a blind infant in interaction with their mothers. In T. Field, S. Goldberg, N. D. Stern, & A. Sostek (Eds.), *High risk infants and children*. New York: Academic.

Altshuler, K. (1974). The social and psychological development of the child. In P. Fine (Ed.), *Deafness in infancy and early childhood*. New York: Medicam Press.

Baldwin, A., Cole, R., & Baldwin, C. (1982). Parental pathology, family interaction and the competence of the child in school. *Monograph of the Society for Research in Child Development, 47*, No. 5.

Battle, C., (1977). Disruption in the socialization of a young severely handicapped child. In R. Marinelli, & A. Dellorto (Eds.), *The psychological and social impact of physical disability*. New York: Springer.

Beckman, P. (1983). Influence of selected child characteristics on stress in families of handicapped infants. *American Journal on Mental Deficiency, 88*, 150–156.

Beckwith, L., Cohen, S., Kopp, C., Parmelee, A., & Marcy, J. (1976). Caregiver infant interaction and early cognitive development in preterm infants. *Child Development, 47*, 579–587.

Bee, H., Barnard, K., Eyres, S., Gray, C., Hammond, M., Spietz, A., Snyder, C., & Clark, B. (1982). Prediction of IQ and language skill from perinatal status, child performance, family characteristics and mother infant interaction. *Child Development, 53*, 1134–1156.

Belsky, J. (1980). Mother-infant at home and in the laboratory. *Journal of Genetic Psychology, 137*, 37–47.

Brassell, W. (1977). Intervention with handicapped infants: Correlates of progress. *Mental Retardation, 15*, 18–22.

Brassell, W., & Dunst, C. (1978). Fostering the object construct. *American Journal of Mental Deficiency, 82*, 507–510.

Brinick, P. (1980). Childhood deafness and maternal control *Journal of Communication Disorders, 13*, 75–81.

Buckhalt, J., Rutherford, R., & Goldberg, K. (1978). Verbal and nonverbal interaction of mothers with their Down's syndrome and nonretarded infants. *American Journal of Mental Deficiency, 82*, 37–343.

Carew, J. (1980). Experience and the development of intelligence in young children at home and daycare. *Monographs of the Society for Research in Child Development, 47*(6).

Cheseldine, S., & McConkey, R. (1979). Parental speech to young Down's Syndrome children. *American Journal of Mental Deficiency, 83*, 612–620.

Cheskin, A. (1981). The verbal environment provided by hearing mothers for their young deaf children. *Journal of Communication Disorders, 14*, 485–496.

Cheskin, A. (1982). The use of language by hearing mothers of deaf children. *Jornal of Communication Disorders, 15*, 145–153.

Cochran, M., & Brassard, J. (1979). Child development and personal social networks. *Child Development, 50*, 601–606.

Cook, J. (1963). Dimension analysis of child rearing attitudes of parents of handicapped children. *American Journal of Mental Deficiency, 68*, 354–361.

Crawley, S., & Spicker, D. (1983). Mother child interactions involving 2 year olds with Down's syndrome. *Child Development, 54*, 1312–1323.

Crnic, K., Friedrich, N., & Greenberg, M. (1983). Adaptation of families with mentally retarded children. *American Journal of Mental Deficiency, 88*, 125–138.

Cronbach, L., & Glaser, G. (1965). *Psychological tests and personnel decisions*. Urbana: University of Illinois Press.

Cruickshank, W., Hallahan, D., & Bice, H. (1976). Personality and Behavioral Characteristics. In W. Cruickshank (Ed.), *Cerebral palsy: A developmental disability*. Syracuse, NY: Syracuse University Press.

Cunningham, C., Reuler, E., Blackwell, J., & Deck, J. (1981). Behavioral and linguistic development in the interaction of normal and retarded children with their mothers. *Child Development, 52*, 62–70.

Curson, A. (1979). The blind nursery school child. *Psychoanalytic Study of the Child, 34*, 51–72.

Daniels, D., & Plomin, R. (1985). Differential experience of siblings in the same family. *Developmental Psychology, 21*, 747–760.

Dingman, H., Eyman, R., & Windle, C. (1963). An investigation of some child rearing attitudes of mothers with retarded children. *American Journal of Mental Deficiency, 67*, 899–908.

Doane, J. (1978). Family interaction and communication deviance in disturbed and normal families. *Family Process, 17*, 357–376.

Edelbrook, C., Costello, A., Dulcan, M., Kalas, R., & Conover, N. (1985). Age differences in the reliability of the psychiatric interview of the child. *Child Development, 56*, 265–275.

Elardo, R., & Bradley, R. (1981). The home observation for measurement of the environment (HOME): A review of research. *Developmental Review, 1*, 113–145.

Epstein, S. (1980). The study of behavior: II. Implications for psychological research. *American Psychologist, 35*, 798–806.

Farran, D., Kassar, C., Yoder, P., Harber, L., Huntington, G., & Smith, M. (1984). *Rating mother child interaction in handicapped and at risk infants*. Paper presented to the first International Symposium on Intervention and Stimulation in Infant Development, Jerusalam, July.

Field, T., & Ignatoff, T. (1981). Videotaping effects on the behaviors of low income mothers and their infants during floor play interactions. *Journal of Applied Developmental Psychology, 2*, 227–236.

Filler, J., & Bricker, W. (1976). Teaching styles of mothers and the match to sample performance of their retarded preschool age children. *American Journal of Mental Deficiency, 85*, 504–511.

Fox, R., & Wise, P. (1981). Infant and preschool reinforcement survey. *Psychology in the Schools, 18*, 87–92.

Fraiberg, S. (1968). Parallel and divergent patterns in blind and sighted infants. *Psychoanalytic Study of the Child, 23*, 264–300.

Fraiberg, S. (1971). Intervention in infancy: A program for blind infants. *Journal of the American Academy of Child Psychiatry, 10*, 381–389.

Freese, M., & Thoman, E. (1978). Assessment of maternal characteristics for the study of mother infant interaction. *Infant Behavior and Development, 1*, 95–115.

Friedrich, W. (1979). Predictors of the coping behavior of mothers of handicapped children. *Journal of Consulting and Clinical Psychology, 47*, 1140–1141.

Friedrich, W., & Friedrich, W. (1981). Psychosocial assets of parents of handicapped and non-handicapped children. *American Journal of Mental Deficiency, 85*, 551–552.

Galenson, E., Miller, R., Kaplan, E., & Rothstein, A. (1979). Assessment of development in the deaf child. *Journal of American Academy of Child Psychiatry, 18*, 128–146.

Gordon, J. (1959). Relationships among mothers achievement, independence training attitudes and handicapped childrens performance. *Journal of Consulting Psychology, 23*, 207–212.

Gottfried, A. (1984). Home environment and early cognitive development: Integration, meta-analysis and conclusions. In A. Gottfried (Ed.), *Home environment and early cognitive development*. New York: Academic.

Green, M., & Durocher, M. (1965). Improving parent care of handicapped children. *Children, 12*, 185–188.

Greenberg, M. (1980). Social interactions between deaf preschoolers and their mothers. *Developmental Psychology, 16*, 465–474.

Greenberg, M. (1983). Family stress and child competence: The effects of early intervention for families with deaf infants. *American Annuals of the Deaf, 128*, 407–417.

Greenberg, M., & Marvin, R. (1979). Attachment patterns and profoundly deaf preschool children. *Merrill-Palmer Quarterly, 25*, 265–279.

Greenberg, R., & Field, T. (1982). Temperament rating of handicapped infants during classroom, mother and teacher interactions. *Journal for Pediatric Psychology, 7*, 387–405.

Guralnick, M. (1981). Prognostic factors affecting child-child social interactions in mainstreamed preschool programs. *Exceptional Education Quarterly, 1*, 71–91.

Henggler, S., & Cooper, P. (1983). Deaf child hearing mother interactions. *Journal of Pediatric Psychology, 8*, 83–95.

Holroyd, J., & Guthrie, D. (1979). Stress in family of children with neuromuscular disease. *Journal of Clinical Psychology, 35*, 734–739.

Holroyd, J., & McArthur, D. (1976). Mental retardation and stress in the parents. *American Journal of Mental Deficiency, 80*, 431–436.

Johnson, D., Breckenridge, J., & McGowan, R. (1984). Home environment and early cognitive development in Mexican-American children. In A. Gottfried (Ed.), *Home environment and early cognitive development*. New York: Plenum Press.

Kagan, J. (1967). On the need for relativism. *American Psychologist, 22*, 131–142.

Kogan, K. (1980). Interaction systems between preschool handicapped or developmentally disabled children and their parents. In T. Field, S. Goldberg, D. Stern, & A. Sostek (Eds.), *High risk infants and children*. New York: Academic.

Kogan, K., Wineberger, H., & Bobbitt, R. (1969). Analysis of mother child interaction in young mental retardates. *Child Development, 40*, 799–812.

Kogan, K., Tyler, N., & Turner, P. (1974). The process of interpersonal adaptation between mothers and their cerebral palsied children. *Developmental Medicine and Child Neurology, 16*, 518–527.

Kubicek, L. (1980). Organization in 2 mother infant interactions involving a normal infant and its paternal twin brother who was later diagnosed as autistic. In T. Field, S. Goldberg, D. Stern, & A. Sostek (Eds.), *High risk infants and children*. New York: Academic.

Lewandowski, L., & Cruickshank, W. (1980). Psychological Development of crippled children and youth. In W. Cruickshank (Ed.), *Psychology of exceptional children and youth*. Englewood Cliffs, NJ: Prentice-Hall.

Lytton, H. (1980). *Parent-child interactions* New York: Plenum Press.

Marshall, N., Hegrenes, J., & Goldstein, S. (1973). Verbal interactions: Mothers and their retarded children versus mothers and their nonretarded children versus mothers and their nonretarded children. *American Journal of Mental Deficiency, 77*, 415–419.

Martini, M. (1980). Structure of interaction between 2 autistic children. In T. Field, S. Goldberg, D. Stern & A. Sostek (Eds.), *High risk infants and children*. New York: Academic Press.

Mash, E., & Terdal, L. (1973). Modification of mother child interactions. *Mental retardation, 11*, 44–49.

McKirdy, L., & Blank, M. (1982). Dialogue in deaf and hearing preschoolers. *Journal of Speech and Hearing Research, 21*, 487–499.

Mink, I., Nihara, K., & Meyers, E. (1983). Taxonomy of family life styles: I. Homes with TMR children. *American Journal of Mental Deficiency, 87*, 484–497.

Moos, R., & Moos, B. (1981). *Family environmental scale manual*. Palo Alto, CA: Consulting Psychologist Press.

Nihara, K., Meyers, C., & Mink, I. (1983). Reciprocal relationship between home environment and development of TMR adolescents. *American Journal of Mental Development, 88,* 139–149.

Nihara, K., Mink, I., & Meyers, C. (1985). Home environment and development of slow learning adolescents. *Developmental Psychology, 21,* 784–794.

Novak, M., Olley, J., & Kearney, D. (1980). Social skills of children with special needs and integrated and separate preschools. In T. Field, S. Goldberg, D. Stern, & A. Sostek (Eds.), *High risk infants and children.* New York: Academic.

Petersen, G., & Sherrod, K. (1982). Relationship of maternal language to language development and language delay of children. *American Journal of Mental Deficiency, 86,* 391–398.

Piper, M., & Ramsey, M. (1980). Effects of early home environment on the mental development of Down's syndrome infants. *American Journal of Mental Deficiency, 85,* 39–44.

Poznanski, E. (1973). Emotional issues in raising handicapped children. *Rehabilitation Literature, 34,* 322–326.

Ragozin, A., Basham, R., Crnic, K., Greenberg, M., & Robinson, N. (1982). Effects of maternal age on parenting role. *Developmental Psychology, 18,* 627–634.

Ricci, C. (1970). Analysis of child rearing attitudes of mothers of retarded, emotionally disturbed and normal children. *American Journal of Mental Deficiency, 74,* 756–761.

Richardson, S. (1969). The effect of physical disability on the socialization of a child. In D. Goslin (Ed.), *Handbook of socialization theory and research.* Chicago: Rand McNally.

Rushton, J., Brainerd, C. & Pressley, M. (1983). Behavioral development and construct validity: The principle of aggregation, *Psychological Bulletin, 94,* 18–38.

Sanders, D. (1980). Psychological implications of hearing impairment. In W. Cruickshank (Ed.), *Psychology of exceptional children and youth* (4th ed.). Englewood Cliffs, NJ: Prentice-Hall.

Schaefer, E., & Bell, R. (1958). Development of parental attitude research instrument. *Child Development, 29,* 339–361.

Schlesinger, H., & Meadow, K. (1972). *Sound and sign: Childhood deafness and mental health.* Berkeley: University of California Press.

Shere, E., & Kastenbaum, R. (1966). Mother child interaction in cerebral palsy. *Genetic Psychology Monographs, 73,* 255–355.

Shores, R., Hester, P., & Strain, P. (1976). The effects of amount and type of teacher-child interaction on child/child interaction in freeplay. *Psychology in the Schools, 13,* 171–175.

Smith, L., & Hagen, V. (1984). Relationships between the home environment and sensory motor development of Down's syndrome and nonretarded infants. *American Journal of Mental Deficiency,*

Suelzel, M., & Keenan, V. (1981). Changes in family support networks over the life cycle of mentally retarded persons. *Amerian Journal of Mental Deficiency, 86,* 267–274.

Terdal, L., Jackson, R., & Garner, A. (1976). Mother and child interactions: A comparison between normal and developmentally delayed groups. In E. Mash, L. Hemerlynck, & L. Handy (Eds.), *Behavior modification in families.* New York: Brunner/Mazel.

Tjossem, T. (1976). Early intervention: Issues and approaches. In T. Tjossem (Ed.), *Intervention strategies for high risk infants and young children.* Baltimore: University Park Press.

Traub, R., & Rawley, G. (1980). Reliability of test scores and decisions. *Applied Psychological Measurement, 4,* 517–545.

Wachs, T. D. (1985). *Measurement of environment.* Symposium presentation Society for Research in Child Development, Toronto, May.

Wachs, T. D., & Gruen, G. (1982). *Early experience and human development.* New York: Plenum Press.

Wachs, T. D., & Gruen, G. (1984). Environmental stimulation and early intervention. *Zero to three: Bulletin of the National Center for Clinical Infant Programs, 5,* 6–10.

Wachs, T. D., Francis, J., & McQuiston, S. (1979). Psychological dimensions of the infants physical environment. *Infant Behavior and Development, 2,* 155–161.

Wedell-Monnig, J., & Lumley, J. (1980). Child deafness and mother child interaction. *Child Development, 51,* 766–774.

Weinraub, M., & Wolf, B. (1983). Effects of stress and social support on mother child interactions in single and two parent families. *Child Development, 54,* 1297–1311.

White, B. (1980). Mainstreaming in grade school and preschool. In T. Field, S. Goldberg, D. Stern, & A. Sastek (Eds.), *High risk infants and children.* New York: Academic.

Wills, D. (1979). The ordinary devoted mother and her blind baby. *Psychoanalytic Study of the Child, 34*, 31–49.

Wulbert, M., Inglis, S., Kriegsman, E., & Mills, B. (1975). Language delay and associated mother–child interaction. *Developmental Psychology, 11*, 61–70.

Yarrow, M., Campbell, J., & Burton, R. (1970). Recollections of childhood: A study of the retrospective method. *Monographs of the Society for Research in Child Development* (Vol. 35).

17

Biophysical Considerations in the Assessment of Young Children with a Developmental Disability

Diane Magyary, Kathryn Barnard, and Patricia Brandt

The primary focus of this chapter is to highlight several important issues about the health care of infants and preschoolers with a disability. Development is a complex ongoing process characterized by physiological and anatomical changes. The physical aspects of health—that is, the physiological and anatomical aspects pertaining to the body—will be specifically discussed in relation to various types of disabilities. Routine primary health care needs, as well as specialty health care needs, will be described. Specific assessment procedures for evaluating the physical aspects of health are also included. The discussion is not meant to be an exhaustive treatment of this topic; rather, it is an illustration of selected issues and examples. The consideration of both physical and developmental processes of health is critical in providing comprehensive, quality health care. In addition, the family unit and the home environment need to be considered for an understanding of how health of children and parents may be supported and fostered.

HEALTH NEEDS: PRIMARY AND SPECIALTY

Children with disabilities often have complex needs requiring the expertise of many specialty professionals, who may be housed within a variety of different institutional systems. The complexity of the health care provided to families with developmentally disabled infants is illustrated by findings from the UCLA Intervention Program for Handicapped Children (Howard & Beckwith, 1980). The majority of the children in the UCLA program were diagnosed as having cerebral palsy, with or without mental retardation. A small percentage of the children had Down syndrome with associated mental retardation or visual or neurological disorders. In addition to child development experts, the families used an average of more than four other health subspecialists, who often included a

DIANE MAGYARY, KATHRYN BARNARD, and PATRICIA BRANDT • Department of Parent-Child Nursing, University of Washington, Seattle, Washington.

pediatric neurologist, a pediatric surgeon, a cardiac surgeon, a cardiologist, an ophthalmologist, an ear–nose–throat specialist, an audiologist, an endocrinologist, a gastroen-
terologist, and a geneticist. The health care needed by these children included the
correction of hearing deficits, surgery to correct orthopedic problems or life-threatening
heart failure, seizure control, and the prevention of amblyopia (Howard & Beckwith,
1980, p. 26). Given the multiplicity of subspecialty services, it became apparent to the
UCLA staff that a designated health professional was needed to coordinate the health-
subspecialty and early-educational-intervention services.

Without a case manager, the long-term specialty care of children with disabilities
may be fragmented or duplicated because of the minimal communication, coordination,
and collaboration among the many professionals and systems involved. This fragmenta-
tion and/or the duplication of specialty services creates frustration for families and may
impact on the quality of care the child receives. Furthermore, the emphasis on the child's
disability and the associated specialty services may result in neglect of the child's primary
health care costs.

According to the Vanderbilt Conference Report on Primary Providers in the Care of
Handicapped Children (Merkens, Burr, & Perrin, 1985), children with disabilities receive subspecialty and tertiary services that often are not coordinated with primary-
health-care services. In fact, many children with disabilities do not have a source of
primary health care (Merkens et al., 1985). A prevalent, but false, assumption is that
subspecialty services optimally provide for preventive child health needs. Coyner (1983)
reported that basic health care for infants with disabilities often consists of episodic visits
to a health provider for the treatment of acute illnesses or chronic conditions associated
with their disabilities. Routine health care is also deficient for children enrolled in many
of the early-intervention programs. Without comprehensive health care that includes prevention and health maintenance, the young child with a disability is often confronted with
additional threats to her or his physical and developmental well-being. As noted by
Blackman (1984d), children with disabilities commonly experience health problems such
as recurring respiratory infections and diarrhea. Because of the many existing structural
or functional abnormalities associated with the child's disability, it is often difficult to
determine the seriousness of the common health problems. Thus, skilled health surveil-
lance and assessment coupled with effective treatment approaches are essential to reduce
the short- and long-term consequences of these common health problems.

PRIMARY HEALTH CARE

Primary-Care Components

Primary health care is defined as the monitoring, maintenance, and promotion of
optimal physical and mental health. Routine primary health care has traditionally been
provided by a health professional, referred to as a *primary-care provider,* who has direct
responsibility and accountability for a designated case load of clients over a period of
time (Zander, 1980). A pediatric primary-care provider is often the initial and regular
source of family-centered health care for children and usually has the most frequent
contact with the child and the family regardless of the presence or absence of particular
health problems (Merkens et al., 1985).

Routine pediatric primary health care should be comprehensive, preventive, continuous, and family-centered. A child's physical and developmental strengths and weaknesses within the context of the family and of other relevant systems need to be addressed to satisfy the *comprehensive* dimension of pediatric primary care. Health care also needs to be *preventive*. In comparison to the overall population, disabled children have a higher prevalence of secondary physiological complications and psychological adjustment problems. Regular monitoring for early detection, possible prevention, or partial remediation of secondary complications is critical. The early detection of secondary cognitive and social-emotional complications requires an understanding of the patterns of development exhibited by infants and preschoolers with a disability. In Chapter 1 of this book, Wachs describes the developmental patterns associated with different disabilities. Evidence suggests that cognitive and social-emotional developmental patterns may be different, depending on the type of disability as well as on the degree or the etiology of the disability. Therefore, assessment protocols should be designed to reflect the fact that not all disabilities are functionally equivalent in their developmental patterns.

Pediatric primary health care also needs to be continuous and family centered. Regularity of contact with the child and the family that is *continuous* over time promotes partnership building with the primary-care provider for the early detection and treatment of developmental problems associated with the disabilities of infants and preschoolers. By a continuous interaction and working together on goals, assessments, and interventions, the development of a therapeutic partnership with the family may be realized. Through this partnership, the family and the primary-care provider develop a more holistic understanding of the infant's needs and are better able to design and revise a *family-centered* comprehensive health plan.

The primary-care provider who has advanced training in the long-term health care of young children with disabilities may serve as a case manager, assessing the family and integrating and coordinating access to subspecialty services (Merkens *et al.*, 1985). This is not to say that the primary-care provider displaces the family as the essential primary caregiver and advocate for their child. However, by maintaining a family-centered approach, the primary-care provider and the parents establish priorities for promoting parental caregiving and case managership of the young child's health care. With support and education as needed for the individual family members, the knowledge and skills required for daily caretaking and coordination are strengthened or developed. The long-term goal of family-centered primary care is for the family to assume the primary responsibility for the child's caretaking and advocacy. The health care professional then acts as a facilitator and a consultant to the family.

If the long-term goal of health care is for the family to assume responsibility for their own health, a logical starting place would be for the family to begin to learn how to assess and monitor their health. Sheehan's model of parental involvement, as discussed in Chapter 5, offers guidelines for making decisions about how to involve parents in the process of assessing their child's development. Because parents vary greatly in their interests and their assessment skills, the extent and type of parental involvement need to be carefully considered by both parents and professionals. Even though Sheehan's model was designed with respect to early-childhood educational assessment, its applicability to health assessment would seem reasonable, given the model's emphasis on developmental assessment. With parents becoming increasingly involved in the assessment of their children and the broadening of this assessment for instructional purposes, a parental involvement model needs to be further tested for its potential usefulness in child health assessment.

Preventive Health Guidelines

As illustrated in Table 1, guidelines for the preventive health supervision of infants and children have been recommended by the American Academy of Pediatrics (1981) Committee on Practice and Ambulatory Medicine. Careful periodic and systematic monitoring of healthy infants is required because the absence of or the recovery from perilous neonatal events or risk factors does not always result in a clean bill of health. In reference to the 1979 Surgeon General's report on Health Promotion and Disease Prevention, Coyner (1983) highlighted the fact that the first year of life is the most hazardous period for physiological stability and integrity before age 65. Health is a dynamic state characterized during infancy by a rapid change in the physiological subsystem as cells rapidly multiply, differentiate and increase in size.

The health supervision guidelines were intended to be used not as absolute standards of health care for all children at all times, but as a general guide for practice. The current guidelines for clinical practice may periodically change, depending on the latest research. In consideration of recent findings from family research, the guidelines in the future may suggest that family screening and assessment procedures are included in primary-health-care protocols. For example, family stress, support, and coping have been found to influence parent–infant interactions, which subsequently impact on the child's health and developmental status (Barnard, Hammond, Mitchell, Booth, Spietz, Snyder, & Elas, 1985; Belsky, 1984; Brandt, 1984).

The American Academy of Pediatrics (1981) routine health-supervision guidelines are currently designed to promote optimal health in essentially well children who receive competent parenting and have satisfactory health and development. Alterations in the content and the schedule of routine health visits would need to be individualized in relation to a particular child's profile as well as the family profile and the broader environmental context. The health supervision protocol may be modified and expanded to include more frequent visits, diagnostic laboratory tests, and more in-depth standardized developmental-assessment procedures and counseling. The primary-care provider considers the biological or environmental risk factors and the preliminary results of child and family screening and assessment procedures when determining how the protocol will be adapted for the individual child. Given the accepted pediatric practice that all healthy children should receive continuous health supervision, it become paramount that children with a disability also obtain continuous health supervision. Not only the generic components required by all children but additional attention is needed to anticipate both the normal and the special health needs of the child with a disability.

The anticipation of a child's normal and special health needs necessitates that the primary-health-care provider obtain measures of the child's environment. As Wachs highlights in Chapter 16, demographic indices such as parental socioeconomic status and educational level are inadequate in providing information about the specific experiences encountered by a particular child within a given environment. More precise environmental measures are needed to generate useful information in designing ways to fulfill a child's health and developmental needs. In Chapter 16, Wachs reviews the various envi-

Table 1. Schedule of Preventive Health Care Recommended by the American Academy of Pediatrics[a]

AGE	Infancy						Early childhood				Late childhood						Adolescence			
	By 1 (mo)	2	4	6	9	12	15	18	24	3 (yr)	4	5	6	8	10	12	14	16	18	20
HISTORY	•	•	•	•	•	•	•	•	•	•	•	•	•	•	•	•	•	•	•	•
MEASUREMENTS																				
Height and weight	•	•	•	•	•	•	•	•	•	•	•	•	•	•	•	•	•	•	•	•
Head circumference	•	•	•	•	•	•														
Blood pressure										•	•	•	•	•	•	•	•	•	•	•
Vision	s	s	s	s	s		s	s	s	o	o	o	o	o	s	o	s	s	o	o
Hearing	s	s	s	s	s		s	s	s	s	o	o	s	s	s	o	s	s	s	o
DEVEL./BEHAV. ASSESSMENT	•	•	•	•	•	•	•	•	•	•	•	•	•	•	•	•	•	•	•	•
PHYSICAL EXAMINATION	•	•	•	•	•	•	•	•	•	•	•	•	•	•	•	•	•	•	•	•
PROCEDURES																				
Hered./metabolic screening	•	↓																		
Immunization		•	•	•			•	•			•						•			
Tuberculin test	↓				•	↑	↓			↑	↓		•		↑		↓	•		↑
Hematocrit or hemoglobin	↓			•		↑	↓			↑	↓		•		↑		↓	•		↑
Urinalysis			•		↑		↓			↑	↓		•		↑		↓	•		↑
ANTICIPATORY GUIDANCE	•	•	•	•	•	•	•	•	•	•	•	•	•	•	•	•	•	•	•	•
INITIAL DENTAL REFERRAL										•										

[a]Any suspected problems should be promptly investigated, regardless of the child's age. Children with disabilities should be seen by a dentist within 6 months from the eruption of the first tooth. Committee on Practice and Ambulatory Medicine, 1981. From *Medical Aspects of Developmental Disabilities in Children Birth to Three* (p. 212), by J. A. Blackman (1984). Rockville, MD: Aspen Systems Corporation. Adapted by permission. Key: • = to be performed; s = subjective by history; o = objective by a standard testing method.

ronmental assessment procedures available for use with developmentally disabled infants and children and discusses the principles to be used when selecting a particular procedure.

PHYSIOLOGICAL AND ANATOMICAL EXPRESSIONS OF DISABILITIES

Healy (1980) noted that there is an epidemiological pattern in childhood disabilities: the more severe the disability, the earlier the manifestation of the disability, and the more the likelihood of associated health problems. The majority of the readily identifiable disabilities evident during the neonatal period are physiologically and/or anatomically expressed in three ways: in a structural deformity, in a neurological dysfunction, or in a metabolic dysfunction, or in a combination of these (Coyner, 1983; Prensky & Palkes, 1982). Examples of these structural, neurological and/or metabolic dysfunctions are as follows (Healy, 1980):

- Visual disorders (e.g., blindness or strabismus).
- Auditory disorders (e.g., deafness).
- Major craniocerebral malformations, for eample, microcephaly (an excessively small head); hydrancephaly (absence of the cerebral hemisphere), or hydrocephaly (an excessively large head).
- Structural musculoskeletal or neuromuscular deformities, for example, spina bifida (a defect in the vertebrae: bones that surround the spinal cord), arthrogryposis (the persistent flexion of a joint), congenital amputations, or limb paralysis.
- Anatomic disorders (e.g., a cleft palate or lip or a congenital heart defect).
- Chromosomal disorders and major malformation syndromes, for example trisomy 21 (down syndrome).
- Metabolic disorders, for example, phenylketonuria (PKU) and hypothyroidism.

As the infant grows older, the expression of disabilities is predominantly manifested as a failure to develop normally (Healy, 1980; Prensky & Palkes, 1982). In the first year of life, one of the early indications of failure to develop normally is an absence or delay in reaching the expected motor milestones within the range of age-appropriate time intervals. Absence of or delayed performance on motor tasks, however, may or may not prove to be diagnostically significant for future development. Motor impairment during infancy does not necessarily predict later intellectual functioning (Prensky & Palkes, 1982). Similarly, the normal achievement of motor milestones does not necessarily mean that intellectual or behavioral functioning will be normal later in childhood. Thus, diagnostic evaluation is often an ongoing process that unfolds as the infant's neuromotor system evolves with higher and more complex central-processing functions. For example, the differential diagnosis of cerebral palsy versus a general developmental delay may become more apparent by 12–18 months of life. The infant with cerebral palsy usually exhibits a history of delayed or poor-quality achievement of motor milestones. Specific abnormal motor movements and reflex patterns are also characteristics of cerebral palsy. In contrast, infants with a general developmental delay may exhibit motor delay as well as depressed development in all areas (Healy, 1984). The differential diagnosis between cerebral palsy and general developmental delay is particularly difficult when cerebral palsy is associated with intellectual impairment, visual or hearing impairment, and/or seizures.

Another type of disability that occurs during the first year of life is seizure disorders. Although convulsions may occur at any age during childhood, the first occurrence is more common during the first 6 months of life and then again at puberty. Typically, the general trend of seizure disorders is that convulsions are more difficult to control and are more likely to be associated with a neurological disability if they occur earlier in life (Prensky & Palkes, 1982). The commonest type of childhood seizure (6 months to 6 years) is febrile seizures, which occur in 3%–5% of the pediatric population (Bresnan & Hicks, 1983). A typical, simple febrile seizure that occurs as a single short episode accompanied by a fever is usually not associated with poor developmental outcome, especially given the absence of further seizures, no childhood history or neurological problems, and no family history of seizures other than febrile seizures (Bresnan & Hicks, 1983; Prensky & Palkes, 1982).

A less frequent disability is an arrest in development or the loss of acquired developmental milestones. Infants may successfully reach developmental milestones normally but then begin gradually to lose the acquired skills (Bernstein, 1981; Prensky & Palkes, 1982). The loss of an acquired skill may be associated with a past or recent severe insult to the brain, such as a tumor, an acute injury, or an infection. In the absence of a brain insult, the underlying pathology may be attributed to an inherited disease in which parts of the nervous system gradually degenerate. Inherited neurological degenerative diseases have important implications, not only for the identified child, but for other family members (Prensky & Palkes, 1982).

EVALUATION PROCESS

As Healy (1980) emphasized, infants who have a disability that is readily discernible at birth require intervention even before the emergence of more complex behavioral dysfunctions in cognition, language, and socioemotional development. Early intervention benefits from an identification of disabilities at birth or soon after. An infant that is suspect on routine health-screening procedures warrants a more in-depth diagnostic evaluation by expert professionals. The early identification process relies on a comprehensive evaluation that includes a thorough health and developmental history, a physical and neurological examination, neuromotor and other developmental assessments, and laboratory tests such as metabolic and genetic screening. The information generated by a diagnostic workup will provide clues to the formulation of a definite or tentative diagnosis and a treatment plan.

Health History

A complete diagnostic evaluation begins with a thorough health and developmental history, which includes questions about a variety of factors that, singly or in combination, may result in a disability. Information is gathered about the suspect infant's extended-family background to help rule out hereditary and historical risk factors. The history from the mother's previous pregnancies is reviewed, as well as the pregnancy, labor, and delivery of the identified infant. What must be remembered in evaluating the utility of this type of history is that, currently, the research results are not clear-cut. Disabilities are not always associated with an abnormal pregnancy and birth history. The reverse may also be true, as newborn complications are not always associated with later disabilities. However, some consensus about risk factors does exist and suggests that an infant has a higher probability of manifesting poor development if exposed to a combination of insults, as opposed to a single insult (Blackman, 1984c; Prensky & Palkes, 1982).

Other components of history taking include the generation of an extensive health and developmental profile on the suspect infant. This profile includes information about any presenting concerns, signs and symptoms, past use of health services, and general information based on a systematic review of the body systems, including illnesses, accidents, immunizations, daily activity patterns, and developmental milestones. Depending on the age of the child, a dental history is included. Day-care and school involvement is considered, as well as other environmental factors (e.g., parent–infant interactions and major family stresses).

A parent-questionnaire health-history form has been designed by Cadol (1981) to systematically review a variety of biological and environmental factors that may contribute to a child's health and developmental profile. Cadol (1981) reported successful experiences with the questionnaire, even with parents whose educational background was limited. The initial time spent with the parents in reviewing and discussing the questionnaire reduces unnecessary time in repeating a history because of missing components or lack of thoroughness.

Parental input into a health history is vital. Parents provide valuable information about how their infant behaves from a day-to-day basis. Parental observations of their infant becomes particularly important when symptoms of poor health and slow development are subtle, borderline, or not likely to be exhibited during a brief exam carried out in a clinical setting. Even before the manifestation of a developmental delay, parents may express a variety of concerns about their infants, such as about a persistent rigidity or limpness, lethargy, irritability, sensitivity and resistance to physical contact, high-pitched or poor cry, constant crying, sleeping difficulties, feeding problems, absence of or poor orientation to light and sound, or an excessive startle reaction to voices or changes in posture. Even if it is difficult for parents to describe the exactness of their concern, they should still be encouraged to share their thoughts and feelings with a professional. Extreme deviations from the normal are likely to be identified for early intervention, whereas more subtle or borderline deviations may be overlooked, and the result may be delayed intervention.

As Sheehan discusses in Chapter 5, parents are likely to view their child's development from a "macroperspective" as contrasted with the "microperspective" often held by professionals. Parents' observation of the child's daily performance on a variety of tasks in a variety of situations yields a more global view of development than that of a professional, who often observes a child in a given test situation with specific tasks. The child's development reported from a parent's "macroperspective," combined with professionals' "microperspective," would reveal the best combination of clues about subtle or borderline deviations from normal development.

Physical and Neurological Examination

A diagnostic evaluation also includes a thorough physical and neurological examination. A physical examination of the bodily state of the child is based on four techniques:

- Auscultation (listening to the sounds produced within the body with the unaided ear or with an instrument)
- Palpation (feeling with the fingers or hands to determine, by use of the tactile senses, the physical characteristics of tissues or organs)
- Percussion (striking directly or indirectly the body surface to produce vibrations in underlying tissues)
- Observation (systematic direct visual inspection)

A general physical examination includes a systematic review of the following bodily components (Barness, 1981):

- Growth measurements, vital signs, and appropriate laboratory procedures
- General appearance, activity level, and responsiveness
- Skin and lymph nodes
- Head and neck (face, nose, mouth, and throat)
- Eyes and ears
- Chest and back (heart and lungs)
- Abdomen
- Extremities, skeletal structure, and muscles
- Genital and anal areas
- Neurological evaluation

Careful monitoring of an infant's growth requires plotting on a growth curve a series of height, weight, and head circumference measurements taken over time. Abnormalities in the shape or size of one's head, if they are not a family characteristic, may reflect an underlying abnormality in the growth and development of the brain (Schor, 1984a).

Throughout the physical examination, particular attention should be given to identifying any of the various minor physical malformations that are frequently related to developmental delays and/or pathology in a particular organ system (e.g., kidneys and heart). These minor physical malformations may include widely spaced eyes; low-set, poorly formed ears; multiple hair whorls; a short or webbed neck; fused fingers; and so on. It is important to remember that any one of the minor physical malformations may be evident in normal individuals (Bernstein, 1981; Prensky & Palkes, 1982). The presence of a cluster of minor physical malformations may be of particular significance if accompanied with a developmental delay. For example, children with Down syndrome typically exhibit a constellation of minor malformations that are evidence of a clinical syndrome associated with a chromosomal abnormality. The constellation of minor malformations may include an upward slant of the eyes, an extra fold at the inner corner of the eye (an epicanthal fold), a small oral cavity, resulting in a protruding tongue; short, broad hands with a single palmar crease; and wide gaps between the first and second toes. The number and extent of these physical stigmata vary from child to child and may be associated with a disturbance in the heart and intestine systems (Blackman, 1984a).

Another important dimension of the physical examination is the assessment of the nervous systems integrity, as evaluated by:

- Cortical functions
- Sensory functions
- Muscle function, tone, strength and symmetry
- Gait and balance
- Cranial nerves
- Autonomic and cerebellar functions
- Reflexes

An evaluation of the neurological system requires hands-on assessment procedures as well as simply observing the child in spontaneous activity. General observation of the child's voluntarily produced activity, behavior, posture, gain, and so on may be as revealing as or more revealing than the actual hands-on assessment procedures used to elicit the more formal responses (Bernstein, 1981; Schor, 1984a).

Observations of general posture and activity, a formal neurological examination, and a neuromotor developmental assessment yield valuable information about the integrity of the nervous system. Especially in infants and young children, the maturation of the nervous system needs to be considered when one is doing a neuromotor development assessment. An age-appropriate profile of how and when motor milestones are performed, as well as the delayed onset or persistence of certain reflexes, provides useful information for detecting neurological disorders.

Although not specifically discussed in this chapter, assessments in other areas of development, such as cognition, language, and social-emotional development, are also critical components of a comprehensive diagnostic workup. In addition, even when the etiology of the disability is biological, as in Down syndrome, the family dynamics and home environment need to be assessed for their support of optimal development and parenting.

The various neurological disorders responsible for a developmental delay are numerous and may manifest themselves in multiple ways. Therefore, it is important that even subtle suspect findings on a physical-neurological examination and a neuromotor development assessment be referred to a specialist (e.g., a pediatrician or a pediatric neurologist). In addition, a formal neurological examination is often difficult to administer and interpret because of the cooperative level of the child. Special expertise and years of experience are often required in the careful and accurate execution of an extensive neurological workup.

Genetic and Metabolic Screening

Disabilities expressed as congenital defects may or may not be of genetic origin. As Sujansky (1981) explained, the term *congenital defect* implies only that the defect is present at birth. The etiology of the defect may or may not be of genetic origin (p. 159). In fact, according to Blackman and Thomson (1984), the majority of birth defects may possibly be the result of an interplay between genetic and environmental factors (e.g., cleft lip and palate, myelomeningocele, and cardiac malformation). Environmental factors may include maternal diseases, infections, and medications. With current advances in genetic evaluation, an understanding of the exact nature of the interplay between environmental and genetic factors may become more apparent.

There is a category of disabilities referred to as *genetic disorders,* which means that the disability was caused by an abnormal single gene or an abnormal set of genes and is referred to as a *chromosomal defects*. Chromosome abnormalities may involve the number of chromosomes (too few or too many) or the actual structure of the chromosome (a missing piece or an extra piece) (Blackman & Thomson, 1984). If a child is suspected of having a chromosomal abnormality, Blackman and Thomson recommended three essential steps: (a) a detailed history of the health and development of individual family members; (b) a physical examination of the identified child with attention given to the signs and symptoms of specific genetic disorders; and (c) specific laboratory tests, which include chromosomal analysis, X rays, and biochemical studies of blood and urine specimens (p. 120). In addition, families of children who have a questionable genetic disorder should be referred to a genetic counseling clinic (Bernstein, 1981; Blackman & Thomson, 1984). The clinical services typically involve not only a diagnostic genetic evaluation of the family but also counseling services to assist families to understand the genetic disorder and the implications for future reproduction and child care.

Advancements in genetic evaluations have coincided with advancements made in large-scale metabolic screening. A newborn may appear normal and may yet be suffering from an inborn error of metabolism, such as phenylketonuria (PKU), that is likely to result in mental retardation if left untreated. As Prensky and Palkes (1982) explained, in most metabolic disorders, the infant, for various reasons, is not able to normally metabolize certain chemicals required for growth. These chemicals are either produced within the body or extracted from food. In certain types of metabolic disorders, the newborn may appear normal because, during pregnancy, the mother's body has properly metabolized certain chemicals for the infant. After birth, the symptoms begin to appear as chemical compounds build up or break down in the body, causing brain damage (Prensky & Palkes, 1982).

Thus, to detect those infants who suffer from metabolic disorders, it is important to repeat metabolic screening procedures a couple of weeks postbirth, even though an initial screening was done during the first days of infancy before hospital discharge. The follow-up screening allows for the careful monitoring of the infant's own metabolic processes without being confounded by the residual effects of pregnancy. However, follow-up screening should not be delayed. The American Academy of Pediatrics (1981) recommends that follow-up metabolic screening for PKU should occur by 2 weeks of life. The earlier the detection and successful treatment of metabolic disorders, the more likely is an optimal prognosis. In fact, for some metabolic disorders, such as galactosemia, prenatal diagnosis is available.

With the advancement of routine metabolic screening, required by most states, infants with inborn errors of metabolism are usually able to be identified before the appearance of symptoms such as delayed growth and development. The routine detection of most metabolic disorders, such as phenylketonuria and hypothroidism, is based on simple, quick, and economical screening procedures. Because these procedures are for screening and are not diagnostic, false negative results may occur. Thus, even when previous screening procedures were negative, it is critical that a metabolic disorder be ruled out for infants who are not exhibiting normal growth and development (O'Brien & McCabe, 1981).

Inborn metabolic errors may involve protein metabolism (e.g., PKU, and maple syrup urine disease), carbohydrate metabolism (e.g., galactosemia), lysosomal storage (e.g., Tay-Sachs) and hormonal biosynthesis (e.g., hypothyroidism). Two of the most prevalent congenital metabolic disorders are hypothyroidism and phenylketonuria. Hypothyroidism is a type of metabolic disorder that is not inherited. Hypothroidism occurs when the thyroid gland fails to develop normally and does not produce sufficient thyroid hormone to support normal growth and development. The treatment involves hormone supplementation, preferably before 1 month of life. Schultz (1984) reported that infants with hypothyroidisms exhibit normal functioning at 5 years of age, if treatment is initiated before 3 months of age.

PKU is an inherited metabolic disorder characterized by a lack of a specific liver enzyme required to convert phenylalanine, an essential amino acid found in high protein food, to tyrosine, another amino acid. Without conversion, the phenylalanine levels become markedly elevated in body tissue, causing brain damage. The name *phenylketonuria* refers to phenylalanines being converted to phenylketones excreted through the urine. The treatment consists of placing the child on a special phenylalanine restricted diet, which consists of a special low-phenylalanine milk-substitute started in infancy and given for life. The special milk substitute is supplemented with other low-phenylalanine foods, including fruits, vegetables, and low-protein bread products. The introduction of meats, dairy products, and other high-protein foods is prohibited because of their high phenylalanine content. Dietary adjustments are made in accordance with blood phenylalanine levels. Dietary restriction continues to be implemented during the preschool years, the formal school years, and even through adulthood (Novelly, & Bapat, 1985. Seashore, Friedman, Schuett, Brown & Michals, 1985). Educators need to be aware of the child's need to comply with the essential dietary treatment. With early and successful treatment, children with PKU generally grow and develop normally (O'Brien & McCabe, 1981; Schultz, 1984). Because PKU is inherited, treatment is extended beyond dietary management to include genetic counseling for the identified child as well as the other family members.

COMMON PHYSICAL-HEALTH PROBLEMS AND RESPONSES

The major emphasis of this section is on the responses of the child to the disability and on the physical health problems often associated with disabilities. Although the primary-care provider is also concerned with the child's socioemotional and developmental needs, as well as the family's adaptation, the illustrations used here will highlight primarily the physical characteristics. However, acknowledgment of the importance of the interrelationships of the child's physical, socioemotional, and developmental responses is needed before proceeding. In addition, it is important to note that, for each response category identified (e.g., feeding and activity), the problems are multifaceted and thus, a comprehensive assessment must include child and environmental factors and the dynamic interplay between these factors. For example, parent–child interaction, inadequate food intake, and child factors such as easy fatigability and poor oral-motor coordination may all contribute to the child's feeding and nutritional problems. The purpose of the following discussion is also to convey information about disabilities (e.g., poor oral-motor coordination) that contribute to the child's vulnerability to developing common health problems.

Coyner (1983) proposed a useful model, as illustrated in Figure 1, for examining the common health problems associated with disabilities identified at birth or shortly thereafter. The model is based on the premise that the pathology of disabling conditions sets into motion a series of biobehavioral responses (physiological, functional, and psychological) that have an impact on the infant's overall health and developmental status. The pathology of disabilities is evidenced by structural deformities and metabolic and/or neurophysiological dysfunctions.

Often, the first major biobehavioral response to the pathology of the disability is the infant's feeding patern. Abnormal suck, swallow, and coordination, for example, result in feding problems and altered nutrient and fluid intake. Inadequate nutritional intake subsequently leads to an overall decline in cell and system integrity, which may be manifested in other biobehavioral responses, such as pattern alterations in growth, elimination, the sleep–wake cycles and/or vulnerability to infections, illnesses, and accidents. Often, these biobehavioral responses are interrelated and thus heighten the complexities involved in diagnosing and treating children with disabilities. In addition, the treatment of the disability may impact on the child's development. For example, an anticonvulsant medication, phenobarbital, used to manage seizure disorders has side effects that may produce alteration in behavior, such as decreased alertness, hyperactivity, or temper outbursts (Bresnan & Hicks, 1983).

The additive and cummulative effects of these biobehavioral responses and corresponding health problems tend to aggravate the pathology involved in the initial disabling condition. Secondary complications may result and often undermine the benefits that the child has derived from early intervention programs. Family functioning may also be threatened by the increase in stress associated with the child's initial disability and secondary complications. In many circumstances, secondary complications are preventable, or at least, the impact of the complication on the child and family can be reduced through routine, systematic evaluation and treatment of the disabled infant's health and development. The family, the primary care provider, and other professionals who interact with the disabled infant make an important contribution to health promotion by identifying the infant's altered biobehavioral responses early and by referring the child for care when needed. The rest of this section describes five types of common physical responses and

health problems experienced by the young child: (a) feeding, nutrition, and growth alterations; (b) activity alterations and safety hazards; (c) hearing and vision alterations; (d)
susceptibility to infections and illness; and (e) sleep–wake alterations. Disabilities that
predispose the child to these complications are also delineated.

Step I. Pathology

    A. Initial—structural, functional, and/or metabolic abnormality

    B. Secondary—added handicaps, complications, and/or chronic illness

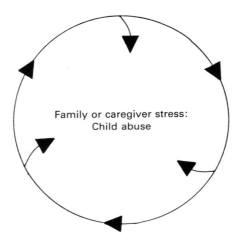

Step II. Feeding problems and decline in nutritional status

Step III. Decline in cell and systems integrity

    A. Physical growth

    B. Activity level

    C. Susceptibility to infection and illness

    D. Elimination

    E. Skin care

    F. Oral health

    G. Biorhythms, response levels

    H. Vision abnormalities

    I. Reduced appetite

Figure 1. The effect of health problems in handicapped infants. From *Developmentally disabled infants and
toddlers: Assessment and interventions* (p. 11) by R. S. Zelle & A. B. Coyner (1983). Philadelphia, PA: F. A.
Davis. Copyright 1983 F. A. Davis. Reprinted by permission.

Feeding, Nutrition, and Growth

Coyner (1983) identified feeding problems and the associated nutritional status as one of the most serious response alterations for both the child and the family. If nutritional intake is not adequate, subsequent alterations, such as in growth, dental health, and elimination and susceptibility to illness, may follow (p. 12). Abnormal feeding patterns are influenced by the feeding process (mechanical action) and nutritional intake (the assimilation of food).

Children with anatomic disorders such as cleft lip and palate may have difficulty with the mechanical actions of feeding. Thr front lip normally develops a suction to transfer liquids and foods to the back of the mouth for swallowing. Both the hard and the soft palates are also important during feeding. The hard palate is a partition between the nasal passage and the mouth; whereas the soft palate muscles function with the upper throat to close the oral and nasal cavities during swallowing (Hardy, 1984). If the child has a cleft lip and palate, these functions are disrupted.

Children with Down syndrome, a chromosomal disorder, have been found to have a reduced growth rate, especially during the first 2 years (Coyner, 1983). Hypotonia, slowness in eating, and persistent spitting up after feedings may contribute to this delayed rate of growth (Blackman, 1984a).

Poor weight gain is also found in children with congenital heart or neuromuscular disorders. Children who have the cardiac or respiratory compromise associated with congenital heart disease often have high caloric needs. However, the energy required during the feeding process may limit the child's capacity to ingest and assimilate enough calories (Ahmann, 1986). Children with conditions such as cerebral palsy or other cerebral–nervous-system disorders also become fatigued because of stressful and time-consuming feedings. The following physical conditions may contribute to a stressed and fatiguing feeding situation: poor coordination of the jaws, lips, tongue, or palate; abnormal head and body postures; oral sensitivity due to past tube feeding; or hypertonic tone of the muscles in cheeks, lips, or tongue (Coyner, 1983).

Infants born preterm may also have nutritional and feeding problems if they have, for example, a poor suck or limited alert times. If the infant is having difficulty coordinating sucking and swallowing, the natural process of suckling through breast feeding appears to be helpful. If bottle feeding is used with the preterm infant, careful selection of the type and size of nipple is needed to allow for the development of effective suck–swallow–breathe patterns (Ahmann, 1986).

Oral and dental problems are commonly interrelated with feeding problems. Structural deformities such as cleft lip and palate may produce an inappropriate alignment of the teeth (Hardy, 1984). Coyner (1983) reported that oral hygiene is complicated when neuromotor dysfunctions produce head and neck involvement or are treated with anticonvulsants that cause gum overgrowth. Dentition is often abnormal and gum disease increased for children with Down syndrome (Blackman, 1984a). Therefore, dental hygiene and monitoring are an important component of a nutritional and feeding evaluation.

Altered patterns in elimination and the corresponding health problems of constipation are also highly interfaced with feeding related issues. Inadequate fluid intake or lack of bulk in the child's diet may contribute to constipation. Although children with Down syndrome or CNS dysfunction are susceptible to constipation, an investigation of sudden changes in bowel patterns is needed (Coyner, 1983). Otherwise, other causes of the child's constipation may be overlooked.

Throughout the management of feeding alterations, it is important to balance the child's nutritional needs with his or her development of feeding skills (Pipes, 1985). An overemphasis on either nutrition or skill development will jeopardize the child's health and development. Lack of proper management contributes to children's developing irregular appetite patterns, food refusal, deficient diets in content (e.g., protein, bulk, iron, and fluids) and calories, resistance to texture, or unnecessarily delayed self-feeding skills.

Deficient nutrition and the corresponding loss of physiological integrity influence the infant's response to the environment and challenges for learning. Abnormal feeding patterns, such as food refusal and irregular appetite, promote behavioral differences in the child and a restriction in the nutrients assimilated. Limited progress in self-feeding skills leads to a delay in self-care or independence for the child. Each step in this cyclical process tends to heighten the impact of the common health problems associated with the child's disability.

State Regulation Alterations

The ability to move from consciousness to sleep is regulated by the central nervous system and by basic hormonal processes. It has been established that children or adults with CNS damage and/or dysfunction often show abnormal sleep–wake patterns. In electrophysiological recordings of sleep, infants with diagnoses of CNS problems do not show the organized patterns of rapid-eye-movement (REM) sleep or of non–rapid-eye-movement (non-REM) sleep instead, they show a disorganized pattern (Schulman, 1969). The available studies also indicate that other signs of neurological abnormality are associated with less control or stability of the processes involved in maintaining conscious and unconscius states (Anders, 1982; Monod & Guidasci, 1976; Prechtl, Theorell, & Blair, 1973). Parmelee (1970) speculated that one of the early indicators of CNS function may be the ability of the infant to maintain a period of non-REM sleep. Children with a diagnosis of mental retardation have been shown to have fewer rapid eye movements during REM sleep (Feinberg, Braun, & Schulman, 1969). These results led to the hypothesis that sleep and cognition are related. There are two possibilities for this relationship. One explanation is that both processes are related to CNS function and thus suffer to similar degrees from lesions of the brain. The second possible explanation is that the processes are intrinsically related and that during sleep, the brain is actively carrying on certain processes complementary to and required for waking cognition.

With the evidence to date, it is reasonable to expect abnormal sleep–wake patterns in children with CNS dysfunction. The normal sleep cycle is about 60–90 minutes in length, and then there is a brief arousal, during which the infant either goes to an awake state or moves back down into another sleep cycle. Even at birth, infants are able to put several cycles together, and by 3 or 4 months they are able to sustain sleep for hours. Typically, infants with CNS immaturity or damage do not show the same ability to modulate these sleep–arousal transitions.

It is not practical or even advisable for all children to have laboratory sleep recordings. However, it is possible to note several features of the sleep–wake patterning from a sleep activity record (Barnard, 1979). These features are the amount of 24 hour sleep, the amount of day sleep, the amount of night sleep, the number of sleep periods, and the amount and frequency of crying. Barnard and Kang (1986) have found that infants under 4 months of age with more total sleep and more day sleep have lower IQ scores at 4 and 8 years of age. Likewise, infants with long amounts of sleep in the earliest months may also demonstrate the difficulty of state transitioning, that is going from sleep to wake. Therefore, when they get to sleep, the organization of their sleep is not as patterned, and they do not move from state to state in as orderly a fashion. These infants are in a constant state of less organized sleep and do not come to arousal periods as well. Preterm infants sleep more in 24 hours than term counterparts and have more sleep during the daytime. This sleep pattern is related to later IQ and also to the amount of time the infant is available for parent–infant interaction (Barnard & Kang. 1986). Parent of high-sleep prematures report less emotional closeness to the infant.

In addition, Barnard & Kang (1986) found that the amount of crying after 4 months is related to behavior problems in later years, so that infants with high amounts and many episodes of crying are reported by their parents and teachers in later years to have more behavioral disturbances. These findings may be associated with a basic ability of the infant and the child to regulate behavior. Perhaps, the infants who cry more are demonstrating the difficulty they have with information processing. It is easier for their systems to get overloaded or disorganized by too much input or by input that comes too fast. Not being able to process the information leads to a system overload for these infants. The resulting discharge is manifested in crying, a tension or overload-release mechanism. Crying as a behavioral index of temperament patterns is discussed by McDevitt in Chapter 13.

In assessing the health of children, it is important to find out about their sleep patterns. Children with developmental problems are more likely to express sleep–wake difficulty, and thus, it is even more critical to assess their sleep patterns. When possible, measures should be instituted that provide the child the environmental structure that facilitates predictable patterns of sleep and activity. For example, recent success has been found in using a "prefeeding treatment." Parents are taught how to wake an infant up before feeding by bringing the infant to a good alert state. Parent–child interaction is improved by a "prefeeding treatment." and infants demonstrate earlier diurnal cycling; that is, they sleep more at night than during the daytime (Barnard, 1985). Also, when a child demonstrates high irritability or tension, it is important to provide more appropriate amounts or timing of stimulation. Zelle (1983) provided good suggestions for approaches in daily care routines to mediate the attention level and the sensory response threshold.

Activity Alterations and Safety Hazards

Children with abnormal muscle tone and reflex responses commonly have alterations in activity patterns. Considerations of safety are also important in relation to these activity differences. As reported by Coyner (1983), examples of the physical health implications of activity differences include (a) fragile bones due to bone tissue demineralization· (b) altered respiratory function due to the predominance of the prone and supine positions and limited movement of the trunk and limbs, and (c) decreased skin temperatures in the extremities because of a reduction in circulation (p. 23). Altered activity patterns interfere with all aspects of the child's development. The hypotonia found in some children with Down syndrome creates difficulties for movement of the infant's arms and the endurance needed to practice movements. The hypertonic muscle patterns exhibited by some children with cerebral palsy may pull the child into exaggerated extension positions that may limit exploration and direct facial interaction with others (Zelle & Coyner, 1983). These abnormal patterns and the compensatory movements that are commonly developed over time for interacting with the environment are often ineffective and tiring for the child. Because of the highly interactive nature of the child's sensory and motor development, abnormal patterns of activity in concert with impaired sensory systems adversively influence the child's exploration (Zelle & Coyner, 1983). An infant with abnormal motor patterns may seldom experience what the normal infant regularly practices.

Children with congenital heart or pulmonary disease are also vulnerable to altered activity patterns and the consequences in development. Because of the fatigue associated with chronic heart or pulmonary illness, the child may have limited movement and/or reduced activity.

In addition to the safety measures applicable to all children, disabled infants and toddlers present some special challenges for accident prevention. In children who have a neuromuscular disorder, sitting balance and upper trunk control may proceed more slowly and may thus create the need for continually adapting seating devices for proper size and stability (Coyner, 1983). Children who have seizure disorders that are not medically controlled may have increased risk of accidents due to falls. The young child with a motor disability is also prone to falls, and his or her environment needs to be regularly inspected for accident hazards as exploration proceeds.

Hearing Alterations

Hearing problems are commonly manifested in children with disabilities. The American Academy of Pediatrics (1982a) Joint Committee on Infant Hearing distributed a position statement that delineates the factors that identify infants who are at risk for having a hearing impairment. According to this statement, the incidence of moderate to profound hearing loss in this at-risk group is 2.5%–5%. The risk criteria developed by the American Academy of Pediatrics are as follows:

- Anatomic malformations involving the head or neck (e.g., cleft palate and Down syndrome).
- Birth weight of 1,500 grams (e.g., prematurity).
- Congenital perinatal infection (e.g., rubella and cytomegalovirus).
- Hyperbilirubinemia that exceeds indications for exchange transfusion.
- Bacterial meningitis (e.g., hemophilus influenzae).
- Severe asphyxia (e.g., Apgar scores of 0–3 and failure to have spontaneous respiration by 10 minutes; hypotonia beyond 2 hours of age).
- Family history of childhood hearing disorder.

According to the America Academy of Pediatrics recommendations (1982a), infants with any of the above risk criteria should be screened by an audiologist by 3 months of age. Electrophysiological or behavioral responses to sound should be used in the initial screening, and any questionable or positive signs of hearing loss indicate immediate referral. However, routine hearing screening by the primary-care provider should begin from birth with testing of the newborn's response to sound.

Hearing loss may be a result of conductive or sensorineural dysfunction or a combination of these. Middle-ear disease is the most common cause of *conductive hearing impairment*, which involves the outer or middle ear (Blackman, 1984b). Intermittent hearing loss characterizes middle-ear infections and produces a decrease in the perceived loudness of sound. Gottlieb (1983) reported that chronic middle-ear infections, if not treated successfully, may cause repeated episodes of hearing loss and may interfere with the development of speech and language skills. The language and cognitive implications for children with a hearing impairment are discussed by Hoffmeister in Chapter 7. If a child is further compromised because of an existing disability such as Down syndrome, hearing loss during the early years makes him or her doubly vulnerable. There is a high incidence of middle-ear disease in children who have Down syndrome, because of the associated deviations in oral-facial structure, such as malformed nasal bones, dysfunction of the eustachian tube, and hyperplasia of the adenoids and tonsils (Blackman, 1984b; Coyner, 1983). Children who have cleft palate also have a high rate of hearing impairment because of eustachian tube dysfunction (Hardy, 1984).

In addition to early screening at 3 months of age for a hearing loss, children who are at high risk need early identification and prompt treatment of middle-ear disease and upper respiratory infections. Regularly scheduled audiological evaluations are also necessary to maximize early treatment. In many situations, promptly applied medical or surgical treatment limits the intermittent hearing loss caused by middle-ear disease and restores the child's hearing to normal.

Sensorineural hearing loss results from damage to the inner ear or the auditory nerve. The cause of sensorineural damage may be losses occurring when the inner-ear structures fail to develop or are damaged after formation. Drugs, infections, birth trauma, and genetically determined factors have been found to produce sensorineural damage (Ahmann, 1986). A sensorineural hearing loss is often associated with children who have cerebral palsy (Taft & Matthews, 1983). Loudness and clarity of sound are decreased. Amplification is the existing mode of treatment, as there are no effective medical or surgical approaches at the present time (Blackman, 1984b).

Visual Alterations

The visual impairments commonly found in children with disabilities include such conditions as blindness, strabismus, refractive errors, and diseases of the eye structure. Having a visual disorder by itself presents unusual challenges for the child. When it is associated with other dysfunctions, the infant is doubly vulnerable to alterations in activity patterns and developmental processes (Coyner, 1983). Deprivation of visual information creates difficulties in the child's social relationships. In Chapter 1 of this book, Wachs reports that blind infants are at risk for alterations in social-emotional-interpersonal development. Wach discusses evidence of divergent, nonparallel patterns of social-emotional development when comparing blind with normal infants and preschool-aged children. The divergent developmental pathway may not be completely adaptable for the blind individual. In view of this pattern of findings, a comprehensive assessment of blind children should include social-emotional factors.

Because few visual impairments result in total loss of vision, early assessment of the infant's functional vision is necessary (Davidson, 1983). Coyner (1983) suggested that, whenever CNS disease is involved in the child's condition, early ophthalmological and regular follow-ups are essential. Primary health care should include visual screening and monitoring of the eye structure and function in routine health evaluations for all children. However, special attention to a regular, ongoing assessment of the visual system of children with disabilities is essential. Thirty percent of children who are multiply handicapped have a visual disorder (Schor, 1984b).

Examples of selected disabilities that place children at risk for visual disorders are provided to highlight the importance of close monitoring of the eye structure and function of children with disabilities. Low-birth-weight infants are vulnerable to refractive errors, muscle imbalance of the eye (strabismus), and blindness (Ahmann, 1986). Children with Down syndrome have an increased incidence of refractive errors, cataracts, and muscle imbalance (Pueschel, 1983).

Susceptibility to Infection and Illness

The gastrointestinal, respiratory, and urinary tract systems are commonly involved when the child with a disability experiences an acute illness. Factors that increase the disabled infant's vulnerability to infections include limited activity, poor coordination of the suck–swallow reflexes and breathing during feedings, inadequate nutrition, and structural differences in the body systems, such as eustachian tube abnormalities (Coyner, 1983). Skin problems are also more prevalent in children with disabilities. Children with ostomies of the stomach (e.g., feeding-tube openings) and colon (e.g., diversion of bowel contents) are susceptible to skin breakdown near the stomas (Henderson & Mapel, 1984). Limited sensation in the lower extremities and inactivity also predispose the child to skin problems.

The premature infant is highly susceptible to infections because its immunological system is more immature than that of the normal newborn infant. In addition, its skin and mucous membranes do not provide the same level of defense as is found in the normal newborn. Therefore, respiratory illness may occur more frequently than in normal infants during the first year (Ahmann, 1986). The immune system of children with Down syndrome is also suspected to be deficient. Levine (1979) suggested that the anatomical differences found, for example, in the respiratory system of children with Down syndrome do not appear to be a sufficient explanation for the increased incidence of respiratory infections. Children with Down syndrome also have a higher incidence of acute lymphatic leukemia and infectious diseases. The mechanisms causing the immunological weakness are under study, and early results indicate some evidence of thymus abnormalities in children with Down syndrome (Levine, 1979). As described in the section on hearing alterations, Down syndrome is often accompanied by structural nasal, mouth, and ear deviations that contribute to the high incidence of middle-ear and/or respiratory disease.

Children with cleft lip and palate are also susceptible to upper respiratory infections and middle-ear disease due to structural disorders. Foods and liquids are in contact with the eustachian tube, predisposing it to inflammation (Gottlieb, 1983).

According to Wolraich (1984), urinary tract infections occur more commonly in children who have myelomeningocele, a midline defect of the skin, the spinal column, and the spinal cord. Neurogenic bladders often accompany this disorder, and thus, these children do not have the urge to urinate or do not have urinary sphincter control. Infections occur when the urine is not emptied totally.

If the child has repeated acute episodes of illness, not only does the likelihood of secondary complications increase, but his or her energy for coping with the primary difficulties of the disability itself is reduced. Bax (1981) reported that preschool children who do not have the additional problems of disabilities are more likely to have developmental and behavioral problems if they have frequent repeated infections.

Special attention must be given to any change in the disabled child's behavior not explained by other factors. Fussiness or behavioral changes may be the only early indications that the child has an infection or an acute illness. Having the parents as well as the primary-health-care provider well informed of the child's symptoms and changes, which need prompt attention, is an important strategy for reducing further unnecessary complications. When providing preventive health care to children with disabilities, the primary-care provider also has a responsibility to be aware of the special recommendations for immunizations for these children (American Academy of Pediatrics, 1982b). The child's parents need to be appropriately included in the decision-making process by having the primary-health-care professional provide sufficient information and opportunity for discussion of the indications for or against immunizations and appropriate alterations. Informed consent of the parents is routinely a component of health care in relation to immunizations and other procedures and is especially important at this time.

SUMMARY

In this chapter, we have emphasized the importance of primary health care for the child with developmental disabilities. All children should have regular health monitoring (Barnard & Douglas, 1974). For children with developmental problems, it is even more important because of the likelihood of functional alterations. It is important that functional status be monitored and that the treatments available be instituted as soon as possible. It makes little sense to have a child in an early intervention program while an ear infection is causing a hearing loss and the infection is using up energy.

The type of approach required is one in which there is an overall case manager who works with the family. This case manager assumes the overall coordination of the child's care, integrating the services required with continued family involvement in planning the total program. Often, the community health nurse or nurse practitioner associated with an early intervention program is best suited to this responsibility. There have been several demonstrations of how effective this case management system is (Kang & Barnard, 1986).

We have summarized the types of functional alterations that are frequently seen in children with developmental disabilities. It is the responsibility of all persons associated with therapeutic efforts to be mindful of these factors and to assess the pattern of function with regard to eating, sleeping, activity, and sensory processing. Augmenting function in these basic daily life activities will increase the success of educational and other therapeutic program goals.

REFERENCES

Ahmann, E. (1986). *Home care for the high risk infant*. Rockville, MD: Aspen Publications.

American Academy of Pediatrics. (1981). *Report of the committee on practice and ambulatory medicine: Guidelines for preventative health supervision of infants and children*. Evanston, IL: Author.

American Academy of Pediatrics. (1982a). Joint committee on infant hearing position statement. *Pediatrics, 70*, 496–497.

American Academy of Pediatrics. (1982b). *Report of the committee on infectious disease* (19th ed.). Evanston, IL: Author.

Anders, T. F. (1982). Neurophysiological studies of sleep in infants and children. *Journal of Child Psychology and Psychiatry, 23*, 75–83.

Barnard, K. E., & Douglas, H. B. (1974). *Child health assessment: I. A literature review*. U.S. Department of Health, Education and Welfare. DHEW publication no. (HRA)75-30.

Barnard, K. (1979). *Nursing child assessment sleep/activity record manual*. Seattle: University of Washington, NCAST Publications.

Barnard, K. E., Hammond, M., Mitchell, S. K., Booth, C. L., Spietz, A., Snyder, C., & Elas, T. (1985). Caring for high-risk infants and their families. In M. Green (Ed), *The psychosocial aspects of the family*. Lexington, MA: Lexington Books.

Barnard, K. (1985). *Nurisng systems toward effective parenting-premature: Final report*. Funded by Maternal and Child Health Training, Grant # MCH-009035, Department of Health and Human Services.

Barnard, K., & Kang, R. (1986). *State modulation concepts for nursing systems toward effective parenting-premature training manual*. Seattle: University of Washington, NCAST Publications.

Barness, L. A. (1981). *Manual of pediatric physical diagnosis*. New York: Yearbook Medical Publishers.

Belsky, J. (1984). The determinants of parenting: A process model. *Child Development, 55*, 83–96.

Bernstein, L. H. (1981). Neurological evaluation. In W. K. Frankenburg, S. M. Thornton, & M. E. Cohrs (Eds.), *Pediatric developmental diagnosis*. New York: Thieme-Stratton.

Blackman, J. A. (1984a). Down's syndrome. In J. A. Blackman (Ed.), *Medical aspects of developmental disabilities in children birth to three*. Rockville, MD: Aspen Systems Corporation.

Blackman, J. (1984b) Middle ear disease. In J. A. Blackman (Ed.), *Medical aspects of developmental disabilities in children birth to three*. Rockville, MD: Aspen Systems Corporation.

Blackman, J. A. (1984c) Perinatal injury. In J. A. Blackman (Ed.), *Medical aspects of developmental disabilities in children birth to three*. Rockville, MD: Aspen Systems Corporation.

Blackman, J. A. (1984d). Routine health care. In J. A. Blackman (Ed.), *Medical aspects of developmental disabilities in children birth to three*. Rockville, MD: Aspen Systems Corporation.

Blackman, J. A., & Thomson, E. (1984). Genetics. In J. A. Blackman (Ed.), *Medical aspects of developmental disabilities in children birth to three*. Rockville, MD: Aspen Systems Corporation.

Brandt, P. (1984). Stress buffering effects of social support on maternal discipline. *Nursing Research, 33*, 229–234.

Bresnan, M., & Hicks, E. (1983). Seizure disorders. In M. Levine, W. Carey, A. Crocker, & R. Gross (Eds.), *Developmental-behavioral pediatrics*. Philadelphia: W. B. Saunders.

Cadol, R. V. (1981). Medical history and physical examination. In W. K. Frankenburg, S. M. Thornton, & M. E. Cohrs (Eds.), *Pediatric developmental diagnosis*. New York: Thieme-Stratton.

Coyner, A. B. (1983). Meeting health needs of handicapped infants. In R. S. Zelle & A. B. Coyner (Eds.), *Developmentally disabled infants and toddlers: Assessment and Intervention*. Philadelphia: F. A. Davis.

Davidson, P. (1983). Visual impairments and blindness. In M. Levine, W. Carey, A. Crocker, & R. Gross (Eds.), *Developmental-behavioral pediatrics.* Philadelphia: W. B. Saunders.

Feinberg, L., Braun, M., & Shulman, E. (1969). EEG sleep patterns in mental retardation. *Electroencephalography and Clinical Neurophysiology., 27,* 128–141.

Gottlieb, M. (1983). Otitis media. In M. Levine, W. Carey, A. Crocker, & R. Gross (Eds.), *Developmental-behavioral pediatrics.* Philadelphia: W. B. Saunders.

Hardy, J. (1984). Cleft lip and palate. In J. Blackman (Ed.), *Medical aspects of developmental disabilities in children birth to three.* Rockville, MD: Aspen Systems Corporation.

Healy, A. (1980). Contemporary theory. In A. Coyner & S. Furuno (Eds.), *Guidelines for early intervention programs.* (Based on a conference entitled Health Issues in Early Intervention Programs.) Salt Lake City: College of Nursing, University of Utah.

Healy, A. (1984). Cerebral palsy. In J. A. Blackman (Ed.), *Medical aspects of developmental disabilities in children birth to three.* Rockville, MD: Aspen Systems Corporation.

Henderson, M., & Mapel, J. (1984). The colostomy and ileostomy. In J. Blackman (Ed.), *Medical aspects of developmental disabilities in children birth to three.* Rockville, MD: Aspen Systems Corporation.

Howard, J., & Beckwith, L. (1980). Child change in an early intervention program for the developmentally disabled. In A. Coyner & S. Furuno (Eds.), *Guidelines for early intervention programs.* (Based on a conference entitled Health Issues in Early Intervention Programs.) Salt Lake City: College of Nursing, University of Utah.

Kang, R., & Barnard, K. (1986). *Evaluation of the child developmental clinical nurse specialist role.* Final report submitted to the Washington State Department of Maternal-Child Health and the Division of Maternal Child Health, DHHS, Rockville, MD.

Levine, S. (1979). The immune system in Down's syndrome. *Down's Syndrome Papers and Abstracts for Professionals, 2,* 2–6.

Merkens, M. J., Burr, C. K., & Perrin, J. M. (1985). *Primary providers in the care of handicapped children.* Unpublished manuscript, Primary Care Center and Department of Pediatrics, Vanderbilt University.

Monod, N., & Guidasci, S. (1976). Sleep and brain malformation in the neonatal period. *Neuropaediatrie, 7,* 229–249.

O'Brien, D., & McCabe, E. (1981). Metabolic evaluation. In W. K. Frankenburg, S. M. Thornton, & M. E. Cohrs (Eds.), *Pediatric developmental diagnosis.* New York: Thieme-Stratton.

Parmelee, A. H. (1970). A panel discussion on sleep cycles in newborn infants: Where might be the gold in these hills? *Neuropaediatrie, 1*(3), 351–353.

Pipes, P. (1985). *Nutrition in infancy and childhood.* St. Louis: Times Mirror/Mosby.

Prechtl, H. F. R., Theorell, K., & Blair, A. W. (1973). Behavioral state cycles in abnormal infants. *Developmental Medicine and Child Neurology, 15,* 606–615.

Prensky, A. L., & Palkes, H. S. (1982). *Care of the neurologically handicapped child.* New York: Oxford University Press.

Pueschel, S. (1983). The child with Down's syndrome. In M. Levine, W. Carey, A. Crocker, & R. Gross (Eds.), *Developmental-behavioral pediatrics.* Philadelphia: W. B. Saunders.

Schor, D. P. (1984a). The neurological examination. In J. A. Blackman (Ed.), *Medical aspects of developmental disabilities in children birth to three.* Rockville, MD: Aspen Systems Corporation.

Schor, D. P. (1984b). Visual impairment. In J. Blackman (Ed.), *Medical aspects of developmental disabilities in children birth to three.* Rockville, MD: Aspen Systems Corporation.

Schuett, V. E., Brown, E., & Michals, K. (1985). Reinstitution of diet therapy in PKU patients from twenty-two U.S. clinics. *American Journal of Public Health, 75,* 39–42.

Schulman, C. A. (1969). Alterations of the sleep cycle in heroin-addicted and suspect newborns. *Neuropaediatrie, 1,* 89–100.

Schultz, F. R. (1984). Phenylketonuria and other metabolic diseases. In J. A. Blackman (Ed.), *Medical aspects of developmental disabilities in children birth to three.* Rockville, MD:Aspen Systems Corporation.

Seashore, M., Friedman, E., Novelly, R. A., & Bapat, V. (1985). Loss of intellectual function in children with phenylketonuria after relaxation of dietary phenylalanine restriction. *Pediatrics, 75,* 226–232.

Sujansky, E. (1981). Genetic evaluation. In W. K. Frankenburg, S. M. Thornton, & M. E. Cohrs (Eds.), *Pediatric developmental diagnosis.* New York: Theime-Stratton.

Taft, L., & Matthews, W. (1983). Cerebral palsy. In M. Levine, W. Carey, A. Crocker, & R. Gross (Eds.), *Developmental-behavioral pediatrics.* Philadelphia: W. B. Saunders.

Wolraich, M. (1984). Myelomeningocele. In J. Blackman (Ed.), *Medical aspects of developmental disabilities in children birth to three*. Rockville, MD: Aspen Systems Corporation.

Zander, K. S. (1980). *Primary nursing development and management*. Germantown, MD: Aspen Systems Corporation.

Zelle, R. S. (1983). Environmental and habilitative approaches to mediate the attention level and response threshhold. In R. S. Zelle & A. B. Coyner, (Eds.), *Developmentally disabled infants and toddlers assessment and intervention*. Philadelphia: F. A. Davis.

Zelle, R. S., & Coyner, A. B. (1983). *Developmentally disabled infants and toddlers*. Philadelphia: F. A. Davis.

From Assessment to Intervention

The most frequently cited purpose of assessing handicapped infants and preschoolers is that such assessment leads to successful intervention. Gradel argues in Chapter 18 that the focus of assessment must be shifted from passive to active. Assessment emphasizing a focus on the ability of children to learn is cited as being preferable to assessment focusing on children's ability to perform. The importance of intervention goals in selecting assessment efforts is also emphasized in this chapter.

In the final chapter, Wachs and Sheehan carefully consider each of the themes that have emerged from earlier chapters each of the themes that have emerged from earlier chapters and attempt to link those themes to assessment and intervention. In this respect, the authors function in the same fashion as the clinicians who will use the text to guide their own assessment efforts. These themes that have emerged—the use of decision rules, the need for carefully articulated assessment purposes, the need for an assessment of learning (as well as of performance), and the need for a broad range of assessment efforts—are general enough to apply across all handicapping conditions, yet specific enough to truly guide practice. The incorporation of these themes into practice should have a positive effect on the assessment of infants and preschoolers with developmental disabilities.

18

Interface between Assessment and Intervention for Infants and Preschoolers with Disabilities

Kathleen Gradel

INTRODUCTION

A casual question such as "What can she do?" posed by a visitor to an infant program for children with disabilities is typically answered by a series of relatively precise, descriptive statements by the teacher, including: "She can say 'hi' by waving her hand and whispering, 'HA'. She can stack three blocks; push a ball on the floor to a friend who is one foot away; put a circle in a three-piece formboard; imitate rocking a baby and hand-clapping . . . " Informal, anecdotal skill profiles such as these offered by practitioners are impressive samples of both the range and the specificity of their knowledge about their charges. Coupled with the pool of information that they have on specific children over time, the breadth of their information base is difficult to synthesize and summarize (Gradel, Thompson, & Sheehan, 1981; Sheehan & Gallagher, 1984).

Attempts of programs to systematize assessment across multiple curricular domains and skill areas have resulted in varied approaches. The four most common are the following:

1. A norm-referenced measure that is economical in administration time and that generates a developmental score or a skill profile on a restricted sample of developmental markers, for example, the Bayley Scales (1969) and the McCarthy Scales (1972).
2. A domain- or criterion-referenced measure consisting of numerous developmentally sequenced items in specific curricular domains, which stands alone without an accompanying curriculum guide, for example, the Vulpé Assessment Battery (Vulpé, 1977), the Learning Accomplishment Profile (LeMay, Griffin, & Sanford, 1977), and the Uniform Performance Assessment System (White, Edgar, Haring, Affleck, Hayden, & Bendersky, 1980).
3. A domain- or criterion-referenced measure, similar to those above, that corre-

---

KATHLEEN GRADEL • Department of Special Education, University of Maryland, College Park, Maryland 20742.

sponds to an available curriculum or activity guide, including, for example, the Hawaii Early Learning Program (Furuno, O'Reilly, Hosaka, Inatsuka, Allman, & Zeisloft, 1979), the Carolina Curriculum for Handicapped Children and Infants at Risk (Johnson-Martin, Jens, & Attermeir, 1986), the Portage Project Checklist (Bluma, Shearer, Frosham, & Hilliard, 1976), and the Early Intervention Developmental Profile (Schafer & Moersch, 1981).

4. A domain- or criterion-referenced measure that provides child performance data that are equally usable in designing interventions across domains and that have some structural or hierarchial foundations, including the Uzgiris-Hunt Scales of Infant Psychological Development (Uzgiris & Hunt, 1975) and the Chicago Infant Neuromotor Assessment (Cech, Josephs, Pearl, & Gallagher, 1983; Gallagher & Cech, this volume).

Assessment activities rarely correspond closely to interventions conducted in infant programs (Sheehan & Gallagher, 1984). Both norm-referenced instruments and criterion-referenced tools often meet neither the basic needs of the interventionist nor the demands presented by the heterogeneous skills and deficits of the baby with mild, moderate, or severe disabilities (see reviews in this book by Robinson & Fieber, Simeonsson & Bailey, and Stagg). The expenditure of time involved in using many instruments may be inordinate compared to the utility of the data generated. Worse, the pool of child performance data gathered may negatively affect the quality of the interventions designed for the child. Examples abound in practice in which standard administrations of a developmental scale such as the Bayley Scales and the subsequent use of a skill profile generated from the test result in a list of intervention objectives consisting primarily of failed items. This is a highly restrictive pool of items on which to base an intervention (Pomerantz & Gradel, 1981).

Practitioners frequently assume that the translation of assessment data into day-to-day intervention plans for infants with mild to severe disabilities is less a problem when they use a criterion-referenced instrument that is packaged with a curriculum. This strategy, used widely by federally funded model infant programs, may provide the necessary breadth of skill assessment not possible with instruments like the Bayley Scales (Fewell & Kelly, 1983; Pefley & Smith, 1976). Unfortunately, the intervention programs resulting from the direct translation of such developmental checklists into daily practice may suffer from other problems.

Early-childhood special educators have designed interventions based largely on items on developmental measures (Kaiser & Hayden, 1977). Child performance on such items is helpful in predicting the extent to which babies with developmental disabilities will parallel the development of nondisabled children. However, interventions based solely on such items tend to ignore the persistent problems associated with using a restricted range of item-specific behaviors. For handicapped children, these items are frequently not representative of the underlying developmental skills presumably being tapped. Further, the items fail to address the broader "survival skills" seen as being critical if young children are to live, play, and go to school in settings with their nondisabled peers and siblings (Sainato & Lyon, 1983; Sheehan & Gradel, 1983; Vincent, Salisbury, Walter, Brown, Gruenewald, & Powers, 1980; Walter & Vincent, 1982).

Practitioners, model developers, and researchers have continued to design, refine, discard, blend, and otherwise experiment with assessment tools and strategies, largely in the context of their particular research or service program. As increased choices in tools and strategies have become available, a parallel emphasis on documentation has emerged (Sheehan, 1982). As a result, the assessment of child progress has become a major concern of infancy–preschool programs for both program evaluation and for aid in implementing interventions. As documentation demands have increased, however, practitioners have continued to press for economical assessments that generate data closely tied to interventions (Sheehan, 1981, 1982).

Assuming that the baby has been identified and placed in a program, the interventionist's concerns typically do not lie in securing diagnostic information, a task that is largely guided by norm-referenced testing (Sheehan & Gallagher, 1984). Rather, the interventionist's task is to design and evaluate educational programs. This focus affords practitioners the potential "luxury" of making assessment decisions with a more process-than product-oriented eye and with a greater degree of flexibility in collecting data that are more directly related to their intervention efforts. This flexibility, however, does not simplify the task of tracking child progress in programs. In fact, it may complicate responsibilities of the teacher, who is expected to be an educational synthesizer, project manager, parent coordinator, and responsive trainer, as well as an assessment specialist (Bricker, 1984). What is clear is that direct-service practitioners must focus on the collection and analysis of data likely to be most useful in making day-to-day decisions about ongoing instruction. The following four qualities characterize such data; they are

1. Discrete, yet qualitatively descriptive of specific skills that are present or that are future intervention targets.
2. Relevant to specific demands of real living and school environments.
3. Useful in the process of instructional decision-making.
4. Likely to convey maximum, nonredundant information with the least amount of time taken from intervention activities.

This chapter focuses on these assessment needs of the practitioner as she or he designs and implements interventions. As the basic day-to-day and longitudinal assessment-related concerns of the infant–preschool special educator are discussed, strategies for meeting those assessment needs are presented and critiqued.

UTILITY OF CRITERION-REFERENCED ASSESSMENT DATA IN DEVELOPING INTERVENTIONS

Administration of Standardized Test Items

Depending on the measure, the information generated by particular items can be viewed as more or less discrete. Interventionists may wish to rely heavily on one or more individual items from standardized tests when designing interventions. Take, for example, an early item on the Bayley Scales, "Reacts to disappearance of face," which appears on many criterion-referenced measures as well. This item is administered by quickly moving out of the baby's range of vision when the child is looking at the examiner's face. A change in facial expression or "other evidence of reaction" (including a smile vanishing, attempts to visually track, or a change in activity level) to the disappearing face is credited as a pass on the item (Bayley, 1969, p. 47). Although most experienced Bayley examiners easily determine whether this item has been passed or failed, the practitioner receiving the protocol is likely to question how the baby performed on the item. When the failed item is incorporated into an educational objective, the teacher would benefit from knowing one or more of the following things about the child's performance while being tested, as he or she designs an intervention:

1. The number of trials attempted to elicit the response.
2. The latency between the disappearance of the face and the response of the baby.
3. Whose face was disappearing (e.g., an examiner's, a parent's, a familiar practitioner's).
4. The distance between the baby's and the examiner's faces.
5. The events that preceded the disappearance of the face (e.g., did the disappearing face coincide with a natural episode of gaze aversion by the baby, following a high-stimulation interaction?).
6. The distance from the baby's focus of attention to the point at which the face disappeared (e.g., 6 inches to the edge of the bassinette or 1½ feet to the edge of the crib).
7. The rate at which the face moved across the "attention zone" and disappeared.

In each case, one or more of these conditions may account for a pass or fail on the part of a baby with moderate or severe disabilities. For example, a slow response latency could account for a failure, depending on either the speed at which the face disappeared or the amount of time the examiner waited for a response once the face disappeared. Knowledge of the nature of the baby's responses and test conditions such as these could assist the teacher in designing instruction. For instance, if the baby were more likely to pass the item when the parent's face moved slowly across a short distance (e.g., when the baby is on a changing table versus in a crib), the teacher could begin instruction under these conditions. Subsequently, he or she could add dimensions of presumed "complexity" for this baby, including increasing the distance and the time the baby was expected to watch, before the disappearance of the face.

Needless to say, it is unlikely that a clinician using the Bayley Scales would document the information suggested in the preceding example. Administration of the Bayley and similar norm-referenced scales (e.g., Cattell, 1949, 1960; Gesell, 1947) is expected to result in a standard test protocol following standardized assessment procedures. Additional information regarding the baby's general responsiveness and overall test performance is usually provided in a narrative format in an assessment summary. Such summaries rarely lend themselves to more discrete item-by-item analysis, nor are they expected to.

Even on criterion-referenced instruments that have many more items and a more lengthy anticipated administration time, there is little additional pay-off to the practitioner in the specificity of the data generated. Because few recording forms or test directions prompt assessors to do otherwise, performance is typically recorded as a "pass" or a "fail," despite the potential utility of added documentation. An additional problem posed by many of the criterion-referenced scales is their less structured directions for item administration. This format potentially increases the flexibility of adapting items to children's specific disabilities. However, it tends to increase the range of interpretation possible by the individual who receives the information, given the qualitative variations in children's responses possible under varied testing conditions. Instrument protocols rarely provide ways to systematically report such information. Despite the objections of practitioners to the restrictiveness of bimodal responses and the amount of intervention-related data lost by such record keeping, they tend to complete instruments in a bimodal fashion in the interest of time economy.

Systematic Item Modification

A recent emphasis by early-childhood special educators and teachers of students with multiple and/or severe disabilities is test adaptation (see the Stagg and the Robinson & Fieber chapters in this book). A prime example is the Adaptive Performance Inventory (API), developed and field-tested by the Consortium on Adaptive Performance Evaluation under an Office of Special Education grant (Gentry, 1980). Borrowing largely from existing developmental instruments, the API consists of 400 sequentially arranged items. It is particularly appropriate for infants and children functioning below age two years.

The API provides a model for systematically modifying test items and for reporting the responses of children to these modifications. For each item on which a sensory or motoric disability is likely to affect a child's performance, one of two types of "standard" adaptations is provided. "Direction adaptations" involve changing item administration, materials, or child position. For example, the item "following comprehensible verbal directions given by an unfamiliar adult" is modified for a deaf and blind child by physically manipulaitng the child through the expected behavior, then repositioning him or her and observing to see if the behavior is repeated independently. "Criterion adaptations" allow modifying the way in which the child responds. For example, "postural orientation to an adult" may replace "makes eye contact with adult" for a child with a visual impairment. Adaptations are provided in this way across items for individuals with motoric, visual, and hearing impairments, as well as for deaf and blind children. The record form allows for notation of the child's passing or failing the item under (a) standard conditions, (b) one or more standard adaptations (i.e., those printed in the manual), or (c) novel adaptations.

The API also provides for record keeping on individual test trials and on consistency of child performance for each skill. For most target behaviors, the record form allows for three assessment trials, for which the assessor records a "pass," a "fail," or a "pass-with-assistance" rating. The pass-with-assistance rating is subject to interpretation, as an assist can include any verbal, model, or physical prompt or cue that is provided and, presumably, one or more of such prompts. In addition to the trial-by-trial record, the child is rated in a pass–fail fashion for overall consistency in the performance of the skill. The assessor is to take into account the child's ability to generalize across persons, materials, and environments (based on general knowledge of the child), as well as the observed or reported stability of the child's performance in the consistency rating. This format for recording more than one trial on an item, as well as the global measure of consistency, is at least an initial attempt to meet the practitioner's needs for systematic record-keeping on multiple assessments of items in light of children's variability.

Unfortunately, only field-test versions of the API were disseminated, in an attempt to assess the instrument's psychometric properties and its utility for direct-service personnel. It is currently being revised and field-tested by Bricker and her colleagues in their work on the Evaluation and Programming System (EPS—Bailey & Bricker, 1986; Bricker & Gentry, 1982). The number of assessment steps included in the API are reduced in the EPS; in addition, a clearer link between assessment data and intervention goals is being incorporated into the new format.

Assessment data generated by the API and the EPS are likely to be a few steps closer to immediate use in interventions because of the modifications in the assessment process, as well as the strategies of documenting consistency in child performance under varied assessment conditions. There are still potentially useful pieces of assessment data that are likely to be lost in the process, including:

1. Which prompt(s) worked when assistance was provided? (I.e., did a verbal reminder ever work alone—or only when paired with a model or a physical prompt?)
2. What was the latency of the response?
3. In a multistep task, which part(s) of the task could the child do alone? On which did she or he need help?

Data like these will be valuable when designing systematic interventions. The following sections provide examples of assessment strategies designed to collect such data.

Provision of Assistance on Items

The API (Gentry, 1980) partially took into account the need of the practitioner for information that describes what happens when the child is assisted in completing an item that he or she failed under standard presentation. As interventions designed to teach emerging skills typically rely on prompting methodologies (Billingsley & Romer, 1983; Wolery & Gast, 1984), it is no surprise that educators are interested in what assistance is necessary for the child to perform a particular behavior. Unfortunately, many practitioners, bound by the protocols for administering even criterion-referenced instruments and by time constraints, rarely assess the efficacy of standard prompts in tested skills.

Strain, Sainato, and Maheady (1984) described a procedure used with preschoolers labeled moderately and severely handicapped that they called a "graduated-prompt/reinforcement" assessment. Borrowing from the "least-prompts" or "least-to-most prompting hierarchies" recently described and experimentally validated in the research literature (as reviewed in Billingsley & Romer, 1983), Strain *et al.* (1984) recommended that comprehensive developmentally referenced instruments (e.g., the LAP and the UPAS) be used as the basis of a modified assessment procedure. This procedure is characterized by the following steps, which are followed with the use of alternating items as described in the test manual:

1. Present the item in the standard fashion.
2. If an item is not performed under standard conditions, reintroduce it, model a correct response, and wait for an imitated correct response from the child.
3. If an item is not passed after the model is presented, reintroduce it, model a correct response, provide a partial physical prompt, and wait for a correct response.
4. Finally, if the child does not demonstrate the skill with the previous assistance (Steps 2 and 3), reintroduce the task, model the response, and provide a full physical prompt.
5. Steps 1 through 4 are repeated, with the assessor using previously identified reinforcers contingent on general attention to and compliance with the test (but not specifically for correct task performance).

This assessment sequence, with appropriately recorded data, generates for the practitioner answers to the following questions:

1. Does the child do the task independently and correctly? (This question is answered in all binary-option tests and is answerd in this procedure following the "pass" on an item after its standard presentation.)
2. If the child does not do the task independently, which prompt is likely to produce correct performance? (This question is answered based on the sequence of Steps 2 through 4.)
3. If the child does not do the task independently, will she or he do it contingent on reinforcement alone? (This question is answered when the assessment is continued through Step 5. Presumably, when a reinforcer is introduced and the task is represented [as in Step 1], the child could be motivated to perform the item without prompts or earlier in the prompting sequence.)
4. If the child does not do the task independently, will she or he do it with a specific prompt and contingent on reinforcement? (This question is answered when the assessment continues through Step 5 (as above), but the child does not perform the task independently when it is presented. Instead, she or he does it with one of the prompts. If the child's performance under the prompt-plus-reinforcement condition results in her or his doing the item with a less intrusive prompt (e.g., a model versus a partial physical prompt) than in the previous sequence, the use of the reinforcer is a possible predictor of improved performance during training).

Practitioners schooled in response-prompting procedures typically use them in the context of systematic training, but rarely in the adaptation of standard assessments. Although it is obvious that such strategies would lengthen assessment time, the pay-off in terms of immediately useful data for planning interventions is unquestionable. Given an assessment of this type, a teacher could design interventions on failed items by using selected response prompts (alone or in a hierarchy) and/or reinforcers that he or she is reasonably certain will be effective.

The next section describes more discrete applications of such methodologies in the direct assessment of skills.

DIRECT ASSESSMENT OF SKILLS:
SKILL-SEQUENCE-BASED ASSESSMENT

Several strategies have been used to directly assess young children's competencies on multistep tasks. With the use of finer grained skill analyses (i.e., skill sequences and task analyses) and observational recording systems, profiles of children's skills and deficits in specific skill areas are possible. Such assessments have come into relatively common use among educators of school-aged children with moderate and severe disabilities. These practitioners have come to rely increasingly on methods of systematic instruction (cf. Snell, 1983). Infant and preschool special educators have used such observational procedures less frequently, perhaps because of their reliance on assessment data gathered from developmental checklists.

This section reviews the use of skill sequences for purposes of assessment and intervention. A skill sequence is a list of component skills that is ordered in an easy-to-difficult fashion. By progressing sequentially through the steps over time, the individual acquires increasingly complex skills that lead to the mastery of a terminal goal. Such a sequence provides the practitioner with a list of instructional steps that can function as a series of short-term objectives. This description has some similarity to the concept of a carefully sequenced curriculum. Basically, that is what a well-designed skill sequence becomes, for discrete skill areas. The concept of skill sequences is not new. Skill lattices (Banerdt & Bricker, 1978; Snell, 1983), concept analyses (Becker, Engelmann, & Thomas, 1975), and skill sequences (Bailey & Wolery, 1984) have been frequently reported in the literature in the context of curriculum development. The notion of using discrete skill sequences as a strategy for focusing instructional and assessment time also fits into prevailing emphases on curriculum-based assessment (Blankenship, 1985; Deno, 1985; Marston & Magnusson, 1985; Ysseldyke & Algozzine, 1982).

A new emphasis on the use of skill sequences has occurred recently, with the direction taken by educators of individuals with severe handicaps in developing "top-down curricula" (cf., Brown, Branston, Hamre-Nietupski, Pumpian, Certo, & Gruenewald, 1979). Basically, practitioners are expected to build "backward" from terminal goals, listing skills in an easy-to-hard order leading to the final, complex goal. Such sequencing may be based on developmental logic (Cohen & Gross, 1979), discrimination learning (Becker *et al.*, 1975), and/or functional remedial logic (Guess, Horner, Utley, Holvoet, Maxon, Tucker, & Warren, 1978; McCormick & Noonan, 1984). Each skill in the sequence is expected to relate directly to the terminal goal. Skills that are not directly related are typically excluded. Presumably, if practitioners develop sequences that are more clearly generated from their long-term objectives, extraneous skills are less likely to occupy teaching and testing time.

To some extent, the use of strictly developmental sequences defies such an assessment strategy, as it is assumed that the child will rarely have acquired more complex skills without demonstrating their prerequisites. In addition, many curricula show a single developmental sequence for each primary domain (e.g., fine motor or gross motor). This structure presumes that all of the skills in a domain are logically ordered, one after the other. An alternative structure is to provide shorter sequences that are more focused on specific skill development—or sequences that integrate across relevant domains. This alternative more closely fits the top-down assessment strategy.

1. Looks at person talking and gesturing.
2. Continues movement if it is imitated by caregiver.
3. Will begin a movement already begun by caregiver.
4. Tries to imitate unfamiliar movement.
5. Imitates unfamiliar movement that is not visible to himself or herself.
6. Imitates new activities, including use of materials.

[Stop here if the child is progressing well with spoken words.]

7. Imitates one sign that stands for a word (e.g., "Daddy," "all gone," "more," "eat," or "drink").
8. Imitates two signs that stand for words.
9. Imitates three signs that stand for words.
10. Imitates sequence of two signs that stand for words.

Figure 1. Gestural-imitation skill sequence. (Source: Johnson-Martin, Jens, & Attermeier, 1986, p. 151.)

Such a sequencing format was adopted by Johnson-Martin *et al.* (1986) in the Carolina Curriculum for Handicapped Infants and Infants at Risk. Curriculum sequences and parallel instructional procedures are provided in 24 skill areas. One example of the specificity used is the cluster of five communication sequences that replaces the traditional domains of receptive and expressive language, including (a) responses to communication from others: (b) gestural imitation; (c) gestural communication; (d) vocal imitation; and (e) vocal communication. Within each sequence, steps are listed from least to most complex. For example, in the gestural imitation sequence, the first step is "Looks at person talking and gesturing," which proceeds to "Imitates new activities, including use of materials" (see Figure 1). At that point, optional additional steps are provided for the imitation of manual signs. Such shorter, focused sequences provide a basis for more discrete assessments.

The skill-sequencing strategies used by educators of individuals with severe disabilities have helped to refine the concept in a way that has not previously occurred in many of the available early-childhood special-education curricula. Figures 2, 3, and 4 illustrate three variations that highlight the utility of skill sequencing. Figure 2 is a teacher-developed sequence representing integrated skills of trunk control in a sitting position and object manipulation (M. Baker & L. Lucas, personal communication, 1986). Figure 3 is an object-performance skill sequence modified from versions by Bailey and Wolery (1984), Uzgiris and Hunt (1975), and Filler, Robinson, Smith, Vincent-Smith, Bricker, and Bricker (1975). Figure 4 is a teacher-developed skill sequence on adaptive switch use (J. Nelson, personal communication, 1986). Each figure shows the skill sequence on an accompanying assessment plan.

Several points become obvious when reviewing these skill sequences. The terminal goal for each appears at the top of the sequence. The steps leading to it are arranged in an order that is easiest (at the bottom of the sequence) to most difficult (progressing toward the top of the sequence, or getting closer to the terminal goal).

Further, *each of the intermediate steps is clearly related to the terminal goal.* This format has been adopted by some practitioners to highlight the "top-down"-assessment–"bottom-up"-intervention process. Although procedures vary, the assessor probes on steps of the skill sequence above the point at which the child is expected to be functioning and proceeds sequentially to less and less complex skills. Depending on the skill and the length of the sequence, top-down assessment can begin from the terminal goal or from

ASSESSMENT PLAN: Use 10-sec latency with least prompts sequence on parallel task analysis. The following prompts apply, in a least-to-most intrusive order: Independent; PP1 = shadow; PP2 = shoulder prompt; PP3 = elbow prompt; PP4 = light physical prompt over hands; FP = full physical prompt over hands.

TERMINAL GOAL: Independent sitting position on floor, supporting self in extended-leg position without losing balance while pivoting to pick up objects, catching self when needed, and returning to midline to play with toy.

8. Sits unsupported, hand bearing weight on side, with other hand manipulating (i.e., picking up or reaching) toy on same side.
7. Sits unsupported, one hand resting at side, with other hand reaching for toy at eye level in front of him or her at midline.
6. Sits unsupported, hands to sides, attention focused in front and laterally (e.g., to watch TV or a peer playing).
5. Sits unsupported, hands at midline manipulating a toy while not bearing weight on his or her hands.
4. Sits unsupported, weight on hands at midline, with attention focused at midline.
3. Sits supported (with bolsters or caregiver's assistance from behind), both hands at one side manipulating a toy.
2. Sits supported (as above), hands to sides, attention focused midline front and laterally.
1. Sits supported (as above), hands in midline, attention focused to front and sides.

Figure 2. Trunk-control–object-manipulation skill-sequence.

ASSESSMENT PLAN: For each step, assess three times and record the number of each of the following: I = Independent response; A = Approximation (and record the form of the response).

TERMINAL GOAL: Tracking of objects of interest following a series of invisible displacements by searching in reverse of the order of hiding, using various screens (e.g., scarves, boxes, or pillows) and toys.

20. Finds object following a series of invisible displacements.
19. Finds object following one invisible displacement.
18. Finds object following one invisible displacement with two screens alternated.
17. Finds object following one invisible displacement with two screens alternated.
16. Searches briefly but unsystematically for objects he or she has not seen being hidden.
15. Finds object under three superimposed screens.
14. Finds object that successive visible displacements.
13. Finds object that is completely covered with a single screen in three places.
12. Finds object that is completely covered with a single screen in two places alternately.
11. Moves around barriers when controlling object is not visible.
10. Finds object that is completely covered with a single screen in two places.
9. Moves around barrier when controlling object is still visible.
8. Searches for objects child has observed being hidden (e.g., in one container or spot, or within reach).
7. Moves object when it is out of reach, to access it.
6. Moves body to put object in reach, to access it.
5. Searches for partially hidden object.
4. Reaches for directly available objects in visually directed manner.
3. Notices the disappearance of a slowly moving object.
2. Visually tracks slow movements of objects or persons.
1. Visually fixates on faces or objects.

Figure 3. Object permanence skill sequence.

ASSESSMENT PLAN: Use task-analytic reposition probe on parallel task analysis.
TERMINAL GOAL: Independent initiation of movement from a rest position to the switch and
   subsequent pressure on the switch for 10 seconds to activate electronic toys, in both a side-
   lying and a seated position.

8. When hand is picked up, moves it 5 inches to the switch and drops hand on switch, then
   maintains pressure for 10 seconds to activate toy.
7. When hand is picked up, moves it 3 inches to the switch and drops hand on switch, then
   maintains pressure for 10 seconds to activate toy.
6. When hand is picked up, moves it 1 inch to the switch and drops hand on switch, then
   maintains pressure for 10 seconds to activate toy.
5. When hand is lifted up above the switch, initiates by dropping hand onto the switch,
   then maintains pressure for 10 seconds to activate toy.
4. When hand is moved to and placed to the switch, maintains pressure for 10 seconds.
3. When hand is moved to and placed on the switch, maintains pressure for 7 seconds.
2. When hand is moved to and placed on the switch, maintains pressure for 5 secons.
1. When hand is moved to and placed on the switch, maintains pressure for 3 seconds.

Figure 4. Skill sequence for adaptive switch use.

some advanced intermediate step. In either case, the order is intended to check for intact
skills that may be present in a form described by a more advanced skill in the sequence.
In this way, an economical assessment is conducted, with a more careful reference to the
clearly operationalized long-term goals seen as functional for the child. Following top-
down assessment, instruction begins at the first point at which the child does not perform
a step to the desired criterion. Intervention proceeds "bottom-up" from that step, progressively through the sequence.

Assessment Procedures

The manner in which each of the sample skill sequences may be used for assessment
by the practitioner can vary. The basic notion is that the sequences can be used as checklists. For greatest utility, however, some discrete observational measurement system
would be used to document the child's performance on the assessed steps. In some cases,
the skill can be rated like a binary-option checklist item (i.e., pass or fail) or with more
descriptive codes. Variations include (a) applying a "least-prompts" or graduated-
prompt–reinforcement-assessment strategy to the skill (cf. Strain et al., 1984); (b) rating
the skill in a fashion similar to that used in the API (previously described); or (c) using a
somewhat more descriptive code than a pass–fail option (e.g., a code indicating that the
child demonstrated the step two out of five times). For example, the assessment plan
adopted for the supported sitting sequence in Figure 2 was a prompt hierarchy constructed
of lesser to greater physical prompts. Alternatively, the assessment plan for the object-
permanence sequence (Figure 3) was to tally each direct-assessment trial and to report a
summary of the number of (a) independent correct responses and (b) approximations, or
responses that involved initiations not resulting in correct performance of the skill in
question.

In some instances, a task analysis can be written for one or more steps of the skill
sequence. This was the option selected by J. Nelson (personal communication, 1986),

who used the task analysis illustrated in Figure 5. In this case, a single task analysis lists the basic behaviors implicit in the skill sequence. This skill breakdown describes the physical movements to be done by the child; the steps are ordered based on what would be observed while the child is actively engaged in operating a switch. A comparison of Figure 4 (the skill sequence) and Figure 5 (the task analysis) illustrates the manner in which the two interface. The task analysis describes the minute behaviors involved in total task performance. The skill sequence incorporates some subtleties not built into the task analysis that mark very gradual steps in skill acquisition by a child with severe multiple disabilities. As is obvious in the skill sequence (Figure 4), there are levels of increasing difficulty based on (a) increasingly less trainer assistance in positioning the child's hand in close proximity to the switch and (b) increased time set as the criterion for the child's maintenance of pressure on the switch to activate an electronic toy. The basis of the skill sequence is a functional longitudinal plan that leads to a terminal goal of maintaining pressure on a switch for at least 10 seconds.

The assessor would select a systematic means of testing using the task analysis. At least three options are commonly used: (a) a least-to-most assistance-prompting hierarchy (commonly referred to as *least prompts*); (b) a reposition probe; and (c) a discontinued probe. Although the details of task-analytic assessment will not be reviewed here, the sense of the collective procedures is that assessment data are gathered to answer the following two questions: (a) If the child cannot do the entire skill, what parts of it can she or he do? (b) If parts of the skill are not performed independently, with what type(s) or degree(s) of assistance can the child accomplish them? Table 1 (p. 386) briefly summarizes the basic steps in conducting systematic assessments of these types.

The reader is referred to Figure 5 for an illustration of a task-analytic reposition-probe on the switch-use task analysis. The assessment procedure allows for each step to

Program: Adaptive switch use to activate asst. electronic toys for 10-sec intervals
Student's Name: R.T.
Instructor: J.N.
Setting: side lying/chair
Instructional Cue: "Let's make the _____ (sing/jump/play)"

Steps (latency = 3 sec)	3/1	3/1	3/1	3/1	3/1								
1. Lifts hand up	P[a]	P	P	P	P								
2. Moves hand 5" to switch	I	A	A	A	A								
3. Drops hand on switch pad	I	I	A	A	A								
4. Applies continuous pressure[b]	P	5"	1"	P	2"								
5. Removes hand	I	I	I	I	P								
6. Puts hand in rest position	I	I	I	I	I								

[a]SCORING CODE: I = independent; A = approximation (which is repositioned during probes); P = physical prompt (put-through)
[b]If doesn't hold down switch for at least 2 sec. (during intervention), provide P for 5 sec. Otherwise, mark seconds switch is activated.

Figure 5. Switch-use reposition-probe data.

be tested. If a step is not done correctly and independently, the child is placed in a "ready" position to perform the subsequent step. It is therefore possible to secure an ongoing record of maximal performance, even in cases in which the child has few skills. As indicated by the data, the child did not lift his hand to initiate movement toward the switch from a resting position (Step 1). In all cases, activation of the switch required the assessor's moving the child's hand to a "ready" position off the surface in order for him to move his hand to the switch (Steps 2 and 3). The maintenance of adequate pressure to activate the toy required sporadic physical assistance by the assessor, as indicated by the variable data on Step 4. The child almost consistently moved his hand from the switch and returned it to a resting position (Steps 5 and 6).

When the minute profile obtained from such an assessment is compared to the overall skill sequence, several points become clear. The most difficult step is the terminal goal; the "easiest" step is the consistent maintenance of pressure on the switch for 3 seconds, when the child is required to make no initiation to the switch. If we compare the child's performance during assessment with the longitudinal plan presented in the skill sequence, it is clear that he has not met a reasonable acquisition criterion; in only one case did he operate the switch for at least 3 seconds. Because the time spent activating the switch is deemed the most critical in this sequence, switch activation would be trained in a bottom-up fashion, proceeding from Step 1 to Step 2 of the sequence, and so on, once criterion had been met on each successive step. Figure 6 (p. 388) is a summary of the intervention plan designed for instruction on Step 1 of the skill sequence.

Interface between Skill Sequence Assessment and Intervention

There are several advantages to writing and using skill sequences. First, a well-designed skill sequence minimizes the need to assume that there are subsequent instructional steps that build toward a usable terminal goal. This is, unfortunately, a problem in many intervention programs; early-childhood special educators assess, train a skill to criterion, and then make a somewhat arbitrary decision about the next skill to test and teach. The practice of constructing curricula by assembling multiple indirectly related skills into sequences representative of broad domains increases this potential problem. In other words, the next step listed in the curriculum in use could well be only indirectly related to the skill just mastered. Nevertheless, it could be targeted as the next step to be taught, even if more logically related skills might more closely match the deficit skill repertoire.

A second related problem potentially solved by using good skill sequences is that of maximally apportioning testing and teaching energies. Two points are pertinent. First, should the child fail to move completely through the sequence to the terminal goal, it is highly likely that she or he will have at least some directly related skills intact. This may not be the case in less clearly defined instructional sequences. Moreover, top-down assessment using skill sequences may better accommodate children's idiosyncratic movement through learning sequences. Interventionists are more likely to "catch" indicators of child change that may not coincide with progress that is tracked strictly developmentally or "bottom-up." Consider, for example, the integrated goals implicit in the steps of the trunk-control–object-manipulation skill-sequence (Figure 2). Especially because fine and gross motor goals are combined in each step, it is possible that a child could demon-

Table 1. Summary of Task-Analytic Assessment Procedures.

Least prompts	Reposition	Discontinued
1. Before assessment, determine which prompts are to be used and in which order.	1. Wait for Step 1 for predetermined latency.	1. Wait for Step 1 for predetermined latency.
2. Wait for Step 1 for predetermined latency.	2. If Step 1 is done correctly, record +, and wait latency for Step 2.	2. If Step 1 is done correctly, record +, and wait latency for Step 2.
3. If Step 1 is done correctly, record "I" for "Independent," and wait the latency for Step 2.	3. If Step 1 is done incorrectly or does not occur within the latency, record a – (incorrect) or NR (no response). In either case, do one of the following:	3. If Step 1 is done incorrectly or not done at all, record – ; if no response, record NR. In this case, stop the assessment and record – for all other steps in the task analysis.
4. If Step 1 is done incorrectly or not within the latency, provide the least intrusive prompt and wait the defined latency, as illustrated below. Record only the letter corresponding to the most intrusive prompt level required to produce correct performance of the step by the child, e.g.,	a. Position the child so that she or he is in a position to do the next step in the chain, or	
a. If incorrect or no response following the latency allowed after the chance for	b. Do the step for her or him so that she or he will be in the "ready" position to initiate the next step in the chain.	
	4. Continue in this fashion, assessing each step of the task analysis.	

independence, give a verbal prompt.
—If correct, record a V, and wait the latency for Step 2.
—If incorrect or no response, proceed to next prompt level (b).

b. Provide a gestural prompt.
—If correct, record a G and wait the latency for Step 2.
—If incorrect or no response, proceed to next prompt level (c).

c. Provide a model prompt.
—If correct, record an M and wait the latency for Step 2.
—If incorrect or no response, proceed to next prompt level (d).

d. Provide a physical prompt.
—If correct, record a P and wait latency for Step 2.

OBJECTIVE: During 10 min of his playtime, while either strapped in his adaptive chair or positioned on his side to free his right arm, with a switch-activated electronic toy in position, R.T. will independently activate the switch for 3 seconds. He will do this within 3 seconds of his hand's being placed on the switch, five randomly selected times during each of three probe sessions spaced over a 2-week period.

INSTRUCTIONAL PROCEDURE: During regularly scheduled playtime, in a nondistracting area of the room, a toy from the sound-and-movement toy group will be put into position within 5 inches of his right hand. For a block of 10 trials, provide full physical assistance to maintain pressure on the switch for 3 seconds. Probe ahead to the next least intrusive level of assistance (3 trials). If he responds at the lower level of assistance, continue with a block of 10 trials at that assistance level. Continue with this sequence, working from higher levels of physical help to lower levels (see graduated guidance levels below). Blocks of 10 trials are distributed across sessions.

NEXT INSTRUCTIONAL STEPS: Increase criterion of hand on switch from 3 to 5 seconds (see skill sequence).

CORRECTION PLAN: Graduated guidance procedures are in effect. If there is an error or no response at a lower level of assistance, return to a full physical prompt to ensure correct responding. (This does not apply to probes).

MAINTENANCE-GENERALIZATION PLAN: Train across different toys in the sound-and-movement toy group ; Mom, teacher, and aide serve as trainers; alternate training in chair and in sidelying; school and home.

SCHEDULE OF DATA COLLECTION: Initial discontinued probe will be followed by a probe series (3 trials) following a training block consisting of 10 successful trials on the prompt level in use. A probe series is on the next, less intrusive level of physical assistance. Levels of graduated guidance assistance (most to least):
    Pressure: 8-with force; 7-gravitational weight; 6-lightly touching.
    Distance: 5-at wrist; 4-at forearm; 3-at elbow.
    Proximity: 2-hand shadowing; 1-hand on table; 0-hand out of sight.

Figure 6. Intervention plan.

strate an idiosyncratic acquisition pattern. For testing purposes, a top-down assessment sequence is a relatively rapid way to check the multiple skills involved (note the assessment plan in Figure 2). From an intervention perspective, training bottom-up on this sequence virtually guarantees instruction on relevant, integrated skills. Even if a child were not to progress to independent sitting with midline toy play, toy retrieval, and trunk control, he or she would have had instruction on directly related skills. Admittedly, the further skill mastery proceeds in the sequence, the more competence will be demonstrated. More important for youngsters with the most severe disabilities, however, mastery of even the lowest steps will result in increased environmental control.

A third factor that is an advantage of such curriculum-referenced assessment is the potential of cross-domain integration of goals within sequences. Although programming that maximizes learning across skill areas is considered exemplary, too little attention is paid to such arrangements in practice. Skill sequences, which are often highly individualized, can serve as the basis of assessing—and programming—such integrated goals. Each of the skill sequences just discussed illustrates such integration, as the steps currently target gross-motor, fine-motor, and cognitive goals.

The next section reviews the use of environmental inventories, another assessment strategy related to ensuring a closer fit between assessment and intervention.

ENVIRONMENTAL ASSESSMENT

The primary emphasis in this chapter is on the direct assessment of youngsters with disabilities. One feature of comprehensive assessment that is often neglected and that directly relates to carefully planned interventions is environmental assessment. Interventions in this field have often used assessments of home environments (a) to describe the context in which an intervention took place; (b) to determine critical deficits that presumably need improvement (e.g., increased interactions or more toys); and, in some cases, (c) to evaluate the generalized effects of intervention programs (Elardo, Bradley, & Caldwell, 1975). In some cases, a specific instrument, such as the HOME (Caldwell, 1970), is used. In others, practitioners may use a program-developed record of observations or one that is idiosyncratic to the ongoing intervention. This second strategy is often used by teachers in home-based programs. The more discrete and systematic the observation system selected, the better the documentation is in such cases.

A growing concern of educators in recent years about the utility of specific intervention goals has led to a variation in these practices. Two complementary trends are relevant:

1. Educators have acknowledged the unsystematic attention given to matching skill instruction in early-childhood special-education settings to expectations and outcomes in children's next educational environments (Vincent et al., 1980).
2. There has been increasing attention to the integral involvement of parents in instructional decision-making (Turnbull & Turnbull, 1982, 1986) and a growing recognition of their potential contributions during the assessment process (Gradel et al., 1981; Sheehan, Chapter 5).

Assessment of Behaviors Needed in Transitions

The first major trend related to the need for a more careful analysis of potential teaching targets is the increasing attention to transition from the early-childhood special-education setting to either a regular or another special-education site (Hutinger, 1981; LeBlanc, Etzel, & Domash, 1978; Vincent & Broome, 1977). Despite the refined assessment data that may be collected on a youngster's progress, he or she is likely to be judged with respect to the criteria defining performance in the next educational setting. Several investigators have analyzed the skills needed by young children in less restrictive educational settings (cf. Brown, 1979; Cobb, 1972; Hops & Cobb, 1973; Sainato & Lyon, 1983; Vincent et al., 1980). Their overarching conclusions suggest that of critical importance are ''survival skills'' that exert social control. These include turn taking, following directions, working and playing independently, working in groups, and making within-classroom transitions independently. This literature is based on observational, interview, and sociometric data. These data, along with special-education placement analyses

(Ysseldyke & Algozzine, 1982), indicate that the mastery of traditional targets is insufficient for success in some next educational settings.

Concerns about such standards are frequently voiced regarding transitions to regular school settings (i.e., kindergarten), as well as to subsequent special-education sites (Turnbull, Winston, Blacher, & Salkind, 1982; Walter & Vincent, 1982). It is not uncommon for an infant educator to visit the expected next school site, to make general observations, and to provide school personnel with information about the students in transition. What appears to be missing from such interactions is that the infant educator must gather both programmatic expectations and clarifications about what the range of acceptable performance is for the enrolled children. What is most important is that such data be available to practitioners on an ongoing basis—not just immediately preceding such a transition. It is possible that such information could make a significant difference in the types of goals targeted for children over time. Minimally, such data could verify for the infant educator that, in fact, he or she is teaching the skills deemed critical by the receiving programs.

There is unfortunately little available relevant instrumentation for use by the practitioner. One viable option is to use existing data bases (e.g., Sainato & Lyon, 1983; Vincent *et al.*, 1980) as a referent. Alternatively, instruments such as those developed by these investigators could be condensed for use. For example, Sainato and Lyon (1983) incorporated 20 coding categories, including time, activity, teacher, physical arrangement, grouping, type of materials, location and access, teaching direction, instructional techniques, type of response, response format, critical dimension, child engagement, response quality, teacher response, frequency of interactions, type and quality of teacher interaction, child–child interaction, transition, and movement. Their descriptive study of special and regular preschool settings provides a reasonable data base to use as a referent for verifying the utility of potential targets in their early-childhood special-education program.

Practitioners may instead wish to isolate the variables most relevant to their programming. J. Nelson and L. Lucas (personal communication, 1986) did this as they designed instructional goals for group functioning in an infant program. Because most of the graduates of the program moved into one of several self-contained toddler rooms in the same school, Nelson and Lucas observed in and inteviewed staff in those rooms to acquire relevant information about expectations for children's participation in groups (see the questions listed in Figure 7).

Parental Input

As Turnbull and Turnbull (1982, 1986) have indicated, parents and professionals are continuing to forge a working relationship in making decisions about educational goal planning and interventions for children with disabilities. Just as the "rules" for doing this are ambiguous, so are the data supporting parental contributions to the assessment process (Sheehan, Chapter 5). Despite such ambiguities, it is clear that practitioners need information about children from their parents, for at least three primary reasons.

First, it is obvious that the most relevant "next environment" for a disabled toddler or preschooler is his or her home. Put simply, most skills being taught in center-based

Time period	Number of children per group or staff	Primary skill or activity instructed	Primary response mode expected or prompted

Additional Questions:
1.a. For your least competent student, how representative was what was observed today?
   b. For your most competent student, how representative was what was observed today?
2.a. For your least competent student, what was the level of grouping primarily used for instruction (not common group times) at the beginning of the year?
   b. For your most competent student, what was the level of grouping primarily used for instruction (not common group times) at the beginning of the year?

Figure 7. Environmental inventory: Group functioning in next setting.

programs should be potentially usable in the child's home—unless there is another defensible rationale for the instruction (i.e., the skills are deemed to be critical in the next school setting). Using such a criterion may help the educators to sort through the pool of possible goals for children, and to set priorities among those that have utility in their homes.

Second, information is needed by practitioners to verify that skills are present or absent in nonschool settings. Given the broad research base indicating that generalization is not a "given" with individuals with disabilities, it has become evident that practitioners must use more pragmatic estimates of what has been learned or not learned. Parental information gives teachers estimates of (a) generalized skill repertoires in children; (b) performance in skills that may not be part of school routines (e.g., at home, at the sitter's, or in the grocery store); and (c) strategies that may be useful in working with

1. How often does B. need a bath?
2. Where do you bathe him (or her)?
3. Do you use shampoo?
4. Do you use soap or baby bath?
5. What kind of tub do you use?
6. Do you like to use a washcloth?
7. Do you use a towel?
8. Can you show me how you hold him (or her) in the tub?
9. How do you rinse his (or her) head?
10. Does anyone help you with bathing him (or her)?
11. What time of the day do you like to bathe him (or her).

Figure 8. Environmental inventory: Bathing baby.

the child across settings. The time required to secure such data in other ways is inordinate and not commonly available to most practitioners. Needless to say, these data appear to be significantly more substantive than the kinds of assessment information often asked of parents (i.e., ''What do you want your child to learn this year at school?'').

One available instrument that has been used for such purposes is the Oliver (MacDonald, 1978), which is a parent-administered inventory for assessing children's communicative repertoires at home and in other natural settings. The Oliver is part of the Environmental Language Program package, which includes two professional assessments and training manuals for both professionals and parents (MacDonald & Horstmeier, 1978). It is a comprehensive questionnaire, intended to document the ways in which the child symbolically and idiosyncratically communicates; recent changes in communication; the child management strategies used; hearing-related behaviors; receptive language; imitation; environmental manipulation by the child; overall expectations; and the interventions used to date.

An additional type of environmental assessment information that caregivers may provide has to do with feasibility. In many programs, practitioners plan to work with caregivers on jointly targeted goals, to facilitate the child's progress. This is often the assumed basis of home-based intervention programs. Thus, it is incumbent on the practitioner that she or he secure at least an informal assessment of the practicality of goals, intervention strategies, and/or timing of interventions in the existing home routines. The questions listed in Figure 8 provide an example of such an informal assessment. They were developed by a home-based teacher to assess the routine followed by a mother with developmental disabilities who was learning to bathe her baby (K. Wilmott, personal communication, 1986).

SUMMARY

This chapter has summarized the primary curriculum-referenced assessment strategies currently in use in exemplary educational settings servicing infants and preschoolers with mild to severe disabilities. The disadvantages of using normative and criterion-referenced instruments in standard ways have been highlighted by offering alternatives that more closely fit intervention practices.

REFERENCES

Bailey, D., & Wolery, M. (1984). *Teaching infants and preschoolers with handicaps*. Columbus, OH: Charles E. Merrill.

Bailey, E. J., & Bricker, D. (1986). A psychometric study of a criterion-referenced assessment instrument designed for infants and young children. *Journal for the Division for Early Childhood, 10*, 124–134.

Banerdt, B., & Bricker, D. (1978). A training program for selected self-feeding skills for the motorically impaired. *AAESPH Review, 3*, 222–229.

Bayley, N. (1969). *Bayley Scales of Infant Development*. New York, Psychological Corporation.

Becker, W. C., Engelmann, S., & Thomas, D. R. (1975). *Teaching cognitive learning and instruction*. Chicago: Science Research Associates.

Billingsley, F. F., & Romer, L. T. (1983). Response prompting and transfer of stimulus control: Methods, research, and a conceptual framework. *Journal of the Association for the Severely Handicapped, 8*, 3–12.

Blankenship, C. S. (1985). Using curriculum-based assessment data to make instructional decisions. *Exceptional Children, 52*, 233–238.

Bluma, S. M., Shearer, M. S., Frosham, A. H., & Hilliard, J. M. (1976). *Portage guide to early education* (No. 12). Portage, WI: Cooperative Educational Agency.

Bricker, D. (1984). *Personnel preparation report: Infant specialist*. Washington, DC: National Council for Exceptional Children.

Bricker, D., & Gentry, D. (1982). *Evaluation and programming system: For infants and young children. Assessment Level I: Developmentally 1 month to 3 years (ESP-1)*. Unpublished manuscript, Center on Human Development, University of Oregon.

Brown, L., Branston, M. B., Hamre-Nietupski, S., Pumpian, I., Certo, N., & Gruenewald, L. A. (1979). A strategy for developing chronological age appropriate and functional curricular content for severely handicapped adolescents and young adults. *Journal of Special Education, 13*, 81–90.

Brown, P. (1979). *Measuring the success of a pre-school special education program using follow-up data*. Unpublished master's thesis, University of Wisconsin, Madison.

Caldwell, B. M. (1970). *Instruction manual inventory for infants (Home observations for measurement of the environment)*. Little Rock: University of Arkansas.

Cattell, P. (1940, 1960). *The measurement of intelligence in infants and young children*. Psychological Corporation.

Cech, D., Josephs, A., Pearl, O., & Gallagher, R. J. (1983). *Chicago neuromotor assessment*. Unpublished assessment instrument. Chicago: Institute of the Study of Developmental Disabilities, University of Illinois.

Cobb, J. (1972). Academic survival skills and elementary academic achievement. In E. Meyer (Ed.), *Strategies for teaching exceptional children*. Denver: Love Publishing.

Cohen, M. A., & Gross, P. J. (1979). *The developmental resource: Behavioral sequences for assessment and program planning*. New York: Grune & Stratton.

Deno, S. L. (1985). Curriculum-based measurement: The emerging alternative. *Exceptional Children, 52*, 219–232.

Elardo, R., Bradley, R., & Caldwell, B. M. (1975). The relation of infants' home environments to mental test performance from six to thirty-six months: A longitudinal analysis. *Child Development, 46*, 71–76.

Fewell, R. R., & Kelly, J. F., (1983). Curriculum for young handicapped children. In S. G. Garwood (Ed.), *Educating young handicapped children: A developmental approach* (2nd ed.). Rockville, MD: Aspen Systems Corporation.

Filler, J. W., Robinson, C. C., Smith, R. A., Vincent-Smith, L. J., Bricker, D.D., & Bricker, W.A. (1975). Mental retardation. In N. Hobbs (Ed.), *Issues in the classification of children* (Vol. 1). San Francisco: Jossey-Bass.

Furuno, S., O'Reilly, K. A., Hosaka, C. M., Inatsuka, T., Allman, T. L., & Zeisloft, B. (1979). *Hawaii early learning profile*. Palo Alto, CA: VORT.

Gentry, D. (1980). *Adaptive performance instrument*. Moscow: CAPE Project, Department of Special Education, University of Idaho.

Gesell, A., & Armatruda, C. S. (1947). *Developmental diagnosis* (2nd ed.). New York: Harper & Row.

Gradel, K., Thompson, M., & Sheehan, R. (1981). Parental and professional agreement in early childhood assessment. *Topics in Early Childhood Special Education, 1*(2), 31–39.

Guess, D., Horner, R., Utley, B., Holvoet, J., Maxon, D., Tucker, D., & Warren, S. (1978). A functional curriculum sequencing model for teaching the severely handicapped. *AAESPH Review, 3*, 202–215.

Hops, H., & Cobb, J. (1973). Survival skills in the educational setting: Their implications for research and intervention. In L. Hamerlynck, L. Hany, & E. Mash (Eds.), *Behavioral change: Methodology, concepts and practice.* Champaign, IL: Research Press.

Hutinger, P. L. (1981). Transition practices for handicapped young children: What the experts say. *Journal for the Division of Early Childhood, 2*, 8–14.

Johnson-Martin, N., Jens, K. G., & Attermeier, S. M. (1986). *The Carolina Curriculum for Handicapped Infants and Infants at Risk.* Baltimore: Paul H. Brookes.

Kaiser, C., & Hayden, A. (1977). The education of the very, very young or but what can you teach an infant? *Educational Horizons, 56*(1), 4–15.

LeBlanc, J. M., Etzel, B. C., & Domash, M. A. (1978). A functional curriculum for early intervention. In K. E. Allen, V. A., Holm, & R. L. Schiefelbusch (Eds.), *Early intervention—A team approach.* Baltimore: University Park Press.

LeMay, D. W., Griffin, P. M., & Sanford, A. R. (1977). *Learning accomplishment profile: Diagnostic edition* (rev. ed.). Chapel Hill, NC: Chapel Hill Training and Outreach Project.

MacDonald, J. D. (1978). *Oliver: Parent-administered communication inventory.* Columbus, OH: Charles E. Merrill.

MacDonald, J. D., & Horstmeier, D. (1978). *Environmental language program.* Columbus, OH: Charles E. Merrill.

Marston, D., & Magnusson, D. (1985). Implementing curriculum-based measurement in special and regular education settings. *Exceptional Children, 52*, 266–276.

McCarthy, D. (1972). *Manual for the McCarthy Scales of Children's Abilities.* New York: Psychological Corporation.

McCormick, L., & Noonan, M. J. (1984). A responsive curriculum for severely handicapped preschoolers. *Topics in Early Childhood Special Education, 4*(3), 79–96.

Pefley, D., & Smith, H., (1976. *It's Monday morning.* Chapel Hill: Technical Assistance Development System, University of North Carolina.

Pomerantz, D., & Gradel, L. (1981). Curricular planning issues in the education of young severely handicapped children. *The Forum, 7*(2), 10, 22.

Sainato, D. M., & Lyon, S. (1983). *A descriptive analysis of requirements for independent performance in special and regular early childhood environments.* Pittsburgh: University of Pittsburgh, Early Childhood Research Institute, Western Psychiatric Institute and Clinic.

Schafer, D. S., & Moersch, M. S. (Eds.). (1981). *Developmental programming for infants and young children.* Ann Arbor: University of Michigan Press, 1981.

Sheehan, R. (1981). Issues in documenting early intervention with infants and parents. *Topics in Early Childhood Special Education, 1*(3), 67–75.

Sheehan, R. (1982). Infant assessment: A review and identification of emergent trends. In D. D. Bricker (Ed.), *Intervention with at-risk and handicapped infants: From research to application.* Baltimore: University Park Press.

Sheehan, R., & Gallagher, R. J. (1984). Assessment of infants. In M. J. Hanson (Ed.), *Atypical infant development.* Baltimore: University Park Press.

Sheehan, R., & Gradel, K. (1983). Intervention models in early childhood special education. In S. G. Garwood (Ed.), *Educating young handicapped children: A developmental approach* (2nd ed.). Rockville: Aspen Systems Corporation.

Snell, M. E. (1983). Developing the IEP: Selecting and assessing skills. In M. E. Snell (Ed.), *Systematic instruction of the moderately and severely handicapped* (2nd ed.). Columbus, OH: Charles E. Merrill.

Strain, P., Sainato, D., & Maheady, L. (1984). Toward a functional assessment of severely handicapped learners. *The Educational Psychologist, 19*, 182–187.

Turnbull, A. P., & Turnbull, H. R. (1982). Parent involvement in the education of handicapped children: A critique. *Mental Retardation, 20*(3), 115–122.

Turnbull, A. P., & Turnbull, H. R. (1986). *Families, professionals, and exceptionality: A special education partnership.* Columbus, OH: Charles E. Merrill.

Turnbull, A. P. Winton, P. J., Blacher, J., & Salkind, N. (1982). Mainstreaming in the kindergarten classroom: Perspectives of parents of handicapped and non-handicapped children. *Journal for the Division of Early Childhood, 6,* 14–20.

Uzgiris, I. C., & Hunt, J. McV. (1975). *Assessment in infancy.* Urbana: University of Illinois Press.

Vincent, L., & Broome, K. (1977). A public school service delivery model for handicapped children between birth and five years of age. In E. Sontag, J. Smith, & N. Certo (Eds.), *Educational programming for the severely and profoundly handicapped.* Reston, VA: Division on Mental Retardation, Council for Exceptional Children.

Vincent, L. J., Salisbury, C., Walter, B., Brown, L., Gruenewald, L. J., & Powers, M. (1980). Program evaluation and curriculum development in early childhood special education. In W. Sailor, B. Wilcox, & L. Brown (Eds.), *Methods of instruction for severely handicapped students.* Baltimore: Paul H. Brookes.

Vulpé, S. G. (1977). *Vulpé Assessment Battery.* Toronto: National Institute on Mental Retardation.

Walter, G., & Vincent, L. B. (1982). The handicapped child in the regular kindergarten classroom. *Journal for the Division of Early Childhood, 6,* 84–95.

White, O., Edgar, E., Haring, N. G., Affleck, J., Hayden, A., & Bendersky, M. (1980). *Uniform performance assessment system.* Columbus, OH: Charles E. Merrill.

Wolery, M., & Gast, D. L. (1984). Effective and efficient procedures for the transfer of stimulus control. *Topics in Early Childhood Special Education, 4*(3), 52–77.

Ysseldyke, J. E., & Algozzine, R. (1982). *Critical issues in special and remedial education.* Boston: Houghton-Mifflin.

19

Issues in the Linkage of Assessment to Intervention

Theodore D. Wachs and Robert Sheehan

It has been argued that humans are designed to categorize information. that is, it may be part of human nature to attempt to group together disparate arrays of stimuli within a single category, as in the use of a symbolic system. Such an attempt will be made in this summary chapter. Our goal in this summary chapter is to highlight what we regard as the major themes and issued that were raised in this book. Given the diversity of viewpoints and populations discussed, such an effort may seem to some readers to be nothing more then a projective test for the editors. Although some editorial ''projection'' may be involved, it also seems clear that certain issues were repeatedly discussed in these chapters. What consistencies exist may be due to the fact that, as clinicians and researchers, the chapter authors are struggling with a common set of problems in the assessment of young developmentally disabled children. In attempting to categorize themes, *three major issues* seem to cut across the majority of chapters in this volume.

THE NATURE OF DEVELOPMENTAL DISABILITIES

One major theme, which has been emphasized by a number of authors, is the lack of *functional equivalence* in developmental pattern and ultimate outcome, even within supposedly homogeneous developmental disabilities. Different children with a specific sensory or motor disability develop in different ways, at different rates, and toward different end points. In good part, the degree of variability, even within supposedly homogeneous disabilities, appears to be due to two factors. First, disabilities are *multidimensional*. Similar developmental disabilities (i.e., visual impairments) can be due to a variety of etiologies, are manifested in varying degrees of severity, and may covary with a number of other conditions. All of these factors are likely to lead to a diversity of developmental pathways and outcomes, even within a given disability condition.

Second, the impact of disabilities on development are *multidetermined*. As was repeatedly noted, the outcome of a disability (i.e., when a disability becomes a handicap) is

THEODORE D. WACHS • Department of Psychological Sciences, Purdue University, West Lafayette, Indiana 47907. ROBERT SHEEHAN • Department of Foundation and Curriculum, College of Education, Cleveland State University, Cleveland, Ohio 44115.

rarely due solely to the disability itself; rather it is mediated by a variety of other factors. For example, for an individual child, the impact of a specific developmental disability may be to limit interaction with the environment. This limited interaction will compound the original problem, and will lead to an outcome that is more serious then would be predicted just on the nature of the disability itself. A second child with the same disability may be reared in a highly supportive environment, that attenuates the long-term impact of the original disability.

A variety of mediating factors have been identified in this book as potentially relevant to outcome. Behavioral style may be one critical mediator. As McDevitt noted in Chapter 13, the potential salience of individual differences in distractibility may be particularly critical for deaf children, for whom there is a stronger need to focus on teacher movements and gestures. Thus, deaf children who are highly distractible may have a poorer outcome than deaf children who are less distractible. Similarly, a developmentally disabled child's motivation level may play an important role in outcome, as noted by Brockman, Morgan, and Harmon (Chapter 14). Disabled children who are more persistent in attempting to get feedback from their environment are more likely to have a better outcome than disabled children who are less persistent. Similarly, the mediating role of biomedical problems associated with developmental disabilities has been documented by Magyary, Barnard and Brandt in Chapter 17. In light of this evidence there are two major implications for the assessment process.

The Selection of an Assessment Strategy

One implication of the multidetermined and multidimensional nature of development disabilities is the need for a wide variety of assessment strategies. In this book, we have seen arguments for the utility of norm-referenced procedures, child-referenced procedures, criterion-referenced procedures with or without specific teaching guides, profile analyses, modifying test or response demands, the use of theoretically based models, and an emphasis on the assessment of critical developmental mediators. The heterogeneity in assessment strategies seen in this book, may, in part, reflect the fact that different disability conditions lead to unique developmental patterns, which may not be assessed by certain types of measures. Concern about the unique developmental patterns associated with different disability conditions has been raised not only in this book but by other authors as well (i.e., Delgardo, 1982).

The heterogeneity of potential assessment approaches may also reflect the fact that different populations are discussed in different chapters. Assessment demands and appropriate assessment strategies are radically different when one is dealing with a mentally retarded child with adequate sensory and motor abilities, as compared to a multiply impaired child, in whom retardation may be compounded by specific sensory and motor disabilities. The problem of different populations needing different assessment approaches is compounded by the fact that there are only a limited number of assessment devices available for use with young developmentally disabled children. Often, what is available is useful only for a specific population or for a specific purpose.

An excellent illustration of why multiple assessment strategies are needed is seen in the search for alternatives to traditional norm-referenced testing procedures. A number of authors in this volume (i.e., Stagg, Chapter 4; Robinson & Fieber, Chapter 8; Dunst &

McWilliam, Chapter 11) have criticized traditional norm-referenced procedures as being inappropriate for the assessment of young developmentally disabled children, particularly in terms of their lack of utility for educational planning. One approach that has been discussed as an alternative to traditional norm-referenced procedures is criterion-referenced assessment. In contrast to norm-referenced assessment, in which individual's level of performance on a sample of items is compared to that of a normative group, criterion-referenced procedures assess *within individual performance* on a presumed population of items (Carver, 1974). Berk (1980) described criterion-referenced measures in two ways: first, as measures that totally represent a behavioral domain, and second, as measures that classify students as masters or nonmasters of an objective, in order to expedite individualized instruction. Typically, criterion-referenced procedures assess what specific skills the individual has mastered, with little or no reference to how the individual compares to a normative group (Duffy & Fedner, 1977). Rather, the examiner is concerned about the profile of skills for the individual child, the appropriateness of those skills, and the performance of that child across time.

In addition to the points raised in this book, proponents of the criterion-referenced approach emphasize that, by the detailing of the precise skills that the individual has mastered and not yet mastered, the transition to intervention becomes much easier (Bagnato & Neisworth, 1981; Salvia & Ysseldyke, 1978). In addition, proponents of the criterion-referenced approach correctly note that a different set of reliability and validity criteria can be used when criterion-referenced procedures are involved (Carver, 1974). This is particularly relevant given the psychometric problems involved in test adaptation for young developmentally disabled children, as documented in this book and elsewhere (Bagnato & Neisworth, 1981; Duffy & Fedner, 1977; Salvia & Ysseldyke, 1978).

Although the use of criterion-referenced assessment procedures appears to neatly sidestep the problems involved in using traditional normative assessment procedures with young developmentally disabled children, these procedures also have their own set of problems. First, as a number or recent papers have stressed, it is all too often *assumed* that, because a test measures whether a child has mastered specific skills, problems with measurement error are minimized (Linn, 1981). However, when criterion-referenced procedures are used to make *decisions* (e.g., whether the child should continue receiving intervention, or whether the child should progress to a higher level of intervention), these assumptions may be incorrect and may lead to inappropriate decisions about the individual child (Linn, 1981; Traub & Rawley, 1980). Thus, in terms of validity, failure on a criterion-referenced measure is usually taken to mean that the child does not have the requisite skill; however, this failure could also be attributed to a variety of nonskill factors, such as motivation, inappropriate item presentation, or a test format that is inappropriate for that particular child or disability. The potential relevance of each of these nonskill factors has been documented in a number of chapters in this book (e.g., chapters by Brockman *et al.* and by Robinson and Fieber).

An additional problem involves the content of the criterion-referenced measure. Most proponents of criterion-referenced assessment (e.g., Bagnato & Neisworth, 1981; Duffy & Fedner, 1977) stress the need for strong links between what is assessed in these measures and what the child is being taught. Although these links may make the skills profile highly teachable, they also raise the risk of assessing the child on relatively trivial skills, *which have little salience in promoting critical developmental changes for the child* (Linn, 1981; MacTurk & Neisworth, 1978). Skills may be chosen for assessment because they are easily measurable and lead to clear instructional objectives (e.g., creeping and crawling performance), but this does not guarantee that these skills represent either the *precursors* or the *critical mediators* of important *developmental processes*.

Even more critically, as a number of reviewers have noted, the use of skills assessment all too often leads to teaching to the test (Sattler, 1980). In teaching to the test, it is *assumed* that the specific skills learned will generalize, or that the skills taught represent the entire behavioral domain. These assumptions of generalizability and representativeness of items cannot be made easily, particularly for the young developmentally disabled child. As Robinson & Fieber have pointed out (Chapter 8), our intervention goal is not to teach specific isolated behaviors, but to teach generalizable skills that children can use in a variety of situations. By encouraging teaching to the test, criterion-referenced procedures may lead to intervention strategies that are inappropriate, *in the long run,* for the young developmentally disabled child.

Clearly, given the points raised above, criterion-referenced procedures cannot be viewed as a panacea for all the difficulties involved in the assessment of young developmentally disabled children. A similar point can be made about each of the assessment approaches discussed in this book. It seems clear that *no single assessment strategy is likely to be particularly useful across the complete range of developmental disabilities,* or even for all children within a single disability category. Rather, as will be discussed below in more detail, greater emphasis needs to be placed on the purpose for which a specific assessment is being used.

The Selection of Test Procedures

A second implication of the multidimensional-multidetermined nature of developmental disabilities in young children is the importance of testing across multiple domains. Currently, there is a clear overemphasis on the assessment of cognitive performance or the assessment of specific skill levels. There is much less interest in assessing noncognitive domains, which may be equally critical in predicting outcome. As noted earlier, these domains may include the environment that the child is living in, as well as individual characteristics like motivation, interpersonal skills, and biomedical history. The potential relevance of these factors to subsequent development cannot be determined through the use of either standard cognitive tests or criterion-referenced procedures.

Historically, the emphasis on a cognitive-skill assessment-strategy is not surprising. The initial development of psychological assessment techniques reflected a need to predict functioning in settings like the school. Not surprisingly, assessment procedures for pre-school populations, which were firmly rooted in this tradition, primarily involved measures of cognitive performance (Brooks & Weinraub, 1976). However, in recent years, it has become increasingly clear that a *multidimensional approach* is necessary to predict outcome for children who are at risk. This approach, involving cognitive, biomedical, social, motivational, temperamental, and environmental assessments (including comparable opportunities for acculturation), applied to groups of infants with known potential risk, may be the only approach with any potential for isolating those infants who will later manifest developmental deficits (Kopp & Krakow, 1983; Ramey, MacPhee, & Yeates, 1982).

Although it could be argued that such a multi-dimensional assessment approach is most relevant to nondisabled risk populations (i.e., premature or low-SES infants), evidence presented in a majority of chapters in this book emphasizes the importance of multidimensional assessments for the developmentally disabled as well. Obviously, not all of the above domains will need to be assessed for a given child for a given purpose (see below). For most cases, however, it seems clear that more than just a cognitive or skills measure is necessary.

WHY IS THIS ASSESSMENT BEING DONE?

A second major theme that has emerged from this book involves the necessity of specifying what types of clinical *decisions* need to be made for an individual child, *before* selecting an assessment strategy and appropriate instruments. As noted by Robinson & Fieber (Chapter 8, p. 127):

> A recurrent theme in this book is the necessity for clarification of the purpose (questions to be answered) for which any assessment of a child is done. This theme is particularly relevant to several topics; the relationships among assumptions underlying an assessment process, the development of an assessment tool, and the use to which a given assessment is put.

There are a number of potential decisions or purposes for which a child is evaluated. These may include assessment of initial risk (screening), confirmation of the existence of significant developmental delay, determination of the most appropriate intervention for a child, or assessment of the effectiveness and/or generalizability of interventions. It seems clear from the various chapters in the book that *different decisions require different types of instruments and different types of assessment strategies.* All too often, however, in the assessment process with young developmentally disabled children, instruments are chosen because they were designed for or adapted to that specific population. In contrast, what has been repeatedly stressed in this book is that it is the *purpose* and not the population that defines the instrument chosen. Thus, although an instrument is designed for a specific population, this does not mean that this instrument will be useful in all decisions that need to be made for children within this population. Similarly, an instrument useful for predicting outcome for a young developmentally disabled child in one situation may not be useful in predicting to other situations. Along the same lines, the validity of adapting a test cannot be put in a yes-or-no framework. Rather, test adaption is seen as valid only when it contributes to making a specific decision about an individual child.[1]

The critical point, repeatedly stressed in this book, is that identification of the types of decisions required have to be made *before* selecting assessment strategies or instruments. Without specific consideration of the types of decisions that need to be made, the choice of an appropriate assessment strategy or instrument becomes a hit-or-miss proposition. An example of the process involved in going from decision specification through

---

[1]An additional advantage of a decision theory framework is that it allows us to use approaches other than classic psychometrics in assessing the utility of assessment procedures. An example of the use of decision theory in this regard is seen in the paper by Swaminathan, Hambleton, & Algina (1974), who reconceptualized reliability as a measure of the degree of agreement on decisions for the individual child, derived from repeating testing.

instrument selection has been detailed by Hubert and Wallander in Chapter 3. To reemphasize this point, two other examples will be given here, one involving the selection of an assessment strategy and the second involving the selection of appropriate instruments.

The Selection of an Assessment Strategy

In discussing this issue, we will again use the question of criterion-referenced versus norm-related procedures. All too often, this question is put into an either-or format: Should disabled children be compared to nondisabled children or to themselves? Should totally new normative measures be developed with content appropriate for developmentally disabled children? Given the emphasis in this book, as well in other writings (i.e., Jones, 1970), the question of whether to use normative or criterion-referenced assessment strategies should not be put in an either-or framework but in decision-theory terms. In such terms, answering the question of what is the appropriate strategy becomes a function of identifying the specific decision that need to be made. For example, if the decision is whether the individual child is *showing impairment* on critical developmental functions, comparison with a nondisabled normative group on content representing normal development is essential to estimate the degree of impairment. Once the question is cast in this framework, the examiner need only decide which norm-referenced instrument is most appropriate for estimating the existence and degree of developmental delay.

Similarly, for the question of whether *intervention is warranted* for the individual child having a specific disability, a *dual comparison*, both with a nondisabled normative group and with a normative group of comparison children with similar disabilities, seems essential. In this decision situation, the disabled child whose level of development is deviant in regard to *both* disabled and nondisabled populations would receive the highest priority for intervention. For the disabled child whose level of functioning is below that of the nondisabled but is within normal limits for the disabled comparison group, the decision of whether or not to intervene would become a function of the domain under investigation. If the available knowledge of child development, as noted in Chapter 1, indicates that developmentally disabled children ultimately (and through routine interaction) achieve adequate functioning in the particular domain under investigation, the individual child showing deficits in this specific domain would have a lower priority for intervention than a child whose domain deficits are in areas where evidence indicates a need for direct intervention.

If a decision involves which domains are to be the focus of intervention, the emphasis is less on the assessment of specific skills and more on assessment of the selected cognitive domains underlying specific skills. In this situation, the most appropriate assessment strategy would be test or response adaptation, as detailed in a number of chapters in this book (e.g., Dunst & McWilliam, Chapter 11; Robinson & Fieber, Chapter 8; Orlansky, Chapter 6). The identification of specific goals within a selected domain and the delineation of rate of progress, could most appropriately be done through intraindividual comparisons of skill performance (e.g., criterion referencing). However, tests for the generalizablility of gains would have to be accomplished through reference to normative groups, involving both disabled and nondisabled children, in appropriate skill areas. As can be seen in the above framework, the *decisions to be made for the individual child or the question being asked about the individual child governs the choice of assessment strategies; the question should not be fit to the strategy chosen.*

The Selection of Test Procedures

In terms of instrument selection, the validity of a decision theory framework is best seen in the choice of appropriate noncognitive instruments. Given the importance of multidimensional assessments, the need arises to decide what noncognitive components should be in a test battery. Again, we would stress the need for decisions to guide the choice of instruments. If the decision to be made involves a prediction of long-term risk (e.g., whether intervention is warranted for this individual child), instruments assessing three noncognitive dimensions would seem to be essential. First, given the demonstrated relevance of environment to long-term functioning for the developmentally disabled (see the chapter by Wachs) it seems clear that some measure of the adequacy of the child's environment must be integrated into the assessment battery. A similar argument can be made for the integration of biophysical procedures, given both the direct and the indirect limitations that biophysical problems place on the disabled child's long-term development (see Chapter 17 by Magyary *et al.*). Finally, given the available evidence on the relevance of socioemotional development to ultimate outcome (see Wachs & Sheehan, Chapter 1; Zentall, Chapter 10), it seems clear that any predictive assessment battery must include measures of the child's social-emotional functioning as well.

Once the decision is made about which noncognitive domains need to be assessed, the question becomes one of selecting the most appropriate instruments within each of these domains. Specific chapters in this book suggest appropriate instruments that would be useful in the assessment of environmental, biophysical, and socioemotional level.

In contrast, if the decision involves selecting the most appropriate intervention strategy, then a potentially different set of noncognitive measures must be identified. To the extent that the intervention is to be carried out at home or by the parent, a measure of the characteristic interactions between parent and child seems warranted. Examples of instruments that would be appropriate for this purpose have been noted in the chapter by Wachs. An intervenor would also want to match the child's characteristics to the types of intervention strategies available, as suggested by McDevitt in Chapter 13. For example, a developmentally disabled child who is highly active may do more poorly in a highly structured classroom; a developmentally disabled child who has problems in sociability or has a low stimulus threshold may do poorly in interventions involving peer-group activities. Accordingly, measures of the child's temperament may also be necessary. Finally, in determining the content of intervention, the child's motivation to engage the intervention must be assessed along with the child's skill level. As noted by Brockman *et al.* (Chapter 14), assessment of a child's motivation may tell us what tasks the child is most likely to persist in, and thus may give the intervention specialist suggestions for which activities are most appropriate for an individual child.

What seems clear from the above is that the initial clinical focus must be the *decision* or *question*, rather than the type of assessment strategy or instrument *per se*. In this framework, assessment procedures and strategies are chosen on the basis of how well they will help the clinician to reach decisions and to answer questions. Ultimately, it is in this decision process that the transition to intervention becomes manifest.

THE ROLE OF THE EXAMINER

For the most part, reviews of assessment deal primarily with test factors. However, in most assessment procedures, tests are given and interpreted by human examiners. A number of chapters in this book have stressed the need for examiners who are knowledgeable about developmental disabilities *and* about assessment procedures. Knowledge about developmental disabilities should go beyond a simple understanding of the types of developmental disabilities, their etiologies, and their characteristics and potential outcomes. Rather, it is also critical that examiners be sensitive to the unique aspects of individual developmental disabilities, what these might mean in terms of alternative developmental pathways, and how these alternative developmental pathways may result in differential outcomes. Said differently, an examiner knowledgeable in developmental disabilities should have an understanding not only of characteristics, but also of the multidimensional and multidetermined nature of developmental disabilities, as discussed earlier.

Examiners knowledgeable about testing procedures would have to have not only a background in test and measurements (i.e., psychometric theory) but also the clinical ability to adequately interpret test results. Additionally, the examiner should also have the ability to understand the possible biasing conditions of test adaptations and how these may influence results.

Unfortunately, what most often occurs is that examiners who are well trained in understanding the nature of developmental disabilities are often poorly trained in assessment. Similarly, examiners who are well trained in assessment skills are often poorly trained in an understanding of developmental disabilities. It is rare to find examiners who not only are sensitive to the unique aspects of an individual child's developmental disabilities, and to what this might mean in terms of alternative developmental pathways, but are also sensitive to the best ways of assessing alternative pathways. Ultimately, as noted by a number of chapters in this book, even when appropriate testing strategies are used, the absence of appropriate examiners results in inadequate assessments.

Given that one of our major weaknesses may be the examiner, what can be done to deal with this problem. Obviously, one approach would be to develop training programs in which developmental disability specialists could be trained in assessment, and assessment specialists could be trained in developmental disabililties. However, this is a long-range solution, and one that will not help current clinicians or intervention specialists faced with the prospect of suddenly having to assess a severely handicapped child, as Stagg has so eloquently noted in Chapter 4. Several authors (e.g., Sheehan, Chapter 5; Kahn, Chapter 9) have suggested the use of alternative assessment procedures, such as parent reports, which require less skilled examiners. However, within a decision theory framework, these approaches are primarily useful for screening. As noted by Gallagher and Cech (Chapter 12), they are much less useful for other types of decisions, such as confirmation of delay or developing specific intervention programs. Thus although some assessment functions may be handled by the use of instruments requiring less training, ultimately, for most decisions, trained examiners will need to be used.

One potential approach, suggested by a number of authors in this book (e.g., Olswang & Bain, Chapter 15; Simeonsson & Bailey, Chapter 2) is greater reliance on multidisciplinary team efforts, *integrating* the skills of those knowledgeable in developmental disabilities and those knowledgeable in assessment techniques. Although ideally such a solution would be most appropriate, in practice what very often results is that assessments are done *individually* by multidisciplinary team members, who come together only to present their results in a staffing. A more appropriate approach, until people can be trained in both developmental disabilities and assessment, would be to integrate the assessment function with the staffing function. In this type of situation, rather than having speech and hearing specialists independently assess these functions, psychologists independently assess cognitive functioning, and physical or occupational therapists independently assess motor functioning, assessments would be done with team members working together *simultaneously* with a given child. This approach would not only facilitate the transmission of information about the characteristics of a given child in particular domains but would also maximize the chances of using the most appropriate test or response adaptation, through on-line communication and feedback among the team members as described by Robinson and Fieber.

The assessment of young developmentally disabled children may be one of the most difficult tasks facing the examiner. Having had training that may be inappropriate to this purpose, having a limited battery of instruments of dubious quality, and facing children for whom standard task demands or response characteristics may be inappropriate, clinicians only naturally often prefer any other type of assessment to that of the young developmentally disabled child. However, in light of advances in medical technology, developmentally disabled children are not only surviving in greater numbers but are also surviving to older ages. Clearly, these children will need appropriate interventions if they are to maximize their developmental potential. Designing the most appropriate interventions for a given child depends on appropriate assessment procedures. What we hope has been demonstrated in this book is that such assessment procedures are possible, *if* examiners appreciate the multidimensional-multidetermined nature of developmental disabilities and attempt to specify why an assessment is necessary (i.e., what questions are being asked) before actually beginning assessment. Under these conditions, the chances of an appropriate assessment are maximized, which, in turn, maximizes the chances of matching available interventions to the unique needs of the individual developmentally disabled child.

REFERENCES

Bagnato, S., & Neisworth, J. (1981). *Linking developmental assessment and criteria.* Rockville, MD: Aspen Corporation.

Berk, R. (1980). Introduction. In R. Berk (Ed.), *Criterion referenced measurement: The state of the art.* Baltimore: Johns Hopkins Press.

Brooks, J., & Weinraub, M. (1976). A history of intelligence testing. In M. Lewis (Ed.), *Origins of intelligence.* New York: Plenum Press.

Carver, R. (1974). Two dimensions of tests. *American Psychologists, 29,* 512–518.

Delgardo, G. (1982). Beyond the norms: Social maturity and deafness. *American Annuals of the Deaf, 127,* 356–360.

Duffy, J., & Fedner, M. (1977). Educational diagnosis with instructional use. *Exceptional Children, 44,* 246–251.

Jones, H. (1970). Principles of psychological assessment. In P. Mittler (Ed.) *The psychological assessment of mental and physical handicaps*. London: Methuen.

Kopp, C., & Krakow, J. (1983). The developmentalist and the study of biological risk. *Child Development, 54*, 1086–1108.

Linn, R. (1981). Issues of validity for criterion referenced measures. *Applied Psychological Measurement, 4*, 537–561.

MacTurk, R., & Neisworth, J. (1978). Norm referenced and criterion referenced measures with preschoolers. *Exceptional Children, 45*, 34–49.

Ramey, C., MacPhee, D., & Yeates, K. (1982). Preventing developmental retardation: A general systems model. in L. Bond & J. Joffe (Eds.), *Facilitating infant and early childhood development*. Hanover: University Press of England.

Salvia, J., & Ysseldyke, J. (1978). *Assessment in special and remedial education*. Boston: Houghton-Mifflin.

Sattler, J. (1980). *Assessment of children's intelligence and special abilities* (2nd ed.). Boston: Allyn & Bacon.

Swaminathan, H., Hambleton, R., & Algina, J. (1974). Reliability of criterion referenced tests. *Journal of Educational Measurements, 1*, 263–267.

Traub, R., & Rawley, G. (1980). Reliability of test scores and decisions. *Applied Psychological Measurement, 4*, 517–545.

Author Index

Subject Index